IIC STUDIES

Studies in Industrial Property and Copyright Law

Volume 23

HART PUBLISHING
OXFORD AND PORTLAND, OREGON
2005

Published by the Max Planck Institute for Foreign and International Patent, Copyright and Competition Law, Munich

Editors
Professor Dr Reto Hilty
Professor Dr Josef Drexl
Professor Joseph Straus

IIC STUDIES

Studies in Industrial Property and Copyright Law

Christopher Heath and Laurence Petit

Patent Enforcement Worldwide

A Survey of 15 Countries

Writings in Honour of Dieter Stauder

Second edition

A joint Research Project by the Max Planck Institute, Munich & CEIPI, Strasbourg

HART PUBLISHING
OXFORD AND PORTLAND, OREGON
2005

Hart Publishing
Oxford and Portland, Oregon

Published in North America (US and Canada) by
Hart Publishing c/o
International Specialized Book Services
5804 NE Hassalo Street
Portland, Oregon
97213-3644
USA

Hart Publishing is a specialist legal publisher based in Oxford, England.
To order further copies of this book or to request a list of other publications please write to:

Hart Publishing, Salter's Boatyard, Folly Bridge,
Abingdon Road, Oxford OX1 4LB
Telephone: +44 (0)1865 245533 or Fax: +44 (0)1865 794882
e-mail: mail@hartpub.co.uk
WEBSITE: http//www.hartpub.co.uk

British Library Cataloguing in Publication Data
Data Available
ISBN 1–84113–538–0 (paperback)

Typeset by Hope Services (Abingdon) Ltd.
Printed and bound in Great Britain on acid-free paper by
Lightning Source, UK Ltd

Preface

A Festschrift, a German tradition that has also made its way to international academia, is normally a one-time event. Second editions are rather uncommon. The Festschrift Dieter Stauder/Writings in Honour of Dieter Stauder/Mélanges dédiés à Dieter Stauder was published under the title "Patent Enforcement in Selected Countries" as a special issue of IIC in October 2000 (31 IIC 625-770). Issues of patent enforcement had been the focus of Dieter Stauder's academic oeuvre since his first publications in the mid-1970s. Perhaps due to the difficulty of the topic as such, positioned somewhere in the area between substantive and procedural law, it has received a broader academic interest only in the last couple of years. This may explain the success of the Festschrift: It sold 1,500 copies in its English version, and was translated into French (La défense des droits de la propriété industrielle en Europe, aux États Unis et au Japon, CEIPI publication No. 48, Litec, Strasbourg 2001), Spanish (La observancia del derecho de patentes, LexisNexis Depalma, Buenos Aires 2003), and Japanese (Shuyôkoku ni okeru tokkyoken kôshi, Keizai sangyô chôsakei, Tokyo 2003). Since October 2000, developments in the field of patent enforcement have been significant and required a major rewriting of all the seven original contributions (the UK, Germany, France, the Netherlands, Italy, Japan and the US): More than 100 decisions have been added. For the second edition, another eight countries have been included: three from Eastern Europe (Poland, the Czech Republic and Hungary), two from Asia (China and Korea), two from Latin America (Argentina and Brazil), and one from Europe (Switzerland). Dieter Stauder was kind enough to contribute an article on European issues of patent enforcement: cross-border litigation, cross-border assistance in obtaining evidence, and the new European Enforcement Directive.

The publication is the result of a co-operation between the Max Planck Institute and CEIPI in Strasbourg. The editors would like to thank Erma Becker from the Max Planck Institute in Munich for competently handling the manuscripts and for compiling the case index. Christine Meder took the photo of Dieter Stauder with the editors. Generous funding for this publication has been provided by the firms Bardehle Pagenberg (Munich), Clifford Chance (London) and Samson & Partner (Munich).

The Editors
Munich and Strasbourg,
September 2004

Preface to the first edition of October 2000

Dieter Stauder, in the honour of whose 60th birthday the following contributions were written, was among the first to realise the importance of enforcement for an effective protection of patent rights. His dissertation on "Patent Infringement in International Commerce", published in 1975, takes up a subject that Dieter Stauder subsequently elaborated in numerous articles and case comments. His groundbreaking fact-finding study on "Patent Infringement Procedure in Germany, the UK, France and Italy" (in German), published in 1988, analyses numerous actual court files from these four countries and highlights the need for harmonisation. Convinced of the latter goal, Dieter Stauder helped to initiate the Symposia of European Patent Judges in 1982, the results of which have been regularly reprinted in this journal. His academic work is crowned by his revision of Romuald Singer's Commentary on the European Patent Convention. Dieter Stauder, engaging personality and fascinating teacher, currently heads the International Section of Strasbourg's CEIPI—for many years to come, we hope.

Als einer der Ersten hat Dieter Stauder, dem die folgenden Beiträge zum 60. Geburtstag gewidmet sind, die Bedeutung der Rechtsdurchsetzung für einen wirksamen Schutz von Patenten erkannt. Dem Thema seiner im Jahre 1975 veröffentlichten Dissertation zur "Patentverletzung im grenzüberschreitenden Wirtschaftsverkehr" ist Dieter Stauder im folgenden noch in zahlreichen Veröffentlichungen nachgegangen. Seine grundlegende rechtstatsächliche Studie zum "Patent- und Gebrauchsmusterverletzungsverfahren in der Bundesrepublik Deutschland, Großbritannien, Frankreich und Italien" von 1988 analysiert zahlreiche Gerichtsakten und macht den Harmonisierungsbedarf in Europa deutlich. Harmonisierung und Informationsaustausch sind auch das Ziel der von Dieter Stauder 1982 mitbegründeten Symposia europäischer Patentrichter, die regelmäßig in dieser Zeitschrift abgedruckt worden sind. Sein eigenes Geburtstagsgeschenk hat sich Dieter Stauder mit der Neubearbeitung des Singerschen Kommentars zum EPÜ gemacht. Dieter Stauder, charmanter Pfälzer und mitreißender Redner, ist derzeit Direktor der internationalen Abteilung des CEIPI in Straßburg—hoffentlich ad multos annos.

C'est en l'honneur de Dieter Stauder et de son 60ème anniversaire que ces articles ont été réunis. Parmi l'un des premiers, Dieter Stauder a su reconnaître l'importance que revêt la mise en oeuvre effective du droit des brevets dans le besoin d'assurer une meilleure protection de ces droits. Cet engouement naissait avec sa thèse, publiée en 1975, qui traitait de „Contrefaçon de brevet et échanges économiques transfrontaliers", et se poursuit encore aujourd'hui au travers de nombreuses publications. L'une de ses plus grandes oeuvres, d'ailleurs, „Etude de droit comparé sur le procès de la contrefaçon de brevet et des dessins et des modèles en République Fédérale d'Allemagne, Grande Bretagne, France et Italie", parue en 1988, mettait en relief la nécessité d'un travail d'harmonisation au sein de l'Europe. Membre fondateur du Colloque des juges européens des brevets, Directeur de la Section Internationale du CEIPI, Dieter Stauder s'est déjà offert son propre cadeau d'anniversaire: la nouvelle édition du commentaire Singer/Stauder sur la Convention sur le brevet européen. Charmant orateur, professeur admiré, directeur au caractère enjoué, et espérons le, pour longtemps encore, ceci est un hommage bien mérité.

Christopher Heath
Laurence Petit

Dieter Stauder with the editors of this volume

Contents

About the Authors and Editors

Ivan B. Ahlert
Fritz Blumer
J.J. (Jan) Brinkhof
Giovanni Francesco Casucci
Prof. W.R. Cornish
Janusz Fiolka
Joaquim Eugenio Goulart
Christopher Heath
David Llewelyn
Timothy P. Maloney
Hans Marshall
Thomas Pattloch
Laurence Petit
Dieter Stauder
Ivo Telec
Monica Witthaus
Jay Yang (Young-June Yang)

Ivan B. Ahlert
Dannemann, Siemsen, Bigler & Ipanema Moreira
R. Marques de Olinda 70, Botafogo
Rio de Janeiro, RJ, 22251-040
Brazil
Telephone: +55 21 2553-1811
Facsimile: +55 21 2553-1812
Email: ahlert@dannemann.com.br
Website: www.dannemann.com.br

Curriculum Vitae

Specialisation:
Patent law, design law, unfair competition; advising; administrative prosecution; assisting litigation.

Professional memberships:
FICPI (member of C.E.T. and reporter of C.E.T. Group 3 on International Patent matters), AIPPI, LES, ICC (former chairman of working group on Deviation of IP registration fees), ABPI (former chairman of the Patent Commission), ABAPI, and member of the advisory board of IDS—Dannemann Siemsen Institute for Intellectual Property Studies.

Career:
Joined Dannemann, Siemsen, Bigler & Ipanema Moreira in 1981, now a partner. Teacher of the Industrial Property Training Course of ABAPI, guest teacher at other courses. Technical assistant and expert of the judge in court actions related to patent infringement and unfair competition. Author of several amendments to the Bill of the new Industrial Property Law. Representative of ABPI, ABAPI and FICPI in working sessions at WIPO concerning the PLT, the SPLT and the PCT reform.

Publications:
Publications on patent topics in Portuguese in national periodicals, books and newspapers and in English in international magazines such as IIC, Managing Intellectual Property, and Latin American Law & Business Report. Former member of the Editorial Commission of ABPI.

Personal:
Degree in Mechanical Engineering by Federal University of Rio de Janeiro. Guest researcher at the Max Planck Institute for Foreign and International Patent, Copyright and Competition Law in Munich (1994). Languages: Portuguese and English, and working knowledge of German, Spanish and French.

Fritz Blumer
Homburger
Weinbergstr. 56|58
8006 Zürich
Switzerland
Telephone: +41 (0)43 222 1000
Facsimile: + 41 (0)43 222 1500
Email: fritz.blumer@homburger.ch

Curriculum Vitae

Born 25 October 1960.

Electrical Engineering Studies at the Swiss Federal Institute of Technology (ETH Zurich, Diploma 1986), followed by a number of years of practice in engineering.

Law Studies at St. Gallen University (PhD 1996) and Harvard Law School (LL.M. 2000).

Visiting researcher at the Max Planck Institute for Foreign and International Patent, Copyright and Competition Law in Munich (1992/93).

Various publications on patent and civil litigation topics, lecturer at the post-graduate program for intellectual property at ETH Zurich (NDS IP). Admitted to the Swiss bar as of 1996, specialising in the fields of patent and other IP litigation and advisory work.

J.J. (Jan) Brinkhof
Stibbe
P.O. Box 75640
1070 AP Amsterdam
Netherlands
Telephone: +31 (0)20 5 460 632
Facsimile: +31 (0)20 5 460 731
Email: jan.brinkhof@stibbe.nl

Curriculum Vitae

Specialisation:
Industrial property law in general and patent law in particular; litigation; arbitration; advising.

Professional memberships:
Board Member AIPPI Dutch Group.

Career:
Patent judge until 2000. Former Presiding Judge IP Chamber of the Court of Appeals, The Hague. Former External member of the Enlarged Board of Appeal of the European Patent Office.

Part-time professor of IP law at Utrecht University. Supervisor and teacher of training courses for patent and trade mark attorneys.

Publications:
Publications on various IP topics in Dutch and international magazines. Editor of the Dutch IP magazine Bijblad bij de Industriële Eigendom.

Personal:
Nijmegen University (1969). PhD. Languages: Dutch, English, German.

Giovanni Francesco Casucci

Clifford Chance
Via Clerici 7,
20121 Milano
Italy
Telephone: +39 02 806341
Facsimile: +39 02 80634200
Email: giovanni.casucci@cliffordchance.com

Curriculum Vitae

Counsel, Head of the IP Dept. of Clifford Chance, Milano, Director of the Master Program Industrial Property Management at the Polytechnic School of Engineering—Milano (www.mip.polimi.it/ipm).

Expertise
Industrial property (litigation, legal opinions and licensing) and commercial law (litigation, legal opinions and commercial agreements).

Director of the Master in Industrial Property Management (IPM), at the MIP- Polytechnic School of Engineering of Milano.

Author of various publications on industrial property.

Frequent lecturer at national and international conferences and seminars.

As an expert on intellectual and industrial property, Dr. Casucci has completed a research contract on "Study on protection and defence of intellectual property rights for the textile and clothing industry" (responsible for the Far East countries) organised by the European Commission, 1997.

Visiting Expert at the US Court Of Appeal for the Federal Circuit (CAFC), with the Honourable Judge Arthur J. Gajarsa, 2000.

STRATA—ETAN expert member at the European Commission DG Research on the research project "Role and strategic use of IPR in international research collaboration", 2000–2001.

Languages: Italian, English and French.

Prof. W.R. Cornish
IP Unit
Faculty of Law
10 West Road
Cambridge
Great Britain
Email: wrc1000@hermes.cam.ac.uk

Curriculum Vitae

Graduated from the Universities of Adelaide and Oxford. Holds LL.D. of Cambridge University and an Honarary Doctorate from Edinburgh University.

Master of the Bench of Gray's Inn, Queen's Counsel and Fellow of the British Academy (chair of Law Section, 2001–2004).

Retired from the Herchel Smith Chair of Intellectual Property Law at Cambridge University in October 2004; President of Magdalene College, Cambridge, 1998–2001. Chair of Centre for European Legal Studies, Cambridge, 1991–1994. Academic Director, British Law Centre, Warsaw University since 1992.

External academic member of the Max Planck Institute for Intellectual Property, Competition and Tax Law in Munich, Germany, as well as co-editor of the Institute's periodical, International Review of Intellectual Property and Competition Law (IIC).

Author of *The Jury* (1968, 1970); *Intellectual Property* (1981, 1989, 1996. 1999, 2003, now with David Llewelyn); (with Fiona Clark, Sir Robin Jacob and others) *Encyclopedia of UK and European Patent Law* (1978 onwards); *Law and Society in England, 1750–1950* (1989); (forthcoming with others) *Oxford History of the Laws of England* (volumes for 1820–1914).

Janus Fiolka
Patent and Trademark Attorney
Ul. Stachowicza 18, V p.
30-103 Cracow
Poland
Email: janusz@dr-fiolka.com

Curriculum Vitae

Specialisation:
Industrial property law, litigation, advising.

Professional membership:
Board Member (Reporter) AIPPI Polish Group.

Career:
1972–1995 researcher at the Intellectual Property Institute, Jagiellonian University. Former Fellow of the Max Planck Institute for Foreign and International Patent, Copyright and Competition Law, Munich. Part time lecturer in intellectual property at Warsaw Business School (Polish Academy of Sciences). Patent and Trademark Attorney, Cracow, Poland.

Publications:
Some 100 publications on various topics in Polish and international magazines. Member of Editorial Board of Copyright World.

Personal:
Born 22 October 1949. Jagiellonian University (1972). PhD (1981). Languages: Polish, English, German, Russian.

Joaquim Eugenio Goulart
Dannemann, Siemsen, Bigler & Ipanema Moreira
R. Marques de Olinda 70, Botafogo
Rio de Janeiro, RJ, 22251-040
Brazil
Telephone: +55 21 2553-1811
Facsimile: +55 21 2553-1812
Email: jgoulart@dannemann.com.br
Website: www.dannemann.com.br

Curriculum Vitae

Specialisation:
Litigation in cases involving Intellectual Property Law.

Professional memberships:
Member of the Brazilian Bar Association, INTA, American Bar Association, ABAPI, AIPPI, LES, ICANN at Large.

Career:
Joined Dannemann, Siemsen, Bigler & Ipanema Moreira in 1997, now a partner and Coordinator of the Litigation Department. Participate in hearings with Judges and Justices from the Higher Courts, including the Supreme Court.

Publications:
Co-author, in Portuguese, of a book commenting the Brazilian Industrial Property Law and author of several articles about intellectual property, published in the Brazilian Intellectual Property Magazine. Regular columnist, in English, for the magazine "IP Litigator".

Personal:
Degree in Law at the Catholic University of Rio de Janeiro, LLM in Intellectual Property Law at The John Marshall Law School, 2002, Master in Corporate Law by the Fundação Getúlio Vargas of Rio de Janeiro, Professor on the LLM in the Industrial Property Law Course of the Catholic University of Rio de Janeiro. Languages: Portuguese and English.

Christopher Heath
Max Planck Institute for Intellectual Property,
Competition and Tax Law
Marstallplatz 1
80539 München
Germany
Email: chh@ip.mpg.de

Curriculum Vitae

Born 16 April 1964.

Studies of law in Konstanz, the LSE and Edinburgh between 1982 and 1989. Qualified as an attorney-at-law in Germany.

Between 1989 and 1992, DAAD scholarship for Japan and work in the law firm of Mori Sôgô, Tokyo.

Since 1992, Head of East Asian Department, Max Planck Institute for Foreign and International Patent, Copyright and Competition Law, Munich,

PhD, University of Salzburg, 2001.

About 100 publications on Japanese, Asian and international intellectual property, competition and antitrust law.

Editor of the Max Planck Series on Asian Intellectual Property Law.

David Llewelyn
White & Case
7-11 Moorgate
London EC2R 6HH, England
Telephone: (44-20) 7600-7300
Facsimile: (44-20) 7600-7030
Email: dllewelyn@whitecase.com

Curriculum Vitae

European Head of Intellectual Property at international law firm White & Case and Senior Visiting Professor at the Intellectual Property Law Unit at Queen Mary College, University of London.

At the beginning of the 1980s he spent nearly two years as a Research Fellow at the Max Planck Institute for Intellectual Property and Competition Law in Munich working with Dieter Stauder among others. He is a co-author of *Kerly's Law of Trade Marks and Trade Names* (13th ed. 2001), the leading practitioners' textbook and speaks regularly at international conferences on IP law.

Timothy P. Maloney
Fitch, Even, Tabin & Flannery
120 South LaSalle Street
Suite 1600
Chicago, IL 60603
U.S.A.
Telephone: (312) 577-7000
Facsimile: (312) 577-7007
Email: tpmalo@fitcheven.com

Curriculum Vitae

Born 12 May 1966.

B.S. Chemical Engineering, University of Illinois 1988.

Process engineer in the oil industry 1988–1990.

J.D. University of Illinois College of Law 1993.

Career:
Partner of Fitch, Even, Tabin & Flannery, a law firm specializing in intellectual property matters. Practice entails all aspects of intellectual property procurement, management and protection. Particular expertise in intellectual property litigation and licensing, including disputes involving patent, trade secret, trademark, unfair competition and antitrust matters. Frequently asked to counsel clients on intellectual property strategy, valua-

tion and management issues, joint technology ventures and intellectual property licensing.

Registered patent attorney, a member of the Illinois Bar, and of numerous federal courts. Active member of the Illinois State and American Bar Associations, the Intellectual Property Law Association of Chicago, the American Institute of Chemical Engineers, the Midwest Entrepreneurs Forum, the International Association for the Protection of Industrial Property, and the Licensing Executive Society.

Author of several publications regarding patent litigation and strategy.

Hans Marshall
Magdalenenstr. 6 a
82131 Gauting
Germany
Email : H2Marshall@aol.com

Curriculum Vitae

Born 22 November 1936 in Karlsruhe, Germany.

Law studies in Munich from 1956 to 1960, ending with the First State Examination. From 1960 to 1964 further training as a junior lawyer. In 1964 passed the Second State Examination

Beginning 1964 work as a public prosecutor and later on as a judge in penal and civil matters at the County Court and District Court in Munich.

As of 1975 presiding judge in a chamber for the enforcement of industrial and intellectual property at the District Court in Munich, dealing with infringement litigation involving patents, utility models, plant varieties, trade marks, design models and copyrights.

From 1987, presiding judge of the corresponding chamber of the Court of Appeal in Munich.

Retired as of April 2000.

Thomas Pattloch
Schulz Noack Baerwinkel
Suite 2302 International Trade Center
2201 Yan An Road (West)
200336 Shanghai
China
Telephone: 0086 21 6219 8370
Fascimile: 0086 21 6219 6849
Email: thomas.pattloch@snblaw.com

Curriculum Vitae

LL.M.(Eur.), German Attorney-at-law

Date and place of birth:	16 February 1971, Offenbach/Main, Germany
Nationality:	German
1991–1997	Law studies in Munich, Germany
1993–1994	Mandarin studies in Taipei, Taiwan
1997	First legal bar exam and training as junior legal barrister with the Munich Higher Civil Court
1998–2002	Legal thesis: "The International Private Law in Respect to the Intellectual Property of the People's Republic of China" at the Max Planck Institute for Intellectual Property, Competition Law and Tax Law, Munich and University of Passau
1998–1999	Research stay at Beijing University
2000	Second legal bar exam; part time work in a China team of an international law firm in Munich
2001	Master of European and International Economic Law program in Munich
2001–2003	Scientific researcher at the Max Planck Institute, responsible for Greater China and Singapore
	Dec. 2001 Admitted to the bar, German Attorney-at-law
Since July 2003	Attorney-at-Law for the Hamburg based German law firm Schulz Noack Bärwinkel in Shanghai; Chairman of the IPR-Working Group of the EU Chamber of Commerce Shanghai since January 2004

Laurence Petit
Centre d'Etudes Internationales de la
Propriété Industrielle
(C.E.I.P.I.)
11, av. du Maréchal Juin
67000 Strasbourg
France
Email: laurence.petit@ip.mpg.de

Curriculum Vitae

1973	Born in Alger, Algeria
1991—1995	Study of Law in Lyon, France

1997	LL.M Augsburg University, Germany
Since 1999	Ph.D. Student, Lyon/Strasbourg Universities
	Assistant at the International Section of the C.E.I.P.I, Strasbourg
	Lecturer at the C.E.I.P.I
	Lecturer at the Faculty of Law of Strasbourg
	Researcher at the Max Planck Institute for Intellectual Property Law
Since 2000	Publications in the field of Industrial Property, especially on Patent Law
Since 2004	Lawyer, DG 5.2.1, European Patent Office, Munich
Membership:	ATRIP

Dieter Stauder
Professeur à la Faculté de Droit de Strasbourg
Directeur de la Section Internationale du
Centre d'Etudes Internationales de la
Propriété Industrielle
11 Avenue du Marechal Juin
67000 Strasbourg
France
Also:
European Patent Office
Section 5.2.1 (International Cooperation)
50331 München
Germany
Email: dstauder@epo.org

Curriculum Vitae

Dieter Stauder, to whom this book is dedicated, was born on 20 October 1940 in Bad Kreuznach, Germany. He studied law at the Universities of Freiburg and Munich, and came to the Max Planck Institute in 1968, first as an assistant to Professor Beier, later to Professor Schricker. During his time at the Max Planck Institute between 1968 and 1992, Dieter Stauder was head of the Commonwealth Department. He finished his PhD on patent infringement in cross-border trade in 1975. A complete bibliography of his works is contained in the French edition of his Festschrift (first edition), published as Volume 48 of the CEIPI collection Strasbourg, 2001. Since 1992, Dieter Stauder has headed the international section of the CEIPI Institute in Strasbourg. There he was made Professor in 1997.

Ivo Telec
Palacky University of Olomouc and
Masaryk University of Brno Czechia
Masaryk University, Law Faculty
Veveří 70, 611 80 Brno, Czechia
Email: Ivo.Telec@law.muni.cz

Curriculum Vitae

Professor of civil law at Palack University of Olomouc and Masaryk University of Brno and attorney-at-law.

Member of permanent civil law commission of the Czech Government Legislative Council and of the board of the legislative and legal advisers of president of the Czech Republic.

Specialisation in intellectual property law in general and copyright and neighbouring rights in particular (legal opinions, licensing).

Publications on various IP topics, particularly Commentary on the Czech Copyright Act.

Monica Witthaus
Goupil Witthaus & Asociados
Tte. Gral. J. D. Perón 1719 1° A
C 1037 ACG Buenos Aires
Argentina
Tel /Facsimile: 00 54 11 4371 8523
Telephone: 00 54 11 4375 5204
Email: mwitthaus@avocats.com.ar

Curriculum Vitae

Attorney at law and patent attorney (agente de Propiedad Industrial) in Argentina.

Specialisation:
Intellectual Property law, contracts, advising, litigation.

Partner of Goupil Witthaus & Asociados

(IP law, corporate law , business law)

Professor of IP law and German (Legal Language) at Universidad de Buenos Aires UBA.

Publications :
Publications on various IP topics and contract law in Argentina and Germany. Lecturer at conferences and Seminars on IP law.

Personal:

Universidad de Buenos Aires (1986),

Scholarship at the Max Planck Institut for Foreign and International Patent, Copyright and Competition Law in Munich (2000),

Stage in Uexküll & Stolberg Patent Attorneys, Hamburg , Germany (1992)

Stage at the EPO , Munich, Germany (1998)

Languages: Spanish, German, English, French.

Jay Yang (Young-June Yang)

KIM & CHANG
Seyang Bldg., 223 Naeja-Dong,
Chongro-Ku, Seoul
Korea 110-720
Telephone: +822 3703 1060
Facsimile: +822 737 9091~3
Email: yjyang@kimchang.com

Curriculum Vitae

Jay (Young-June) Yang is a senior partner at Kim & Chang and has over 20 years of experience in litigation, enforcement and dispute resolution involving intellectual property issues, foreign and domestic customs seizures, and international and domestic licensing and distribution disputes. Mr. Yang has also led IP litigation teams with the goal of obtaining landmark decisions in Korea. He was admitted to the Korean Bar in 1977, and the New York State Bar in 1986. His legal educational degrees include a B. Jur. (1977) from Seoul National University and an LL.M. (1985) from the University of Michigan Law School.

Introduction

DIETER STAUDER

Patent infringement procedures are an instrument whereby the patentee defends his protected invention against unlawful use by third parties. Or, more precisely, the patentee by means of the infringement procedure wants to protect himself against an alleged infringer. After all, there is hardly any other procedure where it is as difficult to ascertain an infringement of the protected right than in the field of patent law. The patent is no solid object whose damage can be easily detected, and even amongst the intellectual property rights, together with trade mark law, it may belong to those rights whose infringement is not easy to determine.

Yet while a trade mark is still visually perceptible to the beholder wanting to determine infringement, the patent is a right described by words, and those words, written into a claim, are so complicated that laymen and lawyers alike fail to understand them. This special feature marks the patent right: It is a technical right of mostly high complexity that even to the informed laymen requires an unusually high degree of expertise to understand the subject matter.

For this reason, this special law requires specialists. Specialists in the field come in the shape of patent attorneys, persons skilled in technical arts or natural sciences and trained in the field of patent law. Furthermore, specialised attorneys trained in the subject matter are necessary, just as especially knowledgeable judges that work daily with the subject matter. It is less important that these non-technical persons have technical knowledge. Rather, with legal knowledge they have to tread in a field where they require counsel and support by experts and where they themselves have enough patience and skill to work with difficult technical problems.

What do the above findings mean for the explanation of patent infringement procedures in a number of different countries? One consequence of the special nature of patent infringement procedures can be found in the country reports: that apart from the rules of ordinary civil procedure, patent infringement procedures have developed their own forms of procedure with special rules and necessities that increasingly show similarities amongst those countries concerned. Only two special features should be mentioned that determine the efficiency of patent infringement procedures: for one, an efficient and possibly speedy safeguarding of evidence regarding the alleged infringement, and, second, the fact that the only sanction of real importance on behalf of the patentee is the grant of speedy injunctive relief. This requires procedures that are quick, but also with a sufficient amount of certainty. Both support the claim for specialised attorneys and judges.

In addition to these two characteristics of infringement procedures, there is a third that is common to all. In principle, patent infringement proceedings revolve around only two disputed issues: first, if in light of the state of the art, the patent is valid and, second, if the allegedly infringing device does indeed fall within the scope of the patent. The identity of these two disputed questions should have led to a uniform court system a long time ago. Especially due to the effect of the European patent and the harmonising effect stemming therefrom, in addition to a generally measurable approximation of legal systems around the world, the practice of effective patent protection in infringement procedures is moving in one direction. The future will show if this will continue.

It should be added that in relation to the number of patents in the individual countries and around the world in general, patent infringement procedures are an extreme exception. It is estimated that only one percent of all patents ever become the object of patent infringement procedures. Patent infringement procedures are thus limited to serious disputes between competitors, but it is also the *ultima ratio* when there is no other way of agreement between the parties. This *ultima ratio* must be effective and deterrent, otherwise prior consultations, especially on the side of the patentee, are unattractive and the value of the right diluted. The interest in patent infringement procedures from a comparative and fact-finding view had its beginning in the 1970s at the Max Planck Institute in Munich. Soon, the topic was picked up and today is the object of discussions, seminars, and writings from academics and practitioners everywhere. After the PCT, the European patent system as well as the other modern patent systems of highly developed countries such as the US, Japan, etc., have brought the granting procedures of patents to a comparatively high level, the interest is now focusing on the effective protection of rights that were often granted and obtained as a result of great cost and effort.

Patent infringement procedures have become an established and recognised legal instrument that is decisively supported by the standards of the TRIPS Agreement. It will be interesting to see if there will be a harmonised European jurisdiction for patent enforcement, be it under the ambit of the European or Community patent. In order to foster European harmonisation, European Patent Judges Symposia for Member States of the European Patent Convention have been held every two years since 1982. The purpose of these meetings is the exchange of information in the field of patent law, and the learning from each other. In a remarkable number of cases, case law in Europe has been harmonised since then. The plans for further European harmonisation and their eventual realisation may well be a model for an even further internationalisation.

A

International Patent Enforcement

1
Comparative Overview and the TRIPS Enforcement Provisions

CHRISTOPHER HEATH

I. Introduction

This chapter is meant to provide a comparative overview of national enforcement mechanisms in light of the TRIPS requirements specified in **Arts. 41–50**. As there is no "international" case law on enforcement, and enforcement mechanisms by their very nature are subject to national law, the TRIPS provisions can only be interpreted in a meaningful manner by making reference to the enforcement mechanisms of individual countries. However, the TRIPS provisions are not commented on in the order they appear in the Agreement, but rather in the sequence of civil procedure: Although the final measures of injunctive relief, damages and other remedies (**Arts. 44–46 TRIPS**) in the TRIPS Agreement precede the provision on interim injunctions (**Art. 50**), the latter already due to their nature have to be decided by a court prior to deciding on final measures.

The term "enforcement" just as the term "intellectual property" is considerably new. "Enforcement" is not a term that would find equivalents in other languages, for which reason it has been difficult to translate. The French may talk about "*la mise en œuvre*", yet it does not have quite the same ring to it. The German term "*Rechtsdurchsetzung*" comes close to enforcement, yet would not only refer to acts against an infringement. "Enforcement" as understood in the modern sense and by the TRIPS Agreement does not relate to any acts necessary for *obtaining* an IP right, but for *putting an end to infringing acts* in order to render the IP right effective.

"Enforcement" does not necessarily determine the means of action. These can be civil, criminal or administrative. *Civil* because private rights are at stake: patents, trade marks, and copyrights may have their administrative sides, particularly where a granting process is involved, yet thereafter would not much differ from real property rights, enforcement of which would also be predominantly civil. But just as acts of vandalism or theft represent criminal offences violating private property, intellectual property infringement may also qualify as a criminal offence, e.g., where committed on a professional scale.[1]

[1] However, a number of free trade agreements, e.g. the US-Singapore Free Trade Agreement, require the introduction of criminal offences even beyond what TRIPS would require. It is questionable if this would lead to an effective strengthening of IP rights. See also below IX.

Administrative enforcement, e.g., by the Patent and Trade Mark Offices, may have advantages due to the often complex nature of intellectual property rights. Administrative agencies that have to determine registrability of an IP right may also be well qualified to determine its scope for the purposes of enforcement.[2] Furthermore, there are no alternatives to administrative enforcement in areas exclusively handled by the administration. For IP matters, this is particularly the case where the export and import of goods is concerned. Border control is thus one of the most important fields of administrative IP enforcement.

The manner of enforcement is also determined by the complexity of the subject matter. Looking at a patent infringement case in, e.g., the UK, an impressive number of highly paid specialists are involved: the judge, two senior barristers (QC) on both sides, aided by two junior barristers. The barristers have been instructed by solicitors, and we may thus well find two solicitors on each side. Because of the technical nature of the patent, barristers and solicitors may be assisted by patent attorneys and/or technical experts. The patentee, often accompanied, would be represented by the head of his patent department. Determining infringement therefore becomes complex, time-consuming and costly. It is not least for this reason that most countries would prefer to leave IP enforcement to the initiative of private parties, e.g., by decriminalising infringements[3] or by public prosecution refusing to take up cases.[4]

Finally, "enforcement" does not refer to any specific remedy. Remedies could be administrative fines, criminal fines or prison terms, or civil remedies such as injunctions (**Art. 44 TRIPS**), compensation (**Art. 45 TRIPS**), destruction of infringing goods or an apology (**Art. 46 TRIPS**). Of all these, the most sought after is the *injunction*. An injunction is meant to put an end to acts of infringement. The importance of injunctive relief for IP infringement stems from three factors: First, to avoid further market confusion and thereby the erosion of the IP owner's competitive position where cases of trade marks or unfair competition are concerned. Second, by upholding the

---

[2] Administrative enforcement mechanisms against infringement can be particularly found in Asia. In Vietnam and China, civil enforcement was not even available until a couple of years ago. In Korea and Japan, the Patent Office can be asked to determine the scope of a patent right in infringement procedures, an avenue fairly common in Korea, but not in Japan. In the Philippines, the Patent Office offers a forum for handling intellectual property disputes that many right owners find preferable to court proceedings due to the expedited nature of proceedings.

[3] E.g., in Taiwan, patent infringement under the revised 2001 Patent Act is no longer a criminal offence, which means that patentees have to rely on private enforcement: See below IX.

[4] While in Germany the first half century of patent law between 1877 and 1917 was dominated by the criminal enforcement of patents, subsequent cases have been almost exclusively civil and reflect the attitude that public prosecution should only take place where public interests are indeed at stake: see below IX.

IP owner's monopoly which (at least for patents and copyrights) has only been granted for a limited period of time: If any infringer could get away with monetary compensation, the IP right would lose its function of excluding all others but the owner from its use. It is only the exclusivity that allows the IP owner to charge a monopoly rent for the protected product. Third, injunctive relief is often the most effective remedy, as damage claims are often difficult to prove.

Last but not least, IP infringement has increasingly become a matter of strategy and tactic. In the same way as strategies for registering IP rights have developed,[5] enforcement has also become an increasingly complex pattern in the commercial strategies of a company.[6]

II. Enforcement and International Law

1. General

Neither in terminology nor in substance did "enforcement" find its way into international agreements on intellectual property rights prior to TRIPS. Arts. 9, 10 Paris Convention contain some rudimentary rules on "seizure on importation", an administrative remedy that can also be found in the Madrid Arrangement for the Repression of False and Deceptive Indications of Source on Goods of 1891. But ensuring seizure upon importation was merely meant to plug a gap in most domestic legislation that did not give special rights of importation and thus made it difficult for the right owner to act on his own behalf in this respect. Furthermore, some provisions of the Paris Convention refer to "effective" remedies, e.g., Art. 10bis ("effective protection against all acts of unfair competition"). More is not specified in the Convention, however.

In addition, there are a number of conventions that deal with the effects of legal disputes. E.g., the Brussels[7] and Lugano[8] Conventions on jurisdiction lay down uniform rules for the EU and EFTA countries regarding jurisdiction

[5] E.g., Rahn, Patentstrategien japanischer Unternehmen (Patent Strategies of Japanese Enterprises), GRUR Int. 1994, 377.

[6] E.g., Moore/Michel/Lupo, Patent Litigation and Strategy, St. Paul, Minn., 2nd ed. 2003.

[7] Convention on Jurisdiction and the Enforcement of Judgments in Civil and Commercial Matters of 27 September 1968, text under www.curia.eu.int; now replaced by the Council Regulation (EC) 44/2001 of 22 December 2001 on jurisdiction and the recognition and enforcement of judgments in civil and commercial matters, O.J. EC of 16 January 2002, L12/1. Denmark is not a participant and remains bound by the Brussels Convention.

[8] Convention on Jurisdiction and the Enforcement of Judgments in Civil and Commercial Matters of 16 September 1988, available at www.curia.eu.int. The Convention was signed between the then EC member states and Norway, Austria, Switzerland, Finland and Sweden. The non-EC members explicitly acknowledged the ECJ's role as interpreting the Convention.

within Europe, and with the purpose of avoiding double litigation. Finally, the Hague Agreements[9] concern assistance in civil procedures.

The scarcity of international rules concerning enforcement stands in marked contrast to what has been achieved in the field of *obtaining* intellectual property rights. Here, a great number of international conventions facilitate the international filing for patents and trade marks: the Paris Convention of 1883 grants a priority period of one year to patents and utility models, and six months to designs and trade marks; the Patent Cooperation Treaty of 1970 defers the requirements of translation and national filing in other countries for another 20 months beyond the one year priority interval in order to provide the applicant with a preliminary search and (for some countries) examination; the Patent Law Treaty 2000 (not yet in force) will further streamline formalities of the application procedure. In the field of trade marks, the Madrid Agreement of 1891 and the Madrid Protocol of 1989 both allow the applicant to obtain protection in other countries on the basis of just one international filing; the Trade Mark Law Treaty of 1994 streamlines application procedures in making certain formal requirements such as the number of copies to be supplied to national patent offices more uniform; and the Nice Agreement on the classification of marks 1957 provides trade mark applicants with a uniform catalogue of goods and services used and applied by all domestic patent offices (the Nice Agreement has 69 members, yet is adhered to by a number of other countries, too).

There is thus a marked contrast between efforts to facilitate and harmonise filing procedures on the one hand and enforcement procedures on the other.

2. Difficulty of Uniform Rules

There are a number of reasons why it has been easier to harmonise rules for *obtaining* IP rights than for *enforcing* them. For one, the basic rules laid down in 1883 by the Paris Convention were negotiated between a very limited number of countries. They required the founding members to change parts of their industrial property laws, yet left most of the application procedures untouched. To this day, there are huge differences in granting procedures, namely between countries that conduct a substantive examination for patents and trade marks (e.g., Japan, the US, the UK and Germany) and those countries with a mere registration system (e.g., France and Italy). When discussions on a uniform system of industrial property rights started in

---

[9] Hague Convention on Private International Law of 17 July 1905, www.hcch.net (French only); Hague Convention on Civil Procedure of 1 March 1954 (www.hcch.net); Hague Convention on the Service Abroad of Judicial and Extra-judicial Documents in Civil or Commercial Matters of 15 November 1965 (www.hcch.net); Hague Convention on the Taking of Evidence Abroad in Civil and Commercial Matters of 18 March 1970 (www.hcch.net) and the attempts to conclude a Hague Agreement on Jurisdiction and Foreign Judgments in Civil and Commercial Matters along the lines of the Brussels and Lugano Conventions that are currently under way (www.hcch.net).

1873, it soon became apparent that a uniform system of world patents or trade marks could not be achieved at that stage due to the national differences in granted and enforcing IP rights.

Next, it was to the advantage of the IP system and its users that granting procedures were undertaken by specialised offices outside the general administration. This meant that harmonising certain principles of application procedure could be undertaken without any repercussions towards the system of administrative law in general. Enforcement procedures on the other hand could not claim such advantage. Rather, civil enforcement in each country is deeply steeped in the domestic system of civil procedure in general. A uniform system of enforcement would have meant specific courts only dealing with such matters – an impractical solution for countries where only a very limited number of IP lawsuits are raised.[10]

A certain harmonisation in matters of infringement only became necessary where uniform patents were granted for several countries, e.g., by an institution such as the European Patent Office. Here, the scope of patent rights had to be specified both for the granting authority and the courts (Art. 69 European Patent Convention). It is not possible for a granting authority to grant patents without knowing how these patents will be interpreted by national courts.[11] This should also be borne in mind where countries are thinking of a reciprocal recognition of patent rights: This only makes sense where the patentee and the granting authority can be certain of the scope given to the patent.

Just to mention some of the issues that a harmonisation of enforcement procedures in civil matters would have to encompass: availability of pre-trial measures; contents of the initial claim; service of such claim and other documents submitted to the court; rules of jurisdiction; rules for obtaining and interpreting evidence; role of the judge and the legal representatives in an action; rules on who should have standing to sue; powers of legal representatives and rules on who would be capable of being a legal representative (patent attorneys?); rules for interim measures; rules on how a trial should be conducted; rules on the interpretation of IP rights; relationship between infringement and nullity; rules on what remedies would be available; rules on appeals.[12] The TRIPS Agreement was the first that tried to set some form of minimum rules for a number of issues mentioned.

---

[10] Which does not mean that an increasing number of countries nowadays refer matters of patent enforcement to specialised courts or specialised divisions within the courts. E.g. in the UK and Thailand, only one first instance court is competent to handle cases of patent infringement. In Japan and the US, there is a common appeal court for these matters. In Indonesia, special commercial courts handle IP cases. In Germany and Italy, a designated number of national courts have jurisdiction over patent enforcement matters.

[11] As was highlighted by the decision of the EPO's Enlarged Board of Appeal of 11 December 1989, OJ 1990, 93 – "Mobil Oil III".

[12] An attempt of harmonising some of these issues has been made by the EC Enforcement Directive, see Chapter 2 for details.

3. History of TRIPS and Enforcement

Interestingly enough, the starting point for including intellectual property rights into the framework of international trade of the GATT Agreement were increasing numbers of pirated or counterfeited goods (for a definition, see below VIII) on markets all over the world. The initial attempt was thus limited to a framework to stop dealing in counterfeit goods.[13] Subsequent negotiations broadened this mandate. As a preparation to a coming GATT round, a 1982 Ministerial Declaration recommended

> "to examine the question of counterfeit goods with a view to determining the appropriateness of joint action in the GATT framework on the trade aspects of commercial counterfeiting, and if such joint action is found to be appropriate, the modalities for such action, having full regard to the competence of other international organisations. For the purposes of such examination, the Contracting Parties request the Director-General to hold consultations with the Director-General of WIPO in order to clarify the legal and institutional aspects involved."[14]

Opposition to such mandate came particularly from Brazil and India with two arguments: First, international trade should deal with tangible rather than intangible goods, and, second, WIPO should handle all issues of intellectual property.[15] Further negotiations, particularly in the first half of 1986 have finally led to the inclusion of both intellectual property rights and services in the new GATT Round that was opened on 20 September 1986 in Punte del Este, Uruguay. In the Common Declaration of 20 September 1986, the mandate to negotiate matters of intellectual property rights was outlined as follows:

> "In order to reduce the distortions and impediments to international trade, and taking into account the need to promote effective and adequate protection of intellectual property rights, and to ensure that measures and procedures to enforce intellectual property rights do not themselves become barriers to legitimate trade, the negotiations shall aim to clarify GATT provisions and elaborate as appropriate new rules and disciplines.
>
> Negotiations shall aim to develop a multilateral framework of principles, rules and disciplines dealing with international trade in counterfeit goods, taking into account work already undertaken in the GATT.
>
> These negotiation shall be without prejudice to other complementary initiatives that may be taken in the World International Property Organization and elsewhere to deal with these matters."[16]

---

[13] Agreement on Measures to Discourage the Importation of Counterfeit Goods, GATT Document L/4817 of 31 July 1979, reprinted in 12 IIC 201 [1981].

[14] 38th Session at Ministerial Level Ministerial Declaration, reprinted in GATT, BISD 30th Supplement, 19 (1983).

[15] Bradley, Intellectual Property Rights, Investment and Trade in Services in the Uruguay Round, 23 Stanford Journal of International Law 57, 66 (1987).

[16] Ministerial Declaration on the Uruguay Round, GATT Document No. MIN.DEC (20 September 1986).

The Ministerial Declaration set the tone for the following negotiations between the opening on 20 September 1986 and the eventual conclusion of the WTO/TRIPS Agreement in Marrakech, Morocco, on 15 April 1994. While the first phase of the negotiations in 1986/87 concerned aspects of counterfeiting and piracy including border measures,[17] a number of European countries wanted intellectual property rights to be strengthened in general.[18]

As a consequence, not only border measures on counterfeit goods, but the whole framework of intellectual property rights became part of the WTO Agreement.

III. TRIPS – General Principles of Enforcement: Arts. 41, 42

1. Procedures in General

Given the fact that the TRIPS Agreement developed out of a framework to combat piracy and counterfeiting, it is no coincidence that one whole part (Part III) of the agreement is dedicated to enforcement, and that this part with 20 provisions is far more detailed than the provisions on, e.g., patents. The high number of provisions also reflects the lack of harmonisation or minimum standards in this area, and the diversity in domestic enforcement systems as described under II above. The emphasis of the TRIPS provision lies in rules for civil enforcement (**Arts. 42–48, 50**) and administrative measures by way of border enforcement (**Arts. 51–60**). **Art. 49** clarifies the fact that infringement can also be dealt with administratively, yet under the same rules as laid down for civil procedures. The structure of **Arts. 42–49** also illustrates that civil enforcement of infringement is regarded as clearly preferable to administrative enforcement. Finally, criminal measures are only mentioned in **Art. 61** and need only be provided for in cases of wilful infringement of patents or copyrights on a commercial scale. This reflects the experience of developed countries that criminal enforcement does not provide a viable alternative to civil procedure.

2. Principles Laid Down in Art. 41

a) **Art. 41.1** requires members to provide a legal framework for effective action against any act of infringement. Such remedies shall be effective against infringing acts, yet also provide safeguards against abuse. In addition, remedies shall constitute a deterrent to further infringement. Already this is difficult to understand, as there is no requirement to provide for punitive sanctions under civil enforcement. **Art. 45.1** states that damages shall be adequate to compensate for the injury, yet this would not have a deterrent

---

[17] Ross/Wasserman, Trade Related Aspects of Intellectual Property Rights – A Negotiating History, Washington 1993, 22.

[18] Ross/Wasserman (above fn. 17) 24, citing the 1988 proposals of the Nordic countries and the EC.

effect. As a deterrent, one can imagine having the infringer pay at least the IP owner's legal expenses, including attorneys' fees. This is set down in **Art. 45.2**, yet only as an optional provision. Within the context of TRIPS, it is thus far from clear what remedies are considered to be deterrent. From an economic point of view, deterrent remedies must be those that go beyond what a lawful user has to invest. If damages are compensatory rather than punitive, these can hardly serve as a deterrent. Burdening the losing party with the winning side's attorney's fees may have a deterrent effect, yet is not mandatory under TRIPS. Providing criminal sanctions can serve as a deterrent, yet is only required in special circumstances as mentioned below (IX). Only injunctive relief is a remedy that a lawful user such as a licensee would not have to face. In the absence of any other "deterrent" provisions, one could thus argue that the legal system should at least provide expedient injunctions (for details, see below V).

The "safeguard against abuse" as mentioned in **Art. 41.1** is further specified in **Art. 48**. Acts against abuse may be the undue exercise of IP rights, e.g., informing third parties of alleged infringements, amounting to unjustified libel or slander. Here, the injured party shall have a right to claim damages that may include attorneys' fees.

b) **Art. 41.2** lays down the basic principles of procedure. These shall be fair and equitable, not unnecessarily complicated or costly, nor entail unreasonable time limits or unwarranted delays. In the wording "fair and equitable", we find the general principle of checks and balances that permeates the enforcement section. Remedies shall be effective, yet take into account the position of both IP owner and alleged infringer. The infringer shall neither be able to continue with his activities undisturbed, nor shall the IP owner be able to harass third parties or initiate unwarranted complaints. The other requirements regarding complexity and delay may be understood in light of what was explained above. By their very nature, IP suits are often complicated. The often necessary involvement of specialists is costly, and the complexity makes delays not uncommon. And still, there are huge discrepancies between certain jurisdictions. Perhaps the most costly IP suits are litigated in the UK and the US. In the latter jurisdiction, an IP lawsuit with an average value of below US$1 million at risk would cost an average of US$400,000 through the end of the suit.[19] In Germany, a comparable lawsuit would only cost a fraction thereof.[20] The average duration of a patent infringement suit in France is six years,[21] while in Japan, it stands at 18.6 months and the target for the district courts Tokyo and Osaka is one year.[22]

---

[19] Maloney, Chapter 15 of this book.

[20] Marshall, Chapter 4 of this book.

[21] Petit, Chapter 5 of this book: "Completely surrealistic" delay. As practically all first instance decisions are appealed, the time of six years refers to first and second instance. If the case goes up to the Supreme Court, 10 years would be the norm.

[22] Heath, Chapter 13 of this book.

Fair and equitable procedures may also encompass some other basic principles. Every party should have the right to be heard and be properly represented in court. Intellectual property being a relatively new subject, many countries have a shortage of qualified lawyers in this field, making professional representation difficult. Also the rules of evidence and the burden of proof should be fair and equitable. In this respect, one rule can be found in **Art. 34** which regards process patents. If the alleged infringer uses a process that the patentee suspects to be covered by the patent, it shall be up to the alleged infringer to prove the contrary. This applies where the final products obtained are identical and the product obtained by the patented process is new and the patentee has made reasonable efforts to enquire about the alleged infringer's process. But fairness also requires the defendant to be protected, particularly where his own trade secrets are concerned. A number of provisions specifically require such protection, even in cases where the information is vital to the IP owner's case. **Art. 34.3** requires the legitimate interests of the defendant in protecting his manufacturing and business secrets to be taken into account, and **Art. 43** requires member states to provide conditions which ensure the protection of confidential information in cases where the defendant is ordered to present evidence. And finally, **Art. 42** requires "means to identify and protect confidential information". Balancing the plaintiff's and the defendant's interests in cases where trade secrets are involved is particularly difficult. The courts in most countries can order *in camera* proceedings that exclude the public from oral hearings. The court can further order the documents of the case to be accessible only to a limited number of persons[23] and impose so-called "gagging orders" on either party.[24] Where the defendant has to produce evidence and claims that trade secrets are at stake, the court must ensure that such an estoppel is not frivolous.[25] Thus, a number of jurisdictions require the relevant documents to be inspected by the judge so as to determine to what extent trade secrets are indeed involved.[26]

Finally, fair and equitable procedures would also require a certain proficiency of judges in deciding IP cases. Due to the specific nature of IP rights, special knowledge and experience in this field is vital in order to ensure timely and well-reasoned decisions. In this respect, **Art. 41.5** provides that there is no obligation to set up special IP courts, and indeed

---

[23] E.g., Sec. 92 Japanese Code of Civil Procedure.

[24] E.g., UK Civil Procedure Rules 1998, Part 31.22.

[25] E.g., Tokyo High Court, 20 May 1997, 30 IIC 452 [1999] – "Sale of Pharmaceuticals": "The intention of protecting trade secrets is not a legitimate reason for refusing an order to produce documents relevant to the other party". See also below.

[26] Such a rule is now contained in Sec. 105(2) Japanese Patent Act. Where evidence is obtained by search orders, similar safeguards are provided by the English Anton Piller (now search) order and the French *saisie contrefaçon*. For details, see IV.

such courts rarely exist for cases of infringement.[27] Many countries, however, have started to limit jurisdiction to only a number of courts: Japan has specific IP divisions at the district courts Tokyo and Osaka, although jurisdiction of these courts in IP matters is not exclusive.[28] In Indonesia, the commercial courts have been given exclusive jurisdiction over IP infringement suits.[29] Not all countries have taken such steps, however. In Italy, until 2004 every one of the about 160 district courts could hear IP cases, making specialised knowledge of the judge unlikely.[30] But even with specialised courts or special divisions, judges will require a number of years of expertise in the field and should thus not be transferred too frequently. Such specialised judges could also be given sufficient career opportunities as an incentive for such specialisation. Judicial expertise is perhaps the most important guarantee for a successful enforcement of IP rights.

c) **Art. 41.3** specifies two further requirements of fair procedure. First, decisions shall be in writing and reasoned, and, second, decisions shall only be based on grounds that the parties had an opportunity to comment on. Having established such a principle, the provision is optional, as are so many in the section on enforcement. While this may be deplorable, one should bear in mind that this is the first international agreement with a section on enforcement, and there are thus no previous agreements or minimum standards which could have been built upon. The requirement of a decision in writing that should be served on both parties could even be broadened. It is regrettable that in many countries, IP decisions are not properly published, making it difficult for users of the IP system to anticipate the results of a possible lawsuit. In addition, publication of decisions also allows academic discussion and international comparison.

d) **Art. 41.4** lays down a very important principle, particularly for those IP rights that are granted by administrative authorities: the right of judicial review of all final administrative decisions, and a right of appeal against any court decision at least regarding the legal aspects. The provision does not use

---

[27] In 1999, Thailand set up a special Intellectual Property and International Trade Court in Bangkok which consists of about 30 full-time and 100 part-time judges: Ariyanuntaka, 30 IIC 360 [1999]. In the US, there is no special IP court in the first instance, yet on appeal. The Court of Appeals of the Federal Circuit hears all appeal cases where intellectual property rights are involved. In addition, some countries provide for specific "patent courts" which do not deal with infringement, but with nullity and revocation of IP rights, thereby functioning as appeal institutions of the patent offices. This would be the case for Germany and Korea. Both countries have in common that the ordinary courts may not hold patents invalid in infringement actions. For details, see below VI.

[28] Heath, Chapter 13 of this book.

[29] Antons, Intellectual Property Law in Indonesia, in: Heath (ed.), Intellectual Property Law in Asia, Kluwer Law London 2002.

[30] Casucci, Chapter 7 of this book.

the word "court", but "judicial authority". Arguably, this includes such quasi-judicial bodies as the European Patent Office's Board of Appeals.[31] That means the judicial review of final administrative decisions must not be confined to legal aspects, but also the facts of the case.[32]

Art. 42 TRIPS specifies the above-mentioned general principles for civil procedures. Even in countries with a prevalence of administrative proceedings, civil procedures have to be made available. This required changes in domestic legislation, particularly for China which had a strong tradition of administrative enforcement.[33] The further requirements of **Art. 42** are more or less self evident and need no further comment.

IV. Rules for Obtaining Evidence: Arts. 43, 50.1(b)

1. TRIPS Provisions Arts. 43, 50.1(b)

More cases may be lost for want of sufficient evidence than for points of substantive law. Issues of evidence feature so prominently in intellectual property cases because of the very subject matter in question. If and to what extent there is damage to tangible property might be the subject of debate between experts, but is rarely a problem of available evidence. This is completely different in the world of intangible rights. If a competitor produces goods that infringe another's patent this would rarely be obvious at first sight. How many infringing goods have been produced and marketed is an issue that can practically only be answered by the inspection of documents in the possession of the infringer. If the infringer has made a profit from such activity, such profit can rarely be determined without further details of the infringer's commercial transactions. For all these reasons, the question of evidence in IP cases basically relates to *obtaining evidence in the possession of the other party*. It is this question that is addressed by **Art. 43 TRIPS** Agreement. Taking into account the above-mentioned problems, the plaintiff has to furnish conclusive proof of the infringement and (where relevant) its scope. But in doing so, the plaintiff is not necessarily confined to the evidence he

---

[31] See the decision EPO Enlarged Board of Appeal, 24 July 1996, OJ 1996, 649; EPO Enlarged Board of Appeal, 10 December 1999, 32 IIC 545 [2002]. It should be noted, however, that the European Patent Office is not bound by the TRIPS provisions, but only by the European Patent Convention.

[32] This position was at least taken by the Korean Constitutional Court, 28 September 1996, 92 Hunga 11 and No. 93 Hunga 8, 9, 10, interpreting a similarly worded constitutional requirement. The Supreme Court's decision led to the setting up of the Korean Patent Court. The Japanese system of appeals against decisions rendered by the Patent Office was already amended in 1948 in order to comply with constitutional requirements. The courts have consistently held that in appeal proceedings the courts can hear all arguments of fact *de novo*: Japanese Supreme Court, 23 June 1991, 24 IIC 523 [1993] – "Evidence of Trade Mark Use".

[33] Details for China are provided by Pattloch in Chapter 12 of this book.

himself can furnish. Rather, the defendant has to comply with orders for submitting relevant evidence, even if this would mean self-incrimination. **Art. 50.1(b) TRIPS** recognises the importance of an order for preserving such evidence if there is a danger that it might otherwise disappear. Particularly because such evidence may well be self-incriminating, defendants may wish to destroy it as soon as they feel pursued. Experience with the production of documents by the defendant has been developed particularly in three countries: the UK, the US and France. While in the US discoveries are available in all sorts of proceedings, the French *saisie contrefaçon* was first introduced in the Patent Act 1844. In the UK, the Anton Piller order was developed particularly for IP cases. In most other countries, such wide-ranging means of discovery are not available, however. This makes the position of the IP owner more difficult, yet to some extent may be compensated by cheaper and speedier trials and a lower threshold of the burden of proof. Arguably, however, countries that still do not provide courts with the power to order the production of documents from the other side may not properly comply with TRIPS.[34]

The TRIPS provisions also indicate the limits of such discovery. For one, the IP owner's request for such evidence must not be frivolous: The plaintiff must have done his utmost to come up with evidence in the first place. In addition, safeguards have to be taken in order to protect the defendant's trade secrets at stake.

In comparing different jurisdictions, measures for obtaining evidence differ both in scope and purpose. While in most jurisdictions that allow an inspection or seizure, the measure would be meant for the preservation of evidence where there is a strong case for infringement, the *saisie contrefaçon* as applied in France and other countries is a measure for ascertaining if an infringement has occurred in the first place. This certainly makes a huge difference. The French concept would not give the defendant any claim for damages for an inspection or seizure if the infringement action as such fails. In addition, the applicant cannot be asked to show strong *prima facie* evidence of infringement if the action is meant to find such evidence in the first place. Consequently, French law does not require the applicant to show any likelihood of infringement (see below 3). If, on the other hand, the measure is meant to prevent the defendant from removing evidence of infringing acts, then such measure can only be justified by a strong *prima facie* case of infringement in the first place, making the applicant liable for damages if the court was misled when granting the order, or if ultimately the defendant is found innocent of infringement.

As to the scope of the order, one can distinguish an order for mere inspection from an actual seizure. A mere inspection is less costly (in contrast to removal and storage of documents or machines), and allows the defendant to continue with his business activities. Seizure, on the other hand, can have the

---

[34] As is argued for the Netherlands by Brinkhof, Chapter 6 of this book.

same result as an interim injunction against the defendant, who in both cases may have difficulties to continue with his commercial activities. Seizure should thus only be granted in circumstances similar to those that would allow issuance of an interim injunction.

Finally, consideration has to be given to the interests of the defendant. Abuse may occur in two ways. For one, such an order can seriously intimidate the defendant and obstruct his business. An English judge once hesitated to grant such an order for obtaining evidence because

> "it seems to me that [such] an order on the lines sought might become an instrument of oppression, particularly in a case where a plaintiff of big standing and deep pocket is ranged against small man who is alleged on the evidence of one side only to have infringed the plaintiff's rights."[35]

In addition, by such order the applicant may obtain knowledge of the defendant's business secrets without any justified reason whatsoever. According to the Düsseldorf High Court,

> "In patent matters, there is no duty to present an object or to permit its inspection according to Sec. 809 German Civil Code in cases where the respondent invokes business secrets in a field that would become apparent upon presentation for inspection, and if the subject matter and the circumstances make it likely that such business secrets exist."[36]

Belatedly, however, even civil law jurisdictions have realised that invoking business secrets by the defendant may be frivolous in itself if invariably used to frustrate the applicant's right of inspection:

> "The intention of protecting trade secrets is not a legitimate reason for withholding relevant documents that may be of importance to the other side. Yet, in order to avoid an unnecessary disclosure of trade secrets, the court should take the necessary steps in each individual case so that no unnecessary damage is done."[37]

Granting the request for obtaining evidence, and properly limiting its extent is thus a difficult but necessary judicial task in order to accommodate the interests of both sides.

2. Details Under National Laws

a) The UK

English law knows a number of preliminary measures aimed at the *preservation* of a certain status quo or the *enabling* of an action against third parties. Preservation of the status quo can be obtained by so-called Mareva injunctions

---

[35] Brightman, quoted in Anton Piller KG *v.* Manufacturing Processes Ltd and others, English Court of Appeal, 8 December 1975, [1976] 1 All E.R. 782.

[36] Düsseldorf High Court, 17 August 1981, Gewerblicher Rechtsschutz und Urheberrecht (GRUR) 1983, 741 – "Interest in Secrecy and Right of Inspection I".

[37] Tokyo High Court, 20 May 1997, 1601 Hanrei Jihô 143 (1997) = 30 IIC 452 [1999] – "Sale of Pharmaceuticals".

or freezing orders that shall prevent the disappearance of the defendant's assets, e.g., off-shore.[38] If it is feared that the defendant himself or a vital witness could make a dash out of the country, a so-called *ne exeat regnum* order can be issued. Evidence can be preserved by the Anton Piller or search order that is further elaborated below.

Finally, a right owner can request the court to order third parties to reveal certain information about others in order that proceedings may be instituted against them. This is particularly useful in cases where the party possessing vital information about infringement is neither a direct nor indirect infringer, e.g., the commissioner of customs, or the owner of a warehouse where infringing goods are stored.[39]

What is currently known as an inspection order under civil procedure rules part 25.1(c)(f), (h) and (l), was developed in a case dating back to 1975, Anton Piller KG *v*. Manufacturing Processes.[40] Instrumental for the order was the plaintiff's barrister and now High Court Judge Hugh Laddie and the then Master of the Rolls, Lord Denning. The order was made without any statutory basis and with very scarce reference to precedents. Some parts of the decision merit a direct quote:

"During the last 18 months the judges of the Chancery Division have been making orders of a kind not known before. They have some resemblance to search warrants. Under these orders the plaintiff and his solicitors are authorised to enter the defendant's premises so as to inspect papers, provided the defendant gives permission. . . . It does not authorise the plaintiffs' solicitors or anyone else to enter the defendants' premises against their will. It does not authorise the breaking down of any doors, nor the slipping in by a back door, nor getting in by an open door or window. It only authorises entry and inspection by the permission of the defendants. The plaintiffs must get the defendants' permission. But it does do this: it brings pressure on the defendants to give permission. It does more. It actually orders them to give permission – with, I suppose, the result that if they do not give permission, they are guilty of contempt of court . . . This is not covered by the rules of court and must be based on the inherent jurisdiction of the court . . . It seems to me that such an order can be made by a judge ex parte, but it should only be made where it is essential that the plaintiff should have inspection so that justice can be done between the parties; and when, if the defendant were forewarned, there is a grave danger that vital evidence will be destroyed, that papers will be burnt or lost or hidden, or taken beyond the jurisdiction, and so the ends of justice be defeated; and when the inspection would do no real harm to the defendant or his case.

---

[38] A very drastic remedy: Tony Willoughby/S. Connal, The Mareva Injunction: A Cruel Tyranny?, [1997] European Intellectual Property Review 479. First decided in English Court of Appeal, Mareva Compania Naviera *v*. International Bulk Carriers, 29 January 1980, [1980] 1 All E.R. 213.

[39] See the relevant cases of Norwich Pharmical *v*. Customs and Excise, House of Lords, [1972] Fleet Street Reports (F.S.R.) 405, and Smith Kline and French *v*. Harbottle, High Court [1980], Report on Patent Cases (R.P.C.) 363.

[40] Anton Piller KG *v*. Manufacturing Processes Ltd and others, Court of Appeal, 8 December 1975, [1976] 1 All E.R. 779. To some extent, this order was already granted by English High Court, EMI Ltd. *v*. Pandit [1975] 1 WLR 302.

Nevertheless, in the enforcement of this order, the plaintiffs must act with due circumspection. On the service of it, the plaintiffs should be attended by their solicitor, who is an officer of the court. They should give the defendants an opportunity of considering it and of consulting their own solicitor. If the defendants wish to apply to discharge the order as having been improperly obtained, they must be allowed to do so. If the defendants refused permission to enter or to inspect, the plaintiffs must not force their way in. They must accept that refusal, and bring it to the notice of the court afterwards, if need be on application to commit. . . . We are told that in two at least of the cases such an order has been effective. We are prepared, therefore, to sanction its continuance, but only in an extreme case where there is grave danger of property being smuggled away or of vital evidence being destroyed. . . . It contains an undertaking in damages which is to be supported (as the plaintiffs are overseas) by a bond for £10,000. It gives an interim injunction to restrain the infringement of copyright and breach of confidential information etc. It orders that the defendants do permit one or two of the plaintiffs and one or two of their solicitors to enter the defendants' premises for the purpose of inspecting documents, files or things, and removing those which belong to the plaintiffs."

It merits pointing out that even such a ground breaking decision was made *ex parte* and was made with surprising speed: The High Court judge refused the *ex parte* application for a search on the same day it was made, 26 November 1975; the Court of Appeal heard the case on 2 December and gave its written decision on 8 December, barely two weeks after the High Court had decided. *Prima facie* evidence of infringement was strong indeed: The defendants were the English agents of the German plaintiff and were suspected of supplying the plaintiffs' German competitors with copyrighted and/or secret drawings of a frequency converter for supplying computers. Danger of misappropriation was corroborated both by two defectors of the defendants and copies of correspondence that indicated the defendants' intention to supply the plaintiffs' competitors with the plaintiffs' latest designs of a new prototype frequency converter. All this evidence was presented by way of a writ of summons and an affidavit.

The decision highlights that the order is not a search warrant in the technical sense. A search warrant could be enforced if necessary by the police. Further, it is an order to allow a third party (the plaintiff) to enter and search the defendant's premises. For that reason, no independent bailiff or solicitor was deemed necessary to carry out the order. The defendant could refuse the order, just as any witness could refuse testimony, yet would be in contempt of court with the consequence of possible imprisonment. Very little thus remains of the defendants' free will to permit or refuse the plaintiffs' entry to the premises.

Already in that case, the first instance judge refused to grant the order as he feared abuse. Some of the following decisions were indeed aimed at specifying the requirements for carrying out the order so as to take the defendants' interests properly into account. Reason for doing so was given by a case argued in the early 1990s.[41] Here, the defendants were alleged to

[41] Universal Thermosensors Ltd *v.* Hibben and others, High Court, 5 February 1992, [1992] 3 All E.R. 257.

have misappropriated certain confidential documents of their former employer, who had obtained an Anton Piller order to search for such documents both in the defendants' private and business premises. After execution of the order, a number of matters had gone awry. First, the affidavit by the plaintiffs' solicitors was open to criticism in several respects, in particular because it was inaccurate. The Anton Piller orders were carried out at 7:30 a.m. at the defendants' private premises with several serious irregularities. The business premises were entered in the absence of any representative of the company. As a consequence, a practice direction was issued by direction of the Lord Chief Justice on 28 July 1994 that laid down the conditions for granting and carrying out an Anton Piller order.

In particular, the new Practice Direction requires a supervising solicitor to be present, limits the time the order can be carried out to between 9:30 a.m. and 5:30 p.m., Monday to Friday, and requires a lady solicitor to be present if premises are entered with only a lady present. The Practice Direction was given a statutory basis in the Civil Procedure Act 1997, Sec. 7 and the above-mentioned Civil Procedure Rules. Already the new terminology of a "search order" indicates the proximity to a search warrant, added by the requirement of a supervising solicitor who has the function (although not the powers) of a French bailiff.

The search order basically allows "access" to the defendant's premises. "Access" would also mean a printout of documents stored in a computer[42] or that keys would have to be provided if cupboards were locked.[43]

Apart from the UK, the Anton Piller or search order can also be requested in a good number of common law countries, e.g., Hong Kong.[44]

b) The French Saisie Contrefaçon

In the absence of other measures for the preservation of a claim such as a Mareva injunction, the *saisie contrefaçon* is the most frequently used measure for obtaining and preserving evidence of infringement. The *saisie contrefaçon* dates back to the first Patent Decrees of 31 December 1791 and 7 January 1792. Subsequently scrapped but living on under French common law, it was recodified by the Patent Act of 5 July 1844 and is now enshrined in Sec. L615-5 Intellectual Property Code. Just as the English Anton Piller order, the *saisie contrefaçon* permits a surprise visit to the defendant's premises and an inspection of all relevant documents or machinery. Yet a number of features make the *saisie contrefaçon* a rather unique instrument of preserving evidence.

It has already been mentioned above that the plaintiff can use the *saisie* even if only for fishing for infringing evidence without a clear case. Distinct

---

[42] English High Court, Gates *v.* Swift, 8 July 1982, [1982] R.P.C. 339.

[43] English High Court, Hazel Grove Music *v.* Elster Enterprises, 4 March 1983, [1983] F.S.R. 379.

[44] Hong Kong Court of Appeal, Tamco Electrical and Electronics (Hong Kong) *v.* Ng Chun Fai and Others, [1994] 1 Hong Kong Law Reports 178.

from the Anton Piller order, a *saisie* has to be granted in principle, even without a good case of likely infringement to be presented. A request for *saisie* has to be made with the presiding judge of the court in whose district the premises to be searched are located.

Two types of *saisie contrefaçon* have to be distinguished: Either one for the *inspection* of documents or machinery. Such *saisie* for inspection is not discretionary, but the plaintiff's right. Or a *saisie* for inspection and *seizure*. Granting a seizure is discretionary and may depend on the plaintiff presenting a *prima facie* case to the judge. In practice, the distinction is less clear. An order for *saisie* granted without any restraint includes the rights of seizure. Thus, limiting the *saisie* to inspection is customary unless the plaintiff can show a good case.

The basis of a request must be an intellectual property right. It is not necessary that such right has been granted, as the application as such would be sufficient.[45] It would even appear possible to base the *saisie* request on a patent in another Member State of the Brussels or Lugano Conventions.[46] A *saisie* order must be carried out within 15 days from being issued and is actually enforced by a bailiff, who may be accompanied by one or more technical experts or the police, but never the applicant himself. The bailiff is chosen by the plaintiff rather than the court.

The scope of the *saisie* has to be described in the court order.[47] In cases of inspection, the bailiff may describe (or copy) products, processes or documents, and can establish their origin. Witnesses cannot be asked in general, yet the defendant's co-operation may be necessary in order to identify certain bar codes, etc. Upon entering the premises, the bailiff must clearly identify himself and furnish the person in possession of the goods or premises to be searched with a warrant.

If an actual seizure is ordered, the objects to be seized and their number have to be defined by the judge who may request the applicant to post a bond.[48] Seizure is normally limited to samples so as to disturb the defendant's business activities as little as possible. This cannot always be achieved, however.

---

[45] It should be noted here that French patent applications are not substantively examined and thus registered far more quickly than would be the case in a system of substantive examination such as under the European Patent Convention, US or Japanese laws. If only applied for, the defendant must at least have received notice of the patent, e.g., by a publication or warning letter: Bordeaux Appeal Court, 27 May 1998, [1998] PIBD-663-III-508 (*saisie* denied due to lack of publication).

[46] Advocated by Petit, Chapter 5 of this book, in the absence of case law. In the reverse, the French courts have accepted proof obtained by a Belgian *saisie contrefaçon* in French infringement procedures: Lille District Court, 4 June 1980, 1980 Dossiers Brevets VI, No. 6. See also Pierre Véron, La saisie contrefaçon, 1999 Dalloz 40.

[47] In the past, *saisie* orders were granted in a rather general fashion, e.g., Lyon Appeal Court, 30 November 1865, 1866 Annales de la propriété industrielle 313.

[48] Lyon District Court, 29 August 1994, 1995 Revue de droit trimestrielle commerciale 415, with comment by Jean Azéma.

What is arguably a very strong measure that favours the IP owner, is not without safeguards for the defendant.

While a court would not interfere in an on-going *saisie* under normal circumstances, the defendant may request a so-called action for revocation (*demande en rétractation*) so as to lift or limit the *saisie* order. A limitation can be particularly justified if trade secrets are involved. Once a defendant insists on confidentiality of documents during the *saisie*, the bailiff would separate these documents from others and then obtain a decision by the judge as to whether the documents or results should be conferred to the plaintiff. The judge may request an expert opinion in such a matter.[49]

The *saisie* may be declared null and void if the formalities are not properly complied with, if the bailiff has not acted on proper instructions, if the *saisie* was abusive, e.g., was only meant to obtain knowledge of a competitor's business or business secrets. Cases where the *saisie* is ruled invalid would make the information obtained by the *saisie* inadmissible in infringement procedures and the applicant liable to any financial harm the respondent can demonstrate.[50]

With a maximum price tag of €15,000 even for complicated *saisie*, the remedy has proved fairly popular and is applied in about 1,000 cases per year.

Apart from France, Belgium, Spain, Italy and Denmark now allow for similar measures. However, one should bear in mind that, e.g., the Italian *saisie* (*descrizione* for a descriptive *saisie*, *sequestro* for a seizure) always requires the applicant to show *fumus boni juris*, in other words, that on the balance of probabilities, the patent is valid and infringed and that there is the likelihood of a good case.[51]

c) The US Discovery System

Unlike the systems in England or France, the US discovery system is not limited to intellectual property cases and gives the IP owner and alleged infringer equal rights of access to information in possession of the other side. The system is far more inquisitive than the ones described above, far more time consuming and costly. It is driven by the idea that the whole truth can be helpful in solving a potential dispute (preferably in the pre-trial stages), and its rigidity must be evaluated in light of the US jury trial system that tends to severely punish those suspected of concealing information. Discoverable in this manner is all information not specifically protected, and directly or

---

[49] It is unclear what is exactly the basis of withholding documents—the mere fact that they contain confidential information, or the fact that they are unrelated to the case the plaintiff wants to prove: Pierre Véron, Documents confidentiels appréhendés lors d'une saisie contrefaçon (Confidential Documents Seized During a *Saisie Contrefaçon*), [1998] RDPI No. 83, 11. For details, see Petit, Chapter 5 of this book.

[50] In 1997, 119 actions for damages based on an invalid *saisie* were brought before the courts, yet only eight were successful: Petit, Chapter 5 of this book.

[51] See Scuffi, Diritto Processuale dei brevetti e dei marchi (Civil Procedure in Patent and Trade Mark Cases), 2001, 237, and Casucci in Chapter 7 of this book.

indirectly relevant to a certain case. Even evidence that would not be admissible in court (e.g., hearsay evidence) is discoverable because it may indicate the names of persons involved who could then be called as witnesses at a trial. Most commonly in IP infringement suits, information concerns the allegedly infringing products or processes, the profit made by the alleged infringer in connection with such activities, issues surrounding negligence or wilfulness on the side of the alleged infringer, and possible defences the alleged infringer may raise against an infringement suit. On the other hand, the alleged infringer can be interested in learning more about the development of the invention and patent application procedures, the patentee's awareness of certain prior art or of issues surrounding the profit made by the patentee of the commercial exploitation of the patented devices. All the above information may be obtained from the plaintiff's and defendant's respective undertakings, their personnel, their advisors (e.g., attorneys or patent attorneys), and also the inventor. Also third parties can be approached for information by issuing a so-called sub poena. The request against third parties has to be reasonable and may not be too broad.

Also the discovery methods go far beyond what would be common or allowed in England or France. These are: requests for production in order to obtain tangible evidence, e.g., documents, photographs or product samples; interrogatories that must be answered in writing under oath and may be used as evidence at the trial; requests to admit certain facts; depositions in order to obtain witness statements before trial; and requests to identify each party's expert witnesses. Each party thus has the opportunity to question the other party's witnesses and expert witnesses, making preparation not only possible but rather highly advisable. To what extent such preparation of witnesses assists in discovering the truth is questionable.

In specific cases, discovery may be refused or limited. Where confidential information is concerned, the court may restrict access to the other party's attorney. Non-compliance with such order is very difficult to prove, however. In addition, any party may refuse to provide information that relates to the communication between the party and an attorney. Thus, legal advice given by patent attorneys during application procedure may not be discoverable.[52] The same holds true for legal advice given by an attorney or patent attorney regarding the alleged infringement. Here, the defendant faces a difficult strategic decision, though. Such communication may after all be useful in order to exonerate a potential infringer from the claim of wilful infringement if it can be shown that reasonable care was taken not to infringe, e.g., by requesting an attorney's or patent attorney's opinion in this matter.

Costs and scope of the discovery procedure make it an unlikely object of exportation to other countries.

---

[52] See, e.g., Advanced Cardiovascular Systems Inc. *v.* C.R. Baird Inc., 5 October 1992, 25 USPQ 2d 1354 (N.D.Cal. 1992).

d) The German Auskunftsanspruch

With the exception of France, civil law systems rarely provide the IP owner with an adequate means of obtaining evidence from the other side. As far as *documents* in the possession of the other side are concerned, courts could certainly order these to be produced, yet would require the document to be described in a manner that would allow a court bailiff to identify it in the event of compulsory execution. This would hold true for, e.g., Germany, the Netherlands and Japan. This is a completely different philosophy from what was described above for France, England and the US. The French system with the *saisie contrefaçon* explicitly allows the IP owner to investigate to what extent an infringement has occurred in the first place. The English Anton Piller order allows the IP owner to actively participate in the search, making the result not least dependent on the IP owner's ingeniousness in uncovering locations where the potential infringer might have squirreled away possibly damaging information. Finally, the US system with its wide-ranging discovery means always puts the addressee between the *scylla* of self-incrimination and the *charybdis* of perjury. Civil law systems as described above would neither allow nor require cooperation of either the IP owner or the alleged infringer in uncovering or presenting evidence.

This position owes less to a reluctance of granting interim remedies – after all, half of the cases of trade mark infringement are dealt with in the interim, somewhat less so in patent cases – than to the belief that every party is obliged to furnish proof for the allegations brought before the court.

As most civil law systems, the German Code of Civil Procedure allows for a request for securing evidence both prior to or during trial, Sec. 485 CCP. If the request is made prior to the main suit, the courts require the likelihood of success in the main action.

Sec. 810 CCP allows inspection of a document under certain circumstances, e.g., it was drafted in the interest of the plaintiff, certifies a legal relationship between the plaintiff and a third person or concerns notes about legal acts between the plaintiff and another person. None of these alternatives is particularly helpful when it comes to proving infringement in IP litigation matters.[53] In addition, Sec. 810 Code of Civil Procedure is quite explicit in stipulating that the court can only order a document to be presented if the plaintiff has a right to see such document.

Sec. 809 Civil Code allows a right of inspection under certain circumstances. The provision reads as follows:

> "He who has a claim against a person in possession of a certain object in regard of such object, or who wants to obtain certainty if he has such a claim, can request that the person in possession of such object presents it for inspection or permits inspection to the extent that such inspection of the object is of interest for the above-mentioned reasons."

---

[53] Already Kammergericht Berlin, 8 March 1919, GRUR 1919, 179.

This provision was interpreted somewhat narrowly by the courts[54] and by academic literature.[55] Not least guided by *Dieter Stauder,*[56] the latest decision of the German Federal Supreme Court makes the provision indeed a meaningful tool of discovery.[57]

Finally, the Anti-Piracy Law of 1990 marked the beginning of a right of information (*Auskunftsanspruch*) in Germany regarding the names of the infringers, suppliers and customers.[58] This right can also be exercised in the interim, and is reinforced by monetary fines in cases of non-compliance, which is considered contempt of court.

e) Obtaining evidence in Japan

The Japanese Code of Civil Procedure in Sec. 234 in connection with the Rules of Civil Procedure, Secs. 152–154, almost literally replicate the German provisions on securing evidence. In addition, Secs. 219–223 specify situations where a party can be requested to produce documents, a claim limited to those circumstances mentioned above for Germany. Perhaps in light of heavy US criticism on the shortcomings of the Japanese discovery procedure (or the absence thereof), the new Code of Civil Procedure, in force since January 1998, now contains a new provision for a certain pre-trial discovery. Here, Sec. 163 reads as follows:

> "A party may, during the pendency of a suit, inquire in writing of the adversary party about matters which are necessary for the preparation of assertions or proof, requesting written responses within an appropriate period to be designated by such party. However, this shall not apply to cases where such inquiry comes under any of the following items.
>
> i. inquiry which is not concrete or particular
> ii. inquiry which insults or embarrasses the adversary party
> iii. inquiry which duplicates an inquiry which has already been made
> iv. inquiry which requests an opinion
> v. inquiry which requires undue expense or time for the adversary party to answer
> vi. inquiry regarding matters similar to such matters as to which testimony may be refused in accordance with the provisions of Sec. 196 or 197."

This section is relatively new and thus untested. In addition, there are no sanctions if the other party does not comply.

---

54 Berlin Royal District Court, 13 April 1910, Mitteilungen 1910, 120; Braunschweig District Court, 20 August 1968, GRUR 1971, 28 – "Abkantpresse"; German Supreme Court, 8 January 1985, GRUR 1985, 512 – "Druckbalken".

55 Hermann Isay, Patentgesetz, 6th ed. 1932, § 4 note 68: "Complete annihilation of trade secrets".

56 Comment on the German Supreme Court Decision, GRUR 1985, 517.

57 German Federal Supreme Court, 2 May 2002, 34 IIC 331 (2003) – "Fax Card".

58 For an in-depth discussion on the *Auskunftsanspruch*, see K. Oppermann, Geld oder Leben – Der Auskunftsanspruch in Extremsituationen (Money or Else – The Right of Information under Pressure), Dorpat 1997.

V. Interim Injunctions: Art. 50

Interim measures under **Art. 50 TRIPS** can be requested either to preserve relevant evidence (**Art. 50.1(b)**, see above V), or to prevent an infringement from occurring, **Art. 50.1(a)**.

1. Provisional Measures to Prevent Infringement, Art. 50 TRIPS

Interim (provisional) injunctions are perhaps the sharpest sword in the area of the IP owner's weapons. Due to their provisional nature, they also spell danger: Due to the time constraints and limits of presenting evidence, the interim decision may not stand up to the scrutiny of a main action. Here again, the interests of both plaintiff and defendant will have to be properly balanced in order to find equitable solutions. These will not least depend upon the IP right in question. In cases of an alleged trade mark infringement, refusing interim measures may cause irreparable harm to the trade mark owner due to market confusion that intensifies every day infringing products are marketed. These considerations are far less relevant in the cases of patents or copyrights, although timely remedies are important here, as the duration of the right is limited. On the other hand, the defendant may suffer irreparable loss if production lines are shut down, employees made redundant and market share is lost without the reasonable prospect that in case the interim decision proves unfounded, such measures can be undone. The considerations contained in **Art. 50 TRIPS** in this respect can be summarised as follows:

(a) The provision does not specify the necessary requirements for issuing provisional measures. Thus, countries are free to specify such requirements in their domestic legislation, e.g., a high likelihood of infringement (as explained under 2) or the question of who is in a better position to compensate possible damages (as elaborated on under 3). **Art. 50.2** specifies, however, that interim measures must be available in procedures where both sides have had the opportunity to be heard or *ex parte*, that is, upon a request of one side without hearing the other. The latter shall be available "where any delay is likely to cause irreparable harm to the right holder". One can thus infer that while urgency is required for an ordinary interim injunction, *ex parte* injunctions require an even higher degree thereof.

(b) The right owner has to supply all available evidence together with his request. The evidence shall indicate both the fact that the applicant is indeed the owner of the IP right, and that the right has been infringed or is likely to be infringed soon. **Art. 50.3** is silent on the question to what extent evidence regarding the validity of the IP right has to be furnished as well. This is understandable given the fact that most jurisdictions would regard registration of a right as *prima facie* evidence of its validity. As mentioned above, **Art. 50.3** does not specify the relationship between irreparable harm and likelihood of infringement.

(c) The provision also contains specific safeguards for the defendant. For one, the court must have the discretion to order the applicant to provide a security "sufficient to protect the defendant and to prevent abuse". The right of a defendant to claim damages in cases where the provisional measure is later revoked is enshrined in **Art. 50.7**. Appropriately, this right of compensation must be available even where there is not fault on the side of the plaintiff: After all, the plaintiff entertains a calculated risk when requesting a provisional measure.[59]

(d) Where a decision has been rendered *ex parte,* the opposition has to be notified without delay and a review of this decision shall be available to the defendant within a reasonable period of time, **Art. 50.4**. Where an *inter partes* measure has been made, the main action shall be initiated within a reasonable period of time not exceeding 20 working days of 31 calendar days, **Art. 50.6**. The latter provision is misguided in view of the practice in many countries: Particularly in matters of trade marks and unfair competition, an interim decision often settles the matter.[60] This is also true for the Dutch *kort geding* that lies somewhere between interim procedures and expedited main action.[61] German and Dutch law would thus not require the plaintiff to initiate a main action in order to obtain a final decision.[62]

2. The Balance of Probability

Most countries require the following elements for issuing interim injunctions:

(1) Urgency. Urgency means that but for the injunction, the IP owner would suffer substantial damages or disadvantages. It is immaterial to

---

[59] So interpreted, e.g., in Sec. 945 German Code of Civil Procedures; Direction 25 English Civil Procedure Rules; Dutch Supreme Court, 16 November 1984, 1985 Nederlandse Jurisprudentie 547 (Ciba Geigy *v.* Voorbraaak). Different, however, San Marino Regulation of Intellectual Property Protection Decree of 29 June 1999, Sec. 102(6): "Damages in respect of the party who obtained the description or seizure if this party is deemed to have been negligent".

[60] See Bastian/Knaak, Trade Mark Infringement Proceedings in the Countries of the European Union, 26 IIC 149 [1995]: The authors arrive at the following figures for interim procedures that conclude the case: 80% for the UK, 65% for the Netherlands, more than 50% for Belgium, 50% for Germany, but only 5% for France and Italy.

[61] The *kort geding* is considered a preliminary measure: European Court of Justice, 16 June 1998, 30 IIC 292 [1999] – "Hermès". Details are provided by Brinkhof, Chapter 6 of this book.

[62] While this does not conform to **Art. 50.6**, the provision cannot be considered self-executing: The question has been left open by the above mentioned "Hermès" decision of the ECJ. However, the Dutch courts which submitted the case held the provision not directly applicable: 30 IIC 295 [1999].

what extent damage has already occurred and is likely to continue or will occur for the first time.

(2) Likelihood that the IP right is valid and infringed. Such likelihood can be proven more easily in cases of trade mark infringement than in cases of patent infringement where difficult technical questions are involved.[63]

The requirement of showing a good case can be considered as a basic issue of justice: No defendant shall be made subject to a measure that presumably would not stand up to a proper trial. Or, put differently, the plaintiff cannot have a legal interest in obtaining a measure that he is unlikely to obtain in proper procedures on the merit. The disadvantage of this approach becomes evident in patent cases. Due to the highly technical and complex nature of infringement procedures, it would be very difficult to persuade the court in the interim that infringement is likely.[64] The alternative in such cases is to conduct a main action *en miniature*.[65]

3. The Balance of Convenience

In order to avoid such summary assessment of the main issues, the English courts have shifted from the balance of probability to the so-called balance of convenience, taking into account the respective commercial situation of plaintiff and defendant. Here such factors such as likely damage of the defendant's continued action would be far more decisive that the likely success in the main action.[66] The question is thus who of the two opponents will be in a better position to pay possible damages according to the outcome of the main action, and to what extent damage suffered by either side can indeed be remedied by monetary relief. According to Cornish/Llewelyn, "The effect of the new emphasis upon the balance of convenience has been somewhat to increase the prospect of an interim injunction in patent cases. But it is difficult to predict how a judge will weigh the particular circumstances, which rarely relate to the issue between the parties".[67]

The most recent case of the otherwise rare interim injunction in patent matters is SmithKline Beecham *v.* Generics (UK).[68] The injunction was

---

[63] For Germany: Marshall, Chapter 4 of this book; for Italy, Casucci, Chapter 7 of this book.

[64] E.g., Marshall, Chapter 4 of this book: "The difficulty in interim proceedings is to convince the court of an infringement, in particular in cases of infringement by equivalents".

[65] This could be the case in the US, where the courts thoroughly examine the issue of likelihood of success: e.g., Hybritech Inc. *v.* Abbott Laboratories, 849 F2d 1446 (Fed. Cir. 1988). The Dutch *kort geding* produces similar effects.

[66] English House of Lords, American Cyanamid *v.* Ethicon, 5 February 1975, 1 All E.R. 504 [1975].

[67] Cornish/Llewelyn, Chapter 3 of this book.

[68] English Patents Court, SmithKline Beecham *v.* Generics (UK), 23 October 2001, Patent World, March 2002, 8.

granted because the plaintiff had a good arguable case and damages would not be an adequate remedy at trial. Due to the complexity of the matter, the court held that it was impossible to side on the relative strengths of the parties' contentions. However, given the well-known fact that once exposed to competition, the price of a patented drug would spiral down very quickly, damages were unable to compensate the plaintiff for loss of market share from which it would be unable to recover. The court also concluded that the defendant's damages would be unquantifiable if the injunction was granted. Yet, "the only thing I think I can say with some certainty is that the order of damage to the claimant is likely to be a good deal greater than that to the defendant . . . [because] claimant's damage is more unquantifiable than that of the defendants, but both are unquantifiable. There are degrees of unquantifiability, just as there are degrees of infinity".

The dangers of this approach may become apparent in the following Portuguese case: A small retailer of glasses had registered a domestic trade mark in his name. At some point, a huge international chain offering similar goods opened three stores in Portugal under a name identical to the registered trade mark, with the opening of additional shops in the offing. Only at that point did the trade mark owner become aware of the likely infringement and requested an interim injunction. The courts denied the injunction with the argument that damage to the international chain would be disproportional even though infringement was highly likely. This in effect means two things: First, the greater the scale of the alleged infringer's operation, the less likely an injunction against him will be granted. And second, in reducing the issue to one of damage compensation, it transforms a monopolistic right into an open licence against payment. The latter consideration has been highlighted in a US decision: "The nature of the patent grant thus weighs against holding that monetary damages will always suffice to make the patentee whole. For the principal value of a patent is its statutory right to exclude".[69] The legitimacy of this view is enhanced by the fact that it will often be highly difficult for the defendant to prove damages in cases where the interim injunction subsequently proves unfounded.

4. Practice in Selected Countries

Just as in the main action (see below VI), interim procedures very much depend on the country, not only in respect to the requirements for granting interim relief.

In the *US*, a request for an interim injunction depends on the following four factors:

(1) a reasonable likelihood of success on the merits;
(2) irreparable harm if relief is not granted;

---

[69] H.H. Robertson *v.* United Steel Deck, 27 May 1987, 820 F.2d 384 (Fed. Cir. 1987).

(3) the balance of hardship tipping in favour of the applicant; and
(4) the impact of the injunction on the public interest.[70]

In *Germany*, about half of the cases in trade mark and unfair competition matters are decided in the interim, without this decision being further challenged.[71] Cases of interim relief in patent actions are fewer due to the difficulty of showing a good case in technically complicated matters. The requirement of urgency is strictly interpreted and requires the IP owner to act quickly, according to some courts within a month's time.[72] In contrast to the US, Japan or the Netherlands, the court would set a hearing for *inter partes* procedures within a couple of days, with a decision being rendered after two to three weeks at the latest. Only evidence that is brought to the trial is considered, and infringement in patent cases may be shown by a private expert opinion. The estoppel of invalidity cannot normally be raised in the interim.

In *France*, interim injunctions are far less important than in Germany, as the *saisie contrefaçon* already acts as a deterrent to further infringement. If not only inspection but also seizure has been ordered, the defendant may have no means of continuing production in any case. Interim injunction can be requested under Art. 615-3 Industrial Property Code, yet requires that the main action is already pending. The measure can be granted "if the substantive proceedings appear well-founded and are instituted within a short time of the day on which the IP owner becomes aware of the facts on which the proceedings are based", Art. 615-3(2). The "short time" is interpreted as not exceeding six months.[73] In judging the balance of probabilities, the judge would have to take into account the likelihood of infringement, the strength of the underlying IP right, and the defences by the alleged infringer. Italy has comparable rules.

The *Dutch kort geding* as explained above comes closer to a pre-emptive decision on the merits and is carried out according to a very strict timetable, normally within two to three months. Although urgency is also required here, the courts do not interpret this too strictly, and even in patent cases, about half of all cases are decided by *kort geding* procedures.[74]

Finally, the *Japanese* procedure in the interim comes closer to an expedited trial on the merits, with hearings being conducted in an interval of two

---

[70] These requirements were set out in the above-mentioned decision Hybritech Inc. *v*. Abbott Laboratories, 17 June 1988, 849 F.2d 1446 (Fed. Cir. 1988).

[71] Bastian/Knaak, Trade Mark Infringement Proceedings in the Countries of the European Union, 26 IIC 149, 165 [1995].

[72] Which would be the case for Munich: Marshall, Chapter 4 of this book.

[73] Paris Appeal Court, 26 February 1992, 1992 Propriété Industrielle Bulletin Documentaire (PIBD)-III-308.

[74] *Kort geding* procedures have become less popular with IP owners after the courts have started to give more consideration to the defendant's interests: Hague Court of Appeal, Hoffman-Laroche *v*. Orgonen, 12 September 1996, 1996 Intellectuele Eigendom en Reclamerecht 237.

weeks rather than one month, as would be the case in the main action. A good part of IP cases are decided in the interim, the main advantage being to exert increased pressure on the defendant.

In all of the above countries except the *Netherlands*, the successful applicant is requested to post security. Injunctive relief is normally accompanied by an order that sets a fine in cases where the injunction is breached by the defendant. All countries allow an appeal either against grant or rejection of an interim injunction.

VI. The Main Action

Interestingly enough, the TRIPS Agreement is silent on the main part of the infringement procedure: the actual trial. This is unsurprising given the fact that procedures are vastly different from country to country, and hardly show any common denominator beyond what could be considered as constitutional requirements such as the right to be properly heard. The actual trial of course depends on how the previous steps of procedure (e.g., means of discovery) are shaped, and what kind of defences the alleged infringer is allowed to introduce. Further, the trial is very much shaped by the position of the judge and the educational background of judges in general: Where a case has to be argued before a lay jury, different skills are required than if the case was decided by a panel of technically and legally trained professionals. It might thus be useful at this stage to briefly introduce the differences in IP infringement trials in the US, Japan and some West European countries.[75]

1. The United Kingdom[76]

As would be expected, the United Kingdom infringement procedure has more in common with the US than with other continental jurisdictions. Particularly the rule making power of the courts allows them to develop procedural rules in accordance with commercial needs.

IP infringement suits are exclusively heard in London, either at the High Court or since 1989 at the Patents County Court, both procedures differing very little in cost or speed. Litigation is shaped by a certain proximity between the bench and the bar, judges being appointed from the ranks of senior counsel. Although no longer mandatory, trials are normally conducted by barristers (often Queen's counsel), assisted by juniors and solicitors.

---

[75] Literature for the countries mentioned below see (XI.). On the enforcement in other countries, the reader is referred to the following: For China, X. Liu, 32 IIC 141 [2001]. For Thailand: Ariyanuntaka, 30 IIC 360 [1999]. For Eastern Europe (Estonia, Latvia, Lithuania, Poland, the Czech Republic, Hungary, Slovenia, Romania and Bulgaria), see The Enforcement of Industrial Property Rights in Eastern Europe, 32 IIC 875-999 [2001].

[76] Nott, Patent Litigation in England [1994] EIPR 3; Civil Procedure, Sweet & Maxwell, 2nd ed. 1999; Cornish/Llewelyn, Chapter 3 of this book.

After the claim is served on the defendant, the judge will hold a case management conference in which issues of fact and law are discussed in order to map out the future trial. The judge will also set a timetable. The change in procedure has considerably speeded up litigation and a decision can now be expected within 12–18 months. Although adversarial in nature, the new rules of civil procedure give the judge far more power over issues such as hearing expert witnesses or limited cross-examination. As cases are normally heard in one go, before the trial the parties have to launch a certificate estimating the length of oral submissions. The new rules of civil procedure introduced in 1998 have also curtailed the right of appeal which is no longer automatic, but that is either granted by the court or more frequently has to be petitioned before the appeal court.

Specifics of the English infringement procedure are the high cost risk involved (see below VII), the concentrated trial, and the importance attached to oral procedures which demands high skills and proficiency from the legal representatives. Perhaps due to the importance of oral pleadings, decisions tend to be more clearly worded than those of other European jurisdictions, thus often serving as important precedents.

2. Germany[77]

German civil procedure is based on the Code of Civil Procedure of 1877 that was significantly amended in 1924 and 1979, in both cases in order to accelerate procedures.

IP infringement suits can be brought before any one of the 16 designated district courts (*Landgericht*), and purchase of even one infringing object at a certain place is sufficient to establish jurisdiction. The result is a concentration particularly in patent matters: Most are litigated either in Düsseldorf or in Munich. Whereas most of the trade mark and unfair competition cases are dealt with in the interim, patent infringement is normally litigated in the main action. The main action even in patent cases does not take more than about 10 months from filing to a first instance decision. This is about the same on appeal before the *Oberlandesgericht*. A final appeal on matters of law lies with the *Bundesgerichtshof*, the Federal Supreme Court. A reform of 2002 has limited the appeal courts' possibilities of reviewing the facts, see below.

Similar to Japan and France, Germany has a system of career judges appointed directly after graduation from the university. Judges are appointed for life and cannot be removed from office or transferred to another court. For the district courts IP divisions, this often means that judges obtain decade-long experience in the field, and would only request promotion to an IP division at a higher court. There are about 100,000 licensed attorneys in Germany, of which about 500 specialise in intellectual property. Patent

---

[77] Schramm, Der Patentverletzungsprozess (Patent Infringement Litigation), 4th ed. Cologne 1999; Marshall, Chapter 4 of this book.

attorneys have not yet been given the right of representation in court, except for the Patent Court (see below).

Cost considerations may make it advisable to commence an infringement action with a warning letter, as the defendant's immediate admittal to the infringement would require the plaintiff to pay all court costs including attorneys' fees. Considerations about "torpedoes" in other European countries may point to the opposite, however (see below 6). For the suit as such, the plaintiff must present all evidence to the court in order to prove infringement, with very limited possibilities of uncovering evidence from the opposite side. The newly inserted Sec. 142 Code of Civil Procedure gives the plaintiff increased rights of obtaining evidence from third parties, yet not from the defendant.

A date for trial would normally be set after an exchange of statements between plaintiff and defendant. The court decides which of the witnesses mentioned by either side would be necessary to prove certain allegations. Ideally, the hearing will be conducted within one day. Before and during the hearing, the court has a more active role than would be the case in other countries. Not only does the court select the witnesses and decide which other evidence is relevant, the Code of Civil Procedure obliges the judge to take an active role during procedure by questioning witnesses (both parties may pose additional questions thereafter), and by pointing out which facts need to be proven or argued further. This kind of judicial "assistance" may help to come to an amicable solution and is also relevant for the grounds of appeal: Facts that the judge requested to be introduced during trial, but that were not sufficiently argued may not be introduced.

Another German characteristic is the separation of infringement and nullity. Appeals against decisions of the Patent Office, or nullity actions per se can only be brought before the Patent Court in Munich, whose decisions can be appealed to the Federal Supreme Court. Infringement courts have no jurisdiction over invalidating patents (although they may do so with designs and utility models, or hold trade marks unenforceable). This has the advantage that the validity question can be argued before a court with both technically and legally trained judges, thus making expert opinions expendable. The infringement court may, but is not obliged to stay proceedings, and this course of action is taken in less than 10% of the cases. Nullity actions would normally be decided within one year. Declaration of nullity during or after infringement proceedings would require the plaintiff to reimburse the defendant for the damages incurred by the enforcement of any court decision. According to Sec. 580(6) Code of Civil Procedure, this also applies if the infringement decision has become final.[78] Comparable systems of nullity actions before a specialised patent court also exist in Austria and Korea.[79]

---

[78] Düsseldorf District Court, 24 June 1986, 1987 GRUR 628 – "Restitutionsklage".

[79] Y.-J. Kim, Das neue Patentverfahren in Korea, GRUR Int. 1999, 417.

3. France[80]

The enforcement procedure of IP rights in France is codified under the French Intellectual Property Code (IPC). IP cases are heard by a number of designated first instance courts (Tribunal de Grand Instance), currently nine. About half of all cases are heard for the courts of Paris, not least due to the fact that a suit can be brought in any place where the tort has occurred, apart from the defendant's residence. Similar to Germany, cases are heard by career judges with normally no previous experience as attorneys. Only attorneys can represent parties before the civil courts, and of the 30,000 French attorneys, about 250 are specialised in intellectual property. French law offers two interesting advantages to potential plaintiffs. First, the above-mentioned *saisie contrefaçon*. Second, the fact that *saisie* and infringement action can already be brought on the basis of a published application of an industrial property right, rather than merely a registered right. Yet, while the above-mentioned jurisdictions of the US, Japan, Germany and the UK have managed to conduct first instance infringement suits in no more than 18 months, the law's delay seems to be a by-word of French justice:

> "Meanwhile the delay of proceedings presents a true problem in France, a situation described by some authors as 'completely surrealistic', in what can be considered 'normal' proceedings, an infringement suit not appealed to the Supreme Court may still take six to seven years for a final verdict . . . If a final appeal is launched before the Supreme Court, which can subsequently remand the case back to another appeal court, a final decision may not be reached before 10 years in total. Although this problem has not escaped public attention, the difficulties involved seem to be insurmountable."[81]

It is not uncommon for a court in Paris to set hearings 15 months in advance. Yet, unlike the UK, the written exchange of statements is more important than the actual oral hearing that may take half a day.

Courts in the UK, France and Italy can revoke intellectual property rights if so requested by way of counterclaim. In France and Italy, this already stands to reason due to the fact that industrial property rights are not substantively examined.

Only in passing should it be mentioned that in Italy, no specific courts have yet been designated for the hearing of IP cases that can thus be brought before any first instance court. Italy further has another specific feature that deserves mention. In all private infringement suits, an opinion regarding the outcome is delivered by the Ministero Publico, the Ministry of Justice. The opinion is only rendered at the end of the oral proceedings, and neither party has the opportunity to know the opinion in advance, or even respond to it. The opinion does not even have to be reasoned.

---

[80] Stenger, L'action Contrefaçon (Patent Infringement Action), Jurisclasseur Brevet, Fasc. 5450, Nos. 35 et seq.; Bertrand, La preuve de la contrefaçon (Proof of Infringement), RDPI No. 49 (October 1993), 11; Petit, Chapter 5 of this book.

[81] Petit, Chapter 5 of this book.

4. Japan[82]

Civil enforcement is based on the Japanese Code of Civil Procedure 1890 which was substantively revised in 1929 and 1996. The revised Code came into force on 1 January 1998. Then and now, the Code and its revisions were drafted on the basis of German models with some modifications made during the US Occupation between 1945 and 1952. In particular, the 1946 Constitution no longer allowed for specialised courts, and Japan has thus a uniform structure of small claims courts, district courts, high courts, and the Supreme Court dealing with all types of cases. With the exception of the Supreme Court, the approximate 3,000 judges in Japan are routinely rotated every three years to a different court, making it difficult for them to attain expertise in a certain field. After the introduction of the system of cross-examination in the late 1940s, the role of the judge has become a rather passive one, making it often difficult for the parties to know which points should be argued further.[83] Procedures tend rather to be in writing, and oral hearings set in intervals of two months sometimes only last a couple of minutes.[84] Decisions are often very detailed on facts and rather brief on the legal issues involved. Particularly Supreme Court decisions tend to be short even if an appeal is allowed. Otherwise, the case would often be dismissed out of hand with the reason that the appellant takes "a peculiar view which cannot be followed".

Japan currently has 18,000 qualified attorneys and 4,800 patent attorneys. Representation is still confined to attorneys, yet patent attorneys are allowed to plead if an attorney has been previously assigned to the case.[85] Increasing the number of patent attorneys and broadening their tasks is also considered expedient in view of the rapidly rising number of intellectual property lawsuits: In 1999, 311 infringement suits were raised, in 2000, already 610. The distribution among the different IP fields was 29% for patents, 23.4% for unfair competition matters, 15.9% for copyrights, 14.5% for trade marks, 9.7% for utility models and 6.2% for designs.

For patents, utility models or computer programs, jurisdiction has been exclusively in the district courts of Tokyo and Osaka, Sec. 6 Code of Civil

[82] Iimura, Current Litigation Practice for IPR Infringement Cases at the Tokyo District Court, AIPPI Japan International Edition 2002, 3 and 143; Heath, Chapter 13 of this book.

[83] S. Ono, Fusei kyôsô hô no shomondai (Problems Related to Unfair Competition Law Suits), 5 Kôgyô shoyûken kenkyû hôgakukai nempô 102, 113 (1982).

[84] Nishiguchi et al., "Teamwork ni yoru hanyôteki soshô un'employees' inventions wo mezashite" (Efficiency of Procedure through Teamwork), 846 Hanrei Times 7, 10 (1994).

[85] The reform of the system of patent attorneys is one of the major issues of current reform. The last amendment to the Patent Attorneys Act was made on 11 June 2002, yet stopped short of giving patent attorneys the full rights to represent clients in infringement procedures: www.jpo.go.jp.

Procedure. An appeal with a complete rehearing of the facts can be launched before the Tokyo High Court, and a final appeal on law in the Supreme Court. Matters are even simpler when it comes to appealing decisions from the Patent Office. The only court competent to hear these appeals is the Tokyo High Court, which allows a complete rehearing of the facts. Also here, a final appeal lies with the Supreme Court. Both the district courts in Tokyo and Osaka have special divisions for intellectual property matters. But even if technical matters are in dispute, expert witnesses, either court appointed or at the request of either party, are uncommon. Under a strangely hybrid system between court appointed experts and technical judges, the special divisions for intellectual property matters at the Tokyo and Osaka District Courts rely on the expertise of persons dispatched from the Patent Office, who are meant to explain technical matters to the judges. Unfortunately, the opinions of these experts are not published or stated in court, and they cannot be questioned by the parties, nor would they lend their signature to the decision in any judicial capacity. Sec. 105bis Patent Act (PA) now gives the court discretion to appoint an expert on the calculation of damages, however. It is likely that Japan will introduce a system of experts for the question of infringement in the next couple of years.

Both under patent and trade mark law, the Patent Office can be requested to give an interpretation of the scope of a patent or trade mark, Sec. 71 PA, 28 Trade Mark Act (TMA). The law now explicitly provides that such a request can also be made by a court, Sec. 71bis PA, 28bis TMA. In such case, three examiners shall be appointed to give an opinion. In order to do so, the Patent Office can also request evidence from the parties. It is not clear to what extent this system is actually used.

The duration of IP infringement suits stood at 18.6 months in the year 2001. Cases handled by the Tokyo and Osaka District Courts are now concluded within one year from the date of filing. Hearings are set at intervals of about one month.

While Art. 22 Japanese Constitution requires proceedings to be conducted in open court, there is an increasing tendency to conduct proceedings *entre nous*. Already ten years ago, the District Court Tokyo had started to conduct hearings in the judge's conference room rather than in the open court. Secs. 168–174 Code of Civil Procedure now explicitly permit hearings where the public can be excluded. A further protection of court documents has been introduced by Sec. 92 which provides that a court decision can authorise only certain persons to have access to court records.

It is up to the right owner to prove that the IP right exists and is infringed. While registered rights carry the presumption of validity, the status of an unregistered right has to be proven, be it well-known or famous. Requirements are fairly high in these cases, and attorneys often face the difficulty that the court fails to express itself as to when proof is sufficient: "If the court is of the opinion that recognition has or has not been conclusively proven, would it not be helpful in such case to give some hint to the parties about this belief?"[86] In some cases, particularly when it comes to proving bad faith, the courts require an unrealistically high level of proof.[87] While written evidence would be the most important means of proof, difficulty in getting hold of documents would result in having parties rely on cross-examining witnesses, delaying proceedings thus making the outcome of evidence more erratic. Further, interim decisions on the merits of a case are notably absent in Japanese civil procedure[88] thus requiring the plaintiff to argue the case for both infringement and damages without knowing if the court would assume infringement in the first place.

In order to speed up infringement procedures and presumably put some pressure on the Patent Office, in a 2000 decision the Supreme Court explicitly allowed the estoppel of invalidity to be considered by the courts in circumstances where the patent was "obviously invalid".[89] Subsequent decisions affirmed that the grounds for holding a patent invalid could relate to a lack of novelty,[90] of inventive step,[91] of insufficient disclosure[92] or of misappropriation.[93] The new approach towards invalidity may have speeded up procedures, but it is not necessarily beneficial to the patentee. According to recent statistics, the patentee's success rate in infringement procedures was a mere 24% of the 70 cases where the estoppel of invalidity was raised after the Supreme Court's decision.[94] The Patent Office is currently trying to come up with solutions that would partly restore its function of determining a patent's validity. The only chance to do so would be a system that is far quicker than the current one.

---

86 S. Ono (see fn. 83 above).

87 E.g., Tokyo High Court, 28 May 1998, [1998] AIPPI Journal of the Japanese Group, Int'l Ed. 247 – "L'Air du Temps", where the court denied bad faith of the defendant despite registration of at least 10 well-known perfume brands in his own name.

88 Criticism is voiced in this respect by S. Ono, "Chiteki zaisanken songai ni okeru songai baishô kyaku no kettei" (On Decisions Regarding the Amount of Damages in Infringement Actions), 111 Kôgyô shoyûken kenkyû 1 (1993). A rare example of an interim decision can be found in Tokyo District Court, 25 May 2001, 15 Law & Technology 61 [2002]. The decision held databases not protectable under copyright law, yet granted the damage claim in principle under tort law. Subsequent proceedings would then relate to the amount of such damages.

89 Supreme Court decision, 11 April 2000, 1710 Hanrei Jihô 68 – "Kilby's Patent III". The principle is perhaps laudable, yet the example is difficult: after all, the patent (covering the basic technology for semiconductors) not only took about 30 years to get granted, but also survived a significant number of oppositions and invalidation requests. It looks as if the courts tried to find reasons for unburdening Japanese semiconductor chip makers from the significant amount of royalties Texas Instruments had demanded for its technology.

90 Tokyo District Court, 14 July 2000 (unreported); Osaka District Court, 5 September 2000 (unreported).

91 Tokyo District Court, 27 September 2000 (unreported).

92 Tokyo District Court, 25 April 2001 (unreported).

93 Tokyo District Court, 30 January 2001 (unreported).

94 111 Japan Patents and Trademarks 12 [February 2002].

5. The United States[95]

The US system may not only be the most costly but also the most complicated when it comes to enforcing IP rights. There are several reasons for this. First, pre-trial discovery procedures are further reaching than in any other jurisdiction; second the decision on the facts by a jury requires different considerations than trials before judges; third, the range of possible defences by the alleged infringer is wider than in most jurisdictions; and fourth, the possibility of claiming increased damages in cases of wilful infringement requires strategic considerations absent in other jurisdictions.

To the extent that an intellectual property right falls under federal jurisdiction (which is not the case for trade secrets or matters of unfair competition), an infringement suit can be brought before one of the 94 federal district courts. In IP matters, appeals are exclusively heard before the Court of Appeals of the Federal Circuit, where also appeals against decisions from the Patent Office are heard. A final appeal lies with the US Supreme Court. Judges in these courts are appointed for life and thus cannot be removed or relocated. Claims of infringement can be brought before any court with jurisdiction over the defendant's residence, place of business or where acts of infringement have been committed. However, in the latter case it is necessary that the defendant has minimum contacts to the forum, which is decided by a sort of rule of reason test.[96] Sometimes reasonable knowledge of distribution chains can be sufficient.[97] Choice of the forum can influence the speed of proceedings, as some courts have gained a reputation for being speedier than others ("rocket docket").

Suits have to be initiated by the IP owner, and in case of co-ownership require a joint suit.[98] Licensees may sue as co-plaintiffs.[99] Suitable defendants can be all those involved in acts of direct or contributory infringement. For strategic considerations, it is not uncommon to sue a small retailer or end user in the first place, since less resistance can be expected. Very few actions reach trial, however. Most are dismissed without court action or disposed of by the

---

[95] Moore/Michel/Lupo, Patent Litigation and Strategy, St. Paul, Minn. 1999; Maloney, Chapter 15 of this book.

[96] See, e.g., Red Wing Shoe Co. *v*. Hockerson-Halberstadt, Inc., 30 June 1998, 148 F.3d 1355 (Fed. Cir. 1998).

[97] See Beverly Hills Fan Co. *v*. Royal Sovereign Corp., 8 March 1994, 21 F.3d 1558 (Fed. Cir. 1994)(holding district court in Virginia had personal jurisdiction over a Chinese corporation which manufactured an allegedly infringing product in Taiwan and sold it to a New Jersey importer because it placed the products in a "stream of commerce" knowing the likely destination of some of the products in Virginia).

[98] Willingham *v*. Lawton, 555 F.2d 1340, 1343 (6th Cir. 1977).

[99] Enzo APA & Sons, Inc. *v*. Geapag A. G., 9 January 1998, 134 F.3d 1090, 1093 (Fed. Cir. 1998); Textile Prods., Inc. *v*. Mead Corp., 28 January 1998, 134 F.3d 1481, 1484 (Fed. Cir. 1998).

court during pre-trial or discovery.[100] Cases will be disposed of without trial by summary judgment where there is no serious dispute about the facts. Particularly after the Supreme Court has held that claim interpretation is a matter of law not of fact,[101] summary judgments have become more common. When issues of fact are concerned, either plaintiff or defendant may opt for a jury trial, an option that particularly in patent cases is questionable due to the lack of technical knowledge on the side of the six to 12 lay persons the jury is comprised of. If anything, juries make the outcome of a trial very difficult to foresee, thus adding to the risk of litigation. Jury trials are on the increase: In the late 1960s, only 3% of all patent cases were decided by juries; in 1999 about 62%.

The defendant may argue that the IP right is invalid, has not been infringed or that its exercise is an abuse. To the extent that patents are concerned, the patentee may request a so-called re-examination before the Patent Office prior to an infringement suit: A re-examined patent is more likely to be upheld. Given the fact that between 1989 and 1996, 46% of all patents in suit were invalidated, importance must be attached to this issue. Particularly in patent cases, many defences concern the patentee's conduct during application procedure, e.g., properly stating the best mode of carrying out the invention, the prior art, or the disclaimers made for the patent to be granted. An IP right may not be enforceable in cases of misuse, antitrust counterclaims or laches.

For remedies such as injunctive relief and damages, see below VII.

6. Intra-European Litigation[102]

Two specific problems of IP enforcement should be mentioned at this stage. The first is the relationship between the European Patent Office's opposition procedures and national infringement litigation, the second, the influence of

---

[100] Out of a total of 2,187 patent cases in 1999, only 98 reached the trial stage. More than half (1,263) were disposed of by the court during discovery. Maloney, Chapter 15 of this book.

[101] Markman *v.* Westview Instruments Inc., 116 Supreme Court 1384 (1996). So-called "Markman hearings" refer to a discussion and ultimate decision on patent claim construction prior to a hearing on damages or liability.

[102] Le contenieux de la propriété industrielle en Europe (Patent Litigation in Europe), Collection CEIPI, Litec 1999; Wadlow, Enforcement of Intellectual Property in European and International Law, Sweet & Maxwell, London 1998; Bertrams, The Cross-Border Prohibitory Injunction in Dutch Patent Law, 26 IIC 625 [1995]; Brinkhof, The Desirability, Necessity and Feasibility of Cooperation in the Field of Patent Law, [1997] EIPR 226; Jacob, The Enlarged Board of Appeal of the EPO: A Proposal, [1997] EIPR 224; von Rospatt, Decisions of German Courts in Patent Infringement Cases with Cross-Border Effect, 29 IIC 504 [1998]; Mousseron/Raynard/Véron, Cross-Border Injunctions – A French Perspective, 29 IIC 884 [1998]; Veron, Thirty Years of Experience with the Brussels Convention in Patent Infringement Litigation, Journal of the Patent and Trade Mark Office Society, June 2002, 432.

the Brussels and Lugano Conventions on the Recognition and Enforcement of Judgments. Both issues for the moment only bear relevancy to Europe. Yet, broadening the ambit of the Brussels and Lugano Conventions to an international convention on the recognition and enforcement of judgments is currently being discussed in the Hague, giving the issue a truly international perspective. Furthermore, separation of granting authority and the court with jurisdiction over the infringement action may well become a more common feature in the future with the advent of more regional patent offices or even the mutual recognition of patent grants. Consequently, also this issue transcends the borders of Europe.

a) European Patent Convention and National Courts

Patent applications before the European Patent Office in Munich are centrally processed until the date of grant, and subsequently divided into a bundle of national patents in those countries that have been designated at the time of application and for which the necessary translation requirements have been fulfilled. Members of the European Patent Convention include not only EU countries but also Switzerland, Slovenia, Hungary, Romania, and others. A decision rendered by the European Patent Office to grant or refuse a patent carries the same weight in EPC member countries as would decisions of their respective national patent offices. Opposition against the grant of a European patent office can be raised up to nine months after grant, well into the phase when the European patent has become effective as a national patent in the designated states. Opposition procedures may well take a couple of years, and any decision can be further appealed to the Board of Appeals.

A good number of European countries grant their national courts jurisdiction over invalidating domestic patents in infringement suits, e.g., England, France or Italy. However, any decision to invalidate a patent is territorially limited. Even where a European patent has been granted, domestic courts cannot invalidate the European patent as such, but only the effect of this patent in the respective member state. In the case where both infringement procedures before national courts and opposition procedures before the EPO are pending and continue in parallel, a number of scenarios are conceivable. If the ultimate decision is the same in both proceedings, this means a considerable waste of time and money due to double procedures. If the European Patent Office ultimately allows the opposition and rejects the patent, then that decision will be binding in the designated countries with the effect that there will be no patent (unless the patentee had opted for a domestic application of the patent in parallel). This result would necessarily have an effect on infringement procedures as these have to be dismissed. If on the other hand the European Patent Office upholds the patent, while a national court revokes it, the effect is that the patent would not be in force in that country, but would be in force in the other designated countries, which might also be undesirable. Given the fact that the invalidation of the national part of the European patent has no influence on the other national parts of the same patent, and the fact that holding a European patent valid in opposition procedures before the European Patent Office has no binding effect on national courts, the question is if under these circumstances, proceedings should be stayed even in countries that give the courts jurisdiction over invalidating a patent. This has been so held both in the United Kingdom and Ireland:

"The fact that there may be proceedings both in the national courts and before the EPO is inevitable as patent rights, both under the Convention and under the Act, are national rights to be enforced by the national courts with revocation and amendment being possible in both the national courts and in certain circumstances before the EPO. That overlap can mean that there are parallel proceedings in this country and the EPO with the potential for conflict. It is desirable for that to be avoided. Therefore the Patents Court will stay the English proceedings pending a final resolution of the European proceedings, if they can be resolved quickly and a stay will not inflict injustice on the party or be against the public interest".[103]

"It is not sensible for a court in this country to allow proceedings to be heard in this country which duplicate those in the EPO unless justice require that to happen. At the time that the 1977 Act was enacted, it was envisaged that proceedings before the EPO would be concluded with reasonable expedition. The consequences would be that any overlap between EPO proceedings and national actions could be prevented by staying the proceedings in this country for a short period. In some cases, the Patents Court has refused to stay proceedings in this country, despite the obvious desirability of taking that action because of the injustice that a stay would cause".[104]

b) Foreign Lawsuits and Their Effect on Domestic Litigation

Two possible scenarios on international civil procedure should be distinguished when it comes to intellectual property litigation. The first is the question to what extent a foreign intellectual property right can be the object of domestic litigation. Intellectual property rights being territorial in nature, such a lawsuit would not only concern a foreign intellectual property right, but also an act of infringement committed abroad. Nonetheless, the defendant's domestic residence may give the courts jurisdiction in this matter. Some countries have been reluctant to take on such cases, however, for the reason that "it would not normally be right for the courts in this country to determine a dispute on infringement of a foreign patent in respect of acts done outside the country provided there is an adequate remedy in the relevant country".[105]

---

[103] English Court of Appeal, Beloit Technologies Inc. *v.* Valmet Paper Machinery, 12 February 1997, [1997] R.P.C. 489, 503.

[104] English Court of Appeal, Kimberly-Clark Worldwide Inc. *v.* Procter & Gamble Ltd., 24 November 1999, [2000] F.S.R. 235–245. In the same vein High Court of Ireland, GD Searle and Companies and Monsantos Company Patent, 14 March 2001, [2002] F.S.R. 24.

[105] English Court of Appeal, Plastus Kreativ *v.* Minnesota Mining, 9 December 1994, [1995] R.P.C. 438. The same conclusion was reached in a US decision: Mars Inc. *v.* Kabushiki Kaisha Nippon Conlux, 29 April 1994, 24 F.3d 1368 (Fed.Cir. 1994).

Other countries have been more flexible in this respect.[106]

The other and widely discussed scenario concerns the influence of foreign litigation on a domestic infringement suit. At first glance, intellectual property rights should offer no particular problems in this respect: Even under the aspect of avoiding double litigation, there should be no serious conflict. After all, an intellectual property right granted in country A can only be infringed in country A, and never in country B. A lawsuit in country B can therefore not be preempted by a lawsuit in country A, as both the intellectual property right and the infringing act are different. To some extent, different rules may apply for matters of unfair competition, if, e.g., a trade secret has been misappropriated in one country and used in the other. Here, double litigation may result in the decision of one country not being enforceable in the other.[107]

The above rules are slightly different within the ambit of the Brussels/Lugano Conventions on jurisdiction and the enforcement of judgments in civil and commercial matters.[108] The Brussels Convention concerns the above-mentioned issues in the following manner. First, a defendant can always be sued at the place of domicile. This would give the court jurisdiction to rule on IP infringements even occurring in other countries provided that the alleged infringer is the defendant domiciled within the jurisdiction of the court. Additional grounds for jurisdiction are the place

[106] Initially, jurisdiction was denied by the German Courts in this respect: Imperial Supreme Court, 2 October 1886, RGZ 18, 28; Imperial Supreme Court, 18 July 1890, Juristische Wochenschrift 1890, 280. Criticism by Isay, Patentgesetz, 5th ed. 1931, 232: "It is incomprehensible why claims of one German company against another German company from infringements [committed abroad] cannot be brought before German courts to be argued there." To the extent that an action can be brought before the court where the defendant has his ordinary residence or business address, the courts have now held that they can indeed rule on foreign property rights: German Federal Supreme Court, 2 October 1997, 30 IIC 227 [1999] – "Spielbankaffaire" for a case of copyright infringement in several countries. However, in this case the German courts would have to inquire to what extent foreign intellectual property rights are infringed according to the laws of these respective countries.

[107] Often, foreign decisions cannot be enforced if there exists a decision about the same matter that contradicts the foreign decision. An example would be Tokyo District Court, 24 September 1991, 1429 Hanrei Jihô 80 – "Manufacture of Plated Copper". In an interim decision in this matter, the Tokyo District Court, 30 May 1989, 1348 Hanrei Jihô 91 had ruled that parallel proceedings on the same subject matter in the US were no impediment to the action as these had not started in earnest. The problem can be limited if the courts were to apply stricter rules on the legal interest for filing a suit for declaration of non-infringement. See also the following explanations.

[108] The Convention originally was not an EC treaty, but a multilaterial treaty. However, subsequently all EC countries acceded to the Convention. The agreement between the EC and the EFTA states led to the conclusion of the Lugano Convention in 1988 which is an almost exact replica of the Brussels Convention. See above.

where the harmful event occurred (Art. 5(3)),[109] and Art. 6(1) which allows a concentration of suits against several defendants domiciled in one or more contracting states. Here, the case can be brought where proceedings are related, and this is the case where several defendants in different European states are sued for infringement of the same European patent.[110] The rules on jurisdiction are not only important in case of possible infringement suits, but also for the declaration of non-infringement. In order to avoid double litigation, Art. 21 Brussels Convention states the following:

> "Where proceedings involving the same course of action between the same parties are brought in the courts of different contracting states, any court other than the court first seized shall of its own motion stay proceedings until such time as the jurisdiction of the court first seized is established.
>
> "Where the jurisdiction of the court first seized is established, any court other than the court first seized shall decline jurisdiction in favour of that court."

According to Art. 22, the same applies to "related actions". If it was held that the same European patent transformed into different national patents was still the same or at least related, there could be no parallel proceedings for infringement over the same patent in different European states, e.g., France and Germany, at the same time. This, in turn, might give rise to concerns of abuse. A company being faced with a potential infringement suit in, say, Germany, could so to speak preempt such infringement suit by filing for a declaration of non-infringement in, say, Italy, where the patentee owns the same European patent. The reason for such a request for declaratory judgment would be the fact that courts in Italy are reputed to be much slower than those in Germany, with the effect that the patentee would not be able to continue or even initiate his suit in Germany, as the matter would fall under Art. 21 or 22 Brussels Convention. This tactic is referred to as the Belgium or Italian torpedo. Its efficiency of course depends on the interpretation of "same (related) cause of action" under Arts. 6(1), 21, 22 Brussels Convention.[111]

---

[109] Which again would only give the court jurisdiction to rule on cases with a foreign connection, which cannot be those of registered IP rights, as the harm can only occur where the patent or trade mark has been registered. This is different in unfair competition cases: e.g., European Court of Justice, 7 March 1995, [1995] 1 All E.R. 289 – "Fiona Shevill", case of tarnishing the reputation of a British plaintiff by a French publisher where the journal was published in several contracting states.

[110] English High Court, Coin Controls *v.* Suzo, 26 March 1997, [1997] F.S.R. 660; The Hague Court of Appeal, 23 April 1998, 1998 Intellectuele Eigendom en Reclamerecht 286 – "Expandable Grafts".

[111] For a broad interpretation: Franzosi, Worldwide Patent Litigation and the Italian Torpedo, [1997] EIPR 382; for a narrow one: Tritton, Intellectual Property in Europe, 2nd ed., London 2002, 1001.

There are further problems with the Brussels Convention related to interim measures and the combination of infringement/nullity actions that cannot be discussed at this stage.

VII. Final Measures: Arts. 44–48

The TRIPS Agreement mentions a number of final measures that have to be provided: injunctions in **Art. 44**, damages in **Art. 45**, destruction of infringing goods in **Art. 46**, and the right of information in **Art. 47**.

1. Injunctive Relief, Art. 44

Injunctive relief is perhaps the most sought after remedy in infringement cases. The remedy would normally not require proof of wilfulness or negligence, as it can only be considered an order for future lawful behaviour. Very few countries would regard injunctive relief only as a discretionary remedy.[112] Ordinarily, the order for injunctive relief is accompanied by a fine that is imposed in the case of contravention.

Countries have different rules on how to word the injunction. While in some countries, it is sufficient for the plaintiff to request the defendant to cease further infringement, other countries require the plaintiff to request a far more detailed order. Thus, in a patent infringement, the plaintiff would have to describe the infringing act and request cessation thereof, sometimes including possible equivalents. In the case of trade marks, the plaintiff would be requested to describe exactly which part of the infringing mark the defendant should no longer use. In general, it is preferable that the request for injunctive relief be particularly tailored to the infringing act. After all, the IP right as such already excludes third parties from using it. If the defendant has unlawfully used the IP right in a certain manner, the remedy should reflect the infringement rather than be a request for lawful behaviour in general, as this could be requested from anyone. It is perhaps not a good idea to limit the injunctive order to a certain infringing type or series, e.g., "The defendant may no longer produce a washing machine of type XY", as this would allow the defendant to merely rename the type or series and continue the infringing activity.

2. Damages, Arts. 45, 48

The calculation of damages is notoriously difficult in intellectual property matters. In most countries, damages are meant "to compensate for the injury the right holder has suffered because of an infringement of his intellectual property right", **Art. 45.1 TRIPS**. Most countries would thus regard damages as compensatory rather than punitive. In the US, cases of wilful

---

[112] As would be the case in the US: Richardson *v.* Suzuki Motor Company, 16 February 1989, 868 F.2d 1226 (Fed. Cir. 1989).

infringement may make the infringer liable to enhanced damage awards "up to three times the amount found or assessed", 35 U.S.C. § 284.[113]

The difficulty of assessing damages is mitigated by the fact that in a good many jurisdictions, the parties settle their case after an infringement is established.[114] It is now common practice in most countries to calculate damages either on the basis of the damages incurred, the infringer's profits or a reasonable royalty. The rationale behind these methods of calculation is the following: Damages are often difficult to quantify. They would include lost sales (difficult to prove causality in competitive markets, however), loss of reputation, sometimes market confusion and consequences of such direct damages, e.g., the closure of production sites. Calculating these damages is often difficult and time consuming. It is often easier to calculate damages according to the principles of *unjust enrichment*. Unjust enrichment would allow the right owner to claim what the infringer has obtained by using an economic position exclusively allocated to the right owner. This is particularly apparent in the case of an ordinary licensing fee: The infringer should at least pay what would have been due had the infringer tried to act lawfully, that is, had he tried to obtain permission to use the right. Yet it is clear that such ordinary licensing fee can only be the bottom line: If an infringer only had to pay an ordinary licensing fee, there would be very little incentive for lawful behaviour, even more so in cases where the right owner would not have granted a licence in the first place. This is different for the claim of the infringer's profits: Also these, it can be argued, have been obtained at the right owner's expense, at least to the extent that without the infringement, those profits should have gone to the right owner. Some examples from national court decisions may illustrate the point.

a) The US

35 USC §284 awards damages for infringement "in no event less than a reasonable royalty". Just as in England and Germany, a trial for establishing infringement often precedes a trial for damages. If the IP owner claims more

---

113 E.g., Read Corporation *v.* Portec, 10 July 1992, 970 F.2d 816 (Fed. Cir. 1992): "The paramount determination in deciding to grant an enhancement and the amount thereof is the egregiousness of the defendant's conduct based on all the facts and circumstance". Another consequence of such wilful infringement is the (discretionary) award of attorneys' fees, Ortho Pharmaceutical Corporation *v.* Smith, 19 March 1992, 959 F.2d 936 (Fed. Cir. 1992).

114 E.g., in Germany, there is a scarcity of decisions on the calculation of damages due to the fact that an interim decision on the infringement as such would cause most parties to settle, particularly as the plaintiff can request all necessary details for the calculation of, e.g., the infringer's profits: Sec. 259 Civil Code. A claim for details is regularly made as a preparation of the damage claim and recognised by the courts as such: Federal Supreme Court, 13 March 1962, GRUR 1962, 398 – "Kreuzbodenventilsäcke II". In France, the fact that courts could order a gross damage amount to be immediately enforceable is an incentive for settling the case.

than reasonable royalties, an expert witness would often be heard as to the exact amount.

Lost profits can be claimed upon proof of the following:

(1) demand for the patented product;
(2) absence of competing and non-infringing products;
(3) ability of the IP owner to actually market the quantity of goods for which lost profits are claimed; and
(4) the amount of profit that would have been made in the absence of infringement.[115]

Lost profits may even be claimed for lost sales of products not manufactured by the patented invention.[116] Where several competing products are on the market, lost profits are limited to the difference between actual market share and market share that would have been realised but for the infringement, plus a reasonable royalty on all products sold beyond this figure.[117] The same decision, however, also affirms the recoverability of damages for the loss of sales of non-patented parts of a patented invention (entire market value).[118] The decisive question is whether the patentee can reasonably expect the sale of non-patented components together with the sale of the patented component.[119] In a competitive market, it is not sufficient merely to compare market shares before and after infringement. Rather, competition must be measured subjectively, i.e., it must be established that consumers had actually diverted their demand. This is not the case

[115] Panduit Corp. *v.* Stahlin Brothers Fiberworks, 25 April 1978, 575 F.2d 1152 (6th Circuit 1978).

[116] Rite-Hite Corp. Kelley, 15 June 1995, 56 F.3d 1538 (Fed. Cir. 1995): Here, the patentee held parallel patents for comparable inventions, one of which was used but not infringed, the other which was not used but infringed. Due to the infringement, sales of products manufactured under the patent that was not infringed had dropped. The court found the loss foreseeable and therefore recoverable. "The basic flaw in the majority's ruling is its rejection of the premise that recovery must be tied to profits from the invention itself": Moore/Michel/Lupo, Patent Litigation and Strategy, St. Paul, Minn. 1999, 529. This becomes apparent in the case where the non-infringed patent had been sold to a third party. Here, it would have been completely clear that the third party was not entitled to damages for the infringement of another's patent. It is similarly questionable if damages would have been granted had the sold products not been protected by another patent. In other words, foreseeability as such is insufficient. Rather the lost profits must be attributable to the achievement that the patent represents.

[117] State Industry Inc. *v.* Mor-Flo Industries, 31 August 1989, 883 F.2d 1573 (Fed. Cir. 1989).

[118] See also Fonar Corporation *v.* General Electric, 25 February 1997, 107 F.3d 1543 (Fed. Cir. 1997): If the infringer uses the advantage of the patented device, this carries the presumption of consumer demand for the whole product.

[119] King Instruments Corp. *v.* Otari Corp., 26 June 1985, 767 F.2d 853 (Fed. Cir. 1985).

where the products may be objectively competing, yet target different consumer groups.[120]

Reasonable royalties are determined by a number of factors, e.g., royalties actually received from other licensees, royalties for comparable patents, licensing policy of the right owner, existence of competition with comparable products, profitability of products sold under the IP right, customary profits in the particular business, and the rate that the IP owner and infringer would have reasonably agreed to when the infringement started.[121] This in effect means that the infringer should still walk away with a profit, as a prudent licensee would have been able to do. Reasonable royalties would not include litigation expenses or attorneys' fees.[122] These expenses can only be recovered upon proof of wilful infringement. The same holds true for the infringer's profits. These can only be taken into account in the discretionary doubling or trebling of damages upon establishing wilful infringement ("egregiousness of the defendant's conduct based on all the facts and circumstances").[123] Interest, however, would normally be awarded.[124]

35 USC § 287 makes a damage award conditional, depending on a proper marking of the product (patented, trademarked) or other knowledge of the infringer about the IP right. Failure to properly mark the products can lead to a loss of damages.[125]

Thus, while providing IP owners with the possibility of obtaining multiple damages in cases of wilful infringement, the US system has also significant limits of damage awards. First, it does not allow IP owners to claim the infringer's profits, and, second, it makes damages conditional, depending on a proper marking of the products. Further, it provides for reimbursement of attorneys' fees only in exceptional circumstances, these being normally wilful infringement.

b) Japan

All intellectual property laws contain a presumption of damages as the profits gained by the infringer or an amount of money the aggrieved party would normally be entitled to receive for the use of the infringed right. This partly helps to ease the plaintiff's burden of proving damages. Damages are

---

[120] BIC Leisure Products *v.* Windsurfing International, 4 August 1993, 1 F.3d 1214 (Fed. Cir. 1993) for the case of up-market and rather down-market surfboards.

[121] Georgia-Pacific Corporation *v.* United States Plywood-Champion Papers, 381 F.Supp. 1116 (Southern District of New York 1970): "In fixing damages on a royalty basis against an infringer, the sum allowed should be reasonable and that which would be accepted by a prudent licensee who wished to obtain a license but was not so compelled and a prudent patentee, who wished to grant a license but was not so compelled".

[122] Mahurkar *v.* C.R. Bard, 29 March 1996, 79 F.3d 1572 (Fed. Cir. 1996).

[123] Read Corporation *v.* Portec Inc., 10 July 1992, 970 F.2d 816 (Fed. Cir. 1992).

[124] General Motors Corporation *v.* Devex Corporation, 24 May 1983, 461 U.S. 648 (1983).

[125] E.g., American Medical Systems Inc. *v.* Medical Engineering Corporation, 4 October 1993, 6 F.3d 1523 (Fed. Cir. 1993).

understood as monetary compensation and may not be punitive.[126] Japanese courts would not bother much with damage calculations based on market share and attribute the right owner's lost profits to the infringing act only where the market structure permitted the conclusion that such loss was directly attributable to the infringing act.[127] As yet only for patent law under the 1999 revision, losses of the right owner can be calculated on a discretionary basis according to the number of infringing goods sold by the defendant, taking into account the right owner's market share and marketing efforts. This would basically mean a calculation based on the infringer's amount of sales multiplied by the right owner's usual profits per item, but limited to the right owner's marketing capacity, Sec. 102(1) Patent Act. The claim is limited to the right owner's marketing capacity, thereby disadvantaging small-scale inventors and universities. Sec. 102(1) also appears applicable where the lost sales are attributable to a different (but unexploited) patent of the patentee.[128] Where claiming lost profits, the right owner has to deduct the expenses saved. Vice versa, the infringer can deduct from his profits the expenses incurred.[129] If the infringer's figures for pure profits seem unrealistically low, the court would simply multiply the infringer's turnover with the IP owner's normal profits, which patent law already provides for on a statutory basis.[130] The infringer's profits cannot be claimed where the IP right in question was not used.[131] In trade mark and unfair

[126] Supreme Court, 11 July 1997, 30 IIC 480 [1999] – "Punitive Damages". Foreign decisions awarding punitive damages may not be enforced in Japan, either.

[127] Tokyo District Court, 12 October 1998, 30 IIC 457 [1999] – "Cimetidine". Tokyo District Court goes even further, 19 March 2002, 4–7 AIPPI Journal 4 – "Pachinko Slot" where the court did not even examine to what extent competing products were on the market, but assumed that but for the infringement, the patentee would have sold a number of products comparable to the infringer's sales.

[128] Tokyo High Court, 15 June 1999, 1697 Hanrei Jihô 96 – "Heat Bank System": Here the patentee held patents A and B, made its turnover by exploiting patent A, while the infringer used the technology of patent B, which then led to a drop in sales of the patentee's products using technology A. The case resembles a similar US case (Rite-Hite Corporation *v.* Kelley Corporation, 15 June 1995, 56 F.3d 1538 (Fed. Cir. 1995) and is open to question: First, the result would doubtlessly be different if patents A and B were held by different owners. Second, if the Patent Act aims at patents being exploited, why should strategic non-exploitation be rewarded?

[129] The infringer's turnover is a presumption for his profits unless otherwise proven: Tokyo District Court, 7 October 1998, 1657 Hanrei Jihô 122 – "Recharging System".

[130] Osaka District Court, 17 September 1998, 282 Hanketsu Sokuhô 17 – "Toaster".

[131] E.g., Osaka District Court, 25 February 1993, 25-1 Chizaishû 56 – "Jimmy'z"; in Tokyo District Court, 31 October 2001, 15 Law & Technology 92 [2002], this principle is affirmed, yet the court stresses that it would apply particularly to trade marks, as no damage to the trade mark owner's goodwill could be detected in such case. The principle is also applied to other IP rights, however: Osaka District Court, 27 March 1981 for a patent. That the courts in trade mark cases require use by the trade mark owner rather than the (registered) licensee is incomprehensible, however: Tokyo District Court, 24 March 1993, 26 IIC 566 [1995] – "Type Chanel No. 5".

competition cases, the plaintiff can also claim damages for loss of reputation[132] or market confusion.[133]

Requesting damages in the amount of an ordinary licensing fee would normally be the fallback provision in cases where neither use of the right, one's own damages, or infringer's profits can be proven.[134] Ordinary licensing fees tended to be rather low and were based on the Inventors Association's figures for contractually negotiated licensing rates in domestic agreements. The highest awards were for the infringement of famous marks such as Snoopy or Chanel, where the courts awarded licensing rates of 10%.[135] Owing to the 1998 amendment of Sec. 102(3) Patent Act, the courts at least in patent cases no longer feel obligated to award only an "ordinary" licensing fee, and recent case law seems to indicate that the courts have become more assertive in arriving at higher figures.[136]

Thus, Japanese law allows for the calculation of damages by way of the right owner's own damage, the infringer's profits or an ordinary licensing fee. The infringer's profits cannot be claimed where the right has not actually been used by the right owner. Japanese patent law further allows for a rather unique calculation of the infringer's profits by multiplying the infringer's actual sales with the profit the IP owner would ordinarily have made from such a sale.

c) Germany

In Germany, damage claims for the infringement of intellectual property rights are now statute based, e.g., Sec. 139 Patent Act. However, no specific method of calculation is given, reflecting the fact that such damage claims have always been a traditional remedy under tort law, and those for intellectual property rights thus follow the same tort law principles. Apart from tort law, the courts also use unjust enrichment as a basis for calculating an appropriate licensing fee, and action without mandate (*Geschäftsführung ohne Auftrag*) to properly calculate and delineate damages based on the infringer's profits. The three calculation methods (the right owner's own damages, infringer's profit and reasonable licence) date back to the 19th century and

---

[132] E.g., Kobe District Court, 23 March 1987, 19-1 Mutaishû 72 – "Love Hotel Chanel". The amount tends to be low, however: between 1 and 3 million Yen.

[133] These cases are rare, however, and the amount is not significant, either: Yokohama District Court, 22 March 1985, 566 Hanrei Times 275 – "Chanel Handbag" (1 million Yen).

[134] It is thus perhaps mistaken if Tokyo High Court, 23 March 1995, 27-1 Chizaishû 171 – "Snack Chanel II", denies the right owner a statutory licensing fee based on the reasoning that a licence would never have been granted. At least the court granted damages for loss of reputation.

[135] Tokyo District Court, 22 December 1978, 378 Hanrei Times 152 – "Snoopy"; Tokyo District Court, 27 April 1988, 20-1 Mutaishû 209 – "Louis Vuitton"; Tokyo District Court, 24 March 1993, 26 IIC 566 – "Type Chanel No. 5".

[136] Tokyo District Court, 30 March 1998, 1656 Hanrei Jihô 143: 7% in a patent infringement case.

were developed by the Imperial Commercial Court (*Reichsoberhandelsgericht*) for cases of copyright infringement. These principles were affirmed by the Imperial Supreme Court in two decisions of 1895[137] and 1898.[138] Damages are meant to restore the *status quo ante*, and may thus not be punitive, the exception being copyright infringements.[139] Apart from monetary damages, the courts can also order other forms of restitution, e.g., delayed market entry if an unlawful time advantage has been achieved by the infringement.[140]

Proof of actual damages can be alleviated by Sec. 287 Code of Civil Procedure that gives the court a certain discretion in assessing damages. Such discretion, however, can only be used once the IP owner has tried everything possible to specify the damages incurred.[141] The three methods of calculation can often lead to different damage amounts. The plaintiff has the choice which method to apply, and may even first sue for an inspection of the relevant commercial documents in the possession of the defendants before deciding how to proceed.[142] Furthermore, the calculation of damages according to a reasonable licensing fee does not preclude the plaintiff from claiming additional damages, as the licensing fee is only regarded as a minimum amount.[143]

The most common form of claiming damages is the reasonable licence, for three reasons. First, this is the only agreeable form of damages where an agreement can be reached. And in most cases an agreement is reached after the court has found for infringement. Second, the other two forms of calculation require far greater efforts by the right owner. Third, many right owners do not wish to lay open their internal cost structures. In addition, to the extent that the claim is based on unjust enrichment (where no negligence is necessary, and where time bar is 30 rather than three years), the amount that can be claimed is also an ordinary licensing fee[144] that is calculated in the same way as under a damage claim.[145] In fact, the reason why an appropriate licensing fee is awarded is far closer to the doctrine of unjust enrichment: By using what is exclusively allocated to someone else, the infringer enriches himself at the right owner's expense. The basis of the calculation is a

[137] Imperial Supreme Court, 8 June 1895, RGZ 35, 63.

[138] Imperial Supreme Court, 31 December 1898, RGZ 43, 56.

[139] In copyright infringement cases, damages are doubled in order to reflect the continuous monitoring efforts of the collecting societies: Federal Supreme Court, 10 March 1972, BGHZ 59, 286 – "Double Tariff".

[140] Federal Supreme Court, 21 February 1989, BGHZ 107, 46.

[141] Federal Supreme Court, 6 March 1980, BGHZ 77, 16 – "Tolbutamid".

[142] Federal Supreme Court, 6 December 1974, GRUR 1975, 434; Federal Supreme Court, 17 June 1992, GRUR 1993, 55 – "Tchibo-Rolex II".

[143] Federal Supreme Court, 6 March 1980, GRUR 1980, 841 – "Tolbutamid".

[144] Federal Supreme Court, 24 November 1981, GRUR 1982, 301 – "Kunststoffhohlprofil II".

[145] Federal Supreme Court, 18 February 1992, GRUR 1992, 599 – "Teleskopzylinder".

percentage of the infringing product's sales price. It is immaterial in this respect that the product has perhaps been sold at a far lower price than the right owner would have wanted, in particular because otherwise it could not be reasonably assumed that the infringer had indeed sold the same quantity of goods at a higher price.[146] The courts are given considerable discretion in the calculation of the licensing fee. One may take into account the commercial importance of the invention, the average licensing fees in the respective technical field (for patents) or comparable marks (for trade marks), but in any case the actual infringement case has to be compared to the situation of a contractual licence. If in the latter case the licensor would receive additional benefits, e.g., by sharing marketing information, this can be a reason for awarding an increased royalty rate against an infringer.[147]

According to Sec. 249 German Civil Code, lost profits can be claimed as the difference between profits but for the infringing act and profits actually made, e.g., as a loss of turnover.[148] This method of calculation requires proof of the causal link between the infringing act and the lost profits, while the burden of proof is on the right owner. Only if the right owner has furnished all facts in his possession can the court make an estimated guess according to Sec. 287 Code of Civil Procedure.[149] It is assumed that the right owner has lost sales in the amount of what the infringer has achieved by the sale of the infringing goods.[150] However, this assumption depends on to what extent potential buyers would have directed their orders towards the right owner, and in this respect third parties offering competing and non-infringing products have to be taken into account.[151] While the right owner does not have to prove every single sale he would have made but for the infringement, he has to show what would have been sold in the normal course of events, i.e., if sales would have continued in the same manner, increased or decreased with a certain likelihood.[152] General overhead cannot be included in lost profits, while costs for research and development can be taken into account to the extent that such costs could have been set off by the profits made for the very product that was subject to the infringement.[153] In the case of composite products, damages for lost sales can be claimed to the extent that these would have been sold together with the patented article.[154]

---

[146] Federal Supreme Court, 6 March 1980, BGHZ 77, 16.

[147] Düsseldorf Appeal Court, 17 April 1980, GRUR 1981, 45.

[148] Imperial Supreme Court, 7 April 1941, RGZ 156, 65.

[149] Imperial Supreme Court, 23 February 1920, GRUR 1920, 103; Federal Supreme Court, 6 March 1980, BGHZ 77, 16 – "Tolbutamid".

[150] Imperial Supreme Court, 29 March 1919, RGZ 95, 220.

[151] Berlin District Court, 25 October 1939, GRUR 1940, 32.

[152] Federal Supreme Court, 16 March 1959, BGHZ 29, 393; Federal Supreme Court, GRUR 1979, 869; Federal Supreme Court, 9 April 1992, GRUR 1992, 530.

[153] Federal Supreme Court, 6 March 1980, BGHZ 77, 16 – "Tolbutamid".

[154] Federal Supreme Court, 30 May 1995 – "Steuereinrichtung II".

German law is fairly generous in awarding attorneys' and patent attorneys' fees (see below). Pre-trial costs are always recoverable as damages.[155] Damages for market confusion or loss of reputation are also acknowledged forms of damages.[156] The right owner's own damages are equivalent to an ordinary licensing fee in cases where the right owner has chosen to exploit the IP right only by licensing.[157]

Finally, the infringer's profits can be claimed based on the assumption that the infringer engaged in a business that only the right owner could have lawfully conducted, and for that reason should surrender to the right owner all the profits made from such business.[158] The infringer's profits cannot be claimed where the right owner would definitely not have used the right at all, while it is insufficient that the right was not actually used.[159] Obviously, the claim for the infringer's profits fails if the infringer has not actually made a profit, a fact that can be ascertained by an inspection of the relevant commercial documents prior to raising such claim. However, the infringer's profits can only be claimed to the extent that such profit was actually made from using the infringed right. Other factors such as adroit advertising, quality, size of the distribution system, reputation of the selling enterprise, special commercial relationships or other factors unrelated to the infringed right bear no conditional relationship to the infringed right and thus cannot be claimed as profits by the plaintiff.[160] Profits made from articles unrelated to the patent infringement can only be claimed under exceptional circumstances. In one case, a patent for slide frames was infringed, and the infringer distributed the slide frames as a free gift together with his cameras. The court held that part of the profit made from such cameras could count as the infringer's profits.[161]

Characteristic for the German method of damage calculation is the necessity of exact calculation mandated by the proportional reimbursement of attorneys' fees (see below): A right owner who claims more than he actually receives in the end partially loses his case and thus has to reimburse the other party for part of the attorneys' fees proportional to the percentage to which the claim is upheld. While the courts are given a significant amount of leeway in the calculation of damages, punitive elements of calculation can only be found in copyright cases.

---

155 Federal Supreme Court, 15 October 1969, GRUR 1970, 189.

156 Federal Supreme Court, 12 January 1966, BGHZ 44, 372 – "Meßmer-Tee II"; Imperial Supreme Court, 28 January 1933, GRUR 1933, 292.

157 Federal Supreme Court, 27 November 1969, GRUR 1970, 296 – "Allzweck Landmaschine".

158 E.g., Imperial Supreme Court, 22 October 1930, RGZ 130, 108; Federal Supreme Court, 29 May 1962, GRUR 1962, 509 – "Dia-Rähmchen II".

159 Imperial Supreme Court, 22 October 1930, RGZ 130, 108.

160 Cologne Appeal Court, 16 March 1990, GRUR 1991, 60 – "Rolex-Imitation"; Federal Supreme Court, 17 June 1992, GRUR 1993, 55 – "Tchibo/Rolex II".

161 Federal Supreme Court, 29 May 1962, GRUR 1962, 509 – "Dia-Rähmchen II".

Just as in the US, the right owner may claim commercial interest rates on the damages or the royalty rate unreasonably withheld during the time of infringement.

d) The United Kingdom

Damage compensation for the infringement of intellectual property rights is now statute based. Damages were introduced as an equitable remedy by the Chancery Amendment Act 1858 (Lord Cairns Act) that conferred on the courts of equity jurisdiction for damages in addition to or in lieu of an injunction or other specific equitable relief. The proper function of damages has been described as follows:

> "As in the case of any other tort (leaving aside cases where exemplary damages can be given) the object of damages is to compensate for loss or injury. The general rule at any rate in relation to 'economic' torts is that the measure of damages is to be, so far as possible, that sum of money which will put the injured party in the same position as he would have been in if he had not sustained the wrong. In the case of infringement of a patent, an alternative remedy at the option of the plaintiff exists by way of an account of profits made by the infringer. There are two essential principles in valuing that claim: First, that the plaintiffs have the burden of proving their loss; second, that if the defendants be wrong-doers, damages should be liberally assessed, but that the object is to compensate the plaintiffs and not punish the defendants. These elemental principles have been applied in numerous cases of infringements of patents. Naturally their application varies from place to place."[162]

Decisions on damages are very rare, and would normally be reached only after a trial on the merits of the case has been concluded:

> "Split trials are very frequently directed, and this is particularly so in intellectual property cases. A split trial is plainly called for in the interest of saving costs. Documents relevant only to quantum are not relevant to the issue of liability".[163]

Damages can thus be claimed either as the right owner's own damages or as the infringer's profits. An ordinary licensing fee would be considered as the right owner's damages and is awarded in cases where sales by the infringer would not have been made by the right owner.

In the last 20 years, there were two notable cases on damage awards: Catnic Component *v.* Hill,[164] and Gerber Garment Technology *v.* Lectra Systems.[165]

After a decision on the merits, the right owner has to decide whether to seek an inquiry as to damages or an account of the infringer's profits. The

---

[162] English House of Lords, General Tyre *v.* Firestone, 16 April 1975, [1976] R.P.C. 197.

[163] English High Court, Baldock *v.* Addison, 22 June 1994, [1995] 3 All E.R. 437.

[164] English High Court, 16 March 1983, [1983] F.S.R. 512.

[165] Patents Court, 20 March 1995 [1995] R.P.C. 383.

decision can be delayed until after a review of the defendant's commercial documents.[166]

The right owner's own damages can be computed as follows:

(1) loss of profits as a direct result of infringement;
(2) loss of profits as an indirect result of infringement (so-called parasitic damages);
(3) notional royalty;
(4) exemplary damages;[167]
(5) compound interest; and
(6) simple interest.

It is well known, however, that computing the right owner's own losses is a difficult matter: "The court must estimate what were the chances that a particular thing would have happened if there had been no infringement and reflect those chances in the amount of damages awarded, and could do no better than reach a figure based on the general impression received from the evidence as a whole" (Gerber *v.* Lectra). The burden of proof in this respect is facilitated by two factors:

(1) Once the existence of infringing articles has been proven, at least some loss of sales can be assumed. If the evidence showed a reasonable commercial exploitation of the genuine product, a comparison of the actual sales with the expectation of future ones could be taken as a measure for such loss;[168] and
(2) Damages would be assessed on the basis that every sale made by the infringer was a lost sale, and the proprietor would be compensated for the lost profit on such sale (Catnic *v.* Hill). However, the latter method can only be reasonably applied in cases where the right owner has a reasonably large market share: In the Catnic decision, the right owner's market share was 90% and the court thus computed 90% of the infringer's sales as lost sales of the right owner. In addition, such assumption can only be applied where the right owner actually has the marketing capacity for the production of articles the lost sales of which shall be calculated as damages. (Catnic Component *v.* Hill; Gerber *v.* Lectra):

---

[166] English High Court, Island Records Ltd. *v.* Tring International, 12 April 1995, [1995] 3 All E. R. 444.

[167] Exemplary damages are in a certain way punitive and can be awarded in the following cases (English House of Lords, Rookes *v.* Barnard, 21 January 1969, 1 All E.R. 367 [1964]: where the defendant's conduct has been calculated to make him a profit which may well exceed the compensation payable to the plaintiff; where the defendant with a cynical disregard for the plaintiff's rights has calculated that the money to be made out of his wrong-doing will probably exceed the damages at risk; where the defendant is seeking to gain at the expense of the plaintiff some objects which either he could not obtain at all or not obtain except at a price greater than he wants to put down.

[168] English High Court, Columbia Pictures *v.* Robinson, 21 August 1987, [1988] F.S.R. 531.

For sales the infringer made, but the right owner could not or would not have made, a reasonable royalty shall be paid.

Apart from direct damages incurred by lost sales, the right owner may further claim:

(1) secondary losses of sales of unpatented articles which went with the patented item as a commercial matter (Gerber *v.* Lectra);
(2) so-called "springboard" losses incurred due to the fact that the infringer by his acts obtains a commercial advantage regarding future sales;[169]
(3) losses incurred by a subsidiary company;
(4) losses for price erosion due to the existence of a competitor.

The difficulty with this item is the fact that price erosion or depression may well have led to larger sales figures. In Gerber *v.* Lectra, the court allowed at least part of the loss due to reduced prices as recoverable damages.

Ordinary licensing fees can be claimed instead of the right owner's own damages in cases where the right owner could not or would not have made the infringer's sales, or where the right owner opts for such calculation method. To the extent that there is sufficient discovery as to the right owner's profit margins, these would be taken into account in arriving at an appropriate licensing fee. The court would also add possible benefits from the sale of accompanied articles not covered by the IP right for which the infringer could also make a profit. In Gerber *v.* Lectra, the court arrived at a royalty rate of 15% where it was established that the right owner would have made a 60% profit from his sales.

As to the claim for account of profits by the infringer, this is an equitable remedy at the discretion of the court. In practice, such an account has rarely been requested due to the difficulty in computation and the possibility that such computation would show little or no profits by the infringer, thereby making any recovery impossible: It is quite clear that in order to compete with the right owner, the infringer has to offer products more cheaply. In addition, expenses actually incurred at the sales of the infringing products can be deducted, e.g., costs of advertising and marketing. There seems to be a fairly liberal attitude allowing deductions from gross profits, especially in respect of skill and labour expended in arriving at the infringing article, provided that there has not been dishonest intent.[170] However, the courts have been reluctant to reduce the amount of infringer's profits in cases where protection only covered part of the article sold:

---

[169] Gerber *v.* Lectra (above); Canadian Supreme Court, Cadbury Schweppes *v.* FBI Foods, 29 January 1999, [2000] F.S.R. 491 for a case of trade secret infringement that gave the infringer a head start of about one year.

[170] Gerber *v.* Lectra (above) for marketing expenses, English High Court, Redwood Music *v.* Chappell, 23 May 1980, [1982] R.P.C. 109 for development costs.

"We are asked to say that there is no interference of any damage resulting from that because the plaintiff's patent was not for the whole article, but merely for something quite trivial and unimportant, which the defendants might easily have got round by slight substitution, as in fact they have got round now, and obtained something better. This seems to be a wholly irrelevant consideration. The fact, admitted in proof, is that this very large sum of money has been received in respect of infringing instruments, and I am entirely unable to accept the view that this invention was of little importance, even if that had been a relevant fact, because the defendant, who had a meter known as the 'plunger' meter, deliberately abandoned that, and deliberately took to making a new meter, called the 'simplex' meter, which was established to be an infringement of the plaintiff's patent . . . I am far from saying that it is all an easy matter to assess damages in a case of this kind".[171]

In summary, English cases on damage calculation are rare and seem to require enormous efforts in time and money, thus strongly discouraging litigation in this respect. As in Germany, interim decisions on the merits are regarded as the most efficient way of dispensing with damage litigation, as the parties would then be expected to settle.

e) France

According to Sec. L. 615-1(2) IPC, "the infringement entails the responsibility of its author". Liability is based on the general tort provisions of Secs. 1382 et seq. Civil Code, which basically means that all damages incurred by the infringement should be properly compensated, yet only to the extent that such damages have been a certain and measurable consequence of the infringement. In particular, the patentee is not allowed to claim the infringer's profits as damages.[172] To the extent that indemnification is based on general principles of civil law mentioned above, the calculation by the judge cannot be made subject to a control by the Cassation Court. The judge may thus arrive at a global figure of indemnification, or request an expert opinion on this matter.[173]

In order to calculate damages incurred by the patentee or the licensee, French law would allow for a calculation of either loss of profits or damages incurred. When calculating lost profits, the courts would make a distinction between the patent being exploited by the patentee or not, before actually determining the amount of counterfeit goods and the extent of infringe-

---

171 English High Court, Meters *v*. Metropolitan Gas Meters, 2 February 1911, [1911] 28 R.P.C. 157.

172 While in the past a good number of courts ruled to the contrary based on the principle of *restitutio in integrum*, an approach also favoured by academics (e.g., E. Pouillet, "Traité des brevets d'invention" (Treaties on Invention Patents), édition Marchal et Billard, 1999, 905), the new Patent Act of 1968 does not leave any doubt about the fact that the infringer's profits cannot be claimed. This was already so held by a decision of the Appeal Court of Paris, 22 February 1963, Annales de la propriété industrielle 1963, 284, and confirmed by the Cassation Court, 13 January 1971, Dalloz 1971, 147.

173 For a critical view on the system of damages, see J.J. Martin, "Brevets d'invention: Une nouvelle politique de l'innovation" (Invention Patents: A New Policy of Innovation), RDPI, No. 95, 1999, 9.

ment.[174] In case the patentee uses his patent, lost profits are calculated based on the amount of counterfeit goods, to which the loss of turnover and the amount of lost profits are added. The extent of infringement is determined by adding up all infringing goods manufactured, sold or imported to France, limited only by the prescription period of three years, according to Sec. L 618-8 IPC. This would also include additional or spare parts for the infringing goods to the extent that these would add to "the whole infringement value" (*le tout commercial*). This is the case where the infringing object would not be sold independently from such parts.[175] The loss of turnover is determined by various factors which are applied quite flexibly, such as the quality of inventive step of the patented products. When the rule of *le tout commercial* is applied, only those profits are taken into account that measure the relative value of the invention in the assembled product. Yet, other elements can also be of importance, such as the market position of the patentee.[176] Finally, the ultimate figure for damages is arrived at by multiplying the amount of lost sales with the profit that would have been made for each product.

If, on the other hand, the patentee does not exploit the patented invention, damages are calculated on the basis of a licensing fee which the infringer would have had to pay in order to use the invention lawfully. Neither can the patentee, who does not exploit the patent, claim any damages incurred by his licensee,[177] who in such cases could intervene in the infringement action in order to claim damages on his own behalf. In such cases, the extent of the infringement is calculated on the basis of the infringer's turnover multiplied by a percentage determined by the court as compensatory fee.[178] In view of a number of academic writers for whom "such handling of matters lends support to infringement",[179] recent decisions have increased the licensing fees awarded.[180]

---

[174] Exploitation is understood as sales of the patented product or a product directly derived therefrom in France. On that subject see J.P. Stenger, "Sanction de la contrefaçon" (Sanctions Against Infringement), Jurisclasseur Brevets 1995, Fascicule 4680, No. 89 *et seq.*

[175] The above principle was established by a decision of the Cassation Court in 1897 and recently affirmed by a decision of the Paris Appeal Court of 19 November 1997, PIBD 1998, No. 651, III, 189.

[176] See J. P. Stenger, Fascicule 4680, No. 113 *et seq.*

[177] Decision of the Paris Appeal Court, 2 March 1971, Dalloz 1972, 45, also reprinted in "Les innovations de la loi du 2 janvier 1968 en matière de brevets d'invention" (The New Patent Act of 2 January 1968), Strasbourg Colloquium, 23 to 25 September 1971, Collection CEIPI, Litec 1972, 194/195.

[178] The court would take into account already existing licensing agreements for the same invention, licensing rates in the same field of technology or simply make an informed guess.

[179] See, e.g., J.Foyer/M. Vivant, "Le droit des brevets" (Patent Law), Collection Thémis, PUF, 1991, 352/353.

[180] The decision of the Cassation Court, 19 February 1991, Annales de la propriété industrielle 1991, 4, is along that line. Yet academic writers do not seem to support this view wholeheartedly. See, e.g., J.M. Mousseron, "Brevets d'invention" (Invention Patents), JCP éd. Entreprise, 1999, 413.

Indemnification for damages actually incurred would take into account two elements: the attack on the monopolistic right as such and the damages incurred in enforcing such right. Yet the patentee would have to show that damages with respect to these two positions as mentioned above can be distinguished from the position of lost profits.[181] As to the expenses for enforcing the patent right, French law distinguishes between the expenses awarded to the successful patentee as court costs – *les dépens* – under Sec. 695 New Code of Civil Procedure, and those the patentee has incurred in addition thereto, *les frais irrépétibles*. The latter are, for example, attorneys' fees, fees of patent attorneys, expenses for expert opinions, etc. Reimbursement of these can be requested based on Sec. 700 New Code of Civil Procedure and is often much lower than the real costs.

On average damages granted by the courts are in the amount of 40,000 Euro. In only nine of the 82 reported cases would the damages and interest exceed 80,000 Euro. [182]

f) Other countries

Most other countries seem to have a less sophisticated manner of calculating damages, often boiling down to what *Casucci* has labelled a "compulsory licence for the past".[183] Taiwan, for example, has introduced treble damages for cases of wilful infringement of copyrights and trade secrets. Korea has adopted the Japanese way of calculating damages by multiplying the infringer's turnover with the right owner's profits on such turnover for patents, trade marks and matters of unfair competition matters.

g) Attorneys' Fees, ***Art. 48***

As has been mentioned above, the *United States* would grant attorneys' fees only in cases of wilful infringement as part of the discretionarily awarded punitive damages. In *Japan*, the losing party has to bear all court costs, yet attorneys' fees have to be borne by each side and only in exceptional circumstances be (partly) awarded as damages where particularly difficult legal questions were involved.[184] In *Germany*, attorneys' fees plus the fees for patent attorneys in cases of, e.g., patent infringement would be part of the litigation expenses which have to be borne by the losing party. However, costs are awarded proportionate to the plaintiff's request. If the plaintiff

---

[181] A more detailed account on the questions involved concerning the attack of a monopolistic right in terms of damages is given by J.P. Stenger, Fascicule No. 4680, No. 149 *et seq*.

[182] P. Véron, *see* "Le contentieux des brevets d'invention, Etude statitique sur 1990–1996 pour la Fédération Nationale des Entreprises (FNDE)-ASPI" (Legal questions Involving Patents in France, Statistics of 1990–1996 compiled on the basis of figures by the Ministry of Justice, (FNDE)-ASPI), November 1997.

[183] Casucci, Chapter 7 of this book.

[184] E.g., Supreme Court, 29 May 1984, 530 Hanrei Times 97 – "American Football Symbol Mark". Amounts tend to be low, e.g, 1 million Yen, and would not represent market rates.

requests 1 million Euro in damages, and the court only awards 600,000, the costs would be split 60:40. An attorney who negligently claims too much would be liable for professional malpractice. Also for this reason German attorneys tend to calculate damage amounts as precisely as possible. In the *United Kingdom*, awarding attorneys fees is discretionary and even in successful cases would not supersede 25% of the successful party's actual attorneys' costs (at market rates).

The above patterns show a fairly complex picture. They reflect the difficulty that has already been mentioned above. On the one side damages should compensate the right owner for an infringement suffered. On the other hand, they should also to some extent constitute a deterrent to further infringement. Particularly in countries where damages are meant to be compensatory rather than punitive, both are almost impossible to reconcile. Yet one should note that the pattern of damage compensation becomes more diverse than just the distinction between punitive damages and compensatory ones. Apart from the US, only *Taiwan* now allows the court to award punitive damages in cases of copyright and trade secret infringement. But damage compensation for copyright infringement in *Germany* comes close to a punitive sanction in that the double amount of compensation is explained by the additional monitoring costs of collecting societies. Further, *Japan* and *Korea* have now opted for a new way of calculating damages by combining the infringer's turnover with the right owner's profits. This, however, is extremely difficult to reconcile with traditional principles of tort law where damages must relate to what the right owner could have achieved but for the infringement.

3. The Right of Information/*Auskunftsanspruch*, Art. 47

Art. 47 TRIPS Agreement requires the courts to order the infringer to inform the right holder of the identity of third persons involved in production and distribution. It has been mentioned above that such a claim is supported in Germany under the *Auskunftsanspruch* and in Great Britain under the Anton Piller Order. In other countries, such a right seems to be more difficult to enforce.

4. Other Remedies, Art. 46

The other remedies as mentioned in **Art. 46 TRIPS** most importantly constitute the destruction of infringing goods. In that respect, **Art. 46** clarifies that in case of a trade mark infringement, it is not sufficient simply to have the infringing marks removed, e.g., from T-shirts. Rather, such goods should be destroyed *in toto* or at least disposed of outside the channels of commerce. Not infrequently, videos are shown where huge steamrollers destroy infringing goods such as watches.

Other possible remedies include apologies or the publication of the decision in a newspaper. According to the Japanese Supreme Court, requiring an apology from the infringer is not unconstitutional.[185] The Korean Supreme Court has held the contrary.[186]

VIII. Administrative Measures, Arts. 49, 51–60

1. Art. 49 TRIPS

The TRIPS Agreement attaches far more importance to civil than to administrative measures, at least to the extent that they relate to infringement procedures. **Art. 42 TRIPS** holds that right holders should be able to resort to civil judicial procedures. This should make clear that enforcement of intellectual property rights is basically seen as a conflict between two parties and not an object of public concern. It thus appears that **Art. 49** only refers to administrative procedures offered in addition to civil ones. In fact, very few countries offer infringement procedures through the administration, for example, Vietnam[187] and China.[188] These countries traditionally have entrusted the national patent offices with intellectual property enforcement. This certainly has the advantage of a competent forum. It has been mentioned above that one of the greatest difficulties in enforcement is the training of judges in specific areas in this difficult field of law. The patent offices, on the other hand, are far more familiar with industrial property law as such. It is equally clear that training and experience in granting industrial property rights does not necessarily qualify for their enforcement. After all, patent offices are not called upon to interpret the scope of an industrial property right in light of an allegedly infringing one, but only in order to determine the requirements of grant.[189] Thus, the patent offices should be aware how courts interpret industrial property rights, but should not do so themselves.[190]

Outside Asia, involvement of the administration in the enforcement of intellectual property rights is thus uncommon.

---

[185] Supreme Court, 4 July 1956, 10-7 Mihshû 705.

[186] Korean Supreme Court, 1 April 1981, 89 Hunma 160.

[187] For details, see Heath, Industrial Property Protection in Vietnam, 30 IIC 419 [1999].

[188] X. Liu, 32 IIC 141 [2001].

[189] However, some countries allow domestic patent offices to render opinions on the scope of an industrial property right. This is namely the case for Korea and Japan, e.g., Secs. 71, 71bis Japanese Patent Act: "A request for interpretation may be made to the Patent Office with respect to the technical scope of a patented invention". However, only in Korea does this system actually appear to be used: See Yang, Enforcement of Intellectual Property Rights in Korea, in: Chang et al., Intellectual Property Law in Korea, Kluwer Law International 2003.

[190] E.g., European Patent Office, Enlarged Board of Appeals, 11 December 1989, EPO Official Journal 1990, 93 – "Friction Reducing Addition".

2. Border Measures, Arts. 51–60

Of far greater importance are border measures that the TRIPS Agreement regulates in considerable detail under **Arts. 51–60**. It has been mentioned above that the TRIPS Agreement developed out of a proposed international agreement on border measures regarding infringing goods. This, in turn, finds its justification and reasoning in previous international agreements that stipulate certain remedies of seizure, in particular the Madrid Arrangement for the Repression of False or Deceptive Indications of Source on Goods that dates back to the year 1891. Border measures have to be provided only for certain infringing goods, however: **Art. 51** only mentions counterfeit trade mark or pirated copyright goods. It is thus necessary to interpret these terms. The TRIPS Agreement itself gives the following definitions:

> "Counterfeit trade mark goods shall mean any goods, including packaging, bearing without authorisation a trade mark which is identical to the trade mark validly registered in respect of such goods, or which cannot be distinguished in its essential aspect from such a trade mark, and which thereby infringes the rights of the owner of the trade mark in question under the law of the country of importation".

> "Pirated copyright goods shall mean any goods which are copies made without the consent of the right holder or person duly authorised by him in the country of production and which are made directly or indirectly from an article where the making of that copy would have constituted an infringement of a copyright or a related right under the law of the country of importation."

This, for one, excludes the whole range of articles that might infringe other rights than trade marks or copyrights, e.g., patents. Measures have thus only to be provided for infringing trade mark and copyright goods. But even here, not all goods that are infringing necessarily fall under the TRIPS definition. A good many countries consider the parallel importation of goods made by the right owner or with his consent abroad as an infringement of domestic intellectual property rights.[191] These goods, however, may be infringing yet do not require border measures, as they have been produced with the authorisation of the right owner.[192] Finally, another aspect merits attention. The criteria "without authorisation" or "without consent" is not without problems. This may be exemplified by the following case: The trade mark owner permits a licensee to produce 1,000 items per day to which the trade mark may be attached. During the licensing period, however, the licensee regularly produces "overruns" that he disposes of in different commercial

---

[191] Particularly in the EU countries, parallel importation of trademarked goods from outside the Community is considered infringing: ECJ, 16 July 1998, 29 IIC 920 [1998] – "Silhouette".

[192] In European countries, right owners would be allowed to invoke border measures against such goods, however: For Germany, e.g., Bundesfinanzgericht (Federal Tax Court), 5 October 1999, case VII R88/98.

channels than the 1,000 "official" items. Or in a copyright case, the licensee receives permission to print 1,000 copies of a certain book within a given period of time. However, he produces 2,000. In both cases, the licensee produces the licensed goods or copies within the licensing period, yet disobeys limitations on the quantity of items that may be produced. Would these overruns be infringing under the TRIPS definition or would these qualify as legitimate goods produced contrary to contractual arrangements and thus only give rise to a contractual dispute between licensor and licensee? The TRIPS Agreement can give no definite answer to this question. It is easy to see that items produced *after* the licensing period would count as infringement. Here, the licensor's authorisation is notably absent. On the other hand, not every breach of licensing agreement should render the goods produced as infringing. Goods certainly do not become infringing because the licensee does not comply with all the terms of the licensing agreement, e.g., does not properly pay his licensing fees, does not purchase the required raw materials, etc. Similar to the above-mentioned factors, third parties are unable to distinguish goods manufactured in compliance with an existing licensing agreement, or beyond it. In the same manner as a third party, e.g., customs, could not distinguish between goods produced under a licence where the licensee duly pays his fees, a customs officer could not distinguish between daylight production and nightly overruns. On the other hand, border measures do not require the possibility of distinguishing infringing from non-infringing goods. According to this author, the distinction should be made as follows: Once a licensing agreement has come to an end, the licensor has a legitimate interest in no longer being associated with any goods being produced by the licensee and passed off as those of the licensor. In that respect, a licensing agreement that has been terminated or come to an end is no different than one that has never been concluded at all. Yet once the licensor gives his authorisation to the licensee for items being produced bearing a certain trade mark or containing certain copyright material, this authorisation for third parties means that all goods produced by the licensee have been authorised. Third parties, after all, hardly have an opportunity to look at the licensing agreement in order to detect what amount of goods the licensee is allowed to produce. In the absence of any publicity of restriction, overruns should qualify as a breach of contract and be actionable as such, but not as an IP infringement.

The procedures set out under the TRIPS Agreement for the seizure of allegedly infringing goods at the border are fairly straightforward. Either the owner of a copyright or trade mark prophylactically asks customs to detain infringing goods, or the goods are detained by customs at their own initiative and the owner of the trade mark or copyright in question thereafter applies for their continued detention.

Customs are the first to come in contact with imported goods, and it is certainly important to have such infringing goods seized already at the border before they disappear into national distribution channels. It is for that reason that the TRIPS Agreement has introduced a right of importation. In the absence of such right, customs would have no means of seizing infringing goods, as only their commercial distribution would amount to an infringement. Thus, the right of importation is vital for customs procedures, but says nothing about, e.g., the lawfulness of parallel imports.[193] In the case of industrial property rights, many countries offer right owners the possibility of listing their registered rights with customs once they suspect that infringing goods might be imported. Due to the high and increasing level of international trade, the chances of customs detecting infringing goods on their own initiative is limited. Most successful operations dealing with the seizure of infringing goods occur once the right owner has received information about an impending shipment of infringing goods and cooperates with customs for the seizure of such goods.

Action by the competent courts or administrative authorities to suspend the release of goods has to be taken if a right holder has "valid grounds for suspecting" infringement and is able to present "adequate evidence" that infringing goods will be imported, **Art. 52**. These requirements are both for a general application to customs, **Art. 52**, as well as for cases where the actual importation of infringing goods is suspected. Because border measures by their very nature are preliminary and may prove unfounded, customs can require right owners to provide security, **Art. 53**. The security is meant to indemnify the importer in cases where the measure has been mistakenly applied, yet shall not act as a deterrent to the request for customs measures, **Art. 53.1**. Once the goods have been detailed at the request of the right owner or at customs' initiative subsequently backed up by the right owner's endorsement, **Arts. 53 and 54** specify what kind of procedure should follow. As detention by customs is preliminary, the right owner has to initiate the main action of infringement within 10 days of the detention, otherwise the goods will be released. It is quite clear that the burden to prove infringement is with the right owner. The 10 day period may seem short, yet it is justified insofar as the importer had no opportunity to be heard while detention was effected. Thus, customs seizure is an explicit case of an *ex parte* measure, and **Art. 50** provides the defendant with similar safeguards. In order to verify an infringement claim, the right owner has a right of inspection and subsequent release of the name and address of the importer.[194] Instead of defending an infringement action, it is quite common for importers to "abandon" their shipments once detention has been ordered. Thus, countries may enact legislation to provide for simplified destruction procedures in these cases, although TRIPS is silent on this matter.

[193] Heath, Parallel Imports and International Trade, 28 IIC 623 [1997].

[194] Here, the European Court of Justice has ruled on an instructive case where the Swedish authorities refused to provide such details: ECJ, 14 October 1999, 31 IIC 591 [2000] – "In re Adidas".

The provisions of the TRIPS Agreement leave open what shall be defined as an act of "importation", in particular if the transit of goods would qualify as such. While the European Court of Justice has so ruled,[195] this is not a foregone conclusion. Rather, the case before the European Court of Justice shows how questionable this can be if detention has only been made on the basis that the goods were infringing due to parallel import restrictions. While there might be a legitimate interest to prevent further circulation of infringing goods as defined under TRIPS, there is far less justification in cases where the goods would be treated as completely lawful and not infringing in the ultimate destination.

Finally, **Art. 60 TRIPS** Agreement exempts the importation of objects for personal consumption from the above-mentioned rules. Even without such explicit mention, it stands to reason that intellectual property rights give rights of commercial exploitation, and acts of private use, as would also be a private importation, would not be deemed infringing at any rate.

IX. Criminal Measures, Art. 61

Finally, the TRIPS Agreement mentions criminal procedures as one method of enforcement. Only one provision is dedicated to criminal procedures (**Art. 61**), thus indicating the TRIPS Agreement's preference for civil enforcement. Criminal procedures even appear less important than administrative ones, thereby reflecting the reality in developed, rather than developing countries. In developed countries, criminal enforcement of intellectual property rights is rare, and if used at all, limited to infringements of trade marks and copyrights. France is a country that to a certain extent uses criminal enforcement of trade mark rights, while for patents, the following statement should be true for all industrialised countries: "For 134 years, criminal protection against infringements has basically brought about nothing."[196] This is none different for, e.g., Germany, where criminal enforcement was the prevailing method in the first 40 years after patent protection was introduced, but subsequently fell into disuse, the last published case dating back to 1933.[197] Criminal enforcement becomes more important where the civil enforcement system shows considerable shortcomings, e.g., with respect to obtaining evidence. Here, right owners prefer to resort to criminal procedure in order to obtain evidence that under civil procedures could not be obtained.[198]

---

[195] ECJ, 6 April 2000, 32 IIC 209 [2001] – "Polo/Lauren".

[196] J.M. Mousseron, "Droit des brevets et loi du 26 novembre 1990" (Patent Law and Act of 26 November 1990), La semaine juridique (JCP) édition Entreprise (E) 1991, 139.

[197] Imperial Supreme Court, 9 January 1933, GRUR 1933, 288.

[198] An example would be, e.g., Taiwan: Generally, criminal actions are seen as more effective for IPR enforcement given the low civil penalties, relative lack of discovery tools, and the history of delay and procedural hurdles in IPR cases: Eastwood/Chen/Weng, Intellectual Property Law in Taiwan, in: Heath (ed.), Intellectual Property Law in Asia, Kluwer Law International 2002, 92.

The TRIPS Agreement only requires members to provide for criminal sanctions in the case of wilful trade mark counterfeiting or copyright piracy on a commercial scale. In these cases, it is arguable that a private dispute over individual rights becomes an issue of public concern.

X. Bibliography

- Ariyanuntaka, TRIPs and the Special IP Court in Thailand, 30 IIC 360 [1999].
- Civil Procedure Rules, Blackstone, 2nd ed. 1999.
- Le contenieux de la propriété industrielle en Europe (Patent Litigation in Europe), Collection CEIPI, Litec 1999.
- The Enforcement of Industrial Property Rights in Eastern Europe, 32 IIC 875-999 [2001].
- X. Liu, Enforcement of Intellectual Property Rights in the People's Republic of China, 32 IIC 141 [2001].
- Moore/Michel/Lupo, Patent Litigation and Strategy, St. Paul, Minn., 2nd ed. 2003.
- Nott, Patent Litigation in England [1994] EIPR 3.
- Schramm, Der Patentverletzungsprozess (Patent Infringement Litigation), 4th ed. Cologne 1999.
- Stenger, L'action Contrefaçon (Patent Infringement Action), Jurisclasseur Brevet, Fasc. 5450, Nos. 35 et seq.
- Wadlow, Enforcement of Intellectual Property in European and International Law, Sweet & Maxwell, London 1998.

B

Patent Enforcement in Western Europe

2
European Issues of Patent Enforcement

DIETER STAUDER IN CO-OPERATION WITH
CHRISTOPHER HEATH

I. Introduction

1. Interests

It is not difficult to imagine the problems a company with its seat outside Europe faces in the case of an action for infringement of a patent in Europe. There are two scenarios to think of in this respect. One is that this company is proprietor of a European patent in certain countries party to the European Patent Convention. The patent proprietor learns that his patent in Europe has been infringed in these countries. The other scenario is that a company with seat outside Europe learns that an action is being taken against its subsidiaries in Europe, possibly even against itself, or against companies selling its product in Europe for infringement of patent, *e.g.* by way of a warning letter or even by way of an action for infringement of patent in a court in Europe.

Both scenarios make it necessary to understand the special situation in Europe. In the first case, the patent owner is interested in knowing the prospects of success and the risks involved in an action in Europe. The questions concern the quality of the courts, the possible choice of courts, the duration and costs of the proceedings, the reliability of the lawyers and patent attorneys, and also, of course, the chances of success with the complaint. If a non-European receives a warning letter or is sued he will want to know whether he can do anything about the court jurisdiction in Europe and what the consequences of a decision are should the court find him guilty of infringing a patent. As an alleged infringer, he will now be particularly interested in knowing how he can contest the validity of the European patent claim being made.

2. Territoriality

To an observer of Europe, the political map of this continent has the appearance of a "patchwork quilt". This equally applies to the European patent[1]

[1] The European patent is granted on the basis of the Convention on the Grant of European Patents (European Patent Convention(EPC)) of 5 October 1973 as amended; the texts in the three official languages of the Convention are published by the European Patent Office in the so-called "blue book", as of July 2002 in its 11th edition.

and jurisdiction. After grant, the European patent falls into territorial parts.[2] Moreover, the courts dealing with patent actions are the national courts of the individual European countries.

Albeit this is no unfamiliar aspect, it does entail an irritating element: the European patent comes into being based on one application and by way of an act of grant of patent, but ends up in the territorial sphere of the countries party to the EPC.

For the territory of the EU and the EFTA countries, the jurisdiction of the court in patent actions is regulated by three different legal acts, which are, however, almost identical. These documents are currently the Council Regulations (EC) No 44/2001 of 22 December 2000, the Conventions of Brussels and of Lugano on Jurisdiction and Enforcement of Judgments in Civil and Commercial Matters.[3]

II. The Central Place of Jurisdiction of the Defendant – Overcoming the Objection of Nullity of Foreign Patents

One should start with an example from case law, a decision of the District Court of Düsseldorf of 1 February 1994.[4] The plaintiff is the owner of a British patent for a conveyor comprising a track. The defendant offered a product at a trade fair in Birmingham (UK) which allegedly infringes a patent. The defendant's seat of business is in North Rhine-Westphalia, a state in Germany. The infringement action was brought before the court of jurisdiction, the District Court of Düsseldorf. The defendant raised the objection that the British patent was not valid. This case contains the first important questions regarding court jurisdiction in Europe.

1. European Law on Jurisdiction and Enforcement of Judgments

The Brussels Convention, which has gained in importance ever since it came into force on 1 February 1973, serves to facilitate the enforcement of judgments in civil and commercial matters – an area to which patent infringement judgments also belong. This European law governs the law of recognition of judgments in civil and commercial matters, and its effectiveness is based on the following:

---

[2] Arts. 2, 3, 64 (1) and (3) EPC.

[3] Brussels Convention on Jurisdiction and the Enforcement of Judgments in Civil and Commercial Matters of 27 September 1968 as amended (European Union); Lugano Convention of 16 September 1988 (EFTA States); the Brussels Convention has been replaced by the Council Regulation (EC) No. 44/2001 of 22 December 2002 on jurisdiction and the recognition and enforcement of judgments in civil and commercial matters, OJ EC of 16 January 2001, L 12/1 *et seq.*, coming into force on 1 March 2002; Denmark is not a participant and remains bound by the Brussels Convention.

[4] District Court Düsseldorf of 1 February 1994, Collection of decisions of the 4th Civil Chamber, 1/1998, 1 *et seq.*

The law directly determines the jurisdiction of the courts. The most important jurisdiction in this respect is the general jurisdiction of the courts of the contracting state where the defendant is domiciled or has its seat as a legal person.[5] The national law of that state then determines which court has specific jurisdiction.

Of decisive importance now is the second characteristic of the convention: if the first court affirms its jurisdiction, this jurisdiction can as a matter of principle no longer be reviewed by another court in a different jurisdiction in the enforcement proceedings.[6] One of the most important reasons for non-recognition, which used to trouble the earlier classical conventions of recognition has thus been eliminated.

The convention is doubly binding, regulating both jurisdiction and enforcement.

Back to our case: The defendant has its seat in Germany. The District Court of Düsseldorf has international jurisdiction according to Article 2 Brussels Convention and local jurisdiction in accordance with German law to render a decision on patent infringement occurring in the United Kingdom. The substantive law to be applied is English patent law, together with European patent law in the case of a European patent.

2. The Objection of Nullity of the Foreign Patent

The objection that the English patent is invalid poses the main obstacle to application of the convention, for "proceedings concerned with the registration or the validity of patents" fall exclusively under the jurisdiction of the courts of the protecting state (the patent state).[7] This provision reiterates the recognised principle that only the courts of the state affording protection of an industrial property right (patent, trade mark, design) whose protection arises by way of registration or nullity may decide on the grant, registration or nullity.

In our original case, the District Court of Düsseldorf decided that it was authorised to judge the validity of the English patent in the context of an objection (defence), *i.e. inter partes*. It justifies this with the fact that English patent law itself allows this kind of estoppel apart from a declaration of nullity with absolute effect (*erga omnes*). The latter would be clearly forbidden by Art. 22 No. 4 EC-Regulation and Art. 16 No. 4 Brussels Convention.

---

5 Art. 2 Brussels Convention and EC Regulation.

6 Art. 35 (3) EC Regulation and 28 (3) Brussels Convention.

7 Art. 22 No. 4 EC Regulation and Art. 16 No. 4 Brussels Convention reads:

> The following courts shall have exclusive jurisdiction, regardless of domicile:
> 4. in proceedings concerned with the registration or validity of patents, trade marks, designs or similar other rights required to be deposited or registered, the courts of the Member-Contracting State in which the deposit or registration has been applied for, has taken place or is under the terms of an international convention deemed to have taken place.

3. English Case Law

English case law points in the opposite direction.[8] The plaintiff is proprietor of a European patent effective in the United Kingdom, Germany and Spain, and brings action against four defendants with seat of business in three different European states. The defendants belong to a joint venture, the Suzo Group. The plaintiff asserts a claim of patent infringement in the three states at the High Court in London. The defendants plead invalidity of the foreign patents; they counterclaim for nullity (revocation) of the English patent.

Justice Laddie declines jurisdiction with regard to the actions for infringement of foreign patents since the question of nullity of the foreign patents, due to the defendants' request in this respect, has rendered the point a main issue in the process.[9] "Infringement and nullity are so closely tied that for purposes of jurisdiction they must be treated as an issue or as a claim".

The Court of Appeal confirmed this view in *Fort Dodge Animal Health Ltd. v. Akzo Novel NV* in its decision of 27 October 1997.[10]

4. Dutch Case Law

One may now turn attention to the country which, when compared to two opposing views above, goes the furthest and was first in progressively advancing the case law associated with the catchword "cross-border injunction". Dutch courts in 1989 rendered a decision which for the first time had effect outside the country in a Benelux trade mark action, and this course was followed by a patent infringement dispute in the early 1990s. The courts of first and second instance at The Hague, which have exclusive jurisdiction over all patent disputes in the Netherlands, further developed this. The proceedings are carried out in a special procedure called the *kort geding*, a summary proceeding which according to the Brussels Convention (and the EC Regulation No.44/2001) can be included under "provisional measures".[11]

---

[8] *Coin Controls v. Suzo International*, [1997] 3 All ER 45; [1997] F.S.R. 660.

[9] The Article to apply: Art. 19 Brussels Convention and 22 EC Regulations which read:

> Where a court of a Contracting Member-State is seized of a claim which is principally concerned with a matter over which the courts of another Contracting State have exclusive jurisdiction by virtue of Article 22 [16], it shall declare of its own motion that it has no jurisdiction.

The question is the interpretation of "principally concerned".

[10] [1998] F.S.R. 22 and 237.

[11] *See*: H. Bertams, "The Cross-Border Prohibitory Injunction in Dutch Patent Law", 26 IIC 618–636 (1995) – an informative report from the time of the beginning; from later publications in English: W. von Meibohm and J. Pitz, "Cross-Border Injunctions in International Patent Infringement Proceedings", [1997] E.I.P.R. 469; short stocktaking by D. Stauder, "Cross-Border Protection of European Patents", 29 IIC 497 *et seq*. (1999).

The Dutch Court declared itself authorised in principle, having been given jurisdiction pursuant to the Brussels Convention, to decide on actions for injunctive relief with effect outside the country and to examine in first instance the validity of the foreign patents as well. The latter is certainly justified with respect to substance insofar as the European bundle patent has the same contents and the parallel foreign patents correspond to the Dutch patent. Also strictly speaking, Art. 16 No. 4 Brussels Convention (and Art. 22 No. 4 EC-Regulation No. 44/2001) prohibits only a declaration of nullity but not examination of the validity or "effectiveness" of the foreign patents.

The proceedings of the *kort geding* appealed to patent owners. It adheres to its own very effective rules that an outsider can only describe with difficulty. In one process of the *kort geding*, for example, a patent owner sued defendants from nine different European countries in the court at The Hague.[12] In these proceedings, however, the appellate court ruled that the foreign patents – the Dutch patent included – would probably have to be deemed invalid, for which reason the plaintiff's claim had to be dismissed.

5. Different Views

It is thus possible to discern the following court views in the case of actions for infringement founded on foreign patents in Europe:

a) In the case of an objection of nullity of the foreign patents the infringement action is automatically barred (United Kingdom).
b) Nullity can be ascertained with effect *inter partes*, if the foreign law allows this (District Court of Düsseldorf).
c) The *kort geding* procedure is in any case not suitable if invalidity is probable (Netherlands).

It should be noted that the ECJ will eventually decide on whether Art. 16-4 Brussels Convention (and automatically Art. 22-4 of the Brussels I Regulation) is applicable where the defendant in a patent infringement action or the claimant in an action for declaration of non-infringement pleads invalidity or nullity of the patent.[13]

---

[12] *Expandable Grafts Partnership v. Boston Scientific*, Court of Appeal The Hague, 23 April 1998.

[13] This reference has been made by the Court of Appeal Düsseldorf on 5 December 2002, 2003 GRUR Int. 1030. *See*: Petit, Nouvelles d'Allemagne: L'heure du glas a-t-elle sonné pour les injonctions transfrontalières de contrefaçon? (News from Germany: Did the Death Knell Sound for Cross-Border Injunctions in Infringement Cases?), Propriété Industrielle 2004, 12. The case is pending under No. C-4/03: OJ of the European Union C 55/14 of 8 March 2003.

III. Jurisdiction Based on the Plurality of the Defendants – The Way to One Single Court?

1. Dutch Case Law

The Dutch courts did not stop at their first step in overcoming the defence of nullity. The court in The Hague allowed claims where the patent owner in the Netherlands not only brought action against the company infringing abroad with its seat in the Netherlands, but also against the subsidiaries established in other European countries and traders in the infringing product. An example using the proceedings mentioned above.[14] The plaintiffs were Expandable Grafts Partnership with its seat in San Antonio (Texas), Ethicon Inc., Somerville (USA) and Cordis Europe S.A. (Belgium); the defendant company's parent name was Boston Scientific with its seat of business in the Netherlands and in eight other European states. Boston Scientific is, by the way, also an American company. The matter concerned the distribution of NIR-Stends.

The court determined that the European offices doing independent business in their state or region were obtaining their supplies from the place of central distribution in the Netherlands and that the Dutch company managed the European companies. The Hague was considered to have jurisdiction for all of the defendants. Thus the "spider in the web" doctrine was born.[15]

2. Legal Basis

The legal basis is a provision of the Brussels Convention allowing defendants domiciled or with their seat of business in different contracting states to be sued collectively in a court of one of the defendants.[16] The European Court of Justice (ECJ) qualified the very broad terms of the jurisdiction regulation in clarifying that the objective of the regulation is to avoid the risk of irreconcilable judgments resulting from separate proceedings in the contracting states.[17]

---

[14] *See* fn. 12.

[15] *See* the short report: District Court refines Case Law on "Spider in the Web" doctrine, 14 WIPR 186 (2002). It is worth mention that the ECJ will decide on whether the "Spider in the Web" doctrine conforms with Art. 6 No. 1 Brussels Convention following a reference recently made by the Dutch Supreme Court: Hoge Raad,19 December 2003, 2004 World Intellectual Property Report, Vol. 18, No. 2, 10. The case is pending under C-539/03: OJ of the European Union of 6 March 2004, C 59/11.

[16] Art. 6 No. 1 Brussels Convention; now Art. 6 No. 1 EC Regulation No. 44/2001 amended by the rule decided by the ECJ, cited in fn. 7.

[17] ECJ, 27 September 1988 – *Kalfelis v. Schröder*, Case 189/87, 1988 E.C.R. 5565.

3. Avoiding Irreconcilable Judgments

Avoiding incompatible judgments presupposes a type of connection that in the view of the ECJ must be autonomously construed on the basis of the Convention. Of course, application of the provision mentioned may not jeopardise the protection afforded by the jurisdiction based on the defendant's domicile or seat.

a) Can incompatibility already be established in that the different claims against the different defendants involve the same European patent and identical infringing subject matter?

The majority of the court decisions up to now recognise that a European patent in its national phase is to be interpreted uniformly in accordance with Art. 69 European Patent Convention which even has a Protocol on Interpretation attached; they accept, however, that the interpretation in different contracting states can vary.[18] The situation is similar with respect to nullity. Even though the grounds for revocation are "Europeanised", it is possible for a European patent to be declared invalid in one state and to be maintained at least in part in another. This possibility for court decisions and application of law to so diverge may cause some to assign a national character to the European bundle patent.

b) Legal Uniformity of Case Law

In the European sphere today, there is still no common court of appeal as there is in the United States with the Court of Appeals of the Federal Circuit (CAFC). Since the beginning of the European patent law movement there have been efforts to create at least a Common European Appeal Court for patents, but the plans have not yet been converted into reality, even though new initiatives are on the way. Jurisdiction based on that of the majority of the defendants has indicated a tendency towards centralisation in one court in Europe.

In attempting to have a common jurisdiction in the ways described, however, the defendants may not be forced to accept an arbitrary place of jurisdiction to which they have no connection. Otherwise the protection afforded the defendants by jurisdiction based on their domicile or seat of business would be undermined. For this reason, there must be requirements beyond those of the same European patent and the same infringing subject matter to make it possible for the defendants to be brought before a court that is, with respect to some of them, in another country.

---

[18] It is a significant discussion especially about the uniform interpretation of the extent of the European Patent: *See* Judges Grabinski and Braendle in: 30 IIC 855 *et seq*. and 875 *et seq*. (1999): Can and may determination of the extent of protection conferred by a European patent in different countries lead to different results?; *Cf*. also Brinkhof, "The desirability, necessity and feasibility of co-operation between courts in the field of European Patent Law", [1997] E.I.P.R. 226 *et seq*.

(1) A possible requirement would be a common action of the defendants as joint tortfeasors in the case of a patent infringement.[19] A vendor-to-buyer supplier relationship, use of a cross-border organisation of distribution and a parent-subsidiary company relationship in different countries could also suffice.

(2) A chain of separate acts of distribution, with each link acting independently, ought not suffice. Purchaser A in country A buying his goods from merchant B in country B, with the latter in his turn receiving the goods from producer P in P, cannot be sued together with producer P. Merchant B, acting independently, breaks the chain and prevents a joint liability of the individuals which could lead to a common place of jurisdiction.

IV. *Forum Delicti Commissi* (Place of Tort)

Today, the jurisdiction of the court where the act occurred presents few difficulties. According to the decision of the ECJ on 30 November 1976 – *Bier v. Mines de Potasse d'Alsace*[20] – the place of the tort is both the place of the causal act as well as the place where the damage was incurred. The plaintiff can choose where he wishes to sue. In the *Fiona Shevill v. Presse Alliance S.A* decision of 7 March 1995,[21] the ECJ handled a cross-border libel case arising from a newspaper article that was circulated in different states. The place of the causal act is the place where the publisher of the publication has his office; in the view of the ECJ, the court there would have jurisdiction over the action to recover complete damages. The libel also occurs in the place where the publication is circulated and the person affected is known, mainly in the United Kingdom. However, these courts only have jurisdiction to rule on the damage incurred in their respective state.

This case law has put an end to the cross-border effect of decisions of courts competent by reason of the place where the act occurred. Forum shopping with cross-border effect is not possible. If action is brought before a court as *forum delicti commissi*, the courts restrict their jurisdiction to decisions on injunctive relief and damages in their state. This case law renders the idea of a unified cross-border infringement in the form of a multistate act almost untenable. Thus, the District Court of Düsseldorf did not consider itself competent as forum of tort in Germany for the infringement in the

[19] *Cf. Coin Controls v. Suzo Int., see* fn. 8; *Sepracor Inc. v. Hochest Marrion Ltd,* [1997] F.S.R. 746 (Patents Court of 14 January 1999), in the case of copyright infringement: *Pearce v. Ove Partnership Ltd,* [1999] All ER 769 (CA of 21 January 1999).

[20] ECJ, 30 November 1976 – *Bier v. Mines de Potasse d'Alsace*, Case 21/76, 1976 E.C.R. 1735; Art. 5 No. 3 Brussels Convention; Art. 5 No. 3 EC Regulation No.44/2001 is amended by clarifying the jurisdiction in relation to the preventive action for infringement.

[21] ECJ, 7 March 1995 – *Shevill v. Presse Alliance*, C-68/93, 1995 I E.C.R. 415.

form of a parallel foreign patent with respect to an export deal from a neighbouring state, which resulted in import to Germany.[22] There is, however, protection by reason of the domestic patent against the threatening foreign import.

V. Provisional Measures

Finally, it is also necessary to examine the place of jurisdiction for provisional measures.[23] Put in simplified terms, this rule of jurisdiction declares that national courts maintain jurisdiction even if pursuant to the European law on jurisdiction another court would have jurisdiction over the main action. Within the framework of the *kort geding* procedure under Dutch law, the question arose whether these special proceedings – which have the character of provisional procedure – justify the Dutch courts' generous foray into cross-border injunctions. The Dutch courts did not follow suit simply in order to prevent another rather weak argument from providing another exception which is already a liberal pro-European one anyway. They concentrated rather on emphasising the basic rules mentioned above and especially in further underlining the protection of the defendant also in the *kort geding*.[24]

VI. The "Torpedoes" against the New Case Law

1. Recent Developments

Legal experts used their innovative skills to provide an antidote to the ingenuity of cross-border judgments. The alleged infringers, who had not yet been sued, but who expected that an infringement action involving cross-border claims was imminent, countered by stipulating the place of jurisdiction themselves. They instituted proceedings against the patent owner in a place of jurisdiction convenient to them, petitioning the court to determine that they did not infringe on the patents. The action for a negative declaratory judgment provides grounds, in accordance with the case law of the ECJ, for the objection of *lis pendens*, a pending lawsuit, with respect to the later infringement action.[25] If the party faced with an imminent infringement action wanted to prevent the patent owner from bringing cross-border

[22] District Court Düsseldorf, 25 March 1999, 1999 GRUR Int. 775 – *Impfstoff II*; of 25 August 1998, Collection of the decisions of the 4th Civil Chamber, 1998/4, 92.

[23] Art. 24 Brussels Convention; identical text Art. 31 EC Regulation No. 44/2001.

[24] *See* Brinkhof, "Geht das grenzüberschreitende Verletzungsgebot zu weit?" GRUR Int. 1997, 489, 493 *et seq.*; *see* for the interpretation of Art. 24 Brussels Convention: ECJ, 17 November 1998 – *Van Uden Maritime BV v. Deco-Line KG*, C-391/95; sensational: Court of First Instance of Brussels, 14 September 2001 – *Colgate v. Unilever.*

[25] Art. 21 Brussels Convention; ECJ, 6 December 1994 – *Tatry v. Maciej Rataj*, C-406/92, 1994 I E.C.R. 5439; now Art. 27 EC Regulation No. 44/2001.

action against him, he was forced to apply for a declaration of non-infringement with effect for the countries where there was threat of an infringement action.

This antidote was dubbed the Italian or Belgian torpedo since the courts there were reputed to be slow, and thus the dilatory effect to the detriment of the patent owner appeared to be great. For in winning time the patent owner came under pressure, because for the time being he could no longer enforce his right by way of an action for injunctive relief.

2. Automatic Suspension

The dilatory effect is reinforced by the fact that the pending suit automatically blocks the second court which cannot even examine whether the first court has jurisdiction to rule on the declaration of cross-border non-infringement.[26] What is supposed to be an advantage of the Brussels Convention (now EC-Regulation No. 44/2001) – that conflicts are avoided by way of this automatic mechanism – turns out to be the opposite.

3. Court Reactions

How do the courts react? In part, they seem to endorse the ECJ's given course of automatic suspension by way of the second court. But there are also rumblings of disapproval.

There are several ways to overcome the dilatory effect: it is possible to regard the issue of the infringement claim and that of the action for a negative declaratory judgment differently or to deny the jurisdiction for the negative declaratory judgment at least for the forum of tort.[27] It would also clearly be possible to view the action for a negative declaratory judgment as an abuse.[28] This would, after all, in the case of obvious abuse, open the way

---

[26] District Court of Düsseldorf, 27 February 1998, 1998 GRUR Int. 804 – *Impfstoff*; the same court, 24 October 2000 – *Wellcome Foundation/Glaxo* – in a case with "auxiliary" claim; request for a preliminary ruling to the ECJ by the 30 September 1999 CA Düsseldorf.

[27] *Cf.* District Court of Liège, 14 October 1997, *Joskin/Vredo*; 2000 Revue de droit intellectuel (Ing.-Cons.) 172 (unfair competition by warning letter (no)); Supreme Court of Sweden (*Högsta Domstollen*) of 14 June 2000 – *Floetek/Kaldnes*; different reasoning by the District Court of Bologna, 16 September 1998, 2000 GRUR Int. 1021 with comment by Stauder. No jurisdiction on the basis of Art. 5 No. 3 Brussels Regulation I: District Court of Milan, 26 March 2003 – *Optigen v. Murchron*; District Court of Milan, 21 March 2002 – *Dade v. Chiron*; District Court of Turin, 13 May 2003 – *GPC v. Filterwork Mann*.

[28] *Cf.* District Court of Paris, 28 April 2000. Reported new case-law: Court of First Instance at Brussels, 12 May 2000, 2001 GRUR Int. 170 and 173 with comment by P. Treichel; and *Roche v. The Wellcome Foundation*, 8 June 2000; District Court of The Hague, 29 September 1999 – *Novo v. DSM*, all to the cross-border declaratory non-infringement claims: *see* report: Remco de Ranitz/Marc van Wijngaarden, IP Litigation Yearbook 2000, 2–4.

for the second court to disregard the automatic suspension and to allow the proceedings. It would, however, be admissible for the second court to come to the assistance of the distressed patent owner with in the framework of a preliminary injunction.[29]

Of course, one must not overlook the fact that there is a risk of diverging judgments. This countermove is as unfinished and unpolished as the attack of cross-border judgments. The overall picture in Europe reveals a lively debate in the courts in the attempt to develop new standards for determining court jurisdiction in Europe. As the ECJ has of yet not given a decision, much is in motion which in the foreseeable future may channel into a calmer course.

VII. The Co-operation Directive

The new EC Regulation 1206/01 of 28 May 2001 on cooperation between the courts of the member states and the taking of evidence in civil or commercial matters is meant to provide the parties in one member state with the right to obtain evidence in another. Upon request of a party, a court in one member state may request a court in another member state to take evidence. It is not clear to what extent this would also allow plaintiffs in, say, Italy or France, to request a *saisie-contrefaçon* to be carried out in countries such as the Netherlands or Germany where this remedy would not be available. After all, Art. 10 No. 3 of the Regulation specifies that the request shall be carried out according to the procedures provided by the requesting country. The seized court in the other country shall then comply with such request unless this procedure is incompatible with its own laws, or due to major practical difficulties. The directive is yet untested and some authors have voiced doubts about their actual scope of application.[30] Further details are provided by G. Casucci in the chapter on Patent Enforcement in Italy.

VIII. The European Enforcement Directive

Of greater relevance in the European context could be the new Directive 2004/48/EC of 29 April 2004 on the enforcement of intellectual property rights. The Directive aims at an approximation of the remedies against IP infringement in the EU member states and requires implementation into national law within two years of its adoption date, Art. 20.

---

[29] *Cf.* District Court of Düsseldorf, 27 January 1998, 1998 GRUR Int. 803 – *Kondensatorspeicherzellen*.

[30] *See* Hattori/Petersen, Shôkô shirabe ni kan suru EU kisoku to kokusaiteki tokkyo shingai sosho (The New European Regulation and Its Implications on International Patent Litigation), 49/6 AIPPI Journal of the Japanese Group (June 2004), 2.

1. Objective

While the Directive acknowledges the progress made in enforcement standards due to the TRIPS Agreement, Recital (7) of the Directive stresses that "there are still major disparities as regards the means of enforcing intellectual property rights." These, as is stated in Recital (8), "are prejudicial to the proper functioning of the internal market and make it impossible to ensure that intellectual property rights enjoy an equivalent level of protection throughout the Community." For that reason, the Directive aims at a "high, equivalent and homogeneous level of protection in the internal market" (Recital (10)).

In substance, the Directive requires implementation of those instruments that the Commission perceived most useful in combating IP infringement in the national context. The Directive may thus be described as a collection of "best", or "most efficient" practices. The Directive does not introduce new measures or instruments that could not be found in any of the member states, *e.g.* punitive damages. Particular emphasis is given to preliminary measures and the preservation and obtaining of evidence.

2. Obtaining Evidence

Particularly, obtaining evidence from the opposing party has been an issue of widely differing practice within the European states, as is further explained in the individual chapters of this book.

It is a general difficulty in the rules of civil procedure that evidence in the control of the opposing party can only be obtained with considerable difficulty and upon exact specification of the documents or objects concerned. This is different in the U.K. due to the instrument of the discovery under Order 26 rules 1–6 of the Rules of the Supreme Court.

Art. 6.1 in this respect tries to balance the interests of both parties in establishing the following rule:

(1) The party wanting to obtain evidence from the other side has to present all reasonably available evidence in order to substantiate his claims;
(2) The party wanting to obtain evidence from the other side must specify such evidence in the possession of the other party;
(3) The protection of confidential information must be assured.

Further commercial documents can be obtained in cases of an infringement committed on a commercial scale, Art. 6.2.

Art. 6 will thus lead to a harmonisation of the widely differing rules on obtaining evidence from the opposing party during the infringement procedure.

Art. 7 concerns the obtaining of evidence from the other side *even before* the commencement of proceedings.

Here, the sweeping instruments of the *saisie-contrefaçon* or the Anton Piller order (now: inspection order) give plaintiffs in France, Belgium, Italy or the UK far better access in this respect than in countries such as Germany or the Netherlands. Here, countries have to "provide provisional measures to preserve relevant evidence in respect of the alleged infringement, subject to the protection of confidential information. Such measures may include the detailed description, with or without the taking of samples, or the physical seizure of the infringing goods, and, in appropriate cases, the materials and implements used in the production and/or distribution of these goods and the documents relating thereto." Unlike the French descriptive *saisie*, the request must only be granted where a party presents "reasonably available evidence to support his claims that his intellectual property right has been infringed or is about to be infringed." The judge thus has to decide to what extent the evidence is capable of supporting the claims. This seems to indicate that the judge can grant or refuse the measure on the balance of probabilities. The judge can exercise his discretion in weighing the evidence presented as follows:

(1) If the evidence is sufficient to support the claims, the measure can be granted *ex parte*, Art. 7.1, third sentence. The other party shall be notified without delay, Art. 7.1, second paragraph, and a review shall take place at the request of the affected party;
(2) If the evidence does not seem sufficiently strong to support the claims, the judge may either order an *inter partes* procedure or dismiss the request.

Art. 7 does not exclude further possibilities of judicial discretion, *e.g.* a deposit of the seized evidence with the court for a subsequent *inter partes* review. Such procedure may be particularly appropriate where the protection of confidential information is of concern.

It is not clear what countries such as Germany or the Netherlands will make of this provision. While the preservation of evidence in these countries is possible, the courts require an exact description of such evidence. The word "specified evidence" that can be found in Art. 6 is missing in Art. 7, however. If Art. 7 is to be regarded as a stand-alone provision, this will speak in favour of introducing broader instruments into Germany or the Netherlands than would be available at present. The question is of huge practical importance, as there certainly is an imbalance between countries in the possibilities of assessing *unspecified* and *ex ante unspecifiable* evidence in the possession of the other party. The authors take the view that Art. 7 shall be interpreted on its own merits, meaning that future European practice will move closer towards a system of *saisie contrefaçon*.

The other conditions mentioned in Art. 7 very much reflect elements of French and English practice: that the court may ask for a security to be posted (common in the U. K.), and that the results of such evidence gathering can only be used if proceedings are initiated within a period not exceeding 20 working days or 31 calendar days, whichever is the longer (in France currently 14 days, which would be consistent with the above rule).

3. The *Auskunftsanspruch*

The right of information mentioned in Section 3 (Art. 8) has been introduced in Germany as the *Auskunftsanspruch* by the 1990 Act Against Combating Piracy. It is a novelty to most other countries in Europe, however. Such *Auskunft* can be ordered as a final remedy, or in the course of interim procedures ("in the context of proceedings"). Article 8 requires persons who are found in possession of infringing goods on a commercial scale or professional service providers to indicate "information on the origin and distribution networks of the goods or services" upon request of the plaintiff. The information shall comprise the names and addresses of the producers, manufacturers, distributors, suppliers and other previous holders of the goods or services. Particularly in the UK, introduction of such an obligation to provide information has caused concern, as this would amount to compulsory self-incrimination. Article 8.3 thus specifies that countries may provide safeguards against misuse, against use in several or criminal proceedings, against misuse of confidential information or in order to "afford an opportunity for refusing to provide information which would force the person to admit his own participation in an infringement."

4. Interlocutory Injunction and Freezing Order

One of the most important remedies, at least in matters of trade marks and unfair competition prevention, is the interlocutory injunction regulated in Art. 9. In fact, the issuance of an interlocutory (interim) injunction more often than not ends the legal dispute for good. The wording of Art. 9.5 is thus following the misguided TRIPS provision of Art. 50.6. The TRIPS provision requires the plaintiff to initiate the main action within the above-mentioned period, as otherwise there is the risk that the defendant subsequently lodges a revocation request.

It is thus necessary to conceive procedures that do not require the plaintiff to raise a main action without necessity. This issue has been adressed by the German practice whereby after the issuance of an interim injunction both parties would formally conclude the lawsuit by contract, the so-called *Abschlußerklärung*.[31] Thereby, the defendant renounces his right to request the revocation of the interim order, or acknowledges the latter's validity.

In addition to the interim injunction as such, the courts may also order the "precautionary seizure of the movable and immovable property of the alleged infringer, including the blocking of his bank accounts and other

[31] Pastor/Ahrens, Der Wettbewerbsprozess, 4th ed. 1999, 1039 *et seq*. Once the defendant has given this declaration, he no longer has a standing to sue to initiate main proceedings. The details are complicated and will not be further elaborated on here.

assets" (Art. 9.2.) This is modelled after the English so-called Mareva injunction (now freezing order).

5. Final Sanctions

The Directive also requires member states to provide for a number of final measures, and specifications as to how these are to be applied. These basically correspond to the TRIPS provisions, that is, the destruction of goods, or their removal from commerce (Art. 10), injunctive relief (Art. 11), damages (Art. 13), and the restitution of attorneys' fees (Art. 14).

The judicial authorities are given discretion to order monetary compensation instead of injunctive relief/destruction of goods against infringers who act unintentionally and without negligence.

In all intellectual property infringement cases, the injunction is the most important relief. Where an injunction has been ordered, non-compliance with the latter shall be subject to a "recurring penalty payment" (Art. 11 sentence 2.) This is unfortunately worded, to say the least. It should rather be understood as a civil sanction comparable to the French *astreinte* with the consequence that such sanction can also be executed in other Member States under the Brussels Regulation. One further argument speaking in favour of interpreting the "penalty" as a civil sanction is the fact that criminal sanctions in general were deleted from the Regulation (see below) not least to due the fact that the Commission had no mandate under the EC Treaty to harmonise those.

6. Calculation of Damages

There are huge discrepancies between member states in the calculation of damages. In many member states, this is little more than a licence for the past, be it due to the difficulties in proving damages, or the reluctance of courts to order high damage amounts. Article 13 specifies that damages shall be the patentee's damages "appropriate to the actual prejudice suffered by him as a result of the infringement" (Art. 13.1, first sentence), calculated by taking into account "all appropriate aspects" such as the right owner's lost profits, the infringer's profits, or an adequate licensing fee. In patent infringement, there are relatively few cases where the courts are required to calculate damages. This might be due to the practice that after an infringement has been established in principle, both parties would settle on the damage amount. In France, the courts have the discretion to order preliminary damages as a lump sum (also mentioned in Art. 13.1.b)) that may also act as a strong incentive to settle.[32]

Art. 14 establishes the principle that the costs of the procedures shall be borne by the unsuccessful party, while discretion is given to take into account reasonableness, proportionality and equity.

---

[32] So-called *condamnation provisoire aux dommages-intérêts (*dommages-intérêts provisionnels). *See* further the chapter on France.

7. Publication of the Decision

Article 15 further obliges member states to introduce the possibility that the decision be published at the infringer's expense. This has been common practice in France and Italy.

8. Analysis

Already in its draft version, the Directive has received prominent criticism for being unnecessary and one-sided.[33] One can indeed wonder why harmonisation in such matters would assist the common market, and why particularly the strengthening of sanctions and remedies should be the appropriate measure to do so.[34] The most egregious provisions in this respect have been deleted in the last minute: the obligation to introduce a damage calculation based on the double licensing fee (procedure in Germany for copyright infringements claimed by collecting societies), and the obligation to introduce criminal sanctions. Both obligations would have appeared premature, if not misguided. A certain one-sidedness still remains. *E.g.*, the defendant's safeguards against the misuse of preliminary measures do not always look satisfactory. It should be noted that in countries where strong preliminary remedies are available, *e.g.* in the United Kingdom, there is also a strict code of conduct for barristers or solicitors presenting scurrilous or insufficiently researched evidence in order to back up their claims. Such safeguards may not be available in other countries that are now obliged to upgrade their enforcement systems in favour of right owners.

IX. European Projects

1. The Situation in the Area of Protection of Invention in Europe

There are many options available in the European sphere for protecting inventions. The instrument which today is particularly interesting for applicants outside of Europe is the European patent, which is based on a central application and after grant converts into a bundle of European patents. The latter are subject in part to European law and in part to national law.

The national patent rights continue to exist alongside the European patent, their substantive content being adapted to European patent law. The legal rules for both patents as far as patentability is concerned are for the most part identical.

---

[33] Most notably: Cornish/Drexel/Hilty/Kur, Procedures and Remedies for Enforcing IPRs: The European Commission's Proposed Directive, (2003) E.I.P.R. 447.

[34] According to Cornish et al. (above fn. 33), "Can it be seriously maintained that current differences over the extent of remedial relief (largely in civil process) is exercising pirates in choosing where to do their buccaneering business? Do they sit down with their lawyers and say 'Let's concentrate on Softland – no double damages there!' 'No no, Secretland would be better – can't be required to reveal our source there!'"

The European patent movement encompassed from the beginning the creation of a Community patent for the European Economic Community as well. The first endeavour included the European patent and the Community patent in the same project. Later this plan fell into two parts: the creation of the European procedure for the grant of patents (the European patent), and the creation of a European patent for the common market (the Community patent). Both conventions were planned as two parts of a whole.

According to the concept that had developed in the course of time, it was also supposed to be possible for the common market to choose between the European bundle patent and the Community patent.

2. The Community Patent

The Community patent, which was the subject three diplomatic conferences, did not come into force in the form agreed upon in 1989. Its demise was probably due in particular to the requirement that the Community patent had to be translated into at least one of the official languages of each of the member states of the European Union.

In 1997, the EU Commission took the initiative and in the year 2000 submitted a proposal for a regulation on the Community patent.[35] In the course of the preliminary work, industry expressed in particular its interest in setting up procedures for litigation that improved on the existing model. The proposal aimed at a central court from the first instance on in order to permit enforcement of the Community patent for the entire area of the common market. This proposal was incorporated partially into the text of the regulation. Proposals containing the details have now been drawn up.[36]

In any case, a project for a centralised system of litigation would be made easier if, initially, only one language was required for the Community patent, regardless of the claims, and translation would only be required in the case that action, especially court action, is taken based on the patent.

3. The European Patent – EPLA

At the same time, there was also a movement to create improved procedures for litigation for the European patent by reason of the resolutions of the Paris Government Conference on 24 and 25 June 1999.[37] A draft agreement was to be submitted, which was supposed to open up the possibility for the contracting states of the EPC to set up their own system for litigation.

[35] Proposal (of the Commission) for a Council Regulation on the Community Patent, Brussels, 1 August 2000, COM (2000) 412 final; new texts up to 2003.

[36] Commission Working Document on the Planned Community Patent Jurisdiction, Brussels, 30 August 2002, COM (2002) 480 final; last version: Proposal for a Council Decision conferring jurisdiction on the Court of Justice in disputes relating to the Community patent, Brussels, 23 December 2003, COM (2003) 827 final.

[37] Report in: 1999 OJ EPO 545 *et seq*.

To this end, a system of European patent court of the first and second instance as common court instances shall be established with European judges presiding. There is currently a controversial discussion taking place among the contracting states as to what extent jurisdiction, at least in the first instance, should remain decentralised in the hands of the regional divisions of the planned European Patent Court. There is no dispute with the view that there must be at least for the second instance a central European Patent Appeal Court. For it is this centralisation that up to now has been so direly needed.

The Agreement on the Establishment of a European Patent Litigation[38] is intended to be open to the contracting states of the European Patent Convention, and it was expected that at least a relevant number of contracting states would be prepared to join this special convention.

The obstacle to continue the work now finished is based on the opinion of the EU Commission that the EU member states no longer have the competence to negotiate jurisdictional agreements. In the diplomatic wording of the Declaration of the Working Party on Litigation of 20 November 2003: "3. The working party is conscious of the fact that the establishment of a litigation system for existing European patents is being paused, in view of the work being done by the European Union to introduce a Community patent with a judicial system of its own."[39]

4. Conclusion

The future results of these ongoing initiatives and discussion will depend largely on how the relationship between the European patent and the Community patent develops and how this relationship is organised. Resolving these questions will also provide the solution for the future system of litigation. One can hope that an effective and user-friendly solution can be found for patent law.

---

[38] Working Party on Litigation of 16 February 2004: Draft Agreement on the Establishment of a European Patent Litigation System, Draft Statute of the European Patent Court, published: w.org: official communications.

[39] *See* the reference in fn. 38 above.

3
The Enforcement of Patent Rights in the United Kingdom

WILLIAM CORNISH AND DAVID LLEWELYN

A. General[1]

I. Enforcing Patents

The only major comparative study of patent litigation in Western Europe was carried out nearly twenty years ago by Professor Dieter Stauder with great perspicuity and unquenched enthusiasm.[2] It cast light on the differences of process and usage in West Germany, England, France and Italy, where previously there had been deep obscurity. Since the research was undertaken quite soon after the signing of the Community Patent Convention, it contributed a great deal towards understanding the difficulties of procuring something like procedural unity for the single Community patent of the future. Now that the Community Patent is coming closer to reality these differences need to be examined afresh. Today European patents, granted by the European Patent Office, take effect separately in each state designated in the application and each is enforceable under the patent law of that state.[3] The Community Patent is to be enforced in separate Community tribunals and in some eclectic manner they will need procedural structures which measure up fully to the requirements of fairness and efficacy enjoined by the TRIPS Agreement, Article 41.

All forms of intellectual property depend for their effect on the availability of court processes for their enforcement. Because patents give rights over

---

[1] This contribution has been written as an introduction to the British system of patent enforcement which seeks to emphasise what is individual about it. It is not intended as a complete commentary on the details of the statute law and rules of practice. For these the reader is directed particularly to F. Clark, Sir R. Jacob, W.R. Cornish, G. Hamer, T. Moody-Stuart and C. May, "Encyclopedia of United Kingdom and European Patent Law" (Sweet & Maxwell, London) looseleaf – cited here as "Encyclopedia PL", and S. Thorley, R. Miller, G. Burkill and C. Birss, "Terrell on the Law of Patents", (15th edition, Sweet & Maxwell, London 2000) cited here as "Terrell". Also, for a more general introduction to UK patent law, *see* W.R. Cornish & D. Llewelyn, "Intellectual Property: Patents, Copyright, Trade Marks and Allied Rights" (5th ed., 2003), Chapters 3–7.

[2] "Patent-und Gebrauchsmusterverfahren in der Bundesrepublik Deutschland, Großbritannien, Frankreich und Italien" (1988).

[3] For the enforcement of foreign patents in the UK, *see* C.II, Transnational Jurisdiction, *infra*.

new products and processes which may prove to be crucial in the advance of an industry, they involve complex legal entitlements which are inherently problematic to enforce. For one thing courts cannot handle the litigation unless they have some real appreciation of the technology involved (the same holds for arbitrators, but they at least can be chosen by the parties). Yet what happens at the stage of enforcement will affect patent agents, lawyers and examining officers during all the stages of application for a patent. The system of enforcement and the procedures involved – including interpretation of legislation and procedural rules – are all crucial to the operation of the patent system as a whole.

Patents are enforceable chiefly by a civil action brought by the patentee. In the UK, patent infringement is not a criminal offence and only in limited circumstances can government services be called in aid by a patentee. Accordingly, when courts hear patent actions, they follow the norms and structures of civil procedure law. Much of the pre-trial and trial process is determined by general principles, but there are also rules which are specific to patent law.

II. Development of English Practice

Nonetheless the United Kingdom has had a long record of providing for patent actions to be tried at first instance in a court of special competence. From 1876, patent actions brought in England[4] were generally heard in the Chancery Division of the newly reorganised High Court. Chancery had no long-standing tradition of using juries, and placing the work in that division ensured that juries would no longer be expected to resolve disputes on technical issues which they were ill-equipped to handle. As a consequence Britain drew apart from the United States and placed patent adjudication in the hands of professional judges. A single judge now decides the case at trial; a bench of three judges hears an appeal to the Court of Appeal; and a bench of five (or possibly more) sits in the third instance provided by the House of Lords. All these judges, following English tradition, have had a first career as barristers[5] and have been appointed by the Crown to the bench only at a relatively late age. So far as experience of patent litigation is concerned, in the Court of Appeal and House of Lords, most of the judges will not have practised earlier as barristers from intellectual property chambers. In the Court of Appeal, however, it is likely, in any technically complex case, that the court will include a Lord Justice of Appeal who came originally from the patents bar.[6]

[4] The superior courts of Scotland and Northern Ireland also have patent jurisdiction, but only occasionally do parties have resort to it. Most patent cases are tried in London. Accordingly this article is confined to English procedure

[5] Or now, on occasion, solicitors.

[6] Until his retirement in 2003, the former patents judge in the Court of Appeal was Lord Justice Aldous. He has been succeeded by Sir Robin Jacob.

In 1949, the Chancery Division acquired a Patents Court as a sub-division with a specialist patents judge.[7] High Court procedure, prescribed in general in the Rules of the Supreme Court, was adapted to the conditions of patent and like litigation by Order 104 of the Rules, which referred specifically to patent litigation. In a move to open patent jurisdiction more readily to small enterprises, in 1989 a Patents County Court (PCC) was set up in London[8] with concurrent jurisdiction. Although section 288 of the Copyright, Designs and Patents Act 1988 provided the mechanism to place limits on the size of claims before the PCC, this was never done.[9] In the event, however, most work has continued to go to the High Court, which, as we shall see, was stimulated into greater efficiency by the lower level competition. There is now little difference in the cost or speed of litigating in either the PCC or the Patents Court. This article is mostly therefore about the present state of patent enforcement through the High Court machinery, and it lays stress on recent changes which attempt to strike a new balance between accessibility, efficiency, thoroughness and cost.

It is possible for English courts to appoint technically qualified persons to assist them as scientific advisers. If they do so, judgment remains a matter for the judge or judges; but they will normally rely very considerably upon the adviser's assessment of the technical evidence given in the proceedings by each party and subjected to cross-examination by the other side.[10] Because at first instance patent cases are tried by technically experienced judges, it is in practice only at the appeal level that experts are used in this way, and then only infrequently.

A contrast therefore arises with those legal systems which regularly leave technical issues for the decision or the advice of court-appointed experts. Not only does this relieve the judges of much of the responsibility in applying the law to the particular facts. It may also influence the way in which legal tests are formulated. It is one thing to use an interpretation of the law as

---

[7] The Chancery Division of the High Court now has five specialists: Laddie, Pumfrey, Neuberger, Patten and Lewison JJ., who sit as patents judges.

[8] It too is a specialised tribunal presided over by a judge with intellectual property experience (currently His Honour Judge Michael Fysh QC). In this Court, for the first time, patent agents were permitted to appear as counsel for parties, as well as solicitors and barristers. For assessments of the Court's work in its early years, *see* R. Nott, "Patent Litigation in England" [1994] EIPR 3; J. Adams, "Choice of Forum in Patent Disputes" [1995] EIPR 497. Since the appointment of Judge Fysh, the case-load of the PCC has increased.

[9] An example of the unfortunate consequence of not doing so is *Optical Laboratories Ltd v. Hayden Laboratories Ltd* [1993] RPC 204, in which Hirst LJ noted that the statement of case comprised 22 pages, the defence and counterclaim 128 pages and the reply 62 pages; this arose partly because of special rules of the PCC which (at the time) required all facts, matters and arguments to be set out in the pleading itself. The judge questioned whether such rules were appropriate for complex cases (at 206) and commented that in the High Court the pleading would have been reduced considerably.

[10] As to expert witnesses, *see* D.III, *infra*.

justification for decisions that the judges are making personally, as is now the case in the United Kingdom; but it is another to formulate propositions of law essentially in order to instruct experts how to go about their task. This is apparent particularly in relation to the assessment of inventive step.

The existence of the patents judges is thus a highly significant feature of the English approach. It makes much practicable which is chancy in a looser system. The one court can be expected to handle questions of the validity of a patent, as well as its infringement. That court can deal with both types of issue by way of claim and counterclaim, thus allowing the issues surrounding validity to affect perceptions of what should amount to infringement. The court can take a firm view of what is significant and what is peripheral or time-wasting. The efficiencies of the English approach deserve to be given full weight as a composite European procedure is hammered into shape for the Community Patent system of adjudication.

The place of professional advisers in patent litigation deserves mention. In the United Kingdom, the profession of patent attorney covers both those who offer their services to the public at large and those who work for particular enterprises. Patent attorneys engage in the business of preparing and pursuing patent applications and they give advice about rights in inventions and other industrial developments, including the licensing of new technology. They may be involved in litigation to enforce the rights, particularly where the technology is complex. However, in the main (although this is changing), that stage is handled by the two branches of the legal profession: solicitors organise the obtaining of evidence and experiments, the filing of court documents, contacting the other parties and so forth. Typically, the advocacy in court and the planning of strategies connected with it is undertaken by a barrister or barristers. As is well known, barristers are not directly commissioned by clients but are instead introduced through solicitors (or patent attorneys). However, it is now possible for solicitors (provided they have undergone advocacy training) themselves to act as advocates in the High Court, and patent attorneys to litigate (*i.e.*, instruct barristers direct and run the litigation but not to be advocate[11]) and in the Patents County Court both solicitors and patent attorneys may appear as advocates for parties. While traditionally judges in the superior courts have been chosen from the ranks of barristers, it is now possible to appoint solicitors as well (Mr Justice Lawrence Collins in the Chancery Division is a former litigation partner in a large firm of solicitors). This conserves the common law balance in which there is no separate judicial profession, and judges are considered to achieve some of their independence from having previously spent a considerable part of their career in a free profession.

[11] The Chartered Institute of Patent Attorneys Higher Courts Qualification Regulations 2000; *see* Fox, "Should patent attorneys litigate?" [2003] CIPA Journal 315.

B. Common Law Process in the English Conception

I. The Accusatorial Inheritance

The special connection between barristers and judges is related to the characterisation of English court procedure as accusatorial, rather than inquisitorial. Traditionally, on both the common law and the chancery sides, litigation has been led by the parties, rather than the court or its officers. The rules of procedure have imposed limits on the freedom of each side to act in what it considers its own best interests, but the character of the rules has been for the most part passive, responding to assertions and requests from one or other of the parties. It was not for the courts to take over the case in any broad sense. They did not, in any general sense, decide what claims should be made by parties and what evidence should be investigated in order to support or deny those claims. In civil litigation, the accusatorial approach has much to be said for it where (as in patent and other commercial litigation) both sides have a reasonable measure of financial support and therefore of independent judgment. They can judge for themselves what to press for, how to get up their case, how to challenge their opponents, when to fight on and when to seek a settlement. As in other business decisions, they are best left to their own devices. However, this is now changing significantly and in a recent case (*Merck v Generics (UK)*[12]) Mr Justice Laddie commented on the impact of the new Civil Procedure Rules (see below under Recent Reforms) "Whatever the position may have been in the past, it is no longer the case that the parties and their lawyers have a free hand to conduct an action as they like . . . Anyone with experience of litigation knows that clients' (and sometimes their lawyers') horns can become so locked with their opponents that their desire to win blinds them as to what is at stake".[13]

The cost of engaging in litigation in Britain has often been criticised as excessive.[14] Its expense certainly is not unrelated to the English version of accusatorial procedure. Each side is at risk, should the other side win, of paying at least a substantial part of the other's costs usually in the region of two-thirds as well as its own; and these costs may include barristers' and solicitors' and patent agents' fees agreed on a free market basis rather than by reference to controlled amounts or scales. The consequence is pressure towards voluntary settlement and for that there is always a strong case, as so much of the modern movement for mediation indicates: the policy in the

---

[12] [2003] EWHC 2842 (Pat).

[13] *Ibid.*, at paras 86–87.

[14] *See* the comments of Lord Esher in *Unger v. Sugg* (1892) 9 RPC 113, referred to recently by Mr Justice Laddie in *Merck v. Generics* [2003] EWHC 2842 at para. 84, "a man had better have . . . anything happen to him in this world, short of losing all his family by influenza, than have a dispute about a patent" at 116.

UK, in the words of Mr Justice Laddie, is "of making litigation a last resort".[15] A difficult balance has to be struck. No sane society considers that the settling of disputes should be costless, otherwise the process would be endless. On the other hand the pressure to make up and mend should not become so relentless that the rich too easily get their way over the poor.

II. Recent Reforms

In Britain there has been a widespread belief that litigation in the superior courts imposes a disproportionate financial risk. A Committee headed by Lord Woolf,[16] recommended a revision of procedure which in essence turns the system in the direction of the inquisitorial, at least so far as to make judges the managers of litigation through its various stages. The new scheme became operative on 26 April 1999, when the Civil Procedure Rules (CPR) were brought into operation: the Rules commence with a statement in Rule 1.1 of the Overriding Objective of "enabling the courts to deal with cases justly".[17] Judges, barristers and other professional litigators have had to learn how to operate the new framework. Although it is still rather early to say whether a real sea-change has taken place, it is fair to say that the amount of litigation proceeding to trial has been reduced and that the cost if it does has been reduced also. The judges, especially at the newly-introduced case management conference which occurs early in the process, have taken a more proactive role in forcing the parties to limit the issues.[18]

Patent litigation is everywhere a particularly costly enterprise if there are serious differences between the parties. Whether the patent is valid and infringed requires full, often lengthy, trial. Partly in response to the creation of the Patents County Court in 1989, the specialist judges in the High Court took it upon themselves to revamp the rules applying to Patents Court proceedings so as to give the judge greater powers of direction over their course. A thoroughgoing re-writing of the Supreme Court Rules, Order 104, was achieved in 1997 in advance of the general "Woolf Reforms," but very

---

[15] *Unilever v. Procter & Gamble* [1999] FSR 849.

[16] At the time, Lord Woolf was Master of the Rolls and so presided over the Court of Appeal. He is now the Lord Chief Justice and so heads the entire judiciary of England and Wales.

[17] Rule 1.1(2) states that this includes: "(a) ensuring that the parties are on an equal footing; (b) sharing expense; (c) dealing with the case in ways which are appropriate (i) to the amount of money involved; (ii) to the importance of the case; (iii) to the complexity of the issues; (iv) to the financial position of each party; (d) ensuring that it is dealt with expeditiously and fairly".

[18] Gentle archaisms have been swept away. Claims are now brought by claimants, not plaintiffs. Latin gives way to English. For more, *see* C.III, Preparation for Trial, *infra*.

much in their spirit.[19] In 1998 the Consolidated Practice Direction (CPD)[20] provided for trials on affidavit evidence (paragraph 13), required parties to narrow the issues (paragraph 22), encouraged admissions (paragraph 23) and required service with pleadings of copies of documents referred to (paragraph 29). As a result, the average length of patent trials in the Patents Court has been reduced from several weeks in the 1980s and before to less than one week in 2002.[21]

Also, in 2003 a new streamlined procedure was introduced, whereby the courts may direct that certain areas of enquiry or dispute are reduced in scope or deleted:[22]

> "Two things should be noted about this procedure. First, although it may be sought by either party, the court has the power to impose it of its own motion. The court will take this power seriously. In some cases that may mean that the court will, at an early stage, require the parties to give it a fuller understanding than normal of what the issues are so that it is better placed to decide whether to impose the streamlined procedure. Second, the [Chancery] Guide makes it clear . . . that the parties' legal advisers are obliged to draw their clients' attention to the availability of this procedure. It must be expected that the court will take that requirement seriously and will monitor compliance with it."[23]

There has been enough of a change in climate and procedure since the Stauder study to make the new conditions of English patent litigation the main subject of this article.

C. *Procedural Steps and Their Problems*

I. Competent Parties and Their Powers[24]

Proceedings alleging the infringement of a patent may be instituted by the proprietor or proprietors of the patent or by an exclusive licensee under the

---

[19] *See* "Laddie J's Practice Direction" [1998] RPC 18. Part 49E of the new Civil Procedure Rules (CPR) replaces Ord 104 and is similar in many respects.

[20] 21 May 1998. The Part 49E Practice Direction (11 March 1999) replaces Ord. 104 RSC but does not revoke the Consolidated Practice Direction, which therefore remains effective.

[21] *See* S. Thorley QC, "Lord Justice Aldous – An Appreciation" [2003] CIPA Journal 537, where Mr Thorley states that "[I]t is perhaps one of the principal tributes that can be laid at William Aldous' door that he and his successors" have achieved this reduction in the length of patent trials.

[22] The Patents Court Guide (12 November 2003), para.10: such a procedure is to be used where all factual and expert evidence is in writing, there is no requirement to give disclosure of documents, there are no experiments, cross-examination is limited, and the duration of the trial will normally not be more than one day.

[23] *Merck v. Generics* (UK), *op.cit.*, at para. 93.

[24] For details, *see* Encyclopedia PL § 10.003–004, 10.101; Terrell § 21.12–12.27.

patent.[25] In the latter case, the patentee may join as claimant, but if it refuses, it must be joined as a defendant. The claim may extend to damages for acts done between early publication of the application and subsequent grant of the patent, but only where the acts would infringe the claims contained in both.[26]

The proceedings may be instituted against any person who is alleged to have performed an act of direct or indirect infringement under the terms of the Patents Act 1977, sections 60(1) and (2), which are based on the Community Patent Convention, Articles 25 and 26.[27] The actual performance may be the defendant itself, its servants or agents. Beyond this, those who collaborate in or instigate infringement by others may be impugned in the infringement itself as a joint tortfeasor, or at least treated as liable for the general torts of conspiring or inducing unlawful acts.[28] The director of a company, or the driving force behind a corporate entity will be personally liable if he expressly authorised or directed the infringements.[29]

When an infringement action is begun in a British court, it is open for a defendant to respond by asserting that his activities do not amount to infringement because they do not fall within the scope of the patent as defined by the claims,[30] or because they do not amount to an infringing activity[31] or because one of the specific defences, such as use for experimental purposes applies.[32] Equally, either by way of defence to the infringement action, or by counterclaim for revocation, the invalidity of the patent may be asserted.[33] The British have been among the most staunch adherents of the

---

[25] *See* Patents Act 1977, s. 60, 61, 67. The proprietor does not have to be registered as such at the commencement of the litigation; but note s. 69. It may rely upon a formally complete assignment to it or upon an enforceable contract to assign ownership: *see Baxter International v. Nederlands Produktielaboratorium voor Bloedtransfusiapparatuur* [1998] R.P.C. 250. For the conditions under which one co-proprietor may institute proceedings by itself, *see* s. 66(2).

[26] Patents Act 1977, s. 69, where further conditions are defined. For the extent to which an assignee may sue in respect of acts occurring before the assignment, *see* s. 30(7).

[27] The British provisions differ somewhat in language but are to be read as far as possible in conformity with the Convention (*see* s. 130(7); and for an instance where this was done so as to exclude the liability of a mere warehouse keeper: *Smith Kline & French v. Harbottle* [1980] RPC 363.

[28] Liability for conspiracy can extend to a person whose own acts are all performed abroad but who secures the commission of an infringement in the UK: *see ABKCo Music v. Music Collection Int.* [1995] RPC 657.

[29] *See, e.g., PLG Research v. Ardon* [1993] FSR 197.

[30] In accordance with EPC, Art. 69 and its Protocol, as given effect in the Patents Act 1977, s. 125.

[31] In the sense outlined in the previous paragraph.

[32] For which *see* Patents Act 1977, s. 60(5), deriving from CPC, Article 27.

[33] Patents Act 1977, s. 74. There are also provisions allowing invalidity proceedings to be commenced independently (possibly ending in the issue of a certificate of contested validity: *see* s. 65); for a person to proceed for a declaration of non-infringement (s. 71) or for relief against groundless threats of infringement proceedings (s. 70).

view that it must be possible in conjoint proceedings to examine whether the patent satisfies all the requirements for patentability, and also the sufficiency of the description of the invention and the propriety of amendments which may have been made to the description or the claims in the specification.[34] As already mentioned, where the court consists of an experienced judge, it is considered highly desirable that the patentee's right should be viewed within the continuum of technical development in the field in question and it is this which the joint trial of infringement and validity aims to achieve.

II. Transnational Jurisdiction in UK Courts[35]

Traditionally courts in the United Kingdom accepted that patents are territorial in nature. Accordingly, actions for infringement of a patent granted by another country in respect of activities occurring on its own geographical territory could not be entertained in a United Kingdom court. (The same applied to proceedings for revocation of foreign patents and other similar issues, such as actions for threats to sue for infringement.[36]) For this two reasons were given. First, the nature of the action was characterised as *local*, not *transitory*, and so restricted to the courts of the locality.[37] Secondly, the cause of action for patent infringement was in nature for a tortious wrong. It was not therefore actionable unless, *inter alia*, the allegedly wrongful act amounted to a tort in the UK jurisdiction.[38] That could not be so, because the patent right was territorial and the act did not occur in that jurisdiction. Behind this somewhat formulaic reasoning lay a clear appreciation of the political dangers, and the probable inefficacy, of intervening in the affairs of other countries through the medium of litigation.[39] Patents give exclusive rights to manufacture and sell commodities, apparatus and processes. A judgment against an infringer will probably include an injunction against activities which provide trade and employment. The effect of an injunction could therefore be of decided economic significance and is unlikely to be palatable

[34] These grounds of objection to the validity of a granted patent, equivalent to the grounds of opposition in EPC, Art. 100, are to be found in Patents Act 1977, s. 72(1).

[35] *See*, in general, Professor Stauder's essay on the subject in this volume, Chapter 2; and further, Wadlow, *Enforcement of Intellectual Property in European and International Law* (London, Sweet & Maxwell, 1998); J. Fawcett and P. Torremans, *Intellectual Property and Private International Law* (London, Butterworths, 1998).

[36] As to the latter, *see Norbert Steinhart v. Meth* (1960) 105 CLR 440 (H.C. Australia).

[37] By extension of the *Moçambique* rule concerning trespass to land: *see Potter v. Broken Hill Pty Ltd* (1906) 3 CLR 479 (H.C. Australia).

[38] This was one aspect of the *double actionability* rule which determined jurisdiction over foreign tort actions by reference to the operative law in both the place of the wrong and England.

[39] For expressions of reluctance to intervene for these reasons, *see, e.g.*, Dillon L.J. in *Mölnlycke v. Procter & Gamble* [1992] RPC 21; Aldous J. (as he then was) in *Plastus Kreativ v. Minnesota Mining* [1995] RPC 438.

when economic activities abroad have in consequence to be closed down – the more so when the defendant is attached to the place, or the claimant belongs to the state asserting jurisdiction; and the merits of the case are far from one-sided.

Yet if contests about the scope or validity of patents covering essentially the same invention take place in different countries and they result in differing outcomes, the results overall may appear inexplicably divergent.[40] This may be particularly apparent where the various patents for EPC countries have been obtained through the single granting procedure of the European Patent Office. In consequence there have been occasions on which Dutch courts in particular have been prepared to embrace a wide extra-territorial jurisdiction to grant injunctions against patent infringement in various European countries.

In contrast British courts have been reluctant to abandon their preference for a strictly territorial approach. They show no readiness to treat EPO patent grants as giving in effect a unitary right over all the designated territories simply because of the single granting procedure. But they, in their turn, have had to bring into account the effects of the EC Regulation on the Recognition and Enforcement of Judgments in civil and commercial matters (formerly the Brussels Convention on the subject). Under this Judgments Regulation (and the Lugano Convention which extends its effects to Switzerland, Norway and other EFTA countries), jurisdiction is conferred by strict rules which are intended to lead to the standard and automatic recognition and enforcement of judgments in the collaborating states. As Professor Stauder explains, the prime rule is this: where the defendant's "domicile" is in a (then) EEA state, the action must be brought in that country.[41] English courts have accepted that, in consequence, they must take jurisdiction to decide a question of intellectual property infringement occurring in any EEA state where the defendant has an English domicile, unless some overriding objection can be raised. The applicable law will then be the law of each country where an infringing act is alleged to take place.[42]

One of the difficulties in the Judgments Regulation is that there is only one provision which directly adapts them to the special characteristics of patent actions. The absence of other modifications has led to significant problems – and these are only beginning to be resolved. The one provision is Article 22(4),[43] which grants exclusive jurisdiction over proceedings

---

[40] Once the right in question is a Community law right extending indivisibly over the whole European Union (as with a Community trade mark), there can in principle be no scope for the application of distinct laws in different member states. Whether this is how matters transpire must be questionable in view of the CTM experience.

[41] Judgments Regulation, Art. 2.

[42] *Pearce v. Ove Arup* [1999] FSR 525 (CA). There is an additional jurisdiction in delict actions – including patent infringement – conferred on a state where the wrongful act is occurring; but then all relief is limited to harm arising in that state: *see* Art. 5(3).

[43] Formerly, Brussels Judgments Convention, Art. 16(4).

concerned with the registration or validity of patents and similar rights to the courts of the country granting the right. It is not a provision which applies in terms to the scope of the rights granted by the patent, though, as we shall see, it may have an indirect effect in any country which allows the invalidity of the patent to be set up as a defence, or as a counterclaim for revocation, in the infringement action.

In some degree British courts have tackled various dilemmas set by the Judgments Regulation for patent jurisdiction. First, the Regulation deals with the case where there are co-defendants of different domicile across EEA states by allowing an action against all to be brought in the courts of any one of them.[44] The object was to prevent too evident opportunities for forum shopping from arising. In the case of allegations that patents over a given invention are being infringed in different member states, it has first to be asked whether each defendant is involved in infringing acts which occur in, or are related to, all the states. In that case it would be proper to apply the Convention provision. However, because there may be a string of national subsidiaries or manufacturing licensees, it can happen that each defendant is in a different state and is alleged only to infringe the local patent. In that situation the English Court of Appeal has not allowed the foreign defendants to be joined in a suit which would encompass infringement by them of their local patents. The danger of inconsistent judgments is held not to arise because of the territorial confines of each patent.[45] As a corollary of this approach, the fact that proceedings have been commenced elsewhere for infringement of the local patent by the local defendant, does not mean that jurisdiction cannot be taken in (say) England to bring an equivalent action against the English defendant.[46] These constraints have seemed appropriate because otherwise the very provisions of the Convention designed to reduce forum shopping could too easily have the obverse effect.

Secondly, a separate jurisdiction arises in the courts of each contracting state to make provisional and protective orders, even though the Conventions give no entitlement to act in the substantive dispute.[47] In intellectual property matters the jurisdiction is probably confined to orders relating to infringing activity within that state.[48] One major difficulty here is to know what procedural steps involve only provisional and protective measures. Clearly they include

---

44 Brussels Convention, Art. 6(1).

45 *Fort Dodge Animal Health v. Akzo Nobel* [1998] FSR 222 at 243; *cf* the decision of the Court of Appeal of The Hague, *Expandable Grafts v. Boston Scientific* [1999] FSR 352, reaching a largely similar result by limiting extra-territorial relief to cases whether the local defendant is "the spider in the web". That seems a sound distinction, even if it is not always easy to apply.

46 *See* the Brussels Convention, Art. 21 (*lis pendens*) and Art. 22 (related actions created a danger of irreconcilable judgments).

47 Brussels Convention, Art. 24.

48 So held by the Court of Appeal of The Hague in *Expandable Grafts* (*supra* note 45), relying upon *Denilauler v. Couchet Frères* [1980] ECR 1553 (ECJ).

ex parte orders for cessation of activities or preservation of evidence. But other forms of relief are more equivocal. Thus British proceedings for an interim injunction which are heard *inter partes* may take into account the substantive allegations in disputes, insofar as the balance of convenience does not settle whether the court will order restraint until trial of the action. The fact, however, that the order is upon this temporary footing may give rise to "provisional and protective" jurisdiction under the Regulation.

Thirdly, whether a Court assumes jurisdiction under Article 2 or under Articles 2 and 6(1) of the Judgments Regulation, there are inherent risks of unfairness in summary proceedings. These may indeed be exacerbated in countries with an inquisitorial tradition, where it is not unknown for the judge to develop his own view of the causes of action open to the parties. He may even act on them after only giving restricted opportunity to the parties to express their own views. If either party is in consequence placed under a temporary restraint which has serious commercial consequences in other EC states, the propriety of the order is likely to seem highly questionable in those states. At least if the order requires recognition and enforcement elsewhere, this may prove difficult, whatever the Conventions may say on the subject. As the English judges have indicated, at least in intellectual property matters it is all too easy to raise doubts about the fairness of procedures and decisions in foreign courts which have an extra-territorial impact.

Fourthly, like most other Contracting States, the United Kingdom allows the defendant in a patent infringement action to impugn the validity of the patent by way of counterclaim (or defence). It is an aspect of trial process which the British strongly favour, since every patent exists within the context of its industrial technology.[49] Since the Regulation expressly limits jurisdiction over the validity of a patent to the courts of the granting state, does this mean that an infringement action to which invalidity is pleaded in response is subject to the same jurisdictional limitation? The English Court of Appeal has held so and, for a time this appeared to be in direct conflict with Dutch interpretation, thereby threatening a major confrontation over speedy cross-border injunctions. However, the Court of Appeal of The Hague has moved closer to the British position. In *kort geding* proceedings for patent infringement, once the defendant has attacked the validity of the patent, cross-border relief is not to be granted unless it is immediately clear that the invalidity claim is without merit.[50]

When an English court is faced with proceedings for enforcement of a patent granted for a country outside the EEA, the Judgments Regulation has no application. It is far from clear whether it would hear infringement proceedings even in the uncommon case where the defendant does not dispute

---

[49] *See* above under Competent Parties and their Powers.

[50] *Expandable Grafts* (*supra* note 45) . In the case, no relief was granted even in respect of the alleged infringements in Holland. It is not yet clear that British courts will adopt the same threshold test, but it is highly desirable that they should do so.

the validity of the foreign patent. In the first place, the legal rationales for refusing jurisdiction – the Moçambique rule concerning local actions and the double actionability rule — are now subject to serious doubt.[51] In any case, there has been a recent willingness to deal with choices between possible jurisdictions for tort actions by reference to the concept of *forum non conveniens* – a discretionary approach that is not accepted when the Jurisdiction Regulation applies. If a challenge to validity is to be a major element in the defence, it is likely that English courts will consider it better to refer the issue to the country of grant.[52]

III. Preparation for Trial

Patent proceedings are rarely straightforward and in recent years the patent judges have attempted to force through very significant procedural change, requiring the parties to such complex litigation to reveal far more of their case and evidence than had historically been so. Thus, in the early 1990s for the first time detailed witness statements had to be served on the opposing party with sufficient notice to enable analysis. This prevented the unsatisfactory practice of ambush by a witness of which the opposing party had no notice and has led to more structured and well-prepared proceedings. In addition the courts require written summaries (or skeletons) of arguments to be filed with the court in advance. Another noteworthy development is the willingness of the patent judges to hear short interim applications (up to 90 minutes) by telephone.[53] On the issue of interim applications generally a major deterrent to one party making spurious or tactical applications in the hope of putting pressure on the other, perhaps not as well funded, is the introduction by the Woolf rules of summary assessment of costs, under which the judge will assess costs immediately (on the basis of reasonableness and proportionality) and the losing party must pay those costs within a short period. However, the level of costs awarded by the court on such summary basis very rarely reflects the actual costs.

IV. Pre-action Procedures

1. Interim Injunctions

In all intellectual property litigation, right owners have the strongest desire for interim relief from courts. An order that an alleged infringer must for the time being close down production, importation, marketing or distribution,

---

[51] Account must now be taken of the Private International Law (Miscellaneous Provisions) Act 1995, preceded by *Red Sea Insurance v. Bouygues* SA [1995] AC 190 and followed by *Pearce v. Over Arup* [2000] Ch. 403.

[52] *See* above.

[53] CPD, para. 35

is often enough to curb or entirely stamp out a damaging outbreak of infringement. So equally is an order that evidence of wrongdoing should be given over to the claimant, or that information be disclosed about channels of supply, and to these we shall come. Britain has seen a great deal of commercial piracy in the last half-century, particularly affecting copyright and trade-marked products and to this the courts have responded by increasing their readiness to provide interim relief of various kinds. These changes have had their influence at many points in the worldwide battle to increase the effectiveness of intellectual property rights against organised piracy and counterfeiting.

Given the complexity of many contests over patents, claimants – and often defendants as well – may particularly desire a foreshortened procedure, rapid and cheap enough to fit commercial realities. But the very fact that there may well be serious arguments on both sides about liability in patent proceedings has led courts in many countries to be cautious in granting this type of relief. In Britain it used to be the case that, once a defendant pleaded a plausible case against liability, the court would rarely grant an interlocutory injunction. Only when the patent was old and generally respected by the industry, or when the patentee had already succeeded in enforcing it against similar defendants, would a court be willing to hold that the claimant had established a *prima facie* case of liability; and this was the first requirement of relief.

In 1975, the House of Lords abandoned this emphasis on making out a *prima facie* case. Instead it placed much greater emphasis on the advantages and disadvantages of restraining the defendant until the issue could be tried in full – this is the so-called balance of convenience.[54] The House of Lords reached this conclusion in patent litigation between major producers of surgical sutures, where clearly it considered that evidence for and against the claimant's *prima facie* case had gone much too far towards seeking a summary assessment of the ultimate issues.

The underlying effect of this shift has been to make the outcome of an application to the court for an interim injunction depend much more upon the respective commercial situations of claimant and defendant. If the patent underpins the patentee's major business activity, the defendant's competition may be specially damaging and this may be a reason in favour of an injunction until trial of the action. On the other hand, if the patent has already been so successful that the defendant's operation is unlikely to inflict major commercial damage, then the latter may be allowed to continue. Of course he faces the risk that if the patentee ultimately wins at trial, the award

[54] *American Cyanamid v. Ethicon* [1975] AC 396. It is still open for a defendant to assert that the claimant has revealed no serious case to be tried, *i.e.* that on the allegations, no liability can as a matter of law arise. This is a more limited than the former inquiry into whether the claimant had made out a *prima facie* case. For more technical treatment of the law affecting interim relief, *see*, *e.g.*, Encyclopedia PL, §§10.005, 10.109.; Terrell, §§ 12.48–69.

of damages or an account of profits will be increased by the losses in the interim period. Overall, the effect of the new emphasis upon the balance of convenience has been somewhat to increase the prospect of an interim injunction in patent cases. But it is difficult to predict how a judge will weigh the particular circumstances, which rarely relate to the issue between the parties.

Any claimant except the Crown must give a cross-undertaking in damages: (now governed by CPR Practice Direction 25 para 5.1(1)) if the claim is not substantiated at a subsequent trial, the innocent defendant's losses must be made good in a monetary award. If it is not clear that the claimants will be able to pay such damages if it loses at trial, it may be ordered that a bank guarantee (or the like) be provided. The enjoined defendant is thus obliged to bear the risk of the claimant's possible insolvency. The need to give such a cross-undertaking is frequently a significant factor in deciding whether to apply for an interim injunction, especially if the claimant has a doubtful case. As such it provides important balancing element to the interim injunction procedure, lacking in, for example, Holland.

2. Securing and Preserving Evidence Before Trial

a) Discovery of names

There are other relatively recent changes of pre-trial procedure which have improved the position of owners of intellectual property. In the 1970s, the House of Lords considerably strengthened the ability of claimants to secure from a court an order that a person who was not a wrongdoer must nevertheless reveal the name or other information about others in order that proceedings may be instituted against them. This can have important implications in the patent sphere. In the leading case,[55] a patentee discovered from government statistics that pharmaceuticals falling within its patent were being imported into Britain, but it could not find out by whom. The Commissioners of Customs and Excise, who had published the information, were ordered to reveal the importer's name. Their protest that if they could not keep the name confidential, they would themselves be fed false information, fell upon deaf ears. Rule 31.17 CPR now makes specific provision for disclosure by a non-party, who need no longer be made a party to the proceedings.[56]

An action for discovery of names can be equally useful against a private party. A company which transports or warehouses infringing goods, but which has no deeper connection with their distribution, is not liable for infringement of the patent.[57] It may, however, be ordered to disclose the

[55] *Norwich Pharmacal v. Customs and Excise* [1972] FSR 405.

[56] The disclosure must be necessary to dispose fairly of the claim or to save costs.

[57] *Smith Kline & French v. Harbottle* [1980] RPC 363.

names of customers who have used the service for their goods. Ultimately, the order is discretionary and would not be used where the result is unduly oppressive.[58]

b) Preservation of assets

Over the same period, the courts have shown greater readiness to grant so-called *Mareva* injunctions (now re-labelled "freezing injunctions").[59] These are aimed at defendants who might otherwise disperse assets or shift them abroad, leaving little or nothing behind from which to satisfy any judgment against them. While these orders have been used in a great variety of litigation, they have been important in the sphere of intellectual property when directed against persons suspected of being "pirate kings". If they can be shown to be holding the profits of illicit activities in assets, such as expensive cars, jewellery or houses, or in bank accounts, orders conserving these can be highly effective. Yet they can have a devastating effect on defendants, since they may find their business credibility destroyed at the launching of the proceedings, rather than at their conclusion. They should therefore be made only when there is the strongest suspicion of liability, and even then should, where possible, be limited in their consequences.[60]

c) Preservation of evidence and provision of information

The best-known enhancement of procedure in the interest of intellectual property owners has been the development by the courts of the *Anton Piller* order for the preservation of evidence and the disclosure of information by the party subject to it. This is now known as a "search order".[61] The order is sought by proceedings held in closed session of which the defendant has no notice, the whole object being to spring a surprise.

The order will require the defendant to admit the claimant – and, all-importantly, the claimant's solicitor – in order (i) to inspect the defendant's premises and seize, copy or photograph material demonstrating the alleged infringement; (ii) to print out infringing computer programs or data and to deliver up infringing goods, and keep infringing stock or incriminating papers; and (iii) in many cases, to require answers to questions concerning sources of supply or the subsequent destination of illicit material. To obtain this relief, the claimant must satisfy the court of three things: (i) that there is an extremely strong *prima facie* case of infringement; (ii) that the damage is likely to be very serious; and (iii) that the defendant possesses incriminating

58 *Sega Enterprises v. Alco Electronics* [1982] FSR 516.

59 Civil Procedure Rules 1999, Part 25.1(1)(f); and *see generally*, "Civil Procedure" 277 *et seq*. (Sweet & Maxwell, 2nd ed. May, 1999).

60 *See* the harsh criticism of court practice by T. Willoughby and S. Connal "The Mareva Injunction: A Cruel Tyranny?" [1997] EIPR 479.

61 *See* Civil Procedure Rules, Part 25.1 (c), (h) and *see also* (l), (f). The Order was given a statutory basis in the Civil Procedure Act 1997, s. 7. The Order can be made by the Patents County Court as well as the High Court: *see McDonald v. Graham* [1994] RPC 407.

articles or documents which otherwise may well be destroyed or removed before any application *inter partes* can be made.

The procedure has been used regularly against evident pirates of copyright material (notably on records, videos and computer games) and counterfeiters of trade marks. It can be effective particularly against small-scale distributors, operating often enough at markets, sports grounds and other fly-by-night venues. Search orders, still made with considerable frequency, are necessarily a rough instrument. The judges seek to avoid unfairly pressurising persons who do not know in advance what is to happen, but they are very much in the hands of the claimant's legal representatives and those who procure the preliminary evidence by trap orders and surreptitious surveillance.

There has been a succession of cases in which judges have certain criticised tactics, including arrangements to involve the police. Various requirements about notification to defendants of what is required of them and what they may do by raising objections to the order in court have been built into the order. The procedure was tightened in 1994, as a result of the decision of Vice-Chancellor Nicholls in *Universal Thermosensors v. Hibben*,[62] notably by requiring in most cases that an independent supervising solicitor be added to the inspection party when it pounces. The order, moreover, should only be served between 9.30 am and 5.30 pm, Monday to Friday. It should identify the supervising solicitor and the persons who will accompany him or her. It should contain undertakings from the supervising solicitor to explain the nature and effect of the order in everyday language and advise the respondent of the right to take legal advice before letting the searching party into the premises and to apply to the Court for discharge of the order.

The law has become detailed and much more could be said on the subject since it operates along a highly sensitive boundary of civil liberties and due process. But by their nature, patented inventions are not so regularly the subject-matter of search orders as are pirate films, records, computer programs and goods of many kinds which bear counterfeit marks and get-up. For one thing, even defendants who are making or distributing direct copies tend to be more substantial concerns than those who deal in compact discs, cosmetics and clothing. Accordingly, we have restricted ourselves to mentioning the basic attributes of the order.

3. Other Pre-Action Procedures

In addition to the interim injunction and the search and freezing orders, the following remedies are also available before as well as after proceedings are commenced: orders for inspection, taking samples of or carrying out experiments on property, delivery up and orders for disclosure of documents.[63]

---

62 [1992] 1 WLR 840.

63 *See* Art. 5 of the Civil Procedure (Modification of Enactment) Order 1998 (SI 1998 No. 2940), which removed the limitation on pre-action disclosure to personal injuries and fatal accident proceedings in Secs. 33 and 34 of the Supreme Court Act 1981.

The latter can assist in allaying suspicions a claimant may have of a defendant and avoid litigation or can lead to rapid settlement prior to issuing of proceedings. More frequent, however, is a tendency for the pre-action procedures to persuade a claimant to drop weaker claims.

D. *Commencement of the Action*

I. Statement and Particulars of Case

Under the new regime prescribed in the CPR Part 7, proceedings for patent infringement are now commenced by issuing a claim form (rather than the writ or petition as previously) under CPR Part 7. Pleadings are now known as "statements of case" and copies of all documents referred to in the statement of case should be served on the defendant.[64] It is preferable to serve the Particulars of Claim at the same time as the claim form, which Particulars must include a concise statement of the facts on which the claimant relies.[65] Defendants are required to give reasons for any denials and put forward any different versions of facts upon which they wish to rely. Both claimant and defendant have to verify their statements of case with a statement of truth, which must be made by an officer of the company (or the individual party, if a natural person) rather than by a legal adviser.

Particulars of Infringement are served with the claim form, stating which of the claims in the specification are alleged to be infringed and giving at least one example of each type of alleged infringement.[66] Where the defendant wishes to challenge validity, either as a defence or in a counterclaim, Particulars of Objections to Validity must be served, stating every ground.[67] A defendant who challenges validity must serve the Particulars within 42 days of the service of the claim form. Also, the CPD requires admissions to be made at an early stage, in the defence or reply (in the case of the former, admissions must be made within 14 days from service of the claim form[68]). This procedure assists greatly in limiting the issues between the parties.

II. Case Management: Directions

A claimant in patent proceedings must apply for directions within 14 days of acknowledgement of service or delivery of defence.[69] The judge to whom

---

64 Para. 29 CPD. Examples would include advertisement referred to in Particulars of Infringements.

65 CPR 16.4(1)(a).

66 PD49E, para. 6.1.

67 PD49E, para. 7.3.

68 CPR 14.2(b). A person who wants to serve a notice to admit facts must do this within 21 days of service of a reply (PD49E, para. 8.1).

69 PD49E, para. 2.5.

the case is assigned will hold a case management conference to consider such issues as: whether the claimant's case is clear, what disclosure of documents is necessary, what and how expert evidence is to be obtained, the factual evidence to be disclosed and whether there are any preliminary issues which can be heard and may therefore limit the scope of the trial.[70] Also, a timetable will be set by the judge, who will also consider whether a scientific adviser should be appointed to assist the court.[71] The timetables set in patent cases tend to be far stricter than hitherto, with little scope for changing deadlines and especially the trial date.

The case management conference is an extremely important change to procedure in patent proceedings and has led to the specialist judges using their many years of experience as patent barristers to intervene and persuade the parties to limit the issues between them and to reduce to the minimum the level of disclosure. However, one problem arising from this judicial intervention is that the parties must prepare for any point which may conceivably be raised at the case management conference and costs are thereby increased. This could be avoided if the judges were prepared to provide the parties in advance with a list of the points they intend raising.

III. Disclosure and Evidence

Once the issues have been delineated clearly through the use of admissions and the case management conference (in which the patent judges will be active in requiring the parties to limit issues), the parties need to give disclosure of documents.[72] At the time of the Stauder study, the English seemed to be adopting the American penchant for ever-wider discovery of documents. This has now been reined in very considerably. A party is required to disclose only (a) those documents on which he relies, (b) documents which adversely affect his own or another's case or which support another party's case, and (c) other documents which he is required to disclose by a practice direction.[73] However, it is important to note that paragraph 9.1 of PD49E exempts disclosure of documents (a) relating to infringement of a patent by a product or process, provided that the alleged infringer serves full particulars of the product or process alleged to infringe, (b) relating to any ground on which the validity of the patent is put in issue, except documents which came into existence within the period beginning two years before the earliest claimed priority and ending two years after that date, and (c) relating to the issue of commercial success, provided that full particulars are served in a schedule directed by the court. These exemptions have reduced considerably the

---

[70] All these issues would be set out in a draft minute of order which has to be filed prior to the conference (PD49E, 11.1(3)) and is then finalised by the judge.

[71] PD49E, 11.3(b). *See* A.II, *supra*.

[72] CPR 31.5(1).

[73] CPR 31.6(c).

amount of disclosure in patent proceedings. However, there have been suggestions that the fact that the trial date is difficult to alter makes it easier for a party to give inadequate disclosure and rely on the clock.

Where experiments are required to prove a fact, the party requiring them must serve a notice giving full details of the experiments. The other party has 21 days in which to serve a notice stating whether or not he admits each fact sought to be proved.[74]

Under CPR 32.1(1) the court may direct the issues on which it requires evidence, the nature of that evidence and may limit cross-examination. Not less than two days before trial in the Patents Court, each party must lodge a certificate estimating the length of its oral submissions, of its examination in chief of its own witnesses and of cross examination. If these estimates start to be overrun the judge at trial will guillotine the advocate accordingly.

The CPR provides for reading guides[75] (comprising the agreed basic documents, and setting out the issues and documents in order) and, in complex cases, for technical primers (containing an agreed background summary of the basic technology).[76] The new civil procedure rules limit expert evidence to what is reasonably required to resolve the issues in the proceedings.[77] Such evidence should be in writing unless the court directs otherwise. Gone are the days when the parties were left free to put forward their own experts who would, in greater or lesser degree, contradict each other at the trial. The parties should agree on the expert wherever possible and it is open to the court to direct that a particular expert be used if the parties cannot agree. The expert's duty is to the court and not to the party or parties choosing him or her,[78] and the letter of instruction to an expert is no longer privileged. The expert remains open to examination in the witness box by either side. He or she therefore has a different function from a court expert who sits with and advises the courts itself. The overriding aim of the new rules is to reduce trial by expert and to date the judges have been rigorous in case management conferences in reducing expert evidence, although they are only rarely limiting the parties to appointing a single joint expert (which the Woolf rules envisage). It had been thought that such a development could lead to the expert effectively becoming the judge but this has certainly not occurred generally and in patent cases the specialist qualifications of the judges has totally negated the possibility.

---

[74] PD49E, para. 10.

[75] Para. 20.

[76] Para. 27.

[77] CPR 35.1.

[78] In *Anglo Group v. Winther Brown* [2000] All ER 296, the judge noted that it is in the interests of the parties that experts give independent evidence to assist in resolution of issues before trial and found on the facts before him that he could not rely on the defendant's expert for independent evidence because he had earlier written an article in which he stated that it was open to an expert to omit or "understate" legitimate points which were adverse to his client's interests.

IV. Trial

The cumulative effect of witness statements and the more interventionist nature of the new rules has meant that patent trials, be they as to validity and/or infringement, are much shorter than in the past and are now on average less than a week. Obviously, this has had a positive impact on the expense, with English proceedings now costing very much less than comparable actions in the US where the cost of a relatively straightforward action runs into millions of dollars.

V. Appeals

A losing party in the Patents Court no longer has an automatic right of appeal but must ask the trial judge for leave. If leave is refused, a petition can be presented to the Court of Appeal, where a single Lord Justice will consider whether to grant permission to appeal. Appeals from the Patents Court are heard by the Court of Appeal which has at present one former patents judge (Lord Justice Jacob) among its members. Unless the court's caseload does not permit, the appeal panel of three judges would usually include that specialist judge on a patent case. An appeal is not a re-hearing from the beginning and in particular witnesses will not be recalled for examination. The facts are taken to be as found by the judge at first instance and the appeal examines whether that judge correctly applied the law to those facts. This leaves considerable scope for arguments, for instance, about the proper interpretation of the patent claims and the assessment of validity in light of evidence on the prior art and on the ability of a skilled person to follow the instructions in the specification on how to perform the invention. Parties may appeal further to the House of Lords but only on an important question of law. Permission to do so is given by either the Court of Appeal itself or, more usually, by the House of Lords on application to it.

E. Remedies for Infringement[79]

English process allows for the following remedies to be awarded to a claimant who has succeeded in establishing infringement of its patent: (i) an *injunction* against future infringements, whether there has already been infringing activity or where it is threatened; (ii) compensation by *damages* for the injury to the claimant or an *account of profits* made by the defendant from its wrongful act; (iii) *delivery up* of infringing material for destruction. An injunction at this stage will ordinarily be permanent, so as to last as long as the patent remains in force. Only in exceptional cases will it be refused, since the

---

[79] *See generally*, Encyclopedia PL, §§ 10.120–132; Terrell §§ 12.02–51.

right is proprietary. The patentee must therefore be provided with the means of ensuring exclusivity in manufacture and trade.

For the same reason, damages (which are assessed at a separate hearing with detailed evidence) can represent not just the losses from sales where the defendant has been in direct competition; in other circumstances they may cover the loss from the defendant's failure to obtain a licence for his activity.[80] If there is evidence that the claimant offers a standard rate for licences that may be the starting point for this second type of assessment, but courts may add to it in order to take account of the defendant's unwillingness to negotiate. If there is no comparable licensing activity, the court will arrive at an amount by the best means it can. The difficulty of doing so is not treated as a reason for awarding only a nominal amount.

The claimant's ability to seek an account of profits is normally an alternative to damages, since there must be no double counting. The nature of the account is restitutionary in character and its existence again stems from the invasion of a property right. It involves an investigation into the actual trading of the defendant (sometimes a useful source of information in itself to the claimant). But the award is not limited to assets which can be specifically identified as representing the actual profit.[81]

Conclusion

It is the earnest hope in the United Kingdom that the courts have now taken effective steps to satisfy the procedural requirements of TRIPS.[82] Not only are patent actions intended today to provide expeditious remedies at the interim and final stages of litigation; they also aim to make the process fair and equitable, without unnecessary complication or cost, unreasonable time-limits or unwarranted delays. The United Kingdom does not expect to have its approach impugned in a dispute raised by another state before the World Trade Organisation. But, as everywhere, its sense of security could turn out to be mistaken. The most pressing question for the British, as for all their partners in the European Union, is now to establish procedures for enforcement of the coming Community patents in the proposed tribunals for them that are determined by considerations of overall fairness and efficiency. The blending of national traditions and respect for national expectations, not least over the languages in which proceedings may be conducted, make this a highly challenging task.

[80] Important statements of principle are to be found in: *General Tire & Rubber v. Firestone Tyre & Rubber* [1976] RPC 197; *Watson Laidlaw v. Potts Cassels* (1914)31 RPC 104; *American Braided Wire v. Thomson* (1890) 7 RPC 152. For a recent consideration, *see* the judgment of Aldous LJ in *SmithKline Beecham v. Apotex* [2003] FSR 544 (CA).

[81] The assessment may well require an apportionment of the profit as a whole in order to estimate the contribution of the patent infringement towards it. *See generally Celanese International v. BP Chemicals* [1999] RPC 203.

[82] *See especially* Art. 41.

4
The Enforcement of Patent Rights in Germany

HANS MARSHALL

A. Outline of the System of Civil Procedure Relating to Patent Litigation

I. Civil Litigation in General

Civil litigation in Germany is based on the German Code of Civil Procedure (*Zivilprozeßordnung*) of 1877. When enacted, the Code of Civil Procedure gave both parties considerable leeway in setting the pace of litigation. Deemed increasingly inappropriate, a major overhaul in the system was made in 1924 in the aftermath of post-war inflation and economic recession. The courts were given much more discretionary power in setting the dates of hearings and determining the place of litigation.[1] After some experiments with a different structure of hearing procedures in the Stuttgart District Courts in the 1970s, another major amendment to the Code of Civil Procedure was passed in 1979. It was last amended in 2001. The purpose of these amendments was to concentrate oral procedures to ideally one hearing, preceded by a thorough exchange of pleadings between the parties. In the alternative, the main hearing date could be preceded by an initial hearing at an early stage in order to clarify the issues in dispute. The result has vindicated such efforts. Litigation even in such complicated matters as patents takes about 10 months from filing of the suit to handing down the court decision in the first instance. This is about the same for appeal proceedings that allow only a limited re-examination of facts.

Civil litigation is in the hands of a legally trained profession. Both judges and attorneys would qualify through legal studies at a university, a first bar exam, to be followed by a two-year apprenticeship at various courts, administrative bodies and law firms, and the second bar exam. Judges would be appointed immediately after such qualification and work in this profession for the rest of their professional lives. The appointment of practising lawyers as judges only occurs at the level of the Constitutional Court.

Legal representation is mandatory in all but the regional courts. Until 1999, only attorneys registered with a certain district court were allowed representation in that court. Since the beginning of 2000, regardless of the place of registration, attorneys can represent clients in civil matters except

---

[1] Goldschmidt, "Die neue Zivilprozeßordnung vom 13. Mai 1924" (The New Code of Civil Procedure of 13 May 1924) (Berlin 1924).

family matters in all German district courts. Permission to represent clients before appeal courts still depends on an enrolment and would be granted after five years of practice. After enrolment, the attorney is able to represent his client in all German courts of appeal. Only especially appointed attorneys can represent clients before the Federal Supreme Court.

There are no specialised courts for patent matters in Germany. Thus, infringement cases involving licensing agreements, employees' inventions and unlawful misappropriation of patent rights[2] and declaratory decisions of non-infringement[3,4] are dealt by a division of judges[5] in the normal civil courts which also decide on general civil matters. In the quest for more efficiency, the courts have established specialised divisions where judges require special knowledge and expertise. These divisions are established by a self governing body of judges discussing such matters once a year. Specialised divisions exist, *e.g.* for construction work cases, medical cases, family and commercial matters, and also IP cases. All the judges of a court may be required to work in any of these divisions when necessary, since all these cases are subject to general civil jurisdiction.

Patent infringement cases have to be decided in a district court (*Landgericht*),[6] but never by a local court (*Amtsgericht*). District courts decide by a bench of three judges with a legal education. One of the main problems of patent litigation is to obtain judges trained to deal with these cases. To become a specialist in patent law, the judges can only learn by experience. A young judge may start by becoming a member in a division of a District Court, working with experienced judges who will help him specialise.

This article will subsequently deal with the civil enforcement of patents only. Criminal enforcement in patent matters is on the books, yet has fallen into disuse. The last criminal prosecution in patent matters was reported in the 1930s.[7]

Apart from criminal enforcement, administrative enforcement through customs control should be mentioned here briefly. On request by the patentee, infringing goods entering the country will be confiscated by customs under Sec. 142a Patent Act. Powers of customs authorities to this effect were introduced by the Anti-Piracy Act of 1990.[8] Seizure of infringing goods by customs authorities becomes more and more important. While figures on

---

[2] Benkard, "Patentgesetz" (Patent Law), Sec. 143, marginal note 4 (9th ed., Munich 1993).

[3] Benkard, "Patentgesetz" (Patent Law), Sec. 139, marginal note 95 (9th ed., Munich 1993).

[4] Federal Supreme Court (BGH), 22 January 1987, Entscheidungen des BGH in Zivilsachen (BGHZ) vol. 99, 340.

[5] Sec. 75 Law on Court Organisation (GVG).

[6] Sec. 142(1) Patent Act (PatG).

[7] Imperial Supreme Court (Reichsgericht), 9 January 1933, 1933 Gewerblicher Rechtsschutz und Urheberrecht (GRUR) 288.

[8] Law of 7 March 1990, Bundesgesetzblatt I, 422.

the seizure of patented items are not available, in 1999 there were 2,200 reported cases of seizure for the alleged infringement of intellectual property rights worth €20.9 million.[9] Request for seizure can be made for goods being exported or imported, and require the patentee to post a bond. A seizure will be carried out by customs authorities only upon request. After a seizure, the patentee will be immediately informed of the goods as such, their quantity, origin, and owner. The patentee may thereupon inspect the goods except in cases where trade secrets are involved. Should the owner of the goods not request their release in two weeks, the goods will be confiscated, otherwise the patentee will be informed. If the patentee insists on seizure despite a request for release, seizure has to be affirmed by a court within two weeks, four weeks at the maximum. If the seizure turns out to be unjustified, the patentee has to compensate the owner of the goods for any damages incurred in connection with the seizure.

II. Stages of Civil Litigation in Germany

When a patent infringement case is brought before the court, upon advance payment of court costs by the plaintiff, the presiding judge of a chamber of the District Court decides on the type of procedure to be followed. He has two main possibilities. Either, he sets a date for an early hearing, limiting the time in which the defendant has to reply to the allegations.[10] When the case has been discussed and when the facts are clear and no further evidence is necessary, the court will render a final decision either immediately or within three weeks.

Otherwise, a written pre-trial procedure may be conducted. Here, a time limit is set for the defendant to answer the allegations.[11] The court may request the parties to reply to the pleadings where there are facts or other procedural questions to be clarified. The court may also ask an expert witness to give a written opinion, to request other authorities to supply records concerning the case, or to request another court to hear a witness.[12] At the end of the written pre-trial procedure, the main hearing takes place, normally followed by the final decision of the court, or an order to hear evidence.

The court has to make sure that complete and correct petitions are filed and that the parties submit complete details concerning the facts of the case.[13] The court must also notify the parties on points of law they may not have been aware of.[14]

---

[9] Reported in Süddeutsche Zeitung, 5 April 2000, 47.

[10] Sec. 275 Code of Civil Procedure (ZPO).

[11] Sec. 276 Code of Civil Procedure.

[12] Sec. 358 a Code of Civil Procedure.

[13] Sec. 139(1) Code of Civil Procedure.

[14] Sec. 139(1) Code of Civil Procedure.

The German courts must ask the plaintiff for a complete and specific description of the infringement, as otherwise a decision could not be enforced.[15] A judgment that merely states that the defendant is not allowed to further infringe the patent is not enforceable – the obligation not to infringe a patent is already sanctioned under criminal law. It is not advisable for a plaintiff to specify the name of the infringing device used by the defendant in his claim, thus escaping enforcement simply by changing the device's name. Therefore, it is necessary to give an exact description of the infringing device in the writ and subsequently in the judgment. Technical features of an infringing embodiment can be specified by adding photos, drawings or brochures to the writ or to the judgment.

Appeals of district court decisions are heard in the Court of Appeals (*Oberlandesgericht*),[16] where a panel of three legally trained judges decides on patent infringement matters.[17] New facts can only be introduced under limited circumstances at this stage,[18] yet the defence of lack of local jurisdiction of the first instance can no longer be raised.[19] Apart from that, there is no substantial difference between procedures in the first instance and on appeal.

A further appeal can be brought before the Federal Supreme Court (*Bundesgerichtshof*) in Karlsruhe when leave of appeal was granted by the Court of Appeals or by the Federal Supreme Court itself.[20] A bench of five judges decides on points of law[21] and no new evidence may be introduced at this stage.

German judgments start with the heading containing the names of the parties, their addresses, their legal representatives and their lawyers. This is followed by the headnote which describes concretely and completely the infringing act or embodiment. This is followed by the facts, both those that are undisputed and disputed, and finally the reasons for the decision.[22] In patent infringement cases, these judgments generally run up to 30 pages. To the extent that judgements deal with points of law, academic writings would be cited to a considerable extent. This reflects an intensive dialogue between academic and practising lawyers in intellectual property matters in Germany.

III. The Profession

In Germany out of about 100,000 licensed attorneys, a small number – perhaps 100 to 150 – specialise in patent infringement suits. As the infringement

[15] Benkard, "Patentgesetz" (Patent Law), Sec. 139, marginal note 32 (9th ed., Munich 1993).

[16] Sec. 119(1)(iii) Law on Court Organisation.

[17] Sec. 177 Law on Court Organisation.

[18] Sec. 531 (2) Code of Civil Procedure.

[19] Sec. 513 (2) Code of Civil Procedure.

[20] Sec. 543 Code of Civil Procedure, 133(i) Law on Court Organisation.

[21] Sec. 139 Law on Court Organisation.

[22] Sec. 313 Code of Civil Procedure.

cases are brought before the normal Civil Court in Germany, patent attorneys may not represent clients or address the Court. They may only advise counsel on the technical questions involved.

B. Problems Related to the Enforcement of Patent Rights:

I. Competent Parties

Generally, the registered patentee or registered exclusive licensee has the right to bring an action for infringement.[23] Registration has only a declaratory effect, however.[24] In case of co-patentees, either all sue together, or one sues on behalf of all regardless of their consent.

If the patent owner is not the original applicant and not registered, he has to prove his rights, for example by presenting the contract of transfer.[25] The same applies to an exclusive, unregistered licence.[26]

A non-exclusive licensee may bring an action for infringement to the court upon proper authorisation by the patent owner.[27]

As to other cases than those mentioned above, a suit can be brought against the misappropriation of a patent or against unjustified threats of alleged infringement.

The right defendant would be the person who infringes the patent.[28] If there are several infringers, the plaintiff should sue them all, either in one single or in separate procedures, since a judgment in an infringement case is effective only *inter partes*. This is also the reason why it is not possible to proceed against one of numerous potential defendants as a representative of all others. The same is true for co-infringers.

For the question of indirect infringement, see below IV.6.

It is the task of the plaintiff to identify the defendant correctly. Even where this is difficult because the defendant tries to disguise his address, business, representatives, etc., the court cannot assist the plaintiff in that matter. Thus it is possible that the plaintiff loses his case for having chosen the wrong defendant.

---

[23] As to the right to sue of the exclusive licensee, *see* Federal Supreme Court, 20 December 1994, 1995 GRUR 338 – *Kleiderbügel.*

[24] Benkard, "Patentgesetz" (Patent Law), Sec. 139, marginal note 16 (9th ed., Munich 1993).

[25] Benkard, *ibid.*

[26] Benkard, "Patentgesetz" (Patent Law), Sec. 139, marginal note 17 (9th ed., Munich 1993).

[27] Benkard, *ibid.*

[28] In a very recent decision, the Federal Supreme Court upheld the liability of a non-resident entrepreneur for the infringement of a national patent right to the extent that the non-resident infringer has supplied the infringing items "knowing the patent at stake and the country of destination, thereby deliberately and intentionally contributing to the marketing in Germany." Federal Supreme Court, 26 February 2002, 34 IIC 432 (2003) – *Radio Clock.*

II. The Competent Court

1. Concentration of Local Jurisdiction

Every District Court has local jurisdiction over acts of infringement.[29] And to the extent that companies are selling and advertising their products throughout Germany, infringement can occur simultaneously in many different places. Patent infringement cases are not very frequent in Germany, with approximately 250 to 300 cases per year. In order to have a number of courts with adequate experience in this area, the Patent Act has authorised concentration of infringement litigation to a limited number of District Courts.[30] Out of a total of about 125 District Courts, currently only 12 are competent to hear patent infringement cases.[31]

In practice, concentration is carried even further. As the plaintiff has a choice between several courts of local jurisdiction, he would choose only the forum with the most experience. That is why about 80 % of all the litigation in patent infringement cases are argued before only three district courts (Düsseldorf, Munich, Mannheim) and the corresponding appeal courts.

This can lead to a certain "forum shopping". When a plaintiff has the choice between several courts, all having local jurisdiction, then he will choose the court most suitable for his action. His motives in choosing a court will be a forum friendly to his case, or the speed of proceedings. Judicial experience with patent infringement cases may also be a motive, as well as a desire to disadvantage the defendant by choosing a court far away from the latter's place of residence.

2. The Brussels and Lugano Conventions and the Regulation (EU) NR 44/2001

The members of the European Union have individual national rules for local jurisdiction of their courts which govern litigation between the nationals of these countries. But in a time of economic globalisation, cross-border connections between companies and persons are on the upswing. A certain degree of legal harmonisation has also been attained in connection with domestic patents, trade marks and community trade marks. In cases of an IP infringement in these countries, it would thus be preferable to sue all infringers in one single action. Under the different laws of civil procedure in the nations concerned, it was difficult to establish local jurisdiction for all infringers in one country. Since 1973, when the Brussels Convention (BC) came into force, the rules for local jurisdiction among the first six members

[29] Sec. 32 Code of Civil Procedure.

[30] Sec. 143(2) Patent Act.

[31] Schulte, "Patentgesetz mit EPÜ" (Patent Law with Cross-References to the EPC), Sec. 143, marginal note 23 (6th ed., Munich 2001).

of the European Union have changed for cases of cross-border infringements involving more than one country.[32] Pursuant to the entry into force of the Amsterdam Treaty, the BC was replaced by the so-called Brussels I Regulation, in force for all EU countries since 1 March 2002.[33]

Neither the Brussels Convention nor the Brussels I Regulation provide specific rules for intellectual property infringement actions. However, it has never been disputed that IP disputes, including patent infringement litigation, fall within the scope of the BC and the Brussels I Regulation. Nevertheless, since the end of the 1980s the practical significance of the BC in cross-border patent infringement litigation has gained in importance. It is beyond the scope of this article to address the system of jurisdiction and enforcement and recognition set up by both legal instruments in their entirety.[34] Only the relevant rules for jurisdiction in cross-border infringement cases will be summarised here, including references to the most important German case law on this issue.

The main principle in determining jurisdiction is the place of the defendant's residence (Art. 2 Brussels I Regulation). In addition thereto, exceptions to that fundamental principle are provided by the BC and the Brussels I Regulation, which, in particular circumstances, provide for alternative fora.

Before examining the relevant jurisdictional rules, a specific and very important provision of both Brussels instruments deserves a brief detour.

According to Art. 22(4) Brussels I Regulation (or Art. 16(4) BC), where the validity of a patent is challenged, exclusive jurisdiction is conferred to "the courts of the Contracting/Member State in which the deposit or registration has been applied for, has taken place or is under the terms of an international convention deemed to have taken place." Clarification on the scope of application of this provision was necessary, and. according the guidance given by the European Court of Justice (ECJ) in *Duijnstee v. Goderbauer*, Art. 22(4) shall be interpreted very narrowly and be limited to actions in which the "dispute itself concerns the validity of the patent or the existence of the deposit or registration."[35] Still disputed, however, is the question whether a distinction should be made as to the application of Art. 22(4) when

---

[32] Zöller, "Zivilprozeßordnung" (Code of Civil Procedure), Art. 2 Reg. 44, marginal note 1 (23rd ed., Cologne 2002).

[33] Council Regulation 44/2001 of 22 December 2000 on jurisdiction and the recognition and enforcement of judgments in civil and commercial matters, OJ L 12, 16 January 2001, 1. The Brussels I Regulation entered into force on 1 March 2002. Denmark is not bound by the Brussels I Regulation, but is still subject to the provisions laid down by the BC. As to the amendments relevant to intellectual property cases *see*: Geschke, "Vom EuGVÜ zum EUGVVO – Ein Überblick – Gibt es Neuerungen für den gewerblichen Rechtsschutz?" (From the Brussels Convention to the Brussels I Regulation – An Overview – Is There Anything New in the Area of IP Protection?) 2003 Mitteilungen der deutschen Patentanwälte 249.

[34] More detailed explanations are provided in Chapter 2, above.

[35] ECJ, 15 November 1983, 1983 ECR 3663 – *Duijnstee/Goderbauer.*

the validity issue is argued as a defence or raised as a counterclaim.[36] Here again, European courts and doctrine voice different opinions.[37]

Initially, German Courts took the view that they should not be deprived of jurisdiction when they have to examine the validity of a foreign patent within an infringement action.[38] In a subsequent decision handed down in 2001, the Düsseldorf District Court confirmed this approach, ruling that the competent court for an infringement action or for a declaration of non-infringement shall not be deprived of jurisdiction when the defendant challenges the validity of the patent where a defence was admissible according to the applicable foreign law.[39] The judges pointed out that an opposite interpretation would be contrary to the interpretation of Art. 16(4) given by the ECJ in the Duijnstee decision. However, a very recent decision handed down by the Düsseldorf Appeal Court seems to put an end to this approach. By giving Art. 22(4) new contours, German judges now appear to be more reluctant to decide infringement cases involving a foreign patent when the validity of the patent at stake is contested.[40] Probably to avoid the risk of an erroneous interpretation, the court preferred to submit this crucial issue to the ECJ.[41]

---

[36] It should be stressed that Art. 25 Brussels I Regulation plays a leading role in this context. By virtue of this provision, a "court seized of claim which is principally concerned with a matter over which the courts of another have exclusive jurisdiction by virtue of Art. 22" shall decline jurisdiction. This begs the question whether this rule is applicable to infringement proceedings within which validity of the patent is raised as a counterclaim.

[37] Stauder, "Die Anwendung des EWG-Gerichtsstand- und Vollstreckungsabkommens auf Klagen im gewerblichen Rechtsschutz und Urheberrecht – Zweiter Teil" (The Applicability of the Brussels Convention to Actions Related to Intellectual Property – Second Part), 1976 GRUR Int. 510; D. Stauder/P. von Rospatt and M. von Rospatt, "Cross-Border Protection of European Patents", 29 IIC 501 (1998); Bragiel, " 'A Funny Thing Happened on the Way of the Forum' – Actionability in the United Kingdom of Infringements of Intellectual Property Rights Committed Abroad", 1999 I.P.Q. 135; Sender Pertegás, "Cross-Border Enforcement of Patent Rights" (Oxford Private International Law Series 2002) (including cross-references to relevant European case law).

[38] Düsseldorf District Court, 1 December 1994, 1998 Entscheidung der 4. Zivilkammer des LG Düsseldorf 1 – *Kettenbandförderer*. In this case, the court of first instance of Düsseldorf was seized with an action for infringement of a British patent. The plaintiff was domiciled in the Netherlands and the defendant was a German based company. To investigate the validity of the patent, the judges applied British patent law.

[39] Düsseldorf District Court, 31 May 2001, 34 IIC 309 (2003) (2001 GRUR Int. 983) – *Flywheel*.

[40] Düsseldorf Appeal Court, 5 December 2002, 2003 GRUR Int. 1030 – *MTD*. *See* comments by Brüning-Petit, "Nouvelles d'Allemagne: l'heure du glas a-t-elle sonné pour les injonctions transfrontalières de cessation de contrefaçon?" (News from Germany: Did the Death Knell Sound for Cross-Border Injunctions in Infringement Cases?), 2004 Propriété Industrielle 12.

[41] This referral was submitted to the ECJ on 6 January 2003 and is pending under No. C-4/03. After several unsuccessful attempts to get the ECJ's opinion on the extent of specific provisions of the Brussels Convention, it remains to be seen whether this referral will lead to a decision.

In addition to Art. 2, the Brussels I Regulation, like the BC, allows the prospective plaintiff to initiate legal proceedings against a person in accordance with Art. 5(3) with respect to unlawful acts, including patent infringements, occurring within the local area of the court's jurisdiction. In this case, provided the defendant has his residence in one of the countries of the Convention/Regulation and the court exercising jurisdiction is a court of a country of the Convention/Regulation, proceedings may be initiated at the place of infringement, even if the defendant resides in a third country.

The wording in Art. 5(3) "where the harmful event occurred", according to the interpretation of the European Court, means the place where the action took place as well as the place where the damage arose.[42] So it follows from this provision that it is possible to have two different local jurisdictions for one infringement action.[43]

On at least two occasions, German courts have taken the view that Art. 5(3) Brussels Convention cannot confer extraterritorial jurisdiction in a cross-border infringement litigation.[44] In the first case, the plaintiff, who was domiciled in Italy, requested an extraterritorial injunction against alleged patent infringement activities of the German and Italian parts of his European patent in both countries against an alleged infringer domiciled in Belgium.[45] The German judges refused to accept jurisdiction over the Italian part of the patent, but, interestingly, before voicing their opinion, felt obliged to point out that their decision did not rely on the mere fact that the patent at issue was a foreign patent. In support of this decision, the judges contended that the jurisdictional rule of Art. 5(3) presupposes that the harm caused has taken place within the territory of the State of the court seized.[46] The same approach was adopted in the subsequent Impfstoff II case.[47]

---

[42] Zöller, "Zivilprozeßordnung" (Code of Civil Procedure), Art 2 Brussels I Regulation, marginal note 26 (23rd ed., Cologne 2002).

[43] It is remarkable that the European Court has not always been consistent in interpreting the above provision. Moreover, in its "Fiona Shevill" decision, where the honour of a British plaintiff was tarnished by a publisher in France that published in several contracting states of the Brussels Convention, the court held that "the place where the harmful event occurred" is the country where the report was published and not the place where the effect of the injury was felt: ECJ, 7 March 1995, (1995) All E.R. 289.

[44] See above Chapter 2, 76 et seq.

[45] Düsseldorf District Court, 25 August 1998, 1999 GRUR Int. 455 – *Schußfadengreifer*, upheld on appeal by Düsseldorf Appeal Court, 22 July 1999, 2001 IPRax 315.

[46] The further arguments put forward by the judges were the role of the territoriality principle and Art. 17(2) of the 1989 Protocol on litigation annexed to the Community Patent Convention. Moreover, it was held that in accordance with the *Shevill* case law and Art. 2 of the Brussels Convention, the plaintiff had the choice to seize the Belgian court which would have had jurisdiction over the whole dispute.

[47] Düsseldorf District Court, 25 March 1999, 1999 GRUR Int. 775 – *Impfstoff II*. In this very complicated case involving defendants domiciled in Germany and in Italy, the Düsseldorf District Court only affirmed jurisdiction with respect to the acts committed in Germany and in violation of the German part of the European Patent.

A further important alternative rule is contained in Art 6(1) Brussels I Regulation which provides an exceptional rule in cases involving a plurality of defendants When several persons are jointly sued, every court in a member state has local jurisdiction with respect to all defendants, provided that one of them has his residence in that jurisdiction. That means in case of the joint infringement of a foreign patent by a person residing in Germany and other persons residing in other member states, that they all could be jointly sued in Germany, even if the infringed patent is valid only in other countries. For such an action to be raised, it is necessary that there is a connection between the different defendants. Hence, it is not permitted to initiate a suit within the local jurisdiction pursuant to Art. 6(1) Brussels I Regulation for the sole purpose of depriving a defendant of having the case dealt with at the local jurisdiction of his residence.[48]

It is submitted that the jurisdictional rule of Art. 6(1) does not pose any problem when the alleged infringers are domiciled in different Member/Contracting States but infringe the same national part of a European patent.[49] More difficult is the case for infringement actions of parallel patents which are issued based on a common European application.

When a plaintiff sues several persons residing in different countries in one action in Germany, according to the above-mentioned rule of the Brussels I Regulation (replacing the Brussels Convention), the court is obliged to follow the German rules of the conflict of laws applying the law of the place where the event occurred when dealing with the question of an infringement of a foreign patent.[50] The same general principle is followed in all member states. In infringement cases, this means that since a patent enjoys protection only in a certain territory, it can only be infringed there. This is also true for a European patent, which after grant becomes a bundle of national patents in those countries the patentee has designated.[51]

This problem was eased after the European Patent Convention (EPC) came into force due to the subsequent harmonisation of patent law. As the

---

[48] To prevent an abuse of Art. 6(1) Brussels I Regulation, the ECJ requires a connection between the claims against several persons sued jointly in one action. In the opinion of the European Court, such a connection exists when a common trial and judgment seem necessary. This is the legal definition of Art. 28 (3) Brussels I Regulation. In another decision, the Court held that this provision is meant to provide better coordination of jurisdiction within the EU and to avoid any inconsistency of decisions. The interpretation of the term "connection" is quite broad and must cover all cases in which the danger of conflicting decisions exists. Zöller, "Zivilprozeßordnung" (Code of Civil Procedure), Art. 6 Brussels I Regulation marginal note 1, and Art. 28 Brussels I Regulation, marginal note 42 (3rd ed., Cologne 2002).

[49] Düsseldorf District Court, 16 January 1996, 1996 Entscheidung der 4. Zivilkammer des LG Düsseldorf 1 – *Reinigungsmittel*.

[50] Art. 40 Introductory Act to the Civil Code (EGBGB).

[51] For the German position on so-called cross-border injunctions, *see* von Rospatt, "Decisions of German Courts in Patent Infringement Cases with Cross Border Effect", 29 IIC 504 (1998).

EPC Contracting States were also Contracting States of the Brussels Convention and now Members of the Brussels I Regulation, a judge who has to apply the relevant foreign law is now able to apply common principles for determining infringement. While this makes the decision on the infringement of a foreign patent easier, the court still has to apply the foreign language and case law of the relevant country. The court is not allowed to use the German interpretation of the EPC's terms for a decision concerning the infringement of a foreign patent. Despite serious attempts to harmonise the interpretation of EPC rules in the contracting states, there still remain certain differences in the interpretation of patents and the determination of the scope of protection.

In conclusion, one cannot fail to mention that hitherto there has been no unanimity in either European case law or in the European doctrinal opinions as to the applicability of Art. 6(1) in such circumstances.[52]

Apart from the jurisdictional provisions mentioned above, both the BC and the Brussels I Regulation include further provisions which also play a crucial role in cross-border litigation. Neither instrument was intended to provide for a harmonised procedural law, and the court seized in such disputes will apply the local rules on procedure. The alternative fora make it indeed possible to bring a suit related to a same dispute before the courts of different States. In order to minimise the risk of irreconcilable decisions, rules as to *lis pendens* and related actions were included in both instruments.

Accordingly, Art. 27 Brussels I Regulation (corresponding to Art. 21 BC) states that when suits on the same subject matter between the same parties are brought before courts of several Contracting/Member States, the actions that were raised later have to be suspended. Once the court where the earliest action was filed has affirmed its jurisdiction, the court subsequently seized has to decline jurisdiction in order to avoid double litigation in the same matter.[53]

However, as already mentioned, the alternative forum provided by the Brussels I Regulation may result in "forum shopping" and give rise to certain misuse of the provisions of both Brussels agreements.

3. Forum Shopping and the "Italian" or "Belgian" Torpedo

The possibility of consolidating separate actions under Art. 6(1) Brussels I Regulation may give rise to some circumvention of the jurisdictional rule stated in the regulation. This might be the case, if, *e.g.* a plaintiff wanting to give local jurisdiction to a court of a certain country would sue a third party together with the true infringers only for the purpose of establishing local jurisdiction of a court in that country for all the defendants.

---

[52] *See, e.g.* UK Court of Appeal, 27 October 1997, 1998 FSR 222 – *Fort Dodge v. Akzo Nobel*; The Hague Appeal Court, 23 April 1998, 1999 FSR 352 – *Expandable Grafts*, reflecting the British and Dutch opinions.

[53] The Lugano Convention applies the same principles as the Brussels I Regulation with regard to the countries of the EFTA.

Another sort of misuse (this time on the side of the possible infringer) results from Art. 27. Certain court systems in Europe have a reputation for being especially slow and ineffective, particularly Italy and Belgium.[54] A plaintiff may have to wait up to three or four years before getting a date for a hearing. The same can be true for appeals, resulting in litigation lasting up to 10 years. The infringer, being faced with a possible request for an interim injunction, *e.g.* in Germany, could quickly initiate an action for a negative declaration of non-infringement before a court in Italy or Belgium. The purpose of this is to have the court declare the plaintiff's activities non-infringing. Should this action be brought before a court prior to the infringement action of the patentee, the latter action must be suspended. This phenomenon, dubbed the Italian or Belgian torpedo,[55] has the effect of delaying clarification of the issue of infringement and the demand for damages for many years, as sure enough, the alleged infringer would launch his action for declaratory judgment in a country with a reputation of dealing with IP cases particularly sluggishly.

Once again, it should be pointed out that Art. 27 Brussels I Regulation is not subject to unanimous interpretation by the European courts and still remains a contentious issue. Clarification of the meaning of Art. 21 Brussels Convention by the ECJ has been requested, but without success.[56]

III. Preparation for Trial

1. Warning Letter

Though not mandatory, the plaintiff would normally send a warning letter to the alleged infringer before starting an infringement action.[57] In the absence thereof, it could happen that the plaintiff has to bear the whole costs of the suit (including attorneys' fees) should the defendant admit to the allegations before the first hearing.[58]

---

[54] This lack of harmonisation of procedures is particularly highlighted by Ryberg, "Procedural Law for Patent Litigation", 28 IIC 904 (1997).

[55] Zöller, "Zivilprozeßordnung" (Code of Civil Procedure), Art. 27 Brussels I Regulation, marginal note 1 (23rd ed., Cologne 2002); Franzosi, "Weltweite Patentstreitigkeiten und ein italienischer Torpedo" (Worldwide Patent Disputes and an Italian Torpedo), 1998 Mitteilungen der deutschen Patentanwälte 300; Tilmann/von Falck, "EU-Patentrechtharmonisierung II: Forum Shopping und Torpedo" (EU-Patent Law Harmonisation II: Forum Shopping and Torpedo), 2000 GRUR 579; Del Corno, "Torpedo Actions: Present and Future", 2002 Italian Intellectual Property 77.

[56] Referral by the Düsseldorf Appeal Court in 1999. Since the parties meanwhile have settled their dispute, the ECJ will no longer have to decide on the matter.

[57] Ullmann, "Die Verwarnung aus Schutzrechten – mehr als eine Meinungsäußerung?" (The Warning Letter for Suspected Infringement of IP rights – Is Such a Letter More Than Just an Opinion?), 2001 GRUR 1027.

[58] Mes, "Patentgesetz" (Patent Law), Sec. 139, marginal note 46 (1st ed., Munich 1997).

In the warning letter, the patent owner must specify what patent he relies on and show why and in what manner his patent has been infringed. Finally, he must request the infringement to stop.[59]

Such a letter can lead to a complaint about unjustified allegations of infringement.[60] Should a patent owner thus not be quite certain that an infringement has occurred, it is preferable to refrain from sending a formal warning letter, but rather inquire for further and better particulars.[61]

According to established case law, the right owner may be liable to compensate the alleged infringer for damages incurred by unjustified allegations of infringement in a warning letter.[62] This is particularly true when a warning letter directly addressed to prospective clients of the alleged infringer discourages the former from buying the accused devices.[63]

The recipient of a warning letter may himself commence an action for a declaration of non-infringement before the IP right owner has taken his case to court.[64] This type of action is useful for an alleged infringer to know if he can continue his activities or not. Should the IP right owner raise his own infringement action, the suit of the former is seen as superfluous and would thus be dismissed.[65]

2. Preserving Evidence

Under the law of civil procedure, in Germany it is possible to start proceedings for the preservation of evidence,[66] either before or after the

---

[59] Schramm, "Der Patentverletzungsprozeß" (Patent Infringement Litigation), 278, (4th ed., Cologne 1999).

[60] Mes, "Patentgesetz" (Patent Law), Sec. 139, marginal note 49 (1st ed., Munich 1997).

[61] Mes, "Patentgesetz" (Patent Law), Sec. 139, marginal note 50 (1st ed., Munich 1997). For the prerequisites to a successful warning letter, *see*: Schulte, "Patentgesetz mit EPÜ" (Patent Law with Cross-References to the EPC), Sec. 139, marginal note 144 (6th ed., Munich 2001).

[62] Federal Supreme Court, 17 April 1997, 1997 GRUR 741 – *Chinaherde*. To be liable, the right owner must act culpably. *See* Schulte, "Patentgesetz mit EPÜ" (Patent Law with Cross-References to the EPC), Sec. 139, marginal note 158 (6th ed., Munich 2001) and Ullmann, "Die Verwarnung aus Schutzrechten – mehr als eine Meinungsäußerung?" (The Warning Letter for Suspected Infringement of IP Rights – Is Such a Letter More Than Just an Opinion?), 2001 GRUR 1027.

[63] Düsseldorf Appeal Court, 20 February 2003, 2003 GRUR 814. In this decision, the case concerned a warning letter addressed to a purchaser who was not only informed of the infringement but also invited to cut off any business relationship with the alleged infringer as far as the suspected infringing devices were concerned. Deviating from the established case law of the Federal Supreme Court, the Düsseldorf judges held that such a warning letter should not be automatically considered unlawful when it subsequently is proven that the patent has not been infringed.

[64] Benkard, "Patentgesetz" (Patent Law), Sec. 139, marginal note 95 (9th ed., Munich 1993).

[65] Benkard, *ibid*.

[66] Secs. 485–494 a Code of Civil Procedure.

infringement suit is raised, the only requirement being that there is a real danger of evidence being destroyed. The procedure for preserving evidence is conducted in the presence of the parties and can concern all types of evidence, such as witness testimonies, inspections, and expert opinions.

There also exists the possibility that a patent owner claiming infringement brings an action before the court requesting the inspection of a device which he assumes is infringing.[67] He may be accompanied by an expert. Until very recently, these so-called *Besichtigungsanspruch* orders were handled very restrictively in Germany. The patent owner was not allowed, *e.g.* to set in motion the device in question or remove the chassis in order to inspect the interior of a product, making such inspection procedures not very important in practice.[68] In a very recent decision the German Federal Supreme Court strained the existing legal rules by a more flexible interpretation of the right of inspection.[69] Overruling the principles laid down in the Pressure Beam case, the judges of the Federal Supreme Court held that a minimum likelihood of infringement should be regarded as sufficient to grant such orders. This important precedent has been met with universal acclaim, inasmuch as the German system has long been considered as falling short of complying with Art. 43 TRIPS. It is a foregone conclusion that the right of inspection under Sec. 809 Civil Code will now become a very useful tool for cases involving evidence of patent infringement.[70] In a subsequent decision, the Federal Supreme Court went a step further, deciding that the rule of good faith should be applied to patent cases. Consequently, a party may be obliged to supply information which may ease the burden of proof of the opposing party when it appears that disclosing such evidence can be done without insuperable difficulty.[71]

---

[67] This right of inspection is provided by Sec. 809 Civil Code. *See* Stauder, "Überlegungen zur Schaffung eines besonderen Beweisverfahren im europäischen Patentverletzungsrecht – Saisie-contrefaçon oder actio as exhibendum als Beispiele?" (Considerations on the Establishment of a Specific Procedure for the Examination of Evidence in European Patent Infringement Litigation – Saisie-contrefaçon or actio as exhibendum as Examples?), 1978 GRUR Int. 230; Marshall, "Der Besichtigungsanspruch" (The Right of Inspection), in: Festschrift Albert Preu (Writings in the Honour of Albert Preu), 151, 157 (Munich 1988) .

[68] Federal Supreme Court, 8 January 1985, 18 IIC 108 (1987) – *Pressure Beam* (*Druckbalken*), with critical comment by Stauder.

[69] Federal Supreme Court, 2 May 2002, 34 IIC 331 (2003) – *Fax Card*. It is worth noting that this decision concerned a copyright infringement case. However, there is no doubt that the solution reached in this case will be applied to cases involving intellectual property rights infringement at a more general level, including for patent rights.

[70] In a subsequent decision, the Federal Supreme Court maintained certain limits to the scope of application of Sec. 809 Civil Code, taking the view that the right of inspection shall be strictly limited to the inspection of specified devices or products and does not open the door to a general right of inspection of the premises of the alleged infringer: Federal Supreme Court, 13 November 2003 – *Kontrollbesuch*, I ZR 187/01, not yet published.

[71] Federal Supreme Court, 30 September 2003 – *Blasenfreie Gummibahn II*, X ZR 114/00, not yet published.

As a general rule, the plaintiff must present all evidence to the court in order to prove infringement.[72] Normally the infringing goods are advertised, offered or sold to the public, thus coming to the attention of the patent owner. The latter may thus purchase the infringing device, obtain a brochure, take a photo or video, and present this to the court as evidence. The costs of such measures must be borne by the losing party of the suit.

German law does not offer the patentee as far-reaching means of discovery as the systems of the UK, the US or France. See, however, below for the patentee's right to request information on the sources of supply, customers, etc. (*Auskunftsanspruch*).

In particular, German law does not allow for the seizure of infringing goods, apart from seizure by the customs authorities (see above) and a seizure under criminal prosecution. Criminal prosecution, apart from being hardly used, would require a specific request by the patentee (Sec. 142 Patent Act). While the results of such a seizure under criminal procedure could be used as evidence in civil proceedings, requests for criminal prosecution are extremely rare in Germany.

Once the plaintiff has substantiated his allegations, an alleged infringer is not allowed to merely deny those facts which happen within his sphere and which he has easy access to, while the owner of a patent may not be able to obtain knowledge of these facts with reasonable efforts.[73] In practice, the alleged infringer may well be obliged to present the allegedly infringing product to the court for inspection, depending on the facts of each case.

Patent law further offers a presumption of infringement to the owner of a process patent. On condition that the product which results from the process patent is new, it is assumed that a comparable product is produced under the process patent, unless otherwise proven by the defendant.[74]

After an infringement has been established (*e.g.* by an interim decision, but also at a preliminary stage), for the purpose of calculating damages, the patent owner can ask the court to order the disclosure of such relevant information as the names of suppliers and customers, the quantity of items bought, produced, sold, imported or exported, purchase and sales prices, profits, costs and the extent of advertising.[75] This request for information (*Auskunftsanspruch*) was initially developed under the common law principle of "good faith" that permeates the whole civil system. Good faith in this particular case required

---

[72] Mes, "Si Tacuisses – Zur Darlegungs- und Beweislast im Prozeß des gewerblichen Rechtsschutz" (Si Tacuisses – Evidence and Burden of Proof in IP Litigation), 2000 GRUR 934.

[73] Schramm, "Der Patentverletzungsprozeß" (Patent Infringement Litigation), 315, 316 (4th ed., Cologne 1999).

[74] Benkard, "Patentgesetz" (Patent Law), Sec. 139, marginal note 119 *et seq*. (9th ed., Munich 1993).

[75] Benkard, "Patentgesetz" (Patent Law), Sec. 139, marginal note 88 *et seq*. (9th ed., Munich 1993).

the infringer to reveal those facts that he had knowledge of, and that the patentee could not establish with reasonable efforts. The *Auskunftsanspruch* was codified by the Anti-Piracy Law of 1990.[76]

3. Preliminary Injunctions

Before starting an action for patent infringement, a patent owner may apply for a preliminary injunction (*einstweilige Verfügung*) in cases of urgency.[77] A preliminary injunction under Sec. 940 German Code of Civil Procedure requires a legal dispute to be settled urgently in order to prevent substantial damages or disadvantages. Case law on this general provision requires the applicant to show a case of urgency. This basically means that a patentee has to act quickly upon receiving notice of an infringement, otherwise the courts would not deem the matter as urgent as to apply preliminary measures. While the lower courts are not completely consistent in the maximum period of delay between positive knowledge of an infringement and a request for preliminary measures, the Munich courts allow a maximum period of one month.[78] Preliminary measures can already be requested before an infringement has actually taken place, yet on condition that there is a real and immediate danger of such an infringement happening.

Preliminary injunctions have become a very important tool in German patent litigation. An empirical study conducted by A. von Falck shows that for the years 1996–2000, more than 100 preliminary injunctions have been requested yearly before the German courts, and that of these more than half have been successful.[79]

In deciding on a request for a preliminary injunction, the courts would have to balance the interests of both parties. In granting the relief, the respondent might incur considerable loss due to the discontinuation of business, etc. On the other hand, the patentee certainly has a valid interest in preventing further infringement. Injunctive relief would be denied in cases where the patentee exploits his patent only through the grant of licences, as in such case, also the main action would normally be aimed at obtaining a licensing fee.

---

[76] For an in-depth discussion on the *Auskunftsanspruch*, see Oppermann, "Der Auskunftsanspruch im gewerblichen Rechtsschutz und Urheberrecht" (The Right of Information in Industrial Property and Copyright Law) (Berlin 1997).

[77] Secs. 935, 940 Code of Civil Procedure.

[78] For the sake of completeness and detailed information about the maximum period requested by the courts to grant preliminary injunctions: *See* Von Falck, "Einstweilige Verfügungen in Patent- und Gebrauchsmustersachen" (Preliminary Injunctions in Patent and Industrial Design Matters), 2002 Mitteilungen der deutschen Patentanwälte 429. More flexible as to the assessment of the "maximum period" are the Frankfurt and Karlsruhe courts. *See e.g.* Frankfurt Appeal Court, 22 January 2001, 2002 GRUR 236.

[79] Von Falck, "Einstweilige Verfügungen in Patent- und Gebrauchsmustersachen" (Preliminary Injunctions in Patent and Industrial Design Matters), 2002 Mitteilungen der deutschen Patentanwälte 429.

Preliminary injunctions may be granted *in* or *ex parte*, depending on the urgency of the case. While according to the general rules of civil procedure, *ex parte* proceedings are the exception, in patent matters they have become the rule. Even if an *ex parte* request is granted, the court would swiftly order a hearing upon request of the respondent. The defendant may further request the applicant to initiate proceedings in the main action within a period of time fixed by the court. While Art. 50(6) of the TRIPS Agreement requires the plaintiff in these cases to commence the main action within a period of one month, this provision has not yet been implemented into domestic law. For this reason, a preliminary injunction does not automatically become ineffective when the main action is not commenced. An *ex parte* decision can be rendered by the court within a few hours. In the case of an *in parte* trial, the court will set a hearing within a few days from the request, and a decision will be handed down within two to three weeks. A plaintiff does not need to supply full evidence for this procedure, it being enough to present affidavits from the witnesses or himself. All that is required is to convince the court that on the balance of probabilities, the patent is valid and has been infringed.[80] The likelihood that the patent is valid is increased if the patentee has succeeded in opposition or revocation proceedings. Cases of infringement can be more easily determined for direct infringement. In the case of an infringement by equivalents, the applicant may present an expert opinion by a private expert. Such an opinion is sufficient at least at the interim stage to decide upon matters of infringement by equivalents.

Even at the interim stage, the appellant may request information from the defendant under the *Auskunftsanspruch* according to Sec. 140b(3) Patent Act. Also the right of inspection can be invoked at that stage, yet is narrowly interpreted by the German courts (see above).

Summary proceedings are not without risk. When it turns out later that the preliminary injunction should not have been granted in the first place, the plaintiff must compensate the defendant for damages suffered in complying with the injunction.[81] Nevertheless, those preliminary injunctions are of great importance and are very often used by patentees, most notably against acts of piracy. The difficulty in interim proceedings is to convince the court of an infringement, in particular in cases of infringement by equivalents. In

---

[80] Thus a preliminary injunction will most likely be dismissed when the patent at stake is being opposed before the EPO: Hamburg Appeal Court, 19 April 2001, 2002 GRUR RR 244 – *Spannbacke*; or even when the validity of the patent may depend on the outcome of a different procedure concerning a different patent: Hamburg District Court, 7 March 2001, 2002 GRUR RR 45 – *Felodipin*. In the latter decision, the case concerned the infringement of a supplementary protection certificate. The court refused to grant a preliminary injunction, stating that the validity of the certificate could only be ascertained after the ECJ had ruled on a referral made by the German Supreme Court as to the nullity grounds of such certificate (Federal Supreme Court, 1 February 2000, 2000 GRUR 392 – *Omeprazol*).

[81] Sec. 945 Code of Civil Procedure.

the Munich courts, about 20 to 30 requests for interim measures in patent infringement cases are made each year.

IV. The Trial

1. The Role of Lawyers

The role of the lawyers in Germany is not restricted to court representation.[82] A great deal of their work takes place in the pre-trial stage of the litigation. Lawyers must gather the facts and evidence. They have to consider what type of action to pursue and in which court. They have to decide whether to start with a preliminary injunction or with the main action. A warning letter must be sent, and possible defences must be considered.

The lawyer representing the defendant has to evaluate the chances of a favourable verdict, and the possible terms of settlement by asking for a licence.

In German district courts and courts of appeal only legally trained attorneys have the right to address the court.[83] They also decide what is presented to the court, prepare the writs and plead in the hearings. As previously mentioned, patent attorneys, having no legal education, may not address the court, but can advise counsel on technical matters. They can also assist in drafting writs where technical questions are concerned, but may not sign them.

2. Experts

Due to the German system of patent infringement litigation, the help of an expert in complicated technical matters may become necessary.[84]

Should a judge himself have the necessary technical expertise, no expert is needed.[85] However, the judge must properly inform the litigants in such case and clearly state so in his decision.[86]

In Germany, experts are called in about 15 % of patent infringement cases. In contrast to a witness, an expert bases his testimony on technical training.

---

[82] Sec. 78(1) Code of Civil Procedure.

[83] Schulte, "Patentgesetz mit EPÜ" (Patent Law with Cross-references to the EPC), Sec. 143 marginal note 24 (6th ed., Munich 2001).

[84] Zöller, "Zivilprozeßordnung" (Code of Civil Procedure), Sec. 402, marginal note 6 b (23rd ed., Cologne 2002).

[85] Although the courts are supposed to interpret the scope of a patent, assistance by an expert is necessary when it is the only way for a judge to be able to assess how a person skilled in the art understands the technical terms used in the patent claim and in the description. This principle applies to all courts, irrespective of their experience in patent matters: *see* Federal Supreme Court, 28 October 2003 – *Geflügelkörperhaltung*, X ZR 76/00, not yet published.

[86] Zöller, "Zivilprozeßordnung" (Code of Civil Procedure), Sec. 402, marginal note 7 (23rd ed., Cologne 2002).

A court expert is regarded as impartial, as he is called and paid for by the court rather than by one of the parties. A private expert can also be heard in an infringement suit, but because of his affiliation to one of the litigants, his impartiality is often questioned. His written expertise may be treated as documentary evidence rather than evidence by an expert.

The expert assists the court in evaluating facts the court has no sufficient expertise about and thus has to rely on the expert's superior knowledge. The expert can only be contradicted by the parties in using additional private expertise, giving the court expert considerable influence over the court's decision. Thus, it is important for the parties to participate actively in the selection of the court expert and in the proceedings after the written expert opinion has been submitted.

Because the expert's opinion may considerably influence a decision in infringement matters, he has to abide by the guidelines set by the court. While making certain that the expert's conclusions properly answer the matters in dispute, the court is ultimately responsible for the final decision.[87]

3. Role of Judges

The role of the judge during trial is an active one. He is not only an observer, but must also guide the litigation. It is his task to make sure that the parties file proper writs and are informed of all the facts relevant to the court's decision.[88] He also has to discuss the legal aspects of the case with the parties.[89] When hearing evidence, the judge is obliged to question the witnesses first, and only afterwards may the lawyers question them. After this stage, the judge discusses the results of the evidence with the parties, asking counsel for oral pleadings before rendering a final decision.[90] The judge is obliged to try to settle the case at every stage of the procedure.[91] Of course, he is not allowed to pressure the parties into a settlement, but can propose what he thinks to be the most preferable solution. Should he not succeed in settling the patent infringement litigation, he must render a decision.

4. Claim Interpretation

A patent can be infringed literally or by equivalents, directly or indirectly. In an infringement procedure, the scope of protection has to be determined. The starting point is an interpretation of the patent claims pursuant to

---

[87] Zöller, "Zivilprozeßordnung" (Code of Civil Procedure), Sec. 402, marginal note 7 a (23rd ed., Cologne 2002).

[88] Zöller, "Zivilprozeßordnung" (Code of Civil Procedure), Sec. 139, marginal notes 1, 5 – 8 (23rd ed., Cologne 2002).

[89] Zöller, "Zivilprozeßordnung" (Code of Civil Procedure), Sec. 139, marginal note 4 (23rd ed., Cologne 2002).

[90] Zöller, "Zivilprozeßordnung" (Code of Civil Procedure), Sec. 285, marginal note 1 (23rd ed., Cologne 2002).

[91] Sec. 278(1) Code of Civil Procedure.

Art. 69(1) European Patent Convention in connection with the Protocol on the interpretation of this provision.[92] In most European countries, this rule applies both to domestic and European patents, as is the case for Germany.[93] According to the Protocol, a patent may not only be interpreted according to the literal wording of the claims, but the claims should not as be interpreted a mere guideline, either.[94]

Patent protection is granted to the inventor as a reward for his intellectual achievement, which will be in the public domain after his monopoly has expired.[95] Competitors, on the other hand, need to be sure of what they are legally permitted to do without infringing the patent.[96] Thus, due reward for the inventor and legal certainty for competitors are the two conflicting interests that have to be reconciled when defining the limits of patent protection.

The purposes of interpreting the patent claims are:

a) elimination of uncertainties;
b) clarification of the technical language;
c) clarification of the importance and scope of the invention;
d) determining possible modifications of the invention;
e) clarifying the extent of equivalents regarded as infringing.

The first step in the interpretation of a patent claim is to determine the subject matter of the patent.[97] This may not exceed the claim language. Matters only mentioned in the description or the drawings do not belong to the subject matter of the patent and cannot be protected as such.[98]

Description and drawings, on the other hand, have to be considered in interpreting a patent claim. Under Sec. 14(2) Patent Act, this is mandatory even in cases where the claim language seems to be clear and understandable by itself. In any event, no protection can be granted for subject matter only based on the description and drawings without being reflected in the claims.

The main function of the description and drawings of a patent specification is to clarify the meaning of the claim language chosen by the

---

[92] *See* Meier-Beck, "Aktuelle Fragen der Schutzbestimmung im deutschen und europäischen Recht" (Current Questions on the Scope of Protection in German and European Law), 2003 GRUR 905.

[93] Federal Supreme Court, 29 April 1986, 18 IIC 795 (1987) – *Moulded Curbstone*.

[94] Benkard, "Patentgesetz" (Patent Law), Sec. 14, marginal note 7 (9th ed., Munich 1993).

[95] Schulte, "Patentgesetz" (Patent Law), Sec. 14, marginal note 17 (6th ed., Cologne 2001).

[96] Schulte, "Patentgesetz" (Patent Law), Sec. 14, marginal note 18 (6th ed., Cologne 2001).

[97] Benkard, "Patentgesetz" (Patent Law), Sec. 14, marginal note 61 (9th ed., Munich 1993).

[98] Schramm, "Der Patentverletzungsprozeß" (Patent Infringement Litigation), 70 (4th ed., Cologne 1999).

patent applicant. The interpretation of those expressions must not always be based on the normal philological meaning of the words used. It is possible to deduct a different understanding of the words used by the patent applicant from the description and the drawings of the patent claim. In this case, the latter meaning is authoritative for the interpretation of the claim. The description of the patent may thus be used like a dictionary.[99]

When interpreting a patent claim, it must also be considered that the drafting language used by persons skilled in the art very often differs from normal language. Authoritative in those cases is always the understanding of a certain expression by a person skilled in the art.[100]

For the interpretation of his patent, the applicant can always refer to the prior art as cited in the description. This may lead to a broader scope of protection in case the contents of disclosure measured against the cited prior art exceeds the mere wording of the claim.[101]

Events occurring during the filing procedure before the patent is granted ("protection history") are in principle of no influence on the determination of the extent of protection:

> "Article 69 of the EPC bases the determination of the extent of protection . . . exclusively on the patent claims, the description and the drawings. Consequently, as a matter of principle the issue does not turn on measures in the grant proceedings that precede the grant of patent. Nor is there any practical need to ascribe protection restricting effects to measures in the grant and opposition proceedings as such that are not reflected in the patent specification or in the amended patent specification. To the extent that they have been reflected in the patent specification, in particular through a restriction of the patent as upheld, their significance derives directly from the provision in Art. 69 of the EPC."[102]

5. The Extended Scope of Protection by the Doctrine of Equivalents

If under the foregoing rules of interpretation, the allegedly infringing embodiment mirrors all the features of the patent claim, infringement is obvious. The average infringer, however, will very seldom identically copy the invention, but will make alterations to circumvent the patent. To prevent this and to secure the inventor the due profit for his achievement, the doctrine of equivalents was developed.

Art. 69 EPC does not preclude an interpretation beyond the wording of the claims in cases when an alleged embodiment which may be a product or

---

[99] Federal Supreme Court, 2 March 1999, 30 IIC 932 (1999) – *Tension Screw.*

[100] Schramm, "Der Patentverletzungsprozeß" (Patent Infringement Litigation), 66 (4th ed., Cologne 1999).

[101] Schulte, "Patentgesetz" (Patent Law), Sec. 14, marginal note 27 (6th ed., Cologne 2001).

[102] Federal Supreme Court, 12 March 2002, 34 IIC 302, 307 (2003); BGHZ 150, 161 – *Plastic Tube Component.*

process is nearly identical to the patented invention, *e.g.* it differs only in one feature.[103]

The doctrine of equivalents is very important in practice. The appeal court in Munich deals with about 40 to 50 patent infringement cases per year, and even though most patentees argue that the allegedly infringing embodiment amounts to a literal infringement of the wording of the claims, in fact more than 80 % of all cases concern questions of equivalents. What, in other words, can qualify as an equivalent?

The standard applied by German courts in determining equivalence is if a person skilled in the art due to his technical expertise was able to identify the modified means employed in the allegedly infringing embodiment as being equally effective in the solution of the problem underlying the invention, based on his knowledge of the meaning and contents of the invention as defined in the patent claims.[104] If the feature, which was changed in the allegedly infringing device could only be arrived at by an inventive activity of a person skilled in the art, this would qualify as a new invention rather than an equivalent infringement,[105] and would be regarded as infringing only in case of a dependent patent.

Vice versa, there is no infringement for a modification so close to the known prior art that the allegedly infringing embodiment would not be patented over prior art. The defendant of a patent infringement case could thus argue that the features of his device, although equivalent to the patented invention, as a whole would not amount to a patentable invention against the known prior art. Even though close to the subject matter of the patented invention, no infringement could be found in such case: the use of prior art or a solution similar thereto cannot qualify as an infringement.[106]

When a patent claim contains numerical specifications or measurements, then a stricter assessment of equivalency is necessary. These specifications limit the protected subject matter in principle.[107]

A special case of equivalence is the dependent patent.[108] This would be, *e.g.* a device that shows all features of a patented invention plus an additional one that qualifies as an improvement. This improvement shows an inventive step and is thus patentable. Although the alteration has inventive quality, the defendant cannot escape infringement in this case as the patented invention

---

[103] Schramm, "Der Patentverletzungsprozeß" (Patent Infringement Litigation), 82 (4th ed., Cologne 1999).

[104] Benkard, "Patentgesetz" (Patent Law), Sec. 14, marginal note 123 (9th ed., Munich 1993).

[105] Schramm, "Der Patentverletzungsprozeß" (Patent Infringement Litigation), 207 (4th ed., Cologne 1999).

[106] Federal Supreme Court, 29 April 1986, 18 IIC 795 (1987) – *Moulded Curbstone.*

[107] Federal Supreme Court, 12 March 2002, 33 IIC 873 (2002) – *Cutting Blade I.*

[108] Schramm, "Der Patentverletzungsprozeß" (Patent Infringement Litigation), 116 (4th ed., Cologne 1999).

is used in full by the subsequent invention. The further development of an inventive idea by adding a new feature may be patentable, but is still infringing.

The same applies to the alteration of one or more features of a patent claim in an equivalent manner and adding further patentable features for improvement. To determine infringement, it is sufficient that the inventive idea of an existing patent is used either literally or by equivalents, regardless if this idea is taken further by adding new patentable features on top.

More difficult to decide are cases where one feature of the patent claim is changed in an inventive manner. Normally, there would be no infringement. Yet, when the change of such feature was known to a person skilled in the art as being equivalent, and only the special embodiment of this feature is inventive, this can still be regarded as an (infringing) improvement invention.[109]

A special case of extending protection of a patent would be the protection of sub-combinations. The German Federal Supreme Court held in several decisions, that the absence of one feature of a patent claim in the allegedly infringing embodiment does not necessarily exclude a patent infringement.[110]

This is true for cases where the feature of the claim that is absent is a superfluous or less important element and this is obvious to a person skilled in the art.[111] Yet where the patent applicant has claimed a feature as essential and a person skilled in the art is able to recognise this as wrong, there is no infringement where the defendant's embodiment omits this feature.

6. Direct and Indirect Infringement[112]

According to Sec. 9 Patent Act, direct infringement refers to the producing, offering, advertising, distributing, selling, using, importing and possessing an infringing device. The same applies to a patented process. Indirect infringement was first codified in Sec. 10 Patent Act (corresponding to Art. 30 Community Patent Convention (CPC) not yet in force), yet had been recognised even by the courts.[113] Sec. 10 Patent Act prohibits offering to

[109] Federal Supreme Court, 12 July 1990, 23 IIC 111 (1992) – *Fixing Device II*; Federal Supreme Court, 17 March 1994, 26 IIC 261 (1995) – *Segmentation Device for Tree Trunks*. On that decision, *see also* Pagenberg, "More Refined Rules of Claim Interpretation in Germany – Are They Necessary?", 26 IIC 228 (1995).

[110] Ullmann, "Schutz der Elemente – elementarer Schutz der immaterialen Güter?" (Protection of Elements – Elementary Protection of IP Rights?), 1993 GRUR 334.

[111] Schramm, "Der Patentverletzungsprozeß" (Patent Infringement Litigation), 194 (4th ed., Cologne 1999).

[112] Mes, "Indirect Patent Infringement", 30 IIC 531 (1999).

[113] Benkard, "Patentgesetz" (Patent Law), Sec. 10, marginal note 1 (9th ed., Munich 1993); first recognised by the Imperial Supreme Court (Reichsgericht), 22 February 1928, Marke und Wettbewerb (MuW) 1927/28, 312. *See also* Isay, "Patentgesetz" (Patent Law), 236 – 238 and 257 – 260 (5th ed., 1931).

supply someone with means that concern an essential element of the invention, for the use of such invention upon knowledge or obviousness that these means are suitable and meant for the use of the invention.

The provision, however, only refers to the essential elements of the invention, and not every screw necessary to assemble the patented device is an essential element. The means must serve to realise the gist of the invention by applying generally accepted standards. The supply with staple products is an "indirect patent infringement" only under two conditions. They must concern an essential element and the supplier must willingly supply the goods for unlawful use.[114]

7. Protection in the Case of Process Patents

In case of a process, protection not only extends to the process itself, but also to the goods produced according to the protected process (Sec. 9(3) Patent Act). In this case the patentee has a great legal relief in giving evidence for the infringement of his patented process according to Sec. 139 (3) Patent Act. If the products from the patented process and those from the alleged infringer are equal, it is assumed that the defendant's products are infringing unless proven to the contrary.

V. Defences

1. Distinction Between Nullity and Infringement Cases

In Germany there is a strict separation between infringement and nullity actions. Nullity cases are exclusively brought before the Federal Patent Court, while infringement cases are heard in the normal civil court. The civil court handling the patent infringement action may interpret the patent, but has no right to ignore or to alter a single word of the patent claim, nor disregard the patent as such.[115]

Once a patent infringement action is commenced, the defendant would often allege nullity of the patent as a defence. This is not admissible, and the alleged infringer has to file a separate nullity action before the Federal Patent Court. In this case the civil court can postpone the proceedings, but it will only do this if there is a high probability that the nullity action will be successful.[116]

Nullity cases are decided in the Federal Patent Court before a bench of five judges.[117] Three of them have a technical rather than a legal back-

---

[114] Benkard, "Patentgesetz" (Patent Law), Sec. 10, marginal note 15 (9th ed., Munich 1993).

[115] Federal Supreme Court, 6 March 1959, 1959 GRUR 320 – *Moped-Kupplung*.

[116] Benkard, "Patentgesetz" (Patent Law), Sec. 139, marginal note 107 (9th ed., Munich 1993). Düsseldorf District Court, 1995 BIPMZ 121 – *Hepatitis C Virus*.

[117] Sec. 67(1) Patent Act.

ground, and exercise full judicial powers. In a nullity action, patent attorneys may represent litigants, while also lawyers with no technical expertise have the right to address the court. Due to the technical training of three of the judges, expert opinions are not deemed necessary.

In 2001, 166 requests for nullity were brought before the Federal Patent Court, in 2000 the number was 189 and in 1999 it was 146.[118] As a rough guess, two thirds of these were brought as a response to an infringement suit. Nullity actions are normally decided within one year by the Federal Patent Court, whose decision can be appealed to the Federal Supreme Court. As the courts require a high likelihood of success for a nullity action in order to suspend infringement proceedings, only 5 to 10% of the latter actions are actually suspended. It has to be mentioned though, that there is no completely uniform pattern for applying this standard among the German district courts.

Declaration of nullity after or during infringement proceedings would require the plaintiff to reimburse the defendant for the damages incurred due to the enforcement of any court decision in this matter. Should the decision affirming infringement have already become final and conclusive, the defendant would nonetheless be able to recover his damages according to Sec. 580(6) German Code of Civil Procedure.[119] In practice, a bailiff or a court would refuse to enforce a decision affirming infringement as soon as the patent has been declared invalid.

2. Other Defences

a) The defence of innocent infringement is not possible in Germany. The objective fact of an infringement is enough. The plea of innocent infringement can only be raised against the claims of information and damages.[120]

b) A defendant can plead prior user rights.[121] The burden of proof for this defence is quite high, though. The defendant has to prove that he had knowledge of the invention before the patent application has been filed and already at that time had made arrangements for the commercial exploitation of the invention. It was unclear, though, if such right would extend to alterations or improvements made by the prior user. In the absence of better guidance by the courts, German doctrine endowed the prior user with the right to make some improvements on the invention to the extent that the patent claims as filed by the patent holder would not be copied or reproduced. This issue was addressed in a recent long-awaited decision by the

---

[118] Statistics in 2002 Bl.f.PMZ 122.

[119] So held by the Düsseldorf District Court, 24 June 1986, 1987 GRUR 628 – *Restitutionsklage*.

[120] Benkard, "Patentgesetz" (Patent Law), Sec. 139, marginal note 27 (9th ed., Munich 1993).

[121] Sec. 12 Patent Act. *See* Keukenschrijver, "Zur sachlichen Reichweite des Vorbenutzungsrechts" (Scope of the Prior User Right), 2001 GRUR 944.

Federal Supreme Court that adopted the approach suggested by the doctrine.[122]

c) When a defendant has an exclusive or non-exclusive licensing contract, he may use the patent and therefore cannot commit infringement. Under special circumstances the defendant can also plead a case for an implied licence.

d) The exhaustion of patent rights also prevents infringement. Although patent rights have territorial limits, exhaustion takes place in the whole EU once a patent owner or his licensee markets the claimed device in one member state.[123] The only exception would be lawful marketing without consent, *e.g.* under a compulsory licence.[124] The burden of proof lies with the alleged infringer.[125] Furthermore, amendments or modifications by which the patented invention is reproduced under an equivalent form are prohibited. According to established case law, such acts would amount to a new manufacturing so that the exhaustion rule is not applicable.[126]

A delay in bringing proceedings can be raised as an estoppel of laches if the plaintiff was aware of the infringer and infringement, but considerably delays the action, thus implying that the contravention will be tolerated. If the infringer's company increased in value due to production and marketing of the allegedly infringing goods, the plea for delay in bringing proceedings may meet with success.[127] Bar such particular circumstances, the normal statute of limitations would apply with a prescription period of three years from the date the patentee obtains knowledge of the infringer and circumstances of the infringement, the infringement was stopped or the patent expired.

---

122 Federal Supreme Court, 13 November 2001, 2002 GRUR 231 – *Biegevorrichtung*. The judges laid great emphasis on the exceptional character of the prior use exemption which makes it impossible for the prior user to extend the scope of his right to embodiments of the invention that he did not recognise at the time of the filing date.

123 ECJ, 31 October 1974, 6 IIC 102 (1975) – *Centrapharm/Sterling Drug*. In a decision handed down in 1999, the German Federal Supreme Court rejected anew the theory of international exhaustion: Federal Supreme Court, 14 December 1999 – *Karate*, 2000 GRUR 635.

124 ECJ, 9 July 1985, 17 IIC 357 (1986) – *Pharmon/Hoechst*.

125 Federal Supreme Court, 14 December 1999, 2000 GRUR 635 – *Karate*.

126 Federal Supreme Court, 8 March 1973, 1976 GRUR 116 – *Spielautomat*, and Federal Supreme Court, 26 September 1996, 1997 GRUR 116 – *Prospekthalter*. The *Prospekthalter* case is the first decision the Federal Supreme Court handed down under the Patent Act 1981 regarding the exhaustion rule.

127 Schramm, "Der Patentverletzungsprozeß" (Patent Infringement Litigation), 269 (4th ed., Cologne 1999).

VI. Remedies

1. Injunctive Relief

The most important remedy in a patent infringement case is the claim for cessation of further infringement (injunctive relief). This remedy is granted even in cases where the defendant bears no direct responsibility for the infringement, *e.g.* when the owner of an enterprise is held responsible for an act of one of his employees even when he had no knowledge of the infringing activity.[128]

On request of the plaintiff, an order for injunctive relief can be accompanied by a fine of up to €250,000 or imprisonment in case of contravention.[129] The limit of the fine, which can be imposed several times and the prison term will be fixed by the court depending on the seriousness of the subsequent contraventions. The fine is not awarded to the plaintiff in lieu of damages, but is paid to the court.

2. Damages

In addition to injunctive relief, the patentee may claim the restitution of damages suffered at the hands of the infringer. Here, at least negligence on the part of the infringer has to be proven.[130]

In order to assess these damages, the infringed IP right owner has the right to request all details necessary for the calculation from the infringer.[131] This can include the names of the suppliers and customers, the quantity of the goods bought, sold, produced, imported or exported, the purchase and sales price of the goods, the profits, the costs and the extent of advertising, etc.

If the defendant does not comply with the above order for information, the court, at the plaintiff's request, may impose a compulsory fine of up to €25,000 and reimposed until the defendant complies. In addition, a prison sentence can be imposed.

In Germany, the infringed patent owner can opt for one of three possibilities for calculating damages.[132] In deciding which of the three would be the

---

[128] Benkard, "Patentgesetz" (Patent Law), Sec. 139, marginal note 23 (9th ed., Munich 1993).

[129] Sec. 890 Code of Civil Procedure.

[130] It is worth noting that wilful infringement is not considered by the judges when assessing the amount of damages to be awarded. Furthermore, the legal requirements as to negligence may be found in Sec. 276(3) Civil Code. *See* Meier-Beck, "Damages for Patent Infringement According to German Law – Basic Principles, Assessment and Enforcement", 35 IIC 115 (2004).

[131] Benkard, "Patentgesetz" (Patent Law), Sec. 139, marginal note 88 (9th ed., Munich 1993).

[132] Schramm, "Der Patentverletzungsprozeß" (Patent Infringement Litigation), 249, (4th ed., Cologne 1999).

best option, he may consider the monetary award, the damage to the defendant, or the simplicity of proof.[133]

The first possibility would be the equivalent of an ordinary licensing fee, the second the infringer's profits, and the third, a reimbursement of lost profits. In practice, most plaintiffs choose the first possibility and ask for the licensing fee because this can be proven with relative ease. The patentee only has to prove what would normally be paid for his product. As a rough guess, about 95% of all plaintiffs would ask for an ordinary licensing fee. The amount of the royalty is calculated analogous to a contractual licence.[134] In the event where only part of the product is patented, the entire commercial entity will serve as the basis for the calculation. But it will depend ultimately on different factors, such as if the patented parts cannot be sold independently from the whole entity, or if the patented parts lead to an increase in value of the whole entity.[135] Even if German courts are still reluctant to allow a penalty surcharge, on a case-by-case basis the discretionary latitude for the judge to grant a higher royalty rate remains.[136]

As to the recovery the infringer's profit,[137] the patentee may only claim the profits which directly result from the infringement. Furthermore, the patentee must have incurred an actual loss.[138] In an important precedent, the Federal Supreme Court recently adopted a new approach defining to what extent the infringer is allowed to deduct his overhead from the profits.[139]

---

[133] The patent owner is not bound by the method of compensation he has first chosen and may opt for another method of calculation during the proceedings, if, *e.g.* he becomes aware that the amount of damages would be higher if another method of calculation were used: *see* Federal Supreme Court, 17 June 1992, 1993 GRUR 55 – *Tchibo/Rolex II*; *see also* Schulte, "Patentgesetz mit EPÜ" (Patent Law with Cross-References to the EPC), Sec. 139, marginal note 65 (6th ed., Munich 2001).

[134] Meaning that the same elements will be considered as those taken into account for calculating a licence: *see*, *e.g.* Federal Supreme Court, 25 May 1993, 1993 GRUR 897 – *Mogulanlage*.

[135] Federal Supreme Court, 30 May 1995, 1995 GRUR 578 – *Steuereinrichtung II*.

[136] Federal Supreme Court, 24 November 1981, 14 IIC 111 (1983) – *Heel Support Device*. As to the factors which may be considered and lead to increased royalties *see* Düsseldorf District Court, 20 May 1999, 2000 GRUR 309 – *Teigportionvorrichtung*.

[137] *See* v. der Osten, "Zum Anspruch auf Herausgabe des Verletzergewinnes im Patentrecht" (Claim for Infringer's Profits in Patent Law), 1998 GRUR 284.

[138] Federal Supreme Court, 2 February 1995, 1995 GRUR 349 – *Objektive Schadensersatzberechnung*. *See* Schulte, "Patentgesetz mit EPÜ" (Patent Law with Cross-References to the EPC), Sec. 139, marginal note 79–81 (6th ed., Munich 2001); Meier-Beck, "Damages for Patent Infringement According to German Law – Basic Principles, Assessment and Enforcement", 35 IIC 115 (2004).

[139] Federal Supreme Court, 2 November 2000, 33 IIC 900 (2002) – *Share of Overheads* (*Gemeinkostenanteil*). Even if this case concerned a design, it is a foregone conclusion that the rulings of this decision will be applied in the realm of patent law. *See also* the comment of Tilmann, "Gewinnherausgabe im gewerblichen Rechtsschutz und Urheberrecht – Folgerungen aus der Entscheidung 'Gemeinkostentanteil'" (Claiming the Infringer's

The Court allowed deduction of costs for the production and distribution of the infringing items, but not the fixed costs which are independent of the particular activity.[140]

Should the plaintiff opt for a calculation based on lost profits, he must show that he would have achieved, partially or totally, the respective sales but for the infringing activities.[141] Expert evidence is mostly served by the plaintiff, which makes such proceedings time-consuming and quite expensive.

No matter what compensation method is chosen, the patent owner has to supply the evidence necessary for calculating the damages he has suffered. For this purpose, it is often necessary to request an expert opinion to determine either the correct percentage of a possible licensing fee, the infringer's profits, or the right owner's loss. In the latter two cases, the expert must be a certified accountant who inspects the balance sheets and accounting methods of the infringer. Interestingly, however, court decisions on the amount of damages are rare due to the fact that once the question of infringement has been decided by an interim decision, the parties would normally settle the case.

Under German law, the losing party to a suit has to bear all expenses related to litigation including the fees for attorneys and patent attorneys.[142] These fees are laid down in an official table of fees (*Gebührentabelle*). Fees basically depend on the value of a case that in infringement cases is determined by the court. The courts determine the average value of patent infringement cases between €500,000 and €5 million. In its decision, the court *ex officio* decides upon the costs of the litigation and to what extent costs have to be split or be borne entirely by one side. In cases where the plaintiff's request is only partially granted (*e.g.* the court only awards half of the damages claimed by the plaintiff) the costs would be split in accordance with the degree of success. This rule makes German attorneys rather hesitant to claim more damages than the court is likely to grant. While the court only decides upon the percentage of litigation costs to be borne by plaintiff and defendant, the exact monetary amount would be fixed by procedures before the registrar of the court. The order of the registrar can be enforced independently from the decision and can also be appealed separately.

Profits in Industrial Property and Copyright Infringement Cases – Consequences of the "Share of Overheads" Decision), 2003 GRUR 647.

[140] For example, the rent costs or the time-related depreciation of fixed assets.

[141] Federal Supreme Court, 13 July 1962, 1962 GRUR 580 – *Laux-Kupplung II. See also* Schulte, "Patentgesetz mit EPÜ" (Patent Law with Cross-References to the EPC, Sec. 139, marginal note 70 (6th ed., Munich 2001); Meier-Beck, "Damages for Patent Infringement According to German Law – Basic Principles, Assessment and Enforcement", 35 IIC 116 (2004).

[142] For detailed information as to the litigation costs at a more general level, *see*: Huber, "Cost of Patent Litigation in Germany", 2001 Managing Intellectual Property No. 107, 57.

To a reasonable extent, the successful plaintiff in an infringement action may also ask for reimbursement of the costs for purchasing an infringing device, or for requesting an initial expert opinion before commencing the action.

3. Other Measures

The successful patentee may further request the infringing products to be destroyed (Sec. 140a Patent Act). The request for destruction may also extend to machinery necessary for producing the infringing goods. Destruction would only be ordered if not out of proportion.

Finally, the successful plaintiff may request the decision to be published in a newspaper. Such a request would only be granted if it is in the legitimate interest of the plaintiff, which is rare in patent matters. Requests for destruction or publication are very rarely made in Germany.

5
The Enforcement of Patent Rights in France

LAURENCE PETIT

A. Patent Law in General

I. Overview

For 125 years patent inventions in France were regulated by the 1844 Patent Act.[1] Owing to the need for modernising its legal system and harmonising it with the provisions of the Strasbourg Convention, that law was replaced by the 1968 Patent Act, which came into force on 2 January 1968. While this Act is still the current basis of patent enforcement, subsequent amendments were necessary, in particular the Act of 13 July 1978, which aligned French law with the Munich Convention. These provisions are codified by Art. L. 611–1 *et seq*. of the French Intellectual Property Code (IPC).[2]

Rules relating to patent litigation, especially patent infringement action, were also covered by these amendments. In this connection, a number of subsequent laws deserve mention. The first was the Act of 27 June 1984 which introduced both preliminary measures and the action for declaration of non-infringement.[3] In addition to this, the Acts of 26 November 1990 and 5 February 1994 which reintroduced the criminal sanctions of infringement (see below) came into force.

---

[1] Nevertheless, the first French Patent Act emerged at the time of the French Revolution and was enacted by means of two decrees of 31 December 1790 and 7 January 1791, both "applicable to the authors of useful discoveries". *See* J. Foyer & M. Vivant, "Le droit des brevets" (Patent Law) 27 *et seq*. (Collection Thémis PUF, 1991).

[2] For the sake of better understanding, it worth noting that the French Code of Intellectual Property contains two main parts: the legislative part and the implementing rules. Accordingly, depending on the part referred to, articles of the Code are identified with L. or R. Furthermore, each part is divided into seven books, each of them providing the legal rules governing a specific intellectual property right. The seventh book is specifically devoted to the protection of inventions and technical knowledge (Art. L. 611 *et seq*. and R. 611 *et seq*.).

[3] For this question *see* the comments of J. M. Mousseron on this new provision in 1984 La semaine juridique (JCP), éd. Entreprise, II, 14335. Up until then the action for declaration of non-infringement was very rarely used. *See, e.g*. Lyon District Court, 3 February 1994, 1996 Dossiers Brevets (DB), IV, 5 and the decision of the Lyon Appeal Court, 4 July 1996, 1997 Propriété Industrielle – Bulletin documentaire (PIBD) 624-III-21.

In France over 80% of patent cases concern infringement litigation and only 25% to 30% of these cases allow for a precise evaluation of damages.[4] All other cases would be subject to settlement in one form or another. The role of patent attorneys in infringement procedures is relatively limited, as only licensed attorneys (avocats) are entitled to plead before the different courts in question. In particular, the "avocats" are the only ones competent to plead in the first instance courts (*Tribunaux de grande instance*), the appeal courts and the courts competent to order interim decisions (Art. 751 New Code of Civil Procedure). Thus, patent attorneys may only assist in preparing a case. Upon request of counsel or the client, a patent attorney may be authorised by the court to take part in the oral hearing as a technical expert. Yet this is somewhat unsatisfactory for a number of reasons, as legal counsel would rarely be specialised in the matters at issue. Unfortunately, at the moment, the position of a patent attorney is somewhat devoid of substance, particularly where his expertise would be most desirable, that is, in infringement procedures. There are about 1,500 patent attorneys licensed in France, while out of 30,000 "avocats" only about 250 are specialised in intellectual property law.[5]

Judges serving on the court are professional magistrates with no special technical training. In order to compensate for this, only certain courts of first instances have jurisdiction to hear patent cases, so that the judges can gain a certain amount of experience in this field. Nevertheless, such expertise can perhaps only be claimed by the Paris Court of First Instance which hears more than 60% of all patent infringement matters (see below).

II. Jurisdiction

Special jurisdiction is provided under Art. L. 615–17 IPC and, in particular, Art. L. 615–19 IPC, if the aspects the judge has to deal with in a patent infringement suit are complex or diverse. Before going into further details in this respect, attention should be drawn to one legal distinction that has found considerable interest in the last couple of years and that concerns what is traditionally referred to as criminal or civil justice.

---

[4] *See* P. Véron, "Le contentieux des brevets d'invention en France, Etude statitique sur 1990–1999 pour la Fédération Nationale des Entreprises (FNDE)-ASPI" (Legal Questions Involving Patents in France. Statistics of 1990–1999 compiled on the basis of figures by the Ministry of Justice), available on Véron's Office homepage: www.veron.com. For statistics prior to 1990, *see* Dieter Stauder, "Patent- und Gebrauchsmusterverletzungsverfahren in der Bundesrepublik Deutschland, Großbritannien, Frankreich und Italien" (Patent Infringement Procedure in Germany, the UK, France and Italy) (Cologne 1988).

[5] P. Véron, "Patent Infringement Litigation in France", 2002 Mitteilungen der deutschen Patentanwälte 390.

Criminalising or decriminalising the infringement of business laws is currently subject to a lively debate[6] that also concerns the field of intellectual property rights, including patents.

While the 1968 Patent Act did not decriminalise patent infringements,[7] the legislature in 1978 finally decided to abolish criminal sanctions owing to the fact that such sanctions had not been used and that a number of other jurisdictions did not provide for criminal sanctions against patent infringement. Subsequent legislation in 1990[8] and 1994[9] reintroduced and even increased the maximum penalty for acts of infringement, a comeback for criminal prosecution in this field.[10] If such attempts will be crowned with success is doubtful. One of the main reasons for abolishing criminal sanctions was the fact that these had gradually fallen into disuse and become dead-letter law, as was stated by Foyer.[11] In fact, no new cases of criminal enforcement under the new law have come to light. As J.M. Mousseron fittingly remarked, "For 134 years criminal protection against infringements has basically brought about nothing, and nonetheless, in order to show that a French patent should not be trifled with, a new provision has been added to the Criminal Code in Art. 423–5."[12]

For these reasons, this article will focus on the civil aspects of an infringement suit.[13] Just for the sake of completeness, it should be added that the rules for a criminal action can be found in Art. L. 615–14 and L. 615–14-1 of the IPC, and the general rules as set out in the Penal Code and the Code of Criminal Procedure.

---

6 C. Mascala, "Vers une dépénalisation des infractions d'affaires? Une réalité?" (Towards Decriminalising the Contraventions of Business Law? A Reality?), 1998 Dalloz Affaires No. 121, 1031.

7 Criminal sanctions for patent infringement were provided for by Art. 52 of the Patent Act of 2 January 1968. Although decriminalisation of patent infringement was not undertaken by legislation in 1968, a number of measures made criminal prosecution almost impracticable: *see* J. Azéma, "Quelques particularités de procédure dans le droit des brevets d'invention" (Procedural Peculiarities in the Field of Patent Law), 1981 Dalloz 1.

8 Law of 26 November 1990, 1990 JCP, III, 64329.

9 Law No. 4-102 of 5 February 1994, 1994 Dalloz 180.

10 The 1990 text, however, does not seem to have adopted the rule of Art. 52(3) Patent Act 1968 on the organisation of civil and criminal justice. According to this section, only a judge in civil matters would be competent to decide upon the question of validity and scope of a patent.

11 J. Foyer, "Proposition de loi No. 2902" (Proposition of Law No. 2902), amending Law 68-1 of 2 January 1968, registered by the presidency of the National Assembly on 17 May 1977 and attached to the minutes of the Session on 18 May 1977.

12 J.M. Mousseron, "Droit des brevets et loi du 26 novembre 1990" (Patent Law and Act of 26 November 1990), 1991 JCP, éd. Entreprise 139.

13 Further information on the criminal aspects is given by Y. Marcellin, "Le droit français de la propriété intellectuelle" (French Intellectual Property Law) (CEDAT, 1999).

Because of the "intrinsic symbiosis of technical and legal aspects",[14] the peculiarities of patent law persist in the field of jurisdiction. According to Art. L. 615–17 IPC, patent matters fall under the special jurisdiction of the district courts with first-instance jurisdiction in this matter.[15] Article 68(1) Patent Act 1968 confirmed this rule, stating that "rights that derive from provisions under this law shall come under the jurisdiction of the courts of first instances and the competent appeal courts". Subsequent rules have designated 10 courts[16] before which patent matters can be adjudicated.[17]

Distinct from some neighbouring countries, such form of specialisation is rather viewed in functional terms. In effect, the French system has not set up special patent courts, but pursued the path of allocating jurisdiction over the subject matter of patents to the major courts. All first instance decisions can be appealed to the appeal courts with jurisdiction over the respective courts of first instances.[18] The final appeal lies with the Supreme Court (*Cour de cassation*).

As mentioned above, about 60% of the patent cases are heard before the *Tribunaux de grande instance* of Paris. About 20% of these cases judged in first instance are subject to appeal.[19]

Meanwhile, the delay of proceedings presents a true problem in France, a situation described by some authors as "completely surrealistic".[20] In what can be considered "normal" proceedings, an infringement suit not appealed to the Supreme Court may still take six to seven years for a final verdict (see below). It is interesting to note that in patent cases, almost all first instance cases are appealed.[21] As a final appeal is launched before the Supreme Court, which can subsequently remand the case back to another appeal court, a final decision may not be reached before 10 years in total. Although this problem

---

[14] J. Azéma, *supra* note 7.

[15] As early as the 1844 Patent Act, the first instance court was given an important role in deciding in patent matters.

[16] Territorial jurisdiction under Art. R 312–2 of the Code of Judicial Organisation (with the same wording in Art. R 631–1 IPC) designates the courts of Paris, Lyon, Marseilles, Bordeaux, Rennes, Strasbourg, Limoges, Nancy and Toulouse.

[17] Such concentration of jurisdiction was meant to be abolished under the 1978 Patent Act, which did not envisage any designation of specific first instance courts. Reducing the number of 10 even further is still a matter of current debate. According to judicial statistics between 1990 and 1995, more than 50% of all patent infringement matters were adjudicated by the courts of Paris, followed by those of Lyon and Rennes. The other courts barely receive 10 cases per year. *See* P. Véron, *supra* note 4.

[18] *See* Art. R 631–1 IPC and the table of territorial jurisdiction therein.

[19] P. Véron, "Patent Infringement Litigation in France", *supra* note 5, 386.

[20] *See* J.P. Martin, "Brevets d'invention, une nouvelle politique de l'innovation" (Invention Patents, a New Policy Innovation), Revue de droit de la propriété industrielle (RDPI), January 1999, 95.

[21] The Paris Appeal Court, which handles about 75% of the patent appeals, is so clogged due to the lack of judges that hearings are set 15 or 16 months in advance: Report of M. Lombard to the French Parliament (Report Lombard).

has not escaped public attention,[22] the difficulties involved seem to be insurmountable.[23] There is currently a vivid discussion concerning the reorganisation of the judiciary, with a number of suggestions by academics and practising lawyers in this field.[24]

Territorial jurisdiction in general is subject to Art. 42 *et seq.* of the new Code of Civil Procedure. According thereto, an action can either be brought at the place where the tort occurred, where the defendant is domiciled, or else where the company is incorporated. In the case of several defendants, jurisdiction can be assumed in total by any of the courts with jurisdiction if there is a sufficient connection.[25] Finally, one last rule deserves mention. According to Art. 14 Civil Code, in cases where the defendant is a foreign national while the plaintiff is French, the suit can be brought before any French tribunal of the plaintiff's choice. This rule does not apply in cases where the provisions of the Council Regulation on the Jurisdiction and Enforcement of Judgments in Civil and Commercial Matters (replacing the Brussels Convention 1968; the Lugano Convention 1988 remains in force) apply.[26] In effect, these two conventions basically supersede the abovementioned privilege of jurisdiction.

Up to now, France did not have to deal much with the concept of the so-called "cross-border injunctions" coming from the Netherlands. Traditionally French courts in several cases have declared themselves exclusively competent to rule on the infringement of French patents.[27] Until

---

[22] *See* J.P. Martin, "Brevets d'invention, une nouvelle politique de l'innovation", *supra* note 20. Judges are well aware of this unsatisfactory situation and the difficulty of providing for speedy justice. *See* the remarks by Belfort, "Le contentieux de la propriété industrielle en Europe" (Industrial Property Rights Litigation in Europe) 77 (Collection CEIPI, Litec, 1999).

[23] The long procedural delays can also heavily influence the costs of proceedings themselves. For an evaluation of these, *see* the remarks in "Deuxièmes rencontres de la propriété industrielle" (The Second Meeting of the Industrial Property Professionals), 1977 PIBD 478.

[24] *See, e.g.* the propositions on a reorganisation of jurisdiction by J.P. Martin, "Brevets d'invention, une nouvelle politique de l'innovation", *supra* note 20. Martin proposes a specialisation of the competent courts by specialised divisions within the first instance courts and only one competent appeal court. *See also* "La spécialisation des tribunaux" (The Specialisation of the Courts), in "Le contentieux de la propriété industrielle en Europe" (Industrial Property Rights Litigation in Europe) 51 (Collection CEIPI, Litec, 1999).

[25] For this question *see* J.P. Stenger, "L'action en contrefaçon" (Patent Infringement Action), Jurisclasseur Brevets, Fasc. 4640, Nos. 35, 39 *et seq.*

[26] The Brussels Convention has been replaced by the Council Regulation (EC) No. 44/2001 of 22 December 2000 on Jurisdiction and Recognition and Enforcement of Judgments in Civil and Commercial Matters, OJEC 16 January 2001, L 12/1. Brussels Convention 1968 on Jurisdiction and the Enforcement of Judgments in Civil and Commercial Matters (consolidated version), including the Protocol on the Interpretation of the 1968 Convention by the Court of Justice, OJEC 26 January 1998, C 27/1.

[27] In particular, Paris District Court, 4 May 1971, 1974 Revue critique de droit international privé 110, with comment by G. Bonet.

recently, French courts merely held that that a "cross-border injunction" can be executed in France, without giving any reasons.[28] That somewhat vague approach has been criticised by some academics.[29]

Three recent decisions have put an end to the "wait-and-see" policy of the French courts. In the first case dated 28 April 2000,[30] the judges of the Court of First Instance of Paris were confronted with an "Italian Torpedo".[31] For the first time, French courts were obliged to interpret some provisions of the Brussels Convention, especially Arts. 21 and 22. This case is of particular interest because it shows how a malicious infringer could benefit from a *saisie-contrefaçon* (see below II.2) by launching a declaration for non-infringement, *e.g.* just after a *saisie-contrefaçon* has been carried out. The factual circumstances of the case were as follows. The plaintiff, the US company General Hospital, was aware of the manufacture of a product infringing its patent by the company Bracco located in Italy, supplied by the company BYK, located in France, which was getting ready to commercialise these products. General Hospital decided to carry out a *saisie-contrefaçon* in the premises of BYK. Shortly before General Hospital filed its claim for infringement, Bracco sought a declaration of non-infringement of the patent before the court of first instance of Milan. When General Hospital sued before the court of Paris, Bracco claimed that the French court should decline jurisdiction based on Art. 21 Brussels Convention or, at least, should stay proceedings under Art. 22.[32]

---

[28] In particular Paris Appeal Court, 28 January 1994, 1996 Dossiers Brevets I and Paris District Court, 11 August 1997, 1997 PIBD 643-III-601.

[29] *See* J.M. Mousseron, J. Raynard & P. Véron, "Cross Border Injunctions – A French Perspective", 29 IIC 884 (1998); J. Passa, "Rejet d'une demande tendant à faire échec en France à une 'Euro-injonction" d'un juge néerlandais saisi d'actes de contrefaçon de brevet" (Rejecting Attempts to Preclude the Effect of "Euro-Injunctions" Granted by a Dutch Judge in Matters of Patent Infringement), Les Petites Affiches, No. 69, 10 June 1998.

[30] Paris District Court, 28 April 2000, 2001 GRUR Int. 173, with comment by P. Treichel.

[31] A "torpedo" is a strategy by potential patent infringer who wants to preclude the patent owner from raising an action for infringement. The mechanism may appear quite simple: the alleged infringer institutes proceedings before a court – mostly before Belgian or Italian courts which have the reputation of being very slow – usually seeking a declaration for non-infringement of the different national parts of a European patent. According the rule of *lis pendens* provided by Art. 21 Brussels Convention, the court seised for the infringement suit may then decline jurisdiction if the judge considers that both proceedings involve the same cause. *See* on the torpedo strategy: G. Del Corno, "Torpedo Actions: Present and Future", 2002 Italian Intellectual Property 77.

[32] Art. 21 Brussels Convention states that any court other than the court first seised shall stay its proceedings until such time as the jurisdiction of the court first seised is established. Should this be the case, the court seised subsequently has to decline jurisdiction in favour of the first seised court. In applying Art. 21, national courts have to consider the rules laid down by the ECJ. (*See i.e.* ECJ, Case 144/86, judgment of 8 December 1987 (Gubisch/Palumbo), [1987] ECR I-4861, where the court held that an action for

In essence, the court ruled that Art. 21 could not apply in the present case considering that claims for a declaration of non-infringement and patent infringement proceedings involved neither the same "object" nor the same cause. It was held that "Proceedings initiated before the present Court by the plaintiffs relate to a declaration of infringement of the patent whose principal aim is to remedy the patent infringement in France, while proceedings begun before the Court of Milan relate to a declaration of non-infringement intended to allow [Bracco] to continue the exploitation of their products." With this ruling, the court of Paris considerably differs from the interpretation of Art. 21 given by the ECJ. Actually, the court based its decision exclusively on the "identity of subject-matter" criterion while the ECJ ruled that this concept "cannot be restricted so as to mean two claims which are entirely identical".[33] Since an appeal against this decision has been lodged, it remains to be seen whether this interpretation of *lis pendens* will become final. What is even more remarkable is that hitherto there has been no consistency in the decisions handed down by other European courts on this issue.[34] As regards Art. 22, the court came to the conclusion that this provision did not oblige the judge to stay the proceedings, but simply gave him the option to do so.[35] This position is very close to those of the Düsseldorf District Court.[36]

In a similar case dated 9 March 2001,[37] the Court of First Instance of Paris reached the same result, as the alleged patent infringer acted in "evident abuse". Here again the judgment was subject of some criticism: some authors wondered whether "the feeling of frustration allows a court to refuse to apply the clear wording of Art. 21 Brussels Convention".[38]

---

termination of the contract and an action to perform the obligations arising out of the same contract have the same cause. Accordingly, the rules of Art. 21 shall apply to those cases "involving the same cause of action and between the same parties".) Following Art. 22 (corresponding to Art. 29 of the Brussels I Regulation), when "related actions" are brought in the courts of different contracting States, any court other than the court first seised may stay its own proceedings or even decline jurisdiction. It follows from the text of Art. 22 that the courts have a certain discretion to apply this rule. *See* M. Pertegás Sender, "Cross-Border Enforcement of Patent Rights", Oxford Private International Law Series, 2002, No. 4.105 *et seq.* – C. Wadlow, "Enforcement of Intellectual Property in European and International Law" 296 *et seq.* (Sweet & Maxwell 1998).

[33] *See* ECJ, Case 144/86, judgment of 8 December 1987 (Gubisch/Palumbo), [1987] ECR I-4861, grounds No. 17.

[34] *See* M. Pertegás Sender, "Cross-Border Enforcement of Patent Rights", *supra* note 32, No. 4.111–4.113.

[35] This decision has been confirmed by a subsequent decision of the Paris Appeal Court, 2001 PIBD 724-III-361.

[36] Düsseldorf District Court, 27 January 1998, 1998 GRUR Int. 803.

[37] *See* Paris District Court, 9 March 2001, 33 IIC 225 (2002) – *Italian Torpedoes*.

[38] *See* P. Véron, "Italian Topedoes: An Endangered Weapon in the French Courts?", 33 IIC 227 (2002).

In a further decision dated 9 February 2001,[39] the Paris Appeal Court confirmed the interpretation of Art. 22 Brussels Convention given by the Paris District Court in the *General Hospital* case and went further to say that "regarding the patents at stake, the subject matter of the pending proceedings in France and in Italy are separate and legally independent even if they claim the same invention. The infringing acts argued in the different proceedings are examined under different national laws, respectively French and the Italian law. Consequently, the decisions of the French and the Italian courts could be divergent but not irreconcilable."[40]

In the absence of a better guidance from the courts hitherto, it is probably premature to comment on the stance of the French courts. One feels, however, tempted to infer from the existing case law that the French judges tend to share the opinion of their English colleagues, who, although falling short of complying with the Brussels Regulation, have traditionally refused to assert jurisdiction on foreign patent infringements.[41] In fact, the reason for the paucity of case law on the interpretation of the Brussels Convention/Regulation in France can be found in the two following reasons: first and foremost, the question of applying the Convention to the interpretation of patent rights has never been clearly established; second, because of the extremely strict rules for issuing interim injunctions and declarations for non-infringement in patent matters and because proceedings in France do not have the reputation of being particularly speedy, one can hardly imagine that French courts represent an attractive forum for strategic users of the Brussels Convention/Regulation.[42]

B. *Enforcement of Patent Rights in Particular*

I. Prerequisites for Patent Infringement Action

An infringement action can only be brought by a plaintiff with proper standing to sue derived from the patent in suit and against the proper defendant who is alleged to have infringed such patent. It must be pointed out that the rules in this respect also apply *mutatis mutandis* to a request for a *saisie-contrefaçon* or the request for an interim injunction.

---

[39] Paris Appeal Court, 9 February 2001, 2002 PIBD 724-III-361.

[40] This decision has been welcomed by the French doctrine: *see* J. Raynard, Comm. to the decision of the Paris Appeal Court, 9 February 2001, 2002 Dalloz 1193.

[41] *See* M. Pertegás Sender, "Cross-Border Enforcement of Patent Rights", *supra* note 32, No. 2.51–2.58; E. M. Kieninger, "Internationale Zuständigkeit bei Verletzung ausländischer Immaterialgüterrechte: Common Law auf dem Prüfstand des EuGVÜ", 1998 GRUR Int. 280.

[42] *See* P. Véron, "Les 'euro-injonctions' devant la justice française" (The "Euro Injunctions" Before the French Courts), 1995 RDPI, No. 57, 13. *See also* the remarks on interim injunctions below. Regarding the scepticism of the French courts to grant a declaration of non-infringement: Paris District Court, 23 June 1999, 2000 PIBD 691-III-55.

1. Patent in Suit

According to Art. L. 613-1 IPC, the exclusive right of exploitation that is granted to the owner of an industrial property right already takes effect with the patent application[43] if two conditions stated in Art. L. 615-4 IPC are met: first, the patent application must have been published or at least been notified to the third party;[44] second, the claims should not have been amended between the publication (or the notification) and the mention of the grant of the patent.[45] The possibility of launching an infringement suit on the mere basis of a patent application is nevertheless limited by Art. L. 615–4 IPC which compels the court to stay its proceedings until the grant of the patent.[46] As Schmidt-Szalewski adequately remarks, "The virtual impossibility of obtaining proper remedies before the grant of the patent renders the right defective up to this date".[47] One of the most important consequence of this rule is the impossibility for the applicant to obtain provisional measures.[48] This system, however, presents the two following advantages: according to Art. L. 615–5 IPC, the proprietor of the patent application can request a *saisie-contrefaçon*;[49] and, when it turns out after grant that the patent has really been infringed, the amount of damages will encompass all the infringing acts since the filing date of the patent application.

---

[43] *See* J.P. Stenger, "L'action en contrefaçon", *supra* note 25, Fasc. 4640, No. 63 *et seq.*; J. Lang, "Zeitliche und strategische Zeitplanung eines Patentverletzungsprozesses in Frankreich", 2002 Mitteilungen der deutschen Patentanwälte 407.

[44] According to standing case law, the notification is valid only with the delivery of a certified copy of the original patent application: Paris Appeal Court, 12 December 1990, 1992 Annales de la propriété industrielle 61; Toulouse District Court, 31 October 1996, 1997 PIBD 626-III-90.

[45] As to the extent of protection conferred by the application, French case law seems to follow the same line as those of the Enlarged Board of Appeal of the EPO. In the G 1/93 decision (1994 OJ EPO, 541), the Board made a distinction between an added feature which makes a technical contribution and one which merely limits the scope of protection. Only the latter is considered allowable, since such an amendment would not represent an unwarranted advantage to the applicant. On this question, French courts ruled that "if the amendment of the claims is made in such a way as to extend the protection conferred by the application as filed or in such a way as to change the subject matter of the claims, these new claims can only be invoked against third parties from the date upon which they have been notified". Nancy Appeal Court, 28 December 1982, 1982 Annales de la propriété industrielle 237; Paris District Court, 21 April 1988, 1988 PIBD 440-III-391; Paris Appeal Court, 3 November 1993, 1994 PIBD 559-III-45.

[46] *See* Paris District Court, 10 April 1990, 1990 PIBD 495-III-537; Lyon District Court, 19 September 1990, 1991 PIBD 496-III-162.

[47] J. Schmidt-Szalewski, "Le droit du breveté entre la demande et la délivrance du titre" (The Right of the Patentee Between the Filing of the Patent Application and the Grant of the Patent), in: "Mélanges Bastian" 389 (Librairies Techniques 1974).

[48] Paris Appeal Court, 12 December 1997, 1997 Annales de la propriété industrielle 137.

[49] It is worth noting that the publication or the notification of the patent application is required, otherwise the *saisie* will be impossible or will be declared invalid.

2. Competent Parties

a) *The competent plaintiff*. The person entitled to raise an infringement action in patent matters under Art. L 615–2 IPC is the patentee. Each of the co-owners may exercise his right "for his own profit" and upon the notification of the writ to the other co-owners.[50] This is different in cases where the patent in suit is the object of a licence or transfer. Standing to sue for licensees is exceptional in principle and subject to strict rules.[51] In that respect, the law distinguishes between contractual and non-contractual licences (Art. L. 615–2, fourth para., IPC). The contractual licensee may only initiate infringement proceedings under the following conditions. First, the licence is an exclusive one, meaning that the licensee must be the only one entitled to use the patent whereas an ordinary licensee has no standing.[52] Second, the above rules only apply to the extent that the licensing contract does not contain a provision that reserves the right of action to the licensor, and that the licensing contract has been properly registered in the Patent Register.[53] Finally, an action can only be considered once the patentee is in default of acting himself. Meanwhile, even if the patentee initially fails to act, this still preserves his right to intervene subsequently in the suit (Art. L. 615–2, third para., IPC).

In case of a transfer, the transferee can naturally pursue all infringing acts subsequent to the transfer, unless otherwise stated in the transfer contract.[54]

b) *The competent defendant*. According Art. L. 615–1 (2) IPC, "An infringement shall imply the civil liability of the infringer." Therefore, an action for patent infringement can be pursued against anyone involved in acts

---

[50] This rule is provided by Art. L. 613–29 CPI, and applied unless an agreement to the contrary exists. *See* Paris Appeal Court, 14 May 2002, 2002 Annales de la propriété industrielle 226.

[51] The 1844 Patent Act did not recognise any rights of licensees.

[52] *See* the decision of the Paris District Court, 14 May 1976, 1977 Dalloz 438. If the patentee decides to act against the infringement and the licensing contract is registered and published in the national Patent Register, the licensee may intervene in the suit. If the patentee remains inactive, the licensee can activate "*l'obligation de garantie*" of the patentee based on the general law of obligations as specified in Art. 1625 Civil Code in the guarantee of the seller to the buyer.

[53] It is understood that the exclusive licensee may only sue against infringement after the date the licensing contract has been published by the registrar. A decision by the Supreme Court has allowed the licensee to launch an infringement action even before a registration of the licensing contract in the Patent Register, applying Art. 126 of the New Code of Civil Procedure, according to which the initially defective action will become admissible upon meeting the necessary requirements. Supreme Court, 29 November 1988, 1989 JCP, ed. Entreprise, I, 18139.

[54] The standing to sue of the transferee requires the registration and the publication of the transfer contract in the Trade and Companies Register (Registre du commerce et des sociétés – RCS): *see* Paris Appeal Court, 29 May 2002, 2002 PIBD 751-III-464 and Paris District Court, 9 March 2001, 2001 PIBD 725-III-394.

detrimental to the patentee's exclusive rights and, in the case of several infringers, the patentee may choose to raise an action against all of them or merely some. However, the third element of Art. L. 615–1 provides for an exception. Where infringing acts, such as offering for sale, are committed by a person other than the manufacturer of the infringing products, this person shall be liable only if these acts have been committed in full knowledge of the facts.[55] A few details related to this rule deserve further mention. In the case of sub-contracting, there is a fairly settled body of case law. For the production of infringing goods, one may distinguish between the person who oversees the production – the manager – and the one who actually manufactures – the sub-contractor. The courts have decided that the infringer in this case is the sub-contractor, who unless otherwise stipulated by contract, has no action himself against the person from whom he has received orders. Yet, it is also settled case law that these two can in fact be viewed as co-infringers, allowing the patentee to pursue his action against each of them.[56]

3. Enforcement

Even though the plaintiff may be in possession of a valid title and may have a right of standing, the title must also be enforceable against third parties. It has already been mentioned above that the patentee who initiates the action must at least comply with the minimum requirement of publication of the patent application, or else have notified the defendant of such application. In this connection three problems should be mentioned. The first concerns the transfer; the second, any subsequent amendments; and the third, patent rights over micro-organisms.[57]

Article L. 613-9 IPC requires all acts of assignment or modifying of rights derived from a patent application or a patent to be duly registered in the National Patent Register in order to be exercised against third parties.[58] Article L. 613-9, second para., IPC makes an exception for the above rule in

---

[55] *See, i.e.* Paris District Court, 30 April 2002, and Paris District Court, 12 April 2002, 2003 PIBD 755-III-1 and 9, where the court ruled that the liability of the retailer or of the fitter of infringing goods may solely be implied when these acts were committed in full knowledge. In the first case in particular, the court considered that the retailer acted in full knowledge since, before the commencement of legal proceedings, he received the patent specification together with a letter from the patent holder permitting him to identify the counterfeiting. It is furthermore noticeable that the courts make a very narrow interpretation of Art. L. 615–1 (3) which does not exempt acts of importation, even if these are not committed in full knowledge: *see* Paris Appeal Court, 12 October 2001, 2002 PIBD 733-III-1.

[56] *See, e.g.* the decision of the Paris District Court, 29 October 1976, 1977 PIBD III-231.

[57] Before the date of making these available to the public, patents on micro-organisms are not enforceable against third parties. *See* Arts. L. 615–4(2), 612–5, second para., and R 612–14, 15 and R 612–42, 43 IPC.

[58] The same applies to European patents under Art. L. 614–11 IPC.

cases where the defendant possesses knowledge of the assignment of rights.[59] Lack of publication has two consequences: the plaintiff is denied standing,[60] and the defendant would only be liable for those acts committed after the transfer or licence was properly registered.[61]

In the event that the patent claims have been amended between the publication of the application and the publication of the grant of the patent, the patent can only be enforced if the amendments do not extend the scope of protection. This rule of Art. L. 615-4 (2) 1° IPC corresponds to Art. 123 (2) EPC. This issue has raised the question of the retroactive character of admissible amendments. It has been decided that such amendments retroactively determine the protection conferred by the application only to the extent that the protection conferred is not extended thereby.[62]

4. Limitations

The writ of summons, which is served by a bailiff on the opposing party, is a central element in patent infringement litigation. It not only constitutes the starting point of the proceedings, but also determines the time frame of the patentee's right to enforce his right.

The prescription period for an infringement action is three years from the date the competent plaintiff obtains knowledge of the circumstances that constitute the infringement (Art. L. 615-8 IPC). According to established case law, infringing acts are considered "successively", so that the prescription period runs from the time each act is committed.[63] It is irrelevant in this respect whether the patent has expired or lapsed before the action is raised. Only the acts committed up to the three years preceding the writ will be taken into consideration.

The rules for prescription follow the common rules as set forth under Art. 2223 *et seq*. Civil Code, although the proper calculation of that period is marked by some particular rules on commencement and interruption.[64]

---

[59] *See*: J.P. Stenger "L'action en contrefaçon", *supra* note 25, Fasc. 4640, No. 81.

[60] This rule again comes under the caveat of Art. 126 New Code of Civil Procedure, according to which the plaintiff will become a competent party once registration and publication is effected in the course of the court action. *See, e.g.* the decision of the Supreme Court, 29 November 1988, 1989 JCP, ed. Entreprise, I, 18139.

[61] *See* the decisions of the Paris Appeal Court, 29 May 2002, 2002 PIBD 752-III-499 and 9 May 2001, 2001 PIBD 725-III-394. *See also*: J.P. Stenger, "L'action en contrefaçon", *supra* note 25, Fasc. 4640, No. 84.

[62] *See* cross-references *supra* note 45.

[63] In a recent decision, the Paris First Instance Court clarified this rule in deciding that when the acts of infringement constitute the selling of infringing goods, the prescription period runs from the date of the last sale: Paris District Court, 5 September 2000, 2001 PIBD 712-III-30.

[64] It has *e.g.* been ruled that if the writ interrupts the prescription period, the request for a *saisie-contrefaçon* has no effect on the prescription period: decision of the TGI Lille, 4 June 1980, 1980 Dossiers Brevets, VI, 6. As to the rules of interruption *see* the explanations by J.P. Stenger, "L'action en contrefaçon", *supra* note 25, Fasc. 4640, No. 104 *et seq*. and

II. Proof of Infringement

1. General Means of Proof

According to a long judicial tradition, proof of infringement can be established by whatever means.[65] This position is now clearly reiterated by Art. 10 of the Law of 26 November 1990, codified as Art. L. 615–5 IPC.[66]

There are various means of proving infringement in an ordinary civil action.[67] One could bring an affidavit issued by a bailiff according to Art. 1317 Civil Code, one could use the presumptions as specified in Art. 1349 *et seq*. Civil Code, or a defendant's admission of having committed a wrong.[68] Other means of proof that can be presented to the judge are, for example, an expert opinion or the court designating a consultant. The latter is a measure specified under Art. L. 615–20 IPC. Here, the judge may either on request or *ex officio* nominate a specialist of his choice who would follow the proceedings and assist in the hearings.[69] In addition, the new Code of Civil Procedure gives also the judge the possibility of requesting an expert opinion as mentioned in Art. 263 *et seq*. Presenting such an expert opinion was extremely common in the past, but has fallen into disuse.[70] Since the function of an expert opinion would be to supply the judge with necessary

---

A. Chavanne & J.J. Burst, "Le droit de la propriété industrielle" (The Industrial Property Law), 1998 Dalloz, No. 450.

[65] This rule was already established by the decision of the Supreme Court, 30 May 1927, 1928 Annales de la propriété industrielle 33 and the Supreme Court took the occasion to confirm this rule in a very recent decision dated 23 April 2003, 2003 PIBD 768-III-362.

[66] The first means for obtaining evidence used in France is the *saisie-contrefaçon*, although legislation should perhaps clarify both for the sake of the parties and the judge that the *saisie-contrefaçon* is by no means the only method of proving infringement. On this subject, *see also* the commentary by P. Mathély, in "Le nouveau droit français des brevets" (New French Patent Law), 1991 JNA (ed.) 454. *See also* A. Bertrand, "La preuve de la contrefaçon" (Proof of Infringement), 1993 RDPI, No. 49, October, 11.

[67] As mentioned above, patent infringement constitutes both a civil and criminal wrong. Proving such wrong can thus take different forms according to the mode of action that is taken. The civil action would be the "normal way" for an infringement suit. For criminal action *see* Y. Marcellin, "La protection pénale de la propriété industrielle" (Criminal Protection of Industrial Property Rights) (Cédat, 1997).

[68] *See* A. Bertrand, "La preuve de la contrefaçon" (Proof of Infringement), 1993 RDPI, No. 49, October, 11.

[69] As introduced by the Law of 26 November 1990, Art. 16. This solution seems to have met with approval by a good many of those who regard such a practice as a flexible and adequate solution. *See* "Le contentieux de la propriété industrielle en Europe" (Patent Litigation in Europe) 57 (Collection CEIPI, Litec, 1999).

[70] Actually the effectiveness of such a measure is regularly called into question. *See* Belfort, *supra* note 22, at 56.

technical information,[71] the prerequisites of such a request are strictly regulated (Art. R. 615–5 IPC). Among these, formal requirements[72] and requirements for the maintenance of trade secrets[73] can be distinguished.

2. "Saisie-contrefaçon"

The French law provides for a special means of proof, which is often described as a privileged and customary implement of French judicial tradition. This measure is the so-called *saisie-contrefaçon* which provides for a means of obtaining evidence that heavily favours the patentee.[74] Generally speaking, the *saisie-contrefaçon* codified in Art. L. 615–5, second and third paras., can be defined as an extraordinary procedure under common law available to the owner of an intellectual property right as a special means of proof.[75] As a preliminary measure prior to an infringement action, the *saisie-contrefaçon* shows the following characteristics. Exempt from common law principles, the *saisie-contrefaçon* allows for a surprise inspection of the domicile or business premises of a competitor by a court bailiff, alone or accompanied, in order to carry out investigations. Because the *saisie* represents only one means for obtaining evidence, the plaintiff may, but not must, request a *saisie* order. The beneficiary of a court order is thus free to have the *saisie* carried out or not, and it is strictly a means of proof. Already at this stage it should be noted that a *saisie* order does not depend on the likelihood of success in the main action. It is the optional and extraordinary character that makes the *saisie-contrefaçon* subject to strict rules when being carried out.

---

[71] *See* J.P. Stenger, "L'action en contrefaçon" *supra* note 25, Fasc. 4640, No. 111. Concerning the judge's discretion *see* the decision of the Rouen Appeal Court, 23 March 1971, 1971 PIBD 63-III-190.

[72] In effect, the judge has to choose an expert from one of the organisations mentioned in a ministerial circular. The request for a technical consultation has to be mentioned in the preliminary or final decision, as otherwise the request for technical expertise and the expertise as such would have to be annulled. *See, e.g.* the Supreme Court, 10 July 1967, 1967 Annales de la propriété industrielle 247.

[73] Precautionary measures also apply to the request of either of the parties or the judge in order to protect private trade secrets. *See* J.P. Stenger, "L'action en contrefaçon", *supra* note 25, Fasc. 4640, Nos. 35, 39 *et seq*.

[74] As mentioned above, the *saisie-contrefaçon* is also provided by the Trade Mark Act (Art. L 716–7 IPC), by the Copyright Act (Art. L 332–1 IPC), by the Design Act (Art. L 521–1 IPC), and by the Plant Varieties Act (Art. L 623–27 IPC). The rules governing the *saisie-contrefaçon* may differ however. *See* P. Véron, "Saisie-contrefaçon", Dalloz 1999.

[75] Historically speaking, the *saisie-contrefaçon* came into existence by the decrees of 31 December 1790 and 7 January 1791. Although abolished a little later, this instrument of proof developed nonetheless further even before its codification by the Patent Act of 5 July 1844. While the 1844 Patent Act lays the foundations for the *saisie-contrefaçon*, this instrument underwent some changes by the Patent Act of 2 January 1968, the Patent Act of 2 November 1990 and the Law of 1 July 1992.

a) *Conditions for carrying out the saisie-contrefaçon*. Carrying out the *saisie-contrefaçon* first of all requires authorisation of a judge. In order to prepare an infringement action, every owner of an intellectual property right would be entitled to request such a procedure.[76] While the *saisie* request is conditional on raising an infringing action, the applicant may proceed with a request for *saisie* even on the basis of a patent that takes no effect in France under Art. 31 Brussels Regulation of 22 December 2000. The Lugano Convention of 16 September 1988 provides for the same rule. This is completely consistent with the *saisie-contrefaçon* being a provisional measure meant to preserve evidence. As yet, there is no French court decision to rule on this matter[77]. Yet, since the reverse has already been accepted by the French courts,[78] there is nothing to suggest that the owner of a foreign patent should not be allowed to obtain evidence of infringement in France by a *saisie-contrefaçon*.[79] And it has already been accepted that verbal evidence obtained by a *saisie-contrefaçon* in France, in order to prove the infringement of a French patent, can be used before a foreign court if there would be similar rules for obtaining evidence in that foreign country.[80]

---

[76] If a patent has not yet been registered, but only applied for, the action would require such application to be enforceable at least by a publication or notification to the defendant. This rule is scrupulously applied by the courts, *e.g.* Bordeaux Appeal Court, 27 May 1998, 1998 PIBD 663-III-508, which ordered the *saisie-contrefaçon* to be revoked since the patent application that formed the basis of the request had neither been published nor properly notified to the defendant at the date the *saisie-contrefaçon* order became effective. The Paris Appeal Court recently gave clear directions which will likely tighten the requirements of proof regarding the notification of the patent application to the alleged infringer: the sole mention of the notification on the *saisie-contrefaçon* request is not sufficient. *See* Paris Appeal Court, 25 April 2001, 2001 Annales de la propriété industrielle 187.

[77] The Ghent Appeal Court confirmed that Belgian courts can order a *saisie-contrefaçon* on the basis of Art. 24 Brussels Convention (replaced by Art. 31 of the Brussels Regulation I) even if the infringement proceedings take place before a foreign court, and even if the European patent at stake has not designated Belgium: Ghent Appeal Court, 17 November 1995, 1996 E.I.P.R., N-66. This position was subsequently confirmed by the Belgian Supreme Court: *See* Supreme Court, 3 September 1999, 2000 Revue de droit commercial belge 128.

[78] French judges have already accepted proof obtained by a *saisie-contrefaçon* abroad (here: Belgium) in order to prove infringement of a French patent: *see* the decision of the Lille District Court, 4 June 1980, 1980 Dossiers Brevets (DB), VI, No. 6.

[79] *See* P. Véron, "Saisie-contrefaçon", *supra* note 74, No. 40 *et seq*. In the absence of a guidance by the French courts, when the patent at stake has no effect in France, P. Véron advises not only requesting the *saisie-contrefaçon* but also a *saisie-conservatoire* (civil seizure) as governed by Law No. 91-650 of 9 July 1991 on Civil Enforcement Measures (the law has been implemented into the New Code of Civil Procedure). Basing the request on the IPC only might risk the request being rejected, as no French patent is at stake.

[80] *See* the legal opinion of the Paris District Court, 24 November 1997, 1998 RDPI, No. 83, 11. However, the court did not allow access to confidential documents in the exclusive possession of the respondent.

Jurisdiction for a *saisie* does not follow the usual rules by subject matter, as stipulated in Art. L. 615–17 IPC, and the territorial rules as specified in Art. 615–17, second para., IPC and Art. R. 312–2 of the Court Organisation Act.[81] Rather, jurisdiction for the *saisie* under Art. R. 615–1 IPC lies with the president of the court of first instance in whose territory the *saisie* will be carried out.[82] The application for a *saisie-contrefaçon* consists of a simple request to the court.[83] The request has to be reasoned and meet a number of other formal conditions necessary to define the object of the request.[84] Particularly, the patent that is the base of the request has to be cited, the person who is allegedly in possession of infringing goods has to be named, the allegedly infringing objects be described and the type of *saisie* specified – *saisie* limited to the description of relevant documents or the infringing product (*saisie description*) or *saisie* which authorises the confiscation of one or more infringing products (*saisie réelle*).[85] If the request is rejected, the petitioner can appeal under Art. 496 New Code of Civil Procedure within 15 days from the publication of the decision. Similarly, the respondent can request the order to be annulled or limited, a course of action also open to the respondent as soon as he obtains knowledge of the *saisie* order. This so-called *demande en rétractation* by the respondent does not stay proceedings, however.[86] The law distinguishes between those measures the judge has to order at the request of the applicant and those that are at his discretion. According to Art. L. 615–5, second para., IPC, the judge may not refuse to grant the *saisie* order. Nor is it up to the discretion of the judge to choose the bailiff or the expert accompanying the latter. On the other hand, the judge has the discretionary power to decide whether he wants to grant a "*saisie confiscation*" or merely a "*saisie description*". The judge is furthermore competent to fix the conditions of the execution of the *saisie*. In particular, the judge can limit the *saisie* to the allegedly infringing products and the number

[81] *See* M. Vivant, "Juge et loi du brevet" (The Judge in Patent Law) 97 *et seq*. (Collection CEIPI, Litec, 1977).

[82] *See* J.P. Stenger, "La saisie-contrefaçon" Jurisclasseur Brevets, Fasc. 4630, No. 15 *et seq*. As it turns out, the judge authorising the *saisie* very often is not the president of the court before which the infringement suit is subsequently brought.

[83] The request has to be made by an attorney registered with the court before which the request is made. If this condition is not properly met, the *saisie* is null and void.

[84] The patentee, however, is not required to furnish *prima facie* evidence of infringement to get the *saisie-contrefaçon* order. This principle has been pointed out by the Douai Appeal Court, 4 February 2002, 2002 Annales de la propriété industrielle 173.

[85] As specified in Arts. 60, 61, 493–498, 797 and 813 of the New Code of Civil Procedure. *See also* P. Véron, "Saisie-contrefaçon", *supra* note 74, Nos. 155–168.

[86] In effect, according to Art. 495(2), New Code of Civil Procedure, the order is carried out then and there, yet on a provisional basis. Remedies against the *saisie* can be requested by any interested person before the judge who ordered the *saisie*, Art. 497 New Code of Civil Procedure. It is unlikely for a judge to interfere in the operation of a *saisie* before it has been carried out. For the powers of a judge in this case, *see* P. Véron, "Saisie-contrefaçon", *supra* note 74, at No. 306 *et seq*.

of items likely to be seized,[87] and may order the applicant to deposit an amount equal to the value of the objects seized.[88] He can also request the applicant to post a bond in the event that the infringement action would fail or the *saisie* as such would be subsequently annulled or declared abusive.

b) *Procedures of the saisie-contrefaçon.* A seizure may only be carried out by a bailiff who may be accompanied by one or more technical experts or the police. If both bailiff and experts can be chosen by the applicant of the *saisie*,[89] the presence of the patent owner is strictly prohibited.[90] The *saisie-contrefaçon* being strictly a means for obtaining evidence, the powers of the bailiff must be clearly defined in the *saisie* order, which in no case may be overstepped. Request for a subsequent *saisie-contrefaçon* by the same applicant for the same case would have to be based on new facts.[91] In order to carry out his mission properly, the bailiff obviously has to be able to access the *locus in quo* and thus the premises where the allegedly infringing objects are located. While the bailiff is not allowed to question witnesses,[92] there might be cases where the bailiff would not be able to carry out his mission without assistance from the respondent. This is the case where, for example, the goods are marked by bar codes and the bailiff has no means of deciphering these. In such cases of difficulty, or in cases of the respondent's non-cooperation in bad faith, the bailiff can always contact the judge who ordered the *saisie* – or the judge otherwise competent for the infringement suit – to order the person found on the premises of the *saisie* to supply the missing goods or information.

The scope of the *saisie* is determined by the judicial order. If the *saisie* is limited to an inspection, the bailiff is confined to a description of the products or processes allegedly infringing, Art. L. 615-5, second para., IPC, or the technical means that would reproduce the contents of a patented invention.

---

87 As to the scope of a *saisie-contrefaçon*, in the 19th century the courts have allowed execution in a rather general fashion, *e.g.* Appeal Court of Lyon, 30 November 1865, 1866 Annales de la propriété industrielle 313. At present, authorisation of a seizure could be limited as to the number of objects actually seized. It is quite settled law that all acts of a *saisie* unrelated to the actual case of infringement would be regarded as abusive, *e.g.* Paris District Court, 22 October 1975, 1977 DB, III.

88 For that aspect, *see* the comment by J. Azéma on Lyon District Court, 29 August 1994, 1995 Revue trimestrielle de droit commercial (RTD com) 415.

89 Frequently the expert would also be the applicant's intellectual property consultant who is bound to maintain professional secrecy.

90 *See* Paris District Court, 15 October 2002, 2003 PIBD 763-III-239, where the court ruled that the presence of the patent owner is not compatible with the requirement of impartiality applicable to this kind of operation.

91 This derives from the old doctrine that once the rights upon which the order was based would be exhausted and could not be used for a new *saisie* request, *e.g.* Paris Appeal Court, 21 December 1870, 1878 Annales de la propriété industrielle 173.

92 Yet, the bailiff can always report so-called "unsolicited statements" of the person in possession of the goods in question.

The bailiff may also be authorised to establish the origin, substance and extent of the infringement. Once the "*saisie description*" is finished, the results will be deposited for the record. The bailiff's report can be accompanied by photocopies of documents, photographs, or even video films that are attached to the record. Both the procedures and the report should be as detailed as possible. If the *saisie* involves the seizure of objects, the bailiff has some additional duties, such as to deposit a sample with a clerk of the court's office where the *saisie* has taken place.[93] The judge may authorise the seizure of plans for the production or composition of goods, advertising material or other documents related to the respondent's business.

With the *saisie-contrefaçon*, legislature has given the patentee significant power at the expense of the respondent. A closer look reveals that this statement has to be qualified. After all, the conditions for granting and carrying out the *saisie* are so strict that in the absence of even one condition, the *saisie* is rendered null and void.

c) *Protection of the interests of the respondent*. In the same way as the judge can impose certain obligations on the bailiff for carrying out the *saisie*, non-compliance with a certain number of legal formalities by the bailiff may entail invalidity of the *saisie*. This already starts with the bailiff having to identify himself properly and his function as a bailiff.[94] The bailiff further has to furnish the person in possession of the goods with one copy of the court order.[95] Compliance with this formality must be on record in the file.[96] At the end of the *saisie*, the bailiff has to note this act in the minutes of proceedings and leave the respondent with a copy of the record (Art. R. 615–2, second para., IPC).[97]

Execution of the *saisie-contrefaçon* frequently raises the ardent question of how to balance the protection of the applicant's property with the protection of the respondent's trade secrets. The principle is that the applicant should be entitled to access all documents that are related to the infringement, regardless of whether they are confidential or not.[98] At the time of the *saisie*, certain secrets of manufacture or commerce may well have to be disclosed, thereby causing a certain detriment to the respondent. The first remedy available to the defendant in such case is the *demande en rétractation*

---

[93] Where only one object is found, the judge may order the applicant to post a bond, or a sequestration of that object in the respondent's hands.

[94] Disregard of this obligation makes the *saisie* void per se, *see* Supreme Court, 20 October 1998, 1998 DB, III, 7 and the comment by J. Azéma, 1999 RTD com. 52, 389.

[95] For details, *see* P. Véron, "Saisie-contrefaçon", *supra* note 74, at No. 200 *et seq*.

[96] If this statement is missing in the records, there is a presumption that the formality has not been complied with, entailing the nullity of the *saisie*. There is no uniform court practice on this point, however. Some courts would assume that the *saisie* is null and void only if the respondent can furnish proof of any damage, while others regard the lack of this formality as rendering the *saisie* void as such.

[97] For form and contents of the minutes, *see* P. Véron, "Saisie-contrefaçon", *supra* note 74, at Nos. 242 *et seq*., 256 *et seq*.

[98] *See* Lyon District Court, 24 November 1988, 1988 DB, V, 6.

suggesting that the judge limit the order meant to prevent the spread of a trade secret. While it is clear that the respondent himself has no right to determine himself which documents are confidential, he may insist on confidentiality. In such case, the bailiff would carry on with the *saisie* regardless, keeping the confidentiality of the documents in his report until a decision by the judge. A judicial decision in that respect can be requested either by the applicant for an order of confidentiality to be lifted or by the respondent for the secrecy to be affirmed. Frequently, the judge may request an expert opinion in order to distinguish those documents necessary for proving infringement from those that are confidential and unrelated to the question of infringement.[99] The bailiff would thus have to make a proposal on how to separate properly the documents seized or inspected. If the parties disagree, a court order would be necessary. Once a decision is made, the sealed documents would be opened and communicated to the parties.

The above should give the reader at least an idea of the conflicts of interest that are triggered by a *saisie-contrefaçon*. It has already been mentioned above that once ordered, the defendant always has the possibility of requesting the order for a *saisie* to be revoked. If a *saisie* is unjustified or otherwise defective, it may subsequently be declared void and entail a claim for compensation.[100] Generally, three types of invalidation of a *saisie* can be distinguished.[101] First the *saisie* is invalid *ex lege* if the infringement suit is not launched out at least 15 days after the *saisie-contrefaçon* order has been granted.[102] According to Art. 117 New Code of Civil Procedure, the *saisie*

[99] There are conflicting decisions on this distinction. Some courts stress the angle of the documents being useful for proving infringement. Others would stress the confidentiality of the documents. *See* P. Véron, "Documents confidentiels appréhendés lors d'une saisie contrefaçon" (Confidential Documents Seized During a *saisie-contrefaçon*), 1998 RDPI, No. 83, 11. Nor have the courts found clear guidelines on who apart from the expert should be allowed to participate in the selection of documents. While some have held that the matter should be open to experts only, *e.g.* Paris District Court, order of 2 October 1997, 1998 RDPI, No. 83, 25, others, while still excluding the parties, would at least allow their legal representatives access, *e.g.* Paris District Court, opinion of 24 November 1997, 1998 RDPI, No. 83, 26.

[100] The record written by the bailiff may directly be challenged by an action for wrongful *saisie* under Arts. 303 to 316 New Code of Civil Procedure. If successful, the bailiff's record would not be used at all.

[101] *See* J.P. Stenger, "La saisie-contrefaçon", *supra* note 82, Fasc. 4630, No. 209 *et seq*.

[102] This rule is stipulated in the fifth element of Art. L. 615–5 IPC. As regards the application of this rule, a distinction has been drawn between the "*saisie-description*" and the "*saisie-confiscation*". In virtue of this distinction, the 15-day rule shall only be observed in case of a "*saisie-confiscation*". *See* Paris Appeal Court, 13 October 2001, 2002 PIBD 733-III-166 and Paris Appeal Court, 14 June 2002, 2002 PIBD 751-III-464. In the latter decision, the Court moreover indicated that the 15-day rule still applies even if the patentee has seised a court which has no jurisdiction over the infringement claim. To put it differently, the patentee who has been granted a "*saisie-confiscation*" order and who fails to launch his infringement suit within this 15-day time limit can no longer use the evidence he obtained from the confiscation; however, he is still allowed to rely on the descriptive part of the *saisie*.

is also invalid if the bailiff has not acted on proper instructions.[103] Invalidity in such cases can be raised as an estoppel and does not require the demonstration of any damages to the respondent. Finally, disrespect for certain formalities in carrying out the *saisie* either imposed by law or judicial order would make the *saisie* invalid if the respondent can show any sort of damage.[104] Invalidity of the *saisie* can however only be successfully claimed if set off as a defence ("*defences au fond*"), that means before challenging the materiality of the infringement.[105] Invalidity of the *saisie* has some unfortunate consequences for the patentee. For one, evidence obtained by an invalid *saisie* is inadmissible.[106] If the *saisie* had authorised the seizure of objects, those have to be returned. Invalidity can be argued by way of counterclaim or as an estoppel.

An action for damages, owing to a wrongful *saisie* brought before the court where the infringement action is raised, can be based on an abuse of rights, an invalid or an unjustified *saisie*. An abuse of rights by the applicant would be a case where a *saisie* is only requested in order to obtain knowledge of a competitor's business, in cases where several *saisies* have been requested, etc. If the *saisie* has been declared invalid, case law is highly inconsistent, but would suggest that the court will only grant damages if financial harm can be demonstrated.[107] The bailiff would also be personally responsible when making errors in the course of his mission, as in such cases he would not have properly abided by the rules of law or the judicial order. Responsibility of the

[103] *See* Supreme Court, 23 April 2003, 2003 PIBD 768-III-362, where the judges declared the *saisie* null and avoid because the bailiff exceeded his power by seizing the hardware of a computer. According the *saisie-contrefaçon* order, the seizure of the hardware would only have been authorised in the event the alleged infringer had refused to communicate his password to the bailiff. In some cases, a partial invalidity of the *saisie-contrefaçon* may be pronounced by the judge. This can be the case when the *saisie-contrefaçon* consists of several distinct operations and the nullity of one of these operations would not affect the others. *See* Paris District Court, 30 May 2003, 2003 PIBD 775-III-571.

[104] This rule follows from Art. 114 New Code of Civil Procedure whereupon lack or disrespect of a certain formality, even if fundamental, can only be argued if there is any grief or damage. Most frequent cases of disrespect of a formal requirement are those where the bailiff does not properly serve a copy of the *saisie* order. Other cases would include the bailiff being accompanied by a person not properly ordered to do so, *e.g.* in cases where the patentee would accompany the bailiff, although the order requires the patentee to choose an expert to do so.

[105] This rule is governed by Art. 112 New Code of Civil Procedure, which states that the nullity of a formal act is only admissible if invoked before any substantive defence. As regards the application of this rule to the *saisie-contrefaçon*, *see* Supreme Court, 25 April 2001, 2001 PIBD 726-III-428, and Supreme Court, 23 April 2003, 2003 PIBD 768-III-361.

[106] *See*, *e.g.* Supreme Court, 22 December 1926, 1927 Annales de la propriété industrielle 82, and more recently, Supreme Court, 6 November 1990, 1991 PIBD 493-III-69.

[107] This does not concern cases of invalidity due to formal requirements, as proof of damages is already necessary to obtain a declaration of invalidity. For details *see* J.P. Stenger, "La saisie-contrefaçon", *supra* note 82, Fasc. 4630, No. 283 *et seq*.

applicant is recognised in three cases: first, when the applicant had no right to request the *saisie*; second, when the *saisie* was abusive; and, finally, when the applicant was solely responsible for any harm caused by an invalid *saisie* due to his own fault (Art. L. 615–5, fourth para., IPC). Compensation of damages would follow the fundamental rules of French law as set out in Art. 1382 Civil Code. Even if brought as an action for damages plus interest, the judge could order other measures of compensation such as the publication of the decision at the expense of the applicant. In all cases, certainly, the respondent would be responsible for proving any damages allegedly incurred. It has to be pointed out that such claims are rarely crowned with success.[108]

The success of the *saisie* is subject to further formalities. It has been mentioned above that, according to Art. L. 615–5 IPC, the *saisie* has to be carried out within 15 days of the request.[109] This requirement was basically imposed by case law, regardless of the exact nature of the *saisie*, and regardless of whether the *saisie* would allow inspection or seizure. A legislative change by Law of 26 November 1990 and its interpretation by the courts disposed of this rule,[110] despite an almost unanimous disapproval of academic writers.[111] According to the courts, a "*saisie description*" would no longer have to be carried out within 15 days to be valid. Following the general rules of procedure, the action for infringement needs a writ of summons served to the defendant and to the competent tribunal.[112] Disregarding this rule would ultimately make the *saisie* invalid even in the absence of any damages. Even if invalidity has no repercussion on the admissibility of the infringement suit, the applicant risks not being able to prove his damages.[113]

---

108 The statistics of 1997 reveal that of 119 actions in this respect, only 8 were successful, *see* P. Véron, *supra* note 4.

109 *See* Arts. R. 615–3 and 623–53 IPC.

110 *See, e.g.* Paris District Court, 12 March 1993, 1993 Dalloz, Summary section 377. This also seems to apply to the law of trade marks, while plant varieties (Art. L. 623–27 IPC) and designs (Art. L. 521–1 IPC) are not concerned.

111 *See* in particular J.P. Stenger, "La saisie-contrefaçon", *supra* note 82, Fasc. No. 4630, No. 140; and also J.P. Martin, "Du délai entre *saisie-contrefaçon* de brevet et assignation" (Some Comments About the Time Limit Between the *saisie-contrefaçon* and the Writ of Summons), 1994 JCP, I, 343. According to Martin "the new text seems to lead to an evident imbalance to the advantage of the patentee".

112 *See* on that subject, P. Mathély, "L'obligation de se pourvoir après une *saisie* contrefaçon" (Obligation to Bring a Suit After the *saisie-contrefaçon*), 1997 Annales de la propriété industrielle 3; and P. Véron, "Le délai de quinzaine imparti au saisissant pour se pourvoir devant le tribunal" (About the Obligation of the Plaintiff to Bring a Suit within 15 Days), 1995 RDPI, No. 65, 35. The Court of First Instance of Paris in a judgment dated 14 June 2002 has to address the issue of the validity of a *saisie* when the infringement suit has not been brought before the competent court and, consequently, the 15-days-time limit could not be respected. In this present case, the court ruled that the failure to this requirement only affects the validity of a *saisie-réelle* (material seizure) and allowed the plaintiff to use the descriptive part of the *saisie*: *see* Paris District Court, 14 June 2002, 2002 PIBD 751-III-464.

113 It should finally be noted that invalidity of the *saisie* would also lead to the invalidity of acts based on the *saisie*, *e.g.* an expert opinion.

III. Preliminary Measures

Under the pressure of interested circles as well as of harmonising French law with that of neighbouring countries, an amendment of 27 June 1984 led to the introduction of Art. L. 615-3 IPC. According to this provision, an especially appointed judge would be competent either to issue an interim injunction against the suspected infringer, or else request the latter to furnish a guarantee. Procedures have been facilitated by legislation enacted on 26 November 1990.[114] Only the president of the court competent for the infringement suit would have jurisdiction in such case.[115] A successful request for interim relief must meet the following conditions. The interim injunction can only be requested within the framework of an infringement action, and thus requires that the infringement action has at least been initiated preliminary. Further, the request shall only be granted "if the substantive proceedings appear well founded and are instituted within a short time of the day on which the patentee becomes aware of the facts on which the proceedings are based" (Art. L. 615-3, second para., IPC).[116]

While the period of this delay is not defined by law, but rather at the discretion of the judge, case law suggests a period not exceeding six months.[117] It further appears that the request can only be made on the basis of a granted patent.[118] Finally, the last condition for an interim order would be the likelihood of success in the main action. The judge would have to take into account the likelihood of infringement, the strength of the underlying patent, and the defences by the alleged infringer.[119] In taking into account

---

[114] Between 1984 and 1990, only two requests out of 100 were actually granted. *See* A. Bertrand, "L'action en interdiction provisoire d'exploitation d'un brevet" (Interim Injunctions in Patent Matters), 1994 RDPI, No. 53, 15.

[115] While Art. L. 615–3 IPC does not specify who could actually request interim relief, it has been suggested by a number of academics that the former should be those persons competent to initiate the main action, in other words, the patentee or licensee. *See* Bertrand, ibid.

[116] *See* C. Le Stanc & L. Petit, "Sanctions for Patent Infringement in France: Injunctive Relief and Damages", 2002 E.I.P.R. 353–354.

[117] Paris Appeal Court, 26 February 1992, 1992 PIBD III-308.

[118] As opposed to the decision of the Supreme Court, 1 March 1994, which allowed the request to be made on the basis of a mere patent application. The decision was heavily criticised by P. Mathély, 1994 Annales de la propriété intellectuelle 197; and Y. Marcellin & J.P. Martin, 1994 RDPI, No. 53, 19. *See e.g.* TGI Rennes, 24 May 2000, 2000 PIBD 705-III-433, where the judges, in conformity with the large part of the doctrine and case law, refused to grant a interim injunction.

[119] The judges seem to be reluctant to grant an interim order when an opposition has been filed with the EPO. The courts commonly substantiate such decision by reliance on the possibility to amend the claims during opposition proceedings: *see* the decision of the Paris District Court, 15 July 2002, 2002 PIBD 752-III-502. *See also*: J. P. Stenger, "L'action en contrefaçon", *supra* note 25, Fasc. No. 4640, No. 200 *et seq.*; *see also* A. Bertrand, *supra* note 114, at 17.

these factors, the judge may refuse the request, or grant the request unconditionally or upon the applicant's posting of a bond.[120] The interim order takes immediate effect, unless otherwise ordered by the judge, and may be accompanied by fine in case of contravention. Both applicant or respondent may be requested to post a bond. The order may be appealed against, and may be repealed or altered by the issuing judge in case of new facts coming to light. Nevertheless, one feels tempted to conclude that the overhaul of the Patent Act in 1990 has not been plainly satisfactory inasmuch as the rules governing the interim injunction remain quite strong.

IV. The Hearing

The defendant is requested to consult counsel within 15 days upon receipt of the writ (Art. 755 New Code of Civil Procedure) and file a defence within six to 12 months. This stage is followed by a lengthy exchange of statements between the parties, the judge being supplied with copies. This stage of exchanging statements may take about two years, after which the judge will fix a date for a hearing. The hearing as such would generally take half a day, in more complicated cases, up to two half-days.[121] After the pleadings in court, each counsel would submit a complete file to the judge in order to have the arguments re-examined for an eventual decision. The decision of the court will normally follow two to three months after the hearing.

The losing party has one month (two months for a foreign party) to launch an appeal against the first instance decision. Once in the hands of the court of appeal, the parties would basically go through the same stages of procedure as in the first instance. Appeal procedures would take between 18 months and three years. A final appeal to the Supreme Court can always be launched but can only be based on points of law.[122] The Supreme Court judges may well take two to three years before reaching a decision.[123]

V. Defences

The defendant of an infringement action would have different means of defending himself against the claim of infringement. First of all the defendant may argue that the action should fail on procedural grounds, such as lack of standing. Defences in law would include, for example, non-commercial use, exhaustion or, of course, non-infringement.

---

[120] In a very recent decision, the Supreme Court confirmed the discretionary power of the judge to freely decide to determine the deposit of a bond: Supreme Court, 20 May 2003, 2003 PIBD 771-III-439.

[121] *See* P. Véron, "Patent Infringement Litigation in France", *supra* note 5.

[122] Chances of success in the Supreme Court are not particularly high. About 85% of all cases are dismissed: P. Véron, *supra* note 4.

[123] For further details on the appeal and the "cassation" proceedings, *see* P. Véron, "Patent Infringement Litigation in France", *supra* note 5, 402–403.

Articles 64–70 New Code of Civil Procedure deal with counterclaims. In particular, the nullity of the patent would customarily be raised as a counterclaim. It should be noted, however, that the defendant can only raise the counterclaim of nullity for those patent claims he is supposed to have infringed. Counterclaims of nullity pose a great risk to the patentee, as the judge has to decide about the counterclaim as a matter of law. A decision on nullity of the patent has absolute effect.[124] Where nullity is alleged as a mere estoppel rather than a counterclaim, matters are less dangerous for the patentee, as the judge in such cases might simply dismiss the action for lack of infringement without expressly examining the validity of the patent.[125]

Among the other defences which may be invoked by the alleged infringer, two deserve particular mention: the right of "prior personal possession" of the invention and the experimental use exception.

The "prior personal possession" exception, as opposed to the right based on prior use of the invention, confers the right to third parties acting in good faith who are in the "intellectual" possession of the invention in order to work it. [126] In other words, proof that the technical knowledge of the invention is the sole requirement. Even if a large part of the academia is still in favour of this traditional solution, a new school of thought advocates the actual prior "use".[127] Existing case law is also inconsistent in this respect.[128] For the Community patent, the rules governing the exemption will be subject to some major amendments.[129]

---

[124] One of the most important changes of the 1978 Patent Act concerned the extent of a declaration of nullity that prior to that date only took effect between the parties, a longstanding principle of French law. *See* J. Mousseron & A. Sonnier, "Le droit français nouveau des brevets d'invention" (The New French Law on Patents) 131 (Collection CEIPI, Litec, 1978). *See also* J. Foyer, "Effets des jugements et autorité de la chose jugée en matière de propriété industrielle" (Effect of Decisions and the Scope of Matters Decided in Intellectual Property Cases), in "Mélanges dédiés à P. Mathély" 157 (Litec, 1990).

[125] From the statistics reported by P. Véron, it follows that when the validity of the patent are in dispute, 23% of the French patents have been declared null, while the figures for European patents is 15%.

[126] The "prior personal use" exemption is ruled by Art. L. 613–9 IPC. The right based on prior use of the invention assumes the effective use or the effective and serious preparation of such use before the filing date of the patent. *See* German Patent Act, § 12.

[127] C. Le Stanc, following Roubier, advocates "if not a real exploitation, at least a clear attempt to implement the invention or its 'industrial' control'", C. Le Stanc, "L'acte de contrefaçon de brevet d'invention" (Patent Infringement), Librairies techniques 1977, 197, No. 224. The opposite is argued by P. Mathély, "Le nouveau droit français des brevets d'invention", *supra* note 66, 298; J. Foyer & M. Vivant, "Le droit des brevets", *supra* note 1, 319; F. Pollaud-Dulian, "Droit de la propriété industrielle" (Industrial Property Law) 235, No. 549 (Montchrestien 1999).

[128] *See* Paris District Court, 31 May 2000, 2001 Dossiers Propriétés Intellectuelles I, 1, where the court required an "industrial" control of the invention for a prior use right. Contrary: Paris District Court, 9 March 2001, 2001 PIBD 728-III-495.

[129] The 2000 Proposal for Council Regulation on the Community Patent gives rise to

The experimental use exemption was introduced in French law in 1968, and is now regulated by Art L. 613–5 IPC. The exemption applies under two conditions. First, the acts must be done for experimental purpose and, second, they must be related to the subject matter of the invention. Traditionally, the first condition excludes acts done with a commercial purpose. While this condition was applied very strictly in the past, the courts will now consider the immediate purpose pursued and the extent of the experiments.[130] More problematical, however, is the assessment of the non-commercial use requirement in the realm of the pharmaceutical industry. The two basic questions being addressed are, first, whether such trials are admissible under the non-commercial use requirement when they are conducted in order to obtain marketing authorisation before the expiration of the patent;[131] and, second, whether such trials comply with the subsequent legal condition requiring the experiments to be "related to the subject matter of the patented invention". At the very outset, French courts denied the experimental character of such experiments due to the commercial purpose of obtaining marketing authorisation.[132] Subsequently, in the Allen & Hanburys cases which ran between 1998 and 1999, the courts adopted a new approach. The crucial starting point for these decisions was the nature of the marketing authorisation that according to the Supreme Court was

---

a certain optimism in this respect. Art. 37 of the Agreement Relating to Community patents done at Luxembourg in 1989 (89/695/EEC, OJ 1989 L 401, 30 December 1989, 1) gave the Contracting States the choice to provide for a right based on a prior use or a right of personal possession. With the 2000 proposal on the Community patent, for the first time, the European legislature has come out in favour of the right based on prior use (Art. 12), coming very close to the German approach. *See* L. Brüning-Petit, "L'exception du droit fondé sur une utilisation antérieure en droit allemand: un modèle pour le droit communautaire des brevets ?" (The Right Based on a Prior Use Exception in Germany: A Model for the Community Law of Patents?), 2003 Propriété industrielle No. 7–8, 10. It remains to be seen if this position will have some influence on French practice.

[130] *See* Lyon Appeal Court, 5 March 1992, Dossiers Brevets 1992, I, 6; Paris District Court, 1 September 1999, 2000 PIBD 691-III-57; Paris District Court, 2 July 1997, 1998 Dossiers Brevets, I, 6.

[131] *See* P. Véron, "Les essais cliniques en vue de la mise sur le marché d'un médicament générique ne peuvent être conduits avant l'expiration des droits de propriété industrielle sur le médicament princeps – Commentaire de l'art. 31 de la loi no. 99-1140 du 29 décembre 1999 de financement de la sécurité sociale pour 2000" (Clinical Trials Seeking the Marketing of Generics Cannot be Carried Out Before the Expiration of the Industrial Property Rights on the Patented Drug – Commentary on the Art. 31 of the Law No. 99-1140 of 29 December 1999 on the financing of the French public welfare system for the year 2000), 2000 RDPI, No. 107, 31; P. Véron, "Contrefaçon de brevets d'invention – Usage expérimental et essais cliniques" (Patent Infringement – Experimental Use and Clinical Trials), 1999 RDPI, No. 104, 15.

[132] *See* the Dioriven case, Paris District Court, 8 July 1982, 1982 PIBD 312-III-235, confirmed by Paris Appeal Court, 27 November 1984, 1985 PIBD 366-III-118.

non-commercial and the tests non-infringing.[133] This stance was adopted based on Arts. L 613–3 and L 613–4 IPC which define the scope of infringing activity by specifying the acts constituting prohibited use of the invention and provide an exhaustive list of the infringing acts: clearly, "marketing authorisation" as such is not an act exclusively reserved to the patentee. The courts then had to interpret which kind of trials would comply with the second legal requirement. This issue is of particular importance for bio-equivalency trials. At a more general level, courts are used to making a distinction between experiments made "on" the invention, which permit testing or improving the invention, and those made "with" the invention. According to established case law, only the first is admissible.[134] Three recent decisions handed down by the Paris District Court have provoked, however, a flurry of protest.[135] In all three cases, the Paris court strained existing legal rules by exempting bio-equivalency trials from infringement. The French doctrine unanimously takes the view that the Court misinterpreted and misapplied the letter of the law. Although all these commentators noted the efforts of the court in striking a balance between the interests of the pharmaceutical industry, the generic industry and public health, they all opine that the decision whether to exempt clinical trials can only be resolved by the legislature.[136] Even if none of these three decisions have been appealed, they undoubtedly are decisions of the greatest importance for the future. This is especially true when one considers the worldwide debates on the lawfulness of bio-equivalency trials and the interest of the European Commission in modifying the European Directive on the Community code relating to medicinal products for human use in order to permit such trials before the expiration of the patent.[137]

---

[133] *See* Supreme Court, 24 March 1998, Bulletin civil IV, No. 110, 88, Paris District Court, 30 January 1998, 1998 PIBD 653-III-244 and Paris District Court 1 September 1999, 2000 PIBD 691-III-57.

[134] *See* the recent decision of the Paris District Court, 3 July 2002, 2003 PIBD 758-III-93.

[135] *See* Paris District Court, 20 February 2001, 2001 PIBD 729-III-530. This approach has been followed in two subsequent decisions: Paris District Court, 12 October 2001, 2002 PIBD 739-III-155, and Paris District Court, 25 January 2002, 2002 PIBD 747-III-342.

[136] *See, i.e.* the very critical commentary of Cousté & Jonquières, "L'exception de recherche en France dans le domaine pharmaceutique: une solution encore à l'essai" (The Research Exemption in France in the Pharmaceutical Sector: A Solution Being Still Tested), 2002 Propriété industrielle 8.

[137] If the overhaul of the Directive on the Community code relating to medicinal product for human use (2001/83/EC of the European Parliament and of the Council of 6 November 2001), and especially of Art. 10-4 proposed by the Commission on 26 November 2001 would succeed, the generic industry could carry out clinical trials on and with the patented substance before the expiration of the patent.

VI. Remedies

The purpose of the whole infringement action is certainly to obtain appropriate remedies. While criminal sanctions were reintroduced in 1993,[138] civil sanctions are the most common. The French system distinguishes between two kinds of sanctions.

1. Sanctions for Restoring the Patentee's Monopoly

There are three remedies which are often granted simultaneously. First, there is injunctive relief as "the natural consequence of finding infringement".[139] In order to give this relief more effect, the injunction is often accompanied by fixed monetary fines in the case of an infringement.[140] Second, follows confiscation of the infringing goods under Art. L. 615–7 IPC, which can be obtained as a remedy to prevent further infringement.[141] For the request to be granted, confiscation has to be necessary in order to stop the infringement, while the value of objects confiscated would be taken into account when calculating damages and interest.[142] The scope of confiscation is limited to those objects in possession of the infringer himself from the time the order is published, and does not extend to infringing objects in the possession of third parties.[143] Finally, the court may order

---

[138] As already explained above, this article does not further elaborate on the enforcement through criminal means. For the sake of completeness, it should be mentioned that criminal sanctions are stipulated in Art. L. 615–14 and L.615-14-1 IPC. The maximum penalty for infringement is a sentence of two years or a maximum fine of 1 million French francs. The higher sanctions would normally be imposed on repeat infringers.

[139] *See* J. Foyer & M. Vivant, "Le droit des brevets" (Patent Law) 349 (Collection Thémis, PUF, 1991).

[140] This particular form of enforcement is currently governed by the Act on the Execution of Decisions of 9 July 1991 (Law No. 91-650, Arts. 33–37). The fine can be calculated in two ways, either through the objects sold or manufactured in defiance of the order, or through the days or months of non-compliance. Contrary to German law, the fine has to be paid to the right holder and not to the court. For this problem, *see* J.P. Stenger, "Sanctions de la contrefaçon – Rétablissement du monopole – Réparation du préjudice – Sanctions pénales (Sanctions for Patent Infringement – Remedies – Criminal Sanctions), Jurislasseur Brevets, Fasc. 4680, No. 13 *et seq*.

[141] Confiscation of infringing goods is pronounced in less than 9% of the cases: *See* E. Belfort, "L'indemnisation des préjudices en matière de contrefaçon: la pratique des tribunaux en France" (Remedies Available for Damages Caused by the Infringement of IP Rights: Practice of the French Courts), 2000 Revue internationale de la propriété industrielle et artistique (RIPIA), No. 201, 17. (This statistic only relates to the cases brought before the Paris court of first instance.)

[142] *See* the decision of the Supreme Court, 27 January 1977, 1977 Annales de la propriété industrielle 14.

[143] Confiscation extends to the objects directly infringing, to objects obtained by using a protected process as well as to objects through which infringement is meant to be committed.

publication of the decision against the infringer.[144] Although no longer explicitly provided for by law,[145] the order for publishing a decision would still be made by the courts. Request for the order must be made by the infringed party at the expense of the infringer. There is a limit on the expenses of publication (€3,850 to €4,600 per publication) to be borne by the infringer and, on average, publication would be ordered in three daily newspapers.[146] Orders for publishing the decision is pronounced in 56% of the cases.[147] Before proceeding with the publication, it is advisable to wait until the decision has become final and the right of review of the defendant is exhausted, otherwise the publication may be qualified as a civil wrong for which the plaintiff might be liable.[148]

2. Damages as Compensatory Measures

According to Art. L. 615–1, second para., IPC, "the infringement entails the responsibility of its author". Liability is based on the general tort provisions of Art. 1382 *et seq.* Civil Code, which basically means that all damages incurred by the infringement should be properly compensated, yet only to the extent that such damages have been a certain and measurable consequence of the infringement. They are no legal provisions relating to the assessment of such damages. In particular, the patentee is not allowed to claim the infringer's profits as damages, and, in practice, French courts are not particularly generous in awarding damages.[149] To the extent that indemnification is based on general principles of civil law mentioned above, the calculation by the judge cannot be made subject to a control by

---

[144] The exact doctrinal nature of an order for publishing a decision is still somewhat disputed. It may either be a preventive measure, or a compensatory one. It might be preferable to review the order as both a sanction against the infringer and a compensatory measure to clear up market confusion. On this debate, *see* C. Lalanne-Gobet, "Publication judiciaire des décisions en matière de contrefaçon" (The Order for Publication of a Decision on Infringement), 1999 JCP, ed. Entreprise 1091.

[145] Contained in the Law of 1844, the remedy was no longer provided for in the Patent Act of 1968.

[146] It is noticeable that these rules are not strictly observed by the courts. *See, i.e.* Strasbourg District Court, 4 February 2002, 2002 PIBD 747-III-343, where the judges ordered the publication of the decision in five newspapers, but limited the expenses of publication to €2,000 per newspaper.

[147] *See* E. Belfort, "L'indemnisation des préjudices en matière de contrefaçon: la pratique des tribunaux en France", *supra* note 141, 17.

[148] *See* Paris Appeal Court, 28 September 2001, 2002 PIBD 732-III-619.

[149] While in the past a good number of courts ruled to the contrary based on the principle of *restitutio in integrum*, an approach also favoured in academic writings (*e.g.* E. Pouillet, "Traité des brevets d'invention" (Commentary on Invention Patents) 905 (ed. Marchal et Billard, 1899), the new Patent Act of 1968 does not leave any doubt about the fact that the infringer's profits cannot be claimed. This was already held by a decision of the Appeal Court of Paris, 22 February 1963, 1963 Annales de la propriété industrielle 284, and confirmed by the Supreme Court, 13 January 1971, 1971 Dalloz 147.

the Supreme Court. The judge may thus arrive at a global figure of indemnification, or request an expert opinion on this matter.[150]

In order to calculate damages incurred by the patentee or the licensee, French law would allow for a calculation of either loss of profits or damages incurred.[151]

a) Lost profits

When calculating lost profits, the courts first and foremost would determine the basis on which damages will be assessed. This operation, consisting of ascertaining the amount of counterfeit goods and the extent of infringement, leads to the assessment of the aggregate infringement value, commonly called the *masse contrefaisante*. This task is virtually always entrusted to a court-appointed expert.[152] The assessment of the *masse contrefaisante* is principally based on the infringer's turnover,[153] including all infringing goods manufactured, sold or imported to France, limited only by the prescription period of three years, according to Art. L. 618-8 IPC. This would also include additional or spare parts in the case of a complex apparatus. In this case, the court will determine whether the apparatus including the patented part can be considered as a "commercial unit" (*le tout commercial*). This is the case where the infringing object would not be sold independently from such parts.[154] In a very recent decision, the French Supreme Court made clear that the *masse contrefaisante* consists of all infringing goods on the date upon which the decision related to the damages was taken and not the date on which the *saisie-contrefaçon* was carried out.[155]

Furthermore, when calculating lost profits, French courts make a distinction between a patent that has been exploited by the patentee and one that has not.

If the patentee uses his patent, lost profits are calculated based on the amount of counterfeit goods to which the loss of turnover and the amount of lost profits are added. The loss of turnover is determined by various factors which are applied quite flexibly, such as the quality of inventive step of the patented products. When the rule of *le tout commercial* is applied, only those

[150] For a critical view on the system of damages, *see* J.P. Martin, *supra* note 20, at 9.

[151] *See* C. Le Stanc & L. Petit, "Sanctions for Patent Infringement in France: Injunctive Relief and Damages", *supra* note 116, 355–357.

[152] However, the courts generally refuse to appoint an expert when the patent right holder fails to prove damages: *see, i.e.* Paris Appeal Court, 27 October 2000, 2002 Revue du Droit de la Propriété Intellectuelle (RDPI), No. 134, 39. In this case, the infringement was characterised by the exhibition of the patented invention at a fair. The invention had not been commercialised.

[153] In a 2000 decision, the Supreme Court took the opportunity of asserting this principle: Supreme Court, 24 October 2000, 2001 PIBD 716-III-125. *See* also Paris Appeal Court, 6 June 2001, 2001 PIBD 730-III-559.

[154] The above principle was established by a decision of the Supreme Court in 1897 and recently affirmed by a decision of the Paris Appeal Court of 19 November 1997, 1998 PIBD 651-III-189.

[155] *See* Supreme Court, 11 February 2003, 2003 PIBD 766-III-313.

profits are taken into account that measure the relative value of the invention in the assembled product. Finally, the ultimate figure for damages is arrived at by multiplying the amount of lost sales with the profit that would have been made for each product. Yet other elements can also be of importance, such as the market position of the patentee, the production capacity, the commercialisation art, etc.[156]

If, on the other hand, the patentee does not exploit the patented invention, damages are calculated on the basis of a licensing fee which the infringer would have had to pay in order to use the invention lawfully. Nor can the patentee, who does not exploit the patent, claim any damages incurred by his licensee,[157] who in such cases could intervene in the infringement action in order to claim damages on his own behalf. In such cases, the extent of the infringement is calculated on the basis of the infringer's turnover multiplied by a rate determined by the court as compensatory fee.[158] In view of a number of academic writers for whom "such handling of matters lends support to infringement",[159] recent decisions have increased the licensing fees awarded.[160] Note that the rate may occasionally be revised downwards in the event the patented invention has been improved by the infringer.[161]

However, the distinction between these two methods of calculating damages is not strictly observed by the courts. It may actually happen that the court grants both a lump sum calculated on the basis of the lost profits and a licensing fee to the patentee who is working its patent. In such cases, the court will consider the production capacity of the patentee, and compensation will be based on royalties even for those infringing items the patentee would never have had the capacity to produce.[162]

---

[156] The same parameters will also be taken into account for the determination of the damages suffered by the exclusive licensee or distributor in cases where the patentee does not work its patent itself. *See* Paris Appeal Court, 12 October 2001, 2002 PIBD 733-III-1.

[157] Decision of the Paris Appeal Court, 2 March 1971, 1972 Dalloz 45, also reprinted in "Les innovations de la loi du 2 janvier 1968 en matière de brevets d'invention. Strasbourg Colloquium, 23 to 25 September 1971" (The New Patent Act of 2 January 1968) 194–195 (Collection CEIPI, Litec, 1972).

[158] The court would take into account already existing licensing agreements for the same invention or licensing rates in the same field of technology, or simply make an informed guess. *See, i.e.* Paris District Court 7 May 2001, 2001 Revue Internationale de la Propriété Intellectuelle et Artistique (RIPIA), No. 204.

[159] *See, e.g.* J. Foyer & M. Vivant, "Le droit des brevets" (Patent Law) 352–353 (Collection Thémis, PUF, 1991).

[160] The decision of the Supreme Court, 19 February 1991, 1991 Annales de la propriété industrielle 4, is along that line. Yet academic writers do not seem to support this view wholeheartedly. *See, e.g.* J.M. Mousseron, "Brevets d'invention" (Invention Patents) 1999 JCP, éd. Entreprise, 413.

[161] *See* Paris Appeal Court, 6 June 2001, 2001 PIBD 730-III-559.

[162] *See* Paris Appeal Court, 13 June 2003, 2003 PIBD 775-III-563. This decision deserves particular mention because it offers very good guidance on how French courts assess damages.

b) Loss

Indemnification for damages actually incurred would take into account two elements: the attack on the monopolistic right as such, including a prospective market confusion and a depreciation of the invention, and the damages incurred in enforcing such right. Yet the patentee would have to show that damages with respect to these two positions as mentioned above can be distinguished from the position of lost profits.[163]

As to the expenses for enforcing the patent right, French law distinguishes between the expenses awarded to the successful patentee as court costs – *les dépens* – under Art. 695 New Code of Civil Procedure, and those the patentee has incurred in addition thereto, *les frais irrépétibles*. The latter are, for example, attorneys' fees, fees of patent attorneys, expenses for expert opinions, etc. Reimbursement of these can be requested based on Art. 700 New Code of Civil Procedure and is often much lower than the real costs. As Mr. Véron outlined, the court costs "become practically symbolic, since the official rate has not been upgraded for more 40 years". In fact, they amount to €200 to €300 in first instance and between €3,000 and €5,000 for appeals.[164]

Most of damages granted by the courts are less than €76,000. In only three of the 94 reported cases would the damages and interest exceed €770,000.[165]

Last but not at least, it should be mentioned that the provisional enforcement of the judgment may be requested by a party. Contrary to the German law, such measure is discretionary, and provisional enforcement will only be pronounced by the judge if the circumstances justify it.[166] Furthermore, when the infringement has been established and when the calculation of compensation requires an expertise, the judge may allow an interim payment of damages to the patentee.[167] The amount of this is freely determined by the

[163] A more detailed account on the questions involved concerning the attack of a monopolistic right in terms of damages is given by C. Le Stanc & L. Petit, "Sanction for Patent Infringement in France: Injunctive Relief and Damages", *supra* note 116, 356 and J.P. Stenger, "Sanctions de la contrefaçon", *supra* note 140, Fasc. No. 4680, No. 149 *et seq*.

[164] *See* P. Véron, "Patent Infringement Litigation in France", *supra* note 5, 401. These costs may be higher in cases where a *saisie-contrefaçon* has been carried out (€1,500–€3,000 corresponding to the bailiff's fees). *See also* C. Viël, "Kosten eines Patentverletzungsprozesses und Berechnung des Schadensersatzes in Frankreich" (Patent Litigation Costs and Calculation of Damages in France), 2002 Mitteilungen der deutschen Patentanwälte 412. Attorney's fees vary between €10,000 and €30,000. Since there are no rules governing lawyer's fees at an official rate as in Germany, the fees are calculated per hour. Consequently, the costs will depend on the complexity and the length of the case, but also on the lawyer.

[165] *See* P. Véron, *supra* note 4.

[166] *See* P. Véron, "Patent Infringement Litigation in France", *supra* note 5, 400.

[167] Such measure follows from the "*principe acquis de la contrefaçon*": *see* Douai Appeal Court, 16 March 1998, 1999 RDPI No. 99, 14.

judge, who will consider the evidence already submitted. According to Art. 514(2) New Code of Civil Procedure, such an order is provisionally enforceable.[168]

[168] *See* Paris Appeal Court, 8 October 1997, 1998 PIBD 646-III-31. The court made a strict interpretation of Art. 514 of the New Code of Civil Procedure which governs the provisional enforcement of judgments and states that provisional enforcement may not be implemented without having been ordered. The second limb of the provision makes an exception for, *i.e.* judge's orders granting an interim payment to a creditor.

6
The Enforcement of Patent Rights in the Netherlands

JAN J. BRINKHOF

A. Introduction

It is not easy to explain briefly how patent rights are enforced in the Netherlands for the benefit of foreign readers. But with the greatest of pleasure I shall attempt to do this for my friend Dieter Stauder who has left his mark in the field of comparative law.

B. Brief Outline of the System

I. Judges

Disputes concerning infringement and nullity of patents are judged in the Netherlands by "ordinary" judges who are not part of any special organisation within the judiciary. They share the same background as other judges and do not have to meet special requirements. They are part of the *Rechtbank* (District Court), the *Gerechtshof* (Court of Appeal) and the *Hoge Raad* (Supreme Court). In practice, judges who deal with patent cases also deal with disputes in other fields of intellectual property such as trade mark law, design law, copyright law, and the law of unfair competition. In general there is always some time left for "ordinary" civil proceedings. One could say that patent judges are so-called semi-professionals.

The Hague District Court has exclusive jurisdiction in cases of disputes concerning infringement and nullity of patents. The consequence is that such disputes in all of the instances are only judged in The Hague by the District Court, the Court of Appeal and Supreme Court. This has been the situation since 1987, before which the judges in The Hague were exclusively competent in nullity cases. Only infringement cases were judged in all of the 19 district courts. Disputes concerning employees' inventions are judged by the *Kantonrechter*[1] who generally deals with minor criminal and civil cases

---

[1] Since the fundamental revision of the Code of Civil Procedure (2002) the *Kantonrechter* is no longer a judge of a special local court but a judge with special tasks within the *Rechtbank*. The purpose of the revision is to make the civil proceedings more efficient, less formal and complicated, while the judges should play a more active role.

and enjoys special competence regarding labour disputes. Since disputes concerning employees' inventions are regarded as pertaining to labour law, the *Kantonrechter* has to judge these disputes.

The concentration of patent disputes in The Hague is a result of the view of the legislature that concentration will at least result in judges being more experienced and hopefully also more professional. The tendency is to concentrate cases concerning intellectual property in The Hague. The judges in The Hague are, for example, exclusively competent in certain disputes concerning trademarks and neighbouring rights. The District Court and the Court of Appeal in The Hague are designated respectively as court of first instance and the court of second instance responsible for dealing with disputes regarding Community trademarks.

In the Netherlands the number of judges dealing with patent cases is small: the district court has about four to five and the court of appeal has three, and each have a number of deputy judges. Lawyers, public servants of ministries, members of the Patent Office and university lecturers can function as deputy judges. The judges of the Supreme Court are regarded as generalists.

The patent judges themselves are convinced that specialisation is inevitable as it takes much time to become acquainted with this field of law. Furthermore, since patent cases are almost exclusively pleaded by specialised lawyers, it would be undesirable if judges lag behind these lawyers with regard to expertise. If they do not keep up, there is a risk that they will not completely understand the pleadings and arguments of the lawyers and will be unable to assess them correctly. Inconsistent and inaccurate judgements might be the result.

The court presidents and the boards responsible for the distribution of cases are not always aware of the special nature of patent disputes. Sometimes they do not realise that dealing with patent cases is more difficult and time consuming than the average civil case. This fact is not always taken into account when standards are set for the number of disputes judges are required to hear. There is also some concern about the recruitment of judges interested in patent cases and about their retaining a sufficiently high level of knowledge and experience. Neither is it recommendable for judges to transfer too quickly to other sectors of the courts, as the return on investment in study and courses is insufficient.

Dutch courts would render an annual of 80 decisions per year on patent infringements.

II. Proceedings

The Code of Civil Procedure contains no special procedures regarding patent disputes. The Patent Acts include some particular provisions of minor importance. In practice, however, some special procedures have developed.

1. Proceedings on the Merits

The Code of Civil Procedure has two main procedures for contentious disputes: the proceedings on the merits and summary proceedings.

Proceedings on the merits are mainly in writing. The basic structure is as follows. The plaintiff issues a writ of summons in which he summons the defendant to appear before the judge at a certain time. In this writ, the plaintiff indicates what he will claim on the day of appearance. Furthermore, the writ indicates extensively the legal and factual basis for the claim. Since the revision of the Code of Civil Procedure (2002) the plaintiff has also the duty to mention the defence of the defendant if he is aware of it. In general, the plaintiff and the defendant are bound to disclose all the relevant information as early as possible. If the defendant decides to put forward a defence he files a written reply. At the same time the defendant could formulate a counterclaim. Subsequent to the defendant's reply, the judge is obliged to examine on his own motion whether the case is suitable for a hearing during which parties can give information and try to secure an amicable settlement: personal appearance of the parties (Sec. 131 in connection with Secs. 87 and 88 Code of Civil Procedure). During this hearing the judge is at the very least passive. Many disputes are settled completely or partially during these hearings. In patent cases such hearings do not occur very often. Usually the judge allows the plaintiff to hand in a counterplea. Generally this opportunity is always used by the plaintiff. Finally, the defendant can draft a rejoinder. The parties can then request a judgement or pleadings. During the pleadings stage, the legal aspects of a case are normally explained. In ordinary cases pleadings are exceptional; in patent cases pleadings are the norm.

In practice the rules of the district courts and courts of appeal regarding procedure have been harmonised. These rules restrict the possibilities for the parties to slow down the proceedings, and have streamlined the proceedings themselves.

There have also been some experiments with accelerated proceedings, aimed at reducing the eternal complaints about slow proceedings. In patent cases there have also been some experiments with proceedings of this kind. Characteristic in patent litigation is that at the beginning of the proceedings a strict timetable is set for the exchange of documents and the hearings. Furthermore, there are rules with regard to the submission of documents. The intention is to know beforehand when the court will deliver its decision.

One has to realise that it is often not possible to hand down a final judgement. It may be necessary to hear witnesses or to have the written opinion of experts.

In general, decisions can be appealed. On appeal, *inter alia* mistakes can be rectified. Parties can reduce the extent of the dispute on appeal. Often the case is again dealt with completely. A final appeal can be brought before the Supreme Court on matters of law.

2. Kort geding

Apart from proceedings on the merits, the Code of Civil Procedure contains provisions concerning the *kort geding*. The *kort geding* (sometimes referred to in English as summary or abbreviated proceedings) originates from the French *référé*, but has developed separately. In urgent cases the presiding judge can be asked to grant a provisional measure. The procedure is extremely simple. The plaintiff serves a writ of summons for the defendant to appear at a certain date before the President of the court. The writ of summons contains the claim of the plaintiff and a concise indication of the basis of the claims. During the hearings there is an oral explanation from the plaintiff where the defendant can defend himself. The presiding judge gives his written decision with the grounds therefore within one or two weeks. Appeal and final appeal are possible. The most important characteristics of *kort geding* are:

- the procedure is informal;
- the presiding judge is active and tries to reach practical solutions with the parties;
- legal rules of evidence do not apply to the *kort geding;*
- orders or injunctions are strengthened by "*dwangsom*" (French: *astreintes*), penalty sums to be paid to the plaintiff by the defendant who breaches the orders or injunctions;
- appeal does not suspend the execution of the judgement.

In general, the law does not require proceedings on the merits after the *kort geding*. However in patent cases (and in cases concerning intellectual property rights mentioned in the TRIPS Agreement) this is different. If injunctions are granted the judge determines a reasonable period within which the plaintiff should commence proceedings on the merits (Sec. 260 Code of Civil Procedure). The provisional measures cease to have effect, if proceedings leading to a decision on the merits of the case are not initiated within that period. This Section was incorporated in the Code of Civil Procedure after the European Court of Justice ruled that the Dutch *kort geding* is a provisional measure within the meaning of Art. 50(6) TRIPS Agreement[2] and after the European Court of Justice ruled that national courts should interpret their law as much as possible in conformity with Art. 50(6) TRIPS Agreement.[3]

The President usually makes a prognosis on the outcome of the proceedings on the merits.[4] This outcome and the balancing of the interests of the

[2] ECJ 16 June 1998 (C-53/96), [1998] E.C.R I-3603, 1999 Nederlandse Jurisprudentie 240 (*Hermès*), 30 IIC 292 (1999).

[3] ECJ 14 December 2000 (C-300/98, C-392/98), [2000] E.C.R. I-11307 – *Tuk v. Dior* and *Assco v. Layher.*

[4] See for example Supreme Court, 21 April 1995, 1996 Nederlandse Jurisprudentie 462 (*Boehringer*), 29 IIC 699 (1998) – *Recormon.*

parties is decisive for the question of whether an immediate measure is appropriate.

The presiding judge uses the *kort geding* to a large extent to meet the requirements of speedy justice. The legal requirement of urgency is not interpreted very strictly, and it seldom happens that a President refers the parties to proceedings on the merits.

For patent cases the *kort geding* is inviting and in fact used in about half of all cases although there is a shift to proceedings on the merits since the introduction of Sec. 260 of the Code of Civil Procedure in 2002. A patentee who sees that his patent is infringed, wishes to stop this infringement as soon as possible. An injunction strengthened with an "*astreinte*" can effectively remove an infringer from the market. An advantage of expeditious injunctions is that complicated proceedings concerning damages can be avoided. The *kort geding* contains some risks. Sufficient attention is not always paid to the complexity of the facts of the case. This can be a huge disadvantage for the defendant. The plaintiff can prepare the case thoroughly and choose the right moment to commence the proceedings. The defendant has no choice but to be ready with his defence in a few weeks time. The defendant will not always succeed in replying adequately to the legal and factual aspects. In the *Hoffmann La Roche v. Organon* case, the court of appeal tried to tighten up the reins.[5] This judgement resulted in the parties opting more frequently for proceedings on the merits.

However, the district court for some time has been aware of the above-mentioned disadvantages of the *kort geding*. The district court started an experiment for factually and technically difficult cases to accept the exchange of documents before the oral hearings (*kort geding* with written phase). Such a *kort geding* is quite similar to proceedings on the merits. The question arises whether it is appropriate to create a special *kort geding* for certain types of cases. Are patentees given preference over other litigants? It is better to act according to the intention of the legislature: if the dispute is too complicated, proceedings on the merits will be required. Accelerated proceedings on the merits are a better alternative, as practice shows. Patentees increasingly use this possibility. Therefore the court now has the problem that it can hardly deal with all the cases in due time.

An infringement action on the merits takes about 12 months until a decision is reached. Accelerated procedures bring this down to eight months, while the *kort geding* might take two to three months. For appeals, these take an average of 12 months for normal and eight months for accelerated proceedings. A final appeal adds between one and two years.

---

[5] The Hague Court of Appeal, 12 September 1996, 1996 Intellectuele Eigendom en Reclamerecht 237.

3. Patent Attorneys and Patent Lawyers

In patent proceedings patent attorneys play an important role. Patent attorneys can be employees or independent professionals. Which type of patent attorney acts in a proceeding depends on the size of the companies involved. Only larger companies have their own patent departments. Often parties submit reports of their patent attorneys in the proceedings. In these reports patent attorneys give their opinion on infringement and validity of the patent. It is not exceptional that patent attorneys give their oral opinion during the hearing. This was allowed by law in 1995 (Sec. 54.3 Dutch Patent Act 1910,[6] Sec. 82 Dutch Patent Act 1995[7]). It will not come as a surprise that the reports of the patent attorneys of the parties contradict each other. Patent lawyers play a major role during the oral pleadings in presenting their oral opinion under the supervision of a lawyer. In general, these lawyers are specialised in the field of industrial property. Some lawyers deal mainly with patent cases. The number of patent lawyers is restricted, and they know each other.

All parties are allowed to conduct their own oral pleadings, though this rarely happens, and aptly so, since oral pleadings are an art.

C. Problems Related to Enforcement of Patent Rights

I. Competent Parties

Because of the fact that most procedures involve infringement, plaintiffs in most cases are the patentees (Sec. 43.1 PA 1910 and Sec. 70.1 PA 1995). Licensees are not allowed to commence infringement proceedings except with an agreement with the patentee. Otherwise the licensee can participate in the process when the patentee claims damages or surrender of profits in the name of the licensee.

It is possible that infringement disputes are commenced by persons other than the patentee. This happens when someone wants to obtain a declaration of non-infringement. Such claims are mentioned separately in the Patent Act (Sec. 54.2 PA 1910, Sec. 80.2 PA 1995). These types of infringement procedure are rather rare.

II. Competent Courts

1. National Jurisdiction

As mentioned earlier, The Hague District Court is exclusively competent to judge disputes concerning infringement and nullity of patents, both based on

---

[6] Hereinafter PA 1910.

[7] Hereinafter PA 1995.

the PA 1910, the PA 1995 or patents granted by the European Patent Office (Sec. 54 PA 1910; Sec. 80 PA 1995). The Hague Court of Appeal is exclusively competent for appeals.

2. International Jurisdiction

a) Even if the judge bases his competence on the Brussels Convention, the Regulation on Jurisdiction and the Enforcement of Judgments or the Lugano Convention[8] and suit is brought at the place of domicile of the defendant (Art. 2 Regulation) or the place where the harmful event occurred (Art. 5.3 Regulation), it is likely that The Hague District Court is exclusively competent, even if the place of residence or the place of damages is outside the district of The Hague. This has not been finally decided upon, but corresponds with the rationale of concentrating patent cases in The Hague.

b) In recent years there has been much discussion about the opinions of Dutch courts concerning international jurisdiction. Therefore, I would like to outline the actual situation.

If in a dispute the Regulation is applicable and if the defendant has his place of domicile in the Netherlands, then according to Dutch courts, there is jurisdiction based on Art. 2 of the Regulation. When the defendant is a legal entity, Art. 60 of the Regulation is applicable. This Article refers to international private law. According to Dutch international private law, the place of domicile of a legal entity is not the "*siège réel*" but the registered seat.[9] If the patentee is of the opinion that a defendant having his place of domicile abroad infringes a Dutch patent, the Dutch judge has international jurisdiction on the basis of Art. 5.3 of the Regulation. In the Netherlands it has been assumed that international jurisdiction is restricted to cases of an (imminent) infringement of a Dutch patent.[10] This is in accordance with the judgement of the European Court of Justice's decision *Shevill v. Presse Alliance.*[11]

Art. 5.3 of the Regulation is interpreted narrowly by the court of appeal. The court of appeal is of the opinion that the article is not applicable to requests for a declaration of non-infringement of a Dutch/European patent against a foreign defendant.[12] Of course one could argue that the defendant has the opportunity to summon the plaintiff based on Art. 5.3 of the Regulation for the infringement of a Dutch/European patent before the

---

[8] Hereinafter reference is only made to the Regulation.

[9] The Hague Court of Appeal, 23 April 1998, 1998 Intellectuele Eigendom en Reclamerecht 286 (*Expandable Grafts v. Boston Scientific*).

[10] *See* for example The Hague District Court, 23 December 1998, Bijblad bij de Industriële Eigendom 1999, 39 (*Chiron v. Roche*).

[11] ECJ, 7 March 1995 (C-68/93), [1995] E.C.R. I – 415 (*Shevill v. Presse Alliance*), 29 IIC 96 (1998).

[12] The Hague Court of Appeal, 22 January 1998, 1998 Intellectuele Eigendom en Reclamerecht 135 (*Evans v. Chiron*).

Dutch judge, and the declaration of non-infringement is a mirror image thereto, and thus the plaintiff can summon the defendant before a Dutch judge to obtain a declaration of non-infringement. The Hague Court of Appeal did not agree with this. The court of appeal held that Art. 5.3 of the Regulation is an exception to the general rule of Art. 2 and has to be interpreted narrowly. The court of appeal found support for its view in Art. 14.5 of the Protocol on the Settlement of Litigation concerning the Infringement and Validity of Community Patents.

There has been much discussion about Art. 6.1 of the Regulation. At first sight this article seems to lend itself to *forum shopping* by the patentee who is confronted with the infringement of parallel patents derived from a single European patent by a multinational with subsidiaries in several Member States. An example can explain this. Assume that a European patent has been granted to Philips in which all member states are designated. Assume furthermore that Philips takes the view that Siemens infringes the parallel patent rights, *e.g.* in the Netherlands, Germany, France and the United Kingdom. Siemens has companies in all of these countries. Can Philips summon Siemens Germany, Siemens the Netherlands, Siemens France and Siemens U.K. jointly before a Dutch, German, French or English court based on Art. 6.1 of the Regulation and require all those Siemens companies to stop infringing the parallel patents in all these countries? The district court answered this question in the affirmative. The district court attached much significance to the rationale of Art. 6.1 of the Regulation – avoiding irreconcilable decisions – and to the character of a European patent.

The Hague Court of Appeal decided in *Expandable Grafts v. Boston Scientific* that this interpretation was too wide. The court of appeal assumed that a European patent was not a single patent valid for all countries it has been granted for. A European patent consists of a bundle of national patents. These separate national patents have much in common as they were granted in a single procedure at the European Patent Office in compliance with the provisions and rules of the European Patent Convention, and subsequently subject to harmonised but not identical national patent laws (Arts. 2.2 and 64.1 EPC). On Art. 6.1 of the Regulation the court of appeal ruled that the literal text of this provision does seem to allow a plaintiff to summon defendants from different countries before a judge in a country chosen by the plaintiff. The plaintiff seems to have as many choices as the number of member states where the defendants have their domiciles. The court of appeal disagreed with the result, however, and referred to the European Court of Justice, *Kalfelis v. Schröder.*[13] The European Court ruled "that there must be a connection between the claims against all parties". Furthermore the court of appeal considered whether there was such a connection where the owner of a Dutch patent from a bundle of European patents requested an injunction against a defendant domiciled in the Netherlands who put certain products on the

[13] ECJ, 27 September 1988 (Case 189/87), [1988] E.C.R. 5565.

market, and against a defendant domiciled in France from infringing a French patent from the same bundle by putting an identical product onto the French market. The court of appeal answered this question negatively. Even if judgements in the Netherlands and France were different – which is possible notwithstanding the fact that the same rules of substantive patent law apply – the decisions cannot be said to be irreconcilable with each other. The national patents of a European bundle of patents exist independently of each other. Therefore it is possible that one patent from a bundle is revoked and the others are not. Furthermore, the scope of protection can be different. Patents resulting from a European patent have their past in common, but not their future. In the example discussed here, the patentee who wants to stop infringement of his patents in France and the Netherlands is forced to commence procedures in both countries with the risk that the outcome in both countries may be different. However, with regard to the fundamental meaning of Art. 2 of the Regulation and the exceptional character of Art. 6, the interests of the defendant summoned before a judge in a country of his domicile or seat is more important than the trouble the patentee incurs, particularly taking into account that diverging decisions are within the nature of a European patent. This might be different in the above-mentioned example where the parties belong to the same concern. When different subsidiaries which belong to the same concern market identical products on different markets, this has to be considered as one common action based on a common business strategy. A proper administration of justice requires a simultaneous examination and judgement in such a situation. This should be permissible under Art. 6. However, it does not mean that the plaintiff has the choice of summoning all the subsidiaries of the concern before the court where one subsidiary is located. According to the court of appeal, this would be contrary to legal certainty. An interpretation of Arts. 2 and 6 in accordance with Art. 5.3, which require the plaintiff to bring the suit where the concern's headquarters are located, might be the most preferable. The claims and the court are connected closest here. The advantage of this solution is that only one forum has jurisdiction, and therefore the possibilities of forum shopping are reduced. Recently, the Supreme Court referred preliminary questions to the European Court of Justice about the interpretation of Art. 6.1 of the Regulation.[14]

Art. 22.4 of the Regulation is interpreted by the Dutch courts as not permitting them to revoke a foreign patent. Yet, Arts. 25 and 22.4 are not understood to mean that Dutch courts no longer have jurisdiction over an infringement case involving a foreign patent when the estoppel/counterclaim of nullity is raised.[15] This is contrary to the opinions of the English High Court and Court of Appeal.[16]

---

[14] Supreme Court 19 December 2003 in the case *Roche v. Primus* (not yet published). See Official Journal of the EU of 6 March 2004, C 59/11.

[15] Case *Expandable Grafts v. Boston Scientific*.

[16] *Fort Dodge v. Akzo*, [1998] F.S.R. 222, 29 IIC 927 (1998).

The Dutch courts in this case will stay the proceedings until the foreign judge (or patent office) has decided on revocation, unless the claim for revocation of the patent clearly has no chance of succeeding.[17]

When a Dutch judge has international jurisdiction in proceedings on the merits based on the Regulation, he also has jurisdiction in the *kort geding*.[18] This means that a judge in *kort geding* can issue orders and injunctions with respect to foreign patents. When the defendant argues that the foreign patent is invalid, the presiding judge will hesitate before granting an injunction against infringement. Recently, the district court has taken the position that it has no cross-border jurisdiction in *kort geding*.[19]

Based on Art. 31 of the Regulation, the presiding judge can even grant a provisional order in cases where the judge in the proceedings on the merits is not internationally competent. The judge here assumes that the provisional order will only have effect in the Netherlands.[20] In this case, the judge will also hesitate before granting injunctive relief when the defendant argues invalidity of the patent.

A problem for which there is currently no solution is the so-called "torpedo". An example is the following situation. A company fears that it will be sued for infringement of parallel patents from a European application. It starts proceedings against the patentee by way of a cross-border declaration of non-infringement. It prefers to bring the case before a forum that presumably does not provide an expeditious procedure because the judicial apparatus has become clogged. What happens if the patentee subsequently summons the potential infringer before the Dutch courts?

The Dutch judge assumes that Art. 27 of the Regulation (*lis alibi pendens*) forces him to stay proceedings until the foreign judge has rendered a decision concerning his international jurisdiction as to a cross-border declaration of non-infringement; this principle is known as the torpedo. It is hoped that there will soon be a preliminary question addressed to the European Court of Justice about international competence concerning cross-border decisions for non-infringement. The torpedo can only be used where a national judge declares himself competent to hand down such decisions.[21]

---

[17] *Expandable Grafts v. Boston Scientific.*

[18] *Cf.* ECJ, 17 November 1998 (C-391/95), [1998] E.C.R. I-7091 (*Van Uden*), para. 19.

[19] It seems that the district court becomes more and more reluctant to grant cross-border injunctions. In a recent decision the district was of the opinion that cross-border injunctions should not be ordered when there is no literal infringement but infringement on the basis of the doctrine of equivalence. See The Hague Court of Appeal, 3 July 2003, *Medinol v. Cordis* (not yet published).

[20] *See* ECJ in *Van Uden*, paras. 37–41.

[21] The Hague Court of Appeal (22 January 1998, 1998 Intellectuele Eigendom en Reclamerecht 135 (*Evans v. Chiron*) held that it has no international jurisdiction as to claims against foreign defendants for a cross-border declaration of non-infringement.

III. Preparation for Trial

In Dutch law no measure such as the Belgian or French *saisie contrefaçon* is available. Neither is discovery. It is unclear whether Sec. 843a Code of Civil Procedure can serve as a basis for ordering the disclosure of documents that can provide evidence of infringement. There is currently no unambiguous case law on this matter. If it turns out that most judges take the view that the provision is insufficient for such an order, I suppose that the legislature has to take action in view of Art. 50(1)(b) TRIPS Agreement.

Pursuant to Art. 46 TRIPS Agreement, Sec. 70(6) PA 1995 allows the patentee to request the seizure or destruction of any infringing products. Furthermore, the patentee can request the confiscation of materials and equipment principally used for the production of those products.[22]

The patentee can request the court to hear witnesses as to the facts and circumstances which are of importance for determining infringement and nullity before commencing infringement proceedings, and before the defendant commences revocation proceedings. The general rules for the testimony of witness hearings (Secs. 186–193 Code of Civil Procedure) apply to these cases. Since 1987 the patentee and third parties may also request the court to order an expert opinion or a provisional visit and inspection before commencing proceedings, Secs. 202–207 Code of Civil Procedure. These procedures are rarely used, however, perhaps due to a lack of awareness by practitioners. Exploring them might be worthwhile, however.

A claim for damages or payment of profits requires an intentional infringement of the patent. It is not sufficient that the supposed infringer is aware of the patent's existence. Rather, he must be aware of infringment, which is a question of intent. It is questionable whether this legal rule is in conformity with Art. 45(1) of the TRIPS Agreement, which contains less strict conditions for liability ("had reasonable grounds to know"). Recently, the Supreme Court has decided that the courts should directly apply Art. 45(1) of the TRIPS Agreement.[23] Adducing intentional infringement is difficult. The legislature has gone some way to ease the patentee's burden of proof in that intentional infringement is assumed when the infringer is alerted by a bailiff's notification that he is infringing the patent (Sec. 43(2) PA 1910, Sec. 73(3) PA 1995). Such notification can be issued before the proceedings commence or before receipt of a writ of summons

Traditionally, the writ of summons is rather brief as to the legal basis of the claims.[24] What is actually being claimed is described comprehensively. Where injunctive relief is claimed, a general wording is sufficient: the patentee requests the judge to stop the defendant from infringing his patent. When

---

[22] Remarkably enough, the PA 1910 has not been changed in this respect.

[23] Supreme Court 19 December 2003 in the case *Roche v. Primus* (not yet published).

[24] This has changed since the revision of the Code of Civil Procedure in 2002.

the judge grants this claim, he normally renders an injunction in such general terms without a more detailed description of the infringement. The Supreme Court concurred with this approach.[25] The scope of such a general injunction is limited to acts which doubtlessly infringe the patent, *inter alia*, by taking into account the grounds on which the judgement is based. Also the reply to the writ used to be rather brief.[26] The written summary of arguments forms part of the procedural documents.

IV. The Trial

The pleadings in a trial follow after the parties have exchanged the written documents. The pleadings are conducted by lawyers rather than patent attorneys.

Occasionally, patent attorneys will give their opinion. The participation of the judge during the pleadings largely depends on his personality. Some judges are active: they ask questions and request that lawyers clarify or explain certain issues. Judges also ask the parties whether they intend to uphold their assertions, claims and defences in full. Some judges ask whether the parties can reach agreement on the whole dispute or parts thereof. Other judges are more passive. They take the view that it is not their task to be active during civil proceedings: the parties determine the scope of the legal dispute, judges render a decision. Without any doubt, the number of active judges is increasing. The legislature has given judges more leeway in taking an active role in proceedings.

The judges can summon the parties in order to request information and to try to settle the dispute amicably (Secs. 87 and 88 Code of Civil Procedure). The judge can request the parties to exchange certain documents. Furthermore, the judge can require evidence as regards certain assertions that are the subject of dispute. There can be evidence by exchanging written documents, but normally witnesses are heard under oath. Normally the judge starts examining the witnesses, followed by questions of counsel for the plaintiff and defence. The witnesses' testimonies are included in the official court report.

The judge can also ask independent experts to testify. In practice, the parties make suggestions as to the experts to be appointed, and the questions to be answered by them. After submitting the (normally) written report, the parties may submit their written comments. The judge can set a hearing for the experts to explain their report and the parties to raise questions. Experts are often appointed when the inventive step of an invention is in dispute. Hearing witnesses would be necessary when infringement and prior use is in dispute. Disputes involving the infringement of a patented process create the

---

[25] Supreme Court, 3 January 1964, 1964 Nederlandse Jurisprudentie 445 (*Lexington*).

[26] This has changed since the revision of the Code of Civil Procedure in 2002.

most problems. The possible infringer here would like to avoid the evidence of witnesses who may inform the patentee about the defendant's trade secrets.

V. Defences

In infringement proceedings some defences are obvious: the defendant will argue that there has been no infringement. A combination of these two defences is most common. The revocation argument can be raised as an estoppel or as a counterclaim aimed at the complete or partial revocation of the patent. In the first case, the infringement suit would simply be dismissed, as infringing an invalid patent is impossible. In the second case, which is more common, the judge would declare the patent completely or partially invalid, *erga omnes*, apart from discussing the infringement claim. In general, the judge will concentrate on questions of validity before determining the question of infringement.

It regularly occurs that proceedings for the revocation of a parallel patent from the bundle of European patents are commenced in another country or before the European Patent Office while an infringement action is pending in the Netherlands. The Dutch judge has several options in such a situation. He can stay the counterclaim of revocation until another judge has decided on the matter of validity. The judge is not obliged to do this, however, and can decide without having regard to cases pending in other countries. When revocation is used as a defence in *kort geding*, the judge can assess whether the patent will be revoked. When there is a real possibility that the patent will be revoked, the judge will refuse the request for an injunction.

When the patent covers a product, infringing devices would normally be in circulation. It is more difficult when the patentee claims that the defendant infringes a patented process: when the allegation is denied, the patentee has to furnish proof.

In revocation proceedings, the question of inventive step almost always has to be answered. Here, the "problem-solution" approach is used. Judges are aware of the disadvantages of this approach, which is, in the words of Lunzer, "tainted with hindsight".[27] Defendants who come up with the same revocation arguments as they have raised without success in opposition procedures or in revocation procedures in foreign countries cannot hope to succeed. It would be necessary to convince the judge that the Opposition Division, the Technical Board of Appeal or the foreign court were erroneous in their decision. Of course, other grounds for revocation under Art. 138 EPC can also be invoked.

---

[27] Singer, "The European Patent Convention", No. 56.05 (revised English edition by Lunzer, London 1995).

When dealing with the question of inventive step, the judge will regularly ask an independent expert to compile a report. The judge will ask the parties for advice on such expertise.

It should be further mentioned that Sec. 56 PA 1910 and Sec. 87 PA 1995 require the Patent Office (Bureau for Industrial Property) to provide the judge with all the information and technical advice necessary in adjudicating a certain case. Such advice and information are deemed equivalent to a technical expertise under Secs. 194–200 Code of Civil Procedure. Such requests are mostly for foreign patents. The advantages are the independence of the Patent Office, and the fact that no additional costs are incurred.

Finally, it should be noted that the European Patent Office is sometimes asked for advice based on Art. 25 EPC.

In infringement proceedings the main question is generally whether the product or the process is within the ambit of the scope of the patent. Case law is based on the Protocol on the interpretation of Art. 69 EPC. Judges try to find a balance between fair protection of the patentee and a reasonable degree of legal certainty for third parties. Judges of the district court and court of appeal are interested in the decisions of their foreign colleagues. They try to arrive at the same results.

The traditional view held by Dutch courts was to determine the scope of patent protection by the "doctrine of the essence of the invention". Under this doctrine the patent claims were not of vital importance. A broad scope of protection was given in accordance with the former German approach. This approach could not be reconciled with Art. 69 EPC, and the Supreme Court changed course in a 1995 decision.[28] The Supreme Court acknowledged that the "doctrine of the essence of the invention" did not sufficiently take into account legal certainty for the benefit of third parties. Based on the Protocol, the scope of patent protection could not be based solely on this doctrine.

Equivalent variants can be covered by patent protection if, under the formula employed in American case law, these have "substantially the same function, way and result". The American "all elements rule" is also applied in Dutch law. An equivalent variant is not per se covered by the scope of protection. In a recent case, the court of appeal held that the doctrine of equivalence is determined by the Protocol and cannot be used to remedy imprecisely worded patent claims.[29] The Supreme Court did not concur. According to the Supreme Court the Court of Appeal's ruling that it would not be fair, in the event that the claim has been carelessly drafted, to afford protection to the patentee for the obvious equivalent embodiments that

---

[28] Supreme Court, 13 January 1995, 391 (*Ciba Geigy v. Oté*), 28 IIC 748 (1995) – *Contact Lens Liquid.*

[29] The Hague Court of Appeal, 30 March 2000 (*Van Bentum v. Kool*), 2003 Bijblad bij de Industriële Eigendom 99.

were known at the time the claim was drafted cannot be reconciled with the third sentence of the Protocol on the Interpretation of Art. 69 EPC.[30]

VI. Injunctive Relief

In almost all cases, the patentee requests an injunction against the infringer (Sec. 43 (1) PA 1910, Sec. 70 (1) PA 1995, Sec. 3:296 Civil Code). Generally, such a claim is coupled with a request for a "*dwangsom*" (French: "*astreinte*"; German: "*Zwangsgeld*") under Sec. 611a Code of Civil Procedure, obliging the infringer to pay a judicially imposed sum to the patentee for every day he acts in contempt of the injunction, or every infringing product manufactured or used in contempt of that injunction. Therefore, an injunction is an effective means for stopping infringements.

In order to implement Art. 46 TRIPS Agreement, PA 1995 (in Sec. 70 (6))[31] allows for the confiscation or destruction of any objects infringing the patent, together with confiscation of materials and equipment that are used for the production of objects that are infringing.

The following remedies are not specifically mentioned in the Patent Act but are recognised in case law:

- order to withdraw infringing products;[32]
- order to submit a list of customers;[33]
- order to submit invoices and data concerning stock, prices, and the like;
- order to name the supplier;[34]
- order to publish the decision in a newspaper or a magazine;
- order to pay an advance on damages.

Granting these orders is discretionary and will be done by balancing the interests of the parties.

Regrettably, it has become almost standard practice to claim all possible forms of relief in every case. One cannot but escape the impression that models for writs of summons are copied indiscriminately. Patentees seem to be unable to distinguish between everyday competitors and pirates.

In general the request for provisional execution of a decision is very common and granted even if there is an appeal. Whoever executes a decision in

---

[30] Supreme Court, 29 March 2002 (*Van Bentum v. Kool*), 2003 Bijblad bij de Industriële Eigendom 100.

[31] The PA 1910 does not contain a comparable provision.

[32] Supreme Court, 23 February 1990, 1990 Nederlandse Jurisprudentie 664 (*Hameco v. SKF*).

[33] *See supra* note 32.

[34] Supreme Court, 27 November 1987, 1988 Nederlandse Jurisprudentie 1988, 722 (*Cloé v. Peeters*).

kort geding and subsequently gets the case dismissed in proceedings on the merits is responsible for any damages.[35]

It is not usual for the infringer to require the plaintiff to post a bond as security when provisionally enforcing a decision.

The party against whom judgement has been given has to pay the costs of the proceedings of the defendant. These are only a small part of the actual costs that are not recoverable. Costs are calculated based on the acts of procedure and the financial interests involved. An advantage of this reimbursement scheme can be that costs are not much of an issue when encouraging an amicable settlement. In general, the parties agree to pay their own costs when a dispute is settled.

VII. Damages

Damages are awarded on condition that intent can be proven (Sec. 42 (2) PA 1910, Sec. 70 (3) PA 1995). The PA 1910 allows for a claim of damages (which could be the damages actually incurred or an ordinary licensing fee) or, in the alternative, the infringer's profits, Sec. 43 (3) PA 1910. The rationale of this provision is to ease the patentee's burden of proof as the infringer has to render his account, and prevent the infringer from keeping the profits. The patentee does not have to make a preliminary choice,[36] as both can be requested, and the higher amount of the two is awarded.

The corresponding section of the PA 1995, Sec. 70 (4), is worded differently. Here, damages and payment of profits can be claimed. It looks as if the judge can award both claims cumulatively. But this is not likely.[37] There is not much case law on damages and the reliquishment of profits. In most cases, the parties reach a settlement after the question of liability is settled and the defendant is ordered to pay damages in principle.

Therefore, there are no clear guidelines, not even on the calculation of an ordinary licensing fee. The absence of such directives might explain why parties prefer to settle the issue of damages among themselves. Judges welcome this practice. It saves difficult and time-consuming proceedings. But, from the point of view of legal certainty and equality before the law, this situation is certainly undesirable.

D. Final Remarks

In this article, the enforcement of patent rights in court proceedings was discussed. It is of course possible to settle disputes by arbitration. However, my

---

[35] Supreme Court, 16 November 1984, 1985 Nederlandse Jurisprudentie 547 (*Ciba Geigy v. Voorbraak*).

[36] Supreme Court, 9 November 1990, 1991 Nederlandse Jurisprudentie 169.

[37] *Cf.* Supreme Court, 14 April 2000, 2000 Rechtspraak van de Week 111, with respect to Sec. 27a Copyright Act, a provision that is worded in similar fashion.

impression is that this happens very rarely. But maybe something is changing. The present author has been involved in several international arbitrations and alternative dispute resolutions concerning European patents.

Literature

- H. Bertrams, "The cross-border prohibitory injunction in Dutch patent law", 26 IIC 625 (1995)
- Jan J. Brinkhof, "Summary proceedings and other provisional measures in connection with patent infringements", 24 IIC 762 (1993)
- Jan J. Brinkhof, "Between speed and thoroughness: the Dutch 'kort geding' procedure in patent cases", (1996) E.I.P.R. 499
- Jan J. Brinkhof, "Cross-border injunctions: a blessing or a curse", in: International law and the Hague's 750th Anniversary, (ed. W.P. Heere), Den Haag, 1999, 103–110
- A.F.M. Brenninkmeijer, "Judicial organization, in: Introduction to Dutch law" (ed. Chorus et al.), 3rd ed., Kluwer Law International, The Hague/London/Boston 1999, 49
- P.A. Stein, "Civil procedure", in: Introduction to Dutch law (ed. Chorus et al.), 3rd ed., Kluwer Law International, The Hague/London/Boston, 1999, 239
- C. Wadlow, "Enforcement of Intellectual Property in European and International Law", Sweet & Maxwell, London 1998.

7
The Enforcement of Patent Rights in Italy*

GIOVANNI CASUCCI

A. The System of Civil Procedure in General

I. Introduction

The Italian system of Intellectual and Industrial property litigation is characterised by the "continental civilistic approach". That means a strict compliance with the formalities regulated by the national Code of Civil Procedure. The disadvantage of this system is that there is a substantial risk for the action to be dismissed by the judge for reasons of formality (*i.e.* the power of attorney not physically joined to the written complaint). Frequently these formal rules are used by defendants and perhaps too easily accepted by the judges in order to avoid having to solve difficult questions on the merits.

In general, patent enforcement is managed in Italy via civil litigation. In principle, even criminal enforcement is available,[1] nevertheless the criminal liability for an IP infringement strictly depends on the evidence of knowledge of the infringement by the alleged infringer. Therefore, in the case of patents, it is very difficult to collect such evidence (for trade marks or designs it is easier), and frequently a lengthy trial will be concluded without a guilty verdict, even though the infringement has been technically proven. The opportunity to benefit from criminal enforcement is usually better for border enforcement under the latest EC Regulation 1383. For reasons of urgency, it could be easier to file a criminal complaint rather than to serve a writ of summons within the deadline of the ten working days available. Nevertheless, even in these cases, it is more than recommended to initiate a subsequent and parallel civil litigation in order to uphold the Custom suspension order.

II. Structure

The structure of the national system of civil justice is organised in three tiers:

---

* Several decisions quoted here are still unpublished. Nevertheless the author will be more than happy to provide them on demand (gfcasucci@virgilio.it).

[1] According to Sec. 88 Italian Patent Act (*Legge sulle invenzioni industriali RD 29.6.1939 No. 1127*).

1. First Instance

At present, according to Sec. 16 of the law of 12 December 2002 No. 273, the Government received the task to create 12 courts having sections specialising in intellectual property rights by June 2003. Accordingly,[2] as of 1 July 2003 the Courts were selected and will now manage all national IP litigation according to territorial jurisdiction

The law confers to the IP Courts an exclusive jurisdiction on "the judicial enforcement of national and community trade marks, patents, plant varieties, utility models, registered designs, copyrights and unfair competition cases related to IP rights". In relation to the last point, there is not a very clear position on the Court having exclusive jurisdiction on pure cases of know-how, unregistered trade marks, slavish imitation or even unregistered design rights.

Thanks to the new institutional approach, the recently appointed IP judges, coordinated by two very renowned Court of Appeal judges, Mr. Massimo Scuffi and Mrs. Marina Tavassi, decided to publish a review, collecting all the decisions rendered from 1 July 2003 onwards. The review will be in Italian and English, with the first edition expected in November 2004.[3]

The average length of a first instance case is about two-and-a-half years.

2. Appeal

The appeal procedure maintains the structure of a collegial body of three judges to review the decisions rendered by the Court of first instance. Both questions of law and of fact can be freshly dealt with by the territorially competent Court of Appeal (*Corte d'Appello*). While it is not possible to change the writ requests (*domande*) as raised in the first instance, it is possible to ask for an instructing phase aimed at examining evidence not completely or only superficially examined in the first instance. There are 26 courts of appeal in Italy. Of these, the 12 specialised Courts will exclusively manage also the appeal phase. The average length of the appeal proceedings is about two years.

---

[2] By Decree n.168 of 27 June 2003, 12 courts in the following towns were designated: Bari, Bologna, Catania, Florence, Genoa, Milan, Naples, Palermo, Rome, Turin, Trieste, and Venice. These designations are preliminary according to Sec. 16(4), and within two years from the entry in force of the Executive Decree, the Government is entitled to review the number and location of these specialised courts. Therefore, up to July 2005, a modification of the number or location of the Courts would be possible. Even now, it is obvious that Sardinia is underrepresented while there is a duplication in Sicily (Palermo and Catania). Moreover, the major area for border controls (Gioia Tauro, near Reggio Calabria) falls under the jurisdiction of Catania for civil enforcement. Therefore, a modification is to be more than recommended.

[3] A link to the related web site will be available at www.mip.polimi.it/ipm.

3. Supreme Court

The Supreme Court (*Corte di Cassazione*) is located in Rome and its aim is to review the decisions rendered by the lower courts exclusively on matters of law. An appeal court's decision could be overturned for an incorrect interpretation of the law, and would thus be remanded to the lower court. If the question does not require a new evaluation of the evidence or interpretation of the facts, the Supreme Court will decide the matter directly without referring the case back. This court is also competent to decide on conflicts concerning jurisdiction or competence arising among lower courts. The decisions of the Supreme Court are final and can be reviewed only in exceptional cases. The average length of Supreme Court proceedings is about two years.

III. Patent Enforcement

As mentioned above, until 1 July 2003, there were no specialised judges or courts dealing with IP rights in Italy. While certain courts in the last 10 to 20 years acquired some experience in patent enforcement matters, it was only possible to expect a specialist approach in exceptionally few cases. Prior to 1 July 2003, any tribunal was competent for patent infringement cases.

There are several elements that should be considered when evaluating patent enforcement.

1. Supra-National Regulations and National Enforcement

First of all, it is evident that IP rights are one of the most harmonised branches of law in Europe. We have international conventions, EU directives, and EU regulations that oblige all the Member States to comply with a more or less defined body of interpretation of substantive and procedural issues. This substantial achievement of harmonisation could, however, be frustrated by ineffective national implementation and/or by an erroneous application of such laws by the national courts that continue to refer to old concepts and interpretations. Therefore, in the area of patent enforcement there is a risk that the judge will not apply EU legislation as implemented by Italian law according to the generally accepted European interpretation. The consequences are easily understandable. It is thus essential for the attorney to inform[4] the court in litigation briefs and during the hearings about the existence of supra-national regulations, their interpretation by the relevant authorities, and the risk of conflicting interpretations.

[4] The sentence "*Jura novit curia*" thus does not mirror reality, although formally that the judge is informed about the law cannot be called into question.

2. Prevailing Urgent Relief Requests

Usually the enforcement of patents is characterised by the patentee's interest in obtaining an interim injunction. A statistic (limited to the Milan court[5]) compiled in 1996[6] shows that in 81% of patent lawsuits preliminary measures are requested and that 34% of the pending proceedings are declared abandoned within four years. That reveals the main significance and relevance of interim measures for patent enforcement in Italy.

3. The "Presumption of Invalidity" of an Italian Patent

Italian patents are granted without substantive examination. The evaluation of the validity of a national patent or an international patent designating Italy is within the jurisdiction of the judicial authority in the case of litigation. This situation (in addition to the fact that Italian patent applications are not effectively published) tends to encourage the prejudice among experts and judges that an Italian patent could not benefit from the presumption of validity stipulated by the Patent Act. Several cases in the past have shown that many domestic patents were enforced, while in fact during litigation it was easily discovered that these patents were completely null and void for lack of novelty or inventive step. Therefore, judges do not easily grant *ex parte* measures so as to avoid the risk of undue damages to the defendant. The situation is considerably different for the EPC or US patents due to substantive examination.[7]

4. Technical Issues

Patent litigation usually involves technical issues that cannot be easily handled without special expertise in the sector concerned (*e.g.* biotechnology, chemistry or electronics). These cases normally are considered too difficult for the courts to decide without the assistance of technical experts. Normally, this intervention takes time and could prejudice the goal of a speedy procedure or even appear incompatible with a preliminary measure

---

[5] According to Franzosi & De Sanctis, "Italy", in "International Patent Litigation" (1997), "Published decisions in proportion to geographical location are approximately as follows: 55% before the court of Milan, 10% before the courts of Rome, 7% before the courts of Turin, and 25% before other courts", para. 6–11.

[6] Research carried out by the S.P.A.C.E. research centre (University Bocconi Milan), with special financial aid from the European Patent Office (EPO), on: "L'emploi du brevet européen et du brevet national par rapport aux politiques de protection du patrimoine technologique dans les entreprises industrielles italiennes, en faisant attention aux spécificités sectorielles". The part related to enforcement is edited by myself, Giovanni F. Casucci, "La Tutela Giudiziaria in Materia Brevettuale (una analisi a campione)", in "Il brevetto quale tutela" (Giuffrè, 1996).

[7] Recently some courts have not even granted a preliminary injunction on the basis of a European Patent in Italy, expressing doubts about the validity of a European Patent as well.

proceeding. In this regard, recently, some courts[8] decided to request technical experts to give their expertise within a short period of time just to give to the court a likelihood about the existence of the infringement and/or about the validity or not of a patent. This would enable the court to decide on the request for a provisional measure in technically complicated cases within an acceptable time frame.

IV. Lawyers

Litigation usually requires the presence of a lawyer admitted to the bar as a representative before the court. The power of attorney must be in writing and, if relating to a particular case, must be physically attached to the writ of summons. The power of attorney covers both first instance and appeal. For the Supreme Court it is necessary to file a new special power of attorney. In case a foreign natural person or a company, citizen of or with registered office in a member country of the Hague Convention of 5 October 1961, wants to act in Italy, the power of attorney must be apostilled under the procedure set forth in the Hague Convention. The proxy shall be legalised and notarised according to the national provisions of the country.[9]

In Italy there is a vast number of lawyers, yet very few specialised in IP matters.[10] Usually, in patent litigation the lawyers are assisted also by a patent attorney giving assistance on technical issues.

V. Patent Attorneys

There are more than 700 patent attorneys admitted to the National Council of Patent Attorneys.[11] Patent attorneys are not admitted to the bar. They usually manage the filing and prosecution procedures related to patents.

---

[8] Court of Prato, 13 August 2003, North Sails Inc. *v.* Veleria Holm Srl, unpublished; Court of l'Aquila, 9 October 2002, Koninklijke Philips Eletronics NV *v.* Opti.Me.S. S.p.a., in Riv. Dir. Ind. 2003, II, 104; Court of Appeal of Milan, 5 May 1995, Boehringer Mannheim Italia Spa and Boehringer Mannheim GmbHh *v.* Ortho Pharmaceutical Co. Cilag Spa and others, in GADI 3311; Supreme Court, 22 October 1997 n. 10388, Soc. Janssen Cilag *v.* Soc. Boehringer Mannheim, in Giust. Civ. Mass. 1997, 1989; Court of Naples, 27 March 2003, Merloni Progetti Spa and Elettroncia Reverberi Srl *v.* Forel Srl, unpublished; Court of Naples, 16 July 1999, Silex Italia Spa *v.* Fratelli Guzzini Spa, Domo Srl and Casamia in GADI 4090.

[9] According to Art. 4(4) EC Regulation 1348/2000, the apostillation is not necessary for the countries which are part of the European Community, except for Denmark.

[10] Counting the members of the associations AIPPI and LES, and considering other databases (*i.e.* PATNET list of experts), it is safe to say that there are about 100 licensed attorneys dealing with IP litigation matters, grouped in a few law firms.

[11] See the web site www.ordine-brevetti.it.

B. Enforcement Issues

The specific actions related to the patent can be divided into:

a) actions against infringement (enforcement action), and
b) actions against the patent (defensive action).

These two actions, of course, have different plaintiffs, different interests, and different fora.

I. Competent Parties

The **plaintiff**, according to the above mentioned classification, could be a) the patent owner for an enforcement action or b) any third party different from the patent owner for a defensive action.

According to a) (enforcement action), the right to commence an action would normally be vested in the patentee. Nevertheless, this right could also be conferred to a licensee by agreement, or could be invoked by the exclusive licensee in cases where the patent owner does not intervene to defend the patent infringement in the licensee's territory.

It is very important to note the fact that in Italy the enforcement of a patent or any other registered right can be initiated even during the application period (with a warning letter giving notice of the existing patent application prior to the publication 18 months after the priority date). This is a significant difference in comparison to other countries (*i.e.* Germany), where it is impossible to enforce a patent before grant.[12]

According to b) (defensive action), the plaintiff could be any party interested in a declaration of nullity or in a declaration of non-infringement. Also the licensee could be interested in contesting the validity of the patent that is the object of a licence. In principle, also the Public Prosecutor could be entitled to ask for nullification or forfeiture of a patent.[13]

Defensive actions, mainly of non-infringement, are well known as "torpedo"[14] actions. This type of action is based on the rule of *lis pendens* according to the Lugano and former Brussels Conventions.[15] The practical

---

[12] For that reason, complex litigation strategies usually start in Italy at the early stages of a patent in order to react immediately against multi-country infringement cases: Court of Vicenza, 7 February 1996, Mariplast Spa *v.* F.lli Costa Spa, in GADI 3464; Court of Naples, 16 July 1999, Silex Italia Spa *v.* Fratelli Guzzini Spa, Domo Srl and Casamia, in GADI 4090; Court of Milan, 27 January 1992, Zaseves di S. Zanetti *v.* Giovanni Luigi Brignoli, in GADI 2792.

[13] Sec. 78 Italian Patent Act.

[14] The "inventor" of this strategy was Prof. Mario Franzosi, whose article, "*Worldwide Patent Litigation and the Italian Torpedo*", was published in [1997] EIPR 7.

[15] Article 21 provides that when the same action is pending before a court of a Member State, the court of another Member State subsequently seized must, on its own motion (*ex*

advantage deriving from such actions is to try to freeze the enforcement actions in "speedy" countries by moving first with a defensive action (mainly of non-infringement) in a "slow" country. Accordingly, in this case, the second action (by the right owner) in principle has to be suspended until the (very slow) decision of the first seized court.[16]

This strategy (mainly implemented in Italy and Belgium) was not greeted enthusiastically and recently some Italian courts denied their jurisdiction on cross-border effects. In particular, in one case[17] concerning an action for declaration of non-infringement of a European patent with respect to several designated states, the Court of Milan denied jurisdiction on the basis of Art. 5.3 Brussels Convention with regard to the foreign portions of the European patent, limiting its competence over the Italian portion of the European patent concerned.

The **defendant** under a) could be any third party infringing the patent, or under b) the patent owner.

Under a) (enforcement action), the defendant would normally be the infringer. In Italy, the infringer could be any person involved in the infringement (also the local distributor, the retailer, the importer). So, normally suits are directed towards the retailer and the main infringer.

Under b) (defensive action), the defendant would be the patent owner.

II. Competent Court

Due to the fact that there were no specialised courts for IP matters in Italy, jurisdiction was and is currently decided exclusively under territorial aspects. In any case, the implementation of the new law related to the specialised IP courts will limit the territorial choice among the possible competent courts following the previous criteria.

There are, therefore, four possible fora:

a) the forum of the defendant;
b) the forum of the infringement;
c) the forum of the nullity action; and
d) the forum of declaration of non-infringement.

---

officio), decline jurisdiction. The case should be pending between the same parties and have the same object and the same cause of action. Article 22 says that when the two cases are not identical but related, the second court may suspend the proceeding. EC Regulation 44/2001 has implemented the provisions contained in the Brussels Convention which are now binding for all Member States with some slight amendments.

[16] The term torpedo in fact was selected in order to express the peculiar concept of the speediness of this strategy: "It is a well-known principle of sea warfare that an escorted convoy should travel at the speed of the slowest ship. If the various ships travel at their own speed, there will be no convoy and no unity."

[17] Court of Milan, 21 March 2002, Dade *v.* Chiron. The same approach was adopted by the Court of Turin, 13 May 2003, GPC *v.* Filterwerk Mann.

Alternative a) concerns an infringement action that can always be initiated at the domicile of the defendant. Alternative b) concerns an infringement action that allows the plaintiff to pursue a so-called "forum shopping" strategy, trying to find the most convenient forum (for any reason: distance, experience of the court, etc.). Alternative c), the case of a defensive action, makes it mandatory to sue the defendant (patentee) in the forum related to the elected domicile, normally of the patent attorney who filed the patent.[18] Alternative d) normally allows the claim to be raised at the forum of the plaintiff, as a declarative action of non-infringement could be filed either in the forum of the defendant or where the possible damage deriving from an infringement action (alleged groundless) might occur.

The possibility of choosing the most convenient court for one's action has several consequences. First, sending a warning letter could entitle the recipient to start a defensive action against the patentee in his own forum. Therefore, it must now be viewed as preferable in Italy to avoid any previous warning and to file for preliminary measures in the forum considered more convenient to the patentee.

III. Preliminary/Interim Measures

As mentioned above, the most important action related to patent enforcement is the action for preliminary/interim measures.

In Italy there are three different types of actions:

1. ***Descrizione***.[19] This order is quite exceptional in the European Union. Only in France can an analogous proceeding be found (*saisie-description*). The "description" is an order granted by the President of the competent court authorising the plaintiff (assisted by the bailiff, eventually by a court expert and usually with a photographer) to inspect and describe the allegedly infringing products/processes. Recently the Italian jurisprudence started to interpret the concept of "evidence of the infringement" more broadly, extending the power of the bailiff even to the collection of the documental and accountancy evidence of the business related to the alleged infringement. Such approach is particularly useful and significant in the enforcement strategies because it offers the opportunity to collect *ex parte* all the elements to quantify the damages suffered, without the risk of manipulation that is typical during the main proceedings.[20] Such an approach is perfectly in line with the policy envisaged by EC Directive 48/2004, Sec. 7 (but see also Chapter 2 VIII for a different view).

---

[18] See Sec. 78 Patent Act and Sec. 28 Code of Civil Procedure.

[19] Sec. 81 Italian Patent Act.

[20] Court of Turin, 8 July 2004, Morellato Spa *v*. Gioie.it Spa, unpublished; Court of Venice, 10 June 2004, Farmitaly Srl *v*. Auchan Spa, unpublished; Court of Turin, 7 April 2004, Nici AG *v*. De Car Due Srl, unpublished; Court of Milan, 27 March 2004, Prada SA *v*. CO.CA.MA Commercio Calzature Mantovane Srl, unpublished.

Although at the moment there are no reported cases, it could be argued that there is a possibility of obtaining such an order in Italy in order to execute it in other Community countries by virtue of EC Regulation 1206/01 of 28 May 2001 on Cooperation between the courts of the Member States in the taking of evidence in civil or commercial matters. According to this Regulation, it is possible for a Court of a Member State to request the competent Court of another Member State to collect evidence.[21] The requesting court may call for the request to be executed in accordance with a special procedure provided by the law of the court's own country (*i.e.* a *descrizione* order), and if so provided by the law of that country, the parties, and, if any, their representatives, have the right to be present at the taking of evidence by the requested court.

The right for the parties to be present is one of the major differences between the French system, where the parties are not allowed to participate in the *saisie-description* proceedings, and the Italian system.

The oral proceedings will contain a detailed description of the operation and the evidence collected. The aim and use of this procedure is to collect official evidence of infringement for the purpose of using it in the trial. Normally, the order can be obtained *ex parte* (*inaudita altera parte*) if there is a risk that the defendant may remove all evidence of the allegedly infringing goods. Normally, no bond is requested. Requests for a description are frequently made during expositions or trade fairs because no civil seizure is allowed in these places. After the order for a description is issued, the plaintiff has 30 days to summon the defendant for an ordinary trial. If this deadline is missed, all the evidence collected will be invalid and cannot be used for any future procedure.

2. ***Sequestro***.[22] The seizure is an order granted by the competent judge, authorising the plaintiff to search and seize all the allegedly infringing goods and all the means for their production. The order does not require the infringer to stop production or sale, but simply freezes the products found. A seizure is carried out by a bailiff under participation of the plaintiff for the correct identification of the goods in question. A seizure can be repeated also in places different from the offices of the defendant within a period of 30 days from being granted. The seizure can also be directed against third parties in possession of the allegedly infringing goods, unless these are meant for private use only. This order can also be granted *ex parte*, whereupon[23] the judge has to fix a hearing within 15 days from the order, obliging the applicant to

[21] This specific strategy (called *Italian Intruder*) to use the *descrizione* and the EC Regulation 1206/01 as a real strategic tool in IP enforcement was announced by the author at the CEIPI 40th annual conference in Strasbourg, 23 April 2004, and will be the subject of a specific article to be published shortly. More sceptical, Stauder in Chapter 2 VII, however.

[22] Sec. 81 Italian Patent Act.

[23] Sec. 669^{sexies} Code of Civil Procedure.

notify the defendant about the hearing within eight days, during which time the seizure can be carried out. At the hearing the judge has to affirm, modify or revoke the order. De facto it is presently very unusual to obtain *ex parte* seizures. Normally, the judge will fix a hearing for an *inter partes* discussion of the case, giving the defendant short notice to organise his defence. After the hearing the judge could either set a time for rendering a decision or fix another hearing for an exchange of pleadings between the two parties. If the matter is complicated, the judge could appoint a court expert to assist the court in the technical matters involved. The function of a seizure order is a double one: to acquire evidence of the infringement, and to stop the circulation of infringing goods. For the latter reason a seizure cannot be limited to some samples, but has to cover all allegedly infringing goods.

3. ***Inibitoria.***[24] The injunction is an order of the Court to cease and desist from using the product or process allegedly infringing the patent by manufacture, promotion, distribution, etc. Since the implementation of the TRIPS Agreement, it is now possible to obtain an injunction also on a preliminary basis. The court can also be requested to impose "*astraintes*" (monetary fines) in case of contempt. Contempt of an injunction granted by the court also constitutes a criminal offence.[25]

4. ***Publication.*** Although not expressly set forth by the law, in many cases Italian courts have, upon request of the applicant, granted an authorisation to publish the order issued.[26] According to part of the doctrine and some case law, publication would amount to a compensative measure, unacceptable during the summary proceedings. It seems that the possibility of being granted authorisation to publish the order very much depends on the facts of the controversy.

5. ***Requirements.*** All the above preliminary measures require two fundamental conditions:

- *fumus boni juris*: the need to show that, on the balance of probabilities, the patent is valid and infringed. There is no need to furnish full evidence, and it is sufficient to show an acceptable likelihood of a good case;

---

[24] Sec. 83 Italian Patent Act.

[25] Sec. 388 Criminal Code "Malicious failure to execute a judicial order".

[26] Court of Modena 20 December 2002, NADIR Snc *v.* Gexon Srl e Arcobaleno Blu, unpublished; Court of Treviso, 4 September 2001, Thun Spa *v.* Zago Adriano Spa, unpublished; Court of Rome, 12 June 2001, Thun Spa *v.* Veroli spa, unpublished; Court of Milan, 14 July 1998, Sacs Srl *v.* Nautica International Inc, unpublished; Court of Rome, 20 April 2001, Louis Vuitton Malletiers SA *v.* Matras Srl, in GADI 4346; Court of Rome, 18 July 2001, GB Carpano Spa and Fratelli Branca Distilllerie Srl *v.* System Liquori, in GADI 4358; Court of Naples, detachment division of Afragola, 13 March 2000, Aceto balsamico del Duca di Adriano Grosoli *v.* Marcello De Nigris, in GADI 4146; Court of Modena, 23 May 2001, Ungaro Srl *v.* Emanuel Ungaro SA, in GADI 4292.

- *periculum in mora*: urgency. It is necessary to demonstrate that the delay incurred in ordinary litigation will generate a irrecoverable loss.

Frequently, preliminary actions are dismissed for the lack of urgency without a discussion on the merits of the case.[27]

It is very important to point out that for a request of preliminary measures, mainly for seizure and injunctive relief, it is necessary in the complaint to anticipate the claims that will be raised in the ordinary action[28] subsequent to the interim procedures. A failure in this respect could cause the preliminary action to be dismissed.

The order granting the preliminary measure (*ordinanza*) should fix a peremptory deadline not exceeding the 30 days for instituting the ordinary action.[29] It is possible that the judge in granting the order will require the applicant to post a security for guarantee of possible damages. If the plaintiff does not comply herewith, the order will not take effect. The decision of the judge concerning the request for preliminary measures (grant or refusal) could be appealed (*reclamo*) before a panel of three judges of the Tribunal of first instance. These judges should re-examine all issues. Against the decision of the panel there is no appeal.

Nevertheless, and due to the fact that the matter concerns a specific case of urgency, it is possible to file a new request once new facts or new juridical reasons have come to light that justify an order.[30] Obtaining a preliminary measure normally opens the way for a settlement. As mentioned above, 34% of all pending cases concerning patents are abandoned during the first two years of litigation. Excluding the 34% of defensive actions (according to the above-mentioned 1996 statistic), one can safely conclude that half of the infringement actions are settled within two years of commencing proceedings.

IV. The Trial

An ordinary action normally starts with the filing and notification of the writ of summons (*atto di citazione*) asking the defendant to appear at a given hearing, no sooner than 60 days from the date of service for a national defendant and 120 for a foreign one.

The writ of summons should contain all the facts, legal arguments and evidence used or relied on during trial. Finally, the writ must contain a precise claim. Writ of summons and claim delimit the subject matter of the litigation. It is not allowed to extend the claim or to introduce new

---

[27] When there is a matter of urgency, it could be better not to wait too long after obtaining knowledge of the infringement to start a litigation: more than six months would be considered a risky delay.

[28] Sec. 669bis and 669^{sexies} Code of Civil Procedure.

[29] Sec. 669^{octies} Code of Civil Procedure.

[30] Sec. 669^{septies} Code of Civil Procedure.

arguments or means of evidence during trial.[31] The defendant must file his defence at least 20 days before the date of the hearing if he makes a counterclaim.[32]

There are three types of hearings:

- the first hearing (*udienza di prima comparizione*) is normally meant to make sure that the formalities of the suit set forth by law are properly complied with (duly served writ, complying with the deadline for filing the defence, etc.);
- the second hearing gives both parties the opportunity to define their claims and points at issue;
- only with the third hearing will the judges start to weigh the evidence offered by the parties and start the real trial.

Civil procedures in Italy are based on written pleadings rather than oral arguments. Therefore, the main work of the attorney is related to drafting written briefs. Nevertheless, in the preliminary proceedings the oral hearings usually play a decisive role in order to present to the judge the arguments.

V. Discovery

With the implementation of the TRIPS Agreement, a new provision was added to the Italian Patent Act. Section 77 now provides that if one party relies on specific documents for its claims and information or documents in the possession of the other party could confirm this claim, the judge could be asked to order such documents to be produced or a questionnaire to be answered. A request can also be based on the "right of information"[33] about third parties involved in the counterfeiting activities. The judge could request compliance with measures necessary to protect confidential information. The above provision for obtaining evidence is seldom applied. Moreover, non-compliance with the request of the judge is not sanctioned. Therefore, the party so ordered can defy the order without any serious consequences other than the judge drawing his conclusions from the party's behaviour.

---

[31] Sec. 184 Code of Civil Procedure allows for a term before trial for the plaintiff to review his claim or requests for evidence in view of the defendant's statements of evidence. After this opportunity, no more changes will be allowed. Nevertheless, the party not complying with the time limits could ask the judge for an extension under exceptional circumstances.

[32] This deadline only applies to counterclaims of the defendant, not for ordinary defences asking for the action to be discussed.

[33] The Court of Turin expressly mentioned the discovery principle when granting two search orders (*descrizione*): Court of Turin, 8 July 2002, Morellato Spa *v.* Gioie.it Spa, unpublished; Court of Turin, 7 April 2004, Nici AG *v.* De Car Due Srl, unpublished.

VI. Technical Expertise

In patent litigation, the judge usually appoints an expert, *Consulenza Tecnica d'Ufficio (CTU)*, to give his opinion in a special expertise phase. The expert is normally selected amongst a list of patent attorneys with experience in the specific field of the case. The judge appointing the expert defines the specific questions that should be answered. In doing so, the expert is given wide powers to investigate the case. The expert could thus examine the products, inspect the production site, make experiments for testing the contents and characteristics of the concerned products/process, etc. Under the Patent Act as amended in 1996,[34] the expert could request the inspection of documents relevant to the questions posed by the judge even if these documents had not been submitted to the court previously.[35] Under Sec. 77(4) Patent Act, the expert could also collect evidence and use this in his expertise. During this phase, the expert will also examine technical briefs by the patent attorneys of both parties. Upon conclusion of his examination, the expert will deliver his opinion to the judge. The expert's advice can be contested by the parties and the expert may be asked for any clarification of or addition to his opinion by the judge. While not frequent, the expert could also be replaced by another expert. It might be useful to note that the judge is not bound by the expert's advice and though this is in practice unusual, he could decide differently from what the expert has suggested.

VII. Post-Expertise Phase

After the CTU phase, the judge will ask the parties to submit their briefs summing up all technical and legal questions in view of the results of the expert's opinion. Normally, after these briefs, the parties have to file their final conclusions (*precisazione delle conclusioni*), after which both parties have 60 days to file their final pleadings (*comparse conclusionali*). Upon the parties request, the judge could fix a final hearing and render a decision, normally within 60 days of the receipt of the final pleadings or this hearing. Italian courts do not provide a guarantee of an "on schedule" service for the proceedings except in particular circumstances. The average length of a suit in the first instance is about two to three years. In some courts, the delay might be less.

---

[34] Sec.77(4) Italian Patent Act .

[35] According to a restrictive interpretation of the provision at issue, the court expert is allowed to take into consideration documents other than those already filed during the previous part of the proceedings only if those documents are provided by the parties. In other words, the court expert is not allowed to search and examine documents on his/her own initiative, but shall limit his/her investigation to the documents provided by the parties.

VIII. Damages

In assessing damages, Italian judges are not particularly generous on average.[36] The plaintiff should provide clear evidence about the actual damages suffered and the loss of profits. During the stage of expertise, one part is devoted to the assessment of damages. Normally, an expert on accountancy is appointed, who frequently does not deal with the evaluation of patents. There is a risk that this opinion is limited to evaluating the sales of infringing goods. If the commercial books or documents are unclear and do not permit an identification of the goods, such an analysis might be absolutely frustrating and ridiculous.

That is why the *descrizione* could play a decisive role, as evidence of infringement is collected by surprise, without many possibilities to hide documents.

The CTU expert rarely feels inclined to infer an average value for the benefit of the court, and neither does the judge give much attention to the plaintiff's request in this respect. The judge usually adopts a sort of paternalistic approach, and from an economical point of view the infringer's risk of having to pay damages frequently is a convenient balance between the *certain* (not officially declared) advantages deriving from the commercial exploitation of the infringement and the *uncertain* risk of being sued and paying just a limited amount of the profits derived from the infringement. This point of view is confirmed by the usual approach of the courts to award compensation for infringement in the amount of a reasonable royalty. This solution seems to be a sort of "compulsory licence for the past" imposed by the judge, thus obliging the patent owner to grant better conditions to the infringer than to contractual licensees. Definitively this system falls short of complying with Art. 41 TRIPS that requires remedies that may serve as a deterrent against infringements. In this author's view, the concept of "adequate compensation" provided by Art. 45 TRIPS should be understood as a warning to dissuade the infringer from infringing. In any event, it is very unsatisfactory for a patent owner to prevail in an infringement action and be awarded a ridiculous amount of damages, giving the infringer a sort of incentive to infringe carefully (perhaps by avoiding clear evidence of invoices, or not declaring the real value of the business). It should be kept in mind that the patent confers an exclusive right to commercially exploit the invention. If the state has to guarantee this exclusivity, it is not sufficient to apply principles of law.

---

[36] Decision of the Court of Vicenza, 17 June 2002, unpublished, in the case Lafer Spa *v.* Fabotex Srl provides an interesting and exhaustive excursus with regard to the criteria for the compensation of damages.

IX. Publication

According to Section 85 Patent Act, the Court can order to publish integrally or partially the judgment declaring the infringement in one or more newspapers at the expense of the infringer.

C. *Final Remarks*

At least formally, Italy implemented all the rules required by TRIPS. In practice, the situation in Italy falls mercifully short of coming up to the expectation of other developed countries. Nevertheless, the Italian system of IP enforcement could show some interesting tools. An appropriate use of the procedural rules (enforcement also during the application period) and the specific judicial remedies (the *descrizione* order, covering also infringer's business information) could offer some strategic advantages in complex enforcement strategies.

At present, a successful strategy for patent enforcement in Italy must take into account the significant investment in legal fees consumed by lawyers specialised in IP litigation, the appropriate selection of the forum of jurisdiction, and the willingness to accept a settlement which, though not completely satisfactory, may be better than an unpredictable decision. Sometimes the best results can be achieved with a complex strategy involving criminal procedures (if these can be instituted), customs procedures and interim measures in civil litigation.

8
The Enforcement of Patent Rights in Switzerland

FRITZ BLUMER

A. System of Civil Procedure

I. Civil Litigation in General / in Patent Matters

Currently in Switzerland, civil litigation is governed by the codes of civil procedure, each code is established by the individual cantons, such codes differ significantly from each other. Under the revised Federal Constitution of 1999, the federation now legislates in the field of civil procedure and court organisation. A Federal Code of Civil Procedure is being drafted and is expected to replace the 26 cantonal codes of civil procedure by 2005 at the earliest.

The court fees are determined both by the value in litigation as well as by the complexity of the case. Patent cases are generally considered to be complex cases.. Courts have considerable discretion in fixing the value in litigation. Depending on the applicable procedural laws of the cantons, courts are bound by the values in litigation jointly specified by the parties or they can choose the higher of any amounts specified by the parties. Parties often declare the value in litigation to be "indefinite but exceeding CHF xy", using rough figures like CHF 500'000 or CHF 1 Mio. It is difficult to calculate the appropriate value in litigation when seeking an injunction under intellectual property laws.

Similar rules are applied to the determination of the compensation for attorney's fees to be paid by the losing party to the winning party. Costs for the consultation of patent attorneys are generally treated as additional expenses that have to reimbursed to the winning party. The attorney's fees can be negotiated between each party and its attorney.

Under the Patent Treaty or Patent Protection Treaty,[1] Switzerland and Liechtenstein constitute a uniform patent territory, which means that, *inter alia*, in European patent applications and PCT applications both countries must be jointly denominated or selected. Thus, in patent matters only, the *Principality of Liechtenstein* has a common court structure with Switzerland. Appeals against Liechtenstein judgments in patent matters can be filed with the Swiss Federal Court.

---

[1] Treaty between the Swiss Confederation and the Principality of Liechtenstein on Patent Protection of 22 December 1978 (OJ EPO 1980, 407).

II. The Profession

Lawyers who have gained admission to the bar of one canton are admitted to the bars of all other cantons and are admitted to represent parties in appeals proceedings before the Federal Court. However, few attorneys regularly handle patent infringement or invalidity cases. There is no formal qualification required for patent attorneys or patent agents who represent clients before the Swiss Federal Institute of Intellectual Property (IPI). Many patent attorneys, however, are qualified as European Patent Attorneys in compliance with Art. 134 European Patent Convention (EPC).

III. Additional Measures for the Enforcement of Patent Rights

Under Article 51 TRIPS Agreement, the customs authority may suspend releasing into free circulation goods suspected of being trade mark counterfeits or pirated copyright goods. This provision provides, that "border measures" may be instituted for other infringements of intellectual property rights. In Switzerland, such measures are available under trade mark, copyright and design law but not under patent law.[2] However, it is planned to introduce border measures against patent infringements.[3]

Criminal proceedings can be instituted against any wilful infringement upon request of the "injured party" (*i.e.*, the patent owner),[4] the maximum penalty is limited to one year imprisonment or a fine of up to CHF 100'000. The right to request criminal proceedings is barred six months after the injured party had knowledge of the identity of the infringer.[5] Criminal proceedings are practically relevant in cases where individuals dealing with counterfeit goods frequently change the legal entities used for the counterfeit trade or such individuals use foreign legal entities that are difficult to sue for practical reasons (such as problems related to the service of action or enforcement issues). Criminal proceedings provide strong measures to procure evidence (such as seizures). However, criminal proceedings are to a large extent beyond the control of the plaintiff.

Only valid patents can lead to a conviction of an infringer and the defence of invalidity of the patent can be raised in criminal proceedings. The criminal court can grant the infringer a sufficient term to bring an action for

---

[2] Secs. 70–72 Trade Mark Act, Secs. 75–77 Copyright Act, Secs. 46–49 Design Act.

[3] Preliminary draft text of 29 October 2001, for an amendment of the Patent Act, Secs. 86a through 86d.

[4] According to Heinrich, "Schweizerisches Patentgesetz / Europäisches Patentübereinkommen" (Swiss Patent Act / European Patent Convention), Zurich 1998, marginal 81.06, the exclusive licensee is not authorised to request criminal proceedings.

[5] Sec. 81 Patent Act.

invalidity of the patent. If the patent had been granted without official preliminary examination (Swiss patents) or if the accused person produces *prima facie* evidence in support of the invalidity, the court may grant the injured party a sufficient term to bring an action for declaratory judgment on the validity of the patent.[6]

B. Enforcement of Patent Rights

I. Competent Parties

1. Plaintiff

Primarily, the registered patent owner is authorised to bring an action for infringement. Also, after a patent has been assigned the unregistered new owner is authorised to bring an action if he or she can prove the assignment with appropriate written evidence.[7] However, the registration of the new patent owner only has declaratory effect. In case of joint ownership, any co-owner is authorised to bring an infringement action.[8]

Under recent case law, it is acknowledged that the exclusive licensee is authorised to bring an infringement action. In a copyright case, the Federal Court held that the exclusive licensee was authorised to bring an infringement action if the licence agreement explicitly or implicitly authorised the licensee to do so.[9] The authorisation of the exclusive licensee to bring an infringement action has been acknowledged in patent cases as well. Moreover, in the preliminary draft of the revised Patent Act such Act explicitly acknowledges the exclusive licensee's authorisation.[10]

For an action for negative declaration of non-infringement, any person having sufficient legal interest in such declaration is authorised to bring the action. The required legal interest is usually founded on the patent owner's allegations of infringement or threatened infringement proceedings. In a recent decision, the Federal Court acknowledged the legal interest of the potential defendant in a patent infringement action that could be foreseen but was not immediately forthcoming. The court further argued that the plaintiff had a legitimate interest in forestalling multiple litigation in various

---

[6] Sec. 86 (1) Patent Act.

[7] *See* Brunner, "Der Patentverletzungsprozess" (Patent Infringement Proceedings), in SMI (Schweizerische Mitteilungen über Immaterialgüterrecht) 1994, 101, 115. Under Sec. 33 (2bis) Patent Act, the contractual assignment of a patent application or patent is valid only if evidenced in writing.

[8] Sec. 33 (2) Patent Act.

[9] Federal Court of 5 May 1987, BGE 113 II 190.

[10] Preliminary draft text of 29 October 2001, for an amendment of the Patent Act, Sec. 73a. Under this draft provision, which is drafted after Sec. 35 (4) Design Act, the exclusive licensee is authorised to bring an infringement action unless the licence agreement explicitly excludes such authorisation.

jurisdictions by initiating an action for negative declaration in Switzerland covering patents in multiple jurisdictions.[11]

2. Defendant

Any person who "unlawfully utilises" a patented invention can be sued under Sec. 66(a) of the Patent Act in infringement proceedings. Any party in a chain of suppliers and resellers can be defendants. If legal entities commit patent infringement, the legal entity as well as its officers can be sued.[12] An infringement action can be brought against a foreign pharmaceuticals manufacturer whose products are sold in Switzerland.[13]

Under Sec. 66 (d) Patent Act, any person who abets any of the offences referred to in Sec. 66 (a) through (c), participates in them, aids or facilitates such offences, is liable as a participant to a patent infringement. Such participation is considered unlawful only if the main offence (that is supported in some way by the participant) is unlawful. The Swiss concept of participation in a patent infringement differs from the German concept of indirect infringement under Sec. 10 German Patent Act insofar as indirect patent infringement under German law can be committed even if there is no unlawful "direct" infringement. If the direct infringement occurs outside Switzerland, the participants are not liable under Swiss patent law even if their participating acts are committed in Switzerland.[14]

II. Competent Courts

1. Courts Designated to Hear Patent Cases

Section 76 Swiss Patent Act provides that each canton must designate one court to be competent for civil actions under the Patent Act as a sole cantonal instance, with this court having jurisdiction for the entire canton. The four cantons which have commercial courts (Zurich, Berne, Aargau and St Gallen) have designated these commercial courts to be competent for patent cases. The four commercial courts handle most patent cases in Switzerland. Among them, the Zurich Commercial Court deals with the largest number of patent cases; such court is composed of judges of the Zurich Appellate Court and commercial judges – part-time judges who are in the division competent for patent cases and are often experienced patent attorneys. In most other cantons the court of appeal is competent to hear patent cases, however such courts may have very little experience in patent matters. For proceedings related to preliminary measures, courts other than those

---

[11] Federal Court of 21 February 2003, BGE 129 III 295.

[12] *See* Brunner (above footnote), 115 s.; *see also* below B.IV.1.

[13] Zurich Commercial Court of 2 July 1996 – Erythropoietin II, sic! 1997, 208.

[14] Federal Court of 21 July 2003, BGE 129 III 588.

competent for the ordinary patent proceedings may be competent, subject to the laws of the respective canton.[15]

Appeals against decisions in patent cases may be brought before the Federal Court, regardless of the value in dispute.[16] While the Federal Court is usually bound by the facts established by the lower court, in patent cases the Federal Court may re-examine the ascertainment of facts by the cantonal instance. The Federal Court may review the technical facts either upon request or *ex officio* and may take further evidence for that purpose. In particular, the Federal Court may ask the expert instituted by the cantonal instance to complete his findings, appoint one or more new experts, or carry out a judicial inspection.[17] However, the Federal Court is reluctant to make use of its authority to re-examine the facts in patent cases.[18] If the establishment of facts is incomplete, the Federal Court regularly makes use of its authority to remand the case to the lower instance to complete the establishment facts and to issue a new decision.[19]

The establishment of a *Federal Patent Court*, which would have exclusive jurisdiction for all patent cases filed in Switzerland as a first instance federal court, has been discussed for decades. The prospects for this project are brightening after the federation has been authorised to legislate in the field of civil procedure and court organisation under the revised Federal Constitution of 1999.[20] The concentration of all patent cases before one court would avoid patent proceedings being brought before courts that lack the necessary experience to handle such cases efficiently.

2. Jurisdiction for Infringement Actions Instituted by the Patent Owner

In *domestic cases*, where both parties have their seat in Switzerland, the plaintiff can choose between either the courts of the seat (domicile) of the defendant or the aggrieved person or the courts at the place where the tortuous act occurred or had its effects.[21] In cases of participation in a patent infringement under Sec. 66 (d) Patent Act, the courts of the place where the participating

---

[15] *See* below B.III.2.

[16] Sec. 76 (2) Patent Act.

[17] Sec. 67 (1) Federal Act on the Organisation of the Federal Judiciary of 16 December 1943 (Bundesgesetz über die Organisation der Bundesrechtspflege, OG).

[18] Federal Court of 21 July 2003, BGE 129 III 588.

[19] Sec. 64 Federal Act on the Organisation of the Federal Judiciary of 16 December 1943 (Bundesgesetz über die Organisation der Bundesrechtspflege, OG).

[20] *See* Hilti, "Ein eidgenössisches Patentgericht (EPG) 1. Instanz in greifbarer Nähe" (A Federal Patent Court of First Instance Near at Hand), sic! 2002, 283; *see also* above A.I.

[21] Sec. 25 Federal Act on Civil Jurisdiction (Gerichtsstandsgesetz, GestG), in force since 1 January 2001.

act was committed can have jurisdiction.[22] In effect, the plaintiff in a patent infringement case has many opportunities for *forum shopping* and in most cases can choose to file an action at the place of his or her Swiss domicile.

In an *international context*, where one or more parties have their domicile outside of Switzerland, jurisdiction of the Swiss courts in intellectual property cases is governed by the Swiss Federal Act on International Private Law (FAIPL). Under Sec. 109 (1) FAIPL, the Swiss courts at the defendant's domicile have jurisdiction over actions concerning intellectual property rights. However, in the absence of such domicile, jurisdiction is at the place where the protection is sought. Under the present Sec. 109 (1) FAIPL, the Swiss defendant can only be sued at his or her domicile whereas the foreign defendant can be sued at any place where the patent is infringed.[23] Political initiative has been taken in order to amend Sec. 109 (1) FAIPL to apply the rules of jurisdiction under the new Federal Act on Civil Jurisdiction, such rules would allow the plaintiff to choose between the court at the defendant's domicile and the court or courts at any place of infringement.

Under the *Brussels Convention*,[24] member states to the European Union established a joint system of jurisdiction and recognition of foreign judgments in civil and commercial matters. This system has been extended to most member states of the EFTA (European Free Trade Association), including Switzerland, under the *Lugano Convention*,[25] which is referred to as a "parallel convention" to the Brussels Convention. On 1 March 2002, the Brussels Convention was replaced by the EU Regulation no. 44/2001 (*Brussels Regulation*).[26] This regulation does not differ significantly in its content from the Brussels Convention. The Lugano Convention remains in force between Switzerland and the states that are both members to the EU and signatories to the Lugano Convention. The Lugano Convention is presently being adapted to the wording of the Brussels Regulation.

The European Court of Justice can review the national courts' interpretation of the Brussels Regulation, however there is no appellate court on an international level to secure uniform application of the Lugano Convention. To minimise the risk of different interpretations of the Brussels Regulation and the Lugano Convention, Protocol 2 to the Lugano Convention requires

---

[22] *See* Romerio in Wirth/Müller (eds.), Gerichtsstandsgesetz (Commentary on the Federal Act on Civil Jurisdiction), Zürich 2001, Section 25 marginal 68. If the direct infringement occurs outside Switzerland, the participant is not liable under Swiss patent law, *see* above B.I.2.

[23] *See* Blumer in Bertschinger/Münch/Geiser (eds.), "Schweizerisches und europäisches Patentrecht" (Swiss and European Patent Law), Basel/Geneva/Munich 2002, marginal 17.17.

[24] Convention on Jurisdiction and Enforcement of Judgments in Civil and Commercial Matters of 27 September 1968, last published in 1998 O.J. (C 27) 1.

[25] Convention on Jurisdiction and Enforcement of Judgments in Civil and Commercial Matters of 16 September 1988, 1988 O.J. (L 319) 9.

[26] Published in 2001 O.J. (L 12) 1.

the courts of the contracting states to take account of the principles laid down in any relevant decision delivered by courts of other contracting states. Through this mechanism, the interpretation of the Brussels Convention by the European Court of Justice has factual relevance for the interpretation of the Lugano Convention in Switzerland. In the course of their application of the Lugano Convention, Swiss courts often refer to the case law of the European Court of Justice on the Brussels Convention and to the respective literature.

The rules on jurisdiction of the Lugano Convention are applicable if the defendant is domiciled in a contracting state, such rules prevail over the respective provisions of the FAIPL.[27] The general rule under Art. 2 Lugano Convention provides jurisdiction in the courts of the contracting state where the defendant is domiciled. As this provision only refers to the national jurisdiction and not to any place of jurisdiction within the respective contracting state, national law determines the jurisdiction within the contracting state.

For intellectual property litigation, Sec. 109 (1) FAIPL is the national provision that establishes jurisdiction under Art. 2 of the Lugano Convention. Under this provision, the court at the defendant's Swiss domicile has jurisdiction for actions concerning the infringement of patent rights. Such jurisdiction is understood to be "comprehensive", *i.e.*, the court at the defendant's domicile has jurisdiction to hear cases based on Swiss patent rights as well as cases based on foreign patent rights.

If a defendant is domiciled in another contracting state to the Lugano Convention, "the courts where the harmful event occurred" have jurisdiction under Art. 5 (3). This provision is understood to refer to both the place where the illegal action was committed as well as to the place where the damage arose.[28] Art. 5 (3) applies if a harmful event has actually occurred before an action is filed or if such harmful event is imminent.[29] Based on the Fiona Shevill decision of the European Court of Justice,[30] it is argued that the jurisdiction of Swiss courts based on Art. 5 (3) Lugano Convention is limited to claims based on the infringement of Swiss patent rights.[31]

---

[27] Art. 4 Lugano Convention; Sec. 1 (2) FAIPL.

[28] European Court of Justice of 30 November 1976, Bier *v.* Mines de Potasse d'Alsace (Case 21/76), 1976 E.C.R. 1735. It is unclear whether in cases of participation in a patent infringement under Sec. 66 (d) Patent Act, the courts of the place where the participating act was committed can have jurisdiction under Art. 5 (3) Lugano Convention. For domestic cases *see* above B.II.2. If the direct infringement occurs outside Switzerland, the participant is not liable under Swiss patent law, *see* above B.I.2

[29] In contrast to the wording of the Brussels and Lugano Conventions, Art. 5 (3) of the Brussels Regulation (above footnote) refers to "the courts for the place where the harmful event occurred *or may occur*".

[30] European Court of Justice of 7 March 1995, Fiona Shevill *v.* Presse Alliance (Case 68/93), 1995 E.C.R. 415.

[31] *See* Heinrich (above footnote) marginal 75.16.

Another exception to the general rule under Art. 2 Lugano Convention (jurisdiction of the courts in the state where the defendant is domiciled) is Art. 6 (1) which provides for jurisdiction of a contracting state over a defendant in another contracting state, namely "where he is one of a number of defendants in the courts for the place where any of them is domiciled." As the wording of the provision suggests, the joint defendants can be sued at a place where at least one of them is domiciled. Art. 6 (1) does not list any conditions under which a plurality of defendants can be sued at the same court. To limit the applicability of the forum of joint defendants, the European Court of Justice used the criterion of Art. 22 (3) of the convention, which defines "related actions" as actions that are "so closely connected that it is expedient to hear and determine them together to avoid the risk of irreconcilable judgments resulting from separate proceedings."[32] In the field of patent litigation, Art. 6 (1) has been applied to joint defendants who sold identical products in different contracting states, thereby infringing the same European patent in different contracting states. However, the developing case law in Europe tends to require additional connections between the joint defendants, such as acting together in a chain from the producer to the distributor to the commercial buyer. With some case law interpreting Art. 6 (1) more broadly, a Dutch Court recently held that foreign defendants can be sued at the Dutch forum as joint defendants only if the foreign co-defendants belong to the same group of companies as the Dutch defendant and the Dutch defendant acts as the European headquarter of the group ("spider in the web").[33]

To summarise, it is acknowledged that a Swiss court, under Art. 2 Lugano Convention (*i.e.*, if the defendant is domiciled in Switzerland), has jurisdiction over claims based on foreign patents. To what extent the Swiss court could have such cross-border jurisdiction over the infringement of foreign patents under other provisions of the Lugano Convention, is uncertain. There is neither Swiss case law nor case law of the European Court of Justice on the respective provisions of the Brussels Convention.

For proceedings related to preliminary measures, courts other than those competent for the ordinary patent proceedings may be competent, subject to the laws of the respective canton.[34]

3. Jurisdiction for Actions for Negative Declaration

In an action for negative declaration under Sec. 74 (3) Patent Act, the potential infringer can seek a declaration of non-infringement. As in any declara-

---

[32] European Court of Justice of 27 September 1988, Kalfelis *v.* Schröder (Case 189/87), 1988 E.C.R. 5565.

[33] *See* above Stauder, section III; Pitz, "Patentverletzungsverfahren" (Patent Infringement Proceedings), Munich 2003, marginal 232; Den Hague Appellate Court of 23 April 1998, Expandable Grafts *v.* Boston Scientific, 1998 European Intellectual Property Review, N-132.

[34] *See* below B.III.2.

tory action, the court has to assess whether the plaintiff has a legitimate interest in such declaration.[35]

In *domestic cases*, jurisdiction for actions for negative declarations of non-infringement under Sec. 25 Federal Act of Civil Jurisdiction is with the court at the domicile of the defendant (*i.e.*, the patent owner). This provision also provides for jurisdiction at the place of the unlawful action, but it is unclear whether it establishes jurisdiction at the place where the alleged infringement took place. As such jurisdiction at the "place of non-infringement" is recognised by the Federal Court in an international context,[36] it is likely that Swiss courts would decide accordingly in domestic cases.

If the defendant and patent owner are not domiciled in either Switzerland or in a contracting state to the Lugano Convention, jurisdiction for negative declarations of non-infringement is governed by Sec. 109 FAIPL. The Federal Court has found that jurisdiction for negative declarations of non-infringement of a Swiss patent should follow the jurisdiction for invalidity actions, that is, at the domicile of the representative in the register or, in the absence of such representative, the courts at the seat of the Swiss registration authority (*i.e.*, Berne).[37]

For declaratory actions related to the non-infringement of Swiss patent rights against a defendant in another contracting state to the Lugano Convention, the question arises whether any Swiss courts can have jurisdiction under Art. 5 (3) or whether the plaintiff can only sue the patent owner at his domicile under Art. 2. The Federal Court found, in connection with a tort action, that Art. 5 (3) shall apply for actions seeking a declaration that the plaintiff is not liable for damages.[38] It would be consistent, therefore, to accept jurisdiction at the "place of non-infringement" under Art. 5 (3). However, the case law on this issue is not uniform.[39]

If the defendant is domiciled in Switzerland, declarations for non-infringement can also be sought with respect to foreign patents. In a recent case, the Federal Court accepted that an Italian plaintiff can sue the Swiss patent owner for a declaration of non-infringement of various patents of third countries before a Swiss court.[40]

---

[35] Federal Court of 24 January 1990, BGE 116 II 196 (with respect to a patent invalidity action).

[36] *See* below in this section, before footnote .

[37] Federal Court of 21 August 1996 – Hitzeschutzschild III, sic! 1997, 331.

[38] Federal Court of 2 August 1999, BGE 125 III 346.

[39] *See* Den Hague Appellate Court of 21 January 1998, Evans Medical *v.* Chiron, 1998 European Intellectual Property Review, N-61, 62; Tribunale di Bologna of 16 September 1998, GRUR Int. 2000, 1021, commented by Stauder.

[40] Federal Court of 21 February 2003, BGE 129 III 295.

III. Preparation for Trial

1. Warning Letters

It is common to ask the infringer in a warning letter to stop the alleged infringement. However, the plaintiff need not warn the defendant before instituting an infringement action; such letter may trigger an action for negative declaration of non-infringement and provide the alleged infringer the legal interest for filing such action.[41] Thus it may be preferable for a patent owner to abstain from warning the infringer before filing an action, thereby avoiding being sued before a court the patent owner would not choose for an infringement action.

However, not warning the alleged infringer before filing an infringement action could result in some additional costs to the plaintiff. If the defendant immediately acknowledges the claims made in the infringement action, such acknowledgment would generally be treated with regard to costs as if the plaintiff won the case. However, a court could consider the proceedings unnecessary and impose some costs on the plaintiff. Under certain procedural laws within Switzerland, the costs are imposed on the plaintiff if the defendant immediately acknowledges the claims.[42] If the defendant had undertaken in writing not to continue the alleged infringement, the court would not admit the action for lack of legal interest, in which case the plaintiff would pay court fees and provide compensation for the defendant's attorneys' fees.

2. Interim Injunctions

Under Sec. 77 Patent Act, a court can, *inter alia*, order provisional measures to: secure evidence, maintain the actual state of facts, or provisionally enforce disputed rights to an injunction. The enumeration of possible provisional measures in this provision is not exhaustive, the court can order any measure that preserves the plaintiff's rights. In a case where the plaintiff invoked Art. 50 TRIPS Agreement to support claims for preliminary measures, the court found that Sec. 77 Patent Act was in compliance with the TRIPS Agreement.[43] In practice, preliminary injunctions (cease and desist orders) are the most relevant provisional measures.

Under Sec. 33 Federal Act on Civil Jurisdiction, the court with jurisdiction over the substance of the matter or the court where the provisional measures are executed shall have mandatory jurisdiction to order provisional measures. The provision also applies in an international context, since the Lugano Convention and the FAIPL do not specify jurisdiction for preliminary

---

[41] *See* below B.IV.1.

[42] *See*, for example, Sec. 60 Berne Code on Civil Procedure.

[43] Superior Court of Basel-Landschaft of 1 October 1997 – Acyclovir, sic! 1998, 78.

measures but allow courts other than those with jurisdiction for ordinary proceedings to issue preliminary measures.[44] In any case, jurisdiction for proceedings related to preliminary measures is both with courts having jurisdiction for ordinary proceedings (*i.e.*, in the substance of the matter) and at the place(s) where preliminary measures are to be enforced. Some cantons require claims for preliminary measures be brought before courts other than those with jurisdiction for ordinary proceedings.[45]

Provisional measures are granted only if the plaintiff produces *prima facie* evidence that the other party has committed or intends to commit an infringing act and the plaintiff is threatened by a loss not easily reparable and can be avoided only by provisional measures.[46] The first prerequisite – often described as the "Verfügungsanspruch" (legal title for the issuance of the preliminary measures) – is met if there is a substantial likelihood that the plaintiff would prevail on the merits in the main proceedings on the infringement issue. The second prerequisite (harm or loss not easily reparable and to be avoided only by provisional measures) is generally referred to as "Verfügungsgrund" (grounds for the preliminary measures). Under the pertinent case law, it is met if the relevant harm later would be difficult to detect, calculate or replace.[47] Financial loss is generally not considered sufficient to establish grounds for preliminary measures, except for cases when the defendant may be unable to pay damages after the judgment in the main proceedings is issued or where damages may be difficult to calculate or prove at that time.[48] Preliminary measures may be justified if the sale of infringing goods causes market confusion, results in an irreversible loss of market shares or if the poor quality of the counterfeits damages the reputation of the plaintiff.[49]

While urgency is not an explicit prerequisite for preliminary measures, the plaintiff may be denied preliminary measures for an unjustified delay and thus should not wait too long after getting knowledge of the infringer and infringement. There are no fixed limits as to what constitutes an unjust delay. Courts apply the concept of "relative urgency", where the time prospectively needed for ordinary proceedings is compared with the delay of the plaintiff's filing for preliminary measures. If a plaintiff waits for a period that would be sufficient to complete ordinary proceedings before filing a motion for preliminary measures, there is no longer a legal interest in obtaining

---

[44] Art. 24 Lugano Convention; Sec. 10 FAIPL.

[45] For example, in the canton of Berne the presidents of the 13 district courts are competent for proceedings on preliminary injunctions whereas ordinary proceedings are within the competence of the Commercial Court.

[46] Sec. 77 (2) Patent Act.

[47] *See* Lutz, "Die vorsorgliche Massnahme" (Preliminary Measures), in "Kernprobleme des Patentrechts"(Basic Problems in Patent Law), Zurich 1988, 328.

[48] *See* Federal Court of 20 July 1982, BGE 108 II 228.

[49] *See* Rubli in Bertschinger/Münch/Geiser (above footnote), marginal 16.41.

preliminary measures.[50] It may be acceptable to wait more than one year before filing a motion for preliminary measures.[51]

The proceedings on preliminary measures are usually summary proceedings with short delays and often only one exchange of briefs. There are no general rules for excluding certain means of evidence but courts may refuse to admit evidence that leads to any unnecessary delay of the proceedings. A summary expert opinion can be ordered by the court to assess technical allegations of the parties in the context of the validity of the patent and its infringement. The summary expert opinion can be delivered orally.[52]

Like the facts on which claims for preliminary measures are based, facts supporting defences against such claims need to be supported by *prima facie* evidence.[53] As in ordinary infringement proceedings,[54] the defendant may invoke the defence that the patent is invalid but the defendant must also provide *prima facie* evidence to prove such defence,[55] When assessing the validity of the patent, the court may take into account examination proceedings for foreign sister patents as well as considerations of the Technical Boards of Appeal of the European Patent Office.[56]

In exceptional cases, "when there is an imminent danger,"[57] provisional measures are granted *ex parte*, *i.e.*, before the defendant is heard. *Ex parte* injunctions that can be immediately enforced are generally referred to as "superprovisorische Verfügungen". They can be justified if the rendering of an injunction is very urgent (for example, if infringing products shall be presented at a forthcoming trade fair) or if the purpose of the measure would be forfeited if the defendant was heard before the measure is ordered (for example, if counterfeits are to be seized).

As a countermeasure to *ex parte* preliminary injunctions, the instrument of "Schutzschrift" (protective letter) is becoming an established practice in Swiss courts. In a protective letter, the potential defendant usually presents a summary of arguments to defend against the allegations of infringement and offers to be available for a hearing or a counterstatement on preliminary injunctions on short notice, should the prospective plaintiff file a motion for preliminary measures. Most courts would keep such protective letter for a few months and consult it in case the prospective plaintiff named in the

---

[50] Zurich Commercial Court of 14 May 1996 – Ski- und Wanderstöcke, Blätter für Zürcherische Rechtsprechung 1996 No. 98.

[51] Fribourg Appellate Court of 5 November 1998 – Förderanlage, sic! 2000, 114 (18 months delay was acceptable).

[52] Zurich Commercial Court of 23 August 1990 – Kurzgutachten, SMI 1991, 208.

[53] Zurich Commercial Court of 25 July 1984 – Aquarius 1, SMI 1986, 215.

[54] *See* below B.V.1.

[55] Federal Court of 13 February 1997 – Erythoropoietin IV, sic! 1997, 408.

[56] St. Gallen Commercial Court of 17 February 1997 – Pulverbeschichtungsanlage I, sic! 1997, 306; Zurich Commercial Court of 10 July 1990 –PR-Lagersystem 1, SMI 1992, 253.

[57] Sec. 77 (3) Patent Act.

protective letter files a motion for *ex parte* measures. Because case law differs from canton to canton, protective letters may not be accepted by all courts.[58] Moreover, in some cantons the courts send the protective letter to the prospective plaintiff immediately whereas in other cantons the protective letter is sent after the prospective plaintiff files a motion for preliminary measures.

Pursuant to Sec. 79 (1) Patent Act, the plaintiff "shall be required to furnish sufficient security". Sec. 80 Patent Act provides security deposits to secure damage claims the defendant may incur if provisional measures are found to be unjustified in subsequent proceedings. The amount of the security is calculated according to the damage potential for the time during which the provisional measures remain in place (*i.e.*, until the final judgment in the main proceedings).[59] However, the amounts fixed by the courts under Sec. 79 (1) vary significantly.

IV. The Trial

1. Prerequisites for Proceedings

If the *"Prozessvoraussetzungen"* (prerequisites for proceedings) are not met, the court must not admit the case. The respective judgment has no binding effect and the parties may bring the case before the same court or another court again. One of the most important prerequisites for proceedings is the jurisdiction of the court seized.[60]

Another prerequisite for proceedings is the *legal interest* of the plaintiff in a judgment. In connection with a request for an injunction, such interest is acknowledged if an infringement is imminent (*e.g.*, very likely to occur). If an infringement has occurred already, it is assumed that the infringement will be repeated.[61] The legal interest in an injunction may cease to exist after the defendant acknowledges the plaintiff's claims and enters into an obligation not to continue the infringing activities.[62]

Under Sec. 74 Patent Act, any person proving an interest may initiate an action to obtain a declaratory judgment on the existence or the non-existence of a matter of fact or legal relationship. An interest in a declaratory judgment is generally acknowledged if all of the following conditions are met: (i) the legal position of the defendant is uncertain, unsecured or endangered, (ii) the

---

[58] For example, the courts in the canton of Zurich, after regularly refusing protective letters, changed their practice in 1997 (Zurich Commercial Court of 2 May 1997, Blätter für Zürcherische Rechtsprechung 1997, no. 46).

[59] Fribourg Appellate Court of 5 November 1998 – Förderanlage, sic! 2000, 114.

[60] *See* above B.II.

[61] Federal Court of 6 June 1990, BGE 116 II 357.

[62] Zurich Commercial Court of 26 September 1995 – Globus II, SMI 1996, 454; Federal Court of 6 June 1990, BGE 116 II 357.

ongoing uncertainty is unbearable for the plaintiff, and (iii) the uncertainty cannot be eliminated by means other than a declaratory action.[63]

In connection with declaratory actions for the non-infringement of patents, the Federal Court recently held that the plaintiff who foresees being sued in another contracting state to the Lugano Convention may have a sufficient interest in a declaratory judgment issued by a Swiss court. The Federal Court left open whether seeking a declaratory judgment in order to block an action before a foreign court could result in a loss of the legal interest.[64]

A court cannot hear a case involving the same parties in the same matter if another action is pending before another court (*lis pendens*). The later court seized must stay its proceedings until the first court seized decides on the merits of the matter.[65] Actions for negative declaration of non-infringement refer to the same claim as the respective infringement action with the legal basis and the subject-matter being the same.[66] Consequently, the potential defendant in an infringement action can forestall the forthcoming infringement action by filing an action for negative declaration, and the plaintiff in such declaratory action may make use of the opportunities for *forum shopping* under the applicable rules on jurisdiction.

Depending on the applicable procedural law of the canton, it may be unclear when an action is considered to be pending.[67] If an action can be filed without conciliation proceedings before the president of the court or before the "Friedensrichter" (justice of peace), the action is pending immediately after the court receives the written complaint. If compulsory conciliation proceedings are required under the applicable procedural law of the canton, an action is considered to be pending until the plaintiff is bound by his action, thereby preventing him from re-filing it after a withdrawal.[68]

Once a judgment has become final, the parties are barred from bringing an action on the same grounds and the court seized with such action must not admit the case. This principle of *res judicata* is limited to identical claims between the same parties. In patent infringement matters, an earlier judgment does not establish *res judicata* if in a later infringement action between the same parties, another infringing embodiment is the basis of the claims.[69]

---

[63] *See* Vogel/Spühler, "Grundriss des Zivilprozessrechts" (Law on Civil Procedure), 7th ed., Berne 2001, ch. 7 marginal 23.

[64] Federal Court of 21 February 2003, BGE 129 III 295.

[65] Sec. 35 Federal Act on Civil Jurisdiction (applicable if both courts are Swiss courts). In international relationships (*i.e.*, if one of the courts seized is a foreign court), similar rules apply (*see* Sec. 9 FAIPL, Art. 21 Lugano Convention).

[66] Federal Court of 21 February 2003, BGE 129 III 295; *see also* European Court of Justice of 6 December 1994, Tatry *v.* Maciej Rataj (Case 406/92), 1994 E.C.R. 5439; above Stauder, section IV.

[67] *See* Vogel/Spühler (above footnote), ch. 8 marginal 35 s.

[68] Federal Court of 26 September 1997, BGE 123 III 414.

[69] Federal Court of 3 November 1995, BGE 121 III 474.

The withdrawal from an action for negative declaration results in a *res judicata* and is equivalent to a judgment on the merits in favour of the defendant.[70] If an invalidity action is withdrawn, the plaintiff in subsequent proceedings may not invoke the invalidity of the patent.[71] Likewise, the party who withdraws an action for declaration of non-infringement may not contest the infringement of the patent if the patent owner subsequently institutes an infringement action based on the same facts.

2. Pleadings and Presentation of Evidence

Pleadings in patent infringement proceedings are generally submitted in writing. The motions should be worded carefully as the plaintiff is required to use language that allows the conversion of the motions into an enforceable judgment.[72] Depending on the applicable law on civil procedure, the parties are forced to present all factual allegations and claims in their first briefs.[73] Under certain codes of civil procedure (for example, in the cantons of Basel-Stadt and Basel-Landschaft), the parties may be barred from using any evidence that has not been referred to in their first briefs.[74] The first briefs (complaint and answer to the complaint) are usually followed by a second set of briefs, the "Replik" (reply) of the plaintiff and the "Duplik" (rejoinder) filed by the defendant.

Counterclaims generally need to be filed with the answer to the complaint. The filing of counterclaims has no other effects than the filing of the respective claims in independent proceedings. However, a court not otherwise having jurisdiction to hear a claim may have jurisdiction if the claim is filed as a counterclaim in proceedings pending before the same court.[75] In patent infringement proceedings, the counterclaim usually concerns the declaration of invalidity of the patent.[76] Accordingly, in invalidity proceedings, the defendant (*i.e.*, the patent owner) may file counterclaims based on the infringement of the patent (for example, damage claims).

Evidence proceedings generally start after the exchange of briefs. In the course of such evidence proceedings, the court will install a court expert, hear witnesses or examine other evidence. The parties have a right to be heard on any piece of evidence introduced in the proceedings. In particular, the parties may comment on the findings of the court expert.

---

[70] *See* Vogel / Spühler (above footnote), ch. 8 marginal 45, ch. 9 marginal 70 s.

[71] Zurich Commercial Court of 28 July 1992 – res iudicata, SMI 1994, 79 s.

[72] *See* below VI for motions for injunctive relief.

[73] So-called "Eventualmaxime" (principle of preclusion of delayed pleaded facts).

[74] *See*, for example, Sec. 107 Code of Civil Proceedings of Basel-Landschaft.

[75] Under Sec. 6 Federal Act on Civil Jurisdiction, a counterclaim can be filed with the court seized for the main claim if a factual connection exists between the original claim and the counterclaim.

[76] *See* below B.V.1.

3. Role of the Parties, the Judge and the Expert

Depending on the patent experience of the judges involved, the court expert may play a crucial role in the proceedings. In a recent decision, the Federal Court stated that only in exceptional cases can the court decide technical issues in patent proceedings without hearing an expert or an expert judge.[77] In any case, the court should carefully review the expert opinion and put it on the "imaginary test stand". In particular, the court should check whether all relevant questions have been addressed, whether the foundations of the expert's findings have been disclosed, whether the reasoning of the expert is logical and whether the expert's conclusions are consistent with the reasoning.[78]

Parties often file expert opinions rendered by experts hired by the parties to support their arguments in the pleadings or to support their criticism on the opinion rendered by the court expert. Courts regularly deny that such "private expert opinions" are of value as evidence. However, depending on the reputation of the private expert and the quality of his statements, the court may still give more weight to private expert opinions than to the statements made by the parties' attorneys.

As in any civil proceedings, the parties determine the scope of the proceedings and the parties to present and prove the relevant facts both in infringement and invalidity proceedings. It is in the interest of the parties to get involved in the proceedings as much as possible, for example, by proposing questions to be asked to the court expert.

The court should take an active role in patent proceedings, in particular, by providing guidance to the parties with regard to a clear and comprehensive presentation of the relevant facts. In practice, it depends both on the experience of the court in patent matters and on the applicable procedural law to what extent and at what stage of the proceedings the court gets materially involved with a case. The Zurich Commercial Court gets materially involved with the merits of a case at an early stage of the proceedings,[79] whereas other courts that are less experienced in patent matters play a less active role and may tend to delay cases. It is in the interest of every court that the parties find an amicable solution to their lawsuits. However, the chance for a court to reach amicable solutions is higher if the court gets involved with the merits of the case early and presents settlement proposals founded on a thorough review of the facts presented and of the legal issues.

---

[77] Federal Court of 9 December 1998, BGE 125 III 29. Expert judges with a qualification as patent attorneys may be involved in patent cases before commercial courts, *see* above B.II.1.

[78] *See* Zürcher in Bertschinger/Münch/Geiser (above footnote), marginal 19.78.

[79] *See* below B.IV.4.

4. Instruction Hearings Held by the Zurich Commercial Court

One peculiarity of the Zurich Commercial Court is its practice to hold "Referentenaudienzen" (instruction hearings) that often lead to an amicable settlement of the case. The court invites the "Referentenaudienz," after the parties filed their first briefs (*i.e.*, the complaint, the answer to the complaint), the counterclaims (if any) and the answer to the counterclaims. The parties are asked to send one or more representatives authorised to enter into a binding settlement agreement. In patent cases, the parties are typically represented by one or two members of their senior management, an internal or external patent attorney and their attorney-at-law. However, the parties may inform the court that they do not wish a hearing if they do not see any chance for a settlement at this stage of the proceedings.

The court delegation at the "Referentenaudienz" is composed of an appellate judge who is often specialised in the field of the case (instructing judge), a law clerk and a commercial judge (a part-time judge who is usually qualified as a patent attorney).[80] In the first part of the hearing, usually short and minutes are taken, the parties are asked whether they want to substantiate any of their arguments and the court delegation often refers to arguments made by the parties that need to be substantiated in its view. In the second part of the hearing, usually informal and no minutes are taken, the court delegation presents its preliminary view on the factual and legal aspects of the case. The assessment of the case may be comprehensive but the court delegation explicitly refers to the provisional character of its assessment. After the presentation of the preliminary views of the court delegation, the instructing judge usually submits a proposal for a settlement, initiates the settlement negotiations and often uses the best of his negotiation skills to convince the parties to settle. These negotiations are confidential and the statements made do not bind the court or the parties if no settlement can be reached.

Only after no settlement can be reached in the *Referentenaudienz*, the court orders the parties to file their second briefs and initiates the evidence proceedings. A settlement in connection with the "Referentenaudienz" at an early stage of the proceedings leads to reduced court fees and allows the parties to avoid considerable cost for attorneys and court experts. On the other hand, the parties need to carefully present all their arguments in their first briefs in order to hear from the court a preliminary assessment as favourable to them as possible.

5. Scope of Protection

In connection with the remedies for patent infringements, the Swiss Patent Act makes a distinction between literal infringement ("Nachmachung") and imitation ("Nachahmung") that may include equivalent infringements and

---

[80] *See* above B.II.1.

infringements where one or more of the features of the patent claim are not realised.[81]

Despite the distinction made between literal infringement and imitations, the wording of the provisions related to claim interpretation are similar to Art. 69 EPC and the Protocol on the Interpretation of Art. 69 of the Convention. Pursuant to Sec. 51 (2) Patent Act, the claims shall determine the extent of the protection conferred by the patent (scope of protection). The description and the drawings shall serve for the interpretation of the claim.[82] The Zurich Commercial Court applies Art. 69 EPC to determine of the scope of protection of a European patent. In the same decision, the court left open whether Art. 69 EPC shall be applied to national patents but pointed out that the Swiss provisions on the scope of protection should apply in the same way as Art. 69 EPC.[83]

The *relevant language version* for the determination of the scope of protection of a European patent is the language of the proceedings before the EPO.[84] Under Swiss law, the patentee is required to provide a translation of the patent if it has not been published in a Swiss official language (German, French or Italian).[85] In compliance with Art. 70 (3) EPC, Sec. 116 Patent Act protects third parties who rely on such translations. They may invoke the translation provided by the patentee in infringement proceedings if the scope of protection is less extensive according to the text of that translation than according to the text in the language of the proceedings.[86]

The interpretation of the patent claims under Sec. 51 Patent Act and Art. 69 EPC can be described as a two-step undertaking. In a first step, the meaning of the patent claims (as understood by the person skilled in the art) is determined to establish the subject-matter of the patent claims. In the second step, the hypothetical person skilled in the art brings its understanding of the subject-matter of the claims in relation to the alleged infringement, taking into account that certain features of the claim may be omitted or replaced by alternative features.[87]

According to a Federal Court decision of 1990, an equivalent infringement is found if the patented solution is achieved by functionally equivalent means that can be derived from the claim by the person skilled in the art,

[81] Sec. 66 lit. a) Patent Act; *see* Blumer in Bertschinger/Münch/Geiser (above footnote), marginal 14.50, 14.55 ss., 14.70 ss.

[82] Sec. 51 (3) Patent Act.

[83] Zurich Commercial Court of 3 December 1991 – Werkzeughalterspindeln II, SMI 1992, 303.

[84] Art. 70 (1) EPC.

[85] Sec. 113 Patent Act.

[86] Sec. 116 (1) Patent Act.

[87] *See* Hilty, "Der Schutzbereich des Patents" (Scope of Protection of Patents), Basel et al. 1990, 229; Brunner (above footnote), 104; Blumer in Bertschinger/Münch/Geiser (above footnote), marginal 14.29 s.

taking into account the prior art.[88] The individual features of the claimed invention are compared with the equivalent features of the alleged infringement.[89] A feature is technically equivalent if its technical contribution to the overall effect of the alleged infringement is the same as the contribution of the corresponding feature of the claimed invention to the overall effect of the invention. The use of such equivalent feature can constitute an equivalent infringement if the person skilled in the art was capable of finding the equivalent feature without performing an inventive step. The prevalence of the claims should be considered and it is not admissible to only use the overall effects of the alleged infringement. *Ex-post-facto* considerations must be avoided, *i.e.*, the hypothetical person skilled in the art is supposed not to know the equivalent feature.

In a Federal Court decision of 1989, the defence was admitted that the alleged infringement was not patentable in view of the prior art.[90] According to this decision, the defendant may not only argue that the alleged infringement is conditioned by the prior art but he may also argue that the accused embodiment would not constitute a patentable invention over the prior art.[91] The decision explicitly refers to the German "Formstein" decision of 1986.[92] However, the Federal Court in a later case argued that the patentee only deserves protection for his or her inventive contribution to the prior art.[93] When assessing the patentability of the alleged infringement over the prior art, the court takes into account only the features of the accused embodiment having a counterpart in the patent claim but not additional features of the accused embodiment lacking any relation to the patent claim and that may contribute to the patentability of the accused embodiment.[94]

V. Defences

1. Invalidity of the Patent in Suit

Claims for a declaration of invalidity of a patent can be brought before the same court as claims against an infringer, moreover claiming the invalidity of the patent in suit can be used as a defence in any infringement proceedings. The defendant in the infringement proceedings may choose between filing either a counterclaim for the declaration of nullity of the patent in suit or raising the invalidity of the patent as a mere defence in the infringement

---

[88] Federal Court of 18 January 1990 – Doxycyclin, SMI 1991, 198.

[89] Zurich Commercial Court of 4 February 1994 – Sicherheitsetikette 1, SMI 1996, 105.

[90] Federal Court of 16 November 1989, BGE 115 II 490.

[91] Federal Court of 16 November 1989, BGE 115 II 490.

[92] German Federal Supreme Court of 29 April 1986 – Formstein, GRUR 1986, 803.

[93] Federal Court of 17 August 2001 – Palettenförderer, sic! 2001, 749.

[94] *See* Busse, "Patentgesetz" (German Patent Act), 5th ed., Berlin / New York 1999, § 14 marginal 105.

proceedings. If a counterclaim is made, a judgment finding that the patent is invalid leads to the deletion of the patent from the register and has effect *erga omnes*. If the court finds the patent invalid after a defence of invalidity, the infringement claims (for injunctive relief, damages etc.) are barred but the finding of invalidity has no effect *erga omnes*.

When choosing between a counterclaim for invalidity and an invalidity defence, the defendant may take into account that an invalidity defence does not affect the value in litigation. On the other hand, a counterclaim for declaration of invalidity is attributed a separate value in litigation that regularly exceeds the value attributed to the infringement claims.

The invalidity of the patent in suit may also be invoked if the infringement action is based on a foreign patent. Because the state for which a patent is registered has exclusive jurisdiction for invalidity proceedings,[95] the declaration of invalidity cannot be the subject of a counterclaim. If the invalidity of a foreign patent is raised as a defence or incidental question in an infringement lawsuit, the Swiss court is free to review the validity of such patent.[96]

The grounds for invalidity of a patent (either a Swiss national patent or the Swiss part of a European Patent) are listed in Sec. 26 Patent Act. These grounds have been harmonised in connection with the European harmonisation efforts that led to the European Patent Convention. Thus, the list of grounds for invalidity in Sec. 26 Patent Act basically follows the list of grounds for revocation in Art. 138 EPC. The grounds for invalidity are the same for Swiss patents and European patents. It must be noted, however, that the extension of the protection conferred by the patent (Art. 138 lit. d) EPC) is no ground for invalidity under Swiss law.

Under Sec. 128 Patent Act, the court may suspend the proceedings, and in particular defer the judgment, when the validity of a European patent has been contested and either one of the parties to the dispute gives proof that an opposition may yet be filed with the European Patent Office or that a final decision has not been taken on the subject of an opposition already filed. While the suspension of the proceedings is considered by the legislature to be the standard practice, the court has to find the balance in the individual case between the interest in expediting proceedings and the interest in avoiding irreconcilable judgments.[97]

---

[95] Art. 16 (4) Lugano Convention.

[96] Zurich Commercial Court of 9 January 1984 – Infringement of Foreign Intellectual Property Rights, SMI 1984, 42.

[97] *See* Walter, "Die Aussetzung des Verletzungs- oder Nichtigkeitsprozesses wegen eines vor dritten Instanzen anhängigen Einspruchs- oder Nichtigkeitsverfahrens nach schweizerischem Recht" (The Suspension of Infringement or Nullity Proceedings due to Opposition or Nullity Proceedings before Third Instances under Swiss Law), GRUR Int. 1989, 441, 443.

2. Exhaustion of Rights

The principle of exhaustion allows the buyer of a patented product to resell it and to use it commercially without the consent of the patent owner.[98] Under Swiss intellectual property law, the principle of exhaustion is generally accepted even though its only statutory basis is in the Copyright Act.[99] There has been a long debate on whether Swiss intellectual property rights shall be exhausted by the sale of the protected product abroad (international exhaustion) or by the sale of the protected product in Switzerland only (national exhaustion). The third alternative would be to introduce regional exhaustion as it applies within the European Union and the European Economic Area (EEA). Switzerland has not become a member to any of these organisations yet. Under the principle of regional exhaustion, the rights in Switzerland would be deemed exhausted after the protected goods have been sold with the right owners consent in any of the member states of the EEA. For non-members of the EU or the EEA, it is unclear under what kind of international agreement Switzerland could introduce the regional exhaustion principle without violating the most-favoured nation principle set forth in Art. 4 TRIPS Agreement.

In landmark decisions stemming from actions against parallel imports of protected goods, the Federal Court has decided in 1996 and 1998 that under trade mark and copyright law, international exhaustion shall apply.[100] For patent law, the Federal Court took a different approach and decided in favour of national exhaustion in the "Kodak" decision of 1999.[101] The debate has not stopped since then. Political initiatives have been taken to allow parallel imports of patented goods.

3. Statute of Limitations, Laches

Like any other tort claims, claims based on patent infringements are subject to the statute of limitations under Sec. 60 Swiss Code of Obligations. Under this provision, claims are barred one year after the injured party learns of the infringing acts, at the latest 10 years after such acts. If tort claims are based on criminal acts, the longer delay also applies to the damage claims under civil law.[102] As the Patent Act provides for criminal sanctions for patent infringement, the applicable statute of limitations under criminal law applies to

[98] *See* Stieger in Bertschinger/Münch/Geiser (above footnote), marginal 12.131 ss.

[99] Sec. 12 (1) Swiss Copyright Act (marginal: "Principle of Exhaustion"): "Where the author has sold a copy of a work or has consented to sale, such copy may be further sold or otherwise distributed."

[100] Federal Court of 23 October 1996 – Chanel, BGE 122 III 469; Federal Court of 20 July 1998 – Nintendo, BGE 124 III 321.

[101] Federal Court of 7 December 1999, BGE 125 III 129.

[102] Sec. 60 (2) Code of Obligations. *See* Stieger, "Verjährung und Verwirkung im Immaterialgüterrecht" (Statute of Limitations and Laches in Intellectual Property Law), Allgemeine Juristische Praxis 1993, 626, 629.

claims based on patent infringements, extending the one year delay under Sec. 60 Code of Obligations to 5 years.[103] To claims for the restitution of the infringer's profits, the same rules apply as to claims for damages.[104]

A long delay in bringing an infringement action can give rise to the defence of laches if the following conditions are met: (i) inactivity of the injured person, (ii) recognisability of the infringement for the injured person, (iii) valuable possessory title of the infringer and (iv) good faith of the infringer.[105] There are no fixed rules on how long the delay in bringing an action may be before the plaintiff is barred from bringing such action, but a court would probably require a delay of several years.

4. Other Defences

The defendant may be in a position to derive rights from a *prior use* of the patented invention. Under Sec. 35 Patent Act, a patent has no effect against a person who, prior to the date of filing of the patent application, was in good faith professionally using the invention in Switzerland or had made special preparations for that purpose. Similar rights to use a patented invention may be based on *intermediate use*, *e.g.*, good faith use between the loss of rights of the applicant or patent holder and the reinstitution in these rights and good faith use during the time before a translation was revised if under the original translation, the scope of protection did not cover the specific use made before the revision.[106]

Private and experimental use are not referred to in the Patent Act in connection with the rights conferred by the patent. It is generally acknowledged that private use for non-commercial purposes does not constitute patent infringement.[107] With regard to experimental use, the situation is less clear. In proceedings related to provisional measures, a court found that the use of a pharmaceutical substance in connection with regulatory proceedings did not infringe the patent. In the reasons, the court found that not allowing the use in connection with regulatory proceedings would, in effect, extend the patent term.[108] It is foreseen to introduce a provision relating to experimental use in the Patent Act.[109]

---

[103] Sec. 81 Patent Act, Sec. 70 (3) Criminal Code.

[104] Federal Court of 17 July 2000, BGE 126 III 382.

[105] *See* Pedrazzini, "Die Verwirkung im schweizerischen Kennzeichenrecht" (Laches in Swiss Trade Mark Law), GRUR Int. 1984, 1984, 502.

[106] Secs. 47, 48, 116 Patent Act. *See* Stieger in Bertschinger/Münch/Geiser (above footnote), marginals 12.212 ss.

[107] *See* Stieger in Bertschinger/Münch/Geiser (above footnote), marginals 12.26 ss.

[108] Superior Court of Basel-Landschaft of 1 October 1997 – Acyclovir, sic! 1998, 78.

[109] Preliminary draft text of 29 October 2001, for an amendment of the Patent Act, Sec. 10a. Under this draft provision, the wording of which is similar to Sec. 11 (2) of the German Patent Act, the effects of the patent shall not extend to acts done for experimental purposes relating to the subject-matter of the patented invention.

The defendant may also raise the defence that the alleged infringement would not be patentable over the prior art. This defence has been discussed in connection with the scope of protection.[110]

VI. Injunctive Relief

In practice, injunctive relief is more relevant than damages. As damages are available only after separate evidence proceedings and in an amount not exceeding the actual loss incurred or the actual profit made by the infringer, the plaintiff regularly concentrates on obtaining an injunction as early as possible and as broadly as possible.

Court orders are usually based on the formal requests and motions worded by the parties. A cease and desist order must be worded in a way that the competent judge may enforce it without another assessment of the defendant's behaviour on the merits.[111] The plaintiff seeking injunctive relief against a patent infringer is therefore required to word the motions in a way that they might be converted into an enforceable order by the court. In many cases, it is not enough to use the wording of the patent claim. The defendant may use only one embodiment of the apparatus defined in the patent claim, in which case the plaintiff may have no legal interest in obtaining injunctive relief covering all embodiments covered by the patent claim. Deviations from the wording of the patent claim in the cease and desist order may also be necessary if the defendant is accused of an equivalent infringement and the court has to decide whether such equivalent infringement falls within the scope of protection.[112]

There are *criminal sanctions* for defendants not complying with a court order issued in civil proceedings. Under Sec. 292 of the Swiss Criminal Code, any person not complying with an order issued by any competent authority can be punished if such order makes reference to this provision. Cease and desist orders in infringement judgments are therefore regularly accompanied by a reference to Sec. 292 Criminal Code. Even though the plaintiffs usually request in their briefs that the cease and desist order include the reference to Sec. 292 Criminal Code, the court should include such reference *ex officio*.

VII. Damages

Under Sec. 73 Patent Act, the defendant who commits any infringing act "wilfully or by negligence", shall be bound to pay damages to the injured party. In practice, the defence that the defendant did not know about the

---

[110] *See* above B.IV.5.

[111] Federal Court of 2 March 1971, BGE 97 II 93.

[112] *See* Blumer in in Bertschinger/Münch/Geiser (above footnote), marginals 17.89 ss.

patent (and therefore did not act wilfully or negligently) is usually not to be heard because, under other provisions, damages are due regardless of whether the infringer acted wilfully or negligently.[113]

Damages may be claimed for the time before the patent is granted, even if the respective lawsuit can be filed only after the grant of the patent. Under Sec. 111 Patent Act, the injured party may invoke the damages caused by the defendant as from the moment at which the defendant became aware of the European Patent Application, but at the latest as from the date of the publication of the European Patent Application. If the European Patent Application was not published in a Swiss official language (*i.e.*, if it was published in English), damages can only be claimed as from the day when a translation of the claims in a Swiss official language was communicated to the defendant or made available to the public by filing it with the Swiss patent authority.[114]

Under consistent case law, the party injured by an infringement of intellectual property rights may choose between damages and the restitution of the infringer's profits. Both claims exist independently of each other but they exclude each other.[115] The plaintiff may claim both damages and restitution of the infringer's profits as alternatives and may choose between the two after the amounts of damages and of the infringer's profits have been determined in evidence proceedings.

For the calculation of damages, three methods are established: (i) the demonstration of the effective or direct damage, (ii) the analogy to a licence fee and (iii) the analogy to the profit made by the infringer. The direct damage incurred by the plaintiff represents his or her lost profits and is best demonstrated by disclosing the profits made by manufacturing or selling the patented products. Since the plaintiff often seeks to avoid such disclosure and it may be difficult to prove that all sales made by the infringer led to a corresponding loss of sales for the injured party, the indirect methods for the calculation of damages often apply. The determination of a licence fee that would be negotiated under market conditions is considered to be an application of the court's discretion to estimate damages under Sec. 42 (2) Swiss Code of Obligations.[116]

The Swiss Patent Act, in Sec. 73 (2) explicitly allows actions for damages to be initiated without specifying the amount of damages, if the injured party is unable to assess the amount of damages to which it is entitled. In such cases, "Stufenklagen" (two-step actions) can be instituted in which the plaintiff combines the claim for damages with an ancillary claim for accounting and

---

[113] Sec. 111 Patent Act (damages for the time before the European Patent issued); Sec. 87 (4) Patent Act (damages for the time after publication of the Swiss patent application if the application was subject to preliminary examination).

[114] Sec. 112 Patent Act.

[115] Federal Court of 16 March 1971, BGE 97 II 169.

[116] Federal Court of 10 October 1996, BGE 122 III 463.

rendering information related to the specification of the main claim.[117] The court first decides whether the damage claim appears founded (*i.e.*, whether the patent has been infringed) and renders a partial judgment on the ancillary claim. Such partial judgment can be appealed before the final judgment (setting the amount of damages) is rendered.[118] After the partial judgment is final and the defendant is ordered to provide information on the infringing actions, and the proceedings continue to determine the amount of damages.

Published decisions regarding courts determining the amount of damages are very rare. After the court, in a partial judgment, grants injunctive relief and orders the defendant to provide the necessary information to calculate the amount of damages, the parties very often prefer to settle the damages issue instead of waiting for the final judgment.

[117] Federal Court of 1 May 1990, BGE 115 II 219.

[118] Federal Court of 17 February 1997, BGE 123 III 140

C

Patent Enforcement in Eastern Europe

9
The Enforcement of Patent Rights in Poland

JANUSZ FIOLKA

A. History

I. Beginnings of Intellectual Property Protection in Poland

The first known inventor's privilege was granted by the Polish Crown between 1418–1421 to a man called Piotr (Peter), who declared that he would build and demonstrate the work of a machine for removing water from mines. The machine would enable the work of twenty horses to be performed by the work of twelve skilled men. So using today's language, the machine would give one man the power of 1.5 horses – not a bad achievement. The background of the invention was obvious. It was much easier at this time and even today to take twelve men to the mine than twenty horses. Under the privilege Piotr had to offer the machine to every mine. As a remuneration, every mine using the machine or which was dried by using the machine should pay to Piotr four *grzywny* per week, that is, four units of the currency in circulation in Poland at the time. This income could be transferred or inherited to other persons and was not limited in time. The miners could use the traditional methods of drying mines, but without permission of Piotr nobody could use his art.[1]

At the end of 18th century Poland had lost its independence and emerged as an independent state only after the First World War. The Treaty of Versailles obliged Poland to join the Paris Convention so as to facilitate Poland's participation in world trade.[2] Soon after, the Patent Office of Polish

---

[1] Wyrozumski, "Zagadnienie poczótków prawnej ochrony wynalazku w Polsce" (Problems at the Beginnings of Legal Protection of Invention in Poland), in: Zeszyty Naukowe Uniwersytetu Jagiellońskiego, Prace z wynalazczości i ochrony własności intelekltualnej (Scientific Bulletin of Jagiellonian University, Works on Inventiveness and Protection of Intellectual Property), Vol. 18, 1978, 24–25, who is quoting *Liber cancellariae Stanislai Ciołek,* published by Caro, Vol. I, Wien 1874, No. 99.

[2] The Polish Government Declaration on Poland's accession to the international association for protection of industrial property, Official Gazette of 4 February 1922, No. 8, item 58, states, that *in execution of Sec. 19 of Annex No. I to the Treaty between the Allied and Confederate Countries, signed in Versailles on 28 June 1919, ratified by Poland on 31 July 1919, . . . the Polish Government has notified accession of Poland to the Paris Convention . . . as revised in Washington on 2 June 1911.*

Republic was created[3] and the first statutes relating to protection of IP were passed by the Polish Parliament (*Sejm*). The statutes were heavily influenced by Dr. Frederic Zoll, professor of Jagiellonian University.

Professor Zoll passed his vision of protecting intellectual property on to many of his pupils, most notably to Professor Stefan Grzybowski (1902–2003), who in 1971 set up *The Institute of Inventiveness and Protection of Intellectual Property*, which became a leading centre of research in intellectual property in Central and East Europe, having contacts with many scientific institutions in foreign countries, particularly the Max Planck Institute for Intellectual Property Protection in Munich.

B. *Brief Outline of the Current System of Intellectual Property Rights*

I. General

The German Civil Code had the strongest influence on a uniform system of civil law in Poland after 1918. This is also true for the industrial property system, as Poland, like Germany, is one of the few countries in which courts in patent infringement cases may not invalidate patents, this being in the exclusive competence of the Patent Office.

On 30 June 2000, the Polish Parliament enacted the new Industrial Property Code (IPC), replacing the Patent Act of 1972,[4] the Trade Mark Act of 1985,[5] the Computer Chip Protection Act of 1992,[6] and the Patent Office Act of 1962.[7] The aim was to unite all aspects of industrial property into one single act. This has not been completely achieved, as the repression of unfair competition still falls within the scope of the Unfair Competition Repression Act of 1993.[8]

---

[3] Provisional Decree of 13 December, 1918 on the Patent Office, Official Gazette No. 21, item 66. According to data published on the web page of the Polish Patent Office, www.uprp.pl, *the Patent Office of the Republic of Poland was established on December 28, 1918. Poland already entered into the Paris Convention for the Protection of Industrial Property on November 10, 1919, joining international cooperation in this field. The first registration of a trade-mark took place on April 11, 1924, and the first patent was granted on April 24, 1924.*

[4] Dziennik Ustaw (Official Gazette later cited as Dz.U.) 1993, No 26, item 117.

[5] Dz.U. No 5, item 16.

[6] Dz. U. No 100, item 498.

[7] Dz.U. 1993, No 26, item 118.

[8] Dz.U. 1993, No. 47, item 211 with later amendments. The draft of this law was prepared by a team of intellectual property researchers using the experience gained during long-term Max Planck fellowships. That is why under prevailing opinion the Polish Unfair Repression Competition Act of 1993 act is in fact codified German court jurisprudence in this field.

The System of Patent Enforcement in Poland

Constitution of Polish Republic of 1977

International agreements to which Poland is a party

The Industry Property Code of 2000 / The Law of Inventive Activity of 1972 (see III below)

	Enforcement before common courts	Enforcement before the Patent Office (PO)	Enforcement before the Customs Office (CO)
Regulations	Civil Code of 1964 and Code of Civil Procedure of 1964	Administrative Code of 1980	Customs Code of 1977
Questions	patent infringement and civil sanctions of patent infringement	nullification	border measures (temporary seizure of goods at the border during customs clearance)
Instances	1st District court judgment, appeal to 2nd Appellate Court 3rd Cassation (II level appeal) to Supreme Court	1st Decision of PO 2nd Motion for reconsidering the case to PO 3rd Appeal to Administrative Court 4th Appeal to Central Administrative Court	1st Decision of Customs Chamber in Warsaw 2nd Appeal to Customs Chamber

II. The Constitution and International Agreements

The new Polish Constitution of 17 October 1997,[9] replacing the one of 1952, outlines the following rights and liberties, which may have an impact on patent enforcement:

a. the right to a just and open hearing of the case without unjustified delay a by a proper, independent, impartial court (Art. 45);
b. the right to appeal a decision (Art. 78);
c. the liberty of artistic creativity, scientific research and publication of its findings, the liberty of teaching and using the achievements of culture (Art. 73);
d. unfair market practices are forbidden and state authorities have a duty to protect consumers against these practices (Art. 76);
e. the right to property and to inheritance (Art. 21).

Only the Constitutional Court may nullify a statute, even retroactively.[10]

[9] Dz. U. No 78, item 483.

[10] *See* Supreme Court judgment of 30 January 2002, file No. *v*. CA 1/102, published in Lex Base under No. 56 019.

Of particular importance for IP enforcement in Poland are Arts. 9 and 91: Article 9 obliges the State to observe international law.

Under Art 91(1), international treaties, once published in the Official Gazette of the Polish Republic, become part of the Polish domestic legal system and are directly applicable unless further legislation is required. Such treaties take precedence over domestic law.

These provisions thus provide the constitutional basis for the courts to directly apply properly ratified and published international conventions or the law of international organisations as domestic law. Also other administrative institutions such as the Patent Office may do so.

Yet under Sec. 6 Polish Language Act, *international agreements ratified by Poland should have a Polish language version, which should constitute the basis for their interpretation, unless the provisions of a law states otherwise.*[11] Poland recently has joined many international agreements. Currently, publication of the text in the Official Journal is only in the Polish language. Previously, the Official Gazette published both the Polish and foreign language versions.

In 2002 the Central Administrative Court (*Naczelny Sąd Administracyjny*)[12] overturned a decision by the Patent Office to refuse an international registration under the Madrid Agreement, as the Patent Office's decision concerning the refusal was based on objections made in French. According to the court, all official acts of public offices should be made in Polish, and the use of French constituted a major legal deficiency, which justified declaring this decision as null and void. Similar views were expressed in other decisions.[13]

Poland has joined many international conventions in the field of protection of industrial property. TRIPS was ratified according to the Polish Government declaration of 31 July 1995, and entered into force on 1 July 1995. However, five month after ratification Poland send a notification to WTO deferring entry of its provisions for four years, or until 1 January

---

[11] The law of 7 October 1999 on Polish language, Dz.U. No. 90, item 999 with later amendments. This law in Sec. 8 provides, that *if a party of an agreement, which execution will take place in Poland is a Polish subject, the agreement shall be executed in the Polish language* (Sec. 8. 1). *The agreement executed in the Polish language may have a version, or versions in a foreign language. Unless the parties of the agreement provided otherwise the interpretation of such agreement shall be done under the Polish version* (Sec. 8. 2).

[12] CA Court (NSA) decision of 21 May 2002, file No. II SA 4033/01, Wokanda 2002/12/39.

[13] *See* CA Court (NSA) decisions of 11 July 2001, file No. *v*. SA 3738/00, LEX Base No. 51274; and February 2001, file No. III SA 2339/99, Przegląd Podatkowy (Tax Review), 2001/11/63, in which decisions were declared invalid, because the files of the case covered documents in a foreign language. In a decision of 6 September 2001, file No. *v*. SA 165/01, LEX Base No. 51 270, the CA Court (NSA) took the view that statements presented to Polish institutions must be made in Polish language. The fact that a given person did not know the Polish language did not justify missing the deadline to launch an appeal by that person.

2000.[14] Of course this begs the question, when TRIPS in fact entered into force in Poland. According to the prevalent view in the Polish literature, the Polish Government had the power to retroactively defer entry.[15] The final word in this matter will belong to the courts.[16]

III. Issues that Require Specific Mention

According to the transitional provisions of the Industry Property Code, *rights granted in respect of inventions, utility models, ornamental designs, topographies of integrated circuits, trade marks and rationalisation proposals existing at the time of entry into force of this Act, shall remain in force. To these rights the previous provisions are applicable, unless the provisions of this Part stipulate otherwise* (Sec. 315. 1).

Furthermore *legal relationships established prior to the entry into force of this Law shall continue to be governed by the previous provisions* (Sec. 315. 2).

This was confirmed by a decision of the Supreme Court.[17]

In the case of patents granted before 22 August 2001,[18] the provisions of the law of 1972 on inventive activity[19] shall apply.

The regulation contained in Sec. 315 creates of course a double standard as to the enforcement of patents, particularly with respect to the term of protection. The law of 1972 provided a 15-year term of patent protection until amended in 1993. There is no possibility of extension even by invoking TRIPS.

Furthermore, the 1972 Act did not deal with the rule of exhaustion, the defence of clinical trials for marketing approval, and gave the Patent Office the right to declare a certain product or process non-infringing.

C. Enforcement of Patents

I. Introduction

Civil litigation in Poland is governed by the provisions of the 1964 Polish Code of Civil Procedure (*Kodeks postępowania cywilnego*), as amended. With

---

[14] The notification is dated 27 December 1995. Barta, Markiewicz: "Prawo autorskie w Światowej Organizacji Handlu" (Copyright in World Trade Organisation), 1996, 74–75.

[15] Ibid., 75.

[16] For instance the Warsaw Customs Chamber's web page reflects the view that Poland has been full member of WTO and TRIPS since 1 July 1995, and there is no word on the declaration made under Art. 65. 3 TRIPS.

[17] Supreme Court decision of 20 December 2001, file No. II CKN 1440/00, published in the Lex Base under item 53 131.

[18] According to Sec. 327, the industrial property law entered into force three months after the date of its publication in the Official Gazette.

[19] The law of 17 October 1972 on inventive activity has been amended many times. The last consolidated text was published in Dz.U. 1993, No 26, item 117.

its 1,153 sections, the CCP is a rather complex piece of legislation that distinguishes between civil litigation in general, and litigation in commercial matters. The latter is the rule in IP matters. Only in exceptional cases would general civil procedures apply, *e.g.* where a single inventor claims ownership over an invention or infringement of his patent. Due to the scarcity of non-commercial cases, general procedures are not further elaborated here.

As a characteristic of patent litigation in Poland, jurisdiction for infringement and nullity/invalidation procedures are split. The Patent Act 1972 gave the Patent Office exclusive jurisdiction over the invalidation of patent rights. In cases where the defendant wished to raise the estoppel of invalidity in an infringement action, a separate action before the Patent Office had to be launched to this end, whereupon the court would stay proceedings. The Patent Office's decision was binding on the courts. In addition, the Patent Office could also be requested to issue declaratory decisions on infringement. For this reason, most cases concerning patent infringement were decided before the Patent Office in determination-of-scope procedures rather than before the courts.

The Industrial Property Code 2000 maintains the split jurisdiction between infringement and invalidity, yet abolishes determination-of-scope procedures.[20] Thus, only the courts are competent to decide if a given embodiment is infringing.

This otherwise clear-cut picture has been somewhat obscured by two Supreme Court decisions in matters of trade mark law, which may be applied *mutatis mutandis* to patent enforcement. In the first decision, *Interagra* I,[21] the court avoided the problem of having to call a trade mark unenforceable vis-à-vis similar use by way of a trade name in holding that use of a trade name per se did not infringe upon another's trade mark right. In the *Cogito*[22] case, the court went even further in that direction. Defendant to the case was the Cogito company that had traded in computer services and obtained a fairly prominent position in the market, yet without ever registering its company name as a trade mark. The plaintiff was a former employee of that company who established his own company under the name Informatic Company Cogito and registered the word trade mark "Cogito", subsequently asking the defendant to refrain from using that name henceforth. While the first instance court persuaded by the fact of registration, granted the plaintiff's

[20] Besler, "Sprawy o ustalenie, ze wskazana produkcja nie jest objeta okreslonym patentem" (Cases for the Determination if a Given Production Is Not Covered by a Given Patent), Ksiega pamiatkowa z okazji 80-lecia rzecznictwa patentowego w Polsce (Commemorative issue 80th Anniversary of Patent Agents in Poland) 287 (2001).

[21] Supreme Court decision of 14 June 1988, file No. II CR 367/87, Orzecznictwo Sądów Polskich i Komisji Arbitrażowych (OSPiKA), item 328, [9/1990] with approving comments by Kępiński.

[22] Supreme Court decision of 30 September 1994, file No. 109/94, Orzecznictwo Sądów Polskich (OSNC), item 18, [1995].

request, the Court of Appeal referred the matter to the Supreme Court. In a highly unusual ruling, the Supreme Court declined to decide the case outright, but gave the opinion that the fact of registration of a mark should not exclude the possibility of the court investigating if the owner of such mark had indeed a right of use. After all, a trade mark was only a "formal right". Even more unusual, the Supreme Court explicitly stated that the above opinion was not binding on the Appeal Court (which of course followed the ruling).

The ruling was subsequently criticised.[23] Others wanted to extend the ruling even further and argued that also a patent right was only a "formal right" giving the court the competence of refusing to enforce an invalid patent.[24] Until now no court decision has addressed this problem.

II. National Jurisdiction and Enforcement of Foreign Judgments

National jurisdiction can be ascertained where the defendant of a suit is domiciled in Poland or where a Polish intellectual property right is infringed. Contracts with a choice of law clause that excludes Polish jurisdiction are enforceable unless jurisdiction is exclusive.

The Polish Patent Office has exclusive jurisdiction in cases of revoking or invalidating intellectual property rights granted in Poland.

For further details, see below VII.1.

III. Procedures in Commercial Matters

The 1989 amendment to the CCP introduced a separate procedure for the civil enforcement of commercial matters in Sec. 479(1)–(27) and establishes that commercial courts have jurisdiction over commercial cases. The purpose of introducing special procedures in commercial matters was to speed up procedures which according to Sec. 479(16) should not take more than three months from the time of raising the claim to the final decision. Within the framework of commercial cases, those related to the conclusion, amendment or recission of agreements and their interpretation should be heard with priority. The reality is somewhat different, however. Since the courts

---

[23] *See* the comments by Supreme Court Judge Żyznowski, "Ochrona nazwy (firmy) i dochodzenie roszczeń na drodze sądowej" (Protection of a Trade Name and Enforcing Claims Before Courts), Aktualne problemy ochrony własności przemysłowej w przemyśle farmaceutycznym (Current Problems of Protection of Industrial Property in the Pharmaceutical Industry), 41–42 seminar proceedings 1996.

[24] Such view is taken by Traple, "Naruszenie patentu a teoria ekwiwalentów" (Patent Infringement and the Theory of Equivalents), Ksiega pamiatkowa z okazji 80-lecia rzecznictwa patentowego w Polsce (Commemorative issue 80th Anniversary of Patent Agents in Poland) 111 (2001), but without mentioning the *Cogito* case.

are clogged with cases, a first instance decision cannot be expected within less than one year, in extreme cases can take up to five years.[25]

To shorten this, Sec. 479(12)(i) was introduced in 2000[26] and requires the plaintiff to present all statements and evidence for their support in the beginning. The plaintiff may not present new statements or evidence during the procedure, unless he proves that the necessity to introduce them became apparent only after launching the petition. There have been no court decisions confirming this practice yet. Sec. 479(12)(i) does not define *statements* (*twierdzenia*). For instance, if the plaintiff in the petition has asked only for injunctive relief, could he later expand his petition and ask also for damages. This is not yet clear.

IV. Style of Decisions

While the judge of course enjoys independence in rendering decisions, precedents such as previous decisions by the Supreme Court in similar cases will be followed. Also appeal court decisions of the same district will be taken into account. To some extent, this also applies to decisions of other courts in similar cases, particularly if consistent with other rulings or views expressed in academic writings. In cases where proceedings take place in a number of counties in parallel, the court may even consider court judgments from these countries, especially from the economic leaders and especially the EU.[27]

In a 1996 amendment to the CCP, Sec. 3. 2 was deleted which obliged the court to examine *ex officio*. The aim of this change was to free the court from emotional engagement in the case should the court be obliged to collect evidence in the case.[28] Since this change the court may rely only on evidence presented by the parties.

V. The Profession

Representation before the courts is not mandatory.

Legal representation in patent infringement matters is somewhat complicated by the fact that there are three different kinds of representatives in legal matters: advocates, legal advisors and patent attorneys.

a) *Advocates*. The profession of advocates (*Adwokaci*) is governed by the 1982 Advocates Act.[29] Advocates may represent a party before the courts and all administrative offices with the exception of the Patent Office, where the

[25] *See* Fiolka, Bolek & Lolek, "Court Decision", 108 Copyright World 10 [2001].

[26] Dz.U. No. 48, item 554.

[27] An example being the Pilsner case.

[28] Szymański, Pietrzak, "Kodeks postępowania cywilnego po nowelizacji z dnia 1 marca 1996" (Civil Procedure Code After the Revision of 1 March 1996), 1996, 30.

[29] Dz. U. No 16, item 124, amended several times.

new Industrial Property Code stipulates exclusive rights of representation for patent attorneys. There is no recognised specialisation of advocates who must have a graduate degree in law, absolve a three-and-a-half year training period and pass the bar exam. In 1990, there were 6,902 advocates, in 1999, 7,166.[30]

b) *Legal advisors*. The profession of legal advisors (*Radcowie Prawni*) is governed by the 1982 Legal Advisors Act.[31] The origin of this profession dates back to the times when legal counsel was employed by state-owned enterprises. When state owned enterprises dwindled due to bankruptcy or privatisation during the 1990s, legal advisors received broader powers of representation. They may now represent business entities or natural persons in all court cases with the exception of family and criminal matters. Requirements are similar to those of attorneys, namely a graduate degree in law, a three-and-a-half year training period and an examination.

Although there are no official statistics, it is estimated that about 20,000 legal advisors are practising in Poland.

c) *Patent attorneys*. The profession of patent attorney (*Rzecznicy Patentowi*) is now governed by the new Patent Attorneys Act of 11 April 2001.[32] Patent attorneys have an exclusive right of representation before the Patent Office, and may represent parties in infringement procedures before the ordinary courts. As such, they enjoy equal rights as attorneys, including launching appeals to the Supreme Court in industrial property protection cases. Professional requirements for patent attorneys are a graduate degree in law or natural sciences, a three-and-a-half-year training period and an examination. Although no official statistics are available, the number of practising patent attorneys is an estimated 1,000.

VI. Competent Parties

1. Apart from the right owner, also the exclusive, registered licensee may launch an action of infringement, unless the licensing agreement provides otherwise (Sec. 76(6) IPC).

2. Should the licensee not comply with the conditions stipulated in the licensing agreement, the licensor may sue the licensee for breach of contract (Sec. 296(4) IPC).

3. In case of direct infringement the infringer may be sued. In addition, Sec. 422 Civil Code also makes contributory infringement actionable as well as inducement to infringement or making profit from the infringement.

---

30 Statistical Yearbook of the Republic of Poland, 2000, 90.

31 Dz. U. No 19, item 145 amended several times.

32 Dz. U. No 49, item 509. The law entered into force on 22 August 2001 to replace the law on patent attorneys of 1993.

VII. The Competent Court

1. Jurisdiction Under the Lugano Convention and Issues Related to Double and Transborder Litigation

Generally speaking, Polish courts and Polish entrepreneurs have little experience with questions of enforcing of the industrial property rights of foreign subjects, and questions of jurisdiction, recognition and enforcing foreign judgments.

Since 1 January 2000, Poland has become a member to the 1988 Lugano Convention on jurisdiction and recognition and enforcement of foreign judgments in civil and commercial matters. The Convention has evoked interest of legal commentators and writers in Poland,[33] however, there have been as yet few known court precedents.

In a decision of 23 August 2001, the Supreme Court held that in a case in which the parties were bound by an agreement stipulating exclusive jurisdiction of a foreign country, the Polish court could not declare lack of domestic jurisdiction before the petition was served on the defendant. [34]

In another decision of 6 April 2001, the Supreme Court dismissed the motion for lifting a temporary injunction against four companies, two of which were seated in Germany and two in Poland. In this case, this suit was launched in the Court of Cologne, Germany. The plaintiff asked for a declaratory judgment that under the contract he had bought stocks on behalf of these four companies. In a motion for granting temporary measures to preserve the assets, the plaintiff asked the Polish court to seize the stocks of the two Polish companies so that these could not be sold and to nominate the guardian of these stocks. The Supreme Court pointed out that even before the Lugano Convention, lack of domestic jurisdiction in the main action did not constitute an obstacle to hearing a motion for granting temporary measures of preservation.[35] However due to the fact that the main action was decided by the Court of Cologne, this court was also competent for granting a temporary measure for preservation. The Polish courts thus could not exercise jurisdiction.

---

[33] *See* for instance Wietz, "Konwencja z Lugano, Wykonalność Zagranicznych Orzeczeń przed Sądami Polskimi" (Lugano Conventions, Execution of Foreign Court Decisions before Polish Courts) (Warsaw 2002); or Włosińska, "Odmowa Uznania Zagranicznego Orzeczenia Sądowego w Świetle Postanowień Konwencji Lugańsiej" (Refusal of Recognition of Foreign Court Decisions in the Lugano Convention) (Zakamycze 2002); Polish National Group Rapport to Q 174 by Fiolka, www.aippi.org.

[34] Supreme Court decision of 23 August 2001, file No. N III CZP 43/01, Orzecznictwo Sądów Polskich 2002, issue 5, item 60 with positive comments by Ciszewski.

[35] Supreme Court decision of 18 February 1993, I CRN 6/93, OSNCP 1993, issue 11, item 204.

There is also no known court precedent regarding the question whether the Polish domestic courts can assume jurisdiction to decide on patent infringements. According to Sec. 1103 Code of Civil Procedure, the decisive factor would be whether the defendant is domiciled or has its headquarters in Poland.

2. National Jurisdiction

IP infringement cases are heard in first instance by one of 29 commercial district courts.

Jurisdiction is determined by the domicile or business establishment of the defendant (Secs. 27, 30 CCP). In addition, jurisdiction can be based on one of the following factors:

(a) A claim for monetary compensation can be launched before a court in the district in which the defendant has a business enterprise to the extent that the claim is linked to the enterprise's activity (Sec. 33 CCP);

(c) Claims related to the existence, execution or nullification of an agreement at the court of the place where performance is due (Sec. 34 CCP);

(d) In cases arising from a tort, the court of the place where such unlawful act took effect (Sec. 35 CCP);

(e) In case several rules of jurisdiction apply, the plaintiff has the right to choose the forum (Sec. 43 CCP).

Since in patent infringement matters often one of the special rules of jurisdiction mentioned above will apply, the plaintiff has a choice of several fora. Procedures in first instance are heard by one judge (Sec. 47(3) CCP), appeal proceedings by a panel of three judges. The final appeal before the Supreme Court is also heard by three judges (Sec. 393(7) CCP).

All judges are professionals with a legal background, yet have no specific technical knowledge.

VIII. Preparation for Trial

1. Measures to Preserve Evidence

General provisions for the preservation of evidence are contained in Secs. 310–315 CCP. Even before raising an action, the plaintiff may ask the court to preserve evidence if there is the danger that the evidence would otherwise be removed or destroyed. The provision should be flexible enough to meet the requirements for preserving evidence in IP enforcement cases.

Requests for preserving evidence should be made before the court that is competent to hear the main action, in cases of urgency and unless a main action has already been launched, in the district where the evidence is located.

Special provisions for the preservation of evidence are contained in the Sec. 80 Copyright Act 1994. Here, the competent court for such request is the one having jurisdiction over the territory where the alleged infringer conducts business or has assets. The court shall decide within three days and can order the alleged infringer to provide all necessary information, documents, etc., relevant to the plaintiff's claim, or can grant an interim injunction. Although there are no known cases, it is well possible that these provisions would be applied *mutatis mutandis* in cases of patent enforcement.

2. Warning Letters

The relevant provisions of the CCP in commercial cases require the plaintiff to enclose all documents related to voluntary attempts to settle the case, and to the defendant's position in this matter (Sec. 479(12)). Lack of the above documents or information is only relevant in cases where the defendant is sued without previous warning and immediately admits to the claim. Here, the court may order the plaintiff to pay all the costs and expenses caused by his action.

3. Interim Injunctions

Interim injunctions are regulated in great detail in Secs. 730–757 CCP. Interim injunctions are granted on the balance of probabilities and on the plaintiff proving a demonstrable loss if the injunction were not granted. An injunction may also be granted in order to safeguard the execution of the judgment, yet may not be aimed at satisfying what the main action should provide. Requests for issuing an interim injunction do not necessarily require launching a petition. However, if the interim injunction is granted before launching the infringement petition, the patent owner will be obliged to do so within 14 days, otherwise the interim measure will lapse.

Somewhat different rules on interim injunctions can be found in Sec. 21 Unfair Competition Repression Act and Sec. 80 Copyright Act. Under these provisions, it is not clear if the court has a right to investigate the validity of the claim. Of course these provisions may be applied *mutatis mutandis* in patent cases.

It is quite common that a patent infringement case begins with an interim injunction to use or sell the patented device. This is a relatively easy matter, as the injunction is granted without hearing the defendant and is based only on arguments presented by plaintiff. The defendant has the right to appeal, which is normally decided within six months.

IX. The Trial

1. In General

The trial is the stage at which the parties can present their claims and evidence is heard. The trial starts with a presentation of the plaintiff's petition, and the defendant's reply. The judge takes an active role in the proceedings and decides on their course. Court sessions may last between half-an-hour and several hours, depending on the case. The current caseload of judges is daunting. According to latest statistics between 1993 and 2003, the number of cases has doubled and the number of judges in courts in the same period grew by only 40%.[36]

2. Expert Opinions

In appropriate cases, the judge can order expert evidence to be heard, which is the norm in IP cases when technical knowledge is required. Experts may be appointed by the court among persons skilled in the art, often from research institutes, universities or other scientific institutions. The parties may present their own experts and expert opinions, yet the court is free to weigh the importance of such expertise. The court will normally follow the opinion of the court-appointed expert. A party dissatisfied with such expertise may request the court to appoint a second expert.

X. Proving Infringement

1. Literal Infringement and Infringement by Equivalents in Patent Matters

Sec. 63(2) IPC provides that the scope of a patent is determined by the claims, while description and drawings may be used as a means of interpretation. As of now, there is no court precedent regarding the doctrine of equivalents. In a Supreme Court decision of 1970, the court held that also a partial use of the patented claims in a certain embodiment would constitute an infringement.[37] In that case, not all elements of the patented device were used. According to the court, the question of infringement depended more on the relative importance of the given element in comparison to the whole invention, and the use of such element in the production process, rather than the fact all elements had to be used. It would indeed constitute a patent infringement if an element was used that could be interpreted as so vital to the whole invention that it constituted the essence thereof. Apart from this decision, cases where patent claims are interpreted are rather rare, and mostly connected with questions regarding the proper remuneration of employed

[36] Główny Urząd Statystyczne (Central Statistical Office), Mały rocznik statystyczny 2002 (Small Statistics' Book 2002) 67 (Warsaw 2002).

[37] Supreme Court decision of 3 February 1970, file No. 615/69, Gazeta Sądowa i Penitencjarna, [20/1970]. Excerpts of this decision are cited in Szwaja, "Prawo wynalazcze. Przepisy, orzecznictwo, piśmiennictwo, objaśnienia" (Law on Inventive Activity. Provisions, Jurisprudence, Literature, Comments) 276–277 (Warsaw 1978).

inventors.[38] These cases often centred around the question of if and to what extent the patented invention was used. Here, the courts were very restrictive and adopted a very literal interpretation of patent claims. In addition, all elements of the patent had to be used in order to constitute infringement, while partial use was not deemed infringing, with the consequence that the inventor had no right to remuneration.[39] In another decision by the Cracow District Court, the latter held that the doctrine of equivalents was not good law in Poland.[40]

2. Protection of Process Patents

A patent granted for a process of manufacture does not only cover that process, but also the products obtained directly therefrom (Sec. 64(1) IPC). Where the alleged infringer manufactures the same products, there is a a reversal of the burden of proof in that the alleged infringer has to prove that the product was produced by a different process (Sec. 64(2)).

XI. Defences

1. Non-Infringement

The most common defence of course is that of non-infringement, in some cases based on the defendant's own IP right. It has been pointed out above that contesting an IP right in court is difficult due to the Patent Office's jurisdiction over the matter. In one case, the Supreme Court has indicated that it might accept the estoppel of abuse of right where such right was obviously obtained contrary to the provisions of law (see the above *Cogito* decision).

2. Invalidity

Polish courts do not have jurisdiction to invalidate a patent, utility model or trade mark. Thus, the defendant cannot raise the estoppel of invalidity in infringement procedures, but only initiate an invalidation action before the Patent Office.

3. Time Bar

An infringement action can be raised before the patent is granted, but will be suspended up to that time. There is no case against infringement prior to the

---

[38] The Polish patent law adopted a system for employees' inventions similar to the German one. The employed inventor of a patented invention in use had a right to remuneration, the amount of which was fixed by law.

[39] Supreme Court, enlarged panel, decision of 23 June 1977, Case No. *v.* PZP 1/77; Supreme Court, decision of 24 November 1978, Case No. IV PR 288/78, OSPIKA 1979; Supreme Court, enlarged panel, decision of 12 March 1987, Case No. III PRN 5/86, OSPIKA 1988, issue 3, item 47,

[40] Cracow District Court, decision of 30 January 1998, Case No. IX GC 536/96.

publication of the application or other knowledge by the infringer. An action for infringement can only be raised within three years from the time the plaintiff obtains knowledge of infringement and infringer. The period of three years is counted separately for each act of infringement, which in practice often means not the action being barred as such, but the plaintiff being able to ask for damages only for the last three years. Yet, there is an absolute time bar of five years from the date of infringement. If the action is based on unfair competition law, the relative time bar of three years is the same, but the action can be raised within 10 years from the date of infringement if the plaintiff had no knowledge of infringement or infringer previously.

4. Other Defences

Other defences include the right of the defendant based on a contractual or compulsory licence, or based on prior user rights. In the case of patents, rights do not extend to acts of experimental use, including experiments made for the purpose of obtaining administrative approval for marketing in the case of pharmaceuticals. The defendant can further rely on exhaustion if the patented or trademarked goods were brought into circulation by the IP owner or with his consent either in Poland or in another country which has concluded a free trade agreement with Poland.

XII. Remedies

The remedies available in cases of IP infringement were established a long time ago, both under general civil law as well as in the separate IP statutes. They are now contained in Secs. 287 and 296 Industrial Property Code. Due to the scarcity of decisions in the field of IP infringement, a lot of ambiguities remain in this area. Basically, six types of remedies are available.

1. Injunctive Relief

Injunctive relief is the most basic remedy in cases of infringement, as in most cases the IP owner is most interested in preventing further acts of infringement. Practice shows that IP owners tend to initiate a claim for injunctive relief as a first stage of a dispute, and only subsequently claim other remedies such as damages once the active infringement has been established.[41] There are also tactical reasons for such procedure, *e.g.* the fairly moderate court fees when claiming injunctive relief when compared to those for claiming damages or unjust enrichment. In addition, the plaintiff can expect far speedier proceedings if only the question of infringement as such has to be

[41] Tomaszek, "Zabezpieczenie roszczeń niepieniężnych w sprawach o naruszenie prawa z rejestracji znaków towarowych" (Interim Injunctions of Non-Pecuniary Claims in Trade Mark Registration Rights Violations Cases), Monitor Prawniczy (MP) 4 [8/1994].

determined. Claiming damages or lost profits often involves lengthier court procedures and far more evidence.

2. Claims for Damages and Infringer's Profits

Damages and infringer's profits can be claimed simultaneously on the assumption that one is subtracted from the other, in other words that the claim for the infringer's profits lowers the IP owner's damages and vice versa.[42] Apart from the Industrial Property Code, the above-mentioned damage claims can also be based on Secs. 415 *et seq*. Civil Code (reimbursement of damages) and Secs. 405 *et seq*. (unjust enrichment). Damages suffered by the IP owner both relate to direct damages and lost profits.

3. Penalty Payments

In cases where the infringement was deliberate, the court may order the infringer to pay a certain sum of money to an organisation whose purpose is to support matters of industrial property. The money should be used for the promotion of industrial property.

4. Reimbursement of Litigation Costs

As a general rule under Polish civil procedure, the losing party has to pay all costs of the case. These costs relate to the court fees, the remuneration of court experts, attorney's fees and other costs related to the case, *e.g.* translator fees. However, in the case of reimbursement of attorney's fees, one should mention that the costs ordered for reimbursement and the actual costs incurred often differ widely. Attorneys are normally paid by the hour, sometimes to an amount of between EUR 100 and 400, and it stands to reason that the courts do not oblige the losing party to pay these, but rather the costs that an attorney would charge according to the official schedule of attorney's, legal advisor's or patent attorney's fees.

5. Destruction of Infringing Goods

The destruction of goods, although available as a remedy, has not been well-received by the public at large. In those few cases where the destruction of counterfeit goods were ordered, press reports were extremely hostile and recommended that these goods should rather be distributed among the homeless or poor. These arguments, of course, have gained weight with the transformation of the economy that widened income disparities. In a very early case of counterfeit goods, the Supreme Court ordered the infringing

[42] This doctrine was endorsed by the Supreme Court, decision of 22 October 1974 published in Orzecznictwo Sądu Najwyższego [1975], No. 10–11, item 153. The view is shared by Markiewicz & Barta in: Czajkowska-Dąbrowska, "Ustawa o prawie autorskim i prawach pokrewnych. Komentarz" (Copyright and Related Rights. Commentary), Barta/ Markiewicz eds., 512–513 (Warsaw 2001). Both relate to copyright infringement.

labels removed from all goods produced by the defendant, already sold or not.[43] The possibility of having the decision executed in relation to those goods already sold to retailers was more than doubtful and reaped criticism.

6. Apology and Publication of Clarifying Statements

According to the explicit provision of Sec. 287(2) IPC, the infringer of a patent has to publish an appropriate statement in the press at the request of the patentee. This provision also applies to other industrial property rights such as trade marks and geographical indications. The text of the statement should be supplied by the plaintiff together with the request.

XIII. Appeal Procedures Before Civil Courts

1. Appeals

Every party to a first instance court decision has the right to launch an appeal to the Appeal Court (Sec. 367 CCP). The deadline is 14 days from receiving written justification of the first instance decision, or if the party did not ask for written justification within seven days from announcement of the decision, 21 days from the announcement (Sec. 368(2) CCP). An appeal after expiry of the deadline will be rejected. Grounds for appellation are violations of substantive law or procedure.

The appeal court will hear the case only within the motions contained in the appeal, but will take into account *ex officio* the fact that the proceedings were null and void (Sec. 378).

The appeal court will take into account evidence collected by the court of first instance. New facts and evidence may presented only if this was not possible before the first instance court, or the need to present these only emerged after the first instance proceedings were closed.

In the appeal proceedings, new claims may not be launched (Sec. 383).

The appeal is heard by the panel of three judges. Appeal proceedings are much speedier, as usually there is only one relatively short trial, after which the decision is announced. There is a *reformationis in peius* bar. As a rule, the appeal court will decide *de novo* if it is accepting the appeal (Sec. 386). In case the first instance decision is overturned, the case is remanded back. In addition to these options, the appeal court may revoke the first instance decision and transfer the case back to the first instance court only if the latter did not decide on the merits of the case *(nie rozpoznał istoty sprawy)* or where evidence has to be taken again. The appeal court decision is immediately

---

[43] Supreme Court, decision of 29 November 1984, IC 357/84, OSN [9/1985], item 131, Jakubecki Postępowanie zabezpieczające w sprawach z zakresu własności intelektualnej (Enforcement Procedures in Cases of Intellectual Property), 2000, 296. The case concerned Wrangler jeans.

executable, unless it defers its execution or requires the plaintiff to place a deposit (Sec. 388).

The appeal court may refer the case to the Supreme Court.

2. Cassation (*kasacja*)

From the appeal court decision, there is a second stage appeal to Supreme Court (Sec. 392 CCP). In commercial matters, the minimal value of the case for cassation is 20,000 Polish zlotys (less than EUR 5,000).

The Supreme Court is not obliged to hear all the cassations. Only if the case presents a major legal problem, or there is a need for interpretation of provisions which are not precise or cause a difference in jurisprudence, will the cassation be taken into account by the Supreme Court (Sec. 393).

According to unofficial statistics, only 25–30% of cassation cases are heard by the Supreme Court. This situation has been widely criticised.

It usually takes one year to get a pre-trial cassation decision.

XIV. Patent Invalidity Procedures Before the Patent Office

The Patent Office's main task is, of course, the grant of industrial property rights. However, it should be noted that Patent Office has also the right to interpret provisions in the field of industrial property.[44]

According to Sec. 255 IPC, the Patent Office is competent to invalidate a patent,[45] a right of protection or a right in registration.

Representation before the Patent Office is not mandatory. However the persons or entities not domiciled or located in Poland must be represented (Sec. 235(3) IPC).

The question of representation before the Patent Office is very strange. According to Sec. 236, the representative of a party in proceedings before the Patent Office in matters connected with filing and maintaining protection of inventions may only be patent attorneys. The Central Attorney's Council (*Naczelna Rada Adwokacka*) argued before the Constitutional Tribunal that this provision was unconstitutional. The Constitutional Tribunal rejected the petition. But it limited the application of Sec. 236 to filing procedures and accepted the right of advocates and legal advisors to represent the parties in so-called adversarial proceedings (*postępowanie sporne*), where the nullification of a patent is decided.[46]

---

[44] Rozporządzenie Rady Ministrów w sprawie szczegółowego zakresu działania Urzędu Patentowego RP z 8 stycznia 2002 r. (Decree of the Council of Ministers on detailed scope of activity of the Patent Office of Polish Republic), Dz.U. No 8, item 59, Paragraph 2. 1. 14).

[45] This text is binding until the entry into force of the amendment referred to in footnote 19.

[46] Constitutional Tribunal decision of 21 May 2002, file No. K 30/01, OTK-A 2002/3/32.

The Patent Office renders an adversarial decision by a panel of three experts. The president of the panel should have legal training (as a judge, attorney, legal advisor or public prosecutor). The other two members of the panel are experts from the Patent Office and representatives of technical associations, both usually having a technical background.

A Patent Office decision may be subject of a motion for reconsidering the case by the Patent Office and then taken (appealed) to the *vojewodship (wojewódzki)* administrative court with appeal to Central Administrative Court *(Naczelny Sąd Administracyjny)*.

XV. Administrative (Border) Measures of Patent Enforcement

There is a possibility of asking the Director of Custom Chamber in Warsaw to seize the goods on the border during customs clearance if the goods violate patent rights. This is regulated by a decree issued under the Polish Customs Code.[47] The protection is granted for a period up to 12 months. The pirate goods may be seized, where after the right owner will be informed and is obliged to launch infringement procedures before the court.

XVI. Conclusion

While the enforcement of patent rights in Poland is certainly not easy, it is not impossible, either. It requires time and patience, but is improving.

[47] *See* Rozporządzenie Rady Ministrów w sprawie sposobu i trybu postępowania organów celnych w wypadku podejrzenia naruszenia przepisów dotyczących ochrony własności intelektualnej z 2 grudnia 2002 r. (Decree on Proceedings of the Customs Office During the Seizure of Goods in the Case of Suspected Infringement of Intellectual Property Rights), Dz.U. No. 12, item 112.

10
The Enforcement of Patent Rights in the Czech Republic

Ivo Telec

A. *Brief Outline of the System of Civil Procedure*

I. General Problems Concerning Industrial Property Rights

Legal disputes over patent and other industrial property rights are neither frequent nor common in the Czech Republic.[1] This is due to their exclusive nature and to the fact that in many cases parties seek a quick, informal and cheap out-of-court settlement. The cases that go to court are often problematic disputes, the outcome of which have many direct or indirect repercussions on development, planning and financing, as well as social implications such as unemployment. There are cases when both parties are interested in an authoritative decision in order to plan future economic activities.

One should also be aware that out of several thousand registered attorneys-at-law, only about 100 are able to give expert legal advice in IP matters because they require a legal specialisation and a creative way of thinking. Often, attorneys-at-law cannot deal with matters of a technical nature by themselves, and therefore cooperate with patent attorneys and vice versa. A coordination between attorneys-at-law and patent attorneys is actually quite common. Patent attorneys and specialised attorneys-at-law give advice based on an increasing number of published court and administrative rulings.

In Czech legal literature we can find no handbook on methods and tactics of patent litigation. There are only a number of articles, mostly on the law against unfair competition, a field also of interest to patents.[2]

---

[1] According to official statistics, 232,101 litigations in civil matters were settled in the Czech Republic in 2001, among them 59 concerning patents and designs (*see* "Statistical Yearbook of the Czech Republic" 654 (1st ed., Prague, Scientia 2002). We cannot rule out the possibility that this statistic, despite its narrow designation, also includes disputes in other matters of industrial property. In addition, there is a separate statistical record of litigation for damages. This may include litigation on the infringement of industrial property rights. The statistical designation thus does not correspond to the legal classification, which is considerably broader.

[2] *See* for instance Hajn, "Předběžné opatření ve sporech z nekalé soutěže" (Interim Injunction in Disputes Concerning Unfair Competition), 1994 Právní rozhledy, No. 10 at 349; and Macek, "Zamyslení nad žalobami či návrhy na vydání předběžného opatření ve sporech z nekalé soutěže z hlediska formulace petitů" (Thoughts on Lawsuits or Proposals for Issuing Interim Injunction in Disputes Concerning Unfair Competition from the Viewpoint of Petits Formulation), 1999 Soudní rozhledy 5, No. 12, at 393.

Pursuing a litigation is usually so costly that it might be more suitable to settle out of court. A large number of disputes are settled out of court with the help of attorneys-at-law, patent attorneys or independent experts. Generally respected experts are often accepted by both parties. An out of court settlement provides no execution title, however.

Patent law is taught at university faculties of law or economics, usually within the framework of intellectual property law. Specialised instruction in patent law is provided by the Institute of Industrial Property Education at the Industrial Property Office in Prague. An educational role is also played by the Bar of Patent Attorneys in Brno, the Czech Bar of Attorneys-at-law in Prague and the Czech national groups of AIPPI and LIDC, both seated in Prague. The Bar of Patent Attorneys is authorised to examine new patent attorney candidates.

There are about 200 patent attorneys, and about 100 attorneys-at-law specialised in industrial property rights. Among other experts there are patent engineers and authorised experts from the administrative branch of patents and inventions, some of whom are also engaged in the evaluation of intangible property. In many cases the same persons handle several jobs.

II. Courts and Jurisdiction

Disputes in industrial property rights generally fall within the jurisdiction of the courts, yet there are also *inter partes* proceedings which fall within the authority of the Industrial Property Office in Prague and are decided in special administrative proceedings. These matters concern the determination of scope both for patents and trade marks, invalidation and compulsory licences, the latter being very exceptional in practice.

The division of powers between courts and the Industrial Property Office is stipulated in the relevant IP laws.

There are no patent courts in the Czech Republic, as there are no specialised courts with the exception of the Constitutional Court. A patent court existed under Austrian and Czechoslovak law, which was applicable in Czech territory in the period between 1872 and 1952.

III. Publication of Decisions

A number of books dealing with selected judicial and administrative decisions in matters concerning patent and other industrial property rights have been published.[3] Commentaries on some judicial decisions have been

---

[3] *See* Anonymus (ed.), "Dusevní vlastnictví" (Intellectual Property), Coll., Vol. I (1st ed., Prague, SEPI 1998) and the following updates; Effenberger (ed.), "Sbírka judikátu ve veci vynálezu a uzitnych vzoru" (Collection of Judicial Decisions in Matters Concerning Inventions and Usable Designs) Vol. I–II (foreign part) (1st ed. Prague, Federální úrad pro vynálezy – Úrad prumyslového vlastnictvì 1991–1994); Jakl (ed.), "Koneená rozhodnutí

published in journals. Some published decisions are of considerable importance because they represent a turning point in legal doctrine.

An example of judicial creativity it is inspiring to read decisions on unfair competition that include scanned photographs of products. Photographs are a simpler, clearer and more suitable means for enforcement purposes than a long description of products.[4]

The Industrial Property Office has made its own recent administrative and judicial decisions accessible to the public via the Internet at www.upv.cz. Also accessible are all decisions of the Constitutional Court in Brno at www.nsoud.cz. All these decisions can be anonymously accessed.

---

ve vecech vynálezu" (Final Decisions in Patent Matters) (1st ed., Prague, Úrad prumyslového vlastnictvì 1994). Sbìrka správnìch rozhodnutì ve vecech prùmyslovych práv (Collection of Administrative Decisions in Industrial Property Matters) Vol. I–III (1st ed. Prague, Úrad prùmyslového vlastnictvì 1994–1999) (Vol. I, 2nd ed., 1996). Macek (ed.), "Rozhodnutí ve vecech obchodního jména a nekalé souteze" (Decisions in Matters of Trade Names and Unfair Competition) (1st ed., Prague, C. H. Beck 2000). Tihelka, "Nad jedním judikátem" (On One Judicial Decision), 1994 Prumyslové vlastnictví No. 10, at 303 an.

From other publications, *see* Cermák & Cermák jr., "Rozhodování o obeanskych právech nebo závazcích *v.* rìzenì pred Úradem prumyslového vlastnictví" (Deciding on Civil Rights or Obligations in Proceedings before the Industrial Property Office), 2001 Prumyslové vlastnictví No. 1/2, at 6. K. Kupka, "K problematice prezkoumávání správních rozhodnutí Úradu prumyslového vlastnictví soudem" (On Problems of Judicial Review of Administrative Decisions of the Industrial Property Office), 1994 Prumyslové vlastnictví No. 7, at 193 an. Mazanec, "Patentovy soud jako soud verejného práva?" (Patent Court as a Public Law Court?), 1994 Prumyslové vlastnictví No. 10, at 289. Strnadov, "Trestní postih pri porusování prumyslovych práv" (Criminal Prosecution of IP Infringement), 2000 Prumyslové vlastnictví No. 5/6, at 111. Telec, "The Enforcement of Industrial Property Rights in the Czech Republic", 32 IIC [2001]. Zamrzla, "Smírcí rízení ve vecech dusevního vlastnictví" (Amicable Settlement in Intellectual Property Matters), 1997 Prumyslové vlastnictví No. 5/6, 85.

There are also references to judicial decisions in various commentaries. *See e.g.* Jezek, "Patentovy zákon. Zákon o uzitnych vzorech. Komentár" (Patents Act. Designs Act. Commentary) (1 ed. Prague, C. H. Beck 1998). Pítra et al., Ochrana prumyslového vlastnictvì. Komentár (Protection of Industrial Property. Commentary) (1 ed., Prague, SEVT – Frances 1992), Vol. I. Zákon o ochrannych známkách. Komentár (Trade Marks Act. Commentary) (1 ed. Prague, C. H. Beck 1996). From earlier publications, *see* Vitásek, "Ceskoslovensky patentní zákon" (Czechoslovak Patents Act) (1 ed. Prague, *v.* Linhart 1933).

Further, *see* various parts of the official Collection of Judicial Decisions and Viewpoints published by the Supreme Court and previous similar collections. *Cf.* also various volumes of the journal Prumyslové vlastnictví (Industrial Property) and earlier journals preceding it.

For academic publications *cf.* Knap, Kunz & Opltová, "Prumyslová práva *v.* mezinárodních vztazích" (Industrial Property Rights in International Relationships) (1 ed. Prague, Academia 1988).

[4] Former Regional Commercial Court Brno, 3 August 1998, No. 11 Cms 92/98-11, 2000 Jurisprudence No. 2, at 29.

B. *Problems Related to the Enforcement of Patent Rights*

I. Competent Parties and Representatives

An action in matters concerning patent rights can be conducted both by the owner of the right and an authorised, registered licensee if the right is likely to be infringed.[5] The same applies to a franchisee. Parties may represent themselves in court but appeal proceedings and proceedings in actions against decisions of administrative bodies, *e.g.* decisions of the Chairman of the Industrial Property Office in Prague have to be heard before the respective district court (since 2003).[6]

Parties are usually represented by attorneys-at-law, but not by notaries public.

Patent attorneys usually do not represent clients in court litigation, yet a number of patent attorneys co-operate with attorneys-at-law on a permanent basis. Patent attorneys have been authorised to represent clients before the court since 2003.

II. The Competent Court

1. First Instance

There is no central jurisdiction in first instance, which makes legal protection more difficult. The regional courts deal with matters concerning patent rights and unfair competition in first instance. This, however, only applies to "business matters" (Sec. 9 (3) (o) Czech Code of Civil Procedure (CCP)). In the case of non-business matters, jurisdiction rests with the respective district court (Sec. 9 (1) CCP). This was probably not intended by the legislature and must be regarded as a legislative error resulting from the abolition of regional business courts as of 1 January 2001.

Making a procedural distinction between "business matters" and "non-business matters" is inappropriate and jeopardises effective and speedy law enforcement.

2. On Appeal

The competent appeal court in patent matters is the Superior Court in Prague for Bohemia and the Superior Court in Olomouc for Moravia. These courts decide in divisions. This also applies to copyright disputes concerning general personality rights pursuant to the Civil Code.

Unfortunately, it often takes a long time for the appeal court to decide a case.

---

[5] Prague Superior Court, 30 December 2000, No. 3 Cmo 382/2000-136.

[6] Supreme Administrative Court in Brno, 3 June 2003, No. 7 A 132/2000.

III. Preparation for Trial

1. Warning letters

It is quite common that the owner of a right in his own interest warns the other party that his/her activities constitute an unauthorised infringement. The owner of a right usually does so by means of a written legal warning drawn up by an attorney in which he briefly describes the state of facts, shows his title to the other party and lays his claim. He also asks the other party to show in writing his/her title. He usually tries to reach an amicable out-of-court settlement. Issuing a legal warning may also clarify misunderstandings or contingent errors concerning rights.

By receiving the warning letter, the other party is made aware that he/she may be infringing someone else's right. Therefore he/she cannot later successfully claim acting *bona fide*. This makes it easier for the injured party to ask the court for an interim injunction.

Still, an attempt for an amicable settlement is not a prerequisite for bringing an action. It sometimes happens that the parties, having reached an amicable settlement, become business partners in the end.

2. Preparation of the Proposal for Interim Injunction or Lawsuit

Requests for interim injunctions need to be well prepared to be successful. Preparation for a suit in general requires not only demanding legal, but also involves organisational and administrative considerations and a number of technical and economic aspects.

The lawsuit is filed in the usual form, which does not differ from other types of lawsuits. What is sometimes different is the style. If the petitioner refers to impending non-proprietary damage, it is often a short "literary essay". Unfortunately, little attention is paid to creative writing in the education of Czech lawyers.

The injured party has a legal right to demand that the other party submit those documents that concern the origin of a product, including information about the product sales. Submitting other documents is a matter of good manners, customs or amicable arrangement.

3. Activities of the Court

a) Settlements

aa) Before starting proceedings

Voluntary and preliminary settlements before the court without starting proceedings (Secs. 67 *et seq.* CCP) are not common in the Czech Republic. Parties either bring their action before the court, claiming also the right to reimbursement of legal costs, or try to reach an agreement with the help of attorneys-at-law or patent attorneys, often repeatedly and without any intervention. In that case, the parties do not reach a settlement approved by the court and thus have no execution title other than by a notary public's or an executioner's record of settlement.

At present, in the area of patent rights we do not quite often come across records of notaries or executioners as execution titles.

bb) Settlements in the course of proceedings
Settlements are more common in the course of the proceedings (Sec. 99 CCP). It happens particularly when it becomes evident that it is suitable or effective for the parties to end the matter with a settlement which may entail a compromise, but results in a cheaper and quicker solution. In IP matters that are legally and factually complicated, time-consuming and costly, the judge usually tries to encourage the parties to reach an amicable arrangement approved by the court. In the end, the judge spares himself work, while the arbitral role of attorneys and their negotiation skills come to the fore.[7]

b) Interim injunctions

aa) General issues
Proposals for court interim injunctions are quite often submitted in matters concerning patent rights, and it follows from their very nature that they cannot be delayed. Attorneys sometimes use this well-tried tactic to "test" the judge's opinion in the respective matter. After the initial hesitations of Czech courts in the early 1990s to issue interim injunctions identical with lawsuits in the same matter, the situation has improved, at least in appeal courts. There was a turning point particularly in matters concerning unfair competition, which are representative of the whole sphere of intellectual property rights.[8] For example, an interim injunction was issued before initiating the main proceedings which ordered the opponent to refrain from using a domain name identical with a business firm and a trade mark of the petitioner.[9]

The general procedure for interim injunctions (Secs. 74 *et seq.* CCP) which is also applicable in patent cases, means that the court has to decide on the proposal for an interim injunction within seven days after the submission of the proposal. This period was defined by a law which entered into force on 1 January 2000, resulting in a considerably shortened period for issuing an

---

[7] In the decision of former Regional Commercial Court in Brno of 9 December 1999, No. 11 Cms 91/97-113, the court approved an amicable arrangement to pay part of a remuneration for an employee's invention. The rest of the remuneration was made subject to further proceedings.

[8] Former Supreme Court No. 30/1993 Coll., court decisions and opinions (civil); Superior Court Prague No. 46/1996 Coll., court decisions and opinions (civil), 1996 Právní praxe *v.* podnikání No. 7/8, at 37; Superior Court Prague No. 49/1997, 1997 Soudní rozhledy No. 3, at 62; from other sources *see* the former Regional Commercial Court Brno No. 56/1998, 1998 Soudní rozhledy No. 7, at 173.

[9] Regional Court Plzen, 21 December 2000, sp.zn. 22 Cm 38/2000.

interim injunction. If ill-founded, a proposal may be rejected (Sec. 75a CCP).

There is a possibility of speeding up procedures by submitting the required duplicates of the requested decision with the proposal (Sec. 9 Ministerial Procedure Suborder), possibly in electronic form on a diskette. This is only used in lawsuits for payments which are to be decided by the court by payment order.

Apart from posting security, which is to be dealt with hereafter, there are no special rules for individual types of industrial property rights. The applicant, however, has to make a formal declaration of validity of the patent or trade mark in question. At least in the interim, the court has to accept the validity of the IP right.

bb) Liability

The petitioner for an interim injunction is objectively liable for the result of the dispute. Therefore, if the main action is lost, he is obliged to compensate the opponent or any third party for any damage arising from the interim injunction. Cases are rare, as the petitioner for interim injunction is usually from the outset certain enough of his right and his ability to prove an unauthorised infringement.

cc) Posting security in interim injunctions

Posting security in an amount sufficient to compensate the other party for possible damages is not usually required, but may be ordered in patent matters. The matter is at the discretion of the respective court, which may order the petitioner to post a security in an amount sufficient for compensation and for preventing abuse.

Disobeying an injunction prohibiting certain commercial activities constitutes the criminal act of obstructing the execution of a court ruling (Sec. 171(1) (c) Penal Code). This applies to any party against whom the injunction was issued.

Occasionally one can come across a criminal law warning in a civil judgment according to Secs. 1 and 3 CCP.[10]

c) Securing evidence

Any relevant evidence can be secured. In patent matters it is important to secure firsthand evidence for an expert to prepare a report. It may be impossible or very difficult to take such evidence later (Sec. 78 CCP). This is, for instance, the case when the manufacturing activity of the defendant changes. The judge may order securing evidence in the form of an expert's report before or after proceedings have been initiated (Secs. 78, 102(2) CCP). The decision will be based on the degree of urgency. While before starting proceedings the court may issue an order only on request, once the proceedings have started, it may do so on its own initiative.

---

[10] Former Regional Commercial Court Brno, 3 August 1998, 11 Cms 92/98-11.

In one case, at the request of the plaintiff and after the proceedings had started, but before ordering the first hearing, the court appointed an expert in patents and inventions to assess the equitable remuneration for an employee's patented invention. Securing evidence in the form of an expert's report was necessary in order to discover how the patent was used in a nuclear plant during the repair of corroded exchangers. It is worth noting that the court ordered the inspection against a third party and considered it necessary to investigate on the spot rather than settle for documents in order to calculate the remuneration.[11]

The participants in proceedings have the right to be present when evidence is taken only when there is no danger of delay.

IV. The Trial

1. Interim Judgments on Preliminary Questions

In patent matters, decisions on the merits for issues important for the later stages of the suit (Sec. 132 (2) CCP) are not uncommon and may even amount to decisions in part. Whether such a procedure is practical is left to the discretion of the court, that can act at its own initiative.

For instance, in cases of innovations, the court may issue a decision ascertaining whether a certain technical innovation is a proposal for improvement or not, whether it is used lawfully by the employer or not, or whether the employer is liable in principle for unjust enrichment at the expense of the innovator. The monetary value of such enrichment would then be determined in the final judgment.

Similar decisions may be made to determine whether a certain creation constitutes an author's work or not, a procedure only adopted in difficult cases.

In other cases, a decision in part is not issued and the court considers the matter only as a prejudicial point of law, *e.g.* whether a certain licence contract is valid or not.

2. Binding Nature of Decisions by the Industrial Property Office

The court is bound to follow a final decision of the Industrial Property Office, *e.g.* whether a certain technical solution falls within the scope of a patented invention, reached in a determination of scope decision. Such procedure is initiated at the request of either the IP owner or a potential infringer. Procedures require both parties to be heard, and are normally conducted in writing. The Industrial Property Office may reach a decision on infringement, yet is not entitled to order any sanctions in such case.

---

[11] Former Regional Commercial Court Brno, 27 May 1997, No. 11 Cms 91/97-20.

Only if the Industrial Property Office, for whatever reason, has not decided upon a matter, may the court itself decide (Sec. 135 (2) CCP) or alternatively stay the proceedings for the Industrial Property Office to decide. The court would take the latter course if there are administrative proceedings in the same matter before the Office. If the Industrial Property Office has not decided the case in determination of scope proceedings, the court usually determines the scope on the basis of an authorised expert's opinion or reports by independent experts.

Separation of jurisdiction between the Industrial Property Office and the courts requires the latter to accept a patent or trade mark registration as a legal fact that may not be disputed. For the estoppel of invalidity, see below at VI.

V. Proving Infringement

1. Presenting Facts and Evidence

For some industrial property matters – but not in patent matters – facts and evidence may be presented together (Sec. 118b CCP). The parties may thus present facts and suggest evidence as proof until the end of the first hearing. Facts and evidence presented later are generally not taken into account by the court. This rule also applies to cases of unfair trade secrets and personality (privacy) rights.

2. Taking Evidence

In patent matters, both participants and judges may suggest suitable evidence, although the decision which evidence will be heard is left to the court's discretion. This strengthens the role of the judge in the proceedings.

3. Types of Evidence

The burden of proof lies with the party alleging a certain fact, but what suggested evidence will be heard is decided by the court. In IP matters, the court may also hear evidence other than what has been submitted, if necessary. In the case of a technical problem, the court may, for example, call for an administrative file of the Industrial Property Office, or for a report of a trading association or the Chamber of Commerce of the Czech Republic. The court may also accept those facts as acknowledged by both parties, *e.g.* statements concerning the marketability of goods.

Proof is usually furnished by documentary evidence, *e.g.* a patent certificate or a certificate on the legal status of a firm, a written licensing contract, a bookkeeping voucher on the purchase of the goods, photographs of products, business catalogues, advertising prospectuses, written analyses of product quality, or various expert reports.

It is common for the plaintiff to present his own documentary evidence before the court and at the same time to ask the court to order the other party to present his/her documentary evidence, *e.g.* bookkeeping vouchers to which the plaintiff has no access. This follows the general procedure of taking evidence and is at the discretion of the court. The plaintiff has no right to have the evidence of the other party presented, but the court usually orders the defendant (or if need be, the plaintiff) to do so.

Products are inspected by the court only in the case of small items, and for illustration when mere photographs, catalogues or other documents are not sufficient.

Proof by hearing witnesses is uncommon. An exception can be disputes related to employment when a hearing of fellow employees seems suitable. This could concern, for example, employees' industrial designs, software programs, innovations or trade secrets.

Quite frequently, evidence is presented by way of an authorised expert's written opinion, *e.g.* for patents and inventions, or computer technology. It makes no difference if the authorised expert is appointed by the court or by one of the parties, sometimes even before proceedings are commenced. The reason for a party to request an opinion may be to assess the chances of success in the respective dispute.

If an authorised expert's opinion was commissioned privately, the other party sometimes challenges not only its content but also the independence of the authorised expert. Moreover, some courts are reluctant to accept privately commissioned opinions, especially when the court intends to request an authorised expert opinion.

Proof by hearing the parties is infrequent in the highly formalised Czech civil procedure. A party may be a witness only when a fact cannot be proven otherwise and when the party who is to be examined agrees. In IP matters, it is an unusual type of proof.

VI. Defences

The defendant may argue that the external appearance of his goods or the technical process used by him in the alleged infringement falls outside the scope of the plaintiff's registered industrial design or patent. The court must solve such a case either implicitly or by issuing a decision in part. But if the case has already been decided by the Industrial Property Office in determination of scope proceedings, the court is bound to follow the administrative decision.

Therefore the procedural tactics of both parties often concern a determination of scope decision which is binding in court proceedings. Court proceedings will become unnecessary if the Industrial Property Office finds the device in question non-infringing. Such an administrative decision can usually be reached more quickly and cheaply than a decision in court proceedings, which are in the hands of the judge.

The defendant cannot counterclaim invalidity of the plaintiff's patent or trade mark, because the invalidation procedure falls under the jurisdiction of the Industrial Property Office and not the court. The defendant thus has to submit a request to the administrative office. In such case, the court could stay proceedings until a decision of the Industrial Property Office on invalidation or revocation of the plaintiff's industrial property right (Sec. 109(2)(c) CCP). The court is obliged to stay proceedings if the invalidation request before the Industrial Property Office has been made prior to the commencement of the suit.

If civil procedures are stayed, the case may only be resolved after a number of years. Therefore, in practice, the parties often prefer determination of scope or revocation/invalidation procedures over civil claims.

In contrast, the defence that the plaintiff himself infringes rights to industrial property is often unsuccessful. The estoppel of "unclean hands" is not recognised. The defendant can, of course, submit a counterclaim, or more common, a request for determination of scope or invalidation of the plaintiff's industrial property in administrative proceedings before the Industrial Property Office.

As a defence, the defendant may also claim exhaustion in appropriate cases.

VII. Remedies

1. Injunctive Relief

The claim for desisting from further infringement or refraining from certain economic or other activities is common in practice. The claim requires that infringement is likely to continue to be repeated or commenced, for instance, if preparations to start a production of infringing goods are under way. Courts will not grant the request if the defendant already refrained from unfair or infringing activities in the course of the proceedings and there is no indication of a danger or repetition. In such case, the plaintiff should withdraw his lawsuit as far as that claim is concerned.

2. Elimination of Consequences/Destruction of Infringing Goods

A restitution claim or an elimination of unlawful consequences is usually requested, but less frequently recognised. Such a claim is usually satisfied not only by withdrawing goods from the market, but by destruction of infringing goods. The claim may also include the destruction of various devices used for infringement or for circumventing technical protection systems. The claim for destruction of infringing goods was only implemented in 2000, hence there is little experience as yet.

A judicial order to destroy infringing goods is not yet common, but lawsuits in that respect do arise. Some laws also state that this claim can be made a supportive remedy if it is not possible to eliminate the infringement otherwise, *i.e.* in a less serious way. Experience with this measure stems predominantly from the area of public law procedures, especially customs law and public consumer law. When ordering the destruction of goods, the judge may also take into consideration whether there is a danger of repeated infringement or of export of infringing goods abroad after their withdrawal from the domestic market, *i.e.* if the goods are only stored and not destroyed.

3. Information as to the Origin of Goods

The right of information as to the origin of goods and their marketing was first acknowledged by law in 2000 and there is not much experience with this instrument yet.

4. Monetary Compensation for Immaterial Losses

Moral compensation is less usual in matters concerning industrial property rights than, for example, for infringement of general personality rights. If moral compensation is also demanded, then the claim is usually directed towards a public apology, for example, in newspapers circulated in the business community.

In addition to the above mentioned claim, the claim for monetary compensation of immaterial loss is most frequent. A pre-condition is proof of an injury of non-proprietary nature, which is not a damage to the goods, a profit loss or a danger of either of these.

By stating in the lawsuit the extent of the claim for monetary compensation of immaterial loss, which is often very high, the plaintiff intends to put the defendant under pressure to settle the dispute by agreement. If the amount of such a claim (or another one) can be quantified only with considerable difficulty or not at all, it is determined by the court (Sec. 136 CCP). It is not an arbitrary judicial consideration, but rather a quantitative consideration based on the merits of the case and subject to assessment and review. There can be difficulties of quantification when the plaintiff does not know all circumstances of an infringement due to a lack of access to the manufacture or commercial premises of the defendant. A case may also require a disproportionately costly expertise by an authorised expert.

Although based on no-fault liability, intent or negligence is taken into consideration by the courts in determining the amount of monetary compensation for immaterial loss.

By claiming monetary compensation for immaterial loss, the plaintiff often intends to recover lost profits. From the legal point of view, however, these two claims are separate and construed on diverse liability principles.

5. Damages

If damages are caused by an IP infringement or by unfair competition, the injured party has a right to compensation of immaterial loss. This can include both the actual damage and the loss of profits. Compensation for actual damage in practice is claimed for damage or destruction of a prototype or a model of a product, or goods in stock, for identifying and determining the amount of damage, for the costs to discover the identity of the infringer, etc.

Generally, the above damages are rarely claimed, as plaintiffs would rather claim monetary compensation, which does not require fault. The amount of damages can also be estimated by the court (Sec. 136 CCP). There is a practical difficulty, though. While damages are decided in first instance by the district courts, IP claims and claims for surrender of unjust enrichment are decided in first instance by regional courts in business matters. Therefore, one cannot entirely rule out the procedural danger of diverging decisions for one and the same infringement of the same right by different courts.

6. Unjust Enrichment

A claim for unjust enrichment is less frequent in IP matters, even though a traditional Roman *actio*. The reason is the preference for monetary compensation of immaterial loss (as above). Nevertheless, surrender of unjust enrichment can be demanded in addition to monetary compensation of immaterial loss and damages in those cases where another person's industrial property is used without legal title, particularly a licence contract, or in the alternative, where such a title existed but no longer does, *e.g.* as a result of discharging the licence contract by the licensor (Secs. 451 et seq. Commercial Code). Where the claim for surrender of unjust enrichment is recognised in IP cases, large sums of money up to many millions of Czech crowns can be at stake.

If the person unjustly enriched did not act in good faith regarding his title, he is liable not only to pay the equivalent of a licensing fee, but also to surrender all his profits (Sec. 458(2) Commercial Code). An example may be the net profit from the unauthorised use of a patented technology regardless of whether the profit was invested or left to a third person, *e.g.* divided among shareholders. The person who was in good faith regarding his title, which is a matter of proof, is entitled to keep the profits. The amount to be restituted can be estimated by the court (Sec. 136 CCP).

In some cases, it may be difficult to make a distinction between profits from unjust enrichment and profits gained lawfully elsewhere. Therefore, attorneys sometimes avoid claims for surrender of profits from unjust enrichment despite the fact that the defendant's bad faith can be proven due to a warning from the plaintiff.

7. Ascertainment/Decision in Part

The court may decide that certain goods are fakes or unauthorised imitations, which has consequences for further proceedings in the the field of public law, especially in customs law and public consumer law.

There is a difficulty in practice that obtaining such a final court decision usually means a considerable loss of time. This may also paralyse the effectiveness of further public law steps and, consequently, the plaintiff's expenditure on protection of his right are increased.

8. Publication of Facts or Decision

a) Private publication of the facts

The injured parties sometimes seek a quick out-of-court redress, which is usually a publication of the facts, *e.g.* in commercial papers. This may be in the form of a paid insertion or expert articles, etc. These measures are usually very effective, often more so than a final court judgment reached after a lengthy and costly litigation with an uncertain result. The costs of such self-defence are sometimes lower than the costs of court proceedings, but have to be borne exclusively by the injured party.

b) Public apology

Moral satisfaction in the form of public apology is possible but it is not usual in IP matters. The primary interest of the injured party is normally monetary compensation.

c) Publication of judgment at the expense of the other party

The right to have a judgment published at the expense of the other party is expressly provided for only in the Copyright Act and in the Commercial Code's section on unfair competition. In other cases, this right is either included in the list of claims under IP rights, or not mentioned at all. Therefore its application is often subject to interpretation, thus requiring a certain determination of the judge.

Heterogeneous regulations of this matter, due to a lack of the legislative and political will in different IP laws, are unhelpful in this respect.

As a claim for publication of judgment is usually only recognised by the court after a considerable lapse of time, the plaintiff may no longer be interested in the matter.

9. Costs of Proceedings

Reimbursement of costs is ordered according to the result of the case. The court will award the winning party the legal costs against the losing party. To this, the losing party will have to add his/her own costs for legal counsel, etc.

a) Reimbursement of attorney's fee

The attorney's fee is included in the parties' costs of proceedings. The deliberation for a reimbursement is decided by the court (Sec. 137 CCP). The amount of reimbursement of attorneys' fees is determined as a lump sum for the proceedings that does not correspond to the attorney's rates. The attorney's rate is only taken into consideration if justified by the circumstances of the case. As the latter rule is new, there is not much experience as yet. Special circumstances of a case may be, for instance, the difficult nature of the matter.

If the participant in proceedings is represented by a patent attorney, the fee for the representation is not part of the costs and cannot be reimbursed even if the party fully succeeds in the respective matter. This is due to the position of a patent attorney as a mere general representative in the proceedings.

Conclusion

Judicial application of patent matters has a long tradition in Czech territory due to Austrian law which was originally in force in the historical provinces of what is today the Czech Republic. Due to political pressures, the period of 1948–1989 witnessed a gradual and temporary deviation from that tradition towards Soviet law. It was reflected, too, in acts of judicial application of the law and in interpretation.

Nevertheless, as early as 1990, considerable progress was made in the former Czechoslovakia in overcoming the Soviet-based IP system. The current problems are once again solved with an international approach in mind. In addition, the influence of EC law and practice, which is a result of the Czech Republic's position as a possible EU member, is evident. Adopting EC law is not always consistent and error free, however.

Since 1 January 2001, all major legal obstacles which would formally block an effective and speedy judicial enforcement of patent rights within the territory of the Czech Republic have been removed, at least as far as the instrument of interim injunctions is concerned. This applies also to unfair competition matters, which apparently follow the earlier Czechoslovakian judicature, from the period of 1918–1939. Another question is the comparatively demanding preparation of the suit. Matters to be considered are legal, technical, commercial, organisational and administrative.

In spite of that, one still encounters delays in proceedings, especially the first hearing for decisions on appeal. One also comes across erroneous legal decisions, especially in first instance courts and an occasional lack of judicial courage to decide matters correctly.

Despite these reservations, there has been a considerable improvement in the Czech Republic as far as the judicial protection of patent rights is concerned. This is largely due to the new laws in that area and the revival of the earlier tradition developed in the 19th century and in the period of 1918–1939.

11
The Enforcement of Patent Rights in Hungary

ZOLTÁN BÉRCESI

Introduction

It stands to reason that the political and economic changes in Hungary in the 1990s also had repercussions on the legal system. Broadening the scope of the market economy and changing the economic framework, *e.g.* by privatisation, the advent of multi-national companies and significant investments, also brought about changes in the field of intellectual property. Changes have also been spurred by Hungary's application to become a member of the European Union and the obligation to harmonise her laws accordingly. The intellectual property system was thus fundamentally overhauled in the 1990s in order to comply with international obligations and the requirements of EU membership as of May 2004. When Hungary became a member to the European Patent Convention (1 May 2003), the Patent Act was substantially revised. Judging from the application figures, intellectual property rights have become of increasing importance. In 2002, 842 domestic and 5,064 foreign application were made.[1]

A. Institutions and Specialists in the Field of Patent Law

I. General

In order to give a comprehensive overview of the patent system in general, it is necessary to describe the decision-making institutions (judges and courts), attorneys and patent attorneys, and the experts or expert organisations that work in the IP field, not least the Hungarian Patent Office.

II. The System of Judicial Procedure in Hungary

1. Judicial Organisation and Jurisdiction

The judiciary consists of four tiers: the local courts (county courts and the District Court in Budapest),[2] the committee courts as courts of first instance

---

[1] Statistics of the Hungarian Patent Office for 2002, reported in Iparjogvédelmi Szemle (ISZ) 2003/1, at 5.

[2] At the local level, there are also special labour courts.

and appeal courts (the Capital Court in Budapest), and finally the Supreme Court.[3]

The first instance county courts have general jurisdiction unless otherwise specified by the Code of Civil Procedure. In particular, matters of industrial property and competition law are heard in first instance by the committee courts, more specifically the Capital Court in Budapest.[4]

Appeals in general matters are heard before the appeal courts in cases where the appeal courts are courts of first instance, the Decision Tribunals. A further appeal to the Supreme Court against appeal decisions by the appeal courts and Decision Tribunals can be brought under certain circumstances.[5]

2. Composition of the Courts

Matters in the county court are decided by a single judge, matters by the appeal court (even at first instance) by a division. When deciding matters at first instance, the appeal court's divisions are composed of one professional and two lay judges, and in appeal matters of three professional judges.[6] The appeal courts and Decision Tribunals have several divisions, *e.g.* criminal, civil, commercial and military. The Supreme Court has divisions on criminal, civil and administrative matters, and those for the uniform application of the law. Industrial property matters are decided by the commercial or civil division. Special provisions apply to the composition of divisions and the training of judges.

3. Type of Civil Procedure

Civil proceedings can be *inter partes* or *ex parte* in nature. A typical example of the latter in the IP field would be an appeal against the Patent Office's decisions. The Code of Civil Procedure recognises three types of decisions: judgments, requests and orders. While the merits of the case are always decided by judgment, matters that arise within a proceeding are mostly decided by order. This is also true for *ex parte* proceedings. In patent matters, all thse procedures are applied.

[3] As of 1 January 2003, Act. No. LXXI/1998, which modifies certain laws regarding the jurisdiction between the Supreme Court and the appeal courts, will introduce yet another tier of courts, the county court tribunals which will be responsible for hearing appeals against decisions of the current appeal courts. This should reduce the workload of the Supreme Court.

[4] Sec. 23 Code of Civil Procedure (Law No. III/1952).

[5] In certain cases, there is no ordinary remedy available against decisions. These first instance decisions become final immediately.

[6] Any Hungarian citizen over 30 with no criminal record is eligible to be a lay judge (Sec. 122(1) Law. No. LXVI/1997 on the organisation and management of the courts).

III. The "Main Players" in the IP Field

1. Judges

There are currently 2,600 judges in Hungary. Judges are independent and are nominated by the President. Judges must be Hungarian citizens with a legal education who have passed a specific examination of civil and commercial law, criminal law and administrative/labour/social security law. No particular importance is attached to matters of intellectual property. Graduation from the university is followed by a three-year internship at the court, followed by the specific examination and another year as secretary of the court. Judges dealing with IP matters need to have another technical qualification. In the Budapest Appeal Court, with exclusive jurisdiction over a number of IP matters, especially for patent cases, at least two of the judges must possess this additional qualification. Of the two IP divisions in the Budapest Appeal Court, four of the six judges thus require a special diploma in a field of technology or natural science. About 500-600 cases are dealt with by these two divisions per year. Until now, the majority of cases concern trade marks. Patent cases are dealt with occasionally.

The two IP divisions sit twice a week. There is an average of four to five court hearings per case, and the cases take two to three years on average. Prior to 2003, appeals had to be argued before the Supreme Court which upheld about 90% of the Appeal Court's decisions. Since 2003, appeals are heard before the Decision Tribunals, while extraordinary further appeals go to the Supreme Court, *e.g.* to guarantee a uniform interpretation of the law.

2. Attorneys

Attorneys may represent a client before the courts, the administration and the Patent Office. Attorneys are required to be members of the local bar association, which must accept any candidate of Hungarian citizenship and Hungarian residence who has a university degree in law and an additional legal qualification, which takes three years both for attorneys and judges. The final examination is the same for judges and attorneys. Attorneys may practice either on their own or as an employee or partner in a law firm. Foreigners are not allowed to practise directly (unless an international treaty allows this), yet may work as "foreign counsel" in co-operation with a Hungarian attorney or law firm. Foreign consultants are allowed to give advice or information on their own jurisdiction, on international or European law. Co-operation agreements between Hungarian firms and foreign consultants are frequent, particularly in Budapest.

While there are about 8,000 attorneys in Hungary (4,000 of them in Budapest), very few of them specialise in IP. Reasons for this may be the high specialisation required in this field, and the technical knowledge necessary to handle patent and utility model cases. The number of IP specialists is thus difficult to ascertain, although most do practice in Budapest. Outside the capital, licensing agreements in particular may require some basic IP knowledge. Most IP matters are handled by attorneys. Due to the technical nature of patents or utility models, attorneys would ask the advice of patent attorneys. A number of law firms also employ patent attorneys.

3. Patent Attorneys

The Patent Attorneys' Act 1996 determines the rights and obligations of patent attorneys.[7] Their main duties are the representation of clients before the courts and administrative bodies in IP matters, the drafting of IP-related contracts and other documents, and advice and counsel in IP matters. Patent attorneys are required to be members of the Patent Attorneys' Association, a public entity that has to accept as members all Hungarian citizens residing in Hungary with a diploma in engineering or natural sciences and a further qualification as a patent attorney. This qualification, the Patent Bar, can be taken after a three-year internship in a patent law firm and is supervised by the Hungarian Patent Office. The Patent Bar consists of the following subject matter: Hungarian law on patents, utility models, know-how, designs, trade marks, geographical indications, copyright and unfair competition law, foreign and international industrial property and certain basic knowledge in criminal, administrative and civil law. Patent attorneys may work either alone, in co-operation, as employees of patent law firms, in a patent law firm organised as a limited company, or as an employee of any other enterprise.

Currently, about 240 patent attorneys are enrolled in Hungary, about 80 of whom work independently. The two largest patent firms with a long-standing reputation are the Danubia Patent and Trade Mark Office, Ltd. and S.B.G. & K. Most of the work is conducted on behalf of foreign clients.

4. The Hungarian Patent Office

The Hungarian Patent Office, the employer of a good many qualified specialists,[8] is responsible for prosecuting all administrative actions in the field of IP. It maintains an official documentation and information service, prepares legislative initiatives and government strategies in the IP field, and co-operates with related institutions on a European and international level. Particularly the latter aspect of "IP diplomacy" is important and has been fairly successful in the past. The Patent Office further fosters teaching and awareness of IP, supervises patent attorneys' associations and assists other associations of specialists for inventions and copyrights. Since 1 January 2001, the President of the Hungarian Patent Office is assisted in his tasks by

---

[7] Law No. XXXII/1995 on Patent Attorneys.

[8] Szabó, "Gondolatok az iparjogvédelem muvelõinek helyzetérõl és jövõjérõl" (Thoughts on Present and Future of Those Involved in Industrial Property Rights), A Magyar Szerzõi Jogi és Iparjogvédelmi Egyesület (MIE) Közleményei, 1998/39, at 110.

a new advisory body, the Council for the Protection of Intellectual Property Rights in Hungary.[9]

5. Other Experts

Expertise in the area of IP may be provided by a number of specialised organisations, institutes, university professors and other experts who can offer relevant information or, in the case of an IP dispute, be nominated as expert witnesses. Particularly with respect to the latter, three problems deserve mention. For one, experts very often lack the specific knowledge of the IP necessary terminology. More often than not, their expertise or witness statements make the judge's task even more difficult. Further, matters of IP infringement combine both technical and legal problems, a distinction which even a skilled expert cannot easily draw. Finally, science is developing at such a pace that experts cannot always keep abreast of new technical fields and thus do not always have the specialised knowledge required.[10]

6. IP Organisations

There is a rich network of private organisations that focus on matters of intellectual property. These are, *inter alia*, the Hungarian Association of Industrial Property and Copyrights, the Hungarian Trade Mark Association, the Hungarian Association of Competition Law, the Hungarian Inventors' Association and several domestic branches of international organisations such as the Hungarian Group of AIPPI. Their activities are manifold and include the organisation of special conferences, the distribution of information, academic research, publication of special periodicals, etc.

IV. Current Situation and Problems Related to Intellectual Property Rights in Hungary

The Hungarian intellectual property system has strong historical foundations on which the modernisation in the 1990s could build. The system thus includes national achievements that are still in conformity with European laws. While the field of industrial property law is still considered as exclusive and not accessible to the public at large, even to lawyers in general, the last five years have seen a marked increase in interest in this field.

At the university level, lectures on intellectual property are part of the general curriculum of civil law and are also offered as an elective subject. The basics of patent and trade mark law are part of the final exam. Notably supported by the Hungarian Patent Office, the law faculties offer a number of

---

[9] The Council consists of a maximum of 15 specialists in the IP field, who are nominated by the Minister for Economic Affairs.

[10] Markó, "A szakértõ szerepe a szabadalommal kapcsolatos eljárásban" (The Role of the Expert in Procedures Regarding Patents), Iparjogvédelmi Szemle (ISZ) 1999/6, at 21.

special courses, also by correspondence. In the academic mainstream, IP related problems do not feature very often. Little is published, and if so, mostly in the "Circular of Industrial Property Rights", edited by the Patent Office or other organisations specialised in this field.[11] General legal periodicals seldom feature IP topics; foreign and international literature on the subject matter can only be found at the Patent Office library due to the high costs of acquisition. No major commentaries exist for patent or trade mark law.

Co-operation between IP specialists is fairly good. Every year a number of special conferences and seminars are jointly organised by the Patent Office, other IP organisations or major law firms or patent firms. Here, an exchange of minds between the members of the Patent Office, the judges, attorneys and patent attorneys specialising in IP, and academics takes place. The Patent Office has entered into a number of co-operation agreements with IP organisations.

B. *The Procedure in Patent-Related Suits*

I. The Parties

While the general rules laid down in the Code of Civil Procedure also apply to patent-related suits, certain special provisions, *e.g.* the Patent Act, apply which modify these general rules.

1. The Admissible Parties in *ex parte* Proceedings

Ex parte IP proceedings are directed at altering a previous decision by the Patent Office. They are initiated on request, in particular by the applicant in a previous proceeding at the Patent Office. However, under certain circumstances, third parties are also allowed standing to sue. Requests to revoke a patent or utility model may be initiated by the true inventor.

In *ex parte* proceedings, the person making the request is party to the proceeding. If in the previous administrative proceeding another party was involved as an opponent, the subsequent proceeding will become *inter partes*. If, in the case of joint ownership, only one of the owners appeals in order to protect the joint patent or utility model, or if proceedings were initiated only against one of the joint owners, the court notifies the others that they may join. Other persons who have a legal interest in the outcome of the proceeding may intervene alongside the appealing party. The general rules of intervention under civil procedure apply (Sec. 48 Code of Civil Procedure).

2. *Inter partes* Proceedings

Inter partes proceedings in patent matters follow the general rules of the Code of Civil Procedure with the following modifications:

---

[11] *E.g.* Trade Mark World, edited by the Hungarian Trade Mark Association, and News of the Society for Industrial Property Rights and Copyright.

(a) In order to preserve, maintain, defend or extend a patent right, each one of the joint owners is entitled to sue even without participation of the others.[12]

(b) In the case of inventions made for hire, the employer as the right owner is entitled to sue. For other inventions made in the course of employment, the employee as the right owner is entitled to sue, while the employer is merely entitled to a non-exclusive licence without standing to sue.

(c) The registered licensee is entitled to raise an infringement action after having given notice to the licensor without the latter having failed to act against the alleged infringement within a period of 30 days from the request.[13]

(d) At the application stage, the applicant is entitled to raise an action, although such action will be suspended until the right is finally and conclusively granted.

(e) In cases of a litigation over the rights over an invention, all registered inventors, owners and those who claim rights over the invention have to be parties to the suit.[14]

3. Role of the Prosecutor

In 1994, the Constitutional Court ruled the general right of the prosecution to intervene in any given suit to be unconstitutional.[15] However, in some suits where only the prosecution can prevent infringements of the law, it is useful and justified to allow participation of the prosecution. In IP matters, the prosecution is entitled to request invalidation of patents, utility models or trade marks in cases of contravention against public order and good morals.

4. Representation in Court

While the general rules of representation as laid down in the Code of Civil Procedure also apply to patent matters, it should be noted that industrial property cases can also be pursued by patent attorneys in court, where they enjoy a position comparable to an attorney. Representation by a patent attorney is rather common in matters of patents and utility models. Larger companies are typically represented by their in-house lawyers or patent attorneys.

---

[12] To that extent, such action also may have negative repercussions on the others, *e.g.* if a deadline is not properly maintained and such omission is not corrected in due course.

[13] The same applies to the registered franchisee. There are no special rules for franchising agreements in Hungarian law.

[14] Supreme Court, Civil Division, decision No. 277, reprinted in Legfelsõbb Bìróság, Bìrósági Határozatok (Supreme Court Decisions) 1988/8.

[15] Constitutional Court decision No. 1/1994.

II. Questions of Jurisdiction

1. General Remarks

The Code of Civil Procedure contains fairly detailed rules on jurisdiction. In patent matters, one should distinguish between *inter partes* and *ex parte* proceedings, between different types of rights and different types of claims.

2. Jurisdiction in *inter partes* Proceedings

a) Exclusive jurisdiction of the Budapest Appeal Court

Certain matters come under the exclusive jurisdiction of the Budapest Appeal Court (Capital Court).[16] These matters are:

(1) for patents and semi-conductor topographies: grants, amendments or revocations of compulsory licences, prior user rights and all suits related to infringement; and
(2) for utility models: grant, amendment or revocation of a compulsory licence, determination of an equitable remuneration in case of use, disputes on prior user rights and/or matters of infringement.

The Budapest Appeal Court, with exclusive jurisdiction in the above matters, decides in a division consisting of three professional judges. In the division that deals with patents, utility models and topographies, at least two of the three judges require an additional technical qualification (*see* above A.III).

b) Other IP matters

For other IP matters not mentioned above, jurisdiction lies with the Appeal Courts as courts of first instance. Other IP matters are, in particular, those that relate to disputes over licensing agreements and possible damage claims ensuing therefrom.[17]

3. Jurisdiction over Unpatented Inventions and Know-How Protection

There are no special rules of jurisdiction for know-how and unpatented innovations. As a consequence, the ordinary county courts are competent to deal with these matters.[18] The Supreme Court has confirmed this, holding

[16] Generally, these matters are regarded as the genuine matters: Németh, "A polgári perrendtartás magyarázata" (Commentary on the Code of Civil Procedure) 148 (1st ed., Budapest 1999).

[17] Supreme Court, decision Gf.VI.32.777/1997, reprinted in: Legfelsõbb Bíróság, Bíròsàgi Hatirozatok (Supreme Court Decisions, subsequently referred to as BH), 2000, at 218.

[18] As of 1 January 2003, matters concerning the protection of know-how and creations not otherwise protected will fall under the jurisdiction of the appeal courts. Matters concerning unprotected innovations will remain under local jurisdiction.

that disputes on the remuneration for innovations in general did not belong to copyright or industrial property disputes, and the general rules of jurisdiction should thus apply.[19]

4. *Ex parte* Proceedings

All appeals against decisions of the Patent Office fall under the exclusive jurisdiction of the Budapest Appeal Court. Decisions of the Patent Office are in particular the grant or revocation of a right, stay of proceedings or ascertainment of a right. Since 2003, also decisions on the publication of translations of European Patents and corrections thereof.

III. Preparation for Trial

1. Preparatory Acts

Once filed, a claim is examined by the court within 30 days for form and content. If incomplete, the claim is either dismissed (rare), or the plaintiff is requested to supply the missing facts or documents. The defendant will normally submit his defence in writing, whereupon the plaintiff will reply. At this stage of the claim, the court may be asked to make an interim decision, or to decide upon the submission of further documents. Interim measures can also be requested at a later stage.

The preparatory phase is very thorough, and it is not uncommon that, in order to clarify the facts or claims, the parties will exchange documents five to six times. The court can request submission of further facts or documents, *e.g.* a copy of the IP right or a power of attorney.[20] The preparatory phase takes between two to five months, whereupon the court will set a hearing date within seven to eight months.

In the preparatory phase, the court quite often suspends proceedings, in particular if the defendant has initiated invalidation proceedings before the Patent Office. This is a particularly popular method of defendants to delay the suit.[21] In order to prevent the defendant from raising an invalidation action prior to the infringement suit, plaintiffs often refrain from sending warning letters to the defendant prior to their suit. Before a suit is filed, the defendant may initiate proceedings of both invalidation and ascertainment of invalidity before the Patent Office, but after commencement of the suit only

[19] Supreme Court, decision Pk. IV.21.275/1993, reprinted in 1994 BH 83; Supreme Court, decision Pf.IV.20.368/1990.

[20] According to the Budapest Appeal Court, it is not sufficient for a foreign company simply to sign a power of attorney, but rather the document has to be properly notarised.

[21] These are often deliberate tactics. If the defendant requests an invalidation trial, the court will decide on preliminary measures independent thereof. *See* Turi, "Az ideiglenes intézkedés elrendelése iránti kérelmek elbìrálásának bìrósági tapasztalatai" (Experiences with Requests for Interim Injunctions), A Magyar Szerzõi Jogi és Iparjogvédelmi Egyesület (MIE) Közleményei, 1998, at 27.

the former. Reasons for invalidation can be that the requirements for protection are not met; reasons for cancellation in connection with a trade mark can be the lack of use or the confusion of consumers.

According to the general rules of the Code of Civil Procedure, the court may, yet does not have to, suspend proceedings (Sec. 152(1) Code of Civil Procedure, Sec. 104(9) Patent Act, and Sec. 95(8) Trade Mark Act). However, it is customary for the court to suspend the proceedings.

2. Interim Measures

Interim measures are among the most important measures in the preparatory stages of a trial. In the 1998 Trade Mark Act, interim measures were particularly mentioned.[22] In about 80% of all trade mark cases, interim measures are requested by the plaintiff. In litigation over patent rights, the request is not as frequent. In trade mark matters, the request for an interim injunction is usually granted, also due to the new provisions concerning customs procedures.[23] In patent matters, courts are more cautious due to the difficulty of proving a likelihood of infringement. Here, the likelihood of success is more difficult to determine, *e.g.* when it comes to comparing chemical processes.[24] Apart from the likelihood of success, the plaintiff needs to show that damages are "imminent".[25] In this respect, the Supreme Court overruled the Budapest Appeal Court in holding that "imminent damages" can also be shown in cases where damages have already occurred, yet further damages are likely due to the continuing infringement. As a third requirement of an interim injunction, the court needs to weigh the pros and cons of the requested relief. In this respect, there are no firm guidelines as to what should be regarded as proportionate. For that reason, the court needs to consider the matter carefully, also when calculating the security the plaintiff has to post.[26]

IV. The Trial

1. Role of Courts and Attorneys

The court plays a very active role in the trial proceedings. The President of the division guides the procedure and determines the sequence of action. As a starting point, the claim is read by the President or the plaintiff. The plaintiff then has to state whether he wishes to uphold or amend the claim, whereupon the defendant has to state his reasoned defence. If necessary the court would then ask that evidence be presented. Although the parties will

---

[22] Law No. XI/1998 on the protection of trade marks and geographical indications.

[23] The most frequent infringement being the importation of goods.

[24] Turi, *supra* note 21, at 26.

[25] *Ibid.*, at 29.

[26] *Ibid.*, at 30 *et seq.*

argue their case orally, thorough preparation in writing is more important in IP matters. That patent attorneys do not always properly present their legal arguments might be a problem at times. Here, it is the task of the court properly to guide proceedings to remedy this.

IP proceedings normally require two to three full days. Five to six months can pass between each hearing due to the participation of experts or the necessity to supplement the claims.

The hearing of evidence is generally more important in cases of technical IP rights, while cases of trade mark infringement can be more easily determined by the court. Evidence would normally be presented in the form of an expertise by the expert witness, documents or other factual evidence.

2. Expert Witnesses

To the extent necessary, the court can request participation of expert witnesses. The expert witness would normally be a member of certain institutions as specified by law, yet someone else can be named if deemed appropriate. The names in fields of expertise of court experts are registered with the Ministry of Justice. In nominating an expert, the court may take requests by the parties into account. The parties very often disagree on the expert and are allowed to present a so-called "private" expertise. It is up to the court to decide to what extent such "biased" expertise is taken into account by the court.

V. Proving Infringement

It is up to the plaintiff to prove that the defendant has made infringing use of his patent. The allegedly infringing device or process must thus correspond to the registered invention, although in the case of process patents, the products directly resulting therefrom are presumed to have been produced under this process. The basis for proving infringement must thus be the patent claim and description. Several decisions have held that a device or process is only infringing if it corresponds to all characteristics of the patented device or process. While the patented invention is not limited to the strict wording of the claims, the claims may not be interpreted as a mere indication of directions for the person skilled in the art to determine the patented invention.[27] In interpreting the contents of the claims, the court very often relies on the expertise of an expert witness from such institutions as the Technical Expert Institution of the Court or the State Pharmaceutical Institute. Infringing use by the defendant can, for instance, be proven by sample purchases or other commercial documents.

---

[27] Supreme Court, decisions Pf.IV.21.139/1992, Pf.IV.20.415/1983.

VI. Defences

Typical defences are the following:

1. Request for Invalidation

It is usual in patent infringement cases that the defendant uses an offensive tactic as the preferred defence. He would thus request an invalidation before the Patent Office. Due to the stay of proceedings in such case, the action might well take four to five years.[28]

2. Better Rights

It is not infrequent that the defendant invokes his own patents as a defence. In this connection, the Supreme Court has held that an unlawful use of one's own patent is not possible in principle, as the owner should enjoy an exclusive right of use. Where the defendant's products thus fall in the ambit of his patent, the act cannot be deemed infringing and the case can only be resolved in the course of a cancellation action.[29]

3. Legitimate Use

Further, the defendant may allege that he or the seller of the goods has a valid licensing agreement. In practice, this defence is mostly unsuccessful.

4. Importation

If the goods have been detained at the border, the defendant cannot argue that because they are in the hands of customs, he has not committed an act of "importation". Such importation is already completed by the physical importation and request for a customs declaration.[30] The defendant may also plead exhaustion of rights, a concept introduced in the Hungarian Patent Act in 1995, without much case law on the matter yet.

VII. Remedies

The plaintiff can request the following remedies: ascertainment of infringement, injunctive relief, request of information about others involved in the infringement (*e.g.* suppliers), and commercial contacts concerning subsequent purchasers. The plaintiff may further request publication of a declaration of infringement in a newspaper determined by the court,

[28] In the course of the cancellation action, the defendant can also argue acts of unfair competition by the plaintiff.

[29] Supreme Court, decision Pf.IV.25.602/1999.

[30] Budapest Appeal Court, decisions III.P.26.236/1998, III.P.28.087/1998.

surrender of the defendant's profits, and seizure and destruction of the goods used primarily to manufacture the infringing products. All the above remedies can be requested cumulatively.

The right owner may of course also request damages. Characteristically, these are not requested in the same procedure that determines the infringement, but rather in a subsequent action. The reasons for this are considerations of the duration and cost of proceedings. Even if successful, the plaintiff cannot claim reimbursement of attorneys' fees from the other side. Attorneys' fees can be freely determined between the parties and are not dependent on the outcome of the case.

C. *Final Remarks*

This article hopes to give the reader some useful information about the current state of affairs on patent enforcement in Hungary. While the legal system was thoroughly modernised in the 1990s, the IP system will be confronted with new challenges caused by Hungary's accession to the European Patent Convention in 2003, and the accession to the EU in 2004. Implications of these developments for the Hungarian IP system will be dealt with in a future article.

D

Patent Enforcement in Asia

12
The Enforcement of Patent Rights in China

THOMAS PATTLOCH

A. Introduction: Dual Enforcement and TRIPS Requirements

Counterfeiting always was and until today remains a rampant problem in the Chinese market. In fact, in all Chinese cities any major Hollywood movie is available on DVD/VCD shortly after its release for about RMB 8 (US$ 0.95).[1] China has revamped the whole system of IP laws and released a totally new set of regulations answering the demand for more and effective claims for right holders. The problems of intellectual property right holders in China today rather than reflecting inadequate legislation, are more a result of the practical difficulties encountered in exercising their rights. Petitioning a court or applying to an administrative department for enforcement can be an ordeal and very often is doomed to fail if not done properly by taking into account the specifics of the Chinese enforcement system.

I. Dual Enforcement

Right holders in China have the choice between civil and administrative enforcement which leads to the description of this system as one of "dual enforcement" which is quite common in Asian countries.

1. Pros and Cons of Dual Enforcement

Many earlier opinions tended to favour administrative enforcement over the courts because this procedure is faster and cheaper.[2] Since the amendments of the IP laws during the accession process of the PRC into the WTO[3] this statement cannot be supported without some reservation. The changes made have been fundamental in many ways: Basically, damage compensation and pre-litigation remedies are now only available from the courts, which will increase their importance tremendously over the long run. Lawsuits can be initiated not only at the place where the infringement took

---

[1] Intellectual Property & Technology Law Journal February 2001 Vol. 13 No. 2, 28; Arjun Subrahmanyan, China Law and Practice ("CLP") May 2002, 18.

[2] Liu Xiaohai, China Patents and Trademarks ("CPT") 1999 No. 3, 17; Dong Jianxiong, CPT 1999 No. 1, 82 *et seq.*; Xu Chao, CPT 1999 No. 2, 59 *et seq.*; Su Chi, Intellectual Property in China Vol. II No. 4 1995, 26 *et seq.*

[3] China has been member of the WTO since 11 December 2001.

place (but where sometimes local interests influence the willingness of the administration to step in), but also at the place of domicile of the defendant.[4] Courts can easily employ experts, investigate themselves, execute evidence preservation measures if necessary and clarify complex matters, which can be more difficult for the administration if legal questions are involved.

In fact, administrative actions are more common in trade mark cases where most cases are clear-cut and infringement is easy to prove. In more complex patent and copyright matters, it is more difficult to prove either the existence of a right (copyright) or the infringement (patents).

Once a choice has been made, it is not possible to switch back to the other method of enforcement when difficulties arise: For example, in patent matters Sec. 5(1) No. 5 Measures for Administrative Enforcement of Patents (hereinafter Patent Enforcement Measures), issued on 17 December 2001 by the State Intellectual Property Office (SIPO) and effective since then, clearly stipulates that once a lawsuit has been filed no request to the administrative authorities for help will be accepted. However, Sec. 25 of the Several Provisions of the Supreme People's Court on Issues Relating to the Application of Law to Adjudication of Cases of Patent Disputes stipulates that courts are not bound by prior findings of infringements by administrative authorities, which indicates that it is possible to take action in court after an administrative decision has been handed down. Sec. 21 of the Interpretation by the Supreme People's Court ("SPC") of Several Issues Relating to the Application of Law to Trial of Cases of Civil Disputes over Trade Marks ("SPC Interpretation Trade Mark Cases"), adopted by the SPC on 12 October 2002 and in force since 16 October 2002, stipulates that where the administrative Administration for Industry and Commerce (AIC) has imposed administrative sanctions on the same act of infringement of a trade mark, the people's court shall not impose any further civil sanctions. The same provision can be found in Sec. 29(2) of the Interpretation by the SPC of Several Issues Relating to the Application of Law to Trial of Cases of Civil Disputes over Copyright, issued on 12 October 2002 by the SPC and in force since 15 October 2002 ("SPC Interpretation of Copyright Cases").

2. TRIPS Compliance

The accession to the WTO has brought about enormous pressure to change and supplement legislation. In theory, TRIPS is directly applicable.[5] In fact, it is still rather unlikely that one might be able to call upon regulations contained in TRIPS to assert a right. The recent changes in the IP laws were meant to meet the requirements of TRIPS which asks for a predictable and impartial judiciary and the grant of rights that are enforceable in legal

[4] Yang Xiaoguang, The China IP Focus 2003, 72.

[5] Thomas Pattloch, Das IPR des Geistigen Eigentums in der VR China, Tübingen 2003, 80, 81.

proceedings. These legal proceedings must allow notice to both parties and their participation in the procedure.[6]

A look at the remodelled IP laws shows that interim injunctions, appeals against administrative decisions and claims for damages have either been newly introduced or substantially remodelled. Assessing the overall framework now in place, it is fair to regard the current set of regulations in theory as compliant with TRIPS. However, it will be up to the courts and administrative organs to prove that the new laws actually no longer lack teeth.

B. *Civil Law Enforcement*

I. General Remarks

Civil law enforcement generally refers to actions in court. The number of IP cases dealt with in Chinese courts is constantly on the rise, prompting most courts in bigger cities to have a specialised chamber for IP matters. It is important to note that court decisions unlike those in Anglo-Saxon jurisdictions do not have a binding effect for other courts (no *stare decisis*). They may serve as reference only.[7]

The usual way to initiate an action is to file a law suit for infringement of right that is based on tort. Other questions such as asserting ownership rather concern contractual matters. It is possible to seek a non-infringement opinion of the courts which is close to a negative declaratory action though not exactly the same: Chinese law until recently did not positively recognise an action for the determination of non-infringement and no explicit stipulations can be found in the Civil Procedure Code. In a recent court decision of 2002, a negative declaratory action was admitted by the court.[8] Other cases of 2003 raise concern that the new development might cause "Chinese local court torpedo" problems to surface in Chinese courtrooms soon.[9] Some scholars tend to recommend such a legal instrument be introduced in order to battle abuse of the new pre-litigation measures.[10] A decision of non-infringement until recently was uncommon in practice, perhaps due to the lack of provisions regarding punitive damages or compensation for attorneys' fees.[11]

---

[6] Chen Wang, Copyright February 2002 Vol. 16, 24.

[7] Chen Yongshun in an interview with Catherine Sun, The China IP Focus 2003, 18.

[8] *See* the written reply of the SPC in 2002 to the Jiangsu Province Higher People's Court in the case Suzhou Longbao Bioengineering Industry Co. *v.* Suzhou Langlifu Health Care Co. Ltd. where a warning letter was answered with a declaratory action of non-infringement in Court which was admitted by the SPC.

[9] *See* the case Eli Lilly *v.* Changzhou Huasheng Pharmaceutical Co. Ltd., reported by Chen Wenping in Asialaw IPReview May 2004, 25.

[10] Dong Wei, CPT 2001 No. 4, 30 *et seq*.

[11] Chen Yongshun in an interview with Catherine Sun, The China IP Focus 2003, 18.

Costs of enforcement in court in comparison to other jurisdictions are much lower though nowhere near cheap.[12] Especially patent litigation can require substantial financial resources if an expert is necessary. At the time of writing, to the knowledge of the author no litigation insurance was available in China.

II. Competent Courts

In the PRC, there exist four levels of courts with a two instance trial system.[13] Judgments of appellate courts are immediately binding and enforceable upon service.[14] On the first level, there are the Basic People's Courts. One tier above are the Intermediate People's Courts. Still higher are the Higher People's Courts. Finally, the highest court in civil and administrative cases is the Supreme People's Court located in Beijing.

1. Basic People's Courts

The basic courts exist at county and city level with more than 3,000 throughout the country.[15] IP matters previously were only heard on this level in domestic copyright and trade mark matters (especially in Beijing and Shanghai), but not if a foreigner or patents was involved. Nowadays there is a tendency to designate the basic courts also more broadly for trade mark matters even if involving foreigners.

2. Intermediate People's Courts (IPC)

These courts, presently numbering close to 400, exist at prefecture level of the provinces and in districts of municipalities directly under the central government.[16] IP matters as well as all matters involving foreigners generally start at this level.[17] In trade mark and copyright cases, actions can be brought to any intermediate court if territorial jurisdiction exists. However, in patent infringement cases, only the intermediate courts in the capitals of the provinces, autonomous regions and municipalities directly under the central government and those specially designated by the Supreme People's Court have jurisdiction.[18] For many IPCs, their territorial jurisdiction coincides

---

[12] *See* the Measures for Fee-Collecting in the People's Courts promulgated by the SPC on 29 June 1989.

[13] Yang Xiaoguang, The China IP Focus 2003, 67; The People's Courts of the PRC, Foreign Affair Bureau of the SPC of the PRC, 1995, 14.

[14] Yang Xiaoguang, The China IP Focus 2003, 67.

[15] The People's Courts of the PRC, Foreign Affair Bureau of the SPC of the PRC, 1995, 4.

[16] The People's Courts of the PRC, Foreign Affair Bureau of the SPC of the PRC, 1995, 3.

[17] Susan Finder, Doing Business in China, Freshfields 2002 Vol. 1, Court system § 2.1.02[05].

[18] Yang Xiaoguang, The China IP Focus 2003, 67.

with the local administrative district. In some areas, one IPC has proven to be not sufficient, and large cities such as Beijing and Shanghai have two IPCs.[19]

3. Higher People's Courts (HPC)

There are 30 HPCs on the provincial level including autonomous regions and municipalities directly under the central government with provincial status such as Beijing or Shanghai. Usually IP cases are heard by the HPC in second instance, where the court reviews facts and legal reasoning. The HPCs also exercise adjudication supervision for the lower courts and must oversee and approve the decision of a lower court not to enforce a foreign arbitration award. A decision for the award to be enforced needs no approval.[20]

4. Supreme People's Court (SPC)

The SPC has a wider power than supreme courts in other countries. Generally, it may review cases not only according to the stipulations in the various laws but also according to a self-assessed need (Sec. 21 No. 2 Civil Procedure Code). This means, that if deemed appropriate, the court may act *ex officio* and delegate itself to hear a particular case no matter at which level according to the law the case should originally be heard.[21] The SPC may review cases not only in respect to legal questions, but also supervise and correct mistakes made by the lower courts as to finding of the facts and evaluation of the findings.[22]

Even more important is the power of the SPC to interpret the application of the law in so-called Explanations, Opinions or Circulars which may include jurisdiction matters.[23] These are legally speaking only directly binding for the courts in the country, but actually do have a very strong influence

---

[19] Susan Finder, Doing Business in China, Freshfields 2002 Vol. 1, Court system § 2.1.02[03].

[20] Johnson Tan, CLP April 2003, 25. When in doubt, the final decision is met by the SPC: *see* the Notice Concerning the Handling of Foreign and Foreign-Related Arbitration, issued on 28 August 1995 by the SPC.

[21] The People's Courts of the PRC, Foreign Affair Bureau of the SPC of the PRC, 1995, 2.

[22] *See* Heilongjiangsheng Jianshe Shejiyuan *v.* Hubeisheng Mianhua Gongsi, Hubeisheng Mianhua Gongsi Rangfan Zhongchuan Chubeiku and Wuhanshi Gongye Daxue Shejiyuan, decided by the Supreme People's Court, Case Number (1998) Zhijianzi No. 37, in the case study Zuigaorenminfayuan Zhishi Chanquan Panli Pingjie, Ed. Jiang Zhipei, Beijing Zhishi Chanquan Chubanshe 2001, 523, and the case, "ZL-9 Multifunction Metal Treatment Fluid" ("ZL-9 Duogongneng Jinshu Chuliye") Jingzhi Zi No. 5, ibid. 527.

[23] Resolution of the NPC Standing Committee Providing an Improved Interpretation of Law, issued 10 June 1981; The People's Courts of the PRC, Foreign Affair Bureau of the SPC of the PRC, 1995, 2.

on legislation and handling of the provisions concerned by the administration. The reason for this widely used power is the lack of detailed provisions in the original source of law, the relevant statutes. Besides the interpretation of existing statutes, the SPC in some cases also submits drafts which adds legislative elements to its powers.[24]

5. Decision Finding, Appeals and Re-trials

Cases generally are to be heard in open trial except for cases involving state secrets, individual privacy cases or offences committed by minors. Open cases should be announced before holding the trial and citizens are allowed to attend freely. Judgments are also publicly announced.[25]

Cases of first instance usually are heard by a panel composed of three to seven judges, in simple cases by one judge only. However, the decision usually has to be approved by the Court President who frequently ignores the proposed decision and reasoning and may change the decision at will.[26]

Cases of appeal are heard by a panel consisting of three to five judges. The presiding judge of the panel is appointed by the president of the court or the chief judge of a court division. Decisions are met by majority with a minority report in case of differing opinions. Major or complicated cases (*i.e.* cases that are controversial, complex, involve important persons, will have influence on the litigants or community or which touch upon vague, absent or inconsistent statutes in respect of which the judges of a court disagree) may also be transferred to a judicial committee set up in the people's courts at all levels which consists of the president of the court, chief judges of the divisions and senior judges.

The judicial committee is the highest authority in the internal court organisation and decides by majority.[27] Litigants cannot know or challenge this mode of deciding a case[28] because it officially only concerns internal affairs of the court and no files are accessible to lawyers of the parties.[29]

A Chinese peculiarity is the system of re-trial. Within two years after a judgment has become legally binding, the SPC or the court on the level

---

[24] Susan Finder, Doing Business in China, Freshfields 2002 Vol. 1, Court system § 2.1.02.

[25] The People's Courts of the PRC, Foreign Affair Bureau of the SPC of the PRC, 1995, 10.

[26] Susan Finder, Doing Business in China, Freshfields 2002 Vol. 1, Court system § 2.1.05[1].

[27] The People's Courts of the PRC, Foreign Affair Bureau of the SPC of the PRC, 1995, 13.

[28] More often than not, the Committee is held even before a trial has been conducted. The judges decide the case without having read the files; instead, a report from a judge in charge is delivered without personal review of the files by the other members of the Judicial Committee.

[29] Susan Finder, Doing Business in China, Freshfields 2002 Vol. 1, Court system § 2.1.05[3].

above the court which gave the final judgment may *ex officio* review a case and order a re-trial at the original level if the case has been decided wrongly. Concerned parties may also apply for retrial within two years although chances that such plea will be successful are very slim.[30]

III. Arbitration

For many years lawyers were set in recommending arbitration proceedings as a more likely and successful way to enforce one's rights. Generally, arbitration is thought to be time and cost saving. An additional advantage is that China is member to the New York Convention of the Recognition and Enforcement of International Arbitration Awards.

Arbitration is regulated in Sec. 257 *et seq*. Civil Procedure Code as of 9 April 1991 and the Arbitration Act of 1995. Sec. 257 Civil Procedure Code stipulates that arbitration clauses in foreign economic contracts or subsequent written arbitration agreements bar the way to the courts. Still, property preservation measures can only be executed by the courts (Sec. 258 Civil Procedure Code) as is the case with recognition and enforcement of foreign arbitration bodies (Sec. 269 Civil Procedure Code). The SPC has decreed that only certain courts have the jurisdiction to deal with enforcement of foreign and foreign-related arbitration awards.[31] This new system seems to have substantially lessened the number of refusals to enforce arbitration awards.[32]

The most popular arbitration commission in China is the China International Economic and Trade Arbitration Commission (CIETAC) with headquarters in Beijing and branches in Shanghai and Hong Kong.[33] As of recently, other national arbitration bodies such as the Beijing Arbitration Commission may also accept cases involving foreigners. Parties of an arbitration agreement naming CIETAC can choose the applicable law and to some extent the procedural rules. Usually each party has to choose one arbitrator from a panel. CIETAC arbitration procedures are relatively informal and typically last for no more than a day. Arbitrators usually take a comparatively broad-brush approach with regard to evidence.[34]

IV. Jurisdiction in IP Cases

Jurisdiction matters generally are regulated in Secs. 18 *et seq*. Civil Procedure Code and for foreign related cases in Secs. 243 *et seq*. Civil Procedure

---

[30] The People's Courts of the PRC, Foreign Affair Bureau of the SPC of the PRC, 1995, 16.

[31] Jurisdiction of Foreign-Related Civil and Commercial Cases, issued by the SPC on 25 December 2001.

[32] Johnson Tan, CLP April 2003, 26.

[33] Johnson Tan, CLP April 2003, 24.

[34] Johnson Tan, CLP April 2003, 26.

Code.[35] Administrative cases such as for patent and customs-related matters are covered by Secs. 13 *et seq*. Administrative Procedure Act.

The SPC has issued a variety of Interpretations for patents, trade marks and copyrights in order to further clarify jurisdiction problems. These are most notably:

- the Several Provisions of the SPC on Issues Relating to the Application of Law to Adjudication of Cases of Patents disputes ("SPC Interpretation Patent Cases"), adopted on 19 June 2001 by the SPC,
- the Interpretation by the SPC on Issues Relating to the Application of Law to Adjudication of Cases of Trade Mark Disputes ("SPC Interpretation Trade Mark Cases"), adopted by the SPC on 12 October 2002 and entering into force on 16 October 2002,
- the Interpretation by the SPC of the Issues Relating to Jurisdiction over and the Scope of the Application of Law to the Hearing of Trade Mark Cases ("SPC Trade Mark Jurisdiction Rules"), adopted on 25 December 2001 and entering into force on 21 January 2002,
- the Several Issues Relating to the Application of Law to Trial of Cases of Civil Disputes over Copyright ("SPC Interpretation Copyright Cases"), adopted by the SPC on 12 October 2002 and entering into force on 15 October 2002,
- and the Interpretation by the SPC of Several Issues Relating to the Application of Law in Adjudication of Cases of Civil Disputes over Domain Names on Computer Network[36] ("SPC Interpretation Domain Names"), adopted by the SPC on 26 June 2001 all contain detailed provisions on jurisdiction.

1. Subject Matter Jurisdiction – Patents

According to Sec. 2 SPC Interpretation Patent Cases, patent disputes in the first instance are subject to the jurisdiction of the Intermediate People's Courts in the places where the provincial governments, governments of autonomous regions or municipalities directly under the central government are located.

Matters to be accepted by the court include disputes over ownership, assignment, infringement, service inventions, pre-litigation, compulsory licences and dissatisfaction with administrative decisions (Sec. 1 SPC Interpretation Patent Cases). The Circular on Several Problems in Patent Trial Work, promulgated by the SPC on 16 February 1985, in its Sec. 1 No. 1 directs all cases concerning the grant of a patent right, its invalidation or its being upheld and all disputes concerning compulsory licence fees to the Intermediate Beijing People's Court in first instance and the Higher Beijing People's Court in second instance.

---

[35] Ye Yonglu, Zhishi Chanquan Susong Shiwu, Guangdong Jingji Chubanshe May 2002, 34 *et seq*.

[36] CPT 2001 No. 4, 94 *et seq*.

Should certain other courts be required to hear the patent disputes, they must gain the approval of the SPC first.

The Civil Procedure Code stipulates in Sec. 39(1) that the Higher People's Courts can act as court of first instance in cases of great impact on the area of jurisdiction. In cases where the claimed amount of compensation reaches a certain level in value, the Higher People's Courts also act as courts of first instance, with the necessary standard in this respect varying from province to province.[37]

A higher court may also transfer a case to a lower court for trial instead. Lower courts may request a higher court to try a case in its place if deemed necessary (Sec. 39(2) Civil Procedure Code).

The Intermediate People's Court according to Sec. 14 No. 1 Administrative Procedure Act has jurisdiction over cases of confirming patent rights of invention and cases handled by the customs, with the Higher People's Court hearing cases in the first instance dealing with grave and complicated issues within their jurisdiction (Sec. 15 Administrative Procedure Act) and the SPC as first instance court in grave and complicated cases having an impact on the whole country (Sec. 16 Administrative Procedure Act).

2. Territorial Jurisdiction

As regards territorial jurisdiction in civil matters, Sec. 29 Civil Procedure Code stipulates that a lawsuit can be initiated in the people's court where the infringing act took place (*i.e.* the place where the acts were undertaken as well as where the infringing results took place) or where the defendant has his domicile.

The various Interpretations described above enlarge and specify the general legal terms concerning territorial jurisdiction.

In patent law, Sec. 5 SPC Interpretation Patent Cases defines places where infringement has occurred as places where acts such as manufacture, use, offer for sale, selling or importing of allegedly infringing products or of a patented process take place, including the places where consequences of the preceding infringing acts are evident.

Sec. 4(1) SPC Interpretation Copyright Cases gives jurisdiction to the court of the place where the infringing goods are kept, seized or detained (Sec. 4 SPC Interpretation Copyright Cases). Sec. 4(2) defines these places as sites where infringing reproductions are stored or hidden away in large quantities on a regular basis. The places where infringing products are seized are deemed to be those where the customs, copyright administrative department or AIC have seized or detained infringing products.

---

[37] For details for all the provinces *see* Ye Yonglu, Zhishi Chanquan Susong Shiwu, Guangdong Jingji Chubanshe May 2002, 283 *et seq.*; Li Yong, The China IP Focus 2003, 55, citing the standard in Beijing at RMB 80 million (equivalent around US$ 10 million).

Sec. 6 SPC Interpretation Trade Mark Cases carries the same meaning as to places where infringing goods are stored away or seized by the AIC.

3. Jurisdiction in Respect to Interim Injunctions

Concerning jurisdiction with interim injunctions, basically the same principles apply as for main actions.

4. Jurisdiction in Actions with Several Defendants / Several Plaintiffs

If a joint action against several defendants for infringing acts in different places of infringement is intended, the plaintiff must choose to bring the case before the competent court of one of the places where the infringing acts by the defendants occurred. Sec. 6 SPC Interpretation Patent Cases covers actions against the manufacturer and/or seller of infringing products or cases involving several defendants.

If several right holders bring an action against one defendant, the people's court of the place where the defendant has committed the infringement has jurisdiction over the case.

5. Administrative Proceedings

In administrative proceedings in relation to patent cases or administrative execution acts, jurisdiction lies with the court in the locality of the administrative organ that initially undertook the specific administrative act. In cases where an administrative decision has been reconsidered and the original decision has been amended, jurisdiction may also lie with the court in the locality of the administrative organ conducting the reconsideration (Sec. 17 Administrative Procedure Act). Between several courts the plaintiff may choose (Sec. 20 Administrative Procedure Act).

V. Procedure in Court

Important legislation governing court procedure are the Evidence in Civil Proceedings Several Provisions (hereinafter "Evidence Provisions"), effective as of 1 April 2002.

The Evidence Provisions provide guidelines for the actual procedure during a trial: A lawsuit is initiated by filing a complaint with the court of jurisdiction. If a party is a foreigner without domicile in the PRC, the power of attorney and evidence obtained or originating from abroad must be notarised and legalised (Sec. 242 Civil Procedure Code).[38] Evidence in a foreign

[38] A more than cumbersome process: Usually after having obtained the notarisation in the home country, the signature of the notary has to be authenticated by his supervising competent government authority whose authentication in turn must be authenticated by its supervising body. The authentication process is taken in a series up to the highest

language must be translated into Chinese. Upon accepting the case the court serves a summons on the defendant. The defendant can then deny the claim or file a counterclaim.

1. General

The length of the procedure as a whole is roughly six months for the first instance and only three months for second instance if no foreigners are involved and the case is not too complex. If the latter is the case, then the total length of the procedure of going through two instances may take up to two years.[39] In China, overall only 30% of the judgments are actually appealed and only 20 to 30% of patent cases are reversed by the higher courts.[40] In patent cases, validity and infringement are bifurcated, but liability and damages are usually decided at the same trial.[41]

2. Preparation

The court first asserts whether or not it has jurisdiction. After that, the parties involved must submit relevant evidence for their claims before the hearing starts. The general principle provides that the burden of proof lies with the party who seeks to substantiate its assertions. The court must inform the parties of the burden of proof with regard to their claims, define the scope of investigation by the court and collecting evidence and issue the bearing of legal consequences if the court fails to obtain the evidence (Sec. 33 Evidence Provisions).

3. Pre-trial Hearing

The court then may organise an exchange of evidence between the plaintiff and the defendant before a date for a hearing is set (Sec. 37 Evidence Provisions). Evidence is exchanged in the presence of the judges with a protocol taken against which the opposing party may raise objection and plead his case. In this pre-trial hearing the court confirms the evidence exchanged, identifies the key issues of the case (*see* the declaration in Sec. 39 Evidence Provisions), examines possible counterclaims, determines the witnesses and fixes the date of the hearing. The court will usually appoint a bench of three judges.

4. Court Hearing

The hearing is open to the public unless the case involves trade or private secrets or state secrets (Sec. 48 Evidence Provisions). The bench has the

---

governmental body whose authentication finally must be legalised with the Chinese consulate or embassy in the person's home country. Such a process may take several weeks and require substantial amounts of time and money.

[39] Chen Yongshun in an interview with Catherine Sun, The China IP Focus 2003, 16.

[40] Chen Yongshun in an interview with Catherine Sun, The China IP Focus 2003, 17.

[41] Chen Yongshun in an interview with Catherine Sun, The China IP Focus 2003, 18.

power to decide whether or not the hearing is to be held openly. Sec. 124 Civil Procedure Code regulates the hearing procedure in general, including statements, witnesses, documentary evidence, reading of conclusions, debate, and final argument.

5. Evidence Examination

During the hearing, the parties will be given the opportunity to cross-examine the evidence, question witnesses and debate the legal issues involved. The investigation of the case by the court is regulated in detail in the SPC provisions, comprising eight steps starting with the plaintiff reading the bill of complaint and ending with the cross-examination of the evidence, (*see* Sec. 47 Evidence Provisions). Only cross-examined evidence may be taken as a basis for a judgment. Before the investigation ends the court sums up the ascertained facts. The judge must encourage the parties to concentrate on the key issues of the case without commenting on the nature of the case or the liabilities of the parties. The procedure in court itself usually lasts four hours or half a day, in complex cases such as patent matters sometimes two full days.[42]

6. Admission and Verification of Evidence

The SPC provisions also contain regulations on the admissibility and verification of evidence. Both are completed in the course of court hearing. To some extent, the judge is free to evaluate the evidence.

7. Collegial Panel

The decision in IP cases is usually met by a collegial panel of three to five judges with one chief judge. He is usually responsible for the report on closing a case and the completion of the judgment. Before and after the hearing he must call together the panel to discuss the case and work on a decision which is theoretically met by the votes of the majority. However, in practice the other judges tend to follow the opinion of the chief judge without further questioning or arguing. This has led to many judgments short on legal reasoning, logic and clear terminology,[43] a situation that needs to be addressed by future legislation. The original idea of Chinese civil procedure law is to hand down the judgment directly after the trial has been closed, but in patent cases it normally takes one to two months (and in more complex cases maybe even three months) to receive the judgment.[44] Once the judgment is served, either party may appeal to the next higher court, in IP matters the Higher People's Court. The appellate court usually decides with a bench of three judges and may rehear a case.

---

[42] Chen Yongshun in an interview with Catherine Sun, The China IP Focus 2003, 16.

[43] For more details *see* Zhou Lin, CPT 2003 No. 3, 7, 8.

[44] Chen Yongshun in an interview with Catherine Sun, The China IP Focus 2003, 16.

The new Evidence Provisions provide for a clearer basis for legal procedure. However, the new system is not identical to the discovery system of common law countries since only evidence on which a party seeks to rely is introduced in the proceedings. A requirement to produce all relevant documents does not exist.[45]

8. Representation

In principle, parties can be represented in court by attorneys-at-law, patent agents or foreign attorneys. Foreign attorneys, however, can act only as citizen representatives, a role which could also be taken by any Chinese citizen.[46]

9. Licensees/Right to Stand

As regards all IP rights, licences do not have to be registered to take legal effect. Concerning the right to stand, *e.g.* in the area of patent law, on 17 December 2001 SIPO promulgated the Measures for the Administration of Recordation of Patent Exploitation Licensing Contracts, which in its Sec. 6 allows licensees to file for an interim injunction together with the right holder in the case of non-exclusive licences[47] or even alone in the case of exclusive licensees.[48] The non-exclusive licensee may also sue alone with the right holder's consent.[49] This basically also holds true for regulations governing trade mark and copyright law.

10. Suspension of Lawsuits in Patent Cases

During a patent infringement lawsuit, the defendant usually claims invalidation of the patent concerned in an effort to suspend the proceedings. Sec. 8 SPC Interpretation Patents Cases even prescribes that besides being required to produce a search report (Secs. 55, 56 PA-ImplR) in a dispute arising from infringement of a patent right for a utility model, a defendant when making his defence applying for suspension must file a request for invalidation of the plaintiff's patent right. Where the defendant requests suspension, he must file for invalidation of the utility model or design patent concerned within the time limit for submitting evidence (Sec. 10 SPC Interpretation Patent Cases).

---

[45] Zhou Lin, China Patents and Trademarks 2002 No. 3, 6 *et seq.*; Chua Eu Jin, China Law and Praxis November 2002, 41 *et seq.*

[46] Chen Yongshun in an interview with Catherine Sun, The China IP Focus 2003, 16.

[47] Or alternatively, if the patentee refuses to take action. This may be difficult to prove in court when challenged by the other side if the patentee gives no reason for his missing action.

[48] Chi Shaojie, CPT 2003 No. 1, 73.

[49] Chen Yongshun in an interview with Catherine Sun, The China IP Focus 2003, 16.

Where utility models and design patents are concerned, suspension is usually granted if applied for within the prescribed time limits. Suspension is not granted in any of the following cases: if no technical documentation is found in the search report produced by the plaintiff that results in the loss of novelty or inventiveness; if the defendant's evidence is sufficient to prove that his technology has been known to the public; if the proof or basis which the defendant has furnished for requesting invalidation is obviously insufficient, or in other circumstances where the court deems fit to proceed (Sec. 9 SPC Interpretation Patent Cases). Additionally, no suspension is granted where in a dispute involving either invention patent, utility model or design patent where the Patent Reexamination Board upon examination has upheld the patent right. In the latter case, the court must proceed (Sec. 11 SPC Interpretation Patent Cases).

When the court suspends, it may at the same time, upon application by the plaintiff, decide to impose a provisional injunction for the defendant to cease and desist (Sec. 12 SPC Interpretation Patent Cases). Such a decision may also involve other measures to preclude additional damages, such as a request for a security deposit. A patent right preservation order shall not last more than six months. The term is counted from the date SIPO receives the notification of assistance for execution. For an extension of the preservation order SIPO must be notified before the term lapses. If no notification is served, the preservation of the patent right is automatically resolved and cannot be revived again (Sec. 13(2) and (4) SPC Interpretation Patent Cases).

VI. Evidence, Burden of Proof, Experts and Protection of Trade Secrets

1. Evidence

Evidence is exchanged in China,[50] but the procedure is by no means as extensive, formal or sophisticated as, for example, in the US or Great Britain. There are no depositions or interrogatory procedures, no real discovery and no extensive obligation to produce all files and documents of possible relevance for the case.[51]

Generally, all evidence submitted must be in original form and in due and enumerated form (Sec. 14 Evidence Provisions). Only if originals are difficult to obtain and the court consents may copies of documents or items be introduced if they are not in dispute (Sec. 10 Evidence Provisions). Evidence originating from abroad must be notarised and legalised in the country of origin before being admitted as evidence (Sec. 11 Evidence Provisions). All documents in a foreign language must be translated into Chinese (Sec. 12 Evidence Provisions).

---

[50] Chua Eu Jin, CLP November 2002, 42.

[51] Chen Yongshun in an interview with Catherine Sun, The China IP Focus 2003, 18.

The time limit for submitting the evidence must be at least 30 days (Sec. 33(3) Evidence Provisions). Witnesses must be indicated to the court ten days before the submission period lapses (Sec. 54 Evidence Provisions). If evidence is not submitted at all in due time, the party is deemed to have relinquished his right to furnish it. Evidence submitted after the deadline will not be taken into the court for cross-examination unless the opposing party agrees.

If the plaintiff applies for evidence preservation measures according to Sec. 74 Civil Procedure Code, he must do so within the evidence submission period and at the latest seven days before the evidence submission period lapses. The court may follow such application and demand a security. Measures to be taken may include sealing, confiscation, taking notes, taping, investigating, copying or getting an expert's opinion. The court may ask both parties or the representative of the plaintiff to be present when taking the measures (Secs. 23, 24 Evidence Provisions).

Any evidence submitted must have been obtained by legal means in order to be introduced in court.[52] Sec. 68 Evidence Provisions says that evidence obtained in a manner prejudicing the legitimate rights and interests of others or prohibited by law should not serve as basis in legal proceedings. Evidence obtained by unlawful means may not be used in cross-examination and serve as basis for a judgment.[53] However, in respect to evidence trap purchases, Sec. 8(2) SPC Interpretation Copyright Cases generally allows this practice. In light of the recent decision, admission in court will depend upon the exact way evidence is collected.

If a case has already been handled by the administration before a lawsuit was initiated, the ascertained facts are not taken as basis of a decision for the court. For example, Sec. 10 SPC Trade Mark Jurisdiction Rules stipulates that where cases of disputes arising from infringement are accepted by the courts and are handled by the AIC, the court shall conduct a hearing nonetheless to ascertain the facts involved.

2. Burden of Proof

Sec. 4 Evidence Provisions stipulate that the interested parties must bear the burden of proof for the facts to support their claim or the facts to rebut the claim of the other party. Sec. 64 Civil Procedure Code reiterates the general rule which places the burden of proof on the party which submits a claim.

In the case where evidence is preserved by competent authorities and cannot be referred to without the involvement of a court, or where state secrets, trade secrets or intimate and private affairs of individuals are involved, or if

[52] Yang Xiaoguang, The China IP Focus 2003, 67.

[53] Beijing Founder Group Corp. *v*. Beijing Gaoshu Tianli Science & Technology Co. Ltd. and Beijing Gaoshu Science and Technology Co. Ltd., Beijing Higher People's Court Judgment No. Gaomingzhongzi 194/2002; Yang Xiaoguang, The China IP Focus 2003, 71.

the claiming party is unable to obtain proof himself for objective reasons, the party may also request the court to collect evidence in his place (Sec. 17 Evidence Provisions).[54]

If it is difficult to decide the burden of proof based on the above principles, the court may, in accordance with the principles of fairness, honesty and good faith, decide who will bear the burden of proof.[55]

For patent disputes there are special rules regarding the burden of proof. In cases concerning patent processes, the entity or individual making the same products shall bear the burden of proof and must provide evidence that the products are made by a different process. Sec. 57 Patent Act provides for the shift of burden in patent litigation onto the defendant, who must furnish evidence that his allegedly infringing product has been produced by a process capable of manufacturing the product at issue, that he actually has used this different process, and that this process is in fact different from the patented process.

3. Experts

In practice, especially in patent cases, calling on an expert is compulsory for a judge who has been mainly trained in legal matters rather than the complicated technical aspects of a given case. However, there is no absolute obligation for the judge to call upon an expert. Parties may apply for an expertise, but, for example, in technology transfer contracts, the judge may well refuse and decide the matter himself should the facts prove not too difficult and the need for an expert is not obvious.[56]

Application for experts must be stated within the deadline for providing evidence (Sec. 25 Evidence Provisions). If the deadline is not met or the expert's fee is not paid to the court or relevant necessary material not provided by the applicant, the latter carries the burden of proof and will not be entitled to an expert opinion.

There are three steps to be followed in order to be able to present a valid expert's appraisal in court. If there exists a designated organisation specialising in appraisals relevant to the case, this organisation usually must be appointed. Otherwise the parties should consult with each other to agree on a suitable expert with the consent of the court. If no consent can be reached, the court will decide who to entrust with this matter (Sec. 26 Evidence Provisions). In doing so, in technical matters the court may rely on the Administrative Department of Science and Technology at or above the provincial level to recommend suitable experts. Chosen experts must be disinterested in the case or be unconnected to either of the parties and may comment only on technical, not legal issues. If a party presents additional

---

54 Chua Eu Jin, CLP November 2002, 42.

55 Li Yong, The China IP Focus 2003, 56.

56 Wuhan Huagong Xueyuan *v*. Shandongsheng Taianshi Jiaoqu Fuli Huagongchang, Case No. (1999) Zhizong Zi No. 20, SPC Case Study, 120.

evidence in the course of the appraisal, it can be taken into account only after it has been verified as to its source and examined by the court and the other party in the hearing.[57]

The expert opinion may be delivered in writing. Where the court feels necessary, the expert must explain his opinion in court and may be cross-examined by the parties.[58]

An expert opinion may be challenged due to lack of qualification of the expert, violation of procedural rules in arriving at the opinion, an obviously faulty opinion, or the use of material facts that are an unsuitable base for the opinion (Sec. 27 Evidence Provisions).[59] Where the opinion is incomplete, an additional opinion may be delivered.

Privately obtained expert opinions can be accepted, but may be challenged by the other side with valid reasons which must be approved by the court which will order a new expert opinion (Sec. 28 Evidence Provisions). Parties may also request one or two experts to explain difficult and decisive questions to the court or question the expert at the expense of the requesting party (Sec. 61 Evidence Provisions). In fact, in many cases this may be a suitable solution, especially where cutting-edge technology is involved.[60]

To appoint an expert in practice has proven to be a major stumbling block for judges and parties alike. Courts feel very insecure about whom to choose and in patent cases usually resort to the Patent Office which already has examined the patent as to substance in the case of invention patents. Where the defendant raises the defence of plea for nullity of the patent, the SIPO would have to re-examine its own former decision. Due to the lack of an adequate number of suitable experts, it may prove difficult to find an acceptable one.[61] It is therefore advisable to present a choice of the parties beforehand[62] and submit sufficient evidence as to qualifications and professional experience of the suggested expert.

4. Protection of Trade Secrets

How to handle the matter of trade secrets raised as a defence by an alleged patent infringer remains difficult in Chinese in legal proceedings, especially when the defendant claims to use a new process which at the same time is a trade secret warranting protection. The general rule in Sec. 66 Civil

---

[57] Jiang Zhipei, CPT 2002 No. 2, 6.

[58] Wang Tong/Hu Zhenyuan, Zhishi Chanquan 2003 No. 2, 43.

[59] In practice, this seems to almost never happen, *see* Wang Tong/Hu Zhenyuan, Zhishi Chanquan 2003 No. 2, 42. If there is a disagreement, the court will invite two additional experts, one from each party, and discuss all three opinions together with the parties before taking the expert's opinions as the basis for the court's decision.

[60] Wang Tong/Hu Zhenyuan, Zhishi Chanquan 2003 No. 2, 42.

[61] Wang Tong/Hu Zhenyuan, Zhishi Chanquan 2003 No. 2, 42.

[62] Experts appointed by the parties must be consented to by both of them, Chen Yongshun in an interview with Catherine Sun, The China IP Focus 2003, 18.

Procedure Act prescribes that evidence shall be presented in court and cross-examined by the parties. However, evidence including state secrets, trade secrets and personal privacy shall be kept confidential.

The Supreme People's Court has issued judicial interpretations relating to cross-examination in 1992, laying down the guidelines empowering the People's Court to decide whether or not a secret should be presented in court session. Where it must be presented, the court session will be held *in camera*.

The problem with current legislation is that the existing statutory legislation restricts only the confidential information from being disclosed to the public, but not to the plaintiff for litigation purposes. He is, in fact, entitled to challenge the evidence involving the trade secret.

Some Chinese courts therefore have adopted confidentiality agreements obliging the parties having access to allegedly confidential parts of a process to use it for litigation purposes only and not to disclose it to third parties.[63] This practice has no clear legal basis and is not applied by all courts throughout the country. Additionally, there are strong controversies on the tactical use of trade secrets in patent litigation. On the one hand, the plaintiff may use his right to cross-examine to spy on opponents' trade secrets and use this notwithstanding any court order. On the other, the defendant may claim certain information to be confidential in an attempt to avoid the burden of proof. It remains to be seen whether new regulations in the future will amend this ongoing uncertainty in practical patent litigation.

VII. Remedies

The General Principles in Sec. 118 stipulate that copyright, patent and trade mark right holders whose rights have been infringed upon by plagiarism, alteration or imitation, may demand that the infringement be stopped, its ill effects eliminated and damages compensated. Various special legislation also contains sections dealing with remedies.

Sec. 134 General Principles serves as the basis for court decisions.[64] Sec. 134(2) General Principles allows confiscation of property used in carrying out illegal activities, which includes infringing goods, fake trade mark labels, materials, tools and equipment used in infringement. Additionally, fines may be imposed. Theoretically, these provisions provide for a wide range of remedies for right holders. However, except for cases of counterfeiting and passing-off, only in rare circumstances will the court order the destruction of infringing goods.

---

63 Wu Yuhe, CPT 2002 No. 2, 21.

64 Jiang Zhipei, Zhongguo Shangbiao Baogao 2003 Vol. 1, 324.

1. Cease and Desist Orders

The main object of right holders in the event of infringement is to have the infringing acts cease immediately. Once an infringement is confirmed by the court, the cease and desist order is regularly sought and granted. Alongside with a cease and desist order the court may disallow further infringement if a risk of repeated infringement exists which is the rule in IP infringement cases.[65]

2. Confiscation and Destruction

Another highly effective remedy is the confiscation and/or destruction of infringing goods. The costs of destruction usually have to be borne by the infringer.[66] In case of patent infringement, goods of lower quality than the original goods are to be destroyed.[67] If the infringing goods are not of lower quality, they can, under certain circumstances, be surrendered to the right holder as damage compensation.[68]

3. Damages

One major drawback in the Chinese system is the very low amount of compensation usually granted. This is gradually changing due to increasing litigation activities by international right holders such as Disney, Toyota, Mitsubishi and others.[69] Damages are generally based on actual damages suffered by the patent holder or actual profits made by the infringer, plus reasonable investigation costs, but do not usually include attorneys' fees or even punitive damages/treble damages.[70]

Chinese law does not recognise punitive damages in spite of recent legislation which allows imposing damages on infringers one to three times the illegal turnover rate.[71] As seen from the Chinese point of view, this does not constitute a punitive element.

Generally speaking, for damages in patent, trade mark and copyright infringement cases, three methods of calculation apply: losses suffered by the right holder, the profits directly gained by the infringer during the period of the infringement, and, if it is difficult to determine the damages in the above two ways, appropriate multiples of royalties for a licence for the right concerned. Where the third way is adopted, one to three times the usual royalties can be granted by the court. Where the court has no means to determine a royalty rate, it may determine a statutory damage from RMB 5,000 to

---

[65] Liu Xiaohai, IIC 2/2001 Vol. 32, 148.

[66] Liu Xiaohai, IIC 2/2001 Vol. 32, 151.

[67] Liu Xiaohai, IIC 2/2001 Vol. 32, 150.

[68] Liu Xiaohai, IIC 2/2001 Vol. 32, 150.

[69] CPT 2002 No. 1, 76 with two cases with higher damage awards.

[70] Chen Yongshun in an interview with Catherine Sun, The China IP Focus 2003, 18.

[71] Liu Xiaohai, IIC 2/2001 Vol. 32, 158 refering to Sec. 49 Consumer Protection Act.

RMB 300,000, with a limit of RMB 500,000 (around US$ 60,000). These basic rules can be found in Secs. 60 PA, 56 TA, 48 CA in liaison with Sec. 24 CSR. The various Interpretations of the SPC define the exact mode of calculation, which may differ in details for patents, trade marks and copyright.

a) Investigation Costs

Starting from the explicit rule in Sec. 20 Competition Act which acknowledges that investigation costs in the case of unfair competition can be reimbursed, this rule has been extended to all cases of infringement of IP rights.[72] Sec. 48(1) CA, Sec. 22 SPC Interpretation Patent Cases, Sec. 17 SPC Interpretation Trade Mark Cases now explicitly state that on the request of the right holder and according to the specific facts of each case, investigation costs may be included if reasonable. They may include reasonable travel and accommodation costs and expenditures for the purchase of the infringing party's product to be used as evidence, as well as the costs of a statement of the injured party in a newspaper to safeguard his interests.[73] The reimbursement of these costs is not subject to the injured party having suffered damage or the infringing party having made a profit.[74] Sec. 17 SPC Interpretation Trade Mark Cases and Sec. 26 SPC Interpretation Copyright Cases reiterate this principle and explicitly list appointed agents and collection of evidence as well as state-fixed lawyers' fees (the latter only upon request and according to the specific circumstances of the case).

b) Court Fees

Generally, court fees depend on the damages claimed according to a formula specified in the law.[75] The costs for appeal are the same as for a trial in first instance.[76]

c) Attorneys' Fees

Attorneys' fees are negotiated by the parties based on the amount of damages and usually range from 10 to 15%.[77] Usually, these fees are not to be paid by the losing side even if the case is fully won. The SPC has allowed in Sec. 17(2) of its Interpretation Trade Mark Cases, Sec. 26 SPC Interpretation Copyright Cases that the court may, according to the circumstances of the case, determine that the defendant shall compensate the plaintiff a reasonable amount of attorneys' fees, the standard of which as set by government

---

[72] Liu Xiaohai, IIC 2/2001 Vol. 32, 156.

[73] Intermediate People's Court of Nanjing, Zuigao Renmin Fayuan Gongbao 1998, 70.

[74] Liu Xiaohai, IIC 2/2001 Vol. 32, 156.

[75] *See* the People's Courts Measures for the Collection of Procedural Fees, promulgated on 29 June 1989 and in force since 1 September 1989.

[76] Chen Yongshun in an interview with Catherine Sun, The China IP Focus 2003, 17.

[77] Chen Yongshun in an interview with Catherine Sun, The China IP Focus 2003, 16. In some cases the attorney may charge even 25% or more.

agencies is very likely to be much lower than the actual costs.[78] Additionally, fees will only be covered if the specific circumstances of the case allow it. Although the various Interpretations of the SPC do not further elaborate on what such circumstances might be, most likely they would be acts of deliberate and wilful infringement, such as clear-cut professional counterfeiting or software pirating cases.

4. Fines

Usually, fines are imposed by courts if a case represents a clear act of counterfeiting or passing-off. However, only the Patent Act contains explicit provisions on it; the Trade Mark Act and Copyright Act only contain comparable provisions in their Implementing Rules.[79] Fines can be imposed not only against infringing companies but also against the persons directly responsible.[80] If the court wants to impose a fine, it will be done after conferring with the Chief Judge of the court and in a separate decision which may be challenged on its own by the defendant within ten days. During the review the fine will not be enforced.[81]

In patent cases, Sec. 19 SPC Interpretation Patent Cases for cases of counterfeiting refers to Sec. 58 PA which allows for fines up to three times of the illegal income; if no income has been obtained, fines up to RMB 50,000 can be imposed. The same limit for statutory damages is valid for passing-off a patent (Sec. 59 PA).

5. Public Apology

As part of the elimination of ill effects the infringing party must issue a declaration in which he admits the infringement committed and promises not to commit further infringements. According to case law, the elimination of ill effects primarily takes place in the form of a public apology in newspapers at the expense of the infringing party. The content of the apology must be approved by the court. If the injured party has not suffered serious damages this specific claim very often is not granted.[82] If a party ordered to make the public apology does not do so, the court can publish the main contents of the decision in a newspaper at the expense of the infringing party.[83]

Interestingly enough, Chinese law makes a distinction between the above described public apology as elimination of ill effects and a apology such as that mentioned in Sec. 120 General Principles (infringement of right of portrait, right of name or honour). The use of such an apology is meant to

---

[78] Ran Ruixie/Zee Wai-Bui, CLP Dec. 2002/Jan. 2003, 28.

[79] Secs. 58 PA, 42 TA-ImplR, 36 CA-ImplR.

[80] Liu Xiaohai, IIC 2/2001 Vol. 32, 160.

[81] Jiang Zhipei, Zhongguo Shangbiao Baogao 2003 Vol. 1, 324.

[82] No. 1 Intermediate People's Court of Beijing, Zuigao Renmin Fayuan Gongbao 1995, 101 *et seq*.

[83] No. 1 Intermediate People's Court of Beijing, CPT 1997 No. 4, 87 *et seq*.

ease tension between the parties and facilitate the settlement of a dispute. It is more common in cases of infringement of personality rights and may therefore occur in cases of infringement of rights of authorship.[84]

6. Executing a Decision

The enforcement of civil judgments which have entered into force is regulated in Secs. 207 *et seq*. Civil Procedure Code. Enforcement is carried out by the courts that tried the cases in first instance. The people's courts all have enforcement bodies which execute the enforcement provisions of the judgments and court orders that have become legally effective, arbitration awards made by China's arbitration bodies and the legally effective judgments of foreign courts which are recognised by the Chinese courts (*see* Sec. 209(3) Civil Procedure Code).

For the enforcement of arbitration awards or notarised documents of obligation together with a compulsory enforcement by the notary public office, the competent court is at the domicile of the party subject to the enforcement procedure or at the location of property owned by this party.[85] The enforcement procedure is initiated only where a party concerned fails to perform its contractual duties in spite of being capable of doing so.[86]

VIII. Preliminary Measures

The Chinese Civil Procedure Code in Secs. 92 *et seq*. does not recognise the institution of the interim injunction as it is defined in other jurisdictions. The law provides two special types of pre-trial procedural measures, the anticipated enforcement (*xianyu zhixing*) and the freezing of assets (*caichan baoquan*).[87]

Usually to obtain a provisional measure from the court a bond must be placed (Sec. 98(2) CPC). Anticipated enforcement according to the Civil Procedure Code in IP cases requires that the plaintiff can convincingly show that the possibility of an infringement by the defendant exists and that the plaintiff would suffer considerable damage difficult to remedy or evidence would be lost without anticipated enforcement.[88] Although theoretically *ex parte* applications without a hearing before the issuing of such orders are possible according to the law and reportedly in practice have been applied,[89]

---

[84] Liu Xiaohai, 32 IIC 145 (2001).

[85] The People's Courts of the PRC, Foreign Affair Bureau of the SPC of the PRC, 1995, 26.

[86] The People's Courts of the PRC, Foreign Affair Bureau of the SPC of the PRC, 1995, 26.

[87] Gao Lulin, Zhishi Chanquan 2003 No. 1, 16.

[88] Liu Xiaohai, 32 IIC 145 (2001).

[89] *See* the cited decision of the Intermediate People's Court Shanghai in: Liu Lu/Gao Yan, Minshi Susongfa lijie shiyong yu anli pingxi, Beijing 1996, 336.

it is rather difficult for a right holder to have the actual advantage of surprise over the defendant after a notice of the original law suit has been served to him.

Before the amendment of the IP laws it was virtually impossible for IP right holders to obtain interim injunctions. Preliminary injunctions according to Secs. 97, 98 Civil Procedure Code require a clear-cut relationship between the parties, which is nearly never the case in infringement proceedings. An *ex parte* application was also not possible since the application for such measure required the previous filing for a lawsuit which deprived the plaintiff of the surprise effect. Property preservation proved difficult due to the necessity to assess the required security and the possibility for the infringer, to post a bond himself to resolve the freezing of his assets (Sec. 95 Civil Procedure Code).

After the revision of the relevant IP-related laws, all statutes contain special provisions citing interim injunctions *expressis verbis*. Additionally, the SPC has issued two special sets of regulations regulating pre-trial measures and evidence preservation, the Several Provisions of the SPC for the Application of Law for Stopping Infringement of Patent Rights before Instituting Legal Proceedings ("SPC Interpretation Interim Injunctions Patents"), adopted on 5 June 2001 and in force since then. In trade mark law, the Interpretation by the Supreme People's Court of the Issues Relating to the Application of Law to Pre-trial Suspension of Acts of Infringement of Trade Marks and to Evidence Preservation, adopted on 25 December 2001 and entered into force on 22 January 2002 ("SPC Interpretation Interim Injunction Trade Marks") is concurrently applicable in copyright cases.

1. Right to Apply

Besides the right holder and his successor in title, the exclusive and sole licensee generally may apply for an interim injunction on his own if the right holder takes no action against infringing activities. Simple licensees cannot apply for such measures without the written consent of the right holder.

2. Procedure

The application must be in written form and in Chinese. The court may not grant more than what has been applied for, *e.g. see* Sec. 5 SPC Interpretation Interim Injunction Patents. The application must contain the specific statement that irremediable damage will be caused to the legitimate rights and interests of the applicant if the relevant act is not stopped immediately (Sec. 3 SPC Interpretation Interim Injunctions Patents). When applying the usual court fees according to the Civil Procedure Code must be paid.

3. Evidence

The applicant must submit documents proving the authenticity and validity of his right, including valid certificates, claims, description, receipt of payment of the annual patent fee and in case of utility models a search report by SIPO (Sec. 4(1) SPC Interpretation Interim Injunctions Patents). An interested party also must submit the patent licensing contract and the proof for filing the contract with SIPO (Sec. 4(2) SPC Interpretation Interim Injunctions Patents). If he does not have this proof, he must submit the certificate of the patentee or other evidence that proves that he enjoys the right. Sole licensees must submit proof that the patentee does not want to file himself for the injunction. Heirs must also prove their legal status. Most notably, the applicant must submit evidence that proves that the respondent is committing or about to commit an act of infringement, including the allegedly infringing product and technical features of the patented technology as well as of the allegedly infringing product (Sec. 4 SPC Interpretation Interim Injunctions Patents).

4. Undertaking

According to Sec. 6 SPC Interpretation Interim Injunctions Patents, a guaranty in the form of a valid pledge or hypothecation must be provided, otherwise the application will be rejected.[90] The necessary amount of the guaranty is determined by the court, taking into account the sales of the product in question, the reasonable costs of storage and stock-keeping, the losses that may be caused to the opponent and other reasonable costs such as wages (Sec. 6 SPC Interpretation Interim Injunctions Patents). Even if an injunction is granted and then executed, where in the process of execution the opponent suffers even greater losses than originally assumed by the court due to the adoption of the measure, the court may ask for an additional surety and resolve the measure if this demand is not met in due time (Sec. 7 SPC Interpretation Interim Injunctions Patents).

5. No Cross Undertaking

As the most important difference to injunctions granted only on basis of the Civil Procedure Code, Sec. 8 SPC Interpretation Interim Injunctions Patents stipulates that any measure taken to execute the ruling of the court to stop the act of infringement will not be stopped because the party against which the application has been filed provides a counter-guaranty.

6. Swift Decision: 48 Hour Rule/*ex parte* Application

When all necessary documents have been submitted, the court must decide within 48 hours and the order must be carried out without delay. Within this time span, the court may verify the facts, summon and consult with one or both parties and then make a decision which the other party is informed of latest within five days (Sec. 9 SPC Interpretation Interim Injunctions

---

[90] Ye Yonglu, Zhishi Chanquan Susong Shiwu, Guangdong Jingji Chubanshe May 2002, 220.

Patents). The wording of the provisions shows that an application can be made *ex parte* if the court does not find it necessary to consult the other side. When deciding, the court must consider whether the alleged or feared act actually is an infringement, whether not taking the advised measure will bring irremediable harm to the rights of the applicant, the content of the information relating to the applicant's provided guaranty, and whether or not ordering the other party to cease the relevant act would be damaging to public interest (Sec. 11 SPC Interpretation Interim Injunctions Patents). Where the applicant institutes legal proceedings against patent infringement and simultaneously requests enjoining an act of patent infringement in advance, the court may first make the ruling on the request which prevents dilatory tactics in proceedings (Sec. 17 SPC Interpretation Interim Injunctions Patents).

7. Main Action

The applicant must initiate legal proceedings within 15 days after the court takes measures to stop the relevant act. If no lawsuit is filed, the measure will be removed (Sec. 12 SPC Interpretation Interim Injunctions Patents). Otherwise the ruling of the court generally remains effective until the final legal instrument has come into effect. The court may deviate from that and order a deadline for the effectiveness of the measure. It may also prolong this deadline after the expiration of the time limit on the request of the interested party (Sec. 14 SPC Interpretation Interim Injunctions Patents).

8. Remedies

If the applicant is not satisfied with the decision of the court, he may apply for reconsideration within 10 days from the date of receipt of the ruling. The execution of the ruling is not suspended during reconsideration (Sec. 10 SPC Interpretation Interim Injunctions Patents).

The party against which the application is filed may, if the right holder does not start legal proceedings as stipulated or if there is an error in the application and losses are caused, initiate legal proceedings with the competent court requesting damage compensation.

9. Evidence Preservation

When executing pre-litigation measures to stop allegedly infringing acts the court may upon application simultaneously preserve the evidence (Sec. 74 Civil Procedure Code and Sec. 16(1) SPC Interpretation Interim Injunctions Patents) or even freeze assets (Sec. 16(2) SPC Interpretation Interim Injunctions Patents and Secs. 92, 93 Civil Procedure Code). The requirements for such a measure therefore are equally high compared to an interim cease and desist order.

Sec. 57 TA and Sec. 50 CA, Sec. 27 SoftReg and the special judicial interpretations of the Supreme People's Court described above cover pre-trial evidence preservation. Parties may apply for such measures in cases where evidence is most likely to be difficult to recover because of the great likelihood that upon initiating the action it will be destroyed or hidden. The courts may ask experts to look into the case before deciding.

IX. Limitation

Limitation in Chinese law does not link limitation to the claim but to the procedural action initiated by a right holder in the courts after awareness of infringement. Sec. 135 General Principles provides for the general limitation period to claim a civil right of two years from the date the right holder has known or has reason to know about the infringement. Sec. 62 PA, Sec. 23 SPC Interpretation Patent Cases reiterate the two-year time limit. In ongoing infringement actions, rulings of the court concerning damages will therefore be computed from two years before the date the right holder instituted legal proceedings.

C. Administrative Law Enforcement

When talking about dual enforcement, "administrative enforcement" is not as homogeneous as one would tend to think. In fact, it depends in the first place on the type of right to determine the competent administrative authority. Among the different administration bureaus are the State Intellectual Property Office (SIPO), the Trade Mark Office within the State Administration of Industry and Commerce (SAIC) with its local offices (AICs), the National Copyright Administration (NCA) with its local copyright bureaus, the State Bureau of Quality and Technical Supervision (head of the Technical Supervisory Bureaus (TSB)), customs, police, prosecutors, judges, the Tobacco Monopoly and the Pharmaceutical Administration.[91]

Patent matters generally are handled by SIPO and its local IP Bureaus. In trade mark matters, the most important agencies are the Trade Mark Office, the police, the TSB and the SAIC with overlapping competencies. For copyright related cases, the NCA and its branches of copyright agencies must be referred to.

Generally, the law allows for action by the administration where public interests are concerned, which is the case in counterfeiting and passing-off cases, *see* Secs. 58, 59 PA, 84, 85 PA-ImplR, 45, 48 TA, (to a much broader extent also referring to infringement of private rights and interests) Sec. 47 CA in liaison with Sec. 37 CA-ImplR and Sec. 24 SoftReg, particularly referring to the public interest. But in patent law, the new legislation encourages the parties to go to court instead of relying on swift administrative raids against infringers.

---

[91] Joseph Simone cited by Ralph Cunningham, The China IP Focus 2003, 12.

I. Competent Administrative Authorities

In patent cases, according to Secs. 2 to 4 Patent Enforcement Measures, promulgated by SIPO and in force since 17 December 2001, special divisions called patent administrative authorities which are defined in Sec. 78 PA-ImplR of the SIPO at county level (usually the local IP Bureau), are competent to handle infringement, mediation and investigation of passing-off and counterfeiting.[92] If a case involves an infringement of a "patent of great influence" by passing-off or counterfeiting, SIPO may provide special rules for the organisation of the administrative authority and, if need be, even provide guidance on how to handle the case (Sec. 4 Patent Enforcement Measures).

II. Procedure in Patent Infringement Cases

Administrative proceedings have the advantage of being less formal and relatively simple, although the same some principles must be followed. For example, if an infringement can be proven, but the infringer cannot be identified, the administration will not accept the case, because it can only decide on clear facts and does not have the power and ability of the police to track down and locate alleged infringers.[93]

Secs. 58 and 59 PA grant administrative authorities of the *locus delicti* to step in *ex officio* in the case of passing-off another person's patent by issuing a cease and desist order and imposing fines (Sec. 22 Patent Enforcement Measures).

Unlike in trade mark and copyright law, in patent law there are detailed administrative provisions as to requirements, procedure and remedies of administrative enforcement laid down in the Patent Enforcement Measures which are supplemented by provincial rules reiterating and sometimes even broadening the procedure.

1. Filing

Right owners, including licensees of exclusive licences if the right holder does not apply and simple licences with the consent of the right holder (Sec. 5(2) Patent Enforcement Measures), need to formulate a request clearly defining the respondent and the specific issues of the case (Sec. 5(1) No. 1 to 5 Patent Enforcement Measures). Sec. 5(1) No. 5 Patent Enforcement Measures limits the general possibility of dual enforcement by stipulating that the administration will not accept a case where the interested party has already instituted proceedings in the People's Courts in respect of the patent dispute.

---

[92] Chen Wang, Copyright February 2002 Vol. 16, 22.

[93] Yang Xiaoguang, The China IP Focus 2003, 73.

Usually the right holder will request the authorities to conduct a raid according to Secs. 27 *et seq.* Patent Enforcement Measures. The law now clearly stipulates that the other side must be informed of the alleged infringement. In practice, at times in clear cut cases, the authorities might go out of their way and order a raid, giving right holders the extremely valuable advantage of getting hold of evidence which otherwise might have been impossible to obtain. In that case, a bond must be placed with the authorities, representing the value of the goods to be seized. Another advantage in such cases is that the infringer is not able to file for invalidation and delay the whole procedure up to currently three years.[94]

2. Acceptance and Procedure

Whether a request is accepted or not will be notified to the applicant within seven days and if it is accepted three or more staff members are appointed to handle the procedure (Sec. 8 Patent Enforcement Measures). Within another seven days after putting the case on file (*i.e.* accepting it) copies of the request are served on the defendant (Sec. 9 Patent Enforcement Measures). This represents a main difference from trade mark law, where a surprise attack may be launched on an alleged infringer by staging a raid with the authorities. According to the law, in patent matters such action would only be possible after notifying the alleged infringer.

Usually the IP Bureau will hold a hearing with a three-day notice before making a decision, although this is not mandatory (Sec. 10 Patent Enforcement Measures). If so, right holders must be well prepared for such a hearing since the authorities may very well be located anywhere in the west of China and local connections may play a role in the procedure. A decision, once made, must contain the facts and reasoning on which the decision is based.

3. Powers of Authorities

Patent administrative authorities may conduct investigations and collect evidence in infringement disputes and passing-off/counterfeiting cases (Sec. 27 Patent Enforcement Measures). In doing so, they may consult and copy contracts, account books and other relevant documents of the case, question interested parties and witnesses and conduct on-site inspections by way of measuring, taking photos and making videotapes.

In infringement cases of patent rights for manufacturing processes they may ask the person who is the object of the investigation to conduct an on-site demonstration. The administration may also take samples (Sec. 29 Patent Enforcement Measures) such as part of the products or in the case of process

---

[94] This is the time frame for going through an invalidation procedure at the Patent Reexamination Board with SIPO in Beijing and the courts after the decision of the Patent Reexamination Board.

patents, a part of the products directly obtained by the process. The quantity must suffice to verify the facts.

The whole procedure is recorded by taking notes which have to be signed by the parties (which if negated is put down in the record as well) and sealed by the staff members (Secs. 28, 29 Patent Enforcement Measures).

Where the evidence is likely to be lost or difficult to obtain afterwards, and where it is impossible to collect evidence by way of sampling, a decision may be met within seven days and a record of the evidence kept. The record may not be destroyed or transferred by the subject of the investigation (Sec. 30 Patent Enforcement Measures). The alleged infringer must co-operate and assist in the investigation (Sec. 31 Patent Enforcement Measures). In case of obstruction, Sec. 41 Patent Enforcement Measures allows imposing penalties or even criminal sanctions may apply.

4. Remedies

The decision of the authorities can be challenged in court where the whole case will be reviewed. The decision may order the infringer to redress his act, confiscate illegal earnings and impose a fine of up to three times the illegal earnings. Parties subject to an administrative penalty can defend themselves before a final decision is met and bring forward evidence (Secs. 23 and 24 Patent Enforcement Measures).

5. Simplified Procedure Against a Repeated Infringer

Sec. 14 Patent Enforcement Measures provides for a significantly simplified procedure in the case of repeated infringement. Where the defendant again commits the same infringing act for the same patent right, the administrative authority upon application by the right holder may directly decide to order the cessation of the infringing act without having to go through the above described procedure. However, it is rather difficult to determine whether an act infringes the same right in the same way. Although the provision is obviously meant to simplify and speed up active enforcement, it may prove counterproductive if challenged in court.

III. Remedies

1. Cease and Desist

Patent administrative authorities may order an infringer to immediately cease the act of manufacture, using, offering for sale, or import of infringing products and to destroy the equipment or moulds especially used for the manufacture of infringing products or exploitation of the patented process and may order the infringer not to sell and/or use the infringing products that have not been sold nor to market them in any form. If such products are difficult to store, their destruction can be ordered; in the case of import, the relevant customs authority may be notified by the Resolution Decision (Sec. 33 Patent Enforcement Measures).

The cease and desist order can be challenged by instituting legal proceedings with the court within 15 days after receiving the official notice of the administration. If 15 days have passed without legal proceedings being initiated, the administration may apply to the courts for compulsory execution. Where the defendant institutes proceedings in the court after the administrative authority establishes the infringement, the enforcement of the decision is not suspended during the proceedings in court (Sec. 34(1) Patent Enforcement Measures).

2. Destruction of Moulds and Tools

In passing-off cases, falsely indicated patent numbers are ordered removed or, if this is not possible, the goods so marked are destroyed. Advertising material must be destroyed as well and the ill effects must be eliminated (*e.g.* by way of public rectification in newspapers). Contracts which contain wrongly "patented" products must be rectified, forged or falsified documents and patent certificates must be handed in to the administration (Sec. 36 Patent Enforcement Measures).

3. Confiscation

Illegal profits may be confiscated in cases of passing-off (Sec. 58 PA). The punishment in patent passing-off affairs and in respect to the illicit income according to Sec. 38 Patent Enforcement Measures is determined in two ways. Where products are sold, the illicit income is determined by the sales price of the passed off products times the quantity of the products sold; or, where a contract is concluded for passing off a patent, the fees collected according to this contract are considered the illicit income (Sec. 38 Patent Enforcement Measures).

4. Fines

Fines must be paid within 15 days of the date of receipt of the decision of punishment, non-observance leads to imposition of additional 3% of the fine per day (Sec. 40 Patent Enforcement Measures).

5. Damages

Before the accession to WTO, damages could also be granted by the administration. In order to strengthen the courts and distinguish between injunctive relief and an in-depth assessment of what damages actually have been caused, only the courts can grant damages. Based on Sec. 57 PA, the administration may now, upon request of the proprietor, only mediate the amount of compensation for infringement. If the mediation fails, legal proceedings can be instituted with the courts in line with the Civil Procedure Code.

6. Publishing of the Decision

In a face-saving society, public announcements can hurt more than fines. According to Sec. 37 Patent Enforcement Measures, cases of passing-off or counterfeiting and their punishment must be published. There are no comparable provisions in trade mark and copyright law which in practice might not exclude the order of such announcement.

D. Criminal Law Enforcement

Chinese law, unlike that of most other countries, heavily relies on criminal enforcement in the battle against counterfeiting. A crucial cornerstone for making this system work is a coordination between the different administrative agencies which are responsible for enforcing IP rights and the Public Security Bureaus (PSBs) attached to the Chinese Procuratorate.

In April 2001, the Supreme People's Court, Supreme People's Procuratorate and the Ministry of Public Security issued two sets of rules intended to establish standards for determining whether counterfeiters may be subject to criminal investigation and public prosecution under the existing two sets of provisions in the Criminal Code:[95] Secs. 140 to 149, which deal with the sale of "fake/inferior goods" and Secs. 213 to 218, which govern the counterfeiting of registered trade marks, patents and copyright infringement.

I. Administrative Authorities, Criminal Prosecution and Related Problems

The above described administrative authorities can impose administrative fines only. The police may get involved with the investigation of, for example, counterfeiting cases in two ways: through petitions directly filed with them by the IP owner, or through the transfer of cases initially handled by the said administrative authorities. The administrative authorities may not investigate cases and prosecute infringing acts under the PRC Criminal Code.

In practice, the transfer of cases from the administrative authorities to the PSBs has not occurred very often for various reasons such as lack of manpower and the unspoken aim of reaping revenue from the administrative fines. Another reason is that the difficulty to determine whether a case merits criminal prosecution.[96]

Reportedly, standards on criminal prosecutions and trade mark cases published in 2001 stated that the police could get involved in cases concerning

---

[95] Hao Yuqiang, CPT 2003 No. 1, 39.

[96] Joseph Simone, CLP May 2002.

well-known marks. However, in practice the police very often refuse to cooperate, citing their heavy workload as a reason.[97] The same holds true for the cooperation between AICs and criminal authorities. Very often, the AIC is asked to do the actual investigation by the competent criminal authorities and the TMO is additionally required to make a statement about the registration of the trade mark and the infringement. This is actually not as the law stipulates. The TA states in Sec. 59 TA that cases which fulfil the requirements of criminal provisions must be transferred to the competent authority and not be left with the AIC. However, prosecution authorities must first actually receive notification by the AIC and then additionally accept the transfer of the case. Both steps very often are not taken and consequently only fines are imposed in a situation where the law calls for criminal prosecution.[98]

II. Basic Principles of Prosecution

Once a case is transferred or accepted, the rules governing criminal law apply, including rules regarding an attempted crime.[99] In Chinese law, individuals may be prosecuted as of age 16 or above.[100] An organisation can also be punished for the commission of a punishable infringement pursuant to Sec. 220 Criminal Code and can be subject to a fine. The distinction between individual and organisation is somewhat unusual to some jurisdictions when it comes to criminal prosecution. If an individual sets up a company (mainly) for the purpose of trade mark infringement, the standards for individuals should apply and not the higher standards for organisations. This is especially the case where other persons commit a crime in the name of the entity and the illegal benefits are divided privately among the individuals.[101] The managers and other persons directly responsible for the criminal act are punished according to the relevant provisions of the Criminal Code.[102]

Only if an individual commits infringing acts knowingly and in full awareness will criminal prosecution be possible. Such awareness and intention will be implied for example in trade mark cases where a well-known trade mark is counterfeited, where infringer and right holder are players in the same local market or are competitors and the negative impact of the counterfeiting is strong, where besides the trade mark also the get-up and trade dress are copied or where infringement continues after warning by the right holder.[103]

---

[97] Joseph Simone cited by Ralph Cunningham, The China IP Focus 2003, 11.

[98] Hao Yuqiang, CPT 2003 No. 1, 42.

[99] Zhou Xiang, Zhishi Chanquan 2002 No. 6, 16, 17.

[100] Zhou Xiang, Zhishi Chanquan 2002 No. 6, 15.

[101] Hao Yuqiang, CPT 2003 No. 1, 40.

[102] Liu Xiaohai, IIC 2/2001 Vol. 32, 161.

[103] Zhou Xiang, Zhishi Chanquan 2002 No. 6, 15.

Offences against IP rights are prosecuted *ex officio*. Private parties may file a private prosecution according to Sec. 170 Criminal Procedure Act[104] with the People's Court if he can prove that the infringing party has injured the victim's body or assets and is therefore liable but that police or state attorneys have failed to prosecute the offence. A negative response can be appealed with the next higher state attorney within seven days after receipt of the decision (Sec. 145 Criminal Procedure Act) or he can file a private prosecution with a second review. Once this has been accepted by the People's Court, the state attorney is obliged to surrender the files in question to the court.

Under the Criminal Procedure Act, the public security authority is responsible for the investigation, arrest and preliminary examination of criminal cases. Right owners may file a complaint either with local competent administrative authority at the place where the defendant resides or even directly institute proceedings with the courts. The court will transfer the case to the public security authority to be placed on file for investigation. Filing for actions involves a choice to make between the different authorities, and may require the right holder to weigh whether his evidence is sufficient for criminal prosecution. Some authors in trade mark infringement cases recommend first starting with the AIC, which is responsible for classical infringement, and then having the case transferred to the public security authority which may handle the case together with the AIC or alone. In serious cases, right holders may consider informing the TMO and the Public Security Ministry.[105]

Filing can be done by the right holder himself, although representation by a patent or trade mark agent is recommended especially for foreigners. Information needs to be accurate and should be treated confidentially. When filing, evidence of the infringement, certificates, trade mark samples or copies of works used by the right holder and those used by the counterfeiter must be submitted. Evidence should best include samples of the original and fake trade marks and goods such as photographs, samples, promotional materials, invoices and others, written and oral statements of witnesses including evidence obtained secretly.[106]

III. Criminal Enforcement of Patent Rights

Sec. 216 Criminal Code punishes any infringement of a patent under serious circumstances with three years of sentence and/or a fine. Sec. 64 Guidelines Criminal Prosecution specifies that individuals with an amount of illegal sales at or above RMB 100,000 and legal persons at or above RMB 500,000 can

[104] Quangao Renmin Daibaio Dahui Changwu Weiyuanhui Gongbao 1996, 246.

[105] Hao Yuqiang, CPT 2003 No. 1, 41.

[106] Hao Yuqiang, CPT 2003 No. 1, 41.

be held criminally liable.[107] If punished by the administration twice or more for such counterfeiting, these limits do not apply. In cases a with serious impact, the above limits are not necessary to result in criminal punishment.

E. *Border Enforcement*

The former Regulations of the PRC regarding Customs Protection of IP Rights have been in force since 1 October 1995.[108] With effect as of 1 March 2004, the revised Regulations of the PRC on the Customs Protection of Intellectual Property Rights ("Customs Regulations") have replaced the prior legislation. New additional Implementing Rules are expected to follow in order to clarify remaining issues and procedures mentioned in the new rules.[109] However, according to the Chinese view, the old regulations already were in compliance with TRIPS and not only cover the import of goods, but also the export.[110]

I. Competent Authorities and Procedures

According to Secs. 12 et seq. Customs Regulations, Customs has the authority to detain imported or exported goods suspected of infringing IP rights entered into records of the State Customs Bureau (SCB) *ex officio* (*see* Sec. 16 Customs Regulations) or upon request of the right holder whose rights (all types of patents, trade marks, copyright) are registered (Sec. 13 Customs Regulations). In contrast to prior legislation, the registration of right is no longer a precondition (Sec. 13(2) Customs Regulations).[111] The SCB has a computerised network connected to all local customs offices of Mainland China. Registration will take 30 days from filing the application to issuing a certificate to the proprietor. The period of validity of such registration has now been extended to ten years from the day of approval of registration with SCB.[112] The cost for each registration is around US$ 1,000.

If the IP right has been recorded, counterfeits may be intercepted when entering the PRC against payment of a bond by the right holder and the payment of a storage fee. The latter has led many companies to refrain from using Customs to battle counterfeiting.[113] Procedures to transfer serious cases for investigation to the Chinese police have not yet been formulated,

---

[107] Sec. 64 Criminal Prosecution Guidelines apparently overlooked by Zhao Guoling/Huang Xu, Zhishi Chanquan 2002 No. 4, 7.

[108] Dong Jiangxiong/Wu Yuhe, The China IP Focus 2003, 65.

[109] *E.g.* Sec. 14 Customs Regulations

[110] Gao Lulin, Zhishi Chanquan 2003 No. 1, 17.

[111] Gao Lulin, Zhishi Chanquan 2003 No. 1, 17.

[112] Dong Jiangxiong/Wu Yuhe, The China IP Focus 2003, 65.

[113] Gao Lulin, Zhishi Chanquan 2003 No. 1, 17 mentions the push of the industry to abolish fees and the necessity of posting a bond.

although Secs. 26, 30 Customs Regulations prescribe the obligation to submit serious cases to the prosecution organs and prosecution according to the Criminal Code. The GAC is working with the Supreme People's Court regarding the issuance of a possible judicial interpretation that would facilitate criminal prosecution against importers and exporters of counterfeits.[114]

II. Fees, Security Bonds, Bonded Zones and Law Enforcement

Usually, detention requires a bond equal to the CIF price of imported or the FOB price of exported suspected goods and must be submitted with the local customs in charge of the case. The bond can be returned after the subtraction of fees such as warehousing, storage and disposal of detained goods, once a decision has been made by Customs or the judicial authorities. If the consignor or consignee contests that the detained goods are infringing, he may apply for clearance, providing a bond equal to the value of the goods (Sec. 19 Customs Regulations), upon which Customs will release the goods (Sec. 24(3) Customs Regulations). He can also provide evidence that the asserted rights have not been infringed after receiving the Customs Detention Receipt. If the evidence is convincing to Customs, the goods will be released (Sec. 24(4) Customs Regulations).

If the right holder fails to place the bond or pay storage fees or fails to come up with a notice of the court concerning the further detainment of goods after 20 or 50 working days, depending on detention upon application or *ex officio*, Customs must release the goods. The bond required to be placed by the right holder must be paid within three working days, otherwise the goods are released. According to the new regulations, right holders in cases of specific applications after detention must turn to the courts to prove infringement. In cases of clear infringement and confiscation *ex officio*, no court order will be required and Customs must decide within 30 working days. This is different again where infringement is not obvious after *ex officio* detention. In such case, again an order from the court must be obtained, which may be an interim injunction (Sec. 23 Customs Regulations).

If goods are found to be infringing, they will mostly be donated to a charitable organisation or sold to the brand owner. If the right holder is not willing to purchase them, the goods will be auctioned off after the infringing features have been removed. Only where the infringing labels, etc., cannot be removed, will the infringing goods be destroyed.

As of yet, no fines are specified by the new regulations, although this power was granted to Customs under the old Customs Regulations. It remains to be seen whether the awaited Implementing Rules will allow for administrative fines to be levied on infringers by Customs.

---

[114] Joseph Simone, CLP May 2002, 22.

III. Possible Counter-measures

The right holder as well as the consignor/consignee can submit the infringement dispute to a related administrative authority or institute legal proceedings with the People's Court within the period of above investigation of the Customs.[115]

If an administrative decision has been reached in respect to an alleged infringement, the cease and desist order to import infringing products may be notified to the relevant customs.[116]

F. Practice of Enforcement

The new possibilities opened up by the law in reality still fall short of its spirit. More often than not, right holders find themselves facing a host of practical problems and obstacles when trying to make the law work.[117] The main problems in battling this phenomenon are local protectionism, limited resources and divided responsibilities between the competent administrative authorities.

- *Local government protectionism*
  Local protectionism occurs in cases of conflicts between interests of local companies and national laws. It is simply applied by ignoring existing legislation or frustrating the actual enforcement of such law.[118] Monopolistic practices and collusion among counterfeit manufacturers and local officials prevent efficient crackdowns on the product pirates.[119]
- *Limited resources and manpower*
  The competent authorities have very limited resources and manpower to tackle the problem. Especially IP Bureaus and Copyright Administrations still lack experience in exercising their new powers, rendering administrative actions more often than not fruitless and daunting.
- *Divided responsibilities*
  The responsibilities in the fight against product piracy are divided, causing confusion in practice. Any attempt to create one competent administrative authority until now has been thwarted by the powerful cadres in the provinces. There exists additionally in some places a strong reluctance of competing government agencies such as the Technical

---

115 Dong Jiangxiong/Wu Yuhe, The China IP Focus 2003, 65.

116 *E.g. see* Sec. 33 No. 5 Patent Enforcement Measures.

117 Ralph Cunningham, IP Asia April 2000, 16 *et seq*.

118 Chen Wang, Copyright February 2002 Vol. 16, 22.

119 Arjun Subrahmanyan, CLP May 2002, 19, 20.

> Supervision Bureau or the Customs to cooperate. This is on the one hand due to the reluctance to forego income generated by administrative fines, on the other due to lack of general knowledge of how and when cases should be transferred. The resulting delay and difficulties also make it more likely that valuable evidence will be "lost".[120]

In practice, it is also increasingly difficult to determine who is actually responsible for manufacturing fakes. Counterfeiters have become increasingly professional and very well organised with sophisticated methods in spreading their fake goods. For example, counterfeited goods exports are subsumed under legitimate export deals and contracts or handled by legally registered foreign trade companies. The only way to successfully battle this process is a strategic approach including the exact quantification of the percentage of fakes in a particular market and an extensive research of the cause and impact of counterfeiting.[121]

Right owners should keep in mind that the new law might not only work in their favour. Enforcement may also very well be used against foreign investors, mainly in design patent or trade mark issues. Practice has shown that recently foreign firms also have been the object of raids initiated by Chinese right holders.[122] The new laws in force will soon need to be further tested in practice. Better understanding the new system of enforcement will then be a prerequisite for success in defending IP rights in China.

---

[120] Arjun Subrahmanyan, CLP May 2002, 20.

[121] Arjun Subrahmanyan, CLP May 2002, 21.

[122] Dong Wei, CPT 2001 No. 4, 30 *et seq.*

13
The Enforcement of Patent Rights in Japan

CHRISTOPHER HEATH

A. Civil Law Enforcement in Japan in General

I. Law Enforcement and Legal Consciousness

"Harmony shall be praised" is the first article of the first Japanese constitution enacted by Prince Shôtoku Taishi as long as 1,350 years ago. Particularly Western models of law enforcement, it is claimed, would be like a sword cutting a thing in two (*Ittô ryôdan ni suru*), exactly the opposite of what should be understood as harmony. Well known is the story of the famous Judge Ôka in the Edo period, who had to adjudicate the following case. A bricklayer found a purse containing three ryô, a lot of money in those days. The purse also contained a little note indicating that a certain carpenter was the purse's owner. The carpenter, however, refused to take the money back – money that had fallen out of his kimono was heartless money that he did not want. The stubborn bricklayer brought the case to court, claiming that the carpenter had to take it back (at this point one may wonder how filing a lawsuit could be in conformity with the rules of harmony in the first place, but let that go). Judge Ôka, renowned for his Solomonic decisions, added one ryô out of his own money to the three ryô in dispute and ruled as follows: "All three of us lose one ryô." The judge lost one because he added one from his own purse. The carpenter received two ryô back, and lost one. The bricklayer received two, and also lost one because he would have been entitled to keep the money. Such judgments have become rare these days, even in Japan.

Still, the eminent Japanese academic and professor of civil law, Kawashima, was convinced that law enforcement through the courts was alien to Japanese legal consciousness:

> I do not think that the costs and long delays of law suits are a sufficient explanation for the low number of law suits in Japan. Rather, the discrepancy between the Japanese legal consciousness and the current legal system is of far greater importance. Traditional legal consciousness in Japan does not regard rights and obligations as clear and defined facts. Yet the current legal system that was adopted from the West aims at clarifying and defining legal rights and obligations of both parties on the basis of established facts. Such a black and white decision destroys the basis of an amicable and cooperative relationship that developed especially because the framework of rights and duties were not clearly defined. In the traditional sense, raising a claim must therefore be regarded as a public challenge or declaration of war.[1]

[1] Kawashima, "Nihonjin no hô ishiki" (The Legal Consciousness of the Japanese People) 139 (Tokyo 1967).

While Kawashima and his thesis on the Japanese legal consciousness has certainly become a classic, a number of academics, both inside and outside Japan, have begged to differ. The main criticism is that Kawashima's thesis, based on Japanese tradition and culture, lacks academic foundation. It would further be a circular argument to conclude that Japanese shun legal proceedings merely from the fact that the number of lawsuits might be small.[2] Not only foreigners, but also the Japanese themselves seem to be dissatisfied with court enforcement in Japan according to a survey conducted in 1985 by the Japanese Lawyers' Association.[3] According to 95.2% of those questioned, court enforcement was too expensive, 90% felt that it took too long, while 75.2% said that only in extreme cases would they sue again.

At any rate, it is a fact that the number of lawsuits in Japan is extremely low when compared to other countries. Including dunning procedures, settlements out of court and disputes in family courts, Japan can count 10 lawsuits per 1,000 inhabitants, while the comparable number in German would be 110.[4]

Apart from that, Kawashima is certainly correct in pointing out that the system of civil and procedural law adopted by Japan from Western countries in the last century did not correspond to the traditional Japanese legal consciousness of clearly defined rights and obligations.[5]

II. Legal System and Enforcement of Laws

1. Japan's Import from the West

Both Japan's civil law and law of civil procedure are structured according to Western models. In modernising its legal system in order to be accepted by Western nations as an equal, Japan faced the choice of modelling her laws on the basis of either the Anglo-American or continental-European system. Due to its development through case law, the Anglo-American system seemed much more difficult to import into and implement in Japan than the codified structure of European law. In order to rid itself of the so-called Unequal Treaties with Western Powers that denied Japan jurisdiction over most foreign nationals, between 1870 and 1900 Japan implemented a legal system

[2] Tanase, "The Management of Disputes: Automobile Accident Compensation in Japan", 24 Law & Society Review, No. 3, 654 (1990). The same opinion is voiced by Miyazawa, in Watanabe, Miyazawa, Kisa, Yoshino & Sato (eds.), "Tekisuto bukku gendai shihô" (Reader on the Current Legal System) 187 *et seq.* (Tokyo 1992); *see also ibid.,* "Taking Kawashima Seriously: A Review of Japanese Research on Japanese Legal Consciousness and Disputing Behaviour", 21 Law & Society Review, 219 *et seq.* (1987); J. Haley, "The Myth of the Reluctant Litigant", 1988 Journal of Japanese Studies, No. 14/1, 111.

[3] K. Ryûzaki, "Soshô sokushin: shinri no jûjitsu to shimin" (Citizen and Speedy Trial), 1988 Jurist, No. 914, 110.

[4] Wollschläger, "Long-Term Economic Development and Civil Litigation in Japan, the U.S. and Germany"; Baum (ed.), "Japan – Economic Success and Legal System" 89 (Berlin 1997).

[5] G. Rahn, "Rechtsdenken und Rechtsauffassung in Japan" (Legal Thinking and Legal Perception in Japan) 369 *et seq.* (Munich 1990).

imported mainly from France and Germany. In particular, the Code of Civil Procedure of 1890 was very much a blueprint of the German *Zivilprozeßordnung* of 1878. That such a wholesale import of a foreign code with the primary purpose of convincing other countries of Japan's "civilised" legal system did not necessarily lead to a fair, efficient and transparent enforcement of civil rights should stand to reason. In particular, Japanese judges were much less willing to take an active role in court proceedings, one of the main conditions for speedy and efficient justice in Germany. For subsequent changes of the Code of Civil Procedure, see below III.1.

2. Industrial Property Rights

Also the concept of industrial property laws was imported from abroad, yet meshed much better with Japan's policy of rapid technological development that became the driving ambition of the Meiji government after 1867: "Knowledge shall be sought throughout the world so as to strengthen the foundations of imperial rule."[6] Not least for that reason, industrial property rights were not regarded as "private rights" as, for instance, the Paris Convention had envisaged,[7] but as tools for industrial development under the jurisdiction of the Ministry of Agriculture and Trade, later the wily Ministry for Trade and Industry (MITI). The main consequence of this approach was a development of IP rights in accordance with Japan's industrial development. The Japanese Patent Act, which was initially enacted in 1871, repealed one year later, and which finally came into force in 1885, was significantly amended in 1888, 1899, 1909, 1921 and 1959. The current Patent Act of 1959 has undergone no fewer than 25 revisions. While often minor, they include such important changes as allowing the patenting of pharmaceutical substances, multiple claims, and the patenting of microorganisms, paving the way for broadening the scope of patent,[8] and increasing damage awards in cases of infringement (see below B.VI). Already in 1905, Japan had taken the bold step of introducing the German-based system of protecting minor inventions by utility models, a system particularly suitable to Japan's small and medium-sized enterprises. Unlike other statutory instruments, no clear preferences for a certain foreign legal system can be detected. While the initial patent statute was based on US law, the revisions of 1921 and 1959 marked a major shift towards the German patent

[6] For an account of the industrial property policies of the Meiji government in Japan, *see* G. Rahn, "The Role of Industrial Property in Economic Development: The Japanese Experience", 14 IIC 449 (1983).

[7] S. Ladas, "International Industrial Property Law" 77 (Cambridge, Mass. 1930).

[8] For details, *see* T. Takenaka, "Interpreting Patent Claims: The US, Germany and Japan Compared" 193 *et seq*. (IIC Studies, Vol. 17, Weinheim 1995). A doctrine of equivalents comparable to the one developed by US and European court law was only recognised by the Supreme Court decision of 24 February 1998, 30 IIC 443 (1999) – *Ball Spline Bearing III*. For subsequent decisions in this respect, *see* the articles by Hattori, Ito and Aoki in Patent 9/1999, 65–92 (in Japanese).

system. And the current Examination Guidelines are often the result of trilateral consultations between the European, US and Japanese patent offices. The current Patent Act of 1959 was amended more than 30 times. Its current version is as of 1 April 2004.

In the last five years, two major changes have been brought about. For one, the enforcement system for patents was completely overhauled, as will be described in the following. Second, the promotion of inventive activity and commercialisation of patents through the Basic Intellectual Property Act of 2003.[9] The strategic IP Commission set up under this statute aims at, *inter alia*, a better exploitation of university inventions and a reduction in the examination time for patents from currently 30 months to only six months in about five years time.

Finally, it should be noted that patent applications and patents have long been used by Japanese companies as strategic business tools. Patent rights in Japan have been regarded less in terms of their court-based enforceability against third parties, than in a multitude of other aspects such as innovative image, potential for cross-licensing, and the like.[10]

3. Statistics

a) *Applications and grants for patents and utility models*

Year	**Patents**		**Utility Models**	
	applications	**grants**	**applications**	**grants**
1930	15,430	4,976	38,487	12,236
	2,862	*1,610*	*382*	*119*
1940	19,827	6,716	31,833	15,703
	1,902	*1,453*	*410*	*357*
1950	16,896	4,272	24,324	8,021
	2,360	*137*	*46*	(–)
1960	43,484	11,252	63,077	22,102
	11,587	*3,576*	*1,069*	*708*
1970	130,831	30,879	142,066	27,718
	30,309	*9,488*	*2,369*	*741*
1980	191,020	46,106	197,785	50,001
	25,290	*8,074*	*1,397*	*533*
1990	367,590	59,401	138,294	43,300
2000	436,865	125,880	9,587	5,372
	49,501	*13,611*	*1,690*	*122*

Numbers in italics indicate applications by or grants to foreigners. The author could not trace the figures for 1990.

[9] Basic Intellectual Property Act, Law No. 122/2002, effective as of 1 March 2003.

[10] G. Rahn, "Patentstrategien in Japan" (Patent Strategies in Japan), 1994 GRUR Int. 377.

b) Number of intellectual property lawsuits between 1993 and 2002

Year	Total	Patents	Utility models	Designs	Trade marks	Copyrights	Unfair competition	Others
1993	**470**	91	130	37	55	70	81	6
1994	**497**	106	98	26	53	72	134	8
1995	**528**	111	61	31	53	87	172	13
1996	**590**	157	77	28	80	85	132	31
1997	**563**	167	70	25	63	94	132	12
1998	**559**	156	58	22	78	112	130	3
1999	**642**	191	72	32	65	117	155	10
2000	**610**	176	59	38	89	97	143	8
2001	**554**	153	34	29	67	127	136	8
2002	**607**	165	38	27	99	113	141	24

c) Requests for preliminary measures

Year	Total	Patents	Utility models	Designs	Trade marks	Copyrights	Unfair competition	Others
1993	**362**	47	38	17	33	138	76	13
1994	**299**	64	21	11	36	76	90	1
1995	**316**	73	28	17	29	68	93	8
1996	**386**	75	36	17	53	106	89	10
1997	**410**	75	30	13	40	139	108	5
1998	**391**	62	19	16	47	142	104	1
1999	**488**	62	25	10	35	275	79	2
2000	**552**	75	22	14	54	283	102	2
2001	**522**	61	15	6	40	321	78	1
2002	**398**	75	3	11	33	200	68	8

d) IP cases on appeal

Year	Total	Patents	Utility models	Designs	Trade marks	Copyrights	Unfair competition	Others
1993	**102**	38	14	10	5	6	25	4
1994	**91**	28	12	7	10	11	21	2
1995	**97**	18	17	4	11	11	32	4
1996	**84**	23	14	3	9	15	19	1
1997	**120**	40	16	11	7	10	31	5
1998	**143**	50	23	10	8	23	24	5
1999	**194**	62	22	7	25	41	36	1
2000	**216**	69	30	2	17	43	55	0
2001	**180**	58	23	9	18	32	38	2
2002	**181**	77	13	7	15	34	33	2

e) Court appeals against decisions by the Patent Office

Year	Total	Patents	Utility models	Designs	Trade marks	Others
1993	**199**	130	37	10	21	1
1994	**285**	201	46	8	30	0
1995	**280**	174	38	24	43	1
1996	**279**	174	45	23	37	0
1997	**328**	179	50	25	74	0
1998	**393**	200	49	34	109	1
1999	**429**	226	54	24	125	0
2000	**478**	273	46	27	132	0
2001	**575**	387	48	30	110	0
2002	**636**	445	22	18	151	0

f) Average duration of IP infringement cases in months

1991	1992	1993	1994	1995	1996	1997	1998	1999	2000	2001
31.1	29.6	31.9	23.1	23.7	22.7	25.0	25.7	23.1	21.6	18.3

III. Basics of Civil Procedure

1. In General

The Japanese Code of Civil Procedure (CPC) of 1890 gave the parties significant latitude in determining the speed of proceedings. Increasingly, however, this was viewed as an obstacle towards efficient justice. In Japan's first major reform of the Code of Civil Procedure in 1926,[11] the judge was granted more authority to set hearings and to reject pleadings that were argued only at a late stage of proceedings. As distinct from the Anglo-American system, the judge had an active role in the hearing of witnesses and conducting of proceedings. The US-American occupation after World War II brought about two changes. For one, no specialised courts were henceforth allowed, which in the case of Japan meant the integration of the administrative courts into the general court structure. Second, the introduction of cross-examination significantly reduced the role of the judge and made it the attorneys' business to question witnesses, who could already be "prepared" beforehand. Both changes, though well meant, did little to improve court

[11] Law No. 61/1926, in force as of 1 October 1929. An excellent overview is provided by Kuno, "Die Novelle der japanischen Zivilprozeßordnung vom 24. April 1926", RabelsZ 3 (1929), 260.

enforcement. The absence of special courts more often than not led to a lack of judicial expertise, aggravated by the fact that judges were routinely rotated every three years to a different court. To this day, it is one of the most serious obstacles to a well-trained body of intellectual property judges that any judge from one of these specialised IP divisions in Tokyo or Osaka may well end up in the family court of Yamagata or the criminal division of Niigata's small claims court. And the introduction of the system of American-style cross-examination of witnesses was of little use without a sufficient means of discovery. As Japan's enforcement system has only very limited mechanisms for obtaining evidence from the other party, cross-examinations Japanese-style often tend to be erratic and resemble the search for a black cat in a darkened room, not knowing if the cat is even there. The last major revision of the CPC to this date, effective as of 1 January 1998,[12] was particularly meant to speed up proceedings.

Civil court enforcement in Japan has encountered the following problems. Not all of these apply to the field of intellectual property rights, however:

a) Prior to the amendment of the Code of Civil Procedure, a "typical" court action was held in about ten hearings with intervals of two months each, and such hearings would often last only three minutes each in order to exchange pleadings and arguments. The old Code of Civil Procedure gave the parties significant leeway regarding the timing of hearings and the presentation of evidence and legal arguments (satirically termed "*samidare*", as hesitantly as Japanese spring rain). The new Code of Civil Procedure 1998 requires more clarity for the writ as such and introduces a preliminary hearing to clarify the issues in dispute. In intellectual property matters, Sec. 104bis introduced an obligation by the defendant to do more than just make a bare denial. Rather, the "other party shall clarify his relevant act in a precise manner". This has significantly helped to speed up procedures. In addition, Sec. 157 CPC allows the court to reject facts or arguments filed unduly late. While this provision was hardly applied prior to 1998,[13] the courts are now more assertive in exercising their discretion in this respect.[14]

---

[12] Law 109/1996, in force since 1 January 1998.

[13] Yoshino, Die neue Diskussion um die Prozeßbeschleunigung in Japan, 8 Recht in Japan 65, 67 (1991).

[14] Tokyo High Court, 31 October 2002, 2003 AIPPI Japan English Edition 359 – *Anti-Allergic Agent*. Here, in a patent infringement suit, the defendant was slow and reluctant in producing relevant documents which caused a tremendous delay in proceedings. In addition, the defendant frequently changed the basis of its argumentation. As this continued on appeal, the appeal court ruled in favour of the plaintiff, as the defendant had failed to overcome the statutory presumption of infringement (the case concerned a manufacturing process) as its arguments in this respect were filed too late.

b) A significant number of problems related to civil procedure centre around evidence and proof. For one, parties in a civil suit have only limited recourse towards obtaining written (documents) or oral (affidavit) evidence from the other party. Systems of pre-trial discovery (the US), the *saisie contrefaçon* (France), the Anton Piller Order (UK) or the *Auskunftsanspruch* (Germany) are alien to the Japanese system. The court can only order evidence "prepared for a certain legal relationship" (Sec. 220 Code of Civil Procedure) which is of course little help in infringement actions. The newly introduced discovery procedure under Sec. 163 Code of Civil Procedure does not specify to what extent the other party has to cooperate, and in any case is without sanctions if there is no cooperation. However, a number of practical measures have eased the plaintiff's burden of proof, particularly in intellectual property cases (*see below* V.3).

c) Court costs[15] normally have to be paid in advance by the plaintiff and can be recovered partly or totally from the defendant, depending on the success of the action. Attorneys' fees are normally not awarded even in successful cases, unless the suit involved a particularly difficult legal question or the successful party was a foreigner and thus would be expected to be represented by counsel in court.[16] Even in these cases, however, attorneys' fees would mostly be awarded to a nominal extent between 200 and 1,000 euro, thus falling way short of covering the actual expenses. With regard to awarding damages, see below.

2. Attorneys and Patent Attorneys

Japan allows both patent attorneys and attorneys to act as representatives in IP matters. Both attorneys and patent attorneys can represent parties before the Patent Office and in appeals against the Patent Office before the Tokyo High Court and the Supreme Court. In matters of IP infringements, patent attorneys have been given the right of representation in court when accompanied by an attorney. The profession of a patent attorney was first introduced in 1890, and patent attorneys numbered 4,278 in 1999.[17] Registration

[15] An overview is provided by M. Akiyama, "Sosho hiyo seidô no gôrika" (On the Appropriateness of Litigation Fees), 1028 Jurist 132; K. Sato, "Ishô no dokusenteki tsûjô jisshikensha to songai baishô" (Exclusive Rights and Damages), 974 Jurist 99.

[16] On average, the parties are represented in less than 50% of all cases. Attorneys fees were awarded due to the difficulty of the legal question involved by the Supreme Court, 29 May 1984, 530 Hanrei Times 97 (1985) – *American Football Symbol Mark*; in case of a foreign plaintiff by Tokyo District Court, 24 March 1993, 26 IIC 566 (1995) – *Type Chanel No. 5*. Interesting, Tokyo District Court, 27 April 1992, 819 Hanrei Times 179 – *Ritz Babywear*: attorneys costs were awarded because the plaintiff, without vigilant enforcement of its well-reputed trade mark right, would not be able to maintain the mark's good reputation. Who there hath shalt be given?

[17] "Benrishi seidô hyaku nenshi" (100 Years of Patent Attorneys, Vol. 3) 259 (Tokyo 2000). The Patent Office (www.jpg.go.jp/saikin) gives a figure of 4,800 at the end of 2001 (accessed 26 April 2002).

as a patent attorney can be based on a successful patent bar examination (annually about 300 candidates are admitted), on the position as a registered attorney or on five years working experience in the Japanese Patent Office. Anyone with a university degree can sit the patent bar examination, and no technical background is required. A successful exam immediately qualifies a candidate for the profession, without an apprenticeship period being necessary. Patent attorneys under the Patent Attorney's Act[18] are allowed representation before the Patent Office and in appeals against the Patent Office's decisions before the Tokyo High Court and the Supreme Court. Patent attorneys are allowed limited representation in infringement suits and can be admitted by the court to plead alongside or in the absence of counsel. Under the new Patent Attorney's Act 2002, they are also allowed to counsel in matters of licensing agreements.

As of 2001, there were 18,246 registered attorneys.[19] Annually, about 1,000 candidates are able to pass the bar exam, which means a passing rate of about 4%. After an apprenticeship period of 18 months, the successful applicant may register at the bar. Very few attorneys specialise in matters of intellectual property; the Patent Office mentions 300.[20]

3. Judges and Decisions

Judges generally tend to take a rather passive role in procedures, which was criticised by the Japanese Bar Association as follows:

> The importance of the judicial weighing of facts cannot be overestimated. Often the result of a case does not depend on a legal question, but rather on the facts established. The attorney has thus to argue his case in accordance with the alleged facts. Despite the principles of oral procedure and party autonomy, the court does very little to clarify facts. Of course, all evidence is subject to judicial discretion in weighing facts. Which efforts have to be made to establish proof and what the judge regards as formally proven or not are a matter of guesswork as there is no clear basis or rule, and also for ascertaining as such there are no clear guidelines.[21]

However, particularly in intellectual property matters, judges have become more active in structuring the procedures and in proposing settlement.

Japanese decisions often go to great lengths to ascertain facts, but fall short on legal argumentation. This is particularly so in Supreme Court decisions, which not only seem to be more timid in breaking new ground than are the

---

[18] Patent Attorney's Act, revised version law No. 49/2000, last amendment as of 17 April 2002.

[19] Japanese Supreme Court, Saibanshô Data Book 2001, 24.

[20] www.jpo.go.jp/saikin (accessible April 2002).

[21] Tokyo Bengoshikai, "Minji sosho shinri no kaizen ni kann suru ikenshô" (Opinion on How to Improve the System of Civil Procedure), 79/80 Tokyo bengoshikai kaihô 71, 92 (1991). Part of this criticism is self-serving, however. As long as civil procedure permits the preparation of a discretionary number of witnesses, judicial discretion in weighing such evidence is the only counterbalance to what would otherwise be the inevitable success of the economically more powerful party.

district and high courts, but also handle cases without much explanation. The Supreme Court consists of only 15 judges, and there has never been an IP specialist among them. Appeals are either dismissed out of hand with the reason that the appellant takes "a peculiar (or particular) view (*dokuji no kenkai*) which cannot be followed", or the court's reasoning is mercifully short. At least for the decisions of the Supreme Court, it is true to say that judges seem to regard it "desirable to write a decision so that the result flows completely naturally from the ascertained facts".[22] Decisions of the lower courts often set out the legal problems involved quite well, while the legal arguments sometimes do not come over too clearly. Academic writings are practically never cited. Here again, matters are somewhat different in intellectual property cases. For one, the judges become more experienced thanks to the specialised courts in Tokyo and Osaka. Groundbreaking decisions mostly originate from these lower courts, in particular the Tokyo and Osaka District Courts rather than the courts on appeal or the Supreme Court.

B. *Enforcement of Patent Rights in Particular*

I. Overview

Patent rights are almost exclusively enforced through the civil courts. Although an ordinary patent infringement is a punishable offence (Sec. 196 Patent Act), criminal cases are almost absent save for a small number of cases of wilfulness.[23] Also the administrative enforcement via border measures is almost negligible for patent rights. Prior to a Supreme Court decision in the year 2000, the Patent Office had a monopoly over invalidating patent rights, as this was regarded as an issue of genuine jurisdiction of the administration having granted the right. This has changed, and the administration has lost a lot of clout in this respect. Patent rights can now be invalidated *inter partes* by the courts in the course of an infringement action, and *erga omnes* by the Patent Office in invalidation procedures to be initiated by anyone.[24] Japanese IP decisions are immediately published on the Internet under www.courts.jp, and many of them are also reported in journals such as Hanketsu Sokuhô, Law & Technology, Chisai Kanri, Patent, Hanrei Jihô and others.

Some attempts have been made to move IP infringement litigation away from the courts to arbitration centres. There is one arbitration centre for industrial property cases that was set up in 2000 and that handled a mere four

---

[22] Y. Nozaki, 756 Jurist 49 (1982); G. Rahn, "Rechtsdenken und Rechtsauffassung in Japan" 337 *et seq*. (Munich 1990).

[23] S. Ishikawa, "Tokkyo hô" (Patent Law), in Hirano et al., "Shukai tokubetsu keihô" 19, part 4 (2nd ed., Tokyo 1991). The cases cited mostly date from pre-1945.

[24] As of 1 January 2004, post-grant opposition and invalidation procedures have been merged.

cases in its first year.[25] As to (court) mediation, in April 1998, a new division meant to mediate IP disputes was set up at the Tokyo District Court. Just as under the normal mediation procedure, an ordinary court can defer a case to the mediation division. In the first year, seven IP cases were referred to this division.

Apart from ordinary civil cases, the courts receive quite a number of requests for preliminary injunctions in patent matters (see statistics above).

The basis of a patent infringement suit, be it as a request for preliminary measures or in the main action, can only be a granted patent. A patent application is not sufficient here. Still, the patent applicant has a right to claim compensation (which is equivalent to a licensing fee) after the patent application has been laid open (*i.e.* 18 months after the filing date) and the alleged infringer has been furnished with a proper warning letter (Sec. 65(1) PA). However, this right can only be exercised after the patent has actually been granted. When raised before, the courts have to suspend proceedings (Sec. 168(2) PA). Prescription starts only once the patent has been registered.

II. Jurisdiction

1. National Jurisdiction

National jurisdiction in patent matters first of all follows the rules of general jurisdiction, that is, a suit can be brought at the residence of the defendant[26] or where the tort has occurred, in other words, in any place infringing articles have been found. Alternatively, the plaintiff can also sue at his place of business or residence, as the courts would regard this as the place where compensation for the infringement of property rights would have to be paid. Sec. 6 of the new Code of Civil Procedure 1998 established a concurrent jurisdiction of the Tokyo and Osaka District Courts for "suits under rights of a patent or utility model, a right of installation or use of data lines, or rights of an author over a program for processing data". Suits concerning this subject matter could thus be brought before the otherwise competent courts, or, if there was jurisdiction in for Eastern Japan, before the District Court of Tokyo, and for Western Japan, before the District Court of Osaka. As of 1 April 2004, the concurrent jurisdiction over this subject matter has become an exclusive one. Patent infringement suits can thus only be brought before the District Court of Tokyo (jurisdiction over the districts of Tokyo,

---

[25] T. Takii, "Nihon chiteki zaisan chûkai center gutaiteki toriatsukai jirei no kentô" (Appraisal of Cases Handled by the IP Arbitration Centre), 54 Chizai Kanri 723 (2004) introduces five cases, but does not give statistics.

[26] In the case of a commercial enterprise, this would normally be the place of registration, yet may also be the place where business is actually conducted: Tokyo High Court, 9 September 1993, 1485 Hanrei Jihô 116 (1994), 27 IIC 108 (1996) – *Cylindrical Cutter.*

Nagoya, Sendai and Sapporo), or Osaka (jurisdiction of the districts of Osaka, Hiroshima, Fukujima and Takamatsu). For all other IP-related subject matter, Sec. 6 Code of Civil Procedure 2004 has introduced a concurrent jurisdiction of the District Courts of Osaka and Tokyo. This would apply to trade mark, copyright and unfair competition cases.

Claims under a patent right under Sec. 6 Code of Civil Procedure also include the interpretation of licensing agreements, the object of which are patents.[27]

As of 1 April 2004, also jurisdiction for appeal cases has changed. For subject matter coming under the exclusive first instance jurisdiction of the District Courts of Tokyo and Osaka, the Tokyo High Court will have exclusive jurisdiction. Legislation passed in April 2004 stopped short of establishing an independent appeal court for intellectual property rights, yet established a separate division within the Tokyo High Court that deals with intellectual property cases. In addition to the exclusive jurisdiction for appeals in patent matters, the Tokyo High Court will also hear appeals for cases brought before the Tokyo District Court under the rules of concurrent jurisdiction. Thus, the other high courts outside Tokyo will still have jurisdiction to hear appeals for cases before the district courts under their jurisdiction.

The Tokyo High Court has exclusive jurisdiction over appeals against decisions rendered by the Patent Office. Appeal procedures basically mean a rehearing of the whole case, including evidence.

A final appeal on questions of law can be brought before the Supreme Court, a body of 15 judges that has wide discretion to allow appeals. The newly inserted Sec. 317(2) CPC allows an *a limine* rejection of the petition to appeal.

2. International Jurisdiction

Two issues have come before the courts regarding international jurisdiction. First, to what extent the infringement of a *foreign* patent can be regarded as an actionable tort or a contributory infringement in Japan. The relevant case concerned acts that were actionable under the extra-territorial provision of § 271(b) and (c) 35 USC, in other words, provisions that allowed the US patentee to bring an action against infringing acts committed abroad (active inducement and contributory infringement). The Japanese courts in three instances denied that such conduct was actionable under Japanese law, basic-

[27] Osaka District Court, 21 September 2001, 1785 Hanrei Jihô 78 (2002) = 35 IIC 324 (2004) – *Jurisdiction in Patent Matters*. According to the court, "matters related to patents" were not limited to questions of infringement and validity, but could also comprise questions of whether a certain patented technology had been worked or not, which was at issue in this case.

ally because the principle of territoriality limited the effects of the US patent to the United States.[28]

Second, to what the extent the infringement of a foreign patent can be determined by the Japanese courts. The latter was affirmed most prominently in the case involving the alleged infringement of a US patent by a Japanese company. The alleged infringer sued the patentee, a Japanese competitor for denigration, actionable under the Japanese Unfair Competition Prevention Act. In the course of determining denigration, the Tokyo District Court used the principles of claim interpretation as applied in the United States in order to determine if there was indeed a patent infringement under US law. The court ultimately denied this, granted the claim under unfair competition prevention law, and awarded the plaintiff (alleged infringer) damages in the amount of almost 2 million Yen plus 1 million Yen in attorneys' fees.[29]

In the case of licensing agreements over a Japanese patent right, jurisdiction can of course be agreed upon between the parties.[30]

Issues of double jurisdiction in patent matters hardly arise in Japan. On a more general level, the courts do not regard court proceedings abroad on the same subject matter as an obstacle to assessing jurisdiction themselves.[31]

As to the *applicable law*, Japanese law would of course be applicable in cases of infringement of a Japanese patent. In the case of licensing agreements, the applicable law might be agreed upon, yet the existence and scope of the underlying (Japanese) patent right would have to be determined under Japanese law. Japanese courts further seem to presume the application of Japanese law over a licensing agreement of a non-registered right (*e.g.* a trade secret), unless otherwise agreed upon.[32]

---

[28] Tokyo District Court, 22 April 1999, 1691 Hanrei Jihô 131 (2000); Tokyo High Court, 27 January 2000, 1711 Hanrei Jihô 131 (2000) = 2001 GRUR Int. 83 with comment by *Petersen*; Supreme Court, 26 September 2002, 19 Law & Technology 81 (2003) – *FM Signal Device*. This is consistent with a previous decision by the Tokyo District Court, 12 June 1953, 4–6 Kakyu Minshû 847, that denied that the infringement of a patent in Manchuria could be qualified as a tort in Japan. *See also* S. Chaen, "Gaikoku tokkyo shingai jiken no kokusai saiban kankatsu" (International Jurisdiction over the Infringement of a Foreign Patent), 21 Kôgyô shoyûken hôgakukai nempô 59 (1997); M. Takabe, "Tokkyoken shingai sosho to kokusai saiban kankatsu" (International Jurisdiction and Patent Infringement), in "Chiteki zaisanhô to gendai shakai" 125 (Tokyo 1999).

[29] Tokyo District Court, 16 October 2003 –*Sango Fossile Powder* (unreported). In a previous case, the Supreme Court had affirmed that the Japanese courts would be competent to determine an alleged copyright infringement in Thailand under similar circumstances: Supreme Court, 8 June 1999, 16 Law & Technology 72 – *Ultraman*.

[30] Tokyo High Court, 16 September 1991, 24 IIC 391 (1993) – *Liquid Fuel Component*. Also reprinted in "Hanrei license hô" 521 (Tokyo 2000), with comment by Nakano.

[31] Tokyo District Court, 24 September 1991, 35 Japanese Annual of Int'l Law 175 (1992) – *Manufacture of Coated Copper*.

[32] Tokyo District Court, 16 September 1991, 24 IIC 391 (1993) – *Liquid Fuel Component*.

3. Composition of Courts

It has been mentioned above that Japan has no specialised courts as such, and up to now no participation of laymen in judicial matters. This of course begs the question of how judges in patent matters would obtain the technical expertise necessary to adjudicate technical questions. Both the courts in Tokyo and Osaka have special divisions for intellectual property matters, three at the Tokyo District Court, one at the Osaka District Court, and one each at the Osaka and Tokyo High Courts. Judges are transferred every three years. Even where technical matters are in dispute, expert witnesses, either court-appointed or at the request of either party, are uncommon. Under a strangely hybrid system between court-appointed experts and technical judges, the special divisions for intellectual property matters at the Tokyo and Osaka District Courts rely on the expertise of persons dispatched from the Patent Office. These are meant to explain technical matters to the judges. The opinion of these Patent Office experts is not published or stated in court, and they cannot be questioned by the parties. Nor would they sign the decision in any judicial capacity. This is of course questionable, particularly in cases appealing the Patent Office's decisions. In such cases, any plaintiff must harbour not unreasonable doubts about the independence of such a person; all the more so since his opinion can in no way be scrutinised by the plaintiff. Currently, there is a discussion to what extent the technical specialists from the Patent Office should give their opinion in court and thus also be questioned by the parties. A newly introduced Sec. 92bis CPC (effective as of 1 April 2004) allows a court to be assisted by an expert member (who is not an expert witness). This provision thus seems to put the current system of the Tokyo and Osaka courts on a firmer legislative basis, and would also allow courts outside the field of IP to ask for expert advice in this manner. Most likely, the provision will thus not influence the composition of IP courts in the future. According to the 2004 amendment to the CPC, the expert dispatched from the Patent Office will be entitled to question the parties and witnesses and make some comments on the date of settlement (Sec. 92^{octies}).

At the level of the Supreme Court, every judge is entitled to two legally trained assistants with experience in sitting as a judge. Of these assistants, one or the other may well have had previous experience with intellectual property matters.

III. Competent Parties

1. The Plaintiff

As the patentee enjoys all the exclusive rights his patent confers to him under the Patent Act, he would certainly be competent to file a suit for any act deemed infringing under Sec. 100 Japanese Patent Act.

The patentee is entitled to launch an infringement action regardless of his entitlement to the patent as such. This is of particular importance for employees' inventions which under Sec. 35 Patent Act belong to the employee, while the employer has a right to a non-exclusive licence. However, the employer can contractually negotiate a transfer of such invention upon payment of a reasonable remuneration.[33] Apparently, only the true inventor could claim estoppel of patent misappropriation when sued by the patentee.[34]

2. Co-Owners of Patents

As a patent in its true construction does not give a right to use, but a right to exclude third parties not entitled to the invention, co-owners should be able to assess their rights independently of each other.[35] Not so in Japan. It is settled case law that Japanese co-owners, at least before grant, have to act jointly to get the patent processed, or to appeal against decisions from the Patent Office.[36] Each co-owner is entitled to individually defend a granted right, though.[37]

According to Sec. 73 Japanese Patent Act, joint owners may work the patented invention without each other's consent,[38] yet not grant any licence or transfer their rights without the other's permission.

---

[33] Reasonableness would depend on the commercial potential of the invention. There are numerous cases on this matter, *e.g.* Tokyo District Court, 23 December 1983, 15-3 Mutaishû 844; Osaka District Court, 26 April 1984, 16-1 Mutaishû 282, and Tokyo District Court, 28 September 1983, 15-3 Mutaishû.

[34] Supreme Court, 20 November 1992, 1050 Jurist 180, AIPPI Journal of the Japanese Group International Edition, 3/1993, 98.

[35] This has been set out for the United Kingdom by the House of Lords in *Steers v. Rogers*, (1893) AC 232: "The truth is that letters patent do not give the patentee any right to use the invention – they do not confer upon him a right to manufacture according to his invention . . . . What the letters patent confer is the right to exclude others from manufacturing in a particular way, and using a particular invention. When that is borne in mind, it appears to me to be very clear that it would be impossible to hold, under these circumstances, that where there are several patentees, either of them, if he uses the patent, can be called upon by the others to pay to them a portion of the profits which he takes by that manufacture, because they are all of them entitled, or perhaps any of them is entitled, to prevent the rest of the world from using it." There seem to be no decisions in Japan, yet the above position is also taken by Matsumoto, in Nakayama (ed.), "Shûkai tokkyo hô" (Patent Law Annotated) 834 (2nd ed., Tokyo 1989). According to Matsumoto, damages by one patentee can only be claimed up to the share he holds in the patent.

[36] Supreme Court, 7 March 1995, 1527 Hanrei Jihô 146 (1995) – *Magnetic Treatment Device*. Also Tokyo High Court, 14 March 1993, Patent 12/1993, 117. The question was decided differently by the Tokyo High Court, 27 January 1994, Patent, 12/1994, 119.

[37] Supreme Court, 25 March 2002, 35 IIC (forthcoming) – *Pachinko Device*.

[38] Despite the mistaken decision of Nagoya District Court, 16 July 1994, 225 Hanketsu Sokuhô, No. 6520.

3. Licensees

Patent law distinguishes between registered and unregistered, exclusive and non-exclusive licences. According to the Patent Act (Sec. 100 *et seq.*) the registered, exclusive licensee is the only one entitled to sue for injunctive relief and damages, while unregistered licences cannot be invoked against third parties. The registered, non-exclusive licence can be used as an estoppel against any subsequent owner of the patent. If an exclusive licence has been registered, the patentee would not be able to work the patent himself, yet could sue any infringer statutorily for an ordinary licensing fee (Sec. 102 Patent Act). Unregistered licensees have no standing to sue, even when empowered by the licensor. Yet, the unregistered exclusive licensee may sue out of his own right for damages.[39] A non-exclusive licensee may sue alongside the patentee.[40]

4. The Defendant

Infringing acts are those that interfere with the exclusive right of the patentee to work the patent under Sec. 68 Patent Act. "Working" is defined in Sec. 2 as acts of manufacture, use, assignment, lease, or import. Producing (non-infringing) parts that can be assembled to create an infringing product are infringing acts in themselves under two circumstances. Either as the manufacture of "substantial" spare parts,[41] or of articles to be used "exclusively" for the manufacture of the patented product under Sec. 101(1) Patent Act. It is sufficient for an infringement that there is no reasonable commercial use for such article other than for the manufacture of infringing products.[42] A claim for patent infringement can be directed against the importer and/or the distributor of infringing goods, yet not against a foreign parent company or foreign developer of infringing goods where the foreign companies lack any connections to the Japanese jurisdiction.[43]

---

[39] Osaka High Court, 20 June 1986, 18-2 Mutaishû 15 – *Permabrush*.

[40] Osaka District Court, 26 December 1964, 15-12 GeMin 3121 – *Polypropylene*. An *agent* who is empowered to grant licences on behalf of the right owner has no independent standing to sue for injunctive relief: Tokyo District Court, 31 January 2002, 1818 Hanrei Jihô 165 – *Tonttu*.

[41] Osaka District Court, 24 April 1989, 21-1 Mutaishû 271 – *Crushing Device*. The case concerned a device consisting of a hammer and a board for crushing stones. While the hammer as such lasted three years, the crushing board had to be replaced at least once a week. The defendant manufactured and sold crushing boards that could qualify as essential parts of the whole device, the manufacture of which could thus qualify as infringing. *See also* K. Matsuo, "Kansetsu shingai no seiritsu to sono kôka" (Structure and Effect of Indirect Infringements), 957 Jurist 248 (1990).

[42] Tokyo District Court, 29 July 1994, 1513 Hanrei Jihô 155 (1995); Tokyo High Court, 23 May 1996, 1570 Hanrei Jihô 103 (1996). *See also* N. Nakayama, "Kôgyô shoyûken hô" (Industrial Property Law) 364–366 (Tokyo 1993).

[43] Tokyo District Court, 14 May 2001, 34 IIC 554 (2003) – *Medicine for Reducing Eye Pressure*.

IV. Preliminary Measures

1. Obtaining Evidence

A complex and comprehensive pre-trial discovery as in US law is alien to the Japanese system. While intellectual property laws contain provisions whereby the court can "order the other party to submit documents necessary for the assessment of damages" (Sec. 105(1) PA), such an order can only be made where the document can be identified with certainty. Yet, this is often not the case, for which reason the US pre-trial discovery procedure, the UK Anton Piller order or the French *saisie contrefaçon* provide the parties with additional rights or disclosure. The new Sec. 163 Code of Civil Procedure has introduced some sort of pre-trial discovery allowing for both parties to request information from the other side about certain facts that have to be specified. Since non-compliance entails no sanctions, it remains to be seen how effective this procedure will be. As of 1 April 2004, provisions related to the pre-trial discovery procedure have been broadened. Secs. 132bis–132^{quater} CPC have been added to allow a party at the pre-trial stage to obtain a court order for a third party (including the presumptive defendant) to submit documents, for a government agency to conduct investigations, for an expert opinion or for an on-site inspection. If granted, the order has to be enforced within four months.

2. Preliminary Injunctions

It has been mentioned in the statistics above that requests for a preliminary injunction are not uncommon in intellectual property matters. Some prominent patent cases have been decided in the interim.[44] Jurisdiction lies with the court that has jurisdiction over the main action, or where the disputed property is located. The latter is not particularly clear in the case of intellectual property rights, in particular it is unclear if all courts have jurisdiction where infringing products have been found or sold. Although technically possible, interim injunctions are hardly granted *ex parte*. In patent matters, the court usually allows the respondent an interval of three weeks to file a response. The whole procedure might take about six months in patent cases. As the case is decided on *prima facie* proof, the request will only be successful where the infringement is a literal one, the validity of the patent is not in question and no possibly novelty destroying documents are filed in response. The court would in substance study the specification of the allegedly infringing product, the technical scope of the invention and compare the structural elements of both.

---

[44] *E.g.*, Tokyo District Court, 6 June 2000, 1712 Hanrei Jihô 175 – *Disposable Camera*; Tokyo District Court. 12 December 2000, 1734 Hanrei Jihô 110 – *Business Model Patent*.

There are no fixed rules about the relationship between a main action and a preliminary action. The latter may be filed before, together with or after the main action. Filing a main action is particularly necessary where damages are sought, or where the request for preliminary measures is unlikely to succeed due to the complexity of the infringement, or due to the fact that the court has to order the respondent to produce a certain document in his possession. The latter is only possible in the main action.

The plaintiff in a case of preliminary injunction has to show that but for the injunction, irreparable harm would occur. In patent matters, this would be the case where the respondent sells large quantities of the allegedly infringing product and/or seriously impedes the patentee's commercial activities. The courts would also look at the financial resources of the defendant to determine if the latter would be able to pay damages in case the injunction was not granted.

As the courts can determine the validity of the patent in an infringement action, the defence of invalidity also bears some weight in preliminary procedures. Here, it is up to the respondent to show a strong *prima facie* case of nullity, *e.g.* by supplying evidence of prior art.

The court may order the plaintiff to post a bond for the execution of the preliminary injunction. The amount of the bond is decided on the basis of the foreseeable damages the respondent would suffer if the injunction turned out to be unjustified. The court may order documents for the calculation of such damages in order to determine the amount of the bond.

A good number of cases are settled during the interim procedures.

V. The Main Action

1. Warning Letters

It is customary, but not strictly necessary, to send a warning letter to the alleged infringer indicating that a patent has been infringed. The letter has no consequences regarding the costs of the action or the question of negligence, yet may influence the court's discretionary power to award damages. Where the patentee wants to initiate an action for preliminary injunction, a warning letter might point to the lack of urgency and for that reason should not be sent. Where a suit is launched on the basis of a patent application rather than a granted right, a claim for compensation can only be made after the defendant has been made aware of the application (Sec. 65ter PA). Here, a warning letter is highly recommended in view of claiming compensation. Warning letters should be sent by registered mail with verified contents.

An interesting phenomenon in Japan are warning letters sent not only to the alleged infringer, but also to customers or suppliers of the accused. Even communications in newspapers have occurred.[45] Such letters can be very damaging to the business reputation of the alleged infringer, and if proved wrong, the right owner is liable for damages.[46]

2. Procedures in the Main Action

Prior to the 1998 amendment of the CPC, procedures in patent infringement cases would take anywhere between two to five years in first instance. The Tokyo and Osaka District Courts now handle such cases within 12 months. The significant improvements made are partly due to the new measures introduced by the CPC and the PA, and partly to the greater expertise of judges handling such cases. After having received the initial claim by the plaintiff and the respondents answer thereto, the judge can convene a pre-trial conference in order to structure the future proceedings regarding the points at issue and the evidence to be presented. Procedures are not conducted "in one go", but in a number of hearings in intervals of about two months. Delaying tactics are less successful than in the past, as the court in such case can either preclude evidence filed too late or use presumptions against the party from which performance is due.

Intermediate decisions on the merits of a case only (leaving the questions of remedies to the final decision) are rare in Japanese civil procedure, yet seem to be increasingly used in IP disputes for an improved structuring of cases.[47]

---

[45] Nagoya District Court, 27 February 1984, 16-1 Mutaishû 91 [1984] – *Walking Beam*; Nagoya District Court, 31 August 1984, 16-2 Mutaishû 568 [1984] – *Magnetic Recorder*, Tokyo District Court, 19 December 1990, 266 Tokkyo To Kigyô 46 – *University Entrance Exam*; Nagoya District Court, 8 October 1992, 1993/10 Patents & Licensing 25 – *Fungus Growing Device*; Tokyo High Court, 26 May 1993, 46/10 Patent 142 [1993] – *Cap Transport Device*; Osaka High Court, 23 February 1993, 1993/10 Patents & Licensing 25, 1994/1 AIPPI Journal (Engl.ed.) 23 – *Fish Processing Device*; Osaka District Court, 22 July 1993, 47/1 Patent 95 [1994] – *Rice Seedling Mat*; Osaka District Court, 27 October 1994, 234 Hanketsu Sokuhô 11 [1994] – *Swinging Doors*; Tokyo District Court, 26 December 1994, 236 Hanketsu Sokuhô 8 [1995] – *Design*; Osaka District Court, 31 August 1995, 244 Hanketsu Sokuhô 4 [1995].

[46] Osaka District Court, 29 June 1979, Tokkyo Kanri Bessatsu 554 [1979], and the other above-mentioned decisions impose a no fault liability in these cases.

[47] *E.g.*, Tokyo District Court, 25 May 2001, 15 Law & Technology 61 [2002]: interim decision on the question to what extent a database could be protected under copyright law (denied) or general tort law (affirmed). A decision on the amount of damages was subsequently rendered by the Tokyo District Court, 21 February 2002, 34 IIC 844 (2003) – *Database*. Also Tokyo District Court, 19 September 2002 (unreported) on the question if an invention was transferred from the inventor to the employer (affirmed). The subsequent decision on the amount of compensation was rendered by Tokyo District Court, 29 January 2004 (unreported) – *Nichia*. Interim decisions have long been advocated as a means of procedural economy: S. Ono, "Chiteki zaisanken songai ni okeru songai baishô kyaku no kettei" (On Decisions Regarding the Amount of Damages in Infringement Actions), 111 Kôgyô shoyûken kenkyû 1 (1993).

3. Obtaining and Introducing Evidence During Trial

While there is a very limited pre-trial discovery in Japan, the courts can order "the other party to produce documents necessary for the proof of alleged infringement or the assessment of damages caused by the infringement" (Sec. 105(1) PA). In the past, submission of documents was often opposed for the reason that trade secrets were involved. After the Tokyo High Court found that "the intention of protection trade secrets is not a legitimate reason for withholding relevant documents that may be of importance to the other side",[48] Sec. 105(2) was introduced that allows the court to inspect documents requested by one party in order to determine if there is good reason for withholding such documents. The assessment of the court is not open to review, as the other party does not see the documents.[49]

Where the other side does not produce evidence, or where evidence is difficult to come by for other reasons, Secs. 248 CPC and 105ter PA entitle the judge to a discretionary calculation of damages.[50]

A considerable improvement for patent infringement cases is the provision of 104bis PA, introduced in 1999 and requiring a defendant to specify his defence of non-infringement in a precise manner, that is, by indicating why his products or processes are not infringing. While the requirement of "substantial denial" puts some burden on the defendant, it is not an outright reversal of the burden of proof. A good example in this respect is a decision where the defendant had not used all elements of the patented invention, yet refused to specify further details. According to the court, it was up to the alleged infringer to prove that his device did not exhibit the same result as the patented invention. As no such proof was furnished, the infringement could be affirmed.[51]

An outright reversal of the burden of proof can be found in the case of process inventions where the defendant produces identical products.[52]

---

[48] Tokyo High Court, 20 May 1997, 30 IIC 452 (1999) – *Sale of Pharmaceuticals*.

[49] *See, e.g.*, Osaka District Court, 4 December 2001, 34 IIC 203 (2003) – *Cogwheel*. Here the court inspected the documents and allegedly infringing device and ultimately decided that the latter was not deemed infringing. It is, of course, difficult for the plaintiff to argue infringement without ever having seen the device. Sec. 105(3) allows for a court inspection of objects and thus complements the provision on an inspection of documents.

[50] Sec. 248 Code of Civil Procedure was applied in Tokyo District Court, 12 October 1998, 30 IIC 457 (1999) – *Cimetidine*. The provision was used in order to determine the amount of the infringer's expenses to be deducted from its turnover in order to arrive a figure for the infringer's profits.

[51] Osaka District Court, 30 October 2001, 34 IIC 311 (2003) – *Aerosole*.

[52] Both Sec. 104 PA and case law (Osaka High Court, 21 June 2001, 34 IIC 433 (2003) – *Electrical Pump*) make the reversal of the burden of proof only apply where the products were not publicly known prior to the filing of the application.

4. Experts

a) *Court experts* are only appointed for issues of damage calculation. Here, Sec. 105bis PA provides a special provision whereby the court upon the request of one party may ask for an expert opinion "with respect to the matters necessary for the proof of the damages caused by the infringement." In such case, "the other party shall explain to the expert the matters necessary for the expert opinion to be given." In other words, the infringing party has to cooperated with the expert for the assessment of damages, failure of which may trigger an award of estimated reasonable damages under Sec. 105ter PA.[53] There is no comparable provision for an expert opinion on infringement, as the Tokyo and Osaka courts are assisted by technical experts dispatched from the Patent Office (*see above* II.3).

b) The parties are of course free to appoint their own experts either on matters of infringement or damage calculation. Their opinions are treated as arguments from the parties, however, and do not enjoy the specific position of a court expert under Secs. 212–218 CPC.[54]

c) Another way of obtaining an expert opinion is contained in Sec. 71 PA. According to this provision, any interested party can ask the Patent Office to provide an expert opinion on the scope of a patent with respect to a certain potentially infringing product or process. The Patent Office renders an expert decision by three members of its Appeal Board. The expert opinion can only decide on the question of infringement as such, yet may not order any sanctions. Courts should seriously take such an opinion by the Patent Office into account,[55] yet are not bound thereby.[56]

Requests for such expert opinions are not particularly frequent. In the year 2002, 75 requests were made.[57] Since 1 January 2000, the procedure for determining infringement is governed by the CPC, and also the courts can request such expertise (Sec. 71bis PA). In May 1998, the Patent Office issued "Guidelines for Filing Hantei Requests".[58]

---

[53] Even prior to the introduction of Sec. 105bis in 1999, there have been court decisions where experts on the calculation of damages were appointed: Tokyo District Court, 9 February 1990, 1347 Hanrei Jihô 111. Here, two financial experts and one tax advisor were appointed to calculate damages incurred over a period of eight years and took 25 days for their expertise.

[54] *See, e.g.* the case Tokyo District Court, 24 March 1995, 1995 AIPPI Japan English edition 238 – *Air Filter*. Here, several expert opinions were presented to the court in order to determine if the defendant's product really consisted of unpolar polymer material, a term that was contained in the patent application. The court affirmed infringement.

[55] Nagoya High Court, 14 June 1967, 18 Kakyu Minshû 676 – *Butylscopoamin Bromide*.

[56] Tokyo High Court, 30 July 1970, 253 Hanrei Times 192 – *Grain Dryer*.

[57] Hinkelmann, "Gewerblicher Rechtschutz in Japan" (Industrial Property in Japan) 288 (Cologne 2004).

[58] www.jpo.go.jp.

5. Contributory, Direct, and Equivalent Infringement

a) Sec. 101 PA distinguishes between direct and contributory infringement. Acts of contributory infringement relate to preparatory acts.[59] It is not a question of indirect infringement if and where the alleged infringer employs subcontractors to commit part of the infringement.[60] Contributory infringement of a process patent can also be affirmed for a product meant to implement the patented process even though not all elements of the process may apply.[61]

b) Acts of direct infringement are the manufacture, importation or offer of products that fall within the scope of the patent right. The latter is determined on the basis of the statement of the claims in the light of the description and drawings (Sec. 70(1) and (2) PA). However, where the scope of an invention cannot be properly determined, there is no liability for infringement even though the allegedly infringing process or device may well fall within the scope of the invention.[62]

c) The Japanese courts acknowledge an equivalent infringement under the following circumstances:

(i) The differences between the patented and allegedly infringing product or process do not concern an essential part of the claimed invention;
(ii) The allegedly infringing product or process, despite the replacement, still attains the same purpose and results;
(iii) A person skilled in the art could have easily anticipated the replacement at the time of production;
(iv) The allegedly infringing product or process at the time of the patent application did not belong to the state of the art or could have been easily anticipated therefrom; and
(v) In the course of patent application proceedings, the scope of the patent claims was not meant to exclude the allegedly infringing product or process.[63]

---

[59] Cases are not particularly frequent, though. The standard commentary of Nakayama, "Shûkai tokkyo hô" (Patent Act Annotated) (3rd ed., 2000) lists 13 cases between 1989 and 1999. It has been mentioned above that preparatory acts for the infringement of a foreign patent are not covered.

[60] Osaka District Court, 20 September 2001 (unreported). The case concerned a process invention.

[61] Osaka High Court, 19 April 2001, 34 IIC 553 (2003) – *Injection Method for Ampules*.

[62] Osaka High Court, 4 December 2001, 34 IIC 554 (2003) – *Scope of Process Invention*. For a product claim, *see* Osaka District Court, 31 January 2002, 34 IIC 822 (2003) – *Washed Rice*. Here, the element of "cleaning" in a patent for a "method for washing and packing rice" was ambiguous and did not necessarily include cleaning methods where no water was used. Use of such cleaning methods by the defendant was thus deemed non-infringing.

[63] Supreme Court, 24 February 1998, 30 IIC 443 (1999) – *Ball Spline Bearing III*.

The burden of proof for the first three elements lies with the patentee, for the elements (iv) and (v), with the alleged infringer.[64] But *see also* 3. above for case where the defendant does not properly state his case.

Subsequent decisions have mostly denied equivalent infringement, particularly because the difference concerned an "essential part" of the invention, a term that finds no interpretation or justification in the current patent law.[65] Equivalents are also excluded where the allegedly infringing device is already contained in prior art (so-called Formstein-defence).[66] The so-called file wrapper estoppel (element (5)) cannot only be invoked where the patent was narrowed in scope in proceeding between the same parties,[67] but also where limitations were made in the initial application procedure.[68] Still, there are cases where equivalent infringement has been affirmed.[69]

VI. Defences

1. Non-Infringement

Sec. 68 gives the patentee the exclusive right to commercially work the patented invention. The exclusive right is limited by statutory or contractual licences, by experimental research, or by exhaustion.

a) Statutory licences are provided for the employer in case of an employee's invention, and for the prior user, Sec. 79. Prior use requires a third party commercially working the invention or having made preparations to this end at the time of filing (see above).

b) Exceptions to the right of exclusive use are always necessary for two purposes: First for a competitor or any third party to verify that the patented invention is working and can indeed by repeated based on the patent specification (experiment). And second, in order to develop further and ultimately better products or processes (research). One of the most contentious issues in the last couple of years related to experiments by manufacturers of generic drugs aimed at obtaining marketing approval. As even generic manufacturers of drugs have to obtain marketing approval, they

---

[64] Tokyo District Court, 7 October 1998 (unpublished).

[65] *E.g.*, Osaka High Court, 1 November 2001, 15 Law & Technology 82 [2002]: replacement of the patented brush with a filter.

[66] Tokyo High Court, 28 November 2001, 15 Law & Technology 83 [2002].

[67] Tokyo District Court, 30 March 2001, 1059 Hanrei Times 195: Here, the patentee had narrowed the scope of the patent in opposition procedures initiated by the defendant to the infringement suit.

[68] Osaka District Court, 9 October 2001, 15 Law & Technology 89 [2002]: Here, the patentee had limited scope of his application during the application procedure and unrelated to the alleged infringer.

[69] *E.g.*, Tokyo District Court, 22 May 2001, 13 Law & Technology 71 [2001]; Tokyo High Court, 26 October 2000, 1738 Hanrei Jihô 97 (2001) – *Isolation of Algae*.

normally prove in a simplified procedure that their own product possesses the same characteristics as the one already proved (so-called bio-equivalency test). These tests are necessary under the Pharmaceutical Act, yet are not or not primarily aimed at improving already existing technology. For that reason, such tests were initially deemed infringing.[70] Subsequent decisions, however, held these tests as not infringing, since Sec. 69(1) PA "is not limited to tests conducted with the aim of proving efficacy or technical limits".[71]

c) Rights for any given product or process covered by a patent are limited to the first act of commercial exploitation (so-called exhaustion). Two questions have been discussed in this respect. First, to what extent marketing a patented product abroad would exhaust the patent rights for this specific product under domestic law in the same way as domestic marketing would, and, second, how the scope of exhaustion should be defined for the repair or reconstruction of products. As to the first question, in 1995 Tokyo High Court held for the first time that also the marketing of patented products abroad would exhaust the domestic patent right over these products with the consequence that the right of importation could no longer be invoked against parallel importers shipping such goods to Japan.[72] On appeal, the Supreme Court did not endorse this theory. It rather held that marketing of patented products abroad did not automatically exhaust the domestic patent right over these products, but that a solution should rather be sought along the lines of contract: To the extent that the seller (patentee) did not reserve any rights, *e.g.*, importation, when selling the products, the purchaser would receive title without any restriction and was thus free to import these goods to Japan. In other words, absence of any notice to the contrary would imply consent. In order to bring home any such restriction on subsequent purchasers, the limitation would have to be clearly printed on the goods.[73] In other words, unless the goods are clearly marked as not for importation to Japan (in which language is still unclear, however), importation is permissible.

Domestic exhaustion would teach that the first commercial marketing of any given patented article does not allow the patentee to control acts of further commercial exploitation. This applies even to cases where the sub-

---

[70] Tokyo District Court, 10 July 1987, 20 IIC 91 (1989) – *Monsanto*; Nagoya High Court, 16 March 1996, 28 IIC 398 (1997) – *Clinical Trials*.

[71] Tokyo High Court, 31 March 1998, 30 IIC 545 – *Procaterole*, and ultimately, Supreme Court, 16 April 1999, 30 IIC 448 (1999) – *Clinical Trials III*: exception of clinical trials limited to what would be required under the Pharmaceuticals Act. "Extending such protection to cover also clinical trials conducted by generic drug makers carried out for the purpose of obtaining governmental approval would effectively prolong the life span of a patent, a benefit that cannot be said to be intended by the Patent Act".

[72] Tokyo High Court, 23 March 1995, 1995 GRUR Int. 417 – *BBS Car Wheels II*.

[73] Supreme Court, 1 July 1997, 29 IIC 331 (1998) – *BBS Car Wheels III*.

sequent use of such article by the purchaser is as unwanted as can be.[74] It is not quite clear to what extent the effects of such exhaustion can be limited by contract.[75] In two cases, the courts held it an infringement for third parties to refill one-way cameras, as the exhaustion doctrine did not cover what according to the court amounted to a reconstruction.[76]

2. Nullity

a) *Prior to the "TI" case*

The estoppel of patent invalidity is one of the most common defences in a patent infringement suit. Once the patentee claims that his patent has been infringed, the defendant counter-argues that, first, there is no infringement, and, second, the patent is invalid anyway and should not have been granted in the first place. Distinct from a good many other jurisdictions such as the US and the UK, but in line with a very similar system in Germany, the estoppel of patent invalidity cannot be raised in an infringement suit in principle. Within the context of a highly formalised system, the Japanese Patent Office, which has granted the patent after a substantive examination, has exclusive first-instance jurisdiction over a request for invalidating the patent that since 1 January 2004 can be raised by anyone[77] for the full life span of the patent upon showing that the conditions for granting the patent have not been met: in other words, that the patent lacks novelty, inventive step or industrial application. Only after the Patent Office has decided upon this request, and

---

[74] In Tokyo High Court, 29 November 2001, 34 IIC 821 (2003) – *Acycrobil*, the defendant had obtained marketing approval for a generic drug containing the same active formula as the one described in the plaintiff's patent. Marketing approval would expire unless the products were actually brought on the market within six months from the date of marketing approval. The defendant thus purchased the plaintiff's pharmaceuticals containing the active ingredient, distilled the latter and used this basic substance for producing the generic drugs. As the patentee had received the economic benefits deriving from the patent by the act of first marketing, he could no longer control further acts of commercial exploitation by the purchaser. The action was thus dismissed.

[75] Osaka High Court, 1 December 2000 (unreported): Here, the plaintiff and patentee had supplied hospitals with tissue paper in patented dispensers. The patentee retained title in the dispensers and obliged hospitals to have the dispensers refilled with tissue paper only through the patentee. The defendant was a company that had refilled the dispensers with tissue. According to the first instance court (Osaka District Court, 3 February 2000), the plaintiff has validly retained title and refilling by third parties thus amounted to an infringement. The High Court found that the retention of title was invalid (as not clearly expressed) and refilling was permissible under the exhaustion doctrine, as the paper as such was not patented.

[76] Tokyo District Court, 6 June 2000, 1712 Hanrei Jihô 175 – *Disposable Camera*; Tokyo District Court, 31 August 2000 (unreported) – *Fuji Film*. The patent in question was for the mechanism to transport the film behind the lens from one storage chamber to the other.

[77] Previously only by an interested party: Tokyo High Court, 28 November 1970, 2-1 Mutaishû 109.

after the appeal board has reviewed such decision, can an appeal be brought before the Tokyo High Court as the court of exclusive jurisdiction in this matter.

Although the Patent Office in a request for invalidation may examine reasons for invalidity *ex officio*, this would be the exception. Customarily, the applicant would have to furnish the Patent Office with reasons for invalidity, also due to the fact that in granting the patent the Patent Office has already conducted an *ex officio* search and examination. In view of the fact that the Patent Office should have first instance jurisdiction over the matter of invalidation, the applicant is allowed to introduce new facts or new potential reasons for invalidity only on appeal before the Tokyo High Court.[78] This is different, however, if the Tokyo High Court remands the case back to the Patent Office. In the re-trial, the applicant would then be entitled to argue new grounds for invalidity. This is even true if the application for invalidity is unsuccessful and has become final and conclusive. The same applicant can bring another invalidity request based on new facts. A decision by the Patent Office on the invalidation of a patent may well take three years. If the decision is appealed before the Tokyo High Court, one may well have to add another 18 months.

The court of the infringement action can, but need not, suspend proceedings where the estoppel of invalidity is raised and an invalidation action brought before the Patent Office.[79] In practice, the court would suspend on the balance of probabilities, yet in the past has also tried to find an equitable means of justice without waiting for the outcome of the Patent Office's decision, particularly in cases where it holds the patent invalid. Three approaches can be distinguished here:

(1) If the invention lacks novelty, the courts have sometimes dismissed the infringement suit, arguing that the defendant and potential infringer could under such circumstances claim a prior user right.[80]

(2) The most common way for the courts to limit the scope of a presumably invalid patent right without challenging the Patent Office's jurisdiction outright would be to limit the scope of the patent right to the examples cited in the description.[81]

(3) Only in rare cases would the courts regard the patent invalid outright.[82]

---

[78] Supreme Court, 4 April 1968, 22/4 Minshû 816.

[79] Sec. 168 (1) Patent Act leaves this open. While the Imperial Supreme Court in one decision held it mandatory to stay the infringement proceedings (15 November 1904, 10 Minroku 1679), the courts were subsequently credited with a discretion in this respect: Takura, in Nakayama (ed.) "Shûkai tokkyo hô" (Patent Law Annotated) 1224 (2nd ed., Tokyo 1989).

[80] *E.g.* Nagoya District Court, 31 July 1991, 15 Tokkyo Kenkyû 3.

[81] *E.g.* Osaka District Court, 25 March 1993, Patent, November 1994 121.

[82] Estoppel of the so-called free state of the art: M. Taneka, 1993 Tokkyo Kanri 1553, citing two decisions of Osaka District Court, 10 February 1976 and 19 July 1990.

In cases of diverging decisions (*e.g.* the infringement court narrows the patent's scope down to the cited examples because it holds the patent invalid, while the Patent Office rejects the invalidation request), these may be remedied on appeal before the Tokyo High Court if the infringement action has been brought before the Tokyo District Court; otherwise only at the Supreme Court level.

b) The "TI" case

The above principles have at least been overturned by a Supreme Court decision of 11 April 2000.[83] The decision concerned the basic patent for semi-conductors filed by Texas Instruments under the pre-1959 Patent Act. The patent was granted only in 1989 in amended form and subsequently survived an action for invalidation before the Patent Office. Most Japanese computer makers thereupon concluded licensing agreements with Texas Instruments, but Fujitsu chose to challenge the patent in an action to ascertain non-infringement. While the Tokyo District Court[84] dismissed the action as the allegedly infringing products were so much advanced over the technology described in the patented invention that they fell outside the scope of the patent, the Tokyo High Court on appeal[85] dismissed the suit because of the obvious invalidity of the patent. The court concluded that, as the original main claim of the patent application was rejected and the sub-claims by law had to concern the same invention, these sub-claims (some of which were subsequently patented) should also have been rejected as lacking inventive step. The Supreme Court confirmed this approach, holding that the enforcement of an obviously *invalid* patent would amount to an unjust enrichment of the patentee, that the suspension of proceedings in the case of an obviously *valid* patent would unjustifiably diminish its value, and that Sec. 168(2) Patent Act did not require a stay of proceedings in the case of an obviously invalid patent. It further held that the court, even in cases where the patent had survived an invalidation action, could hold the patent obviously invalid, and finally, that in such cases enforcing the patent right would mean an abuse. The Supreme Court expressly overturned the above decision of the Imperial Supreme Court of 1904.

Subsequent decisions affirmed that the grounds for holding a patent invalid could relate to a lack of novelty[86] or inventive step,[87] insufficient disclosure[88] or misappropriation.[89] The new approach towards invalidity may

---

[83] Supreme Court, 11 April 2000, 35 IIC 91 (2004) – *Kilby's Patent III.*

[84] 31 August 1994, 1510 Hanrei Jihô 35 (1995) – *Kilby's Patent I.*

[85] Tokyo High Court, 10 September 1997, 1615 Hanrei Jihô 10 (1997) – *Kilby's Patent II.*

[86] Tokyo District Court, 14 July 2000 (unreported); Osaka District Court, 5 September 2000 (unreported).

[87] Tokyo District Court, 27 September 2000 (unreported).

[88] Tokyo District Court, 25 April 2001 (unreported).

[89] Tokyo District Court, 30 January 2001 (unreported).

have speeded up procedures, but is not necessarily beneficial to the patentee. According to recent statistics, the patentee's success rate in infringement proceedings was a mere 24% of the 70 cases where the estoppel of invalidity was raised after the Supreme Court's decision.[90] According to information supplied to the author by presiding Judge Mimura, alleged invalidity was affirmed by the courts in about half the infringement cases. This also had repercussions on the Patent Office's handling of nullity proceedings. While between 1997 and 1999 nullity actions had a success rate of 10–15%, this escalated in 2001 to almost 50%.[91]

Current practice before the courts has shown that the estoppel of invalidity is successful even in cases that are not "obvious". This in effect has given the courts a parallel jurisdiction over patent invalidation matters, albeit limited to an *inter partes* effect. It is thus conceivable that the courts find a patent invalid, yet that the Patent Office in subsequent invalidation proceedings upholds the patent. What should happen in these cases is unclear and, as the law stands at the moment, there is no remedy for the patentee should the court decision already have become final.

VII. Remedies

As remedies against infringement, the Patent Act lists injunctive relief, damages, seizure and destruction of infringing goods.

1. Injunctive Relief

Injunctive relief is the remedy most commonly sought in cases of patent infringement. This remedy is only available during the life span of a patent and cannot be requested beyond the patent's term, even though the action for injunctive relief may have been filed before that date.

Injunctive relief is not available also in cases where a process is infringed, yet the process patent covers only part of the manufacturing process for the products ultimately obtained. In the case at issue, the defendant had manufactured a pharmaceutical and under the Pharmaceutical Act was obliged to test the quality of the substance, which he did using the plaintiff's process patent. Under these circumstances, the Supreme Court denied injunctive relief, arguing that neither manufacture nor sale of the (unpatented) pharmaceutical infringed the plaintiff's patent.[92]

---

[90] 111 Japan Patents and Trademarks 12 (February 2002).

[91] 1997: 184 invalidation requests, upheld in 22 cases; 1998: 252 invalidation requests, upheld in 46 cases; 1999: 293 requests for invalidation, upheld in 27 cases; 2000: 296 requests for invalidation, upheld in 77 cases; 2001: 283 requests for invalidation, upheld in 138 cases. Source: Tokkyo Chô, Tokkyo gyôsei nenji hôkokusho (Annual Report on Patent Administration), at 183 (Tokyo 2002).

[92] Supreme Court, 16 July 1999, 1686 Hanrei Jihô 104. In effect, the Supreme Court made a distinction between process patents for the manufacture of a product and other process patents.

2. Damages in General

Damages under the Japanese Civil Code (Sec. 417) take the form of monetary relief rather than other forms that perhaps more adequately would restore the *status quo ante*. Further, damages are strictly compensatory and in no case punitive, as the Supreme Court has clarified.[93]

3. Calculation of Damages

The usual form of damage calculation as mentioned in Sec. 102 Patent Act is the patentee's loss due to the infringement. In other words, the patentee's (hypothetical) assets but for the infringement, minus the patentee's actual assets after the infringement. While the latter is easy to calculate, the former is certainly not, in particular in the absence of any meaningful discovery as to how the defendant's infringing acts have influenced the patentee's market share, turnover, etc. In the past, the courts were unwilling to make difficult equations as to market share, etc., and outright proof of loss due to the infringing act would only be possible in a market with only two competitors: the patentee and the infringer.[94] A new decision indicates that this has changed.[95] By the amendment of the Patent Act in 1999 (Sec. 102(1)),[96] personal losses can be calculated on a discretionary basis, according to the number of infringing goods sold by the defendant, taking into account the right owner's market share and marketing efforts. For this method of calculation, it does not matter if the defendant did not make a profit from such sales or even distributed items for free. This would basically mean a calculation based on the infringer's amount of sales, multiplied by the right owner's usual profits per item, but limited to the right owner's marketing capacity (Sec. 102(1) Patent Act). The damage claim is limited by the right owner's marketing capacity, thereby putting small-scale inventors and universities at a disadvantage. Sec. 102(1) also appears applicable where the lost sales are attributable to a different (but unexploited) patent

---

[93] Supreme Court, 11 July 1997, 30 IIC 485 (1999) – *Punitive Damages*.

[94] *E.g.* Tokyo District Court, 10 March 1987, 1265 Hanrei Jihô 103 (1988) – *ICS*: No lost profits, as the orders lost by the plaintiff due to the infringement could also have been lost to one of the plaintiff's competitors. Different, the situation in Tokyo District Court, 12 October 1998, 30 IIC 457 (1999) – *Cimetidine*: "The amount of the infringing products sold by the defendant can be said to equal the amount . . . the plaintiff would have sold but for the infringement." Criticism against this "all or nothing" method is voiced by S. Chaen, "Tokkyoken shingai ni yoru songai baishô" (Damages for Patent Infringement), 1162 Jurist 50 (1999).

[95] Tokyo High Court, 15 June 1999, 1697 Hanrei Jihô 96 (2000) – *Heatbank System*. The court calculated the losses in accordance with the plaintiff's market share of 60% even in a case where the patentee did not use the patented technology to manufacture his products that were in competition with the infringing products of the defendant.

[96] Law No. 41/1999.

of the patentee.[97] While the right owner claims lost profits, he has to deduct the expenses saved. Vice versa, the infringer can deduct from his profits the expenses incurred.[98] If the infringer's figures for pure profits seem unrealistically low, the court would simply multiply the infringer's turnover with the IP owner's normal profit, as patent law already provides on a statutory basis.[99] In one notable decision rendered on the amended Sec. 102(1), the Tokyo District Court squarely equated the number of items sold by infringer with what the patentee would have sold but for the infringement. The court refused to take into account competing products on the market, efforts by the infringer to develop the market, advertising expenses by the infringer, or the price differences between the infringer's and the patentee's products.[100]

4. Infringer's Profits

Section 102 Patent Act statutorily regards the infringer's profits as one form of calculating the patentee's damages. How "profits" should be calculated is somewhat in dispute, in particular what the defendant should be permitted to deduct as expenses in this respect in order to arrive at the "pure profit" the courts would allocate. First of all, it is up to the defendant to prove that turnover does not equal profit. In other words, once the defendant's turnover has been established, this figure is presumed to be the amount of profit unless otherwise shown by the defendant.[101] Under Sec. 248 Code of Civil Procedure, the courts would be entitled to a discretionary calculation in cases of "substantial difficulties" in establishing exact proof. One decision on patent infringement allowed for the following deductions:

---

[97] Tokyo High Court, 15 June 1999, 1697 Hanrei Jihô 96 (2000) – *Heat Bank System*: Here the patentee held patents A and B, made its turnover by exploiting patent A, while the infringer used the technology of patent B, which then led to a drop in sales of the patentee's products using technology A. The case resembles a similar US case (*Rite-Hite Corporation v. Kelley Corporation*, 56 F3d 1538 (Fed. Cir. 1995) and is open to question: First, the result would doubtlessly be different if patents A and B were held by different owners. Second, if the Patent Act aims at patents being exploited, why should strategic non-exploitation be rewarded.

[98] Osaka District Court, 17 September 1998, 282 Hanketsu Sokuhô 17 – *Toaster*.

[99] *E.g.*, Osaka District Court, 25 February 1993, 25-1 Chizaishû 56 – *Jimmy'z*; in Tokyo District Court, 31 October 2001, 15 Law & Technology 92 [2002], this principle is affirmed, yet the court stresses that it would apply particularly to trade marks, as no damage to the trade mark owner's goodwill could be detected in such case. The principle is also applied to other IP rights, however: Osaka District Court, 27 March 1981 for a patent. That the courts in trade mark cases require use by the trade mark owner rather than the (registered) licensee is incomprehensible, however: Tokyo District Court, 24 March 1993, 26 IIC 566 (1995) – *Type Chanel No. 5*.

[100] Tokyo District Court, 19 March 2002, 34 IIC 965 – *Pachinko Slot Machine*. The decision is not yet final, as the patent in question was revoked only days after the decision was rendered.

[101] Tokyo District Court, 7 October 1998, 1657 Hanrei Jihô 122 (1999) – *Recharging System*. Details by S. Chaen, 1162 Jurist 50 (1999).

In order to calculate this amount of profit, one should start from the amount of Tagamet tablets and calculate first of all the direct expenses of marketing and producing these (costs of the basic substance, manufacture, packaging, licensing fee, shipping and selling) which have to be deducted. These direct costs over time amount to an average of 45.2% of the sales price, in other words, it would be reasonable to deduct 45% of the tablets' sales price for costs the plaintiff saved due to loss in sales. Further, the plaintiff had other expenses, such as the costs of sales promotion and advertising, wages, research and communication, expenses for entertainment, health and welfare, plus other expenses. Among these expenses are those that are in no way related to the actual sales of Tagamet tablets and the amount that is sold, and should thus not count as deductible expenses.[102]

Things become more complicated if either the infringer makes extremely low profits on his turnover, or if the infringing goods are composite articles of which the patented invention only represents a small part.

As to the first question, the courts increasingly tend to dismiss the infringer's figures for pure profits when deemed unrealistically low. In these cases, the court would multiply the infringer's turnover with the patentee's normal profit on his own devices:

Yet, the profit made by the defendant is extremely small . . . due to the fact that the defendant used the products to promote others of his own. For this reason, the defendant's calculations on prices and profits cannot be taken into account here. Rather, the calculation of profits should be based on what the plaintiff would have made as a profit for the comparable goods he sold.[103]

Under the new Sec. 105bis Patent Act, the court may appoint an expert witness for the calculation of damages (*see above* V.4).

As to the second problem, there is little case material to draw on. In one case of patent infringement where the defendant had only infringed a patent for a composite part of a complex machine, the court awarded damages calculated on the sale of the machine multiplied by a factor corresponding to the relevance of the patented part.[104]

The infringer's profits cannot be claimed where the IP right in question was not used.[105]

5. Ordinary Licensing Fee

Awarding an ordinary licensing fee is the fallback method of calculation if higher damages under other calculation methods fail. Traditionally, in patent

---

[102] Tokyo District Court, 12 October 1998, 30 IIC 457 (1999) – *Cimetidine*.

[103] Osaka District Court, 17 September 1998, 282 Hanketsu Sokuhô 17 (1998) – *Toaster*.

[104] Tokyo District Court, 26 December 2003, 1851 Hanrei Jihô 138 – *Filling Machine*. On the other hand, in a case of copyright infringement, the court awarded the copyright owner the complete profits on the sale of a CD with about 20 different computer games, only one of which was infringing. Tokyo District Court, 31 January 1994, 26-1 Chizaishû 1 – *Pacman*.

[105] Tokyo District Court, 31 October 2001, 15 Law & Technology 92 [2002].

matters the courts awarded extremely low licensing fees based on two studies of the Inventor's Association on licensing fees for certain types of inventions in domestic licensing contracts.[106] In most cases, however, those patents infringed were particularly valuable ones, and often were inventions made abroad. It would thus have been more appropriate to take fees in international licensing agreements as a reference,[107] and award top-end fees rather than across-the-board averages.

In some cases the courts took existing licensing agreements into consideration.[108] Yet the patentee might not be particularly interested in publishing the rates of other licensing agreements on the infringed technology, particularly since there is no reason why an infringer should profit from what an honest user had negotiated. Owing to the 1998 amendment of Sec. 102(2) Patent Act,[109] the courts no longer feel obligated to award only an "ordinary" licensing fee, and recent case law seems to indicate that the courts have become more assertive in arriving at higher figures.[110]

In cases where the above-mentioned damages cannot be claimed, *e.g.* due to time bar, the right owner can base his claim for a licensing fee on the provisions of unjust enrichment (time bar of ten rather than three years).[111]

6. Seizure and Destruction

Seizure of infringing goods by order of a civil court is a provisional measure and may go further than what could ultimately be ordered for destruction.[112] Destruction of goods is relatively easy in cases of finished goods,[113] yet may be more difficult in the case of unassembled or semi-finished products which would only be infringing upon assembly.[114]

---

[106] Hatsumei Kyokai (ed.), "Jisshi ryôritsu" (Use and Compensation) (Tokyo 1980); Hatsumei Kyokai (ed.), "Gijutsu torihiki to royalty" (Technology Transfer and Royalties) (Tokyo 1992).

[107] Which was in fact done in Tokyo District Court, 30 March 1996, 1585 Hanrei Jihô 106 (1996).

[108] Tokyo District Court, 18 October 1996, 1585 Hanrei Jihô 106 – *Concrete Steel Rod.*

[109] Law No. 51/1998.

[110] Tokyo District Court, 30 March 1998, 1646 Hanrei Jihô 143 (1998) awarded an unheard of 7% royalty rate in a patent infringement case.

[111] Tokyo High Court, 13 July 1999, 1696 Hanrei Jihô 137 – *Karaoke.* The court found the damage claim time barred, yet ordered the defendant to pay what a lawful user would have had to pay.

[112] Tokyo District Court, 6 April 1984, 525 Hanrei Times 314 (1985) – *Crystal.* Upon the plaintiff's request the court had ordered the seizure of a high-speed copying machine that commercially copied copyright material without proper permission.

[113] *E.g.* Osaka High Court, 30 November 1993, 25-3 Chizaishû 476 (1993) – *Aluminium Wheels.*

[114] While the request for the destruction of semi-finished goods was initially denied by Tokyo District Court, 28 December 1989, 21-3 Mutaishû 1073 (1989) – *Cable Cover I,* the request was granted in part in appeal: Tokyo High Court, 25 February 1993, 25-1 Chizaishû 33 (1993) – *Cable Cover II.*

7. Court Costs and Attorneys' Fees

The total costs for patent infringement suits are relatively high, at each court level between 8 and 10 million yen (currently 70,000 up to 90,000 euro). Attorneys' fees are freely negotiable and are either calculated per hour or according to a fee table published by the Japanese Bar Association. The latter is divided into an advanced payment and a success fee. Both are calculated according to the economic gains the party makes from winning the suit. Making clear arrangements about attorneys' fees is advised.

While the losing party in a lawsuit has to bear the court costs (although the successful plaintiff would rarely claim these against the defendant in light of the cumbersome procedures), attorneys' fees would have to be borne by each side, and only in exceptional circumstances be (partly) awarded as damages in cases where particularly difficult legal questions are involved.[115]

8. Customs Procedures

Seizure and destruction can be requested under the Customs Tariff Act, last amended in 2003. While the number of registered industrial property rights amounts to about 2.6 million in Japan, customs annually receives more than 9 million requests for blocking unlawful imports. The procedures are regulated in detail in Secs. 21–21^{quater}. Under current procedures for stopping goods allegedly infringing patents, utility models or designs, customs can request the Patent Office for a determination of scope. The Patent Office has to provide such opinion within ten working days. In 2002, customs suspended the importation of goods in almost 7,000 cases concerning about 1 million items. In about 70% of the cases, the allegedly infringing goods came from Korea. Of the 7,000 cases, in 2002 only seven cases concerned patent rights. This number has dropped dramatically after a change in customs regulations that no longer allow a prevention of parallel imports.[116] There are now 13 customs officers specifically responsible for the border enforcement of intellectual property rights, five of them in Tokyo.[117]

---

[115] *E.g.* Supreme Court, 29 May 1984, 530 Hanrei Times 97 – *American Football Symbol Mark*. Amounts tend to be low, *e.g.* 1 million yen.

[116] *Kurakan* (Guideline) 257 of 26 March 1998.

[117] T. Doi, "Customs Control over Importation of Goods Infringing IP Rights in Japan", 192 Patents and Licensing (April 2004), 9.

14
The Enforcement of Patent Rights in Korea

JAY (YOUNG-JUNE) YANG

A. System of Civil Procedure

Jurisdiction over cases involving intellectual property in Korea is divided between civil courts, which have jurisdiction over infringement actions, and the Intellectual Property Tribunal (IPT) of the Korean Intellectual Property Office (KIPO) and the Patent Court, which are responsible for invalidation and cancellation and confirmation-of-scope trials.

The Korean court system can be represented as follows:

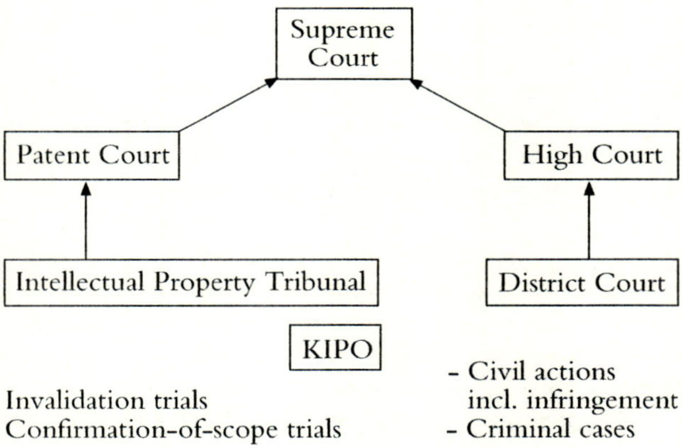

I. The Court System

1. Courts of First Instance

In accordance with Chapter V of the Korean Constitution, the Korean court system is comprised of three tiers: the courts of original jurisdiction, or the district courts; the intermediate appellate courts, or the high courts; and the Supreme Court. Both the district courts and the high courts are divided into geographic districts.

The district courts are the courts of first instance for both civil and criminal matters. The number of judges on a panel in the district court is based on the population of its jurisdiction. Most infringement actions filed with district courts are heard by panels consisting of three judges. However, for infringement actions involving compensation for damages of less than 30 million Won (about US$33,000), the panel consists of only one judge. Judges in district courts are generally transferred to other positions every two years. When a patent is infringed, or when there is a probable threat of infringement, the owner may commence a suit in a civil court seeking preliminary injunction or permanent injunction and damages. The courts, however, do not have authority to invalidate patent registrations. Some district courts have panels of judges who have expertise in intellectual property matters.

2. Courts of Appeal

Appeals from decisions of the district courts are taken to the high courts. The high court undertakes a *de novo* review of the district court's decisions on matters of both law and facts. Therefore, the high court will accept new evidence and arguments in addition to reviewing the record of the district court trial. The high court's panel consists of three judges. Some high courts have panels of judges with expertise in intellectual property matters.

Appeals from the high courts are presented to the Supreme Court, which has discretion as to whether to accept an appeal. The panel will generally consist of four judges. The Supreme Court has judicial assistants who specialise in intellectual property matters having a rank equivalent to that of high court judges.

It is important to note the Republic of Korea follows the civil law tradition, and thus, its judicial system emphasises statutory interpretation over judicial precedent. As a result, a Supreme Court decision is not necessarily a precedent in subsequent cases of a similar nature, but merely persuasive. However, the interpretation of a law rendered in a particular case by the Supreme Court does have a mandatory binding effect on the lower courts when the case is remanded.

3. The Intellectual Property Tribunal of the Korean Intellectual Property Office

The IPT is a first instance tribunal which hears invalidation actions, cancellation actions, confirmation-of-scope trials and other intellectual property matters such as appeals from final rejections of applications for intellectual property rights. The IPT is a body operating within KIPO and was created by combining the Trial Board and the Appellate Trial Board, the two bodies for invalidation actions and confirmation-of-scope trials. The IPT was established contemporaneously with the Patent Court (see below) on 1 March 1998.

The structure of and the procedures required by the IPT are substantially the same as those of the former Trial Board. As with the Trial Board, the IPT will receive new arguments and evidence in addition to reviewing the record, however, the IPT will more actively rely on oral hearings and technical presentations, than did the Trial Board.

4. The Patent Court

The Patent Court, created under the provisions of the Court Organisation Act of 8 July 1994, in force since 1 March 1993, hears appeals from decisions made by the IPT of KIPO. The IPT is not recognised as a court, making the Patent Court equivalent to a court of first instance rather than an intermediate appellate court. However, because the Patent Court only hears cases that have first been decided by the IPT, the Patent Court is an appeal court, at least in practice. As with the high courts, decisions of the Patent Court with respect to matters of law can subsequently be appealed to the Supreme Court. Unlike the other high courts, however, the Patent Court has national jurisdiction.

a) Staffing

The Patent Court is comprised of three panels, each panel consisting of three judges. These judges are appointed by the Supreme Court from the ranks of high court judges who have experience in patent cases or have an academic background in science and/or engineering. Recognising that the judges of the Patent Court would not likely have the scientific background necessary to handle patent issues, the amended Court Organisation Act provides for the appointment of up to fifteen technical examiners, drawn from former KIPO trial examiners, to act as judicial assistants. The judicial assistants' role is to supplement the judges' lack of specialisation in adjudicating intellectual property matters, including preparing reviews of the patent and utility model cases for the judges' review. The judicial assistants may, with the court's permission, make inquiries during a trial or hearing, examine witnesses and parties and clarify any relevant issues, however, they may not vote on the outcome of a case.

b) Jurisdiction

The Patent Court is the only court in Korea that has national jurisdiction, and can review decisions rendered by the IPT regarding patent applications and the validity of patents *de novo*. Any appeals before the Patent Court should be brought within thirty days from the date of receiving a certified copy of the decision from the IPT.

As a court of law, the Patent Court follows the Rules of Civil Procedure and requires compliance with the rules of evidentiary formalities. The Patent Court must also limit its review to the arguments and evidence submitted by the parties. Hearings in the Patent Court concentrate on oral testimony including presentations, demonstrations of prototypes and witness testimony.

The IPT or the Patent Court does not have jurisdiction over patent infringement cases, but rather this lies with the district courts and the high courts, and ultimately the Supreme Court.

II. The Legal Profession

1. Qualifications for and Roles of Attorneys/Patent Attorneys

There are approximately 70 law schools in Korea. Seoul National, Yonsei and Korea University's Colleges of Law rank among the very top. Law school is completed during the four years at the undergraduate level. Students then take the National Bar Exam in order to gain admittance to the National Judicial Training and Research Institute in Seoul. Although students do not need to complete the undergraduate legal coursework in order to be eligible, law school graduates make up the vast majority of those who take the National Bar Exam. At the National Judicial Training and Research Institute, students receive two years training to qualify as a judge, an attorney or a prosecutor. Legal education is completed upon graduation from this institute, after which the graduate is qualified as an attorney-at-law. To become a patent attorney, a person can either pass the Korean Patent Attorney Examination, complete practical training and pass the screening, or be a qualified attorney-at-law who registers as a patent attorney.

Under Korea's dual patent litigation system, attorneys-at-law handle the infringement litigation in the district courts; patent attorneys handle invalidation, confirmation-of-scope and correction trials and prosecution of patents, utility models, designs, and trade marks before KIPO and the IPT, and also handle the appeals of these actions before the Patent Court. Attorneys-at-law and patent attorneys may both handle registration of copyrights and computer programs.

It is advisable to have both patent attorneys and litigation attorneys involved in patent litigation to address the technical and legal issues that may arise. A patent attorney's involvement is necessary because of the validity issues involved in almost every patent infringement action. Even though the courts cannot invalidate a patent, they consider to a certain extent whether the patent should be enforced, and thus look at the novelty and, perhaps to a lesser degree, the inventiveness of a patent.

In addition, the patent attorney, with his or her technical background, can frequently assist technical experts in assessing infringement. Moreover, close coordination is needed between the patent attorney handling an invalidation action or scope trial and the attorney-at-law handling the infringement action to maintain a consistent approach in litigation and KIPO action.

Participation by attorneys in invalidation actions and confirmation-of-scope trials can also be helpful as the Patent Court is a court of law operating under the rules of civil procedure.

2. Qualifications for and Roles of Technical Examiners

The Court Organisation Act, which created the Patent Court, recognised that judges may often lack the technical expertise necessary to understand some of the highly specialised details likely to arise in intellectual property cases. To help remedy this potential problem, the Act also authorised the Supreme Court to appoint up to 15 technical examiners to assist the Patent Court judges. According to Rule 2(2) of the Supreme Court's Rules Concerning Technical Examiners, these technical examiners must have at least one of the following prerequisites:

(1) a Masters Degree in Science and Technology, and ten years subsequent experience in the field;
(2) a Ph.D. in Science and Technology;
(3) five years experience with KIPO; and/or
(4) seven years experience as an official in a technology-related field.

Technical examiners are influential in intellectual property cases, particularly those involving patents and/or utility models. These examiners play an important advisory role, explaining to the judges the technical issues and arguments presented by the parties, and answering any questions that the judges may have regarding the invention. After the oral arguments have been concluded, the technical examiner submits his opinion to the panel. Technical examiners do not have the authority to make decisions in the case.

B. Problems Related to the Enforcement of Patent Rights

I. Competent Parties

1. Standing

In general, the plaintiff to the action is the right owner, and/or the entity suffering damages such as an exclusive licensee. The defendants are the entity directly or indirectly infringing the intellectual property right.

Domestic or foreign individuals, corporations, associations or foundations that are not corporations, but which are provided with a representative or administrator, or an appointed party representing a group having common interest may become a party of a suit in its name.

a) Co-Litigation

If the rights or liabilities which are the subject of a suit are common to two or more persons, or have the same factual and legal basis, such persons may join in a suit as co-litigants (CCP, Sec. 61). The same applies when the rights or liabilities are the same kind or have the same factual and legal basis.

b) Joinder

In the case of infringement of a plaintiff's intellectual property by multiple parties, the district court will enjoin all the defendants if within the court's jurisdiction. Also, a claim for damages is often heard in the same procedure with the claim for permanent injunction in a main action. The IPT and the

Patent Court have been reluctant to join different confirmation-of-scope or invalidation trials where the same parties are involved. In light of this, the problems with the dual litigation system for intellectual property disputes become more apparent, thus making the recent arguments for the consolidation of jurisdiction under the Patent Court much more compelling. For further details, see II below.

c) Defendants

– *Company directors or officers*

Company directors are generally immune unless it can be shown that the decision to infringe was made solely by an individual director or officer. They may, however, be liable for criminal penalties of up to seven years imprisonment or a fine of up to 100 million Won.

– *Parent companies or subsidiaries*

Parent companies or subsidiaries can be sued as a defendant if a common intent existed with the infringer to facilitate infringement, and if they meet the jurisdictional requirement.

II. Competent Court

Most patent infringement actions filed with district courts are heard by panels consisting of three judges. However, for infringement actions involving compensation for damages of less than 30 million Won (about US$33,000), the panel will consist of only one judge. Some district courts have panels of judges who have expertise in intellectual property matters. Judges in district courts are generally transferred to other positions every two years. When a patent is infringed, or when there is a probable threat of infringement, the owner may commence a suit in a civil court seeking preliminary injunction or permanent injunction and damages. The district courts, however, do not have the authority to invalidate an intellectual property right.

As noted earlier, jurisdiction over intellectual property cases is divided between the civil courts, which have jurisdiction over infringement actions, and the IPT and the Patent Court, which are responsible for invalidation and cancellation trials and confirmation-of-scope trials.

This dual patent litigation system has raised significant issues regarding the non-uniform and inefficient application of intellectual property laws. In particular, problems and delays have arisen due to the fact that patent invalidation or confirmation-of-scope actions are often used as defences to infringement actions. As a result, the district court in which the infringement action is filed often waits until the IPT and the Patent Court renders its decision on the validity or the scope of the patent. This delay is amplified if either party decides to appeal the Patent Court's decision to the Supreme Court.

Furthermore, because of the separate claims, issues and jurisdiction, the district court, the IPT or the Patent Court cannot join the claims and/or parties, further increasing the risk of delay or non-uniform application of laws.

In the interest of reducing the inherent delay and overlap caused by the dual litigation system, strong arguments have been posed in favour of giving the Patent Court exclusive jurisdiction over patent, utility model, design and trade mark (collectively "intellectual property") infringement cases.

This has prompted the Chief Judge of the Patent Court to recently announce that the Supreme Court is considering an amendment to the Court Organisation Act. This amendment is expected to give the Patent Court exclusive appellate jurisdiction over intellectual property infringement cases, in addition to its existing jurisdiction over IPT decisions. Furthermore, the Supreme Court is also currently considering the proposition to expand the Patent Court's appellate jurisdiction over infringement cases arising out of other types of intellectual property, such as copyright and software.

III. Preparation for Trial/Pre-Trial Procedures

1. Pre-Trial Discovery

In many other jurisdictions, pre-trial procedures relate primarily to service, discovery and jury selection. The Korean CCP does not provide for pre-trial discovery. There is no trial by jury in Korea. As a result, pre-trial or pre-hearing procedures are considerably abbreviated.

This lack of pre-trial discovery sometimes frustrates the complainant or plaintiff in connection with collecting evidence because it is practically impossible to collect evidence unless a lawsuit is actually filed and proceeds. However, the fact that there is no official pre-trial discovery process does not preclude the plaintiff from collecting evidence on his own. As a result, the party who wishes to initiate a lawsuit may have to exert more effort than in other countries in collecting evidence by conducting a private investigation.

Once the trial begins, the court officially recognises the discovery process, and, the parties can request the court to enforce a request or demand the production of certain evidence. The Korean process of discovery is one that is ongoing throughout the course of the trial, rather than a process that must be concluded before the trial can commence. Accordingly, the complainant or plaintiff often collects supporting evidence during the course of a trial and is able to strengthen his or her arguments or claims against the infringing party.

2. Service

a) Korea

In the absence of special provisions to the contrary, formal communication between the parties is undertaken by the court in conformity with the Korean CCP. The transcripts of documents are delivered to the domicile, place of residence, place of business or office of the person on whom it is to be made. In the event that the location is unknown, or that it is deemed impossible or ineffective, the presiding judge may, upon his own authority or upon motion of parties, order delivery by public notice.

b) Abroad

A Korean court may also serve a claim on a person residing in a foreign country by commissioning a foreign court. Service of proceedings on a Korean national who resides in a foreign country which is a member of the Vienna Convention can be made through the Korean embassy or consulate located in the country unless this violates any law of the country. Service of proceedings on a foreigner out of the domestic jurisdiction is also possible when the foreign country expressly approves. Upon the request of the chief judge of the court concerned, the administrator of the court administration shall entrust the Minister of Foreign Affairs to send the commission to the competent foreign court through diplomatic channels.

The procedures to be taken when service of process from a foreign court is to be effected on a resident of Korea are governed by Korean law. Specifically, when evidence is taken in Korea by a foreign court or administrative office in respect of civil matters, this must be effected under Korean law, in particular the International Civil Judicial Cooperation Act of 8 March 1991, in order to better accommodate the need for the international judicial cooperation and under the Regulations Concerning International Civil Judicial Cooperation promulgated by the Supreme Court. Under the International Civil Judicial Cooperation Act, in order for a foreign court or administrative office to take evidence or effect the service of process in Korea, it must send a request to a competent Korean court through diplomatic channels.

In addition, Korea joined the Hague Conference on Private International Law as of 20 August 1997, and has become a party to the Convention on the Foreign Delivery of Judicial and Extrajudicial Documents in Civil or Commercial Matters on January 2000, which took effect in Korea on 1 August 2000.

3. Preservation of Evidence

Although pre-trial or pre-hearing discovery is virtually non-existent in Korean civil procedure, Chapter 7 of the CCP provides for the "preservation of evidence", which allows a party to file a motion requesting the court to accept evidence prior to the filing of the initial complaint. This is used in cases where there is risk that the evidence will not be available for presentation at a hearing, including situations in which the evidence is likely to be destroyed or a witness will not be available to testify at trial. In such cases, the plaintiff may petition the court to examine the evidence (that is, to inspect documents, inspect and/or seize infringing goods or take testimony) before the filing of the complaint. Courts are generally reluctant to grant requests for such inspections unless the risk of the disappearance of such evidence is substantial.

Because of this, securing samples of the original works or goods as well as of infringing products is recommended before commencing a court action.

Once a court action begins, the infringer often recalls its products from the market, and it thus becomes difficult to secure samples of infringing goods for submission to the court as evidence or for use by an expert or court expert for analysis.

In criminal actions, the prosecutor or police may seize infringing goods. However, as there are many defences and potentially complex technical issues in patent cases, it is difficult to get a prosecutor to act except in a relatively clear and simple case. It may be applied to documents as well as testimony, but the motion must specifically identify the exact evidence that the applicant wishes to preserve.

According to Sec. 377 of the CCP, the following matters shall be made clear in a motion for preservation of evidence:

(a) indication of the other party;
(b) matter requiring proof;
(c) the evidence; and
(d) the reason for requiring preservation of evidence.

The reasons for the preservation of evidence shall be demonstrated by evidence.

If the court grants the motion for preservation of evidence, and the party against whom the motion was filed fails to cooperate, the matters sought to be proved by the requesting party may be presumed against the party failing to cooperate therewith. This procedure may be sought in either *ex parte* or *inter partes* proceedings.

4. Interim or Preliminary Injunctions

To prevent further infringement in the course of the trial, the complainant may request the court to issue a preliminary injunction. Preliminary injunctions provide a relatively prompt method of restraining the infringer from further infringing the intellectual property right.

It usually takes six to 12 months for a preliminary injunction to be issued. Accordingly, instant civil remedies such as a temporary restraining order are practically unavailable in Korea.

Although the law states that a preliminary injunction may be issued with or without a hearing, courts will usually review a petition for a preliminary injunction in *inter partes* proceedings. It is usually possible to obtain an initial hearing on the petition for the preliminary injunction within two to three weeks from the filing date. At the hearing, the petitioner must introduce evidence such as brochures and samples of infringing products and may examine witnesses in support of the petition with the court's permission.

A preliminary injunction is available upon a *prima facie* showing of infringement and of the necessity for provisional relief. In deciding the necessity for provisional relief, courts weigh the irreparable harm to the plaintiff caused by the continuing infringement against the economic harm to the defendant resulting from the grant of injunction. Courts also consider the adequacy of damages to redress the injury to the plaintiff from infringement and the likelihood of invalidation of the relevant IP right, although the validity of the IP right is presumed until it is declared invalid in a final decision of an invalidation action.

The respondent is given an opportunity to present arguments and evidence in rebuttal. At its discretion, the court may hold additional hearing sessions. The parties may request additional sessions to submit further evidence and arguments. When the court decides that the case has been sufficiently reviewed, the hearings are closed and the court renders a decision. The court has broad discretion in deciding whether to issue an injunction.

Although the court may issue a preliminary injunctive order with or without requesting a security deposit, it generally requires the IP right owner to post a security bond before issuing an injunction for the purpose of indemnifying the other party for possible damages. This can be returned either on the basis of the defendant's consent or after a final judgment in the permanent injunction action in favour of the plaintiff.

When a preliminary injunction order is issued, the court may:

(1) prohibit the respondent from continuing the manufacturing or sale of the articles which infringe the petitioner's right;
(2) direct that the infringing articles or other articles used for the infringement be transferred to the custody of a court bailiff; and
(3) instruct the court bailiff to post an appropriate public notice of the order on the premises of the respondent.

If the injunction is granted, it is enforced by the bailiff at the expense of the petitioner. The petitioner's initial court expenses may be recoverable if he subsequently wins the main action.

If the petition for a preliminary injunction is denied by the trial (district) court, the petitioner may appeal the decision to an appellate court. Alternatively, the petitioner may proceed with the filing of an action for a permanent injunction and/or seek other remedies.

If the respondent wishes to appeal the issuance of the preliminary injunction, then he may file an action for cancellation first with the court which issued the injunction or may appeal before an appellate court. If the court decides to uphold the preliminary injunction, the respondent may appeal, although it may still be enforced pending the appeal.

As an alternative to the appeal procedure, the respondent may request that the court direct the petitioner to institute an action for a permanent injunction and/or damages. Upon receipt of such a request, the court will instruct the petitioner to file the complaint within a certain time period (usually within ten days). If the petitioner does not comply, the preliminary injunction will be revoked by the court. If the respondent does not make such a request and the preliminary injunction is upheld in an appeal, the preliminary injunction will remain in force.

5. Warning Letters

Before initiating an action in a civil court, intellectual property owners often send a warning letter to the infringer. These letters generally give notice to the infringer of the infringing nature of his activity and demand that this activity cease immediately. Warning letters are particularly important because damages are usually calculated from the date that the infringer is known to have been aware of the infringing nature of his activity. Although negligence of the infringer is presumed by the existence of a registered IP right, warning letters are advisable especially if the infringing activities occur prior to the registration of the patent right.

Warning letters must be carefully formulated and must be based on supportable allegations. Otherwise, a civil action may be commenced against the sender for tortious interference with business.

IV. The Trial

1. General Procedures

Generally, hearings are held in the manner as mentioned above. Most of the arguments and evidence are presented in the form of briefs and affidavits. Upon examination of witnesses, the court clerk records a summary of the statement made by the witnesses. To avoid errors in the summary, questions to witnesses tend to be leading and call for simple answers. Courtroom stenographers who provide a full transcript of the proceedings are available upon request. It is unusual for more than one witness to testify at a hearing and the testimony generally takes less than 30 minutes. Cross-examination and re-direct examination are also permitted and are similarly brief.

In principle, an intellectual property right holder bears the burden of showing the existence and the likelihood of an infringement by the alleged infringer. As a general rule in Korean civil litigation, all parties must produce their own evidence; court-ordered production of evidence is restricted, and the parties are not obligated to disclose the existence of documents in their possession relating to the case.

Evidence is usually presented at trial in the form of documents or affidavits from witnesses or expert witnesses. Samples or photographs can also be submitted. Oral statements by witnesses can be presented as evidence during in-court witness examinations conducted with the permission of the court. Given the focus on documentary evidence and the limited nature and scope of witness examination in Korean trials, the trials tend to be more inquisitorial than adversarial.

2. Witnesses

Generally, the only information that must be made available by one party to the other is that which is submitted as evidence, either in the form of documents or testimony.

The court may generally call any person as a witness to appear and testify. For purposes of the CCP, however, a "witness" does not include a party to the suit because such testimony is not considered credible. Testimony of a party to a suit will only be permitted if the court "is unable to get a conviction by examination of other evidence" (CCP, Sec. 368). In the case of a company, the "party" for this purpose is the Representative Director, who is the senior representative of a company in Korea (CCP, Sec. 372). Other corporate executives will not be considered to be a "party", but in practice, executives of a company rarely testify, again because they may lack credibility.

In practice, witnesses are called by the court upon petition by a party, and witnesses who are adverse to the petitioner are very rarely called. As described further below, although a witness is generally required to answer questions that are posed at a hearing, the attorney-client privilege may be asserted by attorneys as a defence against this requirement.

The questions to be asked must be submitted to the court in written form prior to the hearing. For this reason, and because the courts do not generally employ court reporters to record the testimony verbatim, the questions are usually leading and require only a very brief answer. Cross-examination and re-examination of witnesses are permitted.

Parties may request the court to call witnesses, including expert witnesses, for testimony.

3. Expert Witnesses

Expert opinions may be submitted to the court in two ways. The first procedure is for either party to introduce expert opinions as evidence in support of its case based on the expert's own findings and knowledge or on other evidence. The parties may submit further evidence rebutting the expert opinion submitted by the opposing side.

The other procedure for obtaining an expert opinion is as a court expert, either as a result of a request by a party or on the court's own initiative. Although the party making such petition may request the court to seek the opinion from a particular source, the opposing party may object, submitting evidence demonstrating the expert's bias. The court has broad discretion with regard to whom it engages as its own expert.

The court may also decline to grant a petition for an expert opinion from a party if unnecessary. In most cases, university professors having expertise in the relevant field are favoured by the courts.

4. Court Ordered Document Production

As a general rule in Korean civil litigation, a party must produce its own evidence; court-ordered production of evidence is unusual, and a party is never obliged to disclose the existence of documents in its possession relating to the case.

Under the CCP, however, a litigant may petition the court to order the other party or a third party to submit a known document which relates to the case. Sec. 343 of the CCP provides that the "submission of documentary evidence shall be made by presenting the document, or by applying for an order of production addressed to the person holding the document".

In other words, a party may either submit documentary evidence that it has in its possession, or may file a motion with a court for an order that a person produce the document. According to Sec. 345 of the CCP, a motion to the court applying for the production of a document must clearly indicate the following:

(1) identification of the document;
(2) gist of the document;
(3) holder of the document;
(4) the fact to be proven by the document; and
(5) the basis for the obligation to produce the document.

Not only must the petitioner have a clear idea as to the existence and content of a document before requesting its submission, he must also show that the holder of the document is obliged to produce it, under one of the following provisions (CCP, Sec. 344):

(1) when the party possesses the document referring to the document in the suit;
(2) when the applicant is entitled to request from the holder of the document the delivery or perusal thereof; and
(3) when the document has been made out for the benefit of the applicant, or the legal relationship between the applicant and the holder thereof.

Unless a document falls into one of the three categories above, the court will not order that it be submitted. One example would be if the document was prepared for the internal use of the holder; in this case the holder may refuse to produce the document. Of course, there may be cases where it is unclear whether the document concerns "the legal relationship between the applicant and the holder" or whether it was prepared for internal use of the holder; however, court precedents and academic writings have not clearly defined this distinction. In practice, petitions for document production are not widely used and the courts often do not grant them.

5. Affidavit Evidence

Having been asked by the presiding judge whether they will accept the authenticity of evidence submitted to the court by the other party, the parties may raise an objection thereto. In case of affidavits, a person who prepared the affidavit can be summoned to court to testify its authenticity.

6. Obtaining Evidence from Abroad

Korea is not a signatory to the Convention on the Taking of Evidence Abroad in Civil or Commercial Matters of 18 March 1970. It may be possible to obtain evidence from abroad based upon a broad interpretation of the International Civil Judicial Cooperation Law, but this has been seldom applied.

7. Presentation at Trial

With the permission of the court, in-court presentation can be made in Korea. In argumentation proceedings, both parties attend and have the opportunity to rebut the opposing party's presentation. Especially in patent litigation, court presentations have been used increasingly and judges have favourably viewed having both parties attend and present their explanations of complex technical issues.

8. Proving Infringement

a) Patents

A patent right is recognised and enforceable only when it has been registered with KIPO. Once granted by KIPO, the term of a patent is 20 years from the filing date of the application, in accordance with the Korean Patent Act (PA).

The PA defines acts that constitute direct infringement of a patent as follows:

> To carry on the business of producing, using, transferring, leasing, importing or, offering for the sale or lease (including displaying for the sale or lease) an article covered by a patent, of using a patented process, or of using, transferring, leasing, importing or, offering for the sale or lease (including displaying for the sale or lease) an article manufactured by a patented process constitutes an infringement of the patent concerned.

Further, according to Sec. 127 of the PA, the following acts are also considered to constitute infringement, and are generally referred to as indirect infringements:

(1) if a patent is related to an invention for a product, an act of producing, transferring, leasing, importing or, offering for the sale or lease (including displaying for the sale or lease), as a business, articles used *exclusively* for the production of the patented product; and
(2) if a patent is related to an invention for a process, an act of producing, transferring, leasing, importing or, offering for the sale or lease (including displaying for the sale or lease), as a business, articles used *exclusively* for the practice of the patented process.

However, there are also exemptions to infringement of a patent:

(1) use of the patented invention for the purpose of research or experiment;
(2) vessels, aircraft or vehicles merely passing through the Republic of Korea or machinery, instruments, equipment or other accessories used therein; or
(3) identical products existing in the Republic of Korea at the time the patent application was filed.

The PA gives a patent applicant a provisional right to recovery of an ordinary royalty after the application has been laid open and the alleged infringer has obtained knowledge of the application. Such compensation cannot be sought until the patent has been granted, after which the patentee has the right to seek full damages and preliminary or permanent injunctive relief.

Infringement is determined by comparing the infringing article or process to the patent claims. There has been only limited recognition of infringement based on the use of equivalents to the elements set forth in the patent claims. The existence of a dependent patent or the modification of a patented product or process by the addition of another element that represents a marked improvement over the patented invention has been given same weight as a defence of non-infringement to an allegation of patent infringement for chemical or pharmaceutical patents, although there is no statutory basis for doing so. The recent trend in patent enforcement appears to be against such non-standard defences. One of the problems hampering patent right holders from enforcing their patent rights in Korea has been the court's tendency to narrowly interpret the claim, basically confining it to specific examples or preferred embodiments given in the specification. However, in *Aktiebolaget Haessle v. Boryung Pharmaceutical Co., Ltd.*,[1] the Supreme Court rejected the infringer's argument to confine the scope of patent protection to the invention disclosed in working examples, declaring that:

(1) as a matter of principle, the scope of patent protection shall be determined by the matters described in the claim;
(2) when the claim wording alone does not render it possible to determine the technical constitution or scope, other disclosures contained in the specification can be used to complement the deficiency; however, in such event, such other disclosures cannot be used to expand the scope of protection beyond the claim language; and
(3) when it is possible to determine the technical scope based on the claim alone, the scope of patent coverage cannot be restricted or reduced by using other disclosures contained in the specification.

[1] Supreme Court, 12 October 1993, 91 Hu 1908.

Furthermore, as is the case in a number of other countries, the doctrine of "prosecution history estoppel" is generally recognised in Korea. In *Cheil Jedang v. Genetics Institute*,[2] the Supreme Court held that prosecution history estoppel should be applied in view of the specification, the opinions of the examiner as expressed from filing of the application to issuance of the patent, the intent of the applicant as indicated in the amendments and arguments made during the prosecution, and the like. Therefore, restrictions raised by the examiner, and amendments or admissions made by the applicant during the patent application procedure concerned, may be used at a later time against the patentee in the interpretation of patent claims.

If a competing article or process falls within a patent claim, it is called literal infringement. To constitute literal infringement, all of the constituents of a claimed invention must be used in the competing article or process. A slight change made in the competing article or process affecting neither the constitution nor the function or effect of the patented invention also constitutes literal infringement.

In Korea, as in some other countries, a patent infringement may also be found to exist under the doctrine of equivalents. According to a Patent Court decision in the *Bayer AG v. Union Quimico Pharmaceutica S.A.* case, the following conditions should be met:[3]

(1) a replaced constitutional element must carry out substantially the same function in substantially the same manner to obtain substantially the same effect as the relevant constitutional element of a patented invention;
(2) such a replacement must have been easily conceivable to one of ordinary skill in the relevant art at the time of the preparation of the competing article;
(3) the competing article was not prior art technology or could not be easily conceived from prior art at the time of filing the application for the patented invention; and
(4) the replaced constitutional element must not have been intentionally excluded from the patent claims during the prosecution history of the patented invention.

Although the doctrine of equivalents was found to apply in relatively few cases, the Korean Supreme Court's recent decision expressly adopting the doctrine of equivalents[4] is anticipated to have a profound effect in broadening the applicability of this doctrine in future cases.

In addition to the literally infringing and equivalent inventions, there may be conflicts between a senior (and basic) invention and a junior (and improvement) invention. In this connection, Sec. 98 of the PA provides that

---

[2] Supreme Court, 6 September 2002, 2001 Hu 171.

[3] Patent Court, 17 September 1998, 98 Heo 2160.

[4] Supreme Court, 28 July 2000, 97 Hu 2200.

if a patented invention utilises another person's patented invention, registered utility model or registered design which was filed prior to the filing date of the patent application concerned, or is in conflict with another person's registered design which was filed prior to the filing date of the patent application concerned, the patentee or his exclusive or non-exclusive licensee may not practise the patented invention without the consent of such other person, nor obtain a non-exclusive license by trial decision. Therefore, the PA clearly recognises the possibility of an infringement of a senior and basic patent by a junior improvement invention.

However, there still exists an uneasy feeling with respect to the enforceability of a senior patent against its junior invention, as exemplified by the decision rendered in *Chevron Research Co. v. Jinheung Fine Chemicals Co.*[5] In this case, the Supreme Court held that a competing process which only adds the use of a conventional catalyst to a patented process does not fall within the scope of the patent simply because the competing process makes a remarkable improvement in the yield and reaction speed over the patented process. This decision resulted in a great deal of controversy. The later *Bayer AG v. Cheil Sugar Co., Ltd.* case[6] made some progress on the issue. In this case, the Supreme Court recognised that the possibility of infringement between a senior basic invention and a junior improvement invention existed, but found no infringement for the reason that using a catalyst constituted a new technical concept, producing superior effects. In the later *Nissan Chemical v. LG Chemical*,[7] however, the Supreme Court conclusively reversed the much criticised "catalyst" precedents. The Court in this case directly addressed the implications of adding a catalyst to a patented chemical reaction and held that mere addition of a catalyst to a patented chemical process does not constitute sufficient grounds for a finding of non-infringement.

b) Utility Models

Utility models are protected under the Korean Utility Model Act. The term of a utility model right is ten years from the filing date of the utility model application.

Under the Utility Model Act, commercial acts of manufacturing, assigning, leasing or importing, or offering for assignment or lease, of goods used exclusively for manufacturing a product relating to utility model registration shall be deemed to constitute an infringement of a utility model right or an exclusive license. The Utility Model Act provides protections similar to those under the Patent Act for infringing activities.

---

5 Supreme Court, 9 April 1985, 83 Hu 85.

6 Supreme Court, 26 November 1991, 90 Hu 1499.

7 Supreme Court, 21 August 2001, 98 Hu 522.

V. General Defences

The most common defences raised in response to an infringement action are a denial of infringement, a claim of invalidity, and a request for a negative confirmation-of-scope trial.

1. Invalidation Action

Unlike in some other countries, the invalidity of a patent is, in principle, not a defence in a patent infringement action. Rather, the validity of a patent should be attacked by bringing a separate patent invalidation action before the IPT when accused of infringement. As invalidation actions are handled by the IPT and the Patent Court whereas infringement actions are handled by the district courts, a decision of invalidity by the IPT or the Patent Court will not have a binding effect on a court until it becomes final and can no longer be appealed. Therefore, a district court which hears an infringement action must proceed with the presumption that the patent is valid until and unless a decision holding the patent invalid has become final and conclusive. Of course, the district court will give close consideration to an invalidation decision made by the IPT or the Patent Court. Moreover, obtaining relief from patent infringement (notwithstanding a non-final decision of invalidity) is difficult.

One exception to this general rule can be found in a number of Supreme Court decisions, including the decisions of *Shindo Mulsan Co., Ltd. v. Hanmi Silup Co., Ltd.*[8] and *Cheiljedang Corporation v. F. Hoffman La Roche AG*,[9] where the Supreme Court held that if every single inventive element constituting a patented invention had been in the public domain prior to the filing date of the patent application, then such a patent cannot assert its patent right. Therefore, upon showing the complete lack of novelty of a patented invention, the court, without having to hold that the patent is invalid, may refuse to enforce the patent and dismiss the infringement action.

2. Confirmation of Scope

As a defence in a patent infringement action, the defendant may make an argument that his product or process does not fall within the scope of the patent concerned. Such an argument is often raised in a separate confirmation-of-scope trial filed by the alleged infringer before or after the initiation of an infringement action, as well as in the infringement action. Confirmation-of-scope trials, which are tried before the IPT and appealed to the Patent Court, are similar to US declaratory judgment actions on non-infringement. Although courts are not bound by the results of confirmation-

[8] Supreme Court, 26 July 1983, 81 Hu 45.

[9] Supreme Court, 22 December 1998, 91 Ma 540.

of-scope trials, the ruling of the IPT or the Patent Court in such trials is highly persuasive. However, there is widespread criticism that confirmation-of-scope trials are redundant and only compound the delay in the legal system.

VI. Final Remedies

The petitioner may bring a "main action" for a permanent injunction and/or other remedies. Other remedies in the main action may include damage compensation and a court order requiring the respondent to publish an apology for infringing the goodwill of the petitioner.

When the court does decide to issue such orders, it may order provisional measures such as injunctive relief before the decision becomes final and can no longer be appealed. Otherwise, the relief will be stayed until the action becomes final and can no longer be appealed.

A claim for damages is often made at the same time as a claim for permanent injunction. Since IP rights such as patents and utility models are presumed valid until declared otherwise by KIPO, civil courts may at their discretion decide to stay the infringement proceedings pending a decision by KIPO on the issue of validity. However, the trend appears to be for courts to proceed with litigation parallel to any KIPO actions.

Other orders, such as orders for disclosure of suppliers or manufacturers, are not generally part of the judgment. It is possible that such information could be obtained through a request during the trial proceedings, but courts are usually highly restrictive in the information that they will seek from a defendant.

1. Financial Compensation/Damages

a) In General

To obtain a damages award in addition to a permanent injunction, the plaintiff is faced with the difficult task of sufficiently proving the amount of damages caused by the infringement. Infringement of an IP right is essentially a tort. Obtaining a damage award requires evidence that the tort was committed wilfully or through negligence. While negligence of the infringer is presumed from the existence of a registered IP right, an infringer may avoid the obligation to pay damage compensation by proving that he had not acted negligently, but rather bona fide. Punitive damages are not recognised under Korean law.

Korean courts were known to be conservative in awarding or calculating damages, and thus, in general, the damage amount were expected to be relatively low. However, damages totaling approximately US$77 million were recently awarded by Korean district courts in two related patent infringement actions, in what is believed to be the largest such damages award in Korean patent litigation history

In most cases, the winning party is only able to recover a nominal amount of litigation costs. Court related costs that are generally recoverable include the Stamp Fee and the cost of expert witnesses. However, only a nominal amount of attorneys' fees are recoverable based on a percentage formula set by Korean civil law.

An action for damages must be filed within three years from the date the plaintiff becomes aware of the damages caused by the infringement and identifies the infringing party or within ten years from the date of the infringement, whichever comes earlier. However, an action for recovering damages based on an infringer's unjust enrichment, can be filed within ten years. An action for recovering damages against a joint tortfeasor can be filed and full damages can be recovered. The joint tortfeasor may recover portions of the damages from other joint tortfeasors.

b) Calculation of Damages

There are currently four methods for calculating damages. One is the amount of actual damages sustained by the plaintiff. If actual damages are difficult to prove, the net profits earned by the infringer can be used to measure damages. The presumption that the infringer's profits are a reasonable measure of damages, however, is rebuttable. Said compensation may not exceed an amount calculated by multiplying the estimated profit per unit by the amount obtained by subtracting the number of articles actually sold from the number of products that the patentee or exclusive licensee could have produced. If the foregoing two methods of calculation of damages are not workable, the IP right owner may seek a normal royalty, which is defined as the royalty which would normally be charged for a license for the same kind of technology. The fourth and most recent method for calculating damages went into effect on 1 July 2001 with the amendment to the PA. This newest method provides that the court may use the profit per unit of the articles that the patentee or exclusive licensee might have sold in the absence of said infringement, multiplied by the defendant's total sales volume of the infringing goods in order to ensure that the plaintiff at least recovers his profit margin for its own products. In such case, said compensation may not exceed an amount calculated by multiplying the estimated profit per unit by the number of products that the patentee or exclusive licensee could have produced, subtracted by the number of articles the patentee or exclusive licensee actually sold. Further, if the patentee or exclusive licensee was unable to sell his or her product for reasons other than infringement, a sum calculated according to the number of articles subject to said circumstances is deducted from the estimated damages. The courts generally will not grant speculative or estimated damages and do not grant punitive damages for infringement of IP rights.

It is often difficult to prove the amount of actual damages or profits earned by the infringer without adequate discovery. Therefore, we view that the courts tend to favour the "reasonable royalty" approach to damages.

However, in one case where the infringer exported most of the infringing goods, the IP right holder was able to prove the infringer's profits by requesting that the Customs Office produce the customs record showing the amount and price of the infringing goods exported by the infringer. Also, the court of the above-mentioned district court case, in calculating the damages awards, allowed the plaintiffs to cite profit margin of the local licensee and manufacturer to arrive at the estimated lost profits incurred by the plaintiff due to patent infringement. In this regard, the courts cited an amended provision of the Korean PA, which was enacted to address the frequently encountered difficulty of obtaining accurate information about an infringer's finances, to authorise such a calculation method.

2. Permanent Injunctions

The procedure for obtaining a permanent injunction is similar to that for a preliminary injunction. However, because the effect of the permanent injunction is permanent, the court is more thorough in reviewing such petitions. Consequently, it usually takes about one to two years to obtain a permanent injunction, which is longer than required for a preliminary injunction action.

The proof necessary for obtaining a permanent injunction and a preliminary injunction differs in two main respects:

(1) in a permanent injunction action, it is not necessary to prove the necessity for preliminary relief; and
(2) the required proof shifts from the presentation of a *prima facie* case to proof by the preponderance of the evidence.

3. Destroying Infringing Materials

Infringing products will be taken into the custody of the bailiff or destroyed as directed by the injunctive order issued by the court.

4. Restoration of Goodwill

When an IP right is infringed, the right holder is also entitled to petition the court for an order to restore the right holder's goodwill.

VII. Criminal Action – Procedure in Criminal Courts

1. General Procedure

Based upon a complaint or other evidence of wrongdoing, the police may commence an informal investigation, which may entail viewing physical evidence and interrogating individuals who may have knowledge of the possible wrongdoing. If as a result of the informal investigation there is sufficient evidence of criminal wrongdoing, the police may charge the alleged wrongdoer with a crime and commence a formal investigation.

While investigating the crime, the police must determine whether to arrest the accused. In order to make an arrest, the police must seek the assistance of the prosecutor's office to obtain a warrant from the court. For this and for other reasons, an individual prosecutor is assigned to the case, although at this stage the investigation is generally conducted by the police investigators. If the police investigators choose to conduct a formal investigation without arresting the individual, they must notify the prosecutor and obtain the prosecutor's approval. If the accused is arrested, the police investigators must complete their formal investigation within ten days following the arrest. Subsequent to and pending completion of the police investigator's formal investigation, the accused may file a petition equivalent to a writ of habeas corpus with the court. If the court permits the accused to be released from custody, pending the completion of the investigation, the accused will not be considered to be under arrest. If the police do not arrest the accused, they have three months to complete their formal investigation, pursuant to internal police guidelines. Regardless of whether the accused is arrested, his passport may be confiscated by the police if he is a foreign national. During this stage, the police investigators may request the prosecutor to obtain a warrant from the court not only for the accused's arrest, but also warrants in relation to other aspects of their investigation, such as the search for physical evidence.

Upon completion of the investigation, the police must refer the case along with their opinion to the prosecutor. Thereafter, the prosecutor will conduct his own investigation. In this regard, we note that it is also possible for the prosecutor to initiate an investigation himself, even in the absence of a prior police investigation.

The prosecutor must first determine whether to arrest the accused pending completion of his investigation (or if the individual is already arrested, whether he should remain in custody). If the accused is arrested, he may file a petition for his release, as mentioned above.

Should an infringer be arrested, the prosecutor must complete his investigation within ten days (which may be extended for an additional ten day period) of the date the police referred the case to the prosecutor. If the alleged wrongdoer is not arrested, the prosecutor has three months to complete his investigation, pursuant to internal guidelines. Upon the completion of the investigation, the prosecutor must determine whether to indict the accused or to drop charges.

2. Summary Offences

The prosecutor may request the court to agree to summary procedures in the event the sanctions sought by the prosecutor are limited to fines. If the court grants this request, the judge may render summary judgment without holding a hearing. A defendant can still request a formal trial within seven days from the date of receiving the summary judgment.

3. Indictable Offences

Any accused person arrested and indicted by the prosecutor is entitled to be tried within six months from the date of the original arrest. The trial is conducted by the relevant district court. If the accused is not arrested, there is no time limit for the completion of the trial. A motion for release on bail may be filed at any time after indictment. As a practical matter, the court will issue a decision on such motion within one week.

4. Appeals

Parties have right of appeal of a district court decision. A notice of intent to appeal the court decision must be submitted to the high court (the next level court) through the district court within seven days following the district court's decision. If the accused has been arrested, the appeal, if granted, must be conducted within four months of the original court judgment. However, there is no time limit for the appeal if the individual is not arrested. The high court's decision may be appealed to the Supreme Court. The procedures to appeal to the Supreme Court are the same as those for the high court appeal.

5. Specifics for Patents

A convicted patent infringer, including a director of a company, may be subject to a sentence up to seven years, or a fine of up to 100 million Won. When a representative officer or employee of a company commits the violation, the company and the individual may each face a penalty. The company may be subject to a fine of up to 300 million Won. A criminal investigation and indictment for patent infringement may only be brought upon the complaint of the patent holder. A criminal action may be initiated either by itself or together with a civil action. Due to the usual complexity of patent cases, the technical issues involved and the various defences that may be raised, the prosecutors are generally reluctant to aggressively investigate patent infringement claims except in very simple and clear cases.

E

Patent Enforcement in the Americas

15
The Enforcement of Patent Rights in the United States

TIMOTHY MALONEY[1]

A. Patent Rights

I. Requirements for Obtaining Patent Rights

Utility patents are generally considered the strongest form of legal protection for intellectual property in the U.S. system. They grant the patent holder a limited legal monopoly on the invention for 20 years after the initial filing date in the United States. During the term of the patent, the patent holder can prevent others from making, using, offering for sale, or selling the patented invention in the U.S. or importing the patented invention into the U.S.

1. The Nature of the Patent Application Proceeding

Obtaining a patent in the United States involves an *ex parte* procedure solely between the inventor or the inventor's assignee and the PTO. As a result of recent changes in U.S. law, pending utility patent applications are now published 18 months after their priority date unless, at the time of filing, the applicant requests that the application not be published and certifies that it will not be filed in any country outside of the United States that provides for publication.[2] If and when the application is published or the patent actually issued, the secrecy of the proceeding ends and the entire written record is open to the public.[3]

The publication of U.S. patent applications brings the U.S. into closer conformity with the procedures of many other countries, and will make it easier for competitors to monitor each other's patenting activity. However, there is currently no procedure available for a party to participate directly in the PTO to oppose the original grant of a patent to another. Such challenges are reserved to the court system and to post issuance PTO reissue and reexamination proceedings, which are discussed later in this article.

Some skeptics lament that the U.S. PTO is in the business of granting patents and lacks sufficient resources to assure that the patents it awards are of

---

[1] The opinions expressed here are solely those of the author.

[2] 35 U.S.C. § 122(b).

[3] 37 C.F.R. § 1.14.

proper scope and provide sufficient disclosure of the invention to benefit the public. However, the entire basis for the patent grant is subject to close scrutiny and frequent challenge during enforcement litigation. The courts provide an important safety net against questionable patents. On the other hand, given the numerous substantive and technical requirements imposed by the U.S. patent laws, the inventor of meritorious technology may nevertheless face many difficulties in attempting to enforce the related patent rights. Proper preparation and prosecution of the patent application in the first instance is crucially important. In artfully drafted patent claims, incomplete disclosure of the invention, and inaccurate characterizations of the prior art are but a few of the types of transgressions during prosecution that can create serious obstacles to successful patent enforcement. The following sections briefly describe the requirements for obtaining a U.S. patent to provide context for the ensuing discussion of patent infringement claims and defenses.

2. Patentable Subject Matter

In the United States, patentable subject matter includes "any new and useful process, machine, manufacture, or composition of matter, or any new and useful improvement thereof."[4] These four classifications are broad and generally encompass the vast majority of technological advances. In recent years, computer software, business methods, and non-naturally occurring biological materials have each been held to be within the broad scope of patentable subject matter.

3. The Patent Specification

The specification of a U.S. patent must meet four general requirements: (1) provide a written description; (2) provide sufficient detail to teach persons of ordinary skill how to make and use the invention; (3) reveal the best mode of making and using the invention known by the inventor at the time the application is filed; and (4) provide at least one claim covering the invention.[5] As discussed below, the failure to meet any one of these requirements can provide invalidity defenses to an accused infringer.[6]

The claimed invention must be the invention described in the specification. In other words, the claims must be supported by the specification as originally filed. Thus, the claims cannot encompass or contain more or different elements, steps, or compositions than are described in

---

[4] 35 U.S.C. § 101.

[5] 35 U.S.C. § 112, ¶ 1.

[6] It is believed that the requirements for a legally sufficient specification are less stringent in many other countries. Thus, U.S. patents based on priority applications filed in another country may be more susceptible to challenge based on an inadequate specification.

the specification. The claims are adequately supported if one skilled in the art could reasonably have found the claimed invention in the specification.[7]

The specification, as filed, must also teach one of ordinary skill in the art how to make and use the invention without undue experimentation. The enablement requirement does not mandate that each and every detail of the invention be included.[8] Rather, the skilled artisan must be able to practice the invention without "undue experimentation." Generally, a considerable amount of experimentation is permissible, if it is merely routine, or if the specification provides a reasonable amount of guidance with respect to the direction in which the experimentation should proceed.[9]

The inventor cannot hide or conceal the best physical mode of making or using the invention. This requirement discourages inventors from applying for patents while at the same time concealing from the public preferred embodiments of their inventions.[10] It is generally immaterial whether the failure to include the best mode in the specification was intentional or accidental. The subjective test is whether the inventor knew of a better mode at the time of the filing date and, if so, whether it is adequately disclosed in the specification.[11] Questions of failure to meet the best mode requirements are rarely addressed during prosecution of a patent in the PTO, but are often raised during litigation to enforce the patent.

The specification must also conclude with one or more claims "particularly pointing out and distinctly claiming the subject matter which the applicant regards as his [or her] invention."[12] The claims, not the specification, define the metes and bounds of the exclusive right granted by the patent. Subject matter disclosed in the patent specification, but not claimed, is dedicated to the public.[13] Generally, the claims may be drafted as broadly as the prior art and the specification allow. Thus, the claims require careful drafting by experienced patent counsel to cover the invention as broadly and comprehensively as possible.

4. Novelty and Non-Obviousness

In the United States, an invention to be patentable must be both new[14] and unobvious[15] over the prior art. Prior art may include other patents from

---

[7] *Texas Instruments v. International Trade Commission*, 871 F.2d 1054, 1062 (Fed. Cir. 1989).

[8] *In re Gay*, 309 F.2d 769, 774 (C.C.P.A. 1962) ("Not every last detail is to be described, else patent specifications would turn into production specifications, which they were never meant to be.").

[9] *In re Jackson*, 217 U.S.P.Q. 804, 807 (Bd. Pat. App. & Int. 1986).

[10] *DeGeorge v. Bernier*, 768 F.2d 1318, 1324 (Fed. Cir. 1985).

[11] *Spectra-Physics, Inc. v. Coherent, Inc.*, 827 F.2d 1524, 1536 (Fed. Cir. 1987).

[12] 35 U.S.C. § 112, ¶ 2.

[13] *Unique Concepts, Inc. v. Brown*, 939 F.2d 1558 (Fed. Cir. 1991).

[14] 35 U.S.C. § 102.

[15] 35 U.S.C. § 103.

anywhere in the world, printed publications or printed patent applications from anywhere in the world, U.S. patent applications which eventually issue as patents, and public uses or offers for sale in the United States of the claimed subject matter. Depending on the circumstances, unpublished and unpatented research activities of others in the United States may also qualify as prior art. Admissions by the inventor as to the content or status of the prior art, even if later shown to be incorrect, are also part of the prior art for that invention.

The determination of novelty of an invention is generally straightforward: the issue is whether the invention is old or new. If a single prior art reference shows identically every element of the claimed invention, the invention is not novel and, therefore, not patentable. The anticipating reference must, however, be enabling. In other words, it must teach one of ordinary skill in the art how to make and practice the invention.

An invention may also not be patentable under § 102 if certain events (so-called statutory bars) occur more than one year before the patent application is filed in the PTO. For example, a published written description of the invention, a public use, or offer of sale of the subject matter of the invention in the United States more than one year before the filing date of the application bars the invention from being patented. Unlike most countries in which absolute novelty is required, an inventor has a one-year grace period after such a public disclosure in which to file a patent application in the United States.

Even if the invention is novel under § 102, the invention may not be patentable under § 103 if "the differences between the subject matter sought to be patented and the prior art are such that the subject matter as a whole would have been obvious at the time the invention was made to a person having ordinary skill in the art to which the subject matter pertains."[16] Obviousness is determined using a three-part inquiry: (1) a determination of the scope and content of the prior art; (2) a determination of the differences between the prior art and the claimed invention; and (3) a determination of the level of ordinary skill in the art.[17] The decision maker must then step back in time and determine whether a person of ordinary skill would have found the invention as a whole obvious at the time the invention was made.

Additionally, so-called secondary considerations or "objective indices of nonobviousness" are often used in determining whether an invention is obvious.[18] Secondary considerations which can be used to support nonobviousness and patentability include, for example, commercial success, a long-standing problem that resisted solution until the invention, failure of others to solve the problem, unexpected results, copying of the invention by others in the art, and initial skepticism in the art concerning the success or value of the invention. For such secondary considerations to be useful in

[16] 35 U.S.C. § 103.

[17] *Graham v. John Deere Co.*, 383 U.S. 1, 17 (1966).

[18] *Id.* at 17–18.

establishing patentability, there must be a direct relationship between the secondary factor and the merits of the claimed invention. Therefore, to be useful in demonstrating nonobviousness, commercial success should be predominately the result of the benefits and merits of the invention rather than, for example, advertising or marketing considerations.[19]

5. The Duty of Candor

Because the proceedings in the PTO are *ex parte* in nature, the applicant has a "duty of candor" to be forthcoming in dealing with the PTO throughout the prosecution of the patent application. This duty of candor includes providing the PTO with all information which may be material to the examination of applicant's patent application. The duty of candor does not require the applicant to carry out a prior art search, but requires disclosure of all prior art of which the applicant or the applicant's representative is aware. The duty to disclose relevant prior art continues throughout the prosecution of the application. Therefore, if the applicant later becomes aware of relevant prior art, including prior art found by patent offices outside the Untied States during prosecution of the corresponding applications filed in other countries, that information must be provided to the PTO. Failure to comply with this duty of candor can result in any patent issuing from the application being declared unenforceable by a trial court.

II. Administrative Correction of Patents

The two mechanisms for making substantive corrections to issued patents in the PTO are the reissue and the reexamination procedures. These administrative procedures enable a patent owner to fix potential problems before enforcing a patent, and also provide alternative avenues for competitors to challenge the validity or restrict the claims of an issued patent.

1. Reissue Proceedings

The reissue procedure is available to correct a defective patent if the owner can establish that (1) the patent is considered "wholly or partly inoperative or invalid" because of a defective specification or drawing or because the inventor claimed more or less than he or she had a right to claim, (2) the defect arose "through error without any deceptive intention," (3) new matter is not introduced into the specification, and (4) the claims in the reissue application meet the legal requirements for patentability.[20] An application for a reissue patent which contains claims enlarging the scope of the original patent must be filed within 2 years of the date of grant of the original patent. The term of a reissue patent is the unexpired portion of the original patent; a reissue patent cannot extend the duration of the original patent.

---

[19] *Pentec, Inc. v. Graphic Controols Corp.*, 776 F.2d 309, 315–316 (Fed. Cir. 1985).

[20] 35 U.S.C. § 251; 37 C.F.R. §§ 1.171–1.179.

Often times the patent owner seeks a reissue patent to expand the scope of the claims to cover a competitor's activities, or to narrow the claims to avoid newly discovered prior art. The reissue file is open to the public. Once the patent owner initiates the reissue proceeding, competitors may participate by filing a written submission protesting the proposed reissue claims on any grounds of patentability. The patent owner must surrender the original patent upon filing the reissue application, and risks the possibility of newly proposed claims and/or the original claims being disallowed. An infringer may have a personal defense of intervening rights to continue an otherwise infringing activity if the activity or preparation for the activity took place before the grant of the reissue patent.[21]

2. Reexamination Proceedings

A patent owner or any interested party can seek a review of an issued patent by the PTO on the basis of patents and/or printed publications that raise a substantial new question of patentability.[22] This procedure allows the PTO to determine the correctness of the original patent grant in light of the newly presented prior art.

Recent changes in rules governing reexamination proceedings allow a third party to request and participate in a reexamination proceeding using either *ex parte* or *inter partes* proceedings. Using *ex parte* proceedings, the third party requestor is limited to responding to an applicant's initial statement concerning patentability if filed.[23] No other input is allowed by the third party. Under *inter partes* proceedings, the third party has the opportunity to respond to arguments and amendments made by the patent owner throughout the reexamination.[24] The third party in the *inter partes* proceeding is limited to issues raised by the patent owner or PTO and cannot raise new issues. The third party is, however, barred from later asserting invalidity in litigation on any ground that was raised, or could have been raised, during the reexamination proceeding.[25]

The PTO can reaffirm the original grant, substitute a new grant by allowing new or amended claims, or withdraw the original grant. The legal presumption of validity of the patent is not strengthened by the successful completion of the reexamination proceeding. However, the practical effect of the reexamination proceeding may considerably strengthen the patent in the eyes of a judge or jury. Courts and juries will generally look with particular favor on a patent which has twice been found patentable by the PTO. On the other hand, the reexamination proceeding provides a potential infringer the possibility of invalidating a patent outside of the court system at a con-

---

[21] 35 U.S.C. § 252.

[22] 35 U.S.C. §§ 301–307.

[23] *Id.*

[24] 35 U.S.C. §§ 311–318.

[25] 35 U.S.C. §315(c).

siderably reduced cost. Considering the potential risk that the patent might actually be strengthened and considering their limited involvement in the reexamination proceeding, it is expected that third parties will use *inter partes* reexamination only where the prior art is believed, to a high level of certainty, to render the patent invalid.

B. The System of Civil Procedure

The U.S. system of justice is an adversary system which relies on the parties and their attorneys to collect evidence and present their dispute before a neutral fact-finder. The Court presides over the presentation of evidence, but does not participate directly in obtaining evidence before or during trial. In theory, the clash of adversaries before the Court is most likely to lead to the truth and a fair resolution of the controversy.

I. The Trial Courts

Pursuant to the authority granted in Article I, Section 8, Clause 8 of the United States Constitution, Congress enacted the patent laws, which are codified at 35 U.S.C. Patent litigation seeks a judicial resolution of the parties' rights regarding the limited monopoly granted by a U.S. patent. It may be initiated by one having rights to enforce a patent against an alleged infringer, or by a party seeking to have the patent declared invalid, unenforceable, or not infringed in response to having been threatened under the patent. Generally speaking, the U.S. civil justice system is comprised of the federal courts and the courts of each of the fifty individual sovereign states. Section 1338(a) of Title 28 of the U.S. Code grants the federal district courts original jurisdiction of all cases arising under the U.S. patent laws, exclusive of the state courts.[26] This jurisdictional grant generally does not extend to claims of infringement of a foreign patent.[27] Actions involving U.S. Patents

---

[26] The first sentence of Section 1338(a) reads as follows: "The district courts shall have original jurisdiction of any civil action arising under any Act of Congress relating to patents, plant variety protection, copyrights and trademarks." Disputes regarding title to patents or contracts regarding patents do not satisfy this standard and must be brought in state court absent some other basis for invoking federal jurisdiction.

[27] *See Mars, Inc. v. Kabushiki-Kaisha Nippon Conlox*, 24 F.3d 1368 (Fed. Cir. 1994). The patent owner in this case sought to enforce both a U.S. and a related Japanese patent against the defendant in one proceeding. Under 28 U.S.C. § 1338(b), a claim of unfair competition may be joined with a substantial and related claim of patent infringement. The Federal Circuit rejected the patent owner's argument that infringement of the Japanese patent constituted unfair competition under this provision. *Id.* at 1373. It also rejected the argument that the Japanese and U.S. patent infringement claims were so related as to permit jurisdiction under a more general supplemental jurisdiction statute, 28 U.S.C. §1367(a). *Id.* at 1375.

are conducted like all other civil actions in the federal courts, and are governed by the Federal Rules of Civil Procedures and the Federal Judiciary Act, 28 U.S.C.

The United States district courts are the trial courts of the federal court system. There are 94 federal judicial districts, including at least one in each state, the District of Columbia and Puerto Rico.[28] The district courts have jurisdiction over nearly all civil and criminal matters arising under federal law.[29] The district courts may also hear controversies involving state law between parties having different state citizenship if the amount in controversy exceeds $75,000.[30]

Pursuant to Article III Section I of the Constitution, district court judges are appointed for life by the President with the advice and consent of the Senate. There are no specific qualifications to become a judge, and most were formerly state court judges, law professors, or accomplished private or government attorneys. Few have any formal training in the sciences or patent law. There are currently 665 authorized judgeships in the district court system, the largest number being in more populous states such as California, Florida, Illinois and Texas.[31]

In view of the broad scope of federal subject matter jurisdiction, these judges are required to handle a wide variety of matters, including contract disputes, personal injury actions, labor disputes, criminal matters, and many others. Patent actions make up only a small percentage of cases in the system at the district court level. In 2002, less than one percent of the total civil cases convened in U.S. district courts were patent cases.

Patent Cases Commenced in U.S. District Court
(1998–2002)

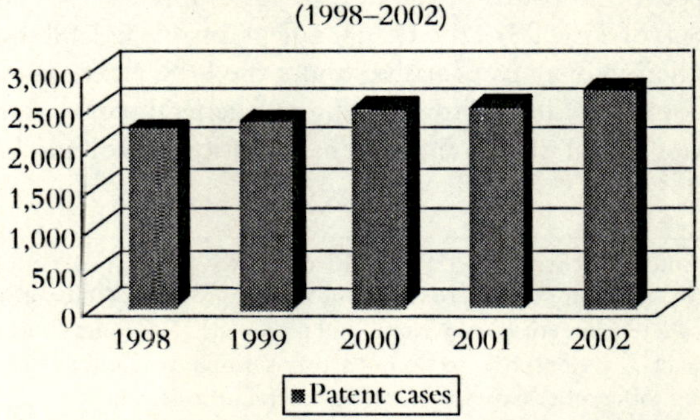

*Sources: www.uscourts.gov and www.fticonsulting.com

[28] The Virgin Islands, Guam and the Northern Mariana Islands, which are U.S. territories, also have district courts that hear patent and other federal cases.

[29] 28 U.S.C. §1131.

[30] 28 U.S.C. §1132.

[31] U.S. District Court Judicial Caseload Profile, *at* www.uscourts.gov (last visited Dec. 3, 2003).

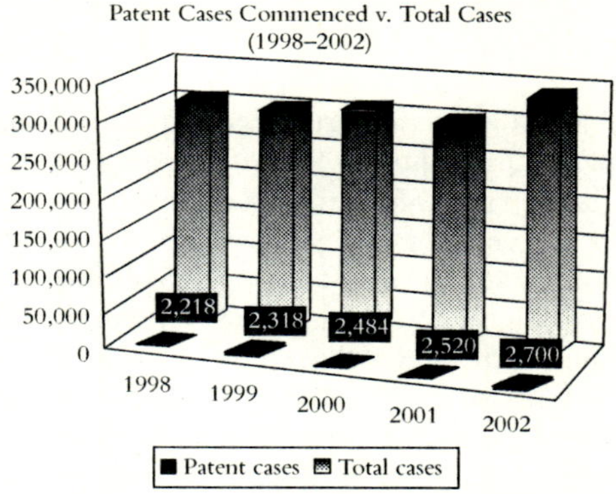

*Sources: www.uscourts.gov and www.fticonsulting.com

Even though there has been a steady upward trend in the number of new patent cases filed each year, these patent cases are still sparsely distributed among the district court judges, such that the typical judge has little experience handling the numerous complex issues involved.[32]

Two other forums for resolving patent infringement suits also deserve mention. The United States Court of Federal Claims has exclusive jurisdiction over patent infringement claims made against the federal government.[33] The United States International Trade Commission ("ITC") has authority to preclude importation of products covered by a U.S. Patent or made abroad by a process covered by a U.S. patent.[34] Significant procedural and substantive differences exist between these forums and the district courts. For example, there is no right to trial by jury in the Court of Federal Claims, nor is injunctive relief available against the government or suppliers to the government.[35] ITC investigations are conducted by ITC staff, whose determinations must consider factors such as the public welfare, competitive economic conditions, and the interests of U.S. consumers which do not necessarily align with the parties' interests.[36] Detailed treatment of these tribunals is beyond the scope of this article.

[32] Judge Cohen, Tenth Annual Judicial Conference of the United States Court of Appeals for the Federal Circuit, 146 F.R.D. 205, 372 (1992) ("[T]here's an under-appreciation of the general lack of experience of district judges [regarding patent matters] . . . [D]istrict judges have to constantly learn and re-learn patent law. They simply cannot keep current with developments in the law.").

[33] 28 U.S.C. § 1498.

[34] 19 U.S.C. § 1337.

[35] *Motorola, Inc. v. United States*, 729 F.2d 765 (Fed. Cir. 1984); *Trojan, Inc. v. Shat-R-Shield, Inc.*, 885 F.2d 854 (Fed. Cir. 1989).

[36] 19 U.S.C. § 1337(a).

II. The Courts of Appeal

The 94 federal judicial districts are organized into 12 regional circuits, each of which has its own court of appeals. With the Federal Courts Improvement Act ("FCIA") of 1982,[37] the U.S. Congress created the Court of Appeals for the Federal Circuit and vested it with exclusive jurisdiction over patent cases. One of its objectives in doing so was to promote uniformity in the area of patent law and diminish the uncertainty created by inconsistent application of the patent law among the regional circuits.[38] The jurisdictional statute, 28 U.S.C. § 1295(a), grants the Federal Circuit exclusive jurisdiction of appeals from final decisions of the district courts in actions where the district court's jurisdiction "was based, in whole or in part, on section 1338 of this title," that is, civil actions arising under the patent law.

The Federal Circuit has inherent authority to determine whether its exercise of jurisdiction in a given case is within the mandate of § 1295(a). The variety of circumstances in which cases have been brought before the Court have raised difficult issues pertaining to the Court's jurisdiction. According to the Court, the inquiry must be addressed on a case-by-case basis by considering whether the plaintiff has asserted "at least some right or privilege that would be defeated by one or sustained by an opposite construction of [the patent] laws."[39] Results in this area have been less than predictable.[40]

The Federal Circuit also hears appeals of patent matters from the PTO, the Court of Federal Claims, and the International Trade Commission, as well as appeals of a variety of non-patent matters. The sixteen appellate judges who sit on the Federal Circuit come from diverse educational and professional backgrounds. Fewer than half have a technical background, but this does not seem to have hindered the Court's ability to grasp technical facts and concepts and in enough depth to apply the governing law in a fair and relatively uniform manner.

---

[37] Federal Courts Improvement Act of 1982, Pub.L. 97-164, 96 Stat 25.

[38] H.R. Rep. 97-312, 97th Cong., 1st Sess. 23 ("[T]he central purpose [of the FCIA] is to reduce the widespread lack of uniformity and uncertainty of legal doctrine that exists in the administration of patent law.").

[39] *Dubost v. United States PTO*, 777 F.2d 1561, 1564 (Fed. Cir. 1985).

[40] Examples of Federal Circuit decisional law regarding the scope of its jurisdiction and the contexts in which such issues arise appear in *Atari, Inc. v. JS&A Group, Inc.*, 747 F.2d 1422 (Fed. Cir. 1984) (jurisdiction exists over appeal from grant of preliminary injunction on copyright count where case also included patent count, even though district court separated patent count for trial); *Schwartzkopf Dev. Corp. v. Ti-Coating, Inc.*, 800 F.2d 240 (Fed. Cir. 1986) (no jurisdiction over remaining state law claim for royalties due under license agreement after counterclaim for declaratory judgment of invalidity and non-infringement dismissed by the counterclaimant); and *Yarway Corp. v. Eur-Control USA, Inc.*, 775 F.2d 268 (Fed. Cir. 1985) (Federal Circuit had jurisdiction over patent licensee's action against patent owner for infringement of licensed patent even though the patent infringement dispute arises between contracting parties).

A party may petition the U.S. Supreme Court to accept an appeal from an adverse decision of the Federal Circuit. The Supreme Court has discretionary control over its docket, and declines to hear the vast majority of cases it is asked to decide. With the authority of its decisions second only to those of the Supreme Court, the Federal Circuit is effectively the court of last resort for most patent litigants.

III. The Use of Juries

The U.S. is unique in using juries to decide commercial civil trials, including patent disputes. The right to a trial by jury is enshrined in the Seventh Amendment to the U.S. Constitution and has been exercised readily by patent litigants. The incidence of jury demands in patent cases has grown from about 3% in the late 1960's to more than 50% in recent years.[41] A civil jury is typically comprised of 6 to 12 persons. The role of the jury is to listen to the evidence presented at trial to determine the true facts, and to determine disputed issues by applying the patent law to those facts. About 66% of patent trials completed year 2001 were tried to a jury.[42] When the evidence presents underlying disputed fact issues, the jury plays a crucial role in determining patent validity, infringement, and damages.

Many have bemoaned the increased resort to juries in patent cases. Opponents of patent jury trials argue that people of only average education, and infrequent technical education, cannot rationally and fairly resolve complex technology disputes involving highly specialized legal doctrines.[43] Others have seemingly unfettered trust in the ability of juries to reach predictably rational and reliable outcomes when properly aided by the Court and trial counsel. Many such jury proponents argue that juries are just as able as judges to decide patent cases, most of who lack technical training and have little experience with patent law.[44] The Federal Circuit has never recognized a "complexity exception" to the Seventh Amendment right to trial by

[41] Hon. P. R. Michel and M. Rhyu, "Improving Patent Jury Trials," 6 Fed.Cir. B.J. 2 (1997).

[42] Kimberly A. Moore, "Jury Demands: Who's Asking?," 17 Berkley Tech. L.J. 847 (Spring 2002).

[43] One line of argument for a "complexity exception" maintains that when it added the Seventh Amendment to the Constitution in 1791, Congress could not have intended juries to handle the complex patent cases that arise today. Others attack the use of "incompetent" juries in patent cases as denying the due process protection of the Fifth and Fourteenth Amendments. They argue that a jury "incapable" of understanding the evidence and governing legal rules provides no safeguard against an erroneous result. *See SRI Int'l v. Matsushita Elec. Corp. of Am.*, 775 F.2d 1107, 1128 (Fed. Cir. 1985) (*in banc*) (Markey, C. J. additional views).

[44] *See* Michel and Rhyu, *supra* note 41, at 3.

jury. For better or worse, juries will likely remain a central element of our system of resolving patent disputes for the foreseeable future.[45]

The proceedings in the U.S. Patent and Trademark Office ("PTO") are restricted to patent attorneys and agents licensed by the PTO. Patent infringement actions in the district courts, and appeals therefrom, may be brought by any attorney licensed by at least one state and admitted to practice in the applicable federal court. With a growing number of patent actions being filed, and the increased awareness of the importance of such cases to their clients, more and more practitioners are entering the arena of patent litigation. A majority of patent litigators have technical degrees and are also licensed to practice before the PTO. However, a growing number of "general" commercial litigators have entered the field of patent litigation, fueling substantial debate regarding the ideal attributes of a lawyer charged with the difficult task of presenting complex patent issues to non-technical, patent novice judges and jurors.[46]

C. Patent Infringement Litigation

Given the relative freedom afforded the parties to investigate and present their cases with relatively little court intervention, the enforcement of patents in the U.S. system is a highly strategic undertaking at all stages of the proceedings. The following discussion of specific procedural and substantive aspects of the enforcement of U.S. patent rights attempts to highlight important tactical and strategic considerations where possible.

---

[45] *See SRI Int'l v. Matsushita Elec. Corp. of Am.*, 775 F.2d at 1130 ("We discern no authority and no compelling need to apply in patent infringement suite for damages a 'complexity' exception denying litigants their constitutional right under the Seventh Amendment."). Two of the most noteworthy patent cases heard by the Supreme Court in recent years have impacted the role of the jury. In *Hilton Davis Chem. Co. v. Warner-Jenkinson Co., Inc.*, 62 F.3d 1512 (Fed. Cir. 1995) (*in banc*), the Federal Circuit held that infringement under the doctrine of equivalents is a question of fact for the jury unless the prior art or the prosecution history prevents the patent owner from asserting a range of equivalents that reaches the accused product or process. The Supreme Court affirmed. *Warner-Jenkinson Co., Inc. v. Hilton Davis Chem. Co.*, 520 U.S. 17, 117 S.Ct. 1040 (1997). Only a year earlier, the Supreme Court also affirmed the Federal Circuit's holding in *Markman v. Westview Instruments, Inc.*, 52 F.3d 967 (Fed. Cir. 1995) (*in banc*), aff'd, 116 S.Ct. 1384 (1996), that the Court, and not the jury, must resolve all issues regarding the interpretation of patent claims. The *Markman* decision has reduced the jury's role by: (1) removing an issue central to both infringement and validity from the jury; (2) permitting more cases to be decided by the Court without a trial when the facts regarding the accused product or process are not disputed; and (3) permitting the Court to facilitate settlement by advising the parties of the scope of the claims prior to trial.

[46] *See, e.g.*, Robert H. Resis, "Benefits of Using an Intellectual Property Firm for Intellectual Property Matters," The Law Works-Intellectual Property Today (August 1996) at 10.

I. Strategic Considerations

Patent licensing in the U.S. is big business. Patent license revenues have grown from about $3 billion in 1980 to roughly $130-140 billion in 2002.[47] Suits to enforce or defeat patents are invariably a component of larger business objectives, and the tactics employed must derive from the underlying business strategy. Patent litigation in the U.S. is a very costly process. Legal fees, expert witness fees, travel expense, photocopy expense, court reporter fees and other costs can mount quickly given the need for careful preparation and presentation of complex legal issues. The following table shows estimated costs through the end of discovery and trial, within ranges of average value at risk. [48]

Median Cost of Patent Litigation (2002)

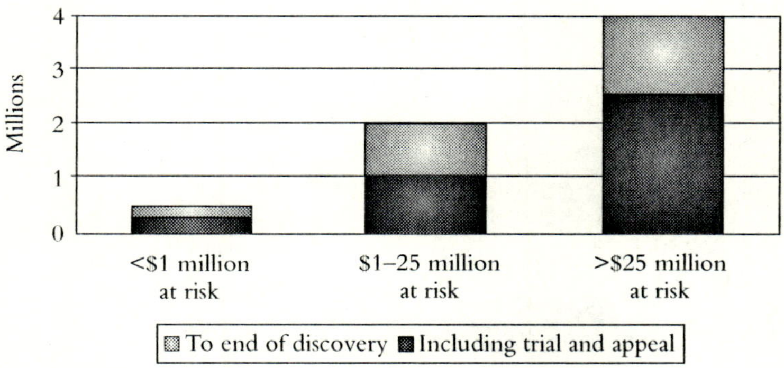

*Source: American Intellectual Property Law Association, *Report of Economic Survey* (2003)

These figures alone compel careful consideration of whether to file suit in the first place, and constant evaluation and reevaluation of discovery, pretrial and trial strategies to maximize the chances of both legal and economic victory.

Many other risk factors necessarily affect the patent owner's and accused infringer's patent strategy. The accused infringer faces not only the risk of being enjoined from continuing the accused commercial activities, but may also be required to pay compensatory damages, as well as enhanced damages and attorney fees, if found to infringe. The financial consequences of an adverse decision of infringement are thus potentially catastrophic. On the

---

[47] Harold Wegner and S. Maebius, "Patent Flooding America's New Patent Challenges," presented at FTC/DOJ Hearing (April 22, 2002).

[48] American Intellectual Property Association, "Report of Economic Survey" (2003).

other hand, a victory for the accused infringer can be a hollow one if it spends all of its profits from the accused activity defending its right to continue.

Because patent invalidity is an absolute defense to an infringement charge, the patent owner risks investing substantial litigation expense and effort only to emerge from trial with a valueless, invalid patent and no means of preventing competitors from practicing the once protected technology. One study reports that from 1983 to 1999 some 1,209 patents were litigated and 35% of those patents were found invalid.[49] This rate of patent invalidity is lower than it was before the Federal Circuit was created, yet remains a significant risk factor to the patent owner.

Each of these risks is magnified by the high degree of uncertainty inherent in the jury trial system. The parties are therefore often motivated to compromise their dispute by entering into a mutually acceptable license relationship. The following chart shows that only about 3% of patent cases terminated in the district courts in fiscal year 2002 reached trial.[50]

Patent Cases Completed in
U.S. District Courts (2002)

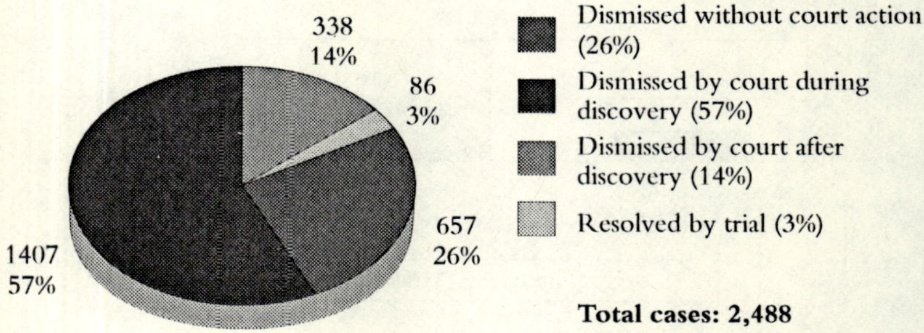

*Source: www.fticonsulting.com

When one considers the number of patent disputes that are resolved before litigation is even initiated, the relative number of controversies left to be determined by trial is indeed very small.

The majority of those cases terminated by court action prior to trial are decided by summary judgment rulings by the trial judge. When there is conflicting evidence regarding the central issues, or when the credibility of witnesses is at issue, the summary judgment procedure is unavailable. Patent cases often settle on the eve of trial; less frequently in the midst of trial. It seems that the uncertainty inherent in the jury system weighs most heavily

[49] *See* Kimberly A. Moore, "Judge, Juries & Patent Cases – An Empirical Peek Inside the Black Box," 99 Mich. L. Rev 365, 386 (2000).

[50] *See* www.fticonsulting.com (last visited Dec. 3, 2003).

on the parties at that juncture, and provides the additional motivation needed to achieve a compromise.

II. Commencement of the Action

A patent infringement action is commenced by filing a complaint in a U.S. district court, upon which the Court issues a summons.[51] The summons and complaint must be served on each adverse party within 120 days of filing in a manner sanctioned by the Federal Rules of Civil Procedure for providing proper notice of the suit to each of them.[52]

1. The Competent Court

A suit to enforce or attack a patent may be filed against a given defendant in any district court in which requirements of personal jurisdiction and venue are met. The rules governing venue in patent cases seek to prevent the defendant from having to litigate in an inconvenient forum. Generally, the proper venue for a patent infringement defendant is any district where the defendant resides or has committed acts of infringement and has an established place of business.[53] Venue is proper for non U.S. citizen defendants in any district court.[54]

The second requirement, that the Court have power to exercise personal jurisdiction over the defendant, depends on whether the defendant has established some minimum contact with the state in which the district court sits and, if so, whether the assertion of jurisdiction over the defendant is fair and reasonable in light of all of the circumstances.[55] All of the defendant's contacts with the forum state, such as offices, employees, bank accounts, product sales, advertising, telephone listings, etc., may be considered. A lesser showing of contacts is necessary if the contacts relate to the course of action (*e.g.*, sales of accused product). Even a non U.S. company with no operations in the U.S. may be subject to jurisdiction if it places an infringing product into distribution channels that it reasonably knows will lead to product sales in the U.S.[56]

If a defendant is sued in a district court where venue or personal jurisdiction requirements are not met, or if there is otherwise a more convenient

---

[51] Fed.R.Civ.P. 3 and 4.

[52] Fed.R.Civ.P. 4.

[53] 28 U.S.C. § 1391(c) and 1400(b).

[54] 28 U.S.C. § 1391(d).

[55] *Red Wing Shoe Co. v. Hockerson-Halberstadt, Inc.*, 148 F.3d 1355 (Fed. Cir. 1998).

[56] *Beverly Hills Fan Co. v. Royal Sovereign Corp.*, 21 F.3d 1558 (Fed. Cir. 1994) (holding district court in Virginia had personal jurisdiction over Chinese corporation who manufactured accused product in Taiwan and sold to New Jersey importer because it placed the products in a "stream of commerce" knowing the likely destination of some of the products in Virginia).

court to hear the case, the district court may transfer the case to the preferred court.[57] Such forum disputes are common in patent actions, and are normally driven by considerations of convenience of the parties and their counsel, how quickly a given court resolves its cases,[58] the attitudes of the judges in each district towards patents, and whether typical jurors in that geographic region are likely to be sympathetic towards either party.[59] The district courts have wide discretion to affect such transfers, and often consider most important the location of key witnesses, the interests in the respective states in the underlying dispute, and the presence of other lawsuits involving the same patent in one of the district courts being considered.

2. The Competent Parties

Article III of the U.S. Constitution limits the federal court jurisdiction to actual cases and controversies. This requirement mandates that the party bringing suit have standing to sue for the alleged injuries.

a) Plaintiffs in suits to enforce patents

The patent statute provides a "patentee" standing to sue for infringement, and defines "patentee" as the original patentee or successors in title to the patent.[60] Thus, an original patent owner clearly may bring suit, as may an assignee of all rights in a patent. An assignee must possess the assigned patent rights at the time that the suit is filed.[61] According to one court, permitting

[57] 28 U.S.C. §§ 1404 and 1406.

[58] As the following statistics from popular patent courts illustrates, some are much slower than others at resolving cases by trial.

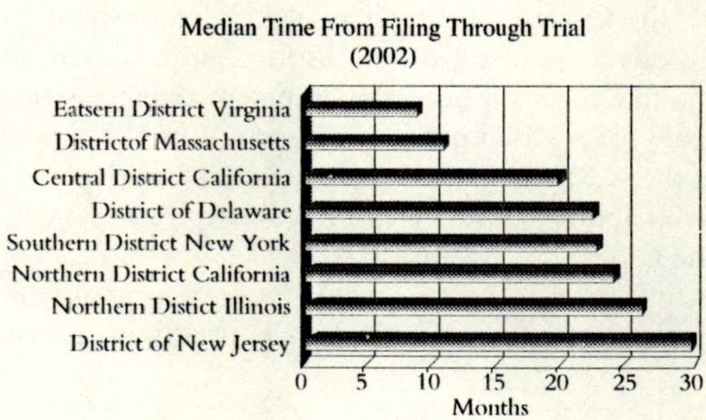

[59] For example, an owner of patented automotive technology may choose to sue a Japanese competitor in Detroit considering the large percentage of persons employed by the U.S. auto industry in that city.

[60] 35 U.S.C. §§ 281 and 100(d).

[61] *Mas-Hamilton Group v. LaGard, Inc.*, 156 F.3d 1206, 1210 (Fed. Cir. 1998). The Federal Circuit clarified in *Mas-Hamilton Group* that a party having standing to sue for infringement when suit was filed maintains standing even though the right to sue for past damages was separately assigned during the lawsuit. The plaintiff's right to seek injunctive relief and future damages at the time of filing suit was sufficient to confer standing.

non-owners the right to sue so long as they subsequently obtain patent ownership would enmesh the courts in abstract disputes, risk multiple litigations, and provide incentives for litigants to expand the scope of pending litigation by acquiring rights in additional patents.[62]

The analysis of standing issues is closely related and often addressed to the rules for joining parties under Rule 19 of the Federal Rules of Civil Procedure. Under Rule 19, a case may not go forward in the absence of a party that is both "necessary" and "indispensable." It is this potential for dismissal that usually motivates parties to bring Rule 19 issues to the Court. A person is necessary if it satisfies the factors of Rule 19(a), which considers: (1) whether the existing parties can resolve their dispute in the person's absence and (2) how the absent person's interests may be affected by the litigation or create inconsistent obligations on the parties. A necessary person should be joined if subject to the Court's jurisdiction. If a necessary party is outside the Court's jurisdictional reach or refuses to be made a party, the Court must dismiss the case if, based on additional factors of Rule 19(b), the case cannot go forward "in equity and good conscience" in the person's absence.

While it is clear that an assignor of all rights in a patent is not required to be joined under Rule 19,[63] more difficult questions arise when less than all of the patent rights are conveyed. Where a patent is co-owned by multiple persons, all must jointly bring suit.[64] Corporations must therefore make certain that each of joint inventors execute an assignment document to avoid subsequent difficulties in bringing an infringement action. A transfer of less than the entire patent, an undivided share of the patent, or all rights in the patent in a geographical region of the U.S. is ordinarily deemed a license, and conveys no right to sue.

A licensee may sue in its own name for patent infringement only if it owns "all substantial rights" under the patent, such that the license operates as a "virtual" assignment. In certain circumstances, a licensee with less than all substantial rights may have standing to sue as a co-plaintiff.[65] The Courts do not consider the use of the word "exclusive" determinative; but rather look to the substance of the agreement to decipher the intent of the parties. To qualify as an exclusive license, an agreement must clearly manifest the patentee's promise not to grant anyone else a license in the area of exclusivity.[66] License provisions expressly granting the licensee a right to sublicense without the licensor's approval, to exclude others from using the technology, to file suit for infringement and to defend the licensor's interest in such a suit

---

[62] *Procter & Gamble Co. v. Paragon Trade Brands, Inc.*, 917 F.Supp. 305, 310 (D.Del. 1995).

[63] *OrthoPharm. Cor. v. Genetics, Inst., Inc.*, 52 F.3d 1026 (Fed. Cir. 1995).

[64] *Willingham v. Lawton*, 555 F.2d 1340, 1343 (6th Cir. 1977).

[65] *Enzo APA & Sons, Inc. v. Geapag A. G.*, 134 F.3d 1090, 1093 (Fed. Cir. 1998); *Textile Prods., Inc. v. Mead Corp.*, 134 F.3d 1481, 1484 (Fed. Cir. 1998).

[66] *Textile Prods., Inc. v. Mead Corp.*, 134 F.3d at 1635–36.

may qualify a license as exclusive. However, a right to sue provision by itself cannot confer standing to an ordinary licensee.[67]

Despite rather clear guidance from the Federal Circuit regarding principles of standing in patent enforcement actions, disputes in this area arise quite frequently. The varied contexts of reported cases regarding standing to sue emphasize the importance of assignments, licenses and other commercial documents that clearly delineate the parties' rights and obligations with respect to litigation against infringers. For example, in *Rite-Hite Corp. v. Kelly Co., Inc.*,[68] independent sales organizations lacked standing to sue for patent infringement of a patented loading dock restraint device because their contracts with the patentee provided only the right to sell the patented restraints in their respective sales territories but no right to exclude others from making, using or selling the invention. As a result, the Federal Circuit vacated the district court's award of damages to the ISO's and dismissed them from the lawsuit.[69] In *OrthoPharmaceutical*,[70] Ortho sought to intervene as a licensee in a patent suit brought by the patent owner, Amgen, against Genetics and Chagai. The license agreement gave Ortho the right to bring suit only if Amgen failed to do so and allowed the party bearing the litigation expense to retain any amount recovered. Other provisions required that Amgen and Ortho consult and sue together if either "finds it necessary to join," and required them to cooperate.[71] Because the license grant itself was nonexclusive, and permitted Amgen to license others, the right to sue provisions did not give Ortho standing to share in the damage award or file a second infringement suit against Genetics.[72]

b) Defendants in suits to enforce patents

Section 271(a) of the Patent Code provides a remedy against those who make, use, sell, offer for sale, or import a patented invention. These are each acts of direct infringement. Those who actively induce infringement by knowingly and actively aiding another's direct infringement can also be held liable.[73] Finally a remedy may also be had against one who contributes to infringement by selling a material part of the invention that he knew was specially adapted to infringe the patent and is not a staple item of commerce suitable for non-infringing use. In order to prove inducement or contributory infringement, a patentee must prove at least one direct infringement.[74] It is

---

[67] *Textile Prods., Inc. v. Mead Corp.*, 134 F.3d at 1636.

[68] *Rite-Hite Corp. v. Kelley Co.*, 56 F.3d 1538 (Fed. Cir. 1995).

[69] *Id.* at 1553–1554.

[70] *OrthoPharm. Cor. v. Genetics, Inst., Inc.*, 52 F.3d at 1026.

[71] *Id.*

[72] *Id.*

[73] 35 U.S.C. § 271(b).

[74] *Aro Manufacturing Co., Inc. v. Convertible Top Replacement Co., Inc.*, 365 U.S. 336 (1961).

not necessary that the direct infringer be named as a party, although doing so often simplifies the task of obtaining evidence sufficient to prove direct infringement.

Section 271(f) creates a cause of action against those who supply components of a patented product in the U.S. intending that the components be assembled into an infringing product abroad. Section 271(g) permits a patentee to sue one who imports, offers to sell or uses in the U.S. a product made abroad by a patented method. Thus, one seeking to enforce U.S. patent rights is afforded substantial flexibility in choosing one's adversaries.

There are often several different entities in the chain of distribution between the manufacture and ultimate sale and use of a competitor's product. The choice of who among them to sue will normally involve consideration of the financial resources of each entity, the commercial realities affecting their interests in defending the suit, each potential party's access to sources of evidence, the basis for assessing damages, and where suit may be brought against each potential party. The manufacturer of an accused product often has the greatest commercial interest in the dispute, control over the most relevant evidence of infringement, and the strongest financial resources to satisfy a settlement or damage award. Numerous courts have therefore recognized a strong public policy favoring patent suits between competing manufacturers.[75] Those who purchase a patented product from the patent owner or a licensee receive an automatic implied license to use and resell the product.[76] Therefore, licensing a competitor to make and sell an otherwise infringing product will also effect a license to the competitor's customers unless such rights are expressly reserved in the license agreement. The lawful owner of a licensed device may also repair it or replace worn parts so long as this does not amount to recreating the patented device.[77]

Notwithstanding the manufacturer's strong interests, suits brought directly against end users of patented technology are a growing trend in the U.S. Such cases often involve relatively inexpensive patented technologies that offer significant efficiencies and cost savings to large enterprises. The potential damages calculated as a percentage of the cost savings achieved by the end user enterprise may far exceed the available damages based on the sales of the vendor who supplied the technology. Also, the small technology vendor may have less ability to pay for a license or awarded damages as compared to its much larger customers. Other considerations, such as the effect

---

[75] *See, e.g., Katz v. Lear Siegler, Inc.*, 909 F.2d 1459, 1464 (Fed. Cir. 1990) ("[T]he manufacturer is the true defendant in the customer suit . . . It is a simple fact of life that a manufacturer must protect its customers, either as a matter of contract, or good business, or in order to avoid the damaging impact of an adverse ruling against its products.").

[76] *Bandag, Inc. v. Al Bolser's Tire Stores, Inc.*, 750 F.2d 903 (Fed. Cir. 1984).

[77] *Aro Mfg. Co. v. Convertible Top Replacement Co.*, 365 U.S. at 336.

of suing customers on the vendor's motivation to settle, may also come into play.[78]

The determination of who the proper defendants are in an infringement action most always involves an analysis of the infringement claim. Consider a patent covering a system that is implemented as an assemblage of components supplied by multiple vendors. Prior to filing suit, the patent owner must carefully consider how each component of the infringing system relates to the patent claims, and which vendors are really responsible for the infringement. It may be necessary to sue multiple vendors and the company using the assembled system in such a circumstance.

Similar complications arise in cases involving products that are customizable by the end user, or products capable of both infringing and non-infringing modes of operation. Consider, for example, a patent covering a method that is practiced only if a machine is set to a particular mode of operation. The statutory cause of action against the machine manufacturer is for indirect infringement, which requires proof of direct infringement by customers.[79] The maker of the machine may deny having knowledge of how each customer uses the machine.

The question of whether the patentee or the vendor should be held accountable for this potential gap in the evidence involves competing practical and policy considerations. The patent owner bears the ultimate burden of proof on the issues of infringement and damages. But requiring the patentee to prove infringement on a customer by customer basis, and limiting its recovery to damages based on sales made to infringing customers, invites large scale litigation involving potentially hundreds of defendants. On the other hand, permitting the patentee to make some lesser showing may work injustice if the infringing mode of operating the machine is seldom used. The Federal Circuit recently provided some guidance on this issue by holding that the mere sale of a device capable of "substantial noninfringing uses" does not constitute indirect infringement.[80] The patentee must therefore prove that the device necessarily infringes when used by customers (*i.e.*, absence of substantial noninfringing uses) in order to cast its claims broadly against the vendor. If the device permits substantial noninfringing uses, the patentee

---

[78] This strategy carries a risk of backfiring, as where the strain created on the manufacturer's customer relations strengthens its resolve to defeat the patent in court. Moreover, the Federal Circuit recently held in *Zenith Electronics Corp. v. Exzec, Inc.*, 182 F.3d 1340, 1353–54 (Fed. Cir. 1999) that infringement allegations directed to customers in bad faith may support a tort claim against the patentee for unfair competition. The statements in *Zenith* were made outside of litigation in various letters and included allegations that the manufacturer could not design around the patent. It is presently unclear what other types of threats will satisfy this bad faith standard, but it does not appear that *Zenith* has had a chilling effect on customer suits.

[79] *Jansen v. Rexall Sundown, Inc.*, 342 F.3d 1329, 1334 (Fed. Cir. 2003).

[80] *Dynacore Holdings Corp. v. U.S. Phillips Corp.*, No. 03-1305 (Fed. Cir. March 31, 2004).

should, at a minimum, present evidence that the vendor instructs and encourages customers to use the infringing mode of operation. Otherwise, the patentee must point to specific instances of direct infringement by individual customers and restrict its suit to liability stemming from those specific instances.[81]

When suspected patent infringement activities occur across an entire industry, the patentee may proceed simultaneously in one or multiple suits against all competitors, or in some logical sequence. Often the first suit is brought against one competitor, in the hope that a ruling of infringement and validity will persuade others to accept a license. Although every defendant is entitled to its own day in court,[82] the Federal Circuit's holding in *Markman* that claim interpretation is an issue of law to be decided by the Court, and not the jury, left it unclear whether a subsequent defendant may re-litigate claim interpretation issues decided in a previous action to which it was not a party. A previous claim construction by a district court is normally binding on the patentee if the determination of claim scope was essential to a final judgment on the question of validity or infringement.[83] A prior interpretation by a district court is not binding on a later defendant who did not have a full and fair opportunity to litigate the issue in the first action.[84] The Federal Circuit recently declined an opportunity to clarify whether an accused infringer is bound by a prior Federal Circuit decision construing a patent's claims in a suit against a different infringer.[85] In the author's view, a final claim construction by the Federal Circuit should govern the same issues raised in subsequent actions unless the later defendant comes forward with new evidence or arguments not addressed in the earlier proceeding that clearly dictate a different construction.

A troubling development for potential infringers is the growing number of patent suits naming multiple competitors as defendants in the same action. The patentee's interest in doing so is to avoid the added expense and potential for inconsistent outcomes associated with piecemeal litigation. The competitor-defendants' interests in avoiding common discovery and trial proceedings involving commercially sensitive technical and financial information is also compelling, particularly the risk that the jury may confuse the features of the different accused products or methods or attribute the actions of one defendant to other defendants. There is also a public interest in not directing the resources of multiple federal judges toward the same patent.

Disputes in this area are governed by Rule 20(a) of the Federal Rules of Civil Procedure, which permits claims against unrelated defendants to be

---

81 *Id.* at pp. 17–21.

82 *Blonder-Tongue Labs Inc. v. University of Illinois Foundation et al.*, 420 U.S. 313 (1971).

83 *In re Freeman*, 30 F.3d 1459, 1466 (Fed. Cir. 1994).

84 *Id.* at 1465.

85 *Tate Access Floors, Inc. v. Interface Architectural Resources, Inc.*, 279 F.3d 1357, 1371 n.3 (Fed. Cir. 2002).

joined only if they arise "out of the same transaction, occurrence, or series of transactions or occurrences" and involve a common question of law or fact. Several district court decisions reject joinder of unrelated competitor-defendants on the theory that the alleged infringements are different transactions or occurrences.[86] With the *Markman* decision emphasizing the need for uniformity in determining the scope and meaning of U.S. patent claims, district courts recently appear more inclined to conduct a common claim construction hearing governing several individual competitor specific actions, while conducting separate discovery and trial proceedings for each defendant.[87] This approach offers benefits of efficiency without prejudicing each defendant's right to defend itself in a separate proceeding.

c) Declaratory judgment plaintiffs

One sufficiently threatened with an infringement suit may file an action in a district court seeking to have the patent declared invalid or not infringed. The Court's jurisdiction over such actions derives from the Federal Declaratory Judgments Act of 1934.[88] The Federal Circuit recognized the importance of the availability of this additional mechanism for resolving patent disputes as follows:

> "Guerilla-like, the patent owner attempts extra-judicial patent enforcement with scare-the-customer-and-run tactics that infect the competitive environment of the business community with uncertainty and insecurity. Before the [Declaratory Judgment] Act, competitors victimized by that tactic were rendered helpless and immobile so long as the patent owner refused to grasp the nettle and sue. After the Act, those competitors were no longer restricted to *in terrorem* choice between the incurrence of a growing potential liability for patent infringement and abandonment of their enterprises; they could clear the air by suing for a judgment that would settle the conflict of interests."[89]

---

[86] *New Jersey Mach., Inc. v. Alford Indus., Inc.*, 21 USPQ2d 2033, 2035 (D.N.J. 1991), aff'd 983 F.2d 1087 (Fed. Cir. 1992) ("[C]laims of infringement against unrelated defendants, involving different machines, should be tried separately against each defendant."); *Paine Weber Jackson & Curtis, Inc. v. Merrill Lynch Pierce Fenner & Smith, Inc.*, 564 F.Supp. 1358, 1371 (D.Del. 1983) ("[A]llegations of infringement against two unrelated parties based on different acts do not arise from the same transaction.").

[87] The notion that the interpretation of patent claims is necessarily an issue common to all cases involving the same patent may be an overstatement. A Court's duty to interpret claims extends only to the claim terms disputed by the parties in the context of their specific infringement dispute. *See Fromson v. Anitec Printing, Inc.*, 132 F.3d 1437, 1442 (Fed. Cir. 1997) ("The analysis of infringement is a two-step progression. In the first step, the Court construes the claim; that is, the Court explains and defines any *disputed* technical terms and sets the scope and boundaries of the claim.") (*emphasis supplied).* Therefore, issues of claim construction would only be common when each defendant's non-infringement position focuses on the same claim limitations.

[88] 28 U.S.C. § 2201.

[89] *Arrowhead Indus. Water, Inc. v. Ecolochem, Inc.*, 846 F.2d 731, 735 (Fed. Cir. 1988).

There are two important limitations on a threatened infringer's ability to avail itself of this mechanism. First, a declaratory judgment action must be based on an "actual controversy" between the parties. The party filing suit must show (1) that it has or is prepared to produce the accused product or use the accused method, and (2) that the patentee's conduct created an objectively reasonable apprehension that the accused infringer would eventually be sued if it continued its activity.[90] An express charge of infringement easily satisfies the "actual controversy" requirement. Accordingly, the patentee should consider omitting such charges when notifying others of patent rights, and focus instead on a desire to discuss a potential license.

However, in light of subtleties of lawyer language, statements falling short of an express infringement charge can give rise to declaratory judgment jurisdiction if the totality of circumstances create a reasonable apprehension of suit.[91] Such circumstances may include, for example, the existence of other litigation involving the patent, statements made to other parties, the status of license negotiations, and the prospect for reaching settlement. Consistent with the purposes of the Declaratory Judgment Act, a manufacturer not directly charged by the patentee may, in some circumstances, bring such a suit based on threats made against its customers. This pragmatic, case-by-case test prevents parties from couching their communications in terms designed to create or defeat declaratory judgment jurisdiction but, by providing less than clear guidelines, adds an additional aspect of uncertainty and risk to legitimate attempts at resolving patent disputes without litigation.

The availability of declaratory judgment relief is also limited by the district court's discretion to decline such cases even when an actual controversy exists.[92] A court may not decline to accept a declaratory judgment action on a whim, and must have a sound reason for doing so.[93] Often such reasoning lies in the existence of other litigation involving the patent. When the other litigation involves the same parties, as when the patentee files an infringement action against the declaratory judgment plaintiff in a different district court, the first filed suit normally takes precedence.[94] The Federal Circuit has recognized an exception to the "first filed rule" which favors a later-filed declaratory judgment suit filed by a manufacturer over an earlier suit by the patentee against the manufacturer's customer.[95] However, in practice, neither the rule nor the exception has been applied rigidly, and outcomes often seem to depend on the deciding judge's interest in handling the underlying patent dispute.

---

[90] *Id.* at 735–36.

[91] *EMC Corp. v. Norrand Corp.*, 89 F.3d 807 (Fed. Cir. 1996).

[92] 28 U.S.C. § 2201states that the Court "may" declare the parties' rights in an actual controversy, which has been interpreted as meaning that the Court may decline to do so. *See also Genentech Inc. v. Eli Lilly & Co.*, 998 F.2d 931 (Fed. Cir. 1993).

[93] *Id.* at 936.

[94] *Id.* at 938.

[95] *Kahn v. General Motors Corp.*, 889 F.2d 1078, 1081–83 (Fed. Cir. 1989).

3. The Pleadings

The parties to a patent action must conform to the procedural pleading requirements of the Federal Rules of Civil Procedure.[96] The principal purpose of these rules is to limit the number of pleadings, to encourage simple and concise allegations, to avoid raising technical barriers to resolving controversies, and to assure that counsel certifies that he or she has good grounds for the allegations made.[97] The pleading rules are construed liberally, and courts freely grant litigants opportunities to correct their errors before dismissing a claim or defense on pleading grounds. A detailed discussion of these procedural requirements is therefore not contemplated here.

a) The complaint

The action is commenced by filing a complaint which must identify the parties, the basis of the Court's jurisdiction, and a "short and plain statement showing that the pleader is entitled to relief."[98] In a patent infringement complaint, the statement will normally allege that the plaintiff owns or otherwise has rights to enforce the patent, that the defendant is infringing the patent by making, using, selling or offering for sale products embodying the patented invention, and that the infringement has damaged plaintiff. The plaintiff may request preliminary and/or final injunctive relief and an accounting for damages. The plaintiff need not specify the amount of damages requested. In a declaratory judgment action, the short and plain statement should include allegations that the patent is invalid, unenforceable and/or not infringed, together with a fairly detailed recitation of the facts and circumstances which gave rise to the accused infringer's reasonable apprehension of suit. The complaint in either type of action should also include a demand for jury trial if a jury is desired.

b) The response to the complaint

The defendant may respond to the patent complaint by filing an answer or by bringing motions challenging the complaint on various procedural grounds.[99] An answer must admit or deny each of the plaintiff's allegations, and raise any "affirmative defenses." Affirmative defenses are matters outside the plaintiff's main case which are in the nature of avoidance, such as invalidity of any patent claim in suit, unenforceability of the patent, laches, and implied license.[100] The defendant may also bring counterclaims for relief against the plaintiff.[101] An accused infringer will normally bring a counter-

---

[96] Fed.R.Civ.P. 7 through 16.

[97] Fed.R.Civ.P. 8 and 11.

[98] Fed.R.Civ.P. 8(a).

[99] Fed.R.Civ.P. 12.

[100] Fed.R.Civ.P. 8(c).

[101] Fed.R.Civ.P. 13.

claim seeking to have the patent declared invalid or not infringed. In a declaratory judgment action, the defendant-patentee is usually seeking a counterclaim for patent infringement.

The most common motions filed in lieu of an answer in patent cases are those challenging the Court's jurisdiction over the defendant, requesting transfer to a more convenient district court, or those alleging that an indispensable party with an interest in the dispute has not been joined.[102] Such motions rarely resolve cases, but may result in tactical advantages such as adding a party with greater access to evidence of the prior art, or avoiding a "rocket docket" court where fast disposal rates provide less time for an accused infringer to investigate the prior art or to develop design changes which would avoid the likely scope of an injunction.

III. The Phase of Discovery

A central feature of the U.S. system of civil justice is its reliance on the parties to prepare their own cases for trial. Each party is to obtain information supporting its case informally, such as by interviewing its own employees or researching public information. Discovery is governed by Fed.R.Civ.P. 26-37 and 45, which provide a formal means for obtaining potential evidence from less accessible sources, converting informally acquired information into admissible evidence, exploring aspects of the opponent's case, and identifying uncontested facts and issues. The rules relating to discovery encourage full disclosure by the parties to avoid potentially unfair surprises at trial.[103]

1. Matters Discoverable

Extensive and invasive discovery is a hallmark of U.S. patent litigation. The scope of permissible discovery is extremely broad. Rule 26(b)(1) allows a party to seek from its opponent or a non-party any information that is not protected by a recognized privilege and is either relevant to an issue in the case or appears "reasonably calculated" to lead to admissible relevant evidence.[104] The Court resolves disputes regarding requested discovery by considering the relevance of the information, whether any privilege is involved, the requesting party's need, and the burden on the objecting party.

It is not possible here to discuss all of the categories of persons and information which may become subject to discovery procedures in patent actions. However, certain discovery can almost be considered routine in patent cases. The patentee will seek evidence regarding the accused product

---

[102] Fed.R.Civ.P. 12(b).

[103] *United States v. Procter & Gamble Co.*, 356 U.S. 677, 683 (1958).

[104] Thus, for example, a memorandum that is inadmissible at trial because of the hearsay rule against out of court statements, may nonetheless be discoverable given its potential to identify witnesses who can testify directly regarding its contents.

or process, the profitability of the infringing activities, the accused infringer's awareness of and intent with regard to the patent, and the accused infringer's defenses. Persons requested to provide such information may include management, engineering and accounting personnel of the accused company, customers and suppliers, former employees, and even competitors. The accused infringer requires evidence regarding the development of the invention and prosecution of the patent application, details of the patented product or process, prior art to the asserted patent and the patentee's awareness of uncited prior art, and the profitability of the patented product or process. Obtaining such information may involve the inventors, the patentee's own engineering, marketing and financial personnel, the patent attorney involved in prosecution, and other companies with prior related technology. Obtaining discovery from a nonparty requires counsel to issue a subpoena which the district court may quash or modify if the subpoena is overbroad or otherwise unreasonable.[105]

Confidential information is commonly subject to a protective order of the Court limiting access to such information. Protective orders often restrict the circulation of trade secret and financial information to the parties' outside counsel, while permitting less sensitive confidential information to be provided to employees of the parties who are assisting trial counsel. Voluntary compliance with the ordered procedures by the parties and their counsel is crucial to the integrity of the process because violations are difficult to prove yet can cause substantial competitive harm.

2. Privileges and Immunities

The two principal limitations on discovery of relevant information in patent actions are the attorney-client privilege and the work product immunity doctrine. The former protects confidential communications between lawyer and client for the purpose of securing legal advice. The latter protects documents prepared by or for counsel in connection with litigation, and counsel's mental impressions.

Perhaps the two most fruitful areas of disputes regarding these discovery limitations in patent cases regard information communicated to or prepared by patent attorneys and information regarding opinions of counsel obtained by the accused infringer. Work product protection is ordinarily not extended to documents prepared by a patent attorney in prosecuting the patent-in-suit. Thus, for example, technical drawings provided to the attorney, results of prior art searches, and drafts of patent applications are not immune from discovery. However, communications between inventors and their patent attorneys regarding legal advice may be subject to the attorney-client privilege.[106]

---

[105] Fed.R.Civ.P. 45.

[106] An earlier line of cases considered the patent attorney a mere conduit of technical information between the applicant and the PTO, and refused to recognize a privilege. More recent cases have rejected this rationale while recognizing the legal nature of the

A finding that an infringement was willful can support a punitive award of multiplication of damages and attorneys fees. These sanctions for the willful infringement of a patent are important deterrents to those willing to disregard a patent owner's legal rights. When an accused infringer offers evidence that it relied in good faith on the advice of counsel that it could legally continue the accused activity, the advice becomes relevant. Under principles of fairness, the Courts have held that relying on evidence of advice of counsel waives the attorney-client privilege as to the subject matter of the advice. Otherwise, a party would rely on favorable documents in its defense while shielding potentially damaging documents behind the privilege.[107]

This puts the alleged infringer in the dilemma of choosing between waiving the privilege or being precluded from using important evidence in its defense. The scope of waiver is unpredictable and depends entirely on district courts' discretion. In some cases, the waiver is narrowly construed, and in others, the waiver is broadly applied to include attorney-client communications and trial counsel work product that, at best, may be tangentially related to the opinions.[108] As a result, clients may be reluctant to openly discuss legally sensitive concerns knowing that their opponents are effectively "listening in" on their discussions with counsel.

When legal advice is sought, records must be appropriately sanitized of any potentially controversial issues. If such precautions are not taken, a defendant may find that records of objective consideration and debate of the issues addressed in counsel's opinion may later be manufactured into alleged admissions in litigation.

The Federal Circuit's early decisions further impose an adverse inference that the defendant received no opinion or received a negative opinion if it does not waive privilege by producing the opinion for use at trial.[109] This adverse inference rule has been criticized as discouraging open, frank and objective discussions between counsel and client, contrary to the public interest.[110] The rule may also unfairly shift the focus away from other factors relevant to the defendant's good faith, such as the existence of substantial

---

dialogue that occurs in preparing a patent application. *In re Spalding Sports Worldwide Inc.*, 203 F.3d 800 (Fed. Cir. 2000); *see also Advanced Cardiovascular Systems Inc. v. C. R. Baird Inc.*, 25 U.S.P.Q.2d 1354 (N.D.Cal. 1992).

[107] *Frazier Indus. Co., Inc. v. Advance Storage Prods.*, 33 U.S.P.Q.2d 1702 (C.D.Cal. 1994).

[108] *Novartis Pharmaceuticals Corp. v. Eon Labs Mfg., Inc.*, 206 F.R.D. 396, 398 (D. Del. 2002) (broad waiver); *Thorn EMI North America, Inc. v. Micron Technology, Inc.*, 837 F.Supp. 616, 621 (D. Del. 1993) (narrow waiver); *See also Steelcase, Inc. v. Haworth, Inc.*, 954 F.Supp. 1195, 1199–2000 (W.D. Mich. 1997) (narrow waiver).

[109] *Underwater Devices Inc. v. Morrison-Knudsen Co.*, 717 F.2d 1380 (Fed. Cir. 1983); *Fromson v. Western Litho Plate & Supply Co.*, 853 F.2d 1568 (Fed. Cir. 1988).

[110] *Lucent Information Management, Inc. v. Lucent Technologies, Inc.*, 186 F.3d 311, 318 (3rd Cir. 1999); *Parker v. Prudential Ins. Co. of America*, 900 F.2d 772, 775 (4th Cir. 1990) (both refusing to apply an adverse inference due to the assertion of privilege).

liability defenses developed during litigation. The Federal Circuit recently invited comment from bar and industry associations in connection with a pending appeal in which the defendant seeks to have the adverse inference rule abolished.[111] The Court's decision could significantly impact one of the most problematic aspects of defending against patent infringement suits under the current state of the law.

3. Discovery Methods

The five discovery procedures employed in patent actions are requests for production, interrogatories, requests to admit, depositions, and facility inspections. Production requests are used to obtain tangible evidence such as documents, drawings, photographs, product samples and digitally stored data. A party may also request to inspect and test the accused or patented products or processes. Technical experts frequently make such inspections to form a basis for the opinions to be presented at trial. Interrogatories are written questions posed to the opposing party that must be answered in writing under oath. The written answers may be used as evidence at trial. Perhaps the most effective interrogatories in preparing a patent case are those which seek identification of potential witnesses, and those which seek to elicit the opponent's contentions regarding the case.[112]

Requests to admit seek written admissions of uncontested matters. Although used somewhat sparingly in patent cases, requests to admit can be effective tools for resolving issues, such as the genuineness of important documents, before trial.

The deposition process permits counsel to obtain sworn testimony from witnesses before trial. Depositions assist counsel in preparing the case by exploring an opponents case, identifying additional documents and witnesses, or obtaining admissions from an important witness. Deposition testimony may be admissible at trial if the witness is unavailable to testify in person. It may also be used to contradict the testimony of a deponent who later testifies at trial. The deposition of a party may be used at trial for any purpose.[113] The deposition is also an important opportunity for each party to assess the strength of their opponent's case, the credibility and demeanor of key witnesses, and to showcase the strengths of their own positions. Because depositions offer both sides a preview of trial, they can be very effective in facilitating settlements.

---

[111] *Knorr-Bremse Systeme Fuer Natzfahrzeuge GMBH v. Dana Corp.*, 344 F.3d 1336 (2003).

[112] For example, properly drafted interrogatories will enable the patentee to learn precisely how the alleged infringer is interpreting disputed terms in the patent claims.

[113] Often used in patent cases, Rule 30(b)(6) permits a corporation to be deposed through one or more designated representatives who speak on the corporation's behalf.

IV. Summary Judgments

Under Federal Rule of Civil Procedure 56, a court may dispose of an action without conducting a trial where the evidence presents no genuine disputed issues of fact. A party may seek summary judgment at any time, but such requests are usually made after the completion of discovery. Courts are frequently requested to resolve patent cases based on summary judgment motions filed by one or both parties. If complex factual issues exist, and expert testimony is required to explain the technology to the Court, such motions should be denied.[114] However, when the facts are not disputed, and an issue such as infringement depends only on the legal construction of the patent claims, summary judgment becomes an effective way to resolve cases quickly and efficiently.

Other issues which may be appropriately resolved by summary judgment in a given case include invalidity due to anticipation and non-infringement because of subject matter relinquished during prosecution (*i.e.*, prosecution history estoppel). Patents ordinarily will not be declared unenforceable for fraud on the PTO, because such an issue of inequitable conduct involves fact issues regarding the applicant's intent to deceive the PTO.

V. Claim Construction Proceedings

As mentioned above, the Federal Circuit's *Markman* decision resolved inconsistencies in prior precedent and held that the Court, and not the jury, has the power and obligation to construe the meaning and scope of patent claims as a matter of law.[115] Claim construction disputes lie at the center of almost every case; their resolution is often dispositive of key validity and infringement issues.

1. Rules for Interpreting Claims

The Court is to construe disputed claim terms to have the meaning that would be understood by one of ordinary skill at the time of the invention. The starting point is the claim language. In determining the ordinary meaning of claim terms, the Court may freely consult dictionaries, encyclopedias or treatises as evidence of the established meanings of claim terms.[116] The Court must also analyze the patent specification to make sure that its interpretation of the claims is consistent with the invention described in the specification. The Court must also determine whether the specification defined a claim term in a way that is different from its ordinary meaning or

---

[114] *Palumbo v. Don-Joy Co.*, 762 F.2d 969, 975 (Fed. Cir. 1985).

[115] *Markman v. Westview Instr., Inc.*, 52 F.3d at 967.

[116] *Texas Digital Sys., Inc. v. Telegenix, Inc.*, 308 F.3d 1193 (Fed. Cir. 2002).

clearly disavowed a particular claim scope. In looking to the specification to construe claims, however, the claims are not normally limited to the embodiment(s) shown in the specification.[117] Thus, the Court is required to walk a fine line between construing the claims consistent with the disclosed invention, without improperly limiting them to that disclosure. The Court also considers the prosecution history record, and looks for statements defining claim terms or unmistakably surrendering claim scope.

A Court has more limited discretion to consider evidence external to the patent and its prosecution history record. It may do so to educate itself about the invention and the relevant technology, but may not use such extrinsic evidence to arrive at a claim construction that contradicts the intrinsic evidence.[118]

2. Procedures for Interpreting Claims

The *Markman* decision did not require the district courts to follow any particular procedure for construing the claims. The Court will frequently conduct a separate evidentiary hearing, known as a "Markman hearing," prior to trial for this purpose. Such hearings may be particularly helpful to the judge when expert testimony is required to understand the relevant technology. The impact of Markman hearings on patent litigation has been substantial. Since Markman hearings began, the percentage of patent infringement cases decided on summary judgment has doubled from 12% to 24%.[119]

Of paramount importance in the claim construction process is the evidence to be presented and the timing of the hearing. Both matters are entirely in the judge's discretion. The hearing may occur at the start of the case, in the middle of discovery, just before trial, or even during trial. Construing the claims early in the litigation process enables the parties' expert witnesses to predicate their opinions on a correct interpretation of the claims and allows the parties to better focus their efforts on pretrial discovery and dispositive motions. An early ruling regarding claim construction may also facilitate settlement. When the case involves particularly complex technology, the Court's preference may be to defer issues of claim construction until the parties have completed sufficient discovery to present a full picture of the relevant technology and prior art.

---

[117] *Anchor Wall Sys., Inc. v. Rockwood Retaining Walls, Inc.*, 340 F.3d 1298 (Fed. Cir. 2003).

[118] *Vitronics Corp. v. Conceptronic, Inc.*, 90 F.3d 1576 (Fed. Cir. 1996).

[119] Robert Weiss, "Markman Practice, Procedure and Tactics," 619 PLI/Pat 117, 148 (September 2000).

VI. Trial

1. General Procedures

The trial of the rare patent action that is not settled or resolved by the Court involves the presentation of evidence, submission of the case to the trier of fact for decision, followed by the entry of judgment. The purpose of the trial is to decide facts based on the testimony of witnesses and examination of evidence, and to apply the governing legal standards to the facts. In a jury trial, factual issues are determined by the jury and legal issues are decided by the judge.[120] In a bench trial, the judge determines both fact and legal issues. The judge also serves the important role of presiding over the trial to assure that the process is fair to the litigants. In carrying out this obligation, the judge will resolve disputes regarding the conduct of the trial, rule on objections to the admissibility of evidence or improper questions asked of witnesses, instruct the jury as to the findings it must make, and control the conduct of the attorneys and witnesses.

Prior to trial, attorneys from both sides meet with the judge in a pretrial conference to determine the approach for the trial and scheduling issues. At this time the parties submit their motions *in limine* to the judge. Such motions request that certain evidence be excluded from the trial for reasons of irrelevance, prejudice or because it is legally inadmissible.

Jury selection is also conducted prior to a trial. The judge and the attorneys question potential jurors to determine if they are able to be fair and impartial; this process is called *voir dire*. The judge may excuse an individual from service in a particular case for various reasons. Each party may also use a limited number of "peremptory challenges" to excuse a potential juror for any reason except race or gender. The process of questioning and excusing jurors continues until 8 to 12 persons are accepted as jurors for the trial.

To the extent possible, the parties are also attempting during the jury selection process to learn the attitudes jurors have about patents, the parties involved in the dispute, and other factors that may affect their view of the dispute. For example, an authoritative juror tends to defend the actions of the PTO, whereas a cynical juror is more likely to see the PTO as a bureaucratic institution of questionable competence. The proficient lawyer will shape the case toward jury attitudes throughout the trial. Jurors often favor inventors that they believe invent for the good of society. However, they are less likely to protect an inventor who they believe is not working to use their

[120] Examples of fact issues include disputes regarding the structure and operation of the accused device, the teachings of the prior art and level of skill in the art, whether the accused device is equivalent to the claims and the amount of damages sustained on account of the infringement. Typical legal issues include claim interpretation, whether inequitable conduct occurred during prosecution, and whether the prior art prevents infringement under the doctrine of equivalents.

invention for the public good. Thus, if an accused infringer is making a product that is better, more efficient, cheaper or safer than the claimed invention, defense counsel will try to emphasize this to draw sympathy from the jury.

After the jury is empanelled, trial begins with opening statement by the parties' attorneys. These statements provide a framework for the case, highlight the points of conflict and issues that the jury will be asked to decide, and attempt to persuade the jury regarding the key issues. After opening statements, the presentment of evidence begins.

Each party may present witnesses, deposition testimony, documents and demonstrative evidence such as charts, photographs, videos, and physical objects. Given the potential for jury confusion, trial counsel must carefully plan a sequence and manner of presenting the evidence which will aid the Court and jury in understanding the complex technical and legal issues involved and sway them toward the desired result. Generally, counsel will attempt to present a simple, straight forward case.

The patent owner has the burden of proving infringement by a preponderance of evidence, which requires showing that the defendant has more likely than not infringed. Techniques the patent owner may use to support the infringement case include: calling the inventor to testify regarding the technology and the merits of the invention, submitting drawings and testimony of the opponent's engineers regarding the accused device, and then utilizing an expert witness to testify regarding infringement. The patent owner must also prove damages, and will normally do so through the testimony of economic and financial experts.

After cross-examining the patentee's witnesses, the accused infringer will attempt to prove its defenses. The most common defenses are non-infringement and invalidity for obviousness or lack of novelty. Any challenge to patent validity must be proven by clear and convincing evidence, thus the accused infringer must prove the defense by presenting evidence that leaves no serious doubt in the mind of the fact finder. The clear and convincing evidence standard is a greater burden than the patent owners' preponderance of evidence standard; this is because a patent is presumed to be valid.

Testimony of the defendant's own witnesses may help demonstrate differences between the invention and the accused device, or show that the invention represents only a small advance over the prior art. Proving the content of the prior art may require introducing documents and testimony from non-party witnesses, often through deposition testimony. The defendant will also invariably introduce testimony from at least one technical expert to make a convincing showing of non-infringement or invalidity. The defendant will also offer its own fact and expert witnesses to counter the patentee's damages evidence.

The patentee will also have an opportunity to rebut the defenses offered, such as by challenging the disclosures of the prior art, showing the tremendous success of the invention, or that the minor differences in the accused device do not affect the way it functions.

Technical, economic and financial experts play a key role. Often, the party with the more credible and convincing experts wins. A trial judge has broad discretion to consider whether a person is qualified as an expert, and whether the expert's knowledge will assist the jury. In response to concerns about the prevalence of "junk science" in federal civil cases, the Supreme Court recently determined that this requires a preliminary assessment of whether the expert's reasoning and methodology is scientifically valid.[121] Technical or financial expert analysis which cannot be tested or does not satisfy accepted standards in the expert's particular field is subject to exclusion.

After the presentation of evidence, the jury listens to closing arguments and then deliberates until a verdict is reached. During the course of the trial, the judge provides instructions to the jury regarding the law that applies to the case, including the proper interpretation of the patent claims. The jury is obligated to apply the law conveyed in the jury instructions to the facts presented at trial to arrive at a verdict.

2. Principle Claims and Defenses

The patent owner in an infringement suit must prove infringement and damages, and may also seek to recover enhanced damages for willful infringement. In addition to defending the infringement charge, the accused infringer may challenge the patent as invalid and/or unenforceable and/or assert other defenses such as laches or implied license. The most commonly asserted claims and defenses are discussed in this section.

a) Infringement

The process for determining patent infringement has two main steps. First, the claims of the patent are interpreted to determine their scope and meaning. Next, the properly interpreted claims are compared to the accused product or process.[122] Patent claim interpretation is performed by the judge based on the words of the claims themselves interpreted in light of the written description and drawings, and the record of proceedings in the PTO. Words in a claim are interpreted to have their ordinary meaning in the applicable field unless they were given a special meaning in the written specification or during prosecution.[123]

In the United States, patent infringement can occur either by literal infringement or under the doctrine of equivalents. Literal infringement of a patent requires that each and every limitation or element of at least one claim be found in the accused product or process. If a single limitation is not present, there is no literal infringement. However, infringement may still be found under the doctrine of equivalents where the differences between the claimed invention and the accused product or process are "insubstantial."

---

[121] *Daubert v. Merrell Dow Pharmaceuticals, Inc.*, 509 U.S. 579 (1993).

[122] *Markman v. Westview Instruments, Inc.*, 52 F.3d at 967.

[123] *Id.* at 979–980.

Evidence that the accused product or process performs "substantially the same function, in substantially the same way, to achieve the same result" as the claimed invention may support a finding of equivalency, but this test is more suitable for analyzing mechanical devices than chemical compositions or processes.

The doctrine of equivalents gives a court the ability to effectively expand the scope of a patent claim beyond the literal language of the claim. Otherwise, a party who copies a patent's inventive concept, but makes some trivial or obvious change, would avoid legal infringement. However, the doctrine of equivalents creates uncertainty as to the scope of patent rights and may thereby discourage legitimate efforts to design around existing patents. Important technical advancements often are the result of such design-around activities.

The courts have struggled to formulate and apply the doctrine in a manner that strikes a proper balance between these competing considerations. In 1995 the Federal Circuit addressed basic issues concerning the doctrine of equivalents and held that (1) the determination of equivalents is a fact issue to be resolved by the jury; (2) the test focuses on the substantiality of differences between the claimed and accused products or processes; and (3) equivalency is determined objectively from the perspective of a hypothetical person of ordinary skill in the relevant art.[124] Two years later, the Supreme Court confirmed equivalents infringement as a viable doctrine, but expressed concern that the doctrine had become "unbounded by the patent claims."[125] The Supreme Court did little to clarify the proper test of equivalency, but required a "special vigilance against allowing the concept of equivalence to eliminate completely any [claim] elements."[126]

Nevertheless, there are important limitations on the doctrine of equivalents intended to prevent patent rights from being extended too broadly. First, the doctrine is applied on an element-by-element basis. Thus, for each claim limitation there must be a corresponding element in the accused product or process that is identical or equivalent to that limitation. Stated differently, if a theory of equivalence would effectively read a claim limitation out of the claim altogether, then there is no infringement. Further, there is no infringement where the scope of equivalents necessary to cover the accused device or process would also cover prior art.[127]

A third important limitation on the doctrine of equivalents is "prosecution history estoppel." This limitation prevents a patent owner from covering subject matter that was relinquished during prosecution of the patent

---

[124] *Hilton Davis Chemical Co. v. Warner-Jenkinson Co., Inc.*, 62 F.3d at 1512 (Fed. Cir. 1995).

[125] *Warner-Jenkinson Co., Inc. v. Hilton Davis Chemical Co.*, 520 U.S. 17 at 28–29.

[126] *Id*. at 40.

[127] *Wilson Sporting Goods Co. v. David Geoffrey & Assoc.*, 904 F.2d 677, 684 (Fed. Cir. 1990).

application. The purpose of prosecution history estoppel is to protect the notice function of the claims. Courts traditionally adopted a "flexible bar" approach under which the subject matter surrendered was determined by what a reasonable competitor would likely conclude from reviewing the prosecution file. However, in its 1999 *Festo* decision (*Festo I*), the Court of Appeals for the Federal Circuit ruled that when a claim limitation is narrowed during prosecution, application of the doctrine of equivalents to that claim element is completely barred.[128] This complete bar approach would eliminate the public's need to speculate as to the subject matter surrendered by a claim amendment. The *Festo I* decision also held that prosecution history estoppel applies to all narrowing amendments made for any reason related to patentability, even those made for purposes of clarification and not in response to a prior art rejection.[129]

Although the *Festo I* decision would lend certainty to the determination of patent scope, there was concern that it represented an overly rigid approach that would, in effect, severely restrict patent rights. The Supreme Court overturned the complete bar approach of *Festo I* and returned the case to the Federal Circuit for further consideration.[130] The claim scope actually surrendered by amendment will remain an important consideration in applying the doctrine of equivalents and prosecution history estoppel. However, according to the Supreme Court, the patent owner should bear the burden of overcoming presumptions that: (1) amendments which narrow a patent claim, for any reason, create prosecution history estoppel; and (2) all coverage between the originally proposed claim and the issued claim was surrendered by the patent owner.

In September, 2003, the Federal Circuit issued its *Festo II* opinion, clarifying its interpretation of the Supreme Court's ruling and the current procedure for analyzing the doctrine of equivalents when prosecution history estoppel is at issue.[131] The Court confirmed that any narrowing amendment made for a reason related to patentability may invoke prosecution history estoppel, even amendments not made to distinguish prior art. If the prosecution record does not reveal the reason for an amendment, then it is treated as an amendment that was made for a substantial reason related to patentability, which creates a second presumption that all equivalents for the amended claim limitation were surrendered. The patent holder may rebut the presumption by showing that the particular equivalent in question was not surrendered. The criteria for determining the scope of surrender may include whether a particular equivalent was foreseeable, whether the

---

128 *Festo Corp. v. Shoketsu Kinzoku Kogyo Kabushiki Co., Ltd.*, 234 F.3d 558 (Fed. Cir. 1999), *remanded and vacated*, 122 S.Ct. 1831 (2002).

129 *Id.* at 566.

130 *Festo Corp. v. Shoketsu Kinzoku Kogyo Kabushiki Co., Ltd.*, 535 U.S. 722, 152 L. Ed. 2d 944, 122 S. Ct. 1831 (2002).

131 *Festo Corp. v. Shoketsu Kinzoku Kogyo Kabushiki Co., Ltd,* 344 F.3d 1359, 68 U.S.P.Q.2d (BNA) 1321 (Fed. Cir. 2003).

amendment was directly relevant to the alleged equivalent, and whether failure to expressly claim the equivalent was due to shortcomings of language. Other criteria may come to light as the district courts gain experience applying the reformulated doctrine.

b) Defenses to infringement

The alleged infringer may assert that the accused product or process does not infringe the patent claims either literally or under the doctrine of equivalence. The burden is on the patent owner to show that the claims cover the alleged infringing device or process. The alleged infringer may also attempt to show that the patent owner is estopped from expanding the claims under the doctrine of equivalents sufficiently to cover the alleged infringing device or process either because of admissions or arguments presented during the prosecution of the patent before the PTO or because the broader reading of the claims would encompass and cover prior art devices or processes. Non-infringement of the patent claims by the accused device or process is almost always raised as a defense in patent infringement suits.

The validity of the patent can also be raised as a defense. Patents are presumed valid. Thus, the alleged infringer must prove the patent is invalid by a more difficult clear and convincing standard of proof. As mentioned above, validity generally involves three components: novelty, utility, and non-obviousness. For a given claim, if the Court finds that a claim lacks any one of the three attributes, that claim is invalid and cannot be infringed by the alleged infringer or anyone else.

The validity of a patent claim is often attacked by a challenger presenting prior art that, in the challenger's opinion, anticipates the patent claims or renders them obvious. If the prior art offered by the challenger is not materially different from that considered by the PTO during examination of the patent, the challenger will have a difficult time showing that the patent is not valid; in effect, the challenger must convince the judge or jury that the PTO failed to do its job properly in granting the patent. If the challenger can present prior art that was not before the PTO examiner, and especially if the new prior art is more relevant to the invention than the prior art before the examiner, the challenger will have an easier time proving invalidity. In important cases, the challenger may be willing to go to great lengths to find additional prior art, including conducting extensive literature searches, hiring technical experts, interviewing other researchers in the field, and even posting rewards for helpful information.

A challenger may also attempt to invalidate a patent by showing sales, offers of sale, or public use of the invention more than one year prior to the effective filing date of the patent application. Evidence of such activity by the patentee or some other party is often not known to the PTO and, thus, if available may pose a serious challenge to patent validity. In other cases, a challenger may also attempt to invalidate a patent by showing that the specification is not enabling or that it fails to disclose the best mode of carrying out the invention which was known at the time the application was filed. These defenses are used less often and are considered less likely to persuade a jury at trial.

The challenger may also assert that the patent owner acted improperly and violated its duty of candor to the PTO in obtaining the patent. This inequitable conduct or fraud defense is raised in many patent infringement suits, oftentimes without sufficient justification. The challenger must show by the difficult evidentiary standard of clear and convincing evidence that the alleged mischaracterization or other inequitable conduct was material to the issue of patentability and that applicant acted with intent to mislead or deceive the PTO. The materiality and intent requirements are interrelated. For example, a high level of materiality can create an inference that the conduct was intentional, and a specific showing of intent can reduce the level of materiality required. Simple negligence or an erroneous judgment made in good faith will generally not support a finding of the necessary intent.

In contrast to invalidity based on the other criteria discussed, a finding of unenforceability based on inequitable conduct affects the entire patent, not just the claims to which the inequitable conduct may specifically relate. It may also render related continuing patents unenforceable.

3. Remedies

a) Injunctive relief

The Court may, pursuant to 35 U.S.C. § 283, grant injunctive relief against future infringing activities. When a clear showing of validity and infringement has been made, the appropriateness of granting injunctive relief is presumed.[132] While the grant of injunctive relief is discretionary, injunctive relief against an infringer is the norm.[133] The district court is given broad discretion to shape injunctions, but must assure that the injunction is narrowly tailored to fit the violation at hand. Often, the injunction is drafted rather broadly to prohibit "further infringement" of the patent. Under such an injunction, further sale of the product adjudged to infringe or a product only insignificantly different would expose the infringer to severe penalties for contempt.

Preliminary injunctions, by which the alleged infringer is forbidden to do certain specified acts before a full trial on the merits of the case, serve to preserve the status quo in the market during the suit. These are rarely granted. In order to obtain a preliminary injunction, the patent owner must show: (1) a reasonable likelihood of success on the merits; (2) irreparable harm to the patentee if the injunction is not granted; (3) hardships favoring the patentee; and (4) that the public interest will be favored by granting the injunction.[134] This showing is often difficult to make at the early stages of the proceeding.

---

[132] *Richardson v. Suzuki Motor Co.*, 868 F.2d 1226 (Fed. Cir. 1989).

[133] *KSM Fastening Sys., Inc. v. H.A. Jones Co.*, 776 F.2d 1522 (Fed. Cir. 1985).

[134] *Atlas Powder Co. v. Ireco Chemicals.*, 773 F.2d 1230, 1231 (Fed. Cir. 1985).

b) Damages

Under § 284, a patentee may recover damages adequate to compensate for the infringement, but in no event less than a reasonable royalty. It is proper to award the patentee's lost profits if they exceed a reasonable royalty. However, the patentee is not entitled to the infringer's profits. To prove lost profits, the patentee will generally try to show: (1) demand for the patented product; (2) ability to meet the demand; (3) absence of non-infringing substitutes; and (4) the amount of profit that would have been earned.[135] However, this is not the exclusive test, and the patentee may find other ways to prove with reasonable probability that it would have made all or some of the infringing sales.[136]

If lost profits cannot be shown, the patentee is entitled to a reasonable royalty. This is calculated as the amount a person would have been willing to pay as a royalty in a hypothetical negotiation at the time infringement began. Some of the factors normally considered in determining the reasonable royalty include the infringer's expected profit, whether the license would have been exclusive, and actual established royalties under the patent or in the particular field.

Prior to enactment of the Federal Circuit, damage awards in patent cases were often relatively small compared to the effort and expense of litigation. A prevailing theme of Federal Circuit jurisprudence has been the need to fully compensate patent owners. As seen in the chart below, several large damages awards have placed potential infringers on notice of the dangers of defending patent litigation.

Case	Damage Award
Polaroid v. Eastman Kodak (1991)	$873,000,000
Haworth v. Stellcase (1996)	$211,000,000
Smith International v. Hughes Tool (1986)	$205,000,000
3M v. Johnson & Johnson Orthopaedics (1992)	$117,000,000
Fonar v. General Electric (1997)	$103,000,000
Stryker v. Intermedics Orthopaedics (1996)	$73,000,000
Mobil Oil v. Amoco Chemicals (1994)	$48,000,000
Shiley v. Bentley Laboratories (1985)	$45,000,000
Schneider v. SciMed Life Systems (1994)	$45,000,000

c) Enhanced damages

Infringement can range from unknowing or accidental to deliberate or reckless disregard of the patentee's legal rights. For willful infringement, damages

[135] *Gyromat Corp. v. Champion Spark Plug Co.*, 735 F.2d 549 (Fed. Cir. 1984).

[136] *Carella v. Starlight Archery & ProLine Co.*, 804 F.2d 135 (Fed. Cir. 1986).

can be increased up to three times the actual damages[137] and may, in exceptional cases, include an award of attorney fees.[138] Willful infringement can be found where an infringer knew of the patent and lacked a reasonable legal justification for the infringing actions. The potential infringer with notice of the patent has an affirmative duty to determine whether any of its actions would constitute infringement. As discussed above, this duty can generally be discharged by obtaining competent legal advice concerning the potential infringement.

VII. Appeal

As mentioned above, appeals involving patent issues are taken to the Court of Appeals for the Federal Circuit.[139] The duty of the Federal Circuit to review the determination in the lower court is limited by the standard of review. The standard of review both determines the power of the Federal Circuit to address claims for error and defines the degree of deference it will accord the findings of fact and conclusions of law made in the district court. The standards of review, ranging from broadest to narrowest, include: *de novo* review, substantial evidence, clear error standard and abuse of discretion.

The "*de novo*" standard of review provides the Federal Circuit the widest latitude in reviewing the lower court decision. Under this standard, the Court exercises its own independent judgment on the evidence of record. Examples of issues that the Federal Circuit reviews *de novo* are claim construction, prosecution history estoppel and determinations of enablement, obviousness, claim indefiniteness.[140]

The Federal Circuit applies a more deferential "substantial evidence" standard of review to the jury's factual findings. Technically, fact finding made by judges enjoy a less deferential "clear error" standard of review; however there is little practical difference between the two. Typically the "substantial evidence" standard is satisfied unless the jury decision requires something a reasonable mind would not accept. Some of the issues that the Federal Circuit reviews under the substantial evidence or clear error standard are literal infringement, equivalency under the doctrine of equivalence, and the factual underpinnings of a finding of inequitable conduct.[141]

---

[137] 35 U.S.C. § 284.

[138] 35 U.S.C. § 285.

[139] 28 U.S.C. § 1295(a).

[140] *Markman v. Westview Instr., Inc.*, 52 F.3d at 997 (claim construction); *Paragon Podiatry Lab, Inc. v. KLM Labs, Inc.*, 984 F.2d 1182 (Fed. Cir. 1993) (validity issues).

[141] *Miles Labs, Inc. v. Shandon Inc.*, 997 F.2d 870 (Fed. Cir. 1993) (literal infringement); *Warner-Jenkinson Co., Inc. v. Hilton Davis Chem. Co.*, 520 U.S. at 17 (1997) (equivalency under the doctrine of equivalence); *Gerber Garment Tech, Inc. v. Lectra Systems, Inc.*, 916 F.2d 683, 686 (factual underpinnings of inequitable conduct).

Under the "abuse of discretion" standard, the Federal Circuit does not reverse the decision below unless it is grossly unsound, unreasonable, or is a clear error of judgment. Examples of issues reviewed under this standard are decisions by a judge to grant enhanced damages and a judge's decision on whether to hold a patent unenforceable due to inequitable conduct based on the jury's fact findings.[142]

Thus, the parties must shape their arguments on appeal to the proper standard or standards of review that apply. The nature of the error claimed, and the applicable standard of review, affects the likelihood of success on appeal. For example, when the legal question of obviousness arises on appeal the Court must apply a multi-step analysis. First the Federal Circuit must construe the claim, which is a question of law governed by the *de novo* standard of review. The ultimate question of obviousness is also freely reviewable *de novo*, but the Court must apply the more deferential substantial evidence standard to the jury's determination of what the prior art in fact teaches. The appealing party has a better chance of prevailing by focusing on an incorrect claim construction, rather than challenging the jury's factual findings regarding the prior art.

The following table summarizes recent tendencies of the Federal Circuit regarding issues frequently raised on appeal.

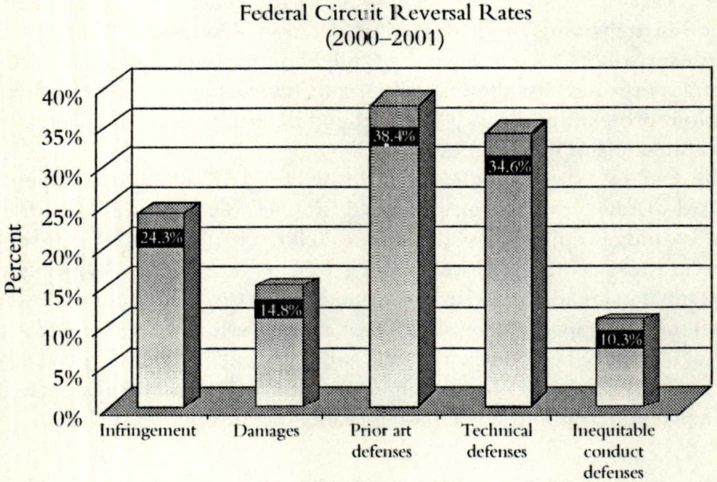

Fig 6

*Source: University of Houston Law Center at www.patstats.org.

[142] *Cybor Corp. v. FAS Tech. Inc.*, 138 F. 3d 1448 (Fed. Cir. 1998) (enhanced damages); *Gerber Garment Tech, Inc. v. Lectra Systems, Inc.*, 916 F.2d at 683 (judge's determination regarding inequitable conduct).

16
The Enforcement of Patent Rights in Argentina

MÓNICA WITTHAUS

A. Introduction

In the Republic of Argentina, patent law has recently undergone radical change, both in theory and in practice. These changes have recently started to bear fruit, as far as the specific point dealt with in this paper is concerned. In fact the recent amendment of the law on patents bringing it into line with the GATT/TRIPS Agreement, has already elicited many rulings on questions of law, such as the term of validity of patents granted before entry into force of the new law, patents of importation, etc. The change is starting to be felt in issues arising from points of fact. Such issues are typical of patent compliance, where the decisions of the courts generally presuppose infringement. Argentina has no courts dedicated exclusively to industrial property. The subject is dealt with by the "federal civil and commercial" and by the "federal criminal and correctional" courts of justice. Nevertheless, in civil cases, at least, industrial property can be said to account for a very large proportion of the matters resolved by the federal civil and commercial courts. It is therefore a major area of specialisation for them.

Industrial property agents representing the interested parties in any matter to be referred to the National Industrial Property Institute (INPI) must use the support of a lawyer if they wish to represent the patent holder before the courts.

In civil claims, proceedings before the courts are written, except for hearings prescribed by the procedural rules on conciliation and on questions of proof. In criminal actions, proceedings are verbal, and their features shall be dealt with in more detail in the corresponding section.

In practice, lawyers generally take the civil option, which is seen as more effective for securing cessation of the use of the patent and any compensation claimed.

The Mediation Act requires a stage of prior mediation to be followed before the court case starts. This stage gives the parties a last chance to reach an out-of-court settlement, in the presence of a registered mediator. The results of this process vary, depending on the conflict concerned. However, in practice, mediation started after interim relief measures have been taken is usually effective, saving the holder of the infringed patent time and money. It also allows the alleged infringer a more face-saving and less expensive exit.

B. *Problems Related to Patent Enforcement*

I. Standing to Sue

1. Regulatory Provisions

The legislation applicable in this field is Law 24 481 on Patents and Utility Models (hereinafter the "Patents Act"), amended by Law 24 572 (vol. 1996) and by Law 25 859 (vol. 2004) with Implementing Decree 260/1996.[1] The GATT/TRIPS Agreement (Law 24 425) also applies.[2] Under this legislation, it is the holders of granted patents and licensees who are the parties with standing to sue to secure compliance with a patent. They may appear as plaintiffs in civil actions for cessation of use, compensation, etc., and can petition for interim relief and advance proof.

Title VI of the Patents Act, "Infringement of Rights Granted by the Patent and Utility Model", Secs. 81 and 83, provide as follows:

Section 81. "In addition to criminal actions, the holder of the patent and its licensee, or the holder of the utility model, may bring civil actions for prohibition of the continued unlawful exploitation and for compensation for the loss incurred."

Section 83. "After submitting title to the patent or utility model certificate, the injured party may petition for the following interim relief, subject to such guarantees as the judge may deem necessary. . . ."

Under Sec. 57 of the former Patent Act 111,[3] a criminal suit was private. The present Act, by contrast, makes no provision in this regard, making such a suit public. This means the party with standing to sue is the Public Prosecutor, who is bound to bring an action officially, as per Sec. 5 Code of Criminal Procedure. Section 82 of that Code allows a patent holder, as an aggrieved party, to become a party seeking damages in criminal proceedings. As such, the patent holder drives the proceedings forward, but they do not thereby lose their public status, since the patent holder has no authority to impose a stay or cessation of the proceedings. Since the offence is actionable by the Public Prosecutor, anyone who suffers loss through, or knows about the offence may report it to the judge, to the police or to the prosecutor concerned.

---

[1] Act concerning Patents and Utility Models, Law 24 481, amended under the same title by Law 24 572 (vol. 1996) and by Law 25 859 published in Official Gazette No. 30 317 of 14 January 2004, regulated by Implementing Decree 260/1996, published in Official Gazette No. 28 360 of 22 March 1996.

[2] Law 24 425, published in Official Gazette dated 5 January 1995.

[3] Patents Act, Law 111 of 1864, inspired by the French law of 1844 (ADLA, 1852–1880, 432).

The right of licensees to sue depends on the patent holder not exercising the right itself.[4] As interpreted by Genovesi,[5] the law limits the right to seek damages in criminal proceedings to holders of exclusive licences. Genovesi does not see a holder of a simple licence as suffering loss through someone else's exploitation of the invention, since the simple licence does not guarantee the licensee exclusivity. Despite the clear distinction drawn between the two types of licensee, it should be pointed out that it is inaccurate to assert that a simple licensee suffers no loss from counterfeiting. While a simple licensee loses less than an exclusive licensee, obviously a simple licensee still suffers economic loss from the presence of an unfair competitor, who places identical products on the market without royalty costs for the licence. Therefore, as the letter of the law makes no distinction between the positions of exclusive and simple licensee, a simple licensee must also be accorded "the right to bring the legal actions which the patent holder is entitled to bring, only if that holder does not exercise it for itself."

2. Patent Applications

a) Owner of a patent application

The law says nothing about the rights of an applicant for a patent. Thus there is no specific regulation of the inventor's rights during the process of granting the patent. To understand how serious this gap in the law is, one need only think of the habitual slowness of the formalities leading to a patent being granted, and the speed of technological progress in certain fields. This means the economic attraction of the invention often peaks before the patent is granted. In that case, a literal (*i.e.* narrow) interpretation of the law will deprive the applicant of protection when it most needs it. Obviously, this will be the time of greatest exposure to counterfeiters and infringers. Since these have no need to invest in research and development, they can afford the luxury of producing (*i.e.* imitating) only those inventions which are on the "crest of a wave".

Opinions in academic writings differ on this point, interpreting the law's silence in various ways.

Breuer Moreno wrote his classic treatise on the matter while Law 111 was in force. Chapter VI of that Law, entitled "On counterfeiting, its prosecution and penalties", likewise only mentioned the rights of the "patent holder" and not those of the "inventor". Breuer Moreno argued that an applicant who suffers loss is entitled to take civil and criminal action against the infringer when conditions exist to do so, provided he gave notice to the infringer of the pending patent application before the patent was granted. Such protection is based on Art. 17 Argentine Constitution, which states: "any author or inventor is the sole owner of his work, invention or discovery for the term granted

[4] Sec. 40 Patent Act.

[5] Genovesi, Luis M., "Acciones civiles y penales", in Correa, Carlos *et al.*, *Derecho de patentes*, Ciudad Argentina, Buenos Aires, 1999, 334.

by Law". This guarantee does not appear conditional upon first obtaining a patent. Instead, it stems from the very fact of the invention.[6]

Also Cabanellas notes the legislature's silence on applicants' rights before granting of the patent. He concludes that "such rights do not exist in Argentine law, because it is constructed on the principle that the patent holder's rights only commence on issue of the patent concerned. There is no legal provision allowing a compensatory right to be granted to the holder of a patentable invention which has not yet been patented." While regretting the gap in protection, Cabanellas maintains that applicants only have the rights which apply to unpatented knowledge, and the rights deriving from the criminal law protection of unpatented inventions under Sec. 77 Patent Act. This system of protection denies unauthorised access to such knowledge, provided the holder takes the necessary precautions to keep it confidential and publicises its intention of doing so. The knowledge must not be disclosed in a manner which enables a normally qualified technician to access it.[7]

Another author, Genovesi,[8] maintains that "the rights granted under a patent exist from the time of granting" and "the criminal provisions of Law 111 referred to infringement of the patent holder's rights". Hence to extend those rights to infringement of an application for a patent or utility model would contravene the prohibition of enforcing criminal laws by analogy. It would also be contrary to Art. 19 of the Constitution, which provides that "no inhabitant of the Nation shall be obliged to do what the law does not command, nor deprived of what it does not prohibit". He also quotes a 1969 judgment of the Argentine National Supreme Court, whereby "the privilege of exploitation of an invention is a concession made by means of the patent. For this reason, to make fraud punishable, Sec. 53 requires that the invention be patented. . . ."[9] While Genovesi contends that this judicial attitude remains valid, he recognises the possibility of a different interpretation, though he certainly does not advocate it. This concerns Sec. 75 of the present Patent Act, which states that "defrauding the inventor of his rights shall be deemed an offence of counterfeiting and punished by imprisonment between six months and three years, and a fine." This refers to "inventor's rights", unlike other provisions, which refer to the right of the holder of a patent or utility model.[10]

---

[6] Breuer Moreno, Pedro, *Tratado de patentes de invención*, Abeledo-Perrot, Buenos Aires, 1957, 600.

[7] Cabanellas, Guillermo, *Derecho de las patentes de invención*, Heliasta, Buenos Aires, 2001, 21–26.

[8] Genovesi, Mariano L., "Acciones . . .", *op. cit.*, 342 *et seq.*

[9] CSJN, "Chinchilla *v.* Bosini", 22 July 1969, *Fallos*, 7:290.

[10] Thus Sec. 76, *e.g.*, punishes the production of objects and the importation, sale, offering for sale, marketing or introduction to Argentina of one or more objects infringing the rights of the holder of the patent or utility model.

Section 77 relates to the penalties for "disclosure and infringement of inventions not yet protected", and sets penalties for:

"c) Whoever breaches the secrecy obligation imposed by this Law".

This indent undoubtedly tends to protect the rights of an applicant for a patent. It makes clear reference to the staff of the National Patent Authority, who are bound by Sec. 70 of the Patent Act to keep the content of patent application files confidential. The one-third increase in the penalty of Sec. 75, to between nine months and four years' imprisonment and a fine, reflects the status of the offenders as civil servants.

b) Owner of an unprotected invention

Further to what has been said above concerning patent applications, it has to be asked what happens in the case of an inventor who has not initiated any procedure to protect his invention.

Undoubtedly, if the broadest interpretation were favoured, what has already been said in connection with Sec. 75 would also be applicable in this case. Indents a) and b) of Sec. 77 concern inventions not yet protected. They punish the behaviour of: "a) whoever is a partner, attorney, adviser, employee or worker of the inventor or his assignees and infringes or discloses the invention as yet unprotected; "b) whoever obtains disclosure of the invention by corrupting the inventor's partner, attorney, adviser, employee worker or his assignees". Here the legislature basically envisages the case of someone who has not submitted an application and is thus particularly vulnerable to such conduct, which would deprive his invention of novelty and thus jeopardise his chances of obtaining the patent. Such conduct is punished with the penalty of Sec. 75 plus one-third, due to such an offender's relationship with the inventor.

II. Competent Courts

Section 89 Patent Act empowers the judges of the Federal Civil and Commercial Court competent to hear civil cases, and the judges of the Federal Criminal Court to hear criminal cases. This competence according to subject-matter is supplemented by the provisions of the Codes of Civil and Criminal Procedure, depending on location. Thus the national federal courts of the Federal Capital (Civil and Commercial or Criminal and Correctional) or their provincial counterparts are competent, as the case may be.

III. Interim Relief and Advance Proof

1. Importance

This point is tremendously important to the subject of concern to us here. When there are no adequate provisions for interim relief or for correct interpretation and application of such relief by the courts the best decisions on the merits of the case will prove totally abstract and merely theoretical, lacking teeth to prevent or compensate for the loss caused by the infringers. The dictum "justice delayed is justice denied" is true in this field as in no other.

Applicable provisions are those of the Patent Act, the formal codes and GATT/TRIPS. Under the Constitution, the last prevail over the first and second.

2. Relief Provided under the Patent Act

a) Sections 83 and 84 Patent Act

Section 83(1) Patent Act provides that:

> "After producing title to the patent or the utility model certificate, the injured party may petition for the following interim relief, subject to such guarantees as the judge may deem fit:
>
> "a) Seizure of one or more examples of the infringing objects, or description of the process complained against;
>
> "b) An inventory or attachment of the forged objects and of the machinery especially designed to manufacture the products or to carry out the process complained against."

In this case, the law clearly requires production of title. Hence, in principle, only the holder of the patent can obtain this kind of protection. The title to the patent serves to prove the "plausibility of the right", which is always required in such cases. An inventor whose invention was not protected by a patent would be denied this kind of protection (*e.g.* an applicant who has not yet obtained the patent).

It is worth asking whether a licensee could apply for such relief if the patent holder did not take the action to which it was entitled. In this case, we think a broad interpretation of Sec. 40 might lead to a positive answer. Otherwise the right granted to the licensee could lack any genuine effectiveness.

Until the enactment of Law 25 859, such relief was granted *ex parte* according to the general principles. The judge thus had to ask the holder of the patent or utility model for whatever guarantee was regarded necessary, either in the form of a promise or a real guarantee. Given its function of ensuring possible compensation for unjustified losses, the amount would depend on the seriousness of the consequences of the requested relief, the plausibility of the applicant's right, etc.

As for the list of measures provided for in this provision, Aracama Zorraquín states that indent b) "should say inventory 'and/or' attachment – one and the other, not one or the other, as the draft says."[11]

---

[11] Aracama Zorraquín, Ernesto, "*El proyecto de ley del Poder Ejecutivo sobre régimen de patentes de invención y modelos de utilidad*", DE, *v.* 147, Buenos Aires, 1992, 811.

The new Section 83(2)[12] stipulates that :

"Judges are allowed to order interim relief regarding a patent granted according to articles 30, 31, 32 Patent Act in order to:

1) Prevent patent infringement, and in particular to prevent the entry of goods into the channels of commerce, including imported goods immediately after customs clearance.
2) Preserve relevant evidence with regard to the alleged infringement

provided the following conditions are met:

a) there is a reasonable probability that a plea of nullity of the patent by the defendant will be rejected; b) the delay in granting relief causes irreparable damage to the holder; c) the loss caused to the holder exceeds damages to the alleged infringer if the relief is wrongly granted; and d) there is a reasonable probability that the patent is being infringed."

If these conditions are met, in exceptional cases, such as a demonstrable risk of destruction of evidence, the judges may order these measures *inaudita altera parte*. In all cases the judge will require an officially appointed expert to give an opinion on points a) and d) above within 15 days. If interim relief is granted, the applicant must provide a sufficient guarantee or bond in order to protect the defendant and to avoid abuses.

According to the new provisions, interim relief will only be ordered when the stipulated conditions – some of them not present in the text of Art. 50 TRIPS[13] – are met.

Previously, interim relief was ordered by the judges *ex parte* according to the principles of the Code of Procedure, and the injunctive relief was ordered on the basis of Art. 50 TRIPS and Sec. 232 Code of Civil and Commercial Procedure.

On 23 May 2000, in the case of "Ishihara Sangyo Kaisha Ltd. *v.* Magan Argentina on discontinuance of patent use", the First Division of the National Federal Civil and Commercial Chamber of Appeals confirmed the finding of the first instance judge. He had ruled that "subject to a real guarantee, which he set at the sum of $35,000 for the loss which the relief might cause if unduly requested, he ordered the defendant", as interim relief in the terms of the Code of Civil and Commercial Procedure, Sec. 232 (*cf.* also Art. 50 TRIPS, points 1 a] and 2]), to refrain from distributing, offering for sale, selling and importing any product infringing patent no. 240 321.[14]

All of the above was the result of a lively discussion in the literature between supporters of the application of Art. 50 TRIPS in case of presumed infringement of a patent holder's rights, and those who took the opposite view, favouring the application of the specific system of Sec. 87 Patent Act,

---

[12] Introduced by Law 25 859.

[13] This refers particuarly to points a) and c).

[14] "Ishihara Sangyo Kaisha Ltd. *v.* Magan Argentina SA on cessation of use of patent", case 895/899, of 23 May 2000, Federal Civil and Commercial Court no. 11, Section 22, of 28 May 1999.

the plea of exploitation,[15] which finally led the National Federal Civil and Commercial Chamber of Appeals to apply Art. 50 TRIPS.[16] They might possibly tighten the requirements for its applicability, ensuring that "in the analysis of the criteria of admissibility, its strict criterion must be observed, since imposing the same implies anticipation of an eventual favourable ruling. Hence the plausibility of the right must be evident from the factors at work in the case, and must require something more than the colour of law."[17] As established by the Second Division, no distinction must be made between enforcement of Art. 50 regarding patents granted under the present system and those granted under Law 111. This is because this "must not be seen at all as a retrospective application of the new provisions, but simply their immediate application, as per Civil Code Sec. 3(1)."[18]

As clearly shown by the comparison of these rulings by the Argentine Courts with the text of the new Sec. 83(2), the amendment was not necessary to meet the goals mentioned in the Explanation of Grounds. This has been pointed out by the literature, which has criticised the new provisions as weakening the protection given to the patent holder.[19]

The conditions listed in points a) and c) of Sec. 83(2) are incompatible with the speed which is essential to interim relief. The existence of those conditions can only be established in a fact-finding process that allows the judge to acquire a detailed knowledge of the facts through a wide range of proof not subject to the constraints of urgency.

---

[15] The institution of the "plea of exploitation" and the arguments of this discussion are dealt with in depth in point c) below, "cessation of exploitation".

[16] "Merial Limited *v.* Afford Especialidades Veterinarias and/or Ricardo Calvo on cessation of exploitation of patent", 24 January 2003, National Federal Civil and Commercial Appeal Chamber, Feria Division; "Eli Lilly and Company on interim relief", case 3289/2001 of 11 October 2001, National Federal Civil and Commercial Appeal Chamber Division 1; "Bayer AG *v.* Agtrol Internac. Arg. SA on interim relief", case 7809/2001 of 12 February 2002, National Federal Civil and Commercial Appeal Chamber Division 2; "Checkpoint systems SA *v.* Sensormatic Arg. SA on indent of Article 250, National Code of Civil and Commercial Procedure", case 10 083, 26 December 2000, National Federal Civil and Commercial Appeal Chamber, Division 3; and "Syngenta Participations-AG *v.* Ipesa on interim relief", case 609/02, 9 April 2002, National Federal Civil and Commercial Appeal Chamber, Division 3. In the latter two cases, Art. 50 was deemed applicable, but the requested relief was denied, because the requirements of admissibility were considered not to have been fulfilled.

[17] "Eli Lilly and Company on interim relief", case 3289/2001, 11 October 2001, National Federal Civil and Commercial Appeal Chamber, Division 1.

[18] "Bayer AG *v.* Agtrol Internac. Argentina SA on interim relief", case 7809/2001, 12 February 2002, National Federal Civil and Commercial Appeal Chamber, Division 2.

[19] Poli, Ivan "Del Dicho al Hecho:Las medidas Cautelares en el Proyecto de Reformas a la Ley de Patentes". Lexis Nexis Jurisprudencia Argentina, JA 2003-IV fascículo n.7, 12 November 2003, p. 3. Otamendi, Jorge, "La Reforma a la Ley de Patentes de Invención y Modelos de Utilidad tan mala como innecearia. Revista Jurídica La Ley, 3 February 2004.

The required determination as to whether "there is a reasonable probability that a plea of nullity of the patent by the defendant will be rejected" according to Sec. 83(2) is a sort of judicial revision of the examination made by the Patent Office before granting the patent, ignoring the presumption of validity of administrative acts which is clearly applicable to the title of the patent holder. Furthermore, a plea of nullity is one of the most time-consuming processes in IP law; it is therefore difficult to see how the patent holder would be able to show that he could succeed in defending his patent if validity of his title is challenged in time to prevent the damage caused by infringers.

Validity of a patent is not an issue that can be decided upon by *summario cognitio*.

On the other hand, one of the main requisites to be fulfilled by a party that applies for interim relief is the guarantee required to assure the compensation of the damage caused by a measure grounded on an invalid patent or otherwise unjustified or wrongly granted.

The conditions provided in point c) "the loss which the holder may suffer exceeds the loss of the alleged infringer if the relief is wrongly granted", are also questions that can only be established, and not easily by proof. Even in long fact-finding processes where payment of damages is sought, the issue of proof of damages caused by the infringer is always a difficult one. This requisite is not compatible with the urgency inherent to interim relief. Furthermore, the right of the patent holder to obtain measures of interim relief cannot depend on a comparison of damages as proposed in point c).

According to point c), when the illegal commercial activity is on a large scale and therefore the losses caused to an infringer by an injunction would be great, he would have many opportunities to avoid the application of the measures contained in Sec. 83; even if the wording of point c) refers to "wrongly granted" relief at this point, it is always difficult to be absolutely sure whether the measures granted are justified (this is why the patent holder is asked for the above-mentioned guarantee), and this point may represent an obstacle for the patent holder seeking interim relief.

Last but not least, it is also important to point out that in many cases the "losses" suffered by the infringer as a consequence of an order to cease exploitation will equal the patent holder's lost earnings.

Pursuant to the amendment, measures can be only granted *ex parte* in exceptional cases, such as the existence of a demonstrable risk of destruction of evidence. This means a perversion of the principles of interim relief. In most cases this sort of legal measures would be deprived of teeth to prevent the damage caused by the infringers if they were not granted *inaudita altera parte*: surprise is one of the mean requisites for their effectiveness.

Even when the Explanation of Grounds of Law 25 859 shows that the referral of this bill is the result of the agreement reached between Argentina and the US during nine rounds of consultations held at the US's request, with a view to resolving differences in the framework of the WTO, and its aim is said to bring Argentina's legislation into line with Art. 50 TRIPS, the amendments introduced in Secs. 83 and 87 Patent Act do not provide a stronger protection of the rights of the patent holder, but, on the contrary, will make it more difficult to obtain the measures authorised by Art. 50 TRIPS.

Section 83 of the Implementing Decree provides that "the interim relief and the guarantees for its appropriateness, as provided by Sec. 83 of the Act, shall not preclude the granting of other interim relief in the terms provided by the substantive or procedural law applicable in each case." This provision is hugely important, and has played a prominent role in the discussion in the literature of the direct application of certain GATT/TRIPS measures and their harmonisation with the provisions of the specific law and surely will be important in the future.

As the literal application of the new Sec. 83 in many cases would not be compatible with Art. 50 TRIPS and would reduce the level of protection conferred to the patent holder, the courts may well have to decide how to interpret these provisions.

b) Expiry of interim relief and prior mediation

Section 86 of the law provides that the relief of Sec. 83 remains ineffective if the applicant does not bring corresponding legal action within 15 days. It is necessary to view this provision in the light of the Mediation Act.[20] This Act subjects all disputes not expressly excluded to its provision of pre-trial mediation. This covers disputes over infringements of the Patent Act. Section 2.6 Mediation Act mentions interim relief as a possible prior procedure excluded from the mediation process. Under the Act, the sequence is as follows: interim relief is granted; a request for mediation is lodged and implemented; if agreement is not reached, the legal action starts. Pre-trial mediation will only start once the ordinary channels of recourse for interim relief have been exhausted. Use of such channels will mean that mediation starts long after the interim relief has lapsed. This is because, under the Procedural Code, a legal action must be brought even if such recourse is pending.[21] This problem has not escaped attention in the literature, which has dealt with the point and outlined possible interpretations with a view to co-ordinating the two provisions.[22]

The root of this difficulty is the Mediation Act's failure to specify terms which could resolve these queries less ambiguously, but compatibly with legal certainty and with the institutions involved, and their purposes.[23]

---

[20] Mediation Act, Law 23 458 and implementing decrees, and Decrees 11/96 and 16/97 of the Federal Civil and Commercial Chamber of Appeals, intended to regulate the application of the new law to industrial property.

[21] Sec. 207 National Code of Civil and Commercial Procedure.

[22] Rebón, Horacio S., "*Medidas cautelares; diligencias preliminares; prueba anticipada y mediación*", LL, 1997-A-1006–1009.

[23] The need for enough time for mediation here comes up against the need to protect the rights of those whose assets or other rights are infringed, by interim relief prior to judgment. For a detailed analysis of the subject, see Witthaus, Mónica, "Mediación y

Obviously, the reasonable solution in this case is to consider the provision of Sec. 86 of the Patent Act fulfilled if mediation started within the 15-day period it allows. Various judicial rulings have established this – and not only with regard to patents.[24] They consider that the start of mediation suspends the term of expiry after interim relief has been granted. Once mediation is complete, the term starts to run again.

c) Cessation of exploitation

Section 87 "plea of exploitation", amended by Law 25 859 states that, "In cases in which interim relief has not been granted as per Sec. 83 Patent Act, the petitioner may request a guarantee from the defendant for non-interruption of its exploitation of the invention."[25] This provision is intended to strike some kind of balance between the rights of the opposing parties – the patent holder and the alleged infringer – in the course of the proceedings to establish whether the alleged infringement has taken place. Accordingly, should this section become applicable, the law will allow two possible alternatives – continuation of the exploitation presumed infringing, with a guarantee by the alleged infringer, or cessation of exploitation. If the alleged infringer decides to continue exploiting the invention for the time needed to obtain a ruling on the merits of the case (certainly a matter of years), the patent holder has no way of stopping it.

Even if henceforward this procedure will only be applied in cases in which the measures of Sec. 83 are not granted, there will be still some problems in harmonising this provision with TRIPS. In fact the difficulties to accomplish points a), b), c) and d) of Sec. 83 may lead to a situation in which Sec. 87 is applied more frequently before.

---

propiedad industrial: críticas e interrogantes a un año de iniciado el camino", *Temas de derecho industrial y de la competencia*, Buenos Aires, 1999, 241 *et seq.*; and Álvarez – Highton – Bestani – Grecco – Kopita – López – Nolasco – Scandale – Witthaus, *Evaluación de la ley de mediación y conciliación después del primer año de vigencia*, Konrad Adenauer Stiftung, CIEDLA, Buenos Aires, 1998.

[24] Federal Civil and Commercial Chamber of Appeals, Division 1: " Mayo Marcos, Daniel *v.* Pelikan SA on Appeal Plea", case no. 2024/2001 of 5 April 2001; Federal Civil and Commercial Chamber, Division 1, "Order de Jaijel, Fanny *et al. v.* Tesis Grupo Editorial Norma on interim relief"; case 22 524 of 10 February 1998; Federal Civil and Commercial Chamber of Appeals, Division 2, "Bodega Navarro Correas S.A. on interim relief", case no. 11 018 of 11 July 2001; National Civil Chamber, Division I, 26 December 1997, "Neyra, José Alberto *v.* Botello, Miguel on interim relief", DE, of 8 July 1998, 6.

[25] Under the former Sec. 87, the criteria for setting the amount of this guarantee were based on various norms, such as the plausibility of the right and the extent of the alleged loss, taking into account of the commercial value of the product in question, the quantity manufactured, etc. The aim is to establish an amount which guarantees that the summonsed person will behave reliably. National Federal Civil and Commercial Chamber of Appeals, Division 2, "American Cyanamid Company *et al. v.* IPESA SA on plea of exploitation", case 172/99, 6 July 1999.

The measures authorised by Art. 50 TRIPS are designed "to prevent an infringement of any intellectual property right from occurring, and in particular to prevent the entry into the channels of commerce in their jurisdiction of goods, including imported goods immediately after customs clearance." They are also intended "to preserve relevant evidence in regard to the alleged infringement." For this purpose, the authorities have authority to "adopt provisional measures *inaudita altera parte* where appropriate, in particular where any delay is likely to cause irreparable harm to the right holder, or when there is a demonstrable risk of evidence being destroyed." The next indents tend to strike a balance, protecting the rights of the alleged infringer. Thus the judge is allowed to require the applicant to prove the reasonability of the right and the imminence of the infringement, and to provide a guarantee or surety. Once the measures have been taken, provision is made for service on the infringer with the possibility of revision, so that it can be decided whether to confirm, revoke or amend the measures. Finally, there is provision for compensation for losses caused by the measures in cases where they are revoked, lapse, or it is found that no infringement or threatened infringement existed.

Comparison of the two provisions mentioned here (Sec. 87 Patent Act and Art. 50 GATT/TRIPS) clearly shows that we have two different solutions. The preventive prohibition of GATT/TRIPS does not contain the option, described above, that the infringer may continue the exploitation. It is clear that Art. 50 appears to be a much more powerful instrument of defence of the patent holder's rights.

Under the former Sec. 87, in the case of "American Cyanamid Co. *et al. v.* Makhteshim Agan Holding BV concerning cessation of use of patent",[26] the judge of first instance decided in favour of the patent holder, ordering suspension of the defendant's exploitation of the patented invention. The Appeals Chamber quashed the judgment, mindful of the existence of the mechanism of the "plea of exploitation" of Sec. 87 Patent Act. The Court found that the intended prohibition of use would entail "premature and hence improper alteration of the situation existing at the time when the relevant petition should be lodged. Thus it would negate the purpose of interim relief, by confusing the subject of the relief sought with the result intended to be achieved by the final judgment." It explained that "this does not mean other interim relief cannot be used in the context of industrial property. But, when the envisaged situation readily fits a legal provision such as that of the said Patent Act Sec. 87, there is no reason in principle to dispense with the specific system."[27] This decision triggered a lively discussion in the literature between

[26] National Federal Civil and Commercial Chamber, Division 1, 23 December 1996, DE, 172–453.

[27] It is worth mentioning that the same Division considered the provisions of Art. 50 TRIPS applicable to a case relating to trade marks, although expressly excepting patents from its opinion. Federal Civil Chamber, Division 1, "Citizen Tokei Kabushiki Kaisha *v.* Trizen Electronics SRL on interim relief", case 1440/97 of 29 May 1997. Division 2 found likewise in the matter of "Pugliese, Francisco Nicolás *v.* Pérez, Carlos Enrique on

defenders of the application of Art. 50 TRIPS in case of presumed infringement of a patent holder's rights,[28] and those who took the opposite view.

The TRIPS supporters based their position on:

- The higher rank of the international treaties, whose provisions prevail over subsequent laws.[29]
- The possibility of granting interim relief other than the measures expressly provided for in the regulations, and of a certain flexibility in granting it, which might justify the application of interim relief beyond the measures expressly provided in the Patent Act.[30]
- The impediment against innovation (Sec. 230 Code of Civil and Commercial Procedure) and the "innovative interim relief" accepted in the legal literature and case law. This is applicable where there is a danger of the situation persisting *de facto* or *de jure*, "thus rendering enforcement of the judgment ineffective or impossible."[31]
- Section 83 of the Implementing Decree authorises imposition of other interim relief allowed in the substantive or procedural law.
- TRIPS requires effective protection of the patent owner's rights. Under Sec. 87 Patent Act, that protection is frustrated if the alleged infringer provides a guarantee (generally insufficient to guarantee the patent holder's rights) and is able to continue to exploit the invention pending a decision on the merits of the case.
- Although Art. 50 does not provide for the involvement of the alleged infringer, as Sec. 87 Patent Act does, the applicant must prove that it has a genuine right, and that there is risk in delay. Section 87 contains no such requirements. Then there are the provisions, described above, intended to uphold the rights of the parties affected by the provisional measures allowed in the indents of Art. 50 TRIPS.

---

interim relief", case 5050/99, of 30 December 1999, concerning conflict between a trade mark and an Internet domain name. Similar judgments at first instance have been given by National Federal Civil and Commercial Court no. 4, Section 8, in "Camuzzi de Argentina SA *v*. Arnedo, Juan Pablo on interim relief", case 2723/99, of 4 June 1999; and "Heladerías Freddo *v*. Spot Network", of 26 November 1997.

[28] The stance of O'Farrell and Chaloupka (O'FARRELL, Ernesto, "El Tratado GATT/TRIPS y el incidente de explotación", LL, 1997-B-1156: "Más sobre las medidas cautelares, el incidente de explotación y el Article 50 of TRIP'S", LL, 1997-D-924; Chaloupka, Pedro, "Efectividad de los derechos de patentes (las patentes impotentes)", LL, 1998-B-1074.

[29] This can be deduced from the National Constitution of the Argentine Republic, from Articles 18, 26 and 27 Vienna Convention on Treaty Law and from the case law of the Argentine Supreme Court (Article 75, indent 22 of the Constitution; Vienna Convention on Treaty Law, 1969, approved by Law 19 865 [ADLA, XXXII-D-6412]; CSJN, "Ekmekdjian *v*. Sofovich", 7 July 1992, LL, 1992-C-540).

[30] Sec. 232, National Code of Civil and Commercial Procedure.

[31] Reimundín – Fassi – Yáñez, quoted by Chaloupka, Pedro, "Efectividad . . .", *op. cit.*, 1077–1078.

- For those who hold this position, the plea of exploitation remains an "imperfect secondary remedy in case such a prohibition cannot be granted or approved".[32]
- Reference is made to the case law of the Supreme Court, which maintains that interpretation of the provisions must also take account of the possible consequences of that interpretation, since denial of the preventive ban on exploitation is tantamount to favouring the infringers, to the detriment of patent holders and consumers.

Some took the opposite stance,[33] favouring the interpretation of the Appeal Court in the case of "American Cyanamid Company". They argue as follows:

- Sections 87 and 50 are compatible because, in the absence of guarantee, the alleged infringer must stop exploitation, which constitutes effective relief.
- The Patent Act was passed after entry into force of the GATT/TRIPS Agreement. The legislature therefore took these provisions into account when drafting the Patent Act.
- Allowance of the option of continuing or halting exploitation is compliant with the constitutional guarantees of lawful trade.

3. Provisional Measures Provided in TRIPS

The interim relief specifically provided by the Patent Act must be supplemented by the provisional measures included in TRIPS. For brevity's sake, we will not list them here, but they are applicable because of the status which international treaties hold in the Argentinean legal order. Despite the discussion generated about the application of Art. 50 to patent disputes, this general principle is unquestioned.

4. Other Provisional Measures

a) The National Code of Civil and Commercial Procedure

Measures of interim relief provided by the National Code of Civil and Commercial Procedure may also be requested. In addition to the attachment and seizure specifically provided under the Patent Act, the Code provides for the following measures:

- judicial intervention, consisting of the appointment of an inspector to collect the seized assets, if these relate to income or proceeds (*e.g.* income from payment of a licence fee). Alternatively, the inspector may provide information about assets, transactions or activities related to the proceedings;

---

[32] Chaloupka, Pedro, "Efectividad . . .", *op. cit.*, 1080.

[33] Among them is the distinguished procedural expert Lino Palacio (Palacio, Lino E., "El incidente de explotación y las medidas cautelares en materia de patentes", ED, 30 May 1997).

- a general freeze of assets, preventing the debtor from selling or encumbering his assets, by entering the measure on the relevant registers. This may take place in cases where there is reason for attachment, but cannot take effect if the debtor's assets are unknown or do not meet the amount of the debt claimed;
- registration of the lawsuit, by entry in the appropriate register of the existence of litigation which may result in amendment of existing entries;
- prohibition of development where there is a danger, if a given situation of fact or of law changes, that this change may affect the judgment or render its enforcement ineffective or impossible;
- prohibition of contracting: when a prohibition of contracting concerning certain assets is necessary by law or by contract, or to ensure forced execution of the assets subject to the order, the judge will order this to be entered on the appropriate registers and notified to the parties concerned;
- general interim relief: under the Code of Civil and Commercial Procedure, Sec. 232, a party having good reason to fear that he may suffer imminent or irreparable harm before judicial recognition of his right, may apply for emergency relief. Depending on circumstances, these measures will be the most apt to ensure provisional compliance with the judgment. The latter measure is particularly important, as it eliminates the rigid and taxative nature of the enumeration.

b) Measures under the National Code of Criminal Procedure

At this point, it is worth mentioning preventive custody, which is intended to ensure that the indicted person complies with the sentence, when there is the possibility of a custodial sentence being imposed. This measure is only applied in cases where the judge considers a suspended sentence inappropriate or if it is inappropriate to allow pre-trial release, because there is good reason to believe that the indicted person will evade justice or hinder the investigations. There is little scope for applying it to the cases of concern to us here, since most of the offences envisaged in the Patent Act do allow suspended sentencing.

5. Measures of Advance Proof

The Argentine procedural order also allows measures of advance proof. This means a given proof may be produced before commencement of the proceedings, if the passage of time may jeopardise such production. Under Sec. 326, the measures which may be requested in advance are the following: a statement by a witness who is very old, seriously disabled or about to leave the country; judicial recognition or expert opinion to record the existence of documents or the state, quality or condition of objects or premises; and a request for information.[34]

[34] Finally, mention should be made of the possibility of applying for preliminary measures tending to facilitate the start of proceedings. Of these measures, the following should be noted: that the person against whom it is proposed to assert the claim must make a

IV. The Judicial Proceedings

As provided by the Patent Act, civil proceedings will follow those of ordinary cases, and criminal actions those of criminal cases, applying the Correction proceedings, a shorter and simpler procedure, ruled in Sec. 405 to 409 of the Code of Criminal Proceedings.

1. Civil Proceedings

The National Code of Civil and Commercial Procedure governs the procedures of an ordinary case. This is the widest of the fact-finding processes, and therefore the one in which the parties have greatest scope for obtaining a ruling based on a detailed knowledge of the facts. This is because it is not subject to the constraints of other, more urgent processes. Therefore it is also the most time-consuming, basically due to the wider scope of the proof and the allowance of longer periods of time.

The Code of Procedure makes the representation by a lawyer compulsory. Any document not signed by a lawyer is deemed not submitted. This is common to all civil proceedings. It means that industrial property agents who can represent patent applicants before INPI by power of attorney or, less often, by authority, cannot do so without the support of a lawyer in court.

Before the trial, the mediation required by Law 24 573 must be carried out. In the case of interest to us here, this is regulated by Decrees 11/96 and 16/97 of the National Federal Civil and Commercial Chamber of Appeals. Recently, in cases of failed mediation, it has been possible to submit the relevant petition.[35]

The stages of ordinary proceedings are:

> First instance: petition, submission of demurrers, defence pleadings and counterclaim, proof, judgment and execution of judgment.

It is important to note that, by virtue of the reforms introduced by the Mediation Act and Law 25 488,[36] once the terms for defence pleadings or counterclaim have elapsed and the demurrers have been resolved, the judge opens the case to evidence. Before starting the stage of production of

---

sworn declaration of any fact relating to its personality. Without corroboration of this, legal action cannot commence. If the eventual defendant has to leave the country, he has to elect domicile. Identification of goods must be carried out, and notice is served for acknowledgement of the obligation to render account, etc. (Sec. 323).

[35] As regards prior mediation in industrial property disputes, including patents, this is analysed in more detail in Witthaus, Mónica, "Mediación y propiedad industrial: Críticas e interrogantes a un año de iniciado el camino", in *Temas de derecho industrial y de la competencia*, Ediciones Ciudad Argentina, Buenos Aires, 1999, 241 *et seq.*

[36] Law 25 488 (Official Gazette of 22 November 2001), in force since 22 May 2002.

evidence tendered, he invites the parties to a hearing at which he enjoins conciliation or another form of conflict resolution. He receives evidence of confessions, if offered by the parties. Then he clarifies the evidence offered, admitting that which deals with disputed or indicative facts. He rules on opposition to opening the case to evidence, and declares the case one of pure law if applicable. He decides on the admissibility of the evidence offered, and resolves the parties' objections in this regard. The judge and the parties may propose conciliatory formulae. If the parties reach agreement, a document is drafted to this effect and approved. If, on the other hand, this conciliatory attempt is unsuccessful, the stage of production of evidence commences.

The Code of Civil and Commercial Procedure, Sec. 377, places the onus of proof on whoever asserts a disputed fact. Each party must prove that it meets the factual precondition of the provision it is invoking as the basis of its claim, defence or plea. This is different for process patents (Sec. 88 Patent Act). Here, the defendant has to prove that the process used by him is different from the patented process; however, the judges are allowed to require the plaintiff to introduce evidence to show that the process used by the defendant infringes the patent and that he is the legal holder thereof in case the product obtained by the protected process is not new.

When obtaining evidence under this section, the legitimate rights of the defendants regarding the protection of their industrial and commercial secrets will be taken into account. Even if the obligation introduced by the amendment seems intended to make the protection stronger, the obligation to prove that the product obtained by the patented process is new in connection with the assumptions of lack of novelty included, is a burden imposed on the patent holder which is harder than the conditions included in Art. 34.2 TRIPS. These provisions are criticised by Poli, who points out that the novelty of the invention has to be established at the moment the application is filed and not at the moment of the infringement and that the requisites introduced may result in the reversal not being applied in the case of parallel imports.[37]

The Code of Civil and Commercial Procedure provides for the following types of evidence, although this listing is not exhaustive:[38] documentary evidence, evidence of records and requested files, evidence of confession (commonly called confessional evidence or close of pleadings), witness evidence, expert evidence and judicially examined evidence.

Most questions arising in patent proceedings are technical. As the parties are assisted by lawyers, whose training is solely legal, like that of the judge, expert evidence is extremely important here. The procedural order allows

---

37 Poli, Iván, *op. cit.*, 9.

38 Under Sec. 378, evidence must be produced by the means expressly provided by law, and by such means as the judge may dispose, at the request of a party or by official order, provided the moral well being and personal freedom of the litigants or third parties are not affected, and no specific ban applies to the case.

each party the right to appoint a technical consultant. This allows parties to present alternative interpretations to the content of the report of the court-appointed expert, or to challenge that report on technical grounds. The result of the expert's report is vastly important because, lacking technical education, the judge will rely on it in most cases to issue his decision.

Once the evidence tendered by the parties has been produced, they are entitled to submit their "alegato", *i.e.* a written pleading on the merits of the evidence. For this purpose, the file is lent to the lawyers in due order.

Having submitted these pleadings, or after the period allowed for this purpose, the judge calls the proceedings for judgment and issues the final judgment.

Second instance: an appeal may be lodged against the judgment of first instance. This opens the proceedings before the second instance, in this case the National Federal Civil and Commercial Chamber of Appeals. Having referred the case to the Chamber, the appellant must submit a written statement of objections justifying the appeal. This will be passed to the opposing party, who will have the opportunity to submit the corresponding defence statement. Resolution of the case proceeds once the statement of objections and the defence statement have been received, or after the period allowed for the latter and (exceptionally[39]), on production of the appropriate evidence. The judgment of second instance will be given by majority: each judge casts his vote in the order in which he was chosen, providing justification or conforming to the vote of another.

The procedural order allows appeal against refusal of leave to appeal. This allows the party to petition directly before the Chamber that the appeal, denied in the first instance, be allowed.

Although the judgment of the court of second instance is normally final, in the cases allowed by Sec. 14 of Law 48,[40] an extraordinary appeal may be made before the Supreme Court.

---

[39] The production of evidence at the second instance is exceptional, and only occurs when probative measures were denied at first instance, when negligence has been declared in relation to the measures, or when new facts arise.

[40] Under Sec. 14 of Law 48, pleading before the Supreme Court is authorised in the following cases: when the action has questioned the validity of a treaty, an act of Congress or an act of an authority executed in the name of the nation, and a ruling has been given against its validity. When the validity of a law, decree or decision of a provincial authority has been questioned on grounds of contravening the national constitution, a treaty or an act of Congress and a ruling has been given in favour of the validity of the provincial law or authority. When the meaning of a clause of the Constitution, of a treaty, an act of Congress or a commission performed in the name of the government has been questioned, and a ruling has been given against the validity of the title, right, privilege or exemption on which the clause in question is based, and that ruling forms the subject of litigation. In addition to the above cases, there is the "praetorian creation" of "arbitrary judgment". This means pleading before the Supreme Court is allowed in cases which, while not concerning any of the legal conditions, nevertheless resulted in a plainly arbitrary ruling, which necessitates a review.

The Court, at its own discretion may reject the extraordinary appeal when the matter at issue proves to be groundless or is of no transcendental importance (Sec. 280, Code of Civil and Commercial Procedure).

It is also possible to file a complaint for rejection of an appeal, which shall be directly submitted to the Supreme Court.

2. Criminal Procedures

The handling of criminal proceedings is governed by the National Code of Criminal Procedure (CPPN). Criminal proceedings may start by specific complaint or police or official warning. The first stage of this process is examination, aiming at investigating the facts of the alleged offence and proving the existence of a punishable fact and the circumstances surrounding it. It will seek to identify those involved, verify the indicted person's personal background, and find out the extent of the injury.

This stage is conducted by a single judge,[41] upon prior request by the Prosecutor [42] which is necessary for the judge to focus on procedures. For cases of illicit acts committed by an unidentified individual, investigations shall be delegated from the beginning of procedures to the Public Ministry, with notice thereof given to the acting judge.[43]

Among the means of proof intended to clarify the facts, the Code lists the following: judicial inspection including the corporal and mental inspection of the indicted person and the identification of corpses; reconstruction of the facts; register of domiciles (specifying the cases in which submission is appropriate) and personal requisition; seizure of objects relating to the offence; interception of correspondence ordered by justified process; opening and examining of such correspondence; telephone tapping; witness evidence; expert evidence; recognition of persons and objects; and confrontation.

Ten days from the preliminary inquiry, the judge will order trial of the indicted person if the evidence is sufficiently convincing to assume that an offence has taken place and that the accused is guilty.

If the examination stage closes by sending the indicted person for trial, the case becomes a legal action.

This is the conclusive stage of the criminal procedure, the course of which culminates in judgment. The principles it must meet are: verbal hearing

---

[41] The judge exceptionally sends the record of proceedings to the prosecutor so that the latter may hear the case, which is known as a delegated hearing or investigation of the case.

[42] The Prosecutor shall make the pertinent request within 24 hours from the time the alleged crime became known by a due report or by police prevention or directly (prosecutor's initiative). Such term can vary in certain cases.

[43] In this case, delegation is directly provided for by the law: Sec. 196bis CPPN, as per text incorporated by Law 25 409, Official Bulletin of 20 April 2001.

(without which it is invalid); directness; concentration; continuity; and openness. It is conducted by a judge,[44] proceeding verbally.

The court summons the Public Prosecutor and the other parties to appear in court within five days to examine the procedural steps, the documents and the seized items. They can offer evidence and make any recusations they consider relevant. The parties and the Public Prosecutor can offer new evidence or indicate that they agree with the inclusion by reading aloud the statements of the witnesses or experts produced at the examination stage. The court will order production of the evidence and will reject what it considers irrelevant or superfluous. If necessary, the court may order production of essential examination measures which were omitted or refused at the earlier stage.

The court sets a hearing for the discussion. It summons the parties, witnesses, experts and interpreters who are to be involved. The discussion is conducted orally and in public (saving exceptional cases involving minors, etc). It resolves the preliminary questions of competence, admissibility of experts and witnesses, formation of the court and nullities. The indicted person's deposition may be taken, though this is optional because he may refuse to declare. The evidence is admitted, and the parties are called upon to plead on the basis of the evidence, to bring charges and offer defences. The Public Prosecutor, the party seeking damages and the defending counsel have the right of reply. Counsel for the defence has the final word.

If the indicted person pleads guilty, and in practice this is rare, the admission of evidence to prove guilt may be omitted. This can only be done by agreement between the court, the prosecutor, the party seeking damages and the defending counsel.

With the admission of evidence completed, the court may move to deliberate or deliver judgment immediately after closure of the discussion. If the case is complex, or time is short, it may be necessary to postpone the drafting of the groundings of the sentence. It will then be read, on pain of nullity, at a public hearing to be held within no more than three days.

V. Defences

1. Pleas Based on the Patent Act and Case Law

In this point we will analyse the pleas which arise from the rules and case law in the specific field. Those based on the rest of the legal order will merely be mentioned in passing, since thorough analysis would exceed the scope of this paper.

---

[44] In this case as it is a "correction proceeding" it is conducted by one Judge, other than in the ordinary criminal proceeding where it is conducted by a collegiate court, consisting in three judges.

First, it is worth mentioning that the allegedly infringing object or process and the patented object or process are not one and the same. The scope of the holder's exclusive right, and hence his right to debar the infringer, rests in the patent claims.[45] It is these which must form the basis of comparison between the objects or processes. As stated, this is where the expert's evidence proves conclusive in nearly all cases. This is the main foundation of nearly all judgments, given the technical nature of the issue and the purely legal training of the judge and counsels of the parties.

Section 65 Patent Act allows opposition to patent nullity or expiry actions by defence or plea. The patent holder's rights lapse in case of nullity or expiry. Hence, in such cases, one of the conditions of infringement is lacking – the existence of a valid patent.

Under Sec. 59, a patent is wholly or partly invalid when granted contrary to the provisions of the Act. This includes absence of the requirements of Sec. 4: novelty (which must be universal),[46] industrial application or inventive activity; as well as the cases mentioned in Sec. 6, which are not considered inventions and those contained in Sec. 7, which are expressly excluded from patentability.[47]

---

[45] Moncayo von Hase, Andrés, "El nuevo régimen de patentes de invención: extensión y límites a los derechos", in Correa, Carlos *et al.*, *Derecho de patentes*, *op. cit.*, 113.

[46] Reference should be made here to the exception of Sec. 5, whereby disclosure of an invention does not affect its novelty when the inventor or its assignees have revealed the invention by any medium of communication or have exhibited it at a national or international exhibition, within one year prior to the date of submission of the patent application or, as the case may be, of recognition of priority. On submission of the appropriate action, documentary evidence must be included on the terms provided by this law.

[47] Pursuant to Sec. 6°, the following are not considered inventions under this Act: a) discoveries, scientific theories and mathematical methods; b) literary or artistic works or any aesthetic creation, as well as scientific works; c) plans, rules and methods for carrying out intellectual activities, for games or for financial-commercial activities, as well as computer programs; d) manners of presenting information; e) methods of surgical, therapeutic treatment or diagnosis applicable on the human body and those related to animals; f) the juxtaposition of known inventions and mixing of known products, variants thereof as to shape, size or materials, except when referred to their combination or fusion in a manner that they cannot be separately operated or when their inherent qualities or functions are modified so as to obtain an industrial result being not obvious to an expert in the art; g) any kind of living matter and pre-existing substances in nature. Pursuant to Sec. 7, the following are not patentable; a) inventions which working within the territory of Argentina should be prevented in order to protect public order or morals, health or the life of people or animals, or to preserve vegetables or to prevent severe environmental damages; b) all biological and genetic material existing in nature or a reproduction thereof, in implicit biological processes in animal, vegetal and human reproduction, including genetic processes related to material likely to lead to its own duplication under normal conditions in nature. Pursuant to Sec. 6 of the decree (which, in the author's opinion, in that regard exceeds the provisions set forth by the law), plants, animals and essentially biological processes for reproduction thereof shall not be considered patentable matter, transgenic plants and animals which exclusion from patentability is not contemplated by the legal text being also thereby excluded from patentability.

Section 62 provides that patents and utility model certificates lapse on expiry of their validity, for waiver by holder thereof (in cases of co-ownership, such waiver shall be made jointly) non-payment of the annual maintenance fees; in addition when use is granted to a third party, but the invention is not exploited for two years, for reasons attributable to the patent holder. According to TRIPS and the Paris Convention, a patent may only be declared expired when a new, compulsory licence is granted. Once this is granted, if the licensee cannot exploit the invention due to the patent holder's behaviour, the patent holder will be penalised by the lapse of the patent. Note that non-exploitation must be the fault of the patent holder, to whom the punishment applies, and not that of the licensee. The licensee may stand to gain, as his obligation to remunerate the patent holder will have lapsed. Law 111 provides for the lapse to be declared (without prior granting of a compulsory licence) if exploitation has not taken place for two years from issue or after suspension of exploitation for a similar period. Both the present Act and Law 111 release the patent holder from the consequences of non-exploitation in case of *force majeure*. The present law expressly defines as *force majeure* "objective difficulties of a technical and legal nature such as delay in obtaining registration, delay by public bodies concerned with authorisation or with placing on the market, beyond the patent holder's control, which render exploitation of the invention impossible." This solution had already been accepted in cases resolved during the validity of the old law.[48]

In practice, nullity and lapse are usually thrashed out by counterclaim, which challenges the plaintiff's valid title, as evidenced by the case law on this point.[49] As both mechanisms are automatic, there is no need for them to be

[48] Thus it has been said that ". . . action for lapse is not viable when the non-use is due to causes of *force majeure*. The fact or principle here is one of the conventional conditions of *force majeure*. Hence 'it is not strange, then, that the administrative permission previously requested for the dispensing of medicinal specialities has been mentioned by authors specialising in industrial law as a typical condition falling within the exemption contemplated in Article 26 of Law 22 362' (*cf.* case 8358 of 30 July 1991). Although, in the precedent described, this doctrine was applied to a case involving the lapse of a trade mark due to lack of use, its conclusions are wholly applicable to the analogous case governed by Article 47 of Law 111. That Article concerns another manifestation of industrial property: the right deriving from the granting of a patent. Under such conditions, the plaintiff's claim cannot be accepted even when – in the best case for the plaintiff – the matter at issue is judged solely in the light of the provisions of the former Law 111" (National Federal Civil and Commercial Chamber, case 11 767 of 10 February 1998, "IPESA SA *v.* Nissan Chemical Industries Ltda. on lapse of patent").

[49] "Hence the ensemble as such, claimed by the plaintiff, is not anticipated either by the patents, which relate solely to mate drinking tube improvements, nor by the patent combining tube and receptacle, but with no link to the suction control system. It follows that, by combining known means, the claimant invented an artefact of sufficient novelty to fall within the scope of Law 111. Thus the deliberate behaviour, noted by the defendants, is clearly unlawful. That fact leads to the judgment being upheld, since the counterclaim was dismissed, and the infringers ordered to refrain from their unfair action" (National Federal Civil and Commercial Chamber of Appeals, Division 2, of 2 April 1996, case 50

judicially declared to place the invention in the public domain. Thus whoever has a legitimate interest can use these defences without awaiting a prior ruling in the matter.

Section 36 states that the right conferred by a patent cannot stand against:

> "a) a third party who carries out scientific or technological investigation purely for experiment, trial or teaching purposes, and for this purpose makes or uses a product or follows a process equal to the one patented."

This exception is common to most legal systems and is designed to avoid exclusive rights deriving from the Patent Act obstructing scientific and technological progress. It may be asked what the exact limit of the permission intended here is, as the growing co-operation between industrial sectors and universities sometimes makes it difficult totally to exclude a commercial purpose, albeit indirect. Examples which come to mind are pre-competitive investigations intended to perfect the product for commercial exploitation after the invention, or applications for an additional patent.

> "b) Habitual preparation of medicaments per unit by authorised professionals, following a medical formulation, nor to acts relating to medicaments thus prepared.
>
> "c) Any person who acquires, uses, imports or in any way markets the patented product obtained by the patented process, once that product has been lawfully placed on the market in any country. It shall be understood that placing on the market is lawful when it conforms to the Agreement on Trade-Related Intellectual Property Rights, Part III, Section IV, TRIPS."[50]

The Implementing Decree explains that a product is considered lawfully placed on the market when the licensee authorised to market it in the country can prove its authorisation from the patent holder in the country of acquisition, or from a third party authorised to place it on the market.[51]

This provision concerns the exhaustion of patent rights. This is one of the most complex issues in the field. The principle is that the holder's right to the patent is "exhausted" when the patented products are first launched on the market. At this time, subsequent transfers of the products are free. The Patent Act adopts the international exhaustion of rights. This means that exhaustion occurs regardless of the country where the first market launch took place. The existence of an export in breach of the territorial exclusivity provided in a distribution agreement or licence in no way affects the legitimacy of placement on the market. This is because, in this case, we are

903/95, "Benítez, Héctor Pedro *v.* Gaya, Miguel *et al.* on cessation of use of models and patterns, and on compensation").

[50] The TRIPS Agreement leaves each state free to decide what system of exhaustion of rights it adopts.

[51] The obscure wording of the Implementing Decree on this point leaves it open to various interpretations. One of these would involve ignoring the international exhaustion adopted by the legislature, banning parallel imports. This provision would be unconstitutional, because it contradicts the law (Moncayo Von Hase, Andrés, "El nuevo régimen . . .", *op. cit.*, 161 *et seq.*).

dealing with breach of contract. This cannot be held against the third party acquiring the products in question. It may give rise to contractual liability, but not to lawsuits based on patent law. Another controversial point is whether the effects of exhaustion of the right occur if there is a compulsory licence since, in that case, there would be legitimacy, but this would ignore the wishes of the patent holder.

Finally, Sec. 36d) governs the use of inventions patented in Argentina on board foreign terrestrial vehicles or sea or air craft accidentally or temporarily in circulation in Argentina's jurisdiction, if used solely for their own needs.

The literature and case law have admitted the defence of "prior use". This is applicable to the case of a first inventor, before the patent holder, who exploits the invention secretly. This activity does not render the patent invalid, since secret exploitation does not destroy novelty. However, it does allow the first inventor to continue that exploitation, since there is no question of an infringement.[52]

According to Ledesma, production of a patented invention is not an offence if it is non-industrial and does not constitute exploitation in economic terms.[53]

Breuer Moreno quotes the case, which he calls "provocation", of a patent holder commissioning its competitors, through an intermediary, to make the patented products, and then taking action against them for counterfeiting. This might be deemed similar to a licence, so that the manufacturer is not breaking the law in any way.[54]

Genovesi cites the instance of manufacture not long after the lapse of the patent. For some authors this is legitimate, since the only way of freely exploiting the patented product since its entry to the public domain is to allow competitors to start production beforehand. Some take the opposite opinion, emphasising that manufacture is one of the patent holder's exclusive rights. Hence, they maintain, any manufacture before expiry of the patent is unlawful, although the objects are only placed on the market after expiry.[55]

2. Defence in Criminal Cases

The crimes contemplated by the Patent Act require positive intent, and the absence of intent is an acceptable defence in this case.[56] However, the

---

[52] Genovesi, Mariano L., "Acciones . . .", *op. cit.*, 350.

[53] Ledesma, Julio C., *Derecho penal industrial,* Depalma, Buenos Aires, 1987, 172.

[54] Breuer Moreno, Pedro, *Tratado de patentes de invención,* vol. II, Abeledo-Perrot, Buenos Aires, 1957, 595.

[55] Genovesi, Mariano L., "Acciones . . .", *op. cit.*, 353.

[56] Pursuant to case law, it has been held that "as an already planned action intended to use the rights derived from ownership of a registration, the absence of fraud implies the absence of such planned action, *i.e.* the absence of the objective element of the legal definition of the offence." (National Federal Civil and Commercial Chamber of

publication of patents leads part of the doctrine to consider that it is viable to assume that infringers know about the patent and therefore commit an intentional infringement.[57] But according to Aracama Zorraquín, Sec. 76 punishes those who "knowingly" perform the enumerated acts, requiring positive proof that the infringer had a prior knowledge of the patent.

3. Formal Defences

The claim for damages is time-barred after two years.[58]

VI. Damages

Under Sec. 81 Patent Act, the patent holder and his licensee may bring civil actions to obtain compensation for loss incurred. This provision is supplemented by Civil Code Secs. 1069, 1077 and 1109, concerning the obligation to make good a loss caused by wilful misconduct or culpable negligence, and the extent of the loss to be compensated.

Action for compensation may be brought in a civil or criminal context. If the criminal option is taken, acquittal of the person on trial does not imply dismissal of the case, since an order to pay compensation may still be given.

As for the rules of compensation, mention should be made of the following:

- Consequential loss, the damage suffered by the patent holder: a fall in sales and therefore of profits; a fall in the prices of the product on the market, reflecting the counterfeiter's lower costs, enabling him to sell them more cheaply; and less possibility of reinvestment, etc.

Appeals, Division 2, "Pezzi, SADI A on litigation", 30 January 1990, Case 6147, reg. 6901, Court No. 3, Sec. No. 9).

[57] "The only circumstance of having an infringing element within the business premises shall render the accused liable for infringement, until the accused proves that a third party manufactured said product and, further, in that case, that he/she had no knowledge of such infringement" (*Gaceta del Foro*, 196–372, cited by Genovesi, Mariano L., "*Acciones . . .*", *op. cit.*, 361. In that sense, also Breuer Moreno, Pedro, *Tratado . . .*, *op. cit.*, 574 and Ledesma, Julio C., *Derecho penal . . .*, *op .cit.*, 170).

[58] In "Continental Plast *v*. Terlizzi SAIC on damages", it is further stated that time limitations run from the moment the corresponding action is originated, *i.e.* at the time the event that generated liability took place, unless damages only become known later by the injured party, and in which case the action for damages may originate at a later date. In the reference case, the appellant had vainly argued that no action could be taken by the appellant until a final decision was passed on proceedings started for discontinuance of use, since it was held that said party was fully able to bring an action for damages in due time (National Federal Civil and Commercial Chamber of Appeals, Division 3, Case 1191/98, 20 May 1999). Breuer Moreno held that the infringer owed to the patent holder the gains, *i.e.* the net benefits, obtained by the undue use of the patent. In that case, a time limitation of ten years should be applicable under Sec. 4023 Civil Code (Breuer Moreno, Pedro, *Tratado . . .*, *op. cit.*, 637 *et seq.*).

- Loss of profit, the earnings of which the injured party is deprived by the infringer's unlawful action. It is caused, *inter alia,* by loss of custom due to the counterfeiter's unfair competition, sometimes to the point of ruin. Some case law has made a distinction between this concept and that of the profits earned by the infringer, which it treats merely as an indication.[59] In some trade mark cases, however, the infringer's earnings have been used as a basis to quantify this heading.[60]
- Pain and suffering as per Civil Code Sec. 1078, applicable without the need for proof, provided an unlawful act has taken place and the claimant holds the right. In this case, pain and suffering take the form of discrediting the legitimate patent holder's business, entailing loss due to the presence of forgeries on the market, possibly of far inferior quality to the legitimate products. In this regard, there has been discussion about the appropriateness of compensation on these grounds if the injured party is a legal person. Orgaz has argued positively on this, saying that legal persons may "experience other pain and suffering, compatible with their nature, and claim appropriate compensation. This applies in

[59] In the case of "Ancase SA *v.* Zugolan SA on cessation of use of patent – compensation in Zugolan SA *v.* Ancase SA on invalidity of patent", it was stated that "what has to be established is the loss suffered by the plaintiff, not the gain procured by the opposing party. Such gain 'can only serve as a guide to gauge the scale of the loss, especially since, as far as making gains is concerned, the use of the trade mark (patent in this case) is but one of many factors contributing to this end . . .' " (National Federal Civil and Commercial Chamber of Appeal, Division 2, case 8072, 30 October 1992). Likewise, concerning infringement of trade mark rights, "the loss cannot be demonstrated in terms of the sales which defendant may have made since, as this Chamber has stated, there is no necessary correlation between income on the one hand and loss of earnings on the other (Division 3, case 2020, of 19 September 1985). This applies especially when it is unproven that the plaintiff's trade mark was so well-known that it can be presumed that the defendant's sales depended on the use of that name" (National Federal Civil and Commercial Chamber of Appeal, Division 3, 29 October 1985, "Vallejo Jiménez, Félix *v.* Traverso Rossi, Ulises Héctor", case 3544). Contrary to this, the Federal Appeals Chamber of Córdoba, Civil and Commercial Division, did use the infringer's profits to calculate this figure in "Brunello, Américo", of 22 August 1977, LL, 1980-A-274.

[60] "While it is certain that the extent of the loss cannot precisely be established, and that part of the price received covers costs and materials, compensation must be estimated. On this subject, Callmann's position, quoted by Otamendi, seems right when he affirms the existence of a definite relation between the defendant's income and the plaintiff's losses, both attributable to the diversion of sales, as evident from the defendant's conviction. Moreover, the amount must be set in terms of the net extra profit which the plaintiff would probably have earned, had it benefited from the infringer's sales . . ." (National Federal Civil and Commercial Chamber of Appeal, Division 3, case 7695/91, "Quimarco SAIC *v.* Dimaca SRL *et al.* on cessation of use of trade mark", 3 March 1995). The rulings quoted by Faerman, on compensation in cases of infringement of trade mark rights, are in line with this (Faerman, Silvia, "La condena al pago de indemnización por infracción a los derechos marcarios", in *Derechos intelectuales*, vol. IV, Astrea, Buenos Aires, 1989, 218).

> cases of usurping good name or damage to reputation."[61] Oscar Etcheverry quotes an old ruling of the National Federal Civil and Commercial Chamber of Appeal that "although the plaintiff suffered no material loss, his pain and suffering cannot but be compensated, since the action derives from an offence of brand imitation, found by firm judgment."[62] Regrettably, since then, judgments have been given which tend to disallow this item when the claimant is a legal person.[63] The literature has criticised this.

In addition to those already listed, this author cites the following items and grounds of compensation: restitution of profits or return of proceeds, as per Sec. 20 of Decree-Law 6673/1963 (industrial patterns and models). Breuer Moreno also favours inclusion of this item. Another is unjust enrichment, which applies if the defendant gets richer at the claimant's expense, a causal relation between the two and lack of good cause justifying the enrichment.[64]

As for admission of the damage claim, it should be said that a new judicial attitude has recently emerged. Echoing the criticism in the literature,[65] it maintains that loss must be presumed to exist in cases where an infringement has been found. The judge must quantify it by applying Sec. 165 Code of Civil Procedure if it cannot be calculated exactly from the evidence in the case. The bases of this new attitude are amply expounded in the case of "Benítez, Héctor Pedro *v.* Gaya on cessation of use of models and patterns, and compensation". This concerned infringement of patent rights:

> "In the context of industrial property difficulties of proof of the loss caused by an infringement are well-known. Often, infringement of a legitimately obtained right originates – as in the records of the proceedings – in malicious conduct. The most modern literature therefore tends – not without firm foundations – to maintain that, as a rule, any usurping of a brand, company name or style, patent or pattern causes a loss. And, as this is generally hard (if not impossible) to prove, the authors favour working from a presumption of loss. To overcome the problems of

---

[61] Orgaz, Alfredo, *El daño resarcible*, 275, quoted by Etcheverry, Oscar, "La reparación de daños en las infracciones de marcas y nombres", in *Derechos intelectuales*, vol. III, Astrea, Buenos Aires, 1988, 17.

[62] Federal Capital Chamber of Appeals, 22 December 1932, JA, 40-348, quoted by Etcheverry, Oscar, "La reparación . . .", *op. cit.*, 17.

[63] It has been ruled that "a petition for compensation of pain and suffering in favour of a commercial company cannot stand . . ." (National Federal Civil and Commercial Chamber of Appeals, Division 2, "Relojes Rolex Argentina SA *v.* Joyería Vía Florida", 2 July 1985, LL, 1986-E-703; JA, 1986-I-346 and that "compensation for pain and suffering does not apply when the claimant is a legal person"; National Federal Civil and Commercial Chamber, Division 3, "Antonio Delgado SA *v.* Alvitos, José M. *et al.*", JA, 1981-IV-240.

[64] Although Etcheverry provides his listing in relation to compensation for undue use of trade marks, the same appears to apply to patents (Etcheverry, Oscar, "La reparación . . .", *op. cit.*, 18 *et seq.*).

[65] Faerman, Silvia, "La condena . . .", *op. cit.*, 218 *et seq.*, applicable to the case, although it refers to trade mark law.

proof and prevent them serving as a means of impunity, especially when the case has connotations of deliberate intent, the judges must use the precautionary ascertainment allowed by the last part of Sec. 165 of the applicable Code. This entails a careful appraisal of the circumstances of each case (*cf.* Otamendi, J., *Derecho de marcas*, 2nd ed., Abeledo-Perrot, Buenos Aires, 1995, p. 325; Etcheverry, O., 'La reparación de daños en las infracciones de marcas y nombres', in *Derechos intelectuales*, Title III, Astrea, pp. 13/20, etc.). Still, it is necessary to warn that, while the case law does not accept certain generalisations of the literature, and allows for the different circumstances of reality, it has recently adopted a certain relaxation of the conventional criteria. In doing so, it approximates to the modern literature, which features a more relaxed mood, in accepting the reality of the loss, and a severe attitude if practices contrary to good faith or to healthy commercial competition are found (*cf.* my vote in case 25 123/94, 'Iurcovich, Natán León *v.* Industrias Bravi SRL on cessation of use of models and patterns', of 28/12/1995). This division ruled that, if a competitor acts unlawfully by usurping, copying or imitating a brand, placing infringing items on the market with the illegitimate purpose of winning a third party's customer by these reprehensible means, that competitor must not be allowed to use the difficulty of proof to evade its civil liabilities. An aura of impunity leads unscrupulous traders into conduct which is ethically and legally wrong. This is seriously detrimental to civilised life and undermines the fundamental pillars of the public good (order, justice and legal security). Therefore, as I said in the case referred to (25 123/1994), in the face of certain activities, it is usually reasonable to assume the existence of losses – in favour of the holder of the violated right – as causally linked to the unlawful act. Though proof is at times fiendishly difficult, the judge still reaches moral certainty that the infringer has caused definite, and not merely conjectured, damage.

My vote in case 7491 of 4/9/1990 was in line with these principles, explicitly or implicitly. This was not an isolated expression, but a manifestation of the juridical realism mentioned above. Ultimately this serves to restrain the unfair advantage and stem the loss unlawfully caused. Thus the aim is to help, as far as possible, towards morality of customs in the complex world of business. Other examples of this laudable trend in the case law are the rulings of Division 1 (case 640 of 8/10/1971), of this Division 2 (case 5221 of 9/10/1987) and of Division 3 (case 4465 of 6/3/1987) (National Federal Civil and Commercial Chamber of Appeals, Division 2, 2/4/1996, case 50 903/95, 'Benítez, Héctor Pedro *v.* Gaya, Miguel *et al.*')."

17
The Enforcement of Patent Rights in Brazil

JOAQUIM EUGENIO GOULART AND IVAN AHLERT

A. Brief Outline of the System of Patents and Civil Procedure

I. Patents

Industrial property rights are governed by the Brazilian Industrial Property Code (IPC), which covers patents, trade marks, service marks, collective and certification marks, indications of origin, industrial designs, trade secrets and unfair competition law. This law, which came in force on 15 May 1997, also covers procedures and lays down criteria for the allocation of damages.

Brazil is a member to the Paris Convention of 1883 (as reviewed in Stockholm in 1967), the TRIPS Agreement and the Patent Cooperation Treaty (PCT).

The applicability of TRIPS has been subject to a great deal of controversy. First, there was dissent between the Government and private practitioners about its date of application: 1 January 2000 for the former, and 1 January 1995 for the latter. Second, there is still some controversy about whether TRIPS requires the extension of patents granted under the preceding legislation with a 15-year term and which were in force at the date of application of the new rule. The Brazilian Patent and Trade Mark Office (Instituto Nacional de Propriedade Industrial (INPI)) has been continuously denying administrative requests for extension of patents. In a decision issued after 1 January 2000 in connection with Brazilian Patent PI 8403932 in the name of Bassani Ticino S.p.A., INPI acknowledged that as a result of a panel proposed by the US against Canada on the issue of the extension of patent term, it was determined by WTO that all patents that are still in force on the "date of application" of TRIPS in a member country should have their term extended to at least 20 years. The same decision added that according to the official position of the Brazilian Government the "date of application" for Brazil should be of 1 January 2000, and finally it refers to the fact that the Ministry of Development, Industry and Commerce, to which the Patent Office is subordinated, has issued an official report in 1997 (CONJUR No. 24/97), which denies the applicability of TRIPS as a ground for extending the term of patents, for which reason the Patent Office is prevented from actually extending patents.

Notwithstanding INPI's position, among several court decisions involving the extension of patent term from 15 to 20 years, the vast majority is in favour of the applicability of TRIPS to this effect. This would mean that those patentees wishing to have their patents extended need to revert to the courts, although it is not possible to predict a positive outcome, as not all courts share the view that the patent period should be extended. There is one decision by a superior court of justice that has indeed endorsed an extension.[1]

Patents are granted by INPI. The basic patentability requirements which are examined by INPI are novelty, inventive step and industrial applicability. Patentable inventions include either products or processes, and include chemicals, pharmaceuticals, foodstuffs and transgenic microorganisms.

Patents of invention are granted for a period of 20 years from the filing date, but no less than 10 years from the date of grant. For utility models, these terms are 15 and 7 years, respectively. One of the major problems encountered in Brazil's IP system is the backlog in applications. Currently, about 500,000 requests for trade mark applications and 24,000 requests for patent applications are pending before INPI. The office requires about four years to proceed with a trade mark application, and seven for a patent application.[2] In this respect, it does not help that the office has been working without a Commissioner for more than a year. One proposal that has been made by the Brazilian Industrial Property Association (ABPI) is to give the office financial independence over its income of more than 100 million Reais (about 30 million Euro).[3]

The current law does not provide for formal pre-grant oppositions, but any interested party – including the applicant – is entitled to submit comments and evidence concerning patentability issues at any time up to the end of examination.

Furthermore, according to Sec. 51 IPC, within 6 months from grant any person having a legitimate interest may file an administrative nullity action before INPI, and INPI may also institute nullity proceedings *ex officio*. Moreover, nullity of a patent can also be judicially requested at any time during the life time of the patent or even after its expiration as a matter of defence in the course of an infringement action.

II. Civil Procedure

There are basically five phases in a civil court action under the Brazilian Code of Civil Procedure: the pleadings phase, clarification, fact-finding, decision, and appeal.

The initial claim commences the action. In the claim, the plaintiff will expose the case and facts, its legal standings and its request for remedy.

---

[1] Superior Court of Justice, 15 March 2004, Special Appeal No. 423.240-RJ.

[2] Figures taken from Folha de São Paulo, 19 March 2004.

[3] Resolution 44 of the ABPI of 20 February 2003.

Once the defendant is duly served with the summons, it will have a 15-day term to respond to the court action (*e.g.*: patent infringement action, patent nullity action). A request for preliminary injunction made by the plaintiff is usually examined by the Court within five days from the filing of the complaint. The defendant must present its arguments in a detailed manner. Subsequently, both parties are requested to amend possible procedural irregularities. The parties then have the opportunity to present further evidence, list their witnesses, request the dismissal of any prejudicial issue on the merits of the court action, such as the competence of the judge to examine the matter. Before handing down a decision, the judge may conduct a trial, which generally takes place in a single day. During the trial, the judge hears the witnesses and the oral arguments of the attorneys and also examines other pieces of evidence. A decision without a hearing is allowed in some specific cases, such as:

(a) where there is a clear case on the evidence, *e.g.* where the limitation period has expired; and/or
(b) when the issue on the merits is solely of law, or when no evidence needs to be heard; or
(c) in cases of default.

The vast majority of the first instance decisions are appealed to the Higher Courts.

If a patent was not granted to the true inventor or to a legitimate successor of the true inventor, instead of requesting nullity of the patent the true inventor or his successor may judicially claim the adjudication of the patent, *i.e.*, the transfer of the rights while maintaining the patent in force.

Unfortunately, the Brazilian court system is not known for its efficiency. Backlogs are huge, and in the last couple of years there have been a number of initiatives on how to improve the judicial system in order to streamline procedures.

III. Patent Nullity and Infringement

Patent nullity actions must be filed at federal courts.[4] During a nullity action, a judge may, as a preventive or incidental measure, determine the suspension of the effects of a patent, provided the relevant procedural requirements are met.

[4] In Appeal No. 9202086737, the 5th Group of the Federal Regional Court (TRF-2R) decided unanimously that in nullity actions of patents and trade marks, INPI should be co-defendant since it is the authority which is responsible for the granting of the rights (DJ of 8 February 2000, 217–218).

A patent may be declared null when granted contrary to the provisions of the IPC, *e.g.* for lack of novelty or inventive step.[5] Alternatively, nullity may apply to only some among the claims (partial nullity), provided the subsisting claims constitute subject matter that is patentable per se.

Nullity of a patent will render it void *ab initio* ("*ex-tunc*").

In the past five years, the number of new court actions aimed at enforcing patent rights has substantially increased. While in 1997, 80 new patent actions were filed before the Brazilian Courts, in 1999 there were 200 new filings and in 2001 more than 100. These numbers are substantially higher when compared with the last decade. However, they are still modest when compared with the number of patent applications filed in Brazil; in the year 2002, 24,098 new patent applications were filed. This is a slight decrease when compared to 2003 (an estimate of 20,000), yet still a significant increase when compared with figures of ten years ago.

There are several reasons for an increase in court actions, including the development of the local market, the significant improvement of the economic situation of the country, the enactment of the new Industrial Property Code (IPC) in 1997 and the TRIPS Agreement. In fact, these new legal tools for enforcing patent rights in Brazil are definitely encouraging patent holders to litigate for the protection of their rights and for claiming monetary compensation for infringement.

This new tendency is also leading the Brazilian Courts to be more thorough when analysing patent infringement cases. For instance, in 2001, the Brazilian Courts in 83% of the decided cases found the patents at issue valid and infringed where the patent owners were foreign companies. This percentage shows that the Brazilian Courts take a very pro-patent view when deciding patent infringement cases.

There are usually two hearings during a civil patent infringement case. The first one takes place after the defendant files its response. It is a conciliatory hearing, in which the judge acts as a mediator and tries to convince the parties to execute a settlement.

The second hearing is the final one, in which the parties hear their witnesses and the judge takes the deposition of the legal representatives of the parties. It is a one-day hearing and it is not mandatory depending on the necessity of the parties to present their evidence.

A patent infringement action usually takes from two to three years to be decided by the first instance court and another two years in the higher courts. In spite of the long duration of the litigation, patent owners may obtain

---

[5] According to a unanimous decision issued by the 1st Group of the Federal Regional Court (TRF-2R), Civil Appeal No. 97.02.14696-8 RJ, published in the Official Gazette of 13 April 1999, a nullity action based on lack of novelty of the patented invention requires the performance of an expert opinion, under penalty of characterising restriction of defence.

preliminary injunctions to stop the infringement until a final decision on the merits is duly rendered.

IV. The Profession

In Brazil, patent applicants can be represented before the INPI by attorneys-at-law or by registered Industrial Property Agents. Before the courts, only attorneys-at-law are qualified to represent applicants or patentees.

The profession of Industrial Property Agent is regulated by Decree-Law No. 8.933 of 26 January 1946.

Nevertheless, following the enactment of the Industrial Property Code of 1971 (Law 5.772/71), INPI assumed that Decree-Law 8.933 had been revoked, thus leaving the field open for any person to act before the office as a representative of patent and trade mark applicants. Not surprisingly, this led to a flood of unqualified persons acting as representatives, thus jeopardising the applicants' right to be represented only by qualified professionals and ultimately also affecting the proper operation of INPI.

The Brazilian Association of Industrial Property Agents (ABAPI) objected to this. Finally on 28 March 1998, a Ministerial resolution[6] was published in the Official Gazette, delegating powers to INPI to regulate the profession of industrial property agents. This regulation was established by Normative Act No. 141 of 4 April 1998 and allowed the registration as "industrial property agents" by those who could prove to have practiced before INPI prior to 24 March 1998. While this Act did not eliminate all unqualified representatives, it established a cut-off date, after which the title of industrial property agent would only be granted to persons passing the exam.

Normative Act No. 141 reinvigorated the provisions of Decree-Law No. 8.933/46, thus establishing that in order to qualify as an industrial property agent one must: (i) be a Brazilian citizen,[7] (ii) 21 years or older, (iii) have an acceptable record with respect to civil and political rights, and (iv) be of good standing. For legal entities, it is required that their partners are all industrial property agents or attorneys-at-law.

According to ABAPI statistics, there are approximately 1,200 industrial property agents registered under the new regulations, while more than 300 have had their registrations cancelled for various reasons. ABAPI has approximately 340 members who are industrial property agents and/or attorneys-at-law.

The vast majority of industrial property agents in Brazil have an expertise in trade mark matters, while only a small portion is truly skilled in patent

[6] Portaria No. 32 of 19 March 1998 of the State Ministry of Industry, Commerce and Tourism.

[7] This requirement was later removed in view of the provisions of the Brazilian Constitution of 1988.

matters, most having degrees in engineering, chemistry, physics or other technical areas.

It should be noted that although a person or legal entity must be qualified to act before the INPI as an applicant representative – *i.e.* one must either be an accredited industrial property agent or an attorney-at-law – Normative Act No. 141 and Law No. 9.279/96 provide that applicants with a domicile or residence in Brazil are also entitled to act before INPI without a representative.

B. Problems Related to the Enforcement of Patent Rights

I. Competent Parties

1. Plaintiff

According to the Code of Civil Procedure 1973 and Brazilian jurisprudence, the plaintiff in an IP court action must be the owner of the intellectual property right. A licensee, exclusive or non-exclusive, can only be a party in a court action as a co-plaintiff.

Only in special cases does the court allow a licensee to act as a sole plaintiff, namely when a written licensing agreement authorises him so.

A court may require a plaintiff domiciled abroad to post a security for the defendant's eventual recovery of its attorney's fees and judicial costs should the plaintiff not prevail in the court action. This does not apply where the plaintiff has a subsidiary company in Brazil which appears as a co-plaintiff. A bond is posted in cash by a deposit in an official bank.

2. Defendant

As already mentioned,[8] wherever the complaint seeks the cancellation of the patent through an independent court action, INPI must be a co-defendant. In an infringement action, the defendants will be persons that are directly or indirectly infringing the patent. INPI will not be a party in infringement actions even if the validity of the patent is challenged by the defendants as a matter of defence.

II. The Competent Court

Infringement actions have to be filed before the state courts (usually, either in the court where the infringer has its domicile or in the court where the infringement took place, *e.g.* where infringing articles are found). According to the Brazilian legislation, the plaintiff is entitled to bring the infringement action before the state court where the tort took place. However, there are

---

[8] *See* A.III on patent nullity.

some situations in which the plaintiff is not able to identify the exact place of the infringement (*e.g.* infringement of a method claim). In these cases, the infringement action will be filed in the court where the infringer is domiciled. If the court action is based on a written agreement, *e.g.* patent licensing agreement, the action will take place in the court indicated in the agreement.

1. Courts of First Instance

a) State Courts

Brazil is a federation of 26 states and one federal district, each of which has its own court structure.

All patent infringement cases are prosecuted before the state courts, which are divided into civil and criminal courts. A decision issued at first instance may be appealed to the state courts of appeal. In 2001, the State Court of Rio de Janeiro created specialised courts to handle IP matters. No other states have yet done so (see below 3).

b) Federal Courts

First instance federal judges sit in each state capital and in the federal district. Only cases involving decisions by federal government agencies go before the federal courts. This includes decisions rendered by INPI (*e.g.* the grant of patents).

2. Courts of Appeal

Each State has its own Court of Appeal. Any appealed decision rendered by a first instance judge will be referred to the local court of appeals.

Decisions rendered by first instance federal judges are subject to appeal before the regional federal courts. The five regional federal courts of appeal are established in the cities of Brasilia, Rio de Janeiro, São Paulo, Recife and Porto Alegre. The Superior Court of Justice only hears appeals against decisions issued by the federal courts of appeal or by the state courts of appeal. The grounds for bringing such appeals are that the decisions violate federal laws or that they are in conflict with previous jurisprudence. The Supreme Court judges only hear constitutional matters. Both the Superior Court of Justice and the Supreme Court are based in Brasilia (the capital of Brazil).

3. Other Courts or Tribunals

The IPC authorises the Judiciary to establish specialised Industrial Property Courts. In view this, four specialised divisions were created by the Federal Court of Rio de Janeiro to judge cases involving decisions of INPI. Subsequently, 12 specialised courts were created by the State Court of Rio de Janeiro to judge intellectual property disputes concerning rights of private parties.

III. Preparation for Trial

1. Warning Letters

In many situations a simple cease and desist letter is enough to stop the infringement. This is a cost-effective way of settling the case and avoiding court actions. However, cease and desist letters may jeopardise the patent owner's rights unless utmost care is taken with procedures.

A warning letter may be served either through the Registry of Titles and Deeds or even by means of a court procedure in which the judge designates a court officer to personally serve the infringing party with the letter. Of course the infringer may or may not comply with the terms of the letter.

In the latter case, the patent owner must seek judicial measures to stop the infringement within ten years or risk losing the case due to the statute of limitations. Moreover, if the patent owner does not act quickly, it may jeopardise its chances to obtain a preliminary injunction to stop the infringement based on a provision similar to laches.

It is important to note that sending a cease and desist letter is not mandatory before initiating court procedures, and if the patentee decides not to serve the infringer with this type of letter beforehand, it will not have any direct effect on the court procedure.

In short, the decision to serve the infringer with a cease and desist letter is a strategic one and has to be analysed on a case-by-case basis. In situations where the patent right holder is seeking an injunction order to seize the infringing goods, such a letter could jeopardise the operation because it will alert the infringer that the patent owner is aware of its illegal activities, giving the infringer adequate time to hide the infringing products.

2. Measures to Preserve Evidence and Preliminary Measures

There are several legal measures that may be taken by the patent owner against an infringer before filing the main civil or criminal action.

Before initiating any patent litigation, it is essential to collect several pieces of evidence to demonstrate the infringement and to preserve evidence. As the infringer may destroy all evidence of the infringement, the best way to proceed is through a preliminary *criminal* search and seizure action.

In Brazil, a patent infringement is both a tort and a criminal offence. In spite of the fact that criminal judges are not familiar with IP matters, criminal procedure is very effective since it does not directly involve a public prosecutor. The patent owner is legally entitled to lodge a criminal action without the interference of the prosecutor. It is only necessary to prove infringement in order to go to a criminal court. The most convenient way to obtain such proof is the preliminary criminal search and seizure action.

This type of preliminary court action is filed before the criminal court and it is based on Secs. 200, 201 and 203 IPC and the Code of Criminal

Procedure. In this procedure, the judge will nominate an expert to accompany the bailiff in the search and seizure procedure. The expert will collect samples of the allegedly infringing products or will verify the existence of the suspected unlawful act in the case of a patent relating to a process. Thereafter, the expert will issue an opinion, which will be examined by the criminal court. This is a very powerful tool, since if the expert finds for patent infringement in his report, the patent holder will have strong evidence to submit before both the civil and criminal courts. This procedure is very cost and time effective, usually taking less than a month. It may also be initiated before the civil courts. Moreover, the Code of Civil Procedure allows an *ex parte* search and seizure order of the infringing products at the defendant's premises, which is also quite important to avoid the continuance of the patent infringement.

After the preliminary search and seizure action, and if the infringement is confirmed by the court-appointed expert, the patent holder may file either a criminal or a civil action, or both. As mentioned above, a public prosecutor is not directly involved in this criminal procedure. Penalties are up to one year of imprisonment. However, the criminal action does not solve the patent infringement problem, since the criminal court is not legally entitled to stop the commercialisation of the infringing product. Therefore, in the majority of cases, the patent holder uses the preliminary criminal search and seizure action only to collect evidence to support its case before the civil court.

When the patent owner has all necessary evidence to lodge its civil action, there are some preliminary measures that may be taken in order to immediately stop the infringement. According to Sec. 209 IPC, in patent infringement cases, the judge is allowed to grant an *ex parte* restraining order to prevent future violations. In this situation, the defendant will not be permitted to sell the infringing goods during the civil action under the threat of a daily fine to be ascertained by the court. This injunction may be granted *inaudita altera parte* and the judge may request the plaintiff to post a bond to guarantee the execution of the injunction. This bond is usually requested by the courts in infringement cases and is not extremely high.

To grant preliminary orders either for collecting evidence or restraining the defendant, the court must apply certain criteria:

(1) *The fumus boni juris*: the plaintiff must demonstrate that it has a good right which deserves protection and that there is a good probability that the defendant is infringing this right (the Letters Patent and an expert report confirming patent infringement would be very powerful pieces of evidence); and
(2) *The periculum in mora*: the judge must be convinced that the plaintiff's right is threatened by an activity of the defendant and could be severely damaged if no action is taken before a final decision on the merits is rendered.

In civil law, a preliminary injunction can be requested at any time and even before the defendant knows of the action. The judge may even grant a preliminary injunction without an express request by the plaintiff if he/she considers that serving the defendant with the summons would risk the integrity of the evidence.

Under the Code of Civil Procedure, it is also possible to obtain a preliminary injunction to freeze the infringer's assets until a final decision on the merits is rendered. However, this type of court order can only be obtained if the patent owner shows that there is an actual risk of not duly recovering damages by the end of the court proceeding.

Furthermore, the plaintiff has to provide the court with a list of the assets of the defendant that it wishes to be frozen. It is not possible to request a general freeze.

Regarding a defendant's bank account, a disclosure is only feasible by means of a court order. In this situation, the financial institution is obliged to reveal the defendant's account, but this type of decision is quite rare, especially in a preliminary injunction.

Besides civil procedures, a criminal investigation of the infringer's assets is also possible. The public prosecutor may request the police to investigate the infringer's assets, which can be very helpful for the right owner in a future civil action seeking damages. In certain specific cases, even the public prosecutor may request the court to freeze the infringer's assets.

IV. The Trial

1. Presenting Evidence and the Importance of Experts

The production of evidence is not confined to a single "discovery-like" phase at first instance.

Documentary evidence should be produced by the parties in the pleading phase. The plaintiff will produce its evidence in the complaint, and the defendant in its response. A request for oral evidence will be considered by the judge at any time or stage of the proceedings.

The types of evidence that may be produced during the action are as follows:

(a) a personal deposition of the parties;
(b) statement of witnesses;
(c) documentary evidence;
(d) sworn written evidence;
(e) evidence from experts;
(f) judicial inspection.

Facts from a non-party can only be discovered by the witnesses' inquiry or when the judge orders a third party to produce a document which may clarify the case.

In patent litigation, a party may submit documentary evidence together with the complaint, but in view of the technical difficulties involved in such disputes, the judges tend to appoint an expert.

The person appointed must be an expert in his/her field, and must prepare a statement attesting to his/her competence to answer technical questions raised by the parties. Both parties are then able to appoint their own expert assistants, who will confirm or oppose the official expert's opinion.

The expert and the parties' assistants may be asked to appear during the hearings to give further clarification to the court. Judges can also request any other evidence that they consider appropriate to the case, *e.g.* experiments.

2. The Role of Lawyers

As mentioned before, in contrast to other countries, in Brazil there are no "patent attorneys". As a matter of fact, any lawyer who is a member of the Brazilian Bar Association can act in a patent infringement case.

The attorney's role in a patent infringement case is quite broad. The attorney is responsible for the collection of evidence, the drafting of all petitions and representation of the client before the court. A non-lawyer cannot act before the Brazilian courts and can only serve an infringer with a privately delivered cease and desist letter.

3. The Role of the Judge

At least in civil cases, there are no jury trials. Even in criminal cases there are jury trials only for capital crimes. Therefore, all patent infringement cases are decided by judges.

In view of this, the judge is the main player in a patent infringement case, since he/she will decide on the granting of a preliminary injunction, the validity of the evidence submitted by the parties, the liability of the parties, the merits of the case, etc. In short, all the steps in the proceeding will be decided by the judge.

The judge also has the responsibility to conduct the hearings, which means he/she has the legal right to take the deposition of the parties and possible witnesses. During the hearings, the judge also has an obligation to encourage the parties to reach a settlement, without, of course, obliging them to do so.

The judges render their decision in writing and the they must base their decision on the facts, the law, the jurisprudence and the doctrine (there are usually several citations in Brazilian decisions). All decisions are published in the Official Gazette (usually a short version), since the deadline to appeal against it only starts running from the date of the official publication of the decision.

4. Scope of Patent Protection

a) Infringing acts

Sec. 42 IPC expressly specifies acts that are considered infringing: manufacturing, using, offering for sale, selling or importing for such purposes without consent a product that is the subject of a patent, or a method, or product directly obtained by a patented method.

Sec. 42(2) provides for the reversal of the burden of proof, whenever the issue concerns a potential infringement of a method claim, which includes products which are obtained directly by the patented method. In such situations, the accused party will bear the burden of establishing that the method it uses does not infringe the method claim and/or that the product being commercialised was not obtained by the claimed method.

Whether or not it is sufficient to establish that an accused product was not "*directly*" obtained by a claimed method is not clear from the law. This is because while Sec. 42(2) contains the expression "directly", Sec. 184 related to crimes against patents refers to a "product (…) obtained by (...) a patented method", without using the expression "directly". Since a crime is also considered to be a civil offence, any act that constitutes a basis for a criminal action will also provide grounds for a civil action.

Unauthorised use of a patented invention is also criminal offence under Secs. 183–185 IPC. There are some differences, however.

Sec. 42	**Secs. 183–185**
Manufacture	Manufacture
Use (product or method)	Use (means or method)
–	Export
Sale	Sale
Offer for sale	Exhibit or Offer for sale
–	Maintain in stock
–	Hide
–	Receive
Import with above purposes	Import (except parallel importation)
–	Supply component
Contribute to perform above acts	–

The acts of maintaining in stock, hiding and receiving listed in Sec. 184 must be performed "*with a view to use for economic purposes*". The importation of a product that was placed on the market in another country by the patentee or with his consent, *i.e.* parallel importation, is not regarded as a crime, although it constitutes a civil tort.

b) Claim interpretation

According to Secs. 41, 186 IPC, infringement will exist whenever an accused product/method contains the features of at least one independent claim, either in a literal manner or by equivalents.

Since an independent claim is taken to define the *essential* features of the patented invention, *as a general principle* an infringement will not occur if the accused product/method does not contain each and every feature of a certain patent claim.

Nevertheless, the provisions concerning infringement by equivalents do not establish whether equivalence is to be determined on an element-by-element basis or if a single element in a claim can be taken to be equivalent to a group of elements in the accused product/method or vice-versa.

The law does not define how equivalence is to be assessed.

c) Indirect infringement

Besides the product/method which is expressly claimed in a patent, also parts of products are protected, whenever those parts only suit the patented product or only have the purpose to perform the patented method.

The corresponding provisions read as follows:

> **Sec. 185** – Supplying a component of a patented product, or material or equipment for carrying out a patented method, provided that the final application of the component, material or equipment necessarily leads to the exploitation of the subject matter of the patent.
> Penalty – detention of one to three months or a fine.

Thus in order to deny an infringement under the above provisions, an accused party must establish that the patentee did not meet his burden to prove that the accused component, material or equipment "*necessarily leads*" to the exploitation of the patented product/method.

This is difficult where:

(i) the component, material or equipment indeed has no other purpose aside from being used in connection with the patented invention; or

(ii) the component, material or equipment can have other purposes aside from being used in connection with the invention, but in the circumstances it is clear that no other use could have been intended when the component, material or equipment was supplied to a third party by the accused party.

V. Defences

1. Invalidity

Since novelty and inventive step are legal requirements for a patent to be valid in Brazil, if the accused product/method can be taken to be fully embraced by the prior art or to be inferred therefrom in an obvious manner, this fact alone would preclude infringement.[9]

Invalidity of a patent is expressly provided in the law as a matter of defence in the course of an infringement action under Sec. 56 IPC in civil and Sec. 205 in criminal matters.

Except if invalidity is argued before a competent federal court, it will only produce legal effects between the parties.

According to the Civil Appeal No. 12754/00 by the 1st Civil Chamber of the city of Rio de Janeiro: "Law No. 9.279/96 [IPC], in its Sec. 56(1) provides for the possibility of arguing nullity of the patent as a matter of defence. Acknowledgement of nullity in this case will only produce effects between the parties which take part in the proceedings, not having the effect, as the appellant seems to believe, of *per se* nullifying the patent itself before the Patent Office".

Moreover, according to a São Paulo court[10] the alleged infringer can argue that the invention is not novel and hence not patentable without the need of requesting nullity of the patent before the competent court, having also established that the competence for judging the case is with the State Court since it refers to subject matter capable of being judged "*incidenter tantum*" and "*inter partes*", whereby the Federal Court is competent for judging the appropriate action for nullifying the patent.

Aside from arguing nullity of the patent as a matter of defence in the course of an infringement action, an accused party may also file a lawsuit before a federal court requesting nullity of the patent with effects *erga omnes*. According to a unanimous decision of the Federal Regional Court,[11] a nullity action based on lack of novelty requires expert evidence.

If there is sufficient evidence about the invalidity of the patent, an injunction can be granted whereby the effects of the patent are suspended before a final decision is issued.[12]

---

[9] In *Vacchi S.A. Ind. e Com. Ltda. v. Master Equipamentos Industriais*, concerning the accused infringement of Brazilian patent PI 8504023, 1st Civil Court of Novo Hamburgo, RS, Civil Appeal No. 594 012 478, 13 April 1994, the court found that the machine manufactured by the defendant was based on the prior art, and was thus entitled to be further manufactured and sold.

[10] 9th Chamber of Private Right of the Justice Court of the State of São Paulo, in Civil Appeal No. 367824 (RJTJESP-215/149–51, April 1999).

[11] 1st Group of the Federal Regional Court (TRF-2R), Civil Appeal No. 97.02.14696-8 RJ (DJ of 13 April 1999). The authors thankfully acknowledge the contribution of Mr. Gert Egon Dannemann in the collection of jurisprudence.

[12] Federal Regional Court of Appeals (TRF-2R), 1st Panel, review No. 9902265138 RJ (DJ-2, 20 July 2000, p. 112). The judge is entitled to determine a suspension of the patent, provided that the proper procedural requirements are fulfilled. Different, the same Court of Appeals, review No. 200202010327488 (DJ-2, 12 September 2002, 379), and review No. 200102010152088 (DJ-2, 2 May 2001, 88): patents issued by the INPI are presumed valid.

2. Non-infringement

Secs. 43 and 45 IPC expressly provide for exceptions to the rights conferred by a patent.

Acts of permissible use under Sec. 43 are: acts done privately and without commercial ends, acts for experimental purposes related to studies or to scientific or technological research, the preparation of a medicine according to a medical prescription for individual cases, and acts of use after domestic exhaustion.

Among the above exceptions, which are mostly self-explanatory, Sec. 43(4) establishes the principle of national exhaustion of rights. A patentee would, however, be entitled to prevent third parties from the parallel importation of patented products.[13]

The research exemption was further clarified by Law 10.196/01 of 14 February 2001 that exempts: acts aimed exclusively at producing information, data and results of tests, intending to obtain marketing approval, in Brazil or in another country, for the exploitation and commercialisation of the patented product after expiry of the patent term.

Prior user rights are granted to a person who in good faith, prior to the date of filing or of priority of a patent application, exploits its object in Brazil.

The application is thus limited to cases in which a certain party has actually used the patented product/method in Brazil before the priority date of another party's patent application. Thus, it is not sufficient for that party to prove that it has reduced the invention to practice before the priority date and/or that it has initiated preparations to use it. This restriction is clear as the prior user is guaranteed the right to continue the exploitation "in the previous form and conditions".

According to available information, prior user rights were claimed for the first time in an infringement action, 8th Civil Court of Porto Alegre, Action No. 109177908. At the time of writing, the expert appointed by the judge had confirmed the prior use, but no decision had been issued.

VI. Remedies

The most common remedies obtained by the patent owner in a patent infringement case are the following:

(1) cessation of the infringement by the defendant under the payment of a daily penalty;
(2) the destruction of all products and material involved in the infringement;
(3) the recovery of damages; and
(4) the payment of attorney fees and judicial (official) costs.

[13] Unless the patentee only uses the patent by importation himself, Sec. 68(4). The provision is questionable under Art. 27(1) TRIPS.

Sec. 209 IPC allows the recovery of damages for losses caused by the infringing act.[14] A judge may, in the formal record of the same action, so as to avoid irreparable damages or damages that would be difficult to recover, grant a preliminary injunctive order before summoning the defendant, against monetary caution or a fiduciary guarantee.

According to Sec. 210 IPC, damages (loss of profits) to the injured party will be determined according to which of the following is most favourable: a) the benefits that would have been gained by the injured party if the violation had not occurred; b) the benefits gained by the infringer; or c) a licensing fee.

In view of this, even if the infringer does not keep records of the illegal operations, it is possible to determine the damages using the different criteria, such as the benefits that would have been obtained by the injured party if the violation had not occurred or a licensing fee.

In addition to losses and damages concerning infringement occurred *after* grant of the patent, the patentee is also entitled to compensation concerning the period of infringement between publication of the respective application and its grant [15] Nevertheless, if the infringer obtained knowledge of the contents of the application prior to its publication – *e.g.* by means of a warning letter – the period of undue exploitation, for the effect of compensation, will be counted from the date of commencement of the exploitation.

Finally, the patent owner may recover attorney fees and the official costs connected with the litigation. However, attorney fees are limited to 10% to 20% of the amount of damages recovered by the patent owner.

[14] Two available second instance decisions, issued unanimously, interpret this provision in different manners. In Civil Appeal No. 28.993-4/0, Ribeirão Preto, DJ of 20 July 1998, the 8th Chamber of Private Right of the Justice Court of São Paulo issued a decision to the effect that the compensation for patent infringement "shall correspond to the profits equivalent to the commercialisation of the patented equipment, in number of units equal to those used by the defendant". In Civil Appeal No. 102.573-4, São Paulo, RJTJ 248, pages 153–159, of August 2001, the 1st Chamber of Private Right of the Justice Court of the State of São Paulo, the decision stressed that "in view of the deficiency of accounting registry by the plaintiff [note: plaintiff in the appeal is the prospective infringer], the calculation shall be performed by articles, being limited to the period in which the commercialisation of the patented product by the defendant has started until the termination of the patent term".

[15] This does not imply that a patent applicant can file an infringement action before grant. According to a unanimous decision issued by the 8th Chamber of Private Right of the Justice Court of São Paulo, in Civil Appeal No. 5.614–4 (RJTJESP-204/119 of 21 May 1998), "the violation of an invention is intrinsically conditioned to the legal existence of the privilege, *i.e.*, the Letters Patent or of the valid patent and not only an expectation of the right derived from a patent application filed at the INPI".

Case List

EU/EPO

31 October 1974, European Court of Justice, 6 IIC 102 (1975) – Centrapharm/Sterling Drug: 4/123
30 November 1976, European Court of Justice, (Case 21/76), 1976 ECR 1735 – Bier *v.* Mines de Potasse d'Alsace: 2/20, 8/28
21 May 1980, European Court of Justice, (Case 125/79), 1980 ECR 1553 – Denilauler/Couchet Frères: 3/48
15 November 1983, European Court of Justice, 1983 ECR 3663 – Duijnstee/Goderbauer: 4/35
9 July 1985, European Court of Justice, 17 IIC 357 (1986) – Pharmon/Hoechst: 4/124
8 December 1987, European Court of Justice, (Case 144/86), – Gubisch/Palumbo, 1987 ECR I-4861: 5/32, 5/33
27 September 1988, European Court of Justice, (Case 189/87), 1988 ECR 5565 – Kalfelis/Schröder: 2/17, 6/13, 8/32
11 December 1989, EPO Enlarged Board of Appeal, OJ 1990, 93 – "Mobil Oil III": 1/11
11 December 1989, EPO Enlarged Board of Appeal, EPO Official Journal 1990, 93 – "Friction Reducing Addition": 1/190
2 February 1994, EPO Enlarged Board of Appeal, G 1/93 decision, 1994 OJ EPO, 541: 5/45
6 December 1994, European Court of Justice, (C-406/92), 1994 ECR 5439 – Tatry/Maciej Rataj: 2/25, 8/66
7 March 1995, European Court of Justice, (C-68/93), [1995] 1 All ER 289, 1995 ECR 415 – Fiona Shevill/Presse Alliance: 1/109, 2/21, 4/43, 4/44, 6/11, 8/30
24 July 1996, EPO Enlarged Board of Appeal, OJ EPO 1996, 649: 1/31
16 June 1998, European Court of Justice, (C-53/96), 1998 ECR I-3603, 1999 Nederlandse Jurisprudentie 240, 30 IIC 292, 295 [1999] – "Hermès": 1/61, 1/62, 6/2
16 July 1998, European Court of Justice, 29 IIC 920 [1998] – "Silhouette": 1/191
17 November 1998, European Court of Justice, (C-391/95), 1998 ECR I-7091 – "Van Uden": 2/24, 6/18, 6/20
14 October 1999, European Court of Justice, 31 IIC 591 [2000] – "In re Adidas": 1/194
10 December 1999, EPO Enlarged Board of Appeal, 32 IIC 545 [2002]: 1/31
6 April 2000, European Court of Justice, 32 IIC 209 [2001] – Polo/Lauren: 1/195

14 December 2000, European Court of Justice, (C-300/98, C-392/98), 2000 ECR I-11307 – Tuk/Dior and Assco/Layher: 6/3

United Kingdom

ABKCo Music *v*. Music Collection Int., [1995] RPC 657: 3/28
American Braided Wire *v*. Thomson, (1890) 7 RPC 152: 3/80
American Cyanamid *v*. Ethicon, 5 February 1975, English House of Lords, [1975] AC 396, [1975] 1 All ER 504: 1/66, 3/54
Anglo Group *v*. Winther Brown, [2000] All ER 296: 3/78
Anton Piller KG *v*. Manufacturing Processes Ltd and others, 8 December 1975, English Court of Appeal, [1976] 1 All ER 782: 1/35, 1/40
Baldock *v*. Addison, 22 June 1994, English High Court, [1995] 3 All ER 437: 1/163
Baxter International *v*. Nederlands Produktielaboratorium voor Bloedtransfusiapparatuur, [1998] RPC 250: 3/25
Beloit Technologies Inc. *v*. Valmet Paper Machinery, 12 February 1997, English Court of Appeal, [1997] RPC 489, 503: 1/103
Catnic Component *v*. Hill, 16 March 1983, English High Court, [1983] FSR 512: 1/164
Celanese International *v*. BP Chemicals, [1999] RPC 203: 3/81
Coin Controls *v*. Suzo, 26 March 1997, English High Court, [1997] FSR 660: 1/110, 2/8, 2/19
Columbia Pictures *v*. Robinson, 21 August 1987, English High Court, [1988] FSR 531: 1/168
EMI Ltd. *v*. Pandit, English High Court, [1975] 1 WLR 302: 1/40
Fort Dodge Animal Health *v*. Akzo Nobel, 27 October 1997, [1998] FSR 222 at 243, 29 IIC 927 (1998): 2/10, 3/45, 4/52, 6/16
Gates *v*. Swift, 8 July 1982, English High Court, [1982] RPC 339: 1/42
General Tyre *v*. Firestone, 16 April 1975, English House of Lords, [1976] RPC 197: 1/162, 3/80
Gerber Garment Technology *v*. Lectra Systems, 20 March 1995, Patents Court, [1995] RPC 383: 1/165, 1/169, 1/170
Island Records Ltd. *v*. Tring International, 12 April 1995, English High Court, [1995] 3 All ER 444: 1/166
Kimberly-Clark Worldwide Inc. *v*. Procter & Gamble Ltd., 24 November 1999, English Court of Appeal, [2000] FSR 235-245: 1/104
Mareva Compania Naviera *v*. International Bulk Carriers, 29 January 1980, English Court of Appeal, [1980] 1 All ER 213: 1/38
McDonald *v*. Graham, 16 December 1993, [1994] RPC 407: 3/61
Merck *v*. Generics, [2003] EWHC 2842: 3/14, 3/23
Meters *v*. Metropolitan Gas Meters, 2 February 1911, English High Court, [1911] 28 RPC 157: 1/171
Mölnlycke *v*. Procter & Gamble, 27 June 1991, [1992] RPC 21: 3/39

Norwich Pharmacal *v*. Customs and Excise, 25 July 1972, [1972] FSR 405: 1/39, 3/55

Optical Laboratories Ltd *v*. Hayden Laboratories Ltd., 15 June 1992, [1993] RPC 204: 3/9

Pearce *v*. Ove Arup, 21 January 1999, [1999] FSR 525 (CA): 2/19, 3/42, 3/51

Plastus Kreativ *v*. Minnesota Mining, 9 December 1994, English Court of Appeal, [1995] RPC 438: 1/105, 3/39

PLG Research *v*. Ardon, 30 July 1992, [1993] FSR 197: 3/29

Red Sea Insurance *v*. Bouygues SA, 18 July 1994, Privy Council, [1996] 3 All ER 749: 3/51

Redwood Music *v*. Chappell, 23 May 1980, English High Court, [1982] RPC 109: 1/170

Rooks *v*. Barnard, 21 January 1969, English House of Lords, 1 All ER 367 [1964]: 1/167

Sega Enterprises *v*. Alco Electronics, 25 May 1982, [1982] FSR 516: 3/58

Sepracor Inc. *v*. Hochest Marrion Ltd, 14 January 1999, English Patents Court, [1997] FSR 746: 2/19

Smith Kline and French *v*. Harbottle, High Court, 7 June 1979, [1980] RPC 363: 1/39, 3/27, 3/57

SmithKline Beecham *v*. Apotex, 14 February 2003, [2003] FSR 544 (CA): 3/80

SmithKline Beecham *v*. Generics (UK), 23 October 2001, English Patents Court, Patent World, March 2002, 8: 1/68

Steers *v*. Rogers, 28 April 1893, House of Lords, (1893) AC 232, 1893 RPC 245: 13/35

Unger *v*. Sugg, 11 February 1892, (1892) 9 RPC 113: 3/14

Unilever *v*. Procter & Gamble, 24 February 1999, [1999] FSR 849: 3/15

Universal Thermosensors Ltd *v*. Hibben and others, High Court, 5 February 1992, [1992] 3 All ER 257 = [1992] 1 WLR 840: 1/41, 3/32, 3/62

Watson Laidlaw *v*. Potts Cassels, 6 February 1914, (1914) 31 RPC 104: 3/80

Germany

2 October 1886, Imperial Supreme Court, RGZ 18, 28: 1/106

18 July 1890, Imperial Supreme Court, Juristische Wochenschrift 1890, 280: 1/106

8 June 1895, Imperial Supreme Court, RGZ 35, 63: 1/137

31 December 1898, Imperial Supreme Court, RGZ 43, 56: 1/138

13 April 1910, Berlin Royal District Court, Mitteilungen 1910, 120: 1/54

8 March 1919, Kammergericht Berlin, 1919 GRUR 179: 1/53

29 March 1919, Imperial Supreme Court, RGZ 95, 220: 1/150

23 February 1920, Imperial Supreme Court, 1920 GRUR 103: 1/149

22 February 1928, Imperial Supreme Court, Marke und Wettbewerb (MuW) 1927/28, 312: 4/113

22 October 1930, Imperial Supreme Court, RGZ 130, 108: 1/158, 1/159

9 January 1933, Imperial Supreme Court, 1933 GRUR 288: 1/19, 4/7

28 January 1933, Imperial Supreme Court, 1933 GRUR 292: 1/156

25 October 1939, Berlin District Court, 1940 GRUR 32: 1/151

7 April 1941, Imperial Supreme Court, RGZ 156, 65: 1/148

6 March 1959, Federal Supreme Court, 1959 GRUR 320 – "Moped-Kupplung": 4/115

16 March 1959, Federal Supreme Court, BGHZ 29, 393: 1/152

13 March 1962, Federal Supreme Court, 1962 GRUR 398 – "Kreuzbodenventilsäcke II": 1/114

29 May 1962, Federal Supreme Court, 1962 GRUR 509 – "Dia-Rähmchen II": 1/158, 1/161

13 July 1962, Federal Supreme Court, 1962 GRUR 580 – "Laux-Kupplung II": 4/141

12 January 1966, Federal Supreme Court, BGHZ 44, 372 – "Meßmer-Tee II": 1/156

20 August 1968, Braunschweig District Court, 1971 GRUR 28 – "Abkantpresse": 1/54

15 October 1969, Federal Supreme Court, 1970 GRUR 189: 1/155

27 November 1969, Federal Supreme Court, 1970 GRUR 296 – "Allzweck Landmaschine": 1/157

10 March 1972, Federal Supreme Court, BGHZ 59, 286 – "Double Tariff": 1/139

8 March 1973, Federal Supreme Court, 1976 GRUR 116 – "Spielautomat": 4/126

6 December 1974, Federal Supreme Court, 1975 GRUR 434: 1/142

10 July 1979, Federal Supreme Court, 1979 GRUR 869 – "Oberarmschwimmringe": 1/152

6 March 1980, Federal Supreme Court, BGHZ 77, 16, 1980 GRUR 841 – "Tolbutamid": 1/141, 1/143, 1/146, 1/149, 1/153

17 April 1980, Düsseldorf Appeal Court, 1981 GRUR 45: 1/147

17 August 1981, Düsseldorf High Court, 1983 GRUR 741 – "Interest in Secrecy and Right of Inspection I": 1/36

24 November 1981, Federal Supreme Court, 1982 GRUR 301, 14 IIC 111 (1983) – "Heel Support Device": 1/144, 4/136

8 January 1985, German Supreme Court, 1985 GRUR 512 – "Druckbalken": 1/54, 4/68

29 April 1986, Federal Supreme Court, 1986 GRUR 803, 18 IIC 795 (1987) – "Moulded Curbstone": 4/93, 4/106, 8/19

24 June 1986, Düsseldorf District Court, 1987 GRUR 628 – "Restitutionsklage": 1/78, 4/119

22 January 1987, Federal Supreme Court, BGHZ 99, 340: 4/4

21 February 1989, Federal Supreme Court, BGHZ 107, 46: 1/140

16 March 1990, Cologne Appeal Court, 1991 GRUR 60 – "Rolex-Imitation": 1/160

12 July 1990, Federal Supreme Court, 23 IIC 111 (1992) – "Fixing Device II": 4/109

18 February 1992, Federal Supreme Court, 1992 GRUR 599 – "Teleskopzylinder: 1/145

9 April 1992, Federal Supreme Court, 1992 GRUR 530: 1/152

17 June 1992, Federal Supreme Court, 1993 GRUR 55 – "Tchibo/Rolex II": 1/142, 1/160, 4/133

25 May 1993, Federal Supreme Court, 1993 GRUR 897 – "Mogulanlage": 4/134

1 February 1994, Düsseldorf District Court, Collection of decisions of the 4th Civil Chamber, 1/1998, 1 *et seq.*: 2/4

17 March 1994, Federal Supreme Court, 26 IIC 261 (1995) – "Segmentation Device for Tree Trunks": 4/109

1 December 1994, Düsseldorf District Court, 1998 Entscheidung der 4. Zivilkammer des LG Düsseldorf 1 – "Kettenbandförderer": 4/38

20 December 1994, Düsseldorf District Court, 1995 BIPMZ 121 – "Hepatitis C Virus": 4/116

20 December 1994, Federal Supreme Court, 1995 GRUR 338 – "Kleiderbügel": 4/23

2 February 1995, Federal Supreme Court, 1995 GRUR 349 – "Objektive Schadensersatzberechnung": 4/138

30 May 1995 – Federal Supreme Court, 1995 GRUR 578 – "Steuereinrichtung II": 1/154, 4/135

16 January 1996, Düsseldorf District Court, 1996 Entscheidung der 4. Zivilkammer des LG Düsseldorf 1 – "Reinigungsmittel": 4/49

26 September 1996, Federal Supreme Court, 1997 GRUR 116 – "Prospekthalter": 4/126

17 April 1997, Federal Supreme Court, 1997 GRUR 741 – "Chinaherde": 4/62

2 October 1997, Federal Supreme Court, 30 IIC 227 [1999] – "Spielbankaffaire": 1/106

27 January 1998, Düsseldorf District Court, 1998 GRUR Int. 803 – "Kondensatorspeicherzellen": 2/29, 5/36

27 February 1998, Düsseldorf District Court, 1998 GRUR Int. 804 – "Impfstoff": 2/26

25 August 1998, Düsseldorf District Court, 1999 GRUR Int. 455 – "Schußfadengreifer": 4/45

2 March 1999, Federal Supreme Court, 30 IIC 932 (1999) – "Tension Screw": 4/99

25 March 1999, 1999 Düsseldorf District Court, 1999 GRUR Int. 775 – "Impfstoff II": 2/22, 4/47

20 May 1999, Düsseldorf District Court, 2000 GRUR 309 – "Teigportionvorrichtung": 4/136

22 July 1999, Düsseldorf Appeal Court, 2001 IPRax 315 – "Schußfadengreifer II": 4/45

5 October 1999, Federal Tax Court, case VII R88/98: 1/192

14 December 1999, Federal Supreme Court, 2000 GRUR 635 – "Karate": 4/123, 4/125

1 February 2000, Federal Supreme Court, 2000 GRUR 392 – "Omeprazol": 4/80

24 October 2000, Düsseldorf District Court, (unreported) – "Wellcome Foundation/Glaxo": 2/28

2 November 2000, Federal Supreme Court, 33 IIC 900 (2002) – "Share of Overheads": 4/139

22 January 2001, Frankfurt Appeal Court, 2002 GRUR 236: 4/78

7 March 2001, Hamburg District Court, 2002 GRUR RR 45 – "Felodipin": 4/80

19 April 2001, Hamburg Appeal Court, 2002 GRUR RR 244 – "Spannbacke": 4/80

31 May 2001, Düsseldorf District Court, 34 IIC 309 (2003), 2001 GRUR Int. 983 – "Flywheel": 4/39

13 November 2001, Federal Supreme Court, 2002 GRUR 231 – "Biegevorrichtung": 4/122

26 February 2002, Federal Supreme Court, 34 IIC 432 (2003) – "Radio Clock": 4/28

12 March 2002, Federal Supreme Court, 34 IIC 302, 307 (2003), BGHZ 150, 161 – "Plastic Tube Component": 4/102

2 May 2002, Federal Supreme Court, 34 IIC 331 (2003) – "Fax Card": 1/57, 4/69

5 December 2002, Düsseldorf Appeal Court, 2003 GRUR Int. 1030 – "MTD": 2/13, 4/40

20 February 2003, Düsseldorf Appeal Court, 2003 GRUR 814: 4/63

30 September 2003 Federal Supreme Court, X ZR 114/00, (unreported) – "Blasenfreie Gummibahn II": 4/71

28 October 2003, Federal Supreme Court, X ZR 76/00, (unreported) – "Geflügelkörperhaltung": 4/85

13 November 2003 Federal Supreme Court, I ZR 187/01, (unreported) – "Kontrollbesuch": 4/70

France

30 November 1865, Lyon Appeal Court, 1866 Annales de la propriété industrielle 313: 1/47, 5/87

21 December 1870, Paris Appeal Court, 1878 Annales de la propriété industrielle 173: 5/91

22 December 1926, Supreme Court, 1927 Annales de la propriété industrielle 82: 5/106

30 May 1927, Supreme Court, 1928 Annales de la propriété industrielle 33: 5/65

22 February 1963, Paris Appeal Court, 1963 Annales de la propriété industrielle 284: 1/172, 5/149

10 July 1967, Supreme Court, 1967 Annales de la propriété industrielle 247: 5/72

13 January 1971, Supreme Court, 1971 Dalloz 147: 1/172, 5/149

2 March 1971, Paris Appeal Court, 1972 Dalloz 45: 1/177, 5/157

23 March 1971, Rouen Appeal Court, 1971 PIBD 63-III-190: 5/71

4 May 1971, Paris District Court, 1974 Revue critique de droit international privé 110: 5/27

22 October 1975, Paris District Court, 1977 Dossiers Brevets, III: 5/87

14 May 1976, Paris District Court, 1977 Dalloz 438: 5/52

29 October 1976, Paris District Court, 1977 PIBD III-231: 5/56

27 January 1977, Supreme Court, 1977 Annales de la propriété industrielle 14: 5/142

4 June 1980, Lille District Court, 1980 Dossiers Brevets VI, No. 6: 1/46, 5/64, 5/78

8 July 1982, Paris District Court, 1982 PIBD 312-III-235: 5/132

28 December 1982, Nancy Appeal Court, 1982 Annales de la propriété industrielle 237: 5/45

27 November 1984, Paris Appeal Court, 1985 PIBD 366-III-118: 5/132

21 April 1988, Paris District Court, 1988 PIBD 440-III-391: 5/45

24 November 1988, Lyon District Court, 1988 Dossiers Brevets, V, 6: 5/98

29 November 1988, Supreme Court, 1989 JCP, ed. Entreprise, I, 18139: 5/60

10 April 1990, Paris District Court, 1990 PIBD 495-III-537: 5/46

19 September 1990, Lyon District Court, 1991 PIBD 496-III-162: 5/46

6 November 1990, Supreme Court, 1991 PIBD 493-III-69: 5/106

12 December 1990, Paris Appeal Court, 1992 Annales de la propriété industrielle 61: 5/44

19 February 1991, Supreme Court, 1991 Annales de la propriété industrielle 4: 1/180, 5/160

26 February 1992, Paris Appeal Court, 1992 PIBD III-308: 1/73, 5/117

5 March 1992, Lyon Appeal Court, 1992 Dossiers Brevets I, 6: 5/130

12 March 1993, Paris District Court, 1993 Dalloz, Summary section 377: 5/110

3 November 1993, Paris Appeal Court, 1994 PIBD 559-III-45: 5/45

28 January 1994, Paris Appeal Court, 1996 Dossiers Brevets I: 5/28

3 February 1994, Lyon District Court, 1996 Dossiers Brevets (DB), IV, 5: 5/3

1 March 1994, Supreme Court, 1994 Annales de la propriété intellectuelle 197: 5/118

29 August 1994, Lyon District Court, 1995 Revue de droit trimestrielle commerciale 415: 1/48, 5/88

4 July 1996, Lyon Appeal Court, 1997 PIBD 624-III-21: 5/3
31 October 1996, Toulouse District Court, 1997 PIBD 626-III-90: 5/44
2 July 1997, Paris District Court, 1998 Dossiers Brevets, I, 6: 5/130
11 August 1997, Paris District Court, 1997 PIBD 643-III-601: 5/28
2 October 1997, Paris District Court, 1998 RDPI, No. 83, 25: 5/99
8 October 1997, Paris Appeal Court, 1998 PIBD 646-III-31: 5/168
19 November 1997, Paris Appeal Court, 1998 PIBD 651-III-189: 1/175, 5/154
24 November 1997, Paris District Court, 1998 RDPI, No. 83, 26: 5/80, 5/99
12 December 1997, Paris Appeal Court, 1997 Annales de la propriété industrielle 137: 5/48
30 January 1998, Paris District Court, 1998 PIBD 653-III-244: 5/133
16 March 1998, Douai Appeal Court, 1999 RDPI No. 99, 14: 5/167
24 March 1998, Supreme Court, Bulletin civil IV, No. 110, 88: 5/133
27 May 1998, Bordeaux Appeal Court, 1998 PIBD 663-III-508: 1/45, 5/76
20 October 1998, Supreme Court, 1998 Dossiers Brevets, III, 7: 5/94
23 June 1999, Paris District Court, 2000 PIBD 691-III-55: 5/42
1 September 1999, Paris District Court, 2000 PIBD 691-III-57: 5/130, 5/133
28 April 2000, Paris District Court, 2001 GRUR Int. 173: 5/30
24 May 2000, Rennes District Court, 2000 PIBD 705-III-433: 5/118
31 May 2000, Paris District Court, 2001 Dossiers Propriétés Intellectuelles I, 1: 5/128
5 September 2000, Paris District Court, 2001 PIBD 712-III-30: 5/63
24 October 2000, Supreme Court, 2001 PIBD 716-III-125: 5/153
27 October 2000, Paris Appeal Court, 2002 RDPI, No. 134, 39: 5/152
9 February 2001, Paris Appeal Court, 2001 PIBD 724-III-361, 2002 Dalloz 1193: 5/35, 5/39, 5/40
20 February 2001, Paris District Court, 2001 PIBD 729-III-530: 5/135
9 March 2001, Paris District Court, 2001 PIBD 725-III-394, 33 IIC 225 (2002) – "Italian Torpedoes": 5/37, 5/54
25 April 2001, Paris Appeal Court, 2001 Annales de la propriété industrielle 187: 5/76
25 April 2001, Supreme Court, 2001 PIBD 726-III-428: 5/105
7 May 2001, Paris District Court, 2001 RIPIA, No. 204: 5/158
9 May 2001, Paris Appeal Court, 2001 PIBD 725-III-394: 5/61
6 June 2001, Paris Appeal Court, 2001 PIBD 730-III-559: 5/153, 5/161
28 September 2001, Paris Appeal Court, 2002 PIBD 732-III-619: 5/148
12 October 2001, Paris Appeal Court, 2002 PIBD 733-III-1: 5/55, 5/156
12 October 2001, Paris District Court, 2002 PIBD 739-III-155: 5/135
13 October 2001, Paris Appeal Court, 2002 PIBD 733-III-166: 5/102
25 January 2002, Paris District Court, 2002 PIBD 747-III-342: 5/135
4 February 2002, Douai Appeal Court, 2002 Annales de la propriété industrielle 173: 5/84

4 February 2002, Strasbourg District Court, 2002 PIBD 747-III-343: 5/146

12 April 2002, Paris District Court, 2003 PIBD 755-III-9: 5/55

30 April 2002, Paris District Court, 2003 PIBD 755-III-1: 5/55

14 May 2002, Paris Appeal Court, 2002 Annales de la propriété industrielle 226: 5/50

29 May 2002, Paris Appeal Court, 2002 PIBD 751-III-464: 5/54

29 May 2002, Paris Appeal Court, 2002 PIBD 752-III-499: 5/61

14 June 2002, Paris Appeal Court, 2002 PIBD 751-III-464: 5/102, 5/112

3 July 2002, Paris District Court, 2003 PIBD 758-III-93: 5/134

15 July 2002, Paris District Court, 2002 PIBD 752-III-502: 5/119

15 October 2002, Paris District Court, 2003 PIBD 763-III-239: 5/90

11 February 2003, Supreme Court, 2003 PIBD 766-III-313: 5/155

23 April 2003, Supreme Court, 2003 PIBD 768-III-362: 5/65, 5/103

23 April 2003, Supreme Court, 2003 PIBD 768-III-361: 5/105

20 May 2003, Supreme Court, 2003 PIBD 771-III-439: 5/120

30 May 2003, Paris District Court, 2003 PIBD 775-III-571: 5/103

13 June 2003, Paris Appeal Court, 2003 PIBD 775-III-563: 5/162

Netherlands

3 January 1964, Supreme Court, 1964 Nederlandse Jurisprudentie 445 – Lexington: 6/25

16 November 1984, Supreme Court, 1985 Nederlandse Jurisprudentie 547 – Ciba Geigy *v.* Voorbraak: 1/59, 6/35

27 November 1987, Supreme Court, 1988 Nederlandse Jurisprudentie 1988, 722 – Cloé *v.* Peeters: 6/34

23 February 1990, Supreme Court, 1990 Nederlandse Jurisprudentie 664 – Hameco *v.* SKF: 6/32, 6/33

9 November 1990, Supreme Court, 1991 Nederlandse Jurisprudentie 169: 6/36

13 January 1995, Supreme Court, 391 (Ciba Geigy *v.* Oté), 28 IIC 748 (1995) – Contact Lens Liquid: 6/28

21 April 1995, Supreme Court, 1996 Nederlandse Jurisprudentie 462 (Boehringer), 29 IIC 699 (1998) – Recormon: 6/4

12 September 1996, The Hague Court of Appeal, 1996 Intellectuele Eigendom en Reclamerecht 237 – Hoffman-Laroche *v.* Orgonen: 1/74, 6/5

22 January 1998, The Hague Court of Appeal, 1998 European Intellectual Property Review, N-61, 62, 1998 Intellectuele Eigendom en Reclamerecht 135 – Evans Medical *v.* Chiron: 6/12, 6/21, 8/39

23 April 1998, The Hague Court of Appeal, 1998 Intellectuele Eigendom en Reclamerecht 286, 1999 FSR 352, 1998 European Intellectual Property Review, N-132 – Expandable Grafts *v.* Boston Scientific: 1/110, 2/12, 2/14, 3/45, 3/48, 3/50, 4/52, 6/9, 6/15, 6/17, 8/33

23 December 1998, The Hague District Court, 1999 Bijblad bij de Industriële Eigendom 39 – Chiron *v.* Roche: 6/10

30 March 2000 The Hague Court of Appeal, 2003 Bijblad bij de Industriële Eigendom 99 – Van Bentum *v.* Kool: 6/29

14 April 2000, Supreme Court, 2000 Rechtspraak van de Week 111: 6/37

29 March 2002, Supreme Court, 2003 Bijblad bij de Industriële Eigendom 100 – Van Bentum *v.* Kool: 6/30

3 July 2003, The Hague Court of Appeal, (unreported) – Medinol *v.* Cordis: 6/19

19 December 2003, Supreme Court – Roche *v.* Primus, (unreported): 6/14, 6/23

Italy

27 January 1992, Court of Milan, GADI 2792 – Zaseves di S. Zanetti *v.* Giovanni Luigi Brignoli: 7/12

5 May 1995, Court of Appeal of Milan, GADI 3311 – Boehringer Mannheim Italia Spa and Boehringer Mannheim GmbHh *v.* Ortho Pharmaceutical Co. Cilag Spa and others: 7/8

7 February 1996, Court of Vicenza, GADI 3464 – Mariplast Spa *v.* F.lli Costa Spa: 7/12

22 October 1997, Supreme Court, n. 10388, Giust. Civ. Mass. 1997, 1989 – Soc. Janssen Cilag *v.* Soc. Boehringer Mannheim: 7/8

14 July 1998, Court of Milan, (unreported) – Sacs Srl *v.* Nautica International Inc: 7/26

16 September 1998, District Court of Bologna, 2000 GRUR Int. 1021: 2/27, 8/39

16 July 1999, Court of Naples, GADI 4090 – Silex Italia Spa *v.* Fratelli Guzzini Spa, Domo Srl and Casamia: 7/8, 7/12

13 March 2000, Court of Naples, detachment division of Afragola, GADI 4146 – Aceto balsamico del Duca di Adriano Grosoli *v.* Marcello De Nigris: 7/26

20 April 2001, Court of Rome, GADI 4346 – Louis Vuitton Malletiers SA *v.* Matras Srl: 7/26

23 May 2001, Court of Modena, GADI 4292 – Ungaro Srl *v.* Emanuel Ungaro SA: 7/26

12 June 2001, Court of Rome, (unreported) – Thun Spa *v.* Veroli spa: 7/26

18 July 2001, Court of Rome, GADI 4358 – GB Carpano Spa and Fratelli Branca Distilllerie Srl *v.* System Liquori: 7/26

4 September 2001, Court of Treviso, (unreported) – Thun Spa *v.* Zago Adriano Spa: 7/26

21 March 2002, Court of Milan – Dade *v.* Chiron: 2/27, 7/17

17 June 2002, Court of Vicenza, (unreported) – Lafer Spa *v.* Fabotex Srl: 7/36

8 July 2002, Court of Turin, (unreported) – Morellato Spa *v.* Gioie.it Spa: 7/33

Switzerland

26 September 1995, Zurich Commercial Court, SMI 1996, 454 – "Globus II": 8/62

3 November 1995, Federal Court, BGE 121 III 474: 8/69

14 May 1996, Zurich Commercial Court, Blätter für Zürcherische Rechtsprechung 1996 No. 98 – "Ski- und Wanderstöcke": 8/50

2 July 1996, Zurich Commercial Court, sic! 1997, 208 – "Erythropoietin II": 8/13

21 August 1996, Federal Court, sic! 1997, 331 – "Hitzeschutzschild III": 8/37

10 October 1996, Federal Court, BGE 122 III 463: 8/116

23 October 1996, Federal Court, BGE 122 III 469 – "Chanel": 8/100

13 February 1997, Federal Court, sic! 1997, 408 – "Erythoropoietin IV": 8/55

17 February 1997, Federal Court, BGE 123 III 140: 8/118

17 February 1997, St. Gallen Commercial Court, sic! 1997, 306 – "Pulverbeschichtungsanlage I": 8/56

2 May 1997, Zurich Commercial Court Blätter für Zürcherische Rechtsprechung 1997, No. 46: 8/58

26 September 1997, Federal Court, BGE 123 III 414: 8/68

1 October 1997, Superior Court of Basel-Landschaft, sic! 1998, 78 – "Acyclovir": 8/43, 8/108

20 July 1998, Federal Court, BGE 124 III 321– "Nintendo": 8/100

5 November 1998, Fribourg Appellate Court, sic! 2000, 114 – "Förderanlage": 8/51, 8/59

9 December 1998, Federal Court, BGE 125 III 29: 8/77

2 August 1999, Federal Court, BGE 125 III 346: 8/38

7 December 1999, Federal Court, BGE 125 III 129: 8/101

17 July 2000, Federal Court, BGE 126 III 382: 8/104

17 August 2001 – Federal Court, sic! 2001, 749 – "Palettenförderer": 8/93

21 February 2003, Federal Court, BGE 129 III 295: 8/11, 8/40, 8/64, 8/66

21 July 2003, Federal Court, BGE 129 III 588: 8/14, 8/18

Poland

3 February 1970, Supreme Court, file No. 615/69, Gazeta Sądowa i Penitencjarna, [20/1970]: 9/37

22 October 1974, Supreme Court, Orzecznictwo Sądu Najwyższego [1975], No. 10–11, item 153: 9/42

23 June 1977, Supreme Court, enlarged panel. Case No. *v.* PZP 1/77: 9/39

24 November 1978, Supreme Court, Case No. IV PR 288/78, OSPIKA 1979: 9/39

29 November 1984, Supreme Court, IC 357/84, OSN [9/1985], item 131, Jakubecki Postępowanie zabezpieczające w sprawach z zakresu własności intelektualnej (Enforcement Procedures in Cases of Intellectual Property), 2000, 296: 9/43

12 March 1987, Supreme Court, Case No. III PRN 5/86, OSPIKA 1988, issue 3, item 47: 9/39

14 June 1988, Supreme Court, Case No. II CR 367/87, OSPIKA 1990, item 328: 9/21

18 February 1993, Supreme Court, Case I CRN 6/93, OSNCP 1993, issue 11, item 204: 9/35

30 September 1994, Supreme Court, Case No. 109/94, Orzecznictwo Sądów Polskich (OSNC) 1995, item 18: 9/22

30 January 1998, Cracow District Court, Case No. IX GC 536/96: 9/40

February 2001, CA Court (NSA), Case No. III SA 2339/99, Przegląd Podatkowy (Tax Review), 2001/11/63: 9/13

11 July 2001, CA Court (NSA), Case No. *v*. SA 3738/00, LEX Base No. 51274: 9/13

23 August 2001, Supreme Court, Case No. N III CZP 43/01, Orzecznictwo Sądów Polskich 2002, issue 5, item 60: 9/34

6 September 2001, CA Court (NSA), Case No. *v*. SA 165/01, LEX Base No. 51 270: 9/13

20 December 2001, Supreme Court, Case No. II CKN 1440/00, published in the Lex Base under item 53 131: 9/17

30 January 2002, Supreme Court, Case No. *v*. CA 1/102, published in Lex Base under No. 56 019: 9/10

21 May 2002, CA Court (NSA), Case No. II SA 4033/01, Wokanda 2002/12/39: 9/12

21 May 2002, Constitutional Tribunal, Case No. K 30/01, OTK-A 2002/3/32: 9/46

Czech Republic

Former Supreme Court No. 30/1993 Coll., court decisions and opinions (civil): 10/8

Superior Court Prague No. 46/1996 Coll., court decisions and opinions (civil), 1996 Právní praxe *v*. podnikání No. 7/8, 37: 10/8

Superior Court Prague No. 49/1997, 1997 Soudnì rozhledy No. 3, 62: 10/8

27 May 1997, Former Regional Commercial Court Brno, No. 11 Cms 91/97-20: 10/11

Former Regional Commercial Court Brno No. 56/1998, 1998 Soudní rozhledy No. 7, 173: 10/8

3 August 1998, Former Regional Commercial Court Brno, No. 11 Cms 92/98-11, 2000 Jurisprudence No. 2, at 29: 10/4, 10/10

9 December 1999, Former Regional Commercial Court in Brno No. 11 Cms 91/97-113: 10/7

21 December 2000, Regional Court Plzen, sp.zn. 22 Cm 38/2000: 10/9

30 December 2000, Prague Superior Court, No. 3 Cmo 382/2000-136: 10/5

3 June 2003, Supreme Administrative Court in Brno, No. 7 A 132/2000: 10/6

Hungary

Supreme Court, decision Pf.IV.20.415/1983: 11/27
Supreme Court, Civil Division, decision No. 277, 1988 Legfelsõbb Bìróság, Bìrósági Határozatok (Supreme Court Decisions) 8: 11/14
Supreme Court, decision Pf.IV.20.368/1990: 11/19
Supreme Court, decision Pf.IV.21.139/1992: 11/27
Supreme Court, decision Pk. IV.21.275/1993, reprinted in 1994 BH 83: 11/19
Constitutional Court decision No. 1/1994: 11/15
Supreme Court, decision Gf.VI.32.777/1997, 2000 BH 218: 11/17
Budapest Appeal Court, decision III.P.26.236/1998: 11/30
Budapest Appeal Court, decision III.P.28.087/1998: 11/30
Supreme Court, decision Pf.IV.25.602/1999: 11/29

China

No. 1 Intermediate People's Court of Beijing, Zuigao Renmin Fayuan Gongbao 1995, 101 *et seq.*: 12/82
Intermediate People's Court Shanghai in: Liu Lu/Gao Yan, Minshi Susongfa lijie shiyong yu anli pingxi, Beijing 1996, 336: 12/89
No. 1 Intermediate People's Court of Beijing, CPT 1997 No. 4, 87 *et seq.*: 12/83
Intermediate People's Court of Nanjing, Zuigao Renmin Fayuan Gongbao 1998, 70: 12/73
Heilongjiangsheng Jianshe Shejiyuan *v.* Hubeisheng Mianhua Gongsi, Hubeisheng Mianhua Gongsi Rangfan Zhongchuan Chubeiku and Wuhanshi Gongye/Daxue Shejiyuan, Supreme People's Court, Case Number (1998) Zhijianzi No. 37: case study Zuigaorenminfayuan Zhishi Chanquan Panli Pingjie, Ed. Jiang Zhipei, Beijing Zhishi Chanquan Chubanshe 2001, 523: 12/22
Wuhan Huagong Xueyuan *v.* Shandongsheng Taianshi Jiaoqu Fuli Huagongchang, Case No. (1999) Zhizong Zi No. 20, SPC Case Study, 120: 12/56
Beijing Founder Group Corp. *v.* Beijing Gaoshu Tianli Science & Technology Co. Ltd. and Beijing Gaoshu Science and Technology Co. Ltd., Beijing Higher People's Court Judgment No. Gaomingzhongzi 194/2002; Yang Xiaoguang, The China IP Focus 2003, 71: 12/53
Eli Lilly *v.* Changzhou Huasheng Pharmaceutical Co. Ltd., reported by Chen Wenping in Asialaw IPReview May 2004, 25: 12/9

Japan

15 November 1904, Imperial Supreme Court, 10 Minroku 1679: 13/79
12 June 1953, Tokyo District Court, 4-6 Kakyu Minshû 847: 13/28

4 July 1956, Supreme Court, 10-7 Mihshû 705: 1/185

26 December 1964, Osaka District Court, 15-12 GeMin 3121 – "Polypropylene": 13/40

14 June 1967, Nagoya High Court, 18 Kakyu Minshû 676 – "Butylscopoamin Bromide": 13/55

4 April 1968, Supreme Court, 22/4 Minshû 816: 13/78

30 July 1970, Tokyo High Court, 253 Hanrei Times 192 – "Grain Dryer": 13/56

28 November 1970, Tokyo High Court, 2-1 Mutaishû 109: 13/77

10 February 1976, Osaka District Court, 1993 Tokkyo Kanri 1553: 13/82

22 December 1978, Tokyo District Court, 378 Hanrei Times 152 – "Snoopy": 1/135

29 June 1979, Osaka District Court, Tokkyo Kanri Bessatsu 554 (1979): 13/46

27 March 1981, Osaka District Court, 13-1 Mutaishû 336: 1/131, 13/99

28 September 1983, Tokyo District Court, 15-3 Mutaishû: 13/33

23 December 1983, Tokyo District Court, 15-3 Mutaishû 844: 13/33

27 February 1984, Nagoya District Court, 16-1 Mutaishû 91 (1984) – "Walking Beam": 13/45

6 April 1984, Tokyo District Court, 525 Hanrei Times 314 (1985) – "Crystal": 13/112

26 April 1984, Osaka District Court, 16-1 Mutaishû 282: 13/33

29 May 1984, Supreme Court, 530 Hanrei Times 97 (1985) – "American Football Symbol Mark": 1/184, 13/16, 13/115

31 August 1984, Nagoya District Court, 16-2 Mutaishû 568 (1984) – "Magnetic Recorder": 13/45

22 March 1985, Yokohama District Court, 566 Hanrei Times 275 – "Chanel Handbag": 1/133

20 June 1986, Osaka High Court, 18-2 Mutaishû 15 – "Permabrush": 13/39

10 March 1987, Tokyo District Court, 1265 Hanrei Jihô 103 (1988) – "ICS": 13/94

23 March 1987, Kobe District Court, 19-1 Mutaishû 72 – "Love Hotel Chanel": 1/132

10 July 1987, Tokyo District Court, 20 IIC 91 (1989) – "Monsanto": 13/70

27 April 1988, Tokyo District Court, 20-1 Mutaishû 209 – "Louis Vuitton": 1/135

24 April 1989, Osaka District Court, 21-1 Mutaishû 271 – "Crushing Device": 13/41

30 May 1989, Tokyo District Court, 1348 Hanrei Jihô 91: 1/107

28 December 1989, Tokyo District Court, 21-3 Mutaishû 1073 (1989) – "Cable Cover I": 13/114

9 February 1990, Tokyo District Court, 1347 Hanrei Jihô 111: 13/53

19 July 1990, Osaka District Court, 1993 Tokkyo Kanri 1553: 13/82

19 December 1990, Tokyo District Court, 266 Tokkyo To Kigyô 46 – "University Entrance Exam": 13/45

23 June 1991, Supreme Court, 24 IIC 523 (1993) – "Evidence of Trade Mark Use": 1/32

31 July 1991, Nagoya District Court, 15 Tokkyo Kenkyû 3: 13/80

16 September 1991, Tokyo District Court, 24 IIC 391 (1993) – "Liquid Fuel Component": 13/30, 13/32

24 September 1991, Tokyo District Court, 1429 Hanrei Jihô 80, 35 Japanese Annual of Int'l Law 175 (1992) – "Manufacture of Plated Copper": 1/107, 13/31

27 April 1992, Tokyo District Court, 819 Hanrei Times 179 – "Ritz Babywear": 13/16

8 October 1992, Nagoya District Court, 1993/10 Patents & Licensing 25 – "Fungus Growing Device": 13/45

20 November 1992, Supreme Court, 1050 Jurist 180, AIPPI Journal of the Japanese Group International Edition, 3/1993, 98: 13/34

23 February 1993, Osaka High Court, 1993/10 Patents & Licensing 25, 1994/1 AIPPI Journal (Engl.ed.) 23 – "Fish Processing Device": 13/45

25 February 1993, Osaka District Court, 25-1 Chizaishû 56 – "Jimmy'z": 1/131, 13/99

25 February 1993, Tokyo High Court, 25-1 Chizaishû 33 (1993) – "Cable Cover II": 13/114

14 March 1993, Tokyo High Court, Patent 12/1993, 117: 13/36

24 March 1993, Tokyo District Court, 26 IIC 566 (1995) – "Type Chanel No. 5": 1/131, 1/135, 13/16, 13/99

25 March 1993, Osaka District Court, Patent 11/1994, 121: 13/81

26 May 1993, Tokyo High Court, Patent 10/1993, 142 (1993) – "Cap Transport Device": 13/45

22 July 1993, Osaka District Court, Patent 1/1994, 95 – "Rice Seedling Mat": 13/45

9 September 1993, Tokyo High Court, 1485 Hanrei Jihô 116 (1994), 27 IIC 108 (1996) – "Cylindrical Cutter": 13/26

30 November 1993, Osaka High Court, 25-3 Chizaishû 476 (1993) – "Aluminium Wheels": 13/113

27 January 1994, Tokyo High Court, Patent, 12/1994, 119: 13/36

31 January 1994, Tokyo District Court, 26-1 Chizaishû 1 – "Pacman": 13/104

16 July 1994, Nagoya District Court, 225 Hanketsu Sokuhô, No. 6520: 13/38

29 July 1994, Tokyo District Court, 1513 Hanrei Jihô 155 (1995): 13/42

31 August 1994, Tokyo District Court, 1510 Hanrei Jihô 35 (1995) -- "Kilby's Patent I": 13/84

27 October 1994, Osaka District Court, 234 Hanketsu Sokuhô 11 (1994) – "Swinging Doors": 13/45

26 December 1994, Tokyo District Court, 236 Hanketsu Sokuhô 8 (1995) – "Design": 13/45

7 March 1995, Supreme Court, 1527 Hanrei Jihô 146 (1995) – "Magnetic Treatment Device": 13/36

23 March 1995, Tokyo High Court, 27-1 Chizaishû 171 – "Snack Chanel II": 1/134

23 March 1995, Tokyo High Court, 1995 GRUR Int. 417 – "BBS Car Wheels II": 13/72

24 March 1995, Tokyo District Court, 1995 AIPPI Japan English edition 238 – "Air Filter": 13/54

31 August 1995, Osaka District Court, 244 Hanketsu Sokuhô 4 (1995): 13/45

16 March 1996, Nagoya High Court, 28 IIC 398 (1997) – "Clinical Trials": 13/70

30 March 1996, Tokyo District Court, 1585 Hanrei Jihô 106 (1996): 13/107

23 May 1996, Tokyo High Court, 1570 Hanrei Jihô 103 (1996): 13/42

18 October 1996, Tokyo District Court, 1585 Hanrei Jihô 106 – "Concrete Steel Rod": 13/108

20 May 1997, Tokyo High Court, 1601 Hanrei Jihô 143 (1997), 30 IIC 452 (1999) – "Sale of Pharmaceuticals": 1/25, 1/37, 13/48

1 July 1997, Supreme Court, 29 IIC 331 (1998) – "BBS Car Wheels III": 13/73

11 July 1997, Supreme Court, 30 IIC 480 (1999) – "Punitive Damages": 1/126, 13/93

10 September 1997, Tokyo High Court, 1615 Hanrei Jihô 10 (1997) – "Kilby's Patent II": 13/85

24 February 1998, Supreme Court, 30 IIC 443 (1999) – "Ball Spline Bearing III": 13/8, 13/63

30 March 1998, Tokyo District Court, 1646 Hanrei Jihô 143 (1998): 1/13, 13/110

31 March 1998, Tokyo High Court, 30 IIC 545 – "Procaterole": 13/71

28 May 1998, Tokyo High Court, (1998) AIPPI Journal of the Japanese Group, Int'l Ed. 247 – "L'Air du Temps": 1/87

17 September 1998, Osaka District Court, 282 Hanketsu Sokuhô 17 (1998) – "Toaster": 1/130, 13/98, 13/103

7 October 1998, Tokyo District Court, (unreported): 13/64

7 October 1998, Tokyo District Court, 1657 Hanrei Jihô 122 (1999) – "Recharging System": 1/129, 13/101

12 October 1998, Tokyo District Court, 30 IIC 457 (1999) – "Cimetidine": 1/127, 13/50, 13/94, 13/102

16 April 1999, Supreme Court, 30 IIC 448 (1999) – "Clinical Trials III": 13/71

22 April 1999, Tokyo District Court, 1691 Hanrei Jihô 131 (2000): 13/28

8 June 1999, Supreme Court, 16 Law & Technology 72 – "Ultraman": 13/29

15 June 1999, Tokyo High Court, 1697 Hanrei Jihô 96 (2000) – "Heat Bank System": 1/128, 13/95, 13/97

13 July 1999, Tokyo High Court, 1696 Hanrei Jihô 137 – "Karaoke": 13/111

16 July 1999, Supreme Court, 1686 Hanrei Jihô 104: 13/92

27 January 2000, Tokyo High Court, 1711 Hanrei Jihô 131 (2000) = 2001 GRUR Int. 83: 13/28

3 February 2000, Osaka District Court, (unreported) – "Tissue Paper": 13/75

11 April 2000, Supreme Court, 1710 Hanrei Jihô 68, 35 IIC 91 (2004) – "Kilby's Patent III": 1/89, 13/83

6 June 2000, Tokyo District Court, 1712 Hanrei Jihô 175 – "Disposable Camera": 13/44, 13/76

14 July 2000, Tokyo District Court, (unreported) – "Lack of novelty": 1/90, 13/86

31 August 2000, Tokyo District Court, (unreported) – "Fuji Film": 13/76

5 September 2000, Osaka District Court, (unreported) – "Lack of novelty": 1/90, 13/86

27 September 2000, Tokyo District Court, (unreported)– "Lack of inventive step": 1/91, 13/87

26 October 2000, Tokyo High Court, 1738 Hanrei Jihô 97 (2001) – "Isolation of Algae": 13/69

1 December 2000, Osaka High Court, (unreported) – "Tissue Paper II": 13/75

12 December 2000, Tokyo District Court. 1734 Hanrei Jihô 110 – "Business Model Patent": 13/44

30 January 2001, Tokyo District Court, (unreported) – "Misappropriation of patent": 1/93, 13/89

30 March 2001, Tokyo District Court, 1059 Hanrei Times 195: 13/67

19 April 2001, Osaka High Court, 34 IIC 553 (2003) – "Injection Method for Ampules": 13/61

25 April 2001, Tokyo District Court, (unreported) – "Insufficient disclosure of patent": 1/92, 13/88

14 May 2001, Tokyo District Court, 34 IIC 554 (2003) – "Medicine for Reducing Eye Pressure": 13/43

22 May 2001, Tokyo District Court, 13 Law & Technology 71 (2001): 13/69

25 May 2001, Tokyo District Court, 15 Law & Technology 61 (2002): 1/88, 13/47

21 June 2001, Osaka High Court, 34 IIC 433 (2003) – "Electrical Pump": 13/52

20 September 2001, Osaka District Court, (unreported) – "Process invention": 13/60

21 September 2001, Osaka District Court, 1785 Hanrei Jihô 78 (2002), 35 IIC 324 (2004 – "Jurisdiction in Patent Matters": 13/27

9 October 2001, Osaka District Court, 15 Law & Technology 89 (2002): 13/68

30 October 2001, Osaka District Court, 34 IIC 311 (2003) – "Aerosole": 13/51

31 October 2001, Tokyo District Court, 15 Law & Technology 92 (2002): 1/131, 13/99, 13/105

1 November 2001, Osaka High Court, 15 Law & Technology 82 (2002): 13/65

28 November 2001, Tokyo High Court, 15 Law & Technology 83 (2002): 13/66

29 November 2001, Tokyo High Court, 34 IIC 821 (2003) – "Acycrobil": 13/74

4 December 2001, Osaka District Court, 34 IIC 203 (2003) – "Cogwheel": 13/49

4 December 2001, Osaka High Court, 34 IIC 554 (2003) – "Scope of Process Invention": 13/62

31 January 2002, Osaka District Court, 34 IIC 822 (2003) – "Washed Rice": 13/62

31 January 2002, Tokyo District Court, 1818 Hanrei Jihô 165 – "Tonttu": 13/40

21 February 2002, Tokyo District Court, 34 IIC 844 (2003) – "Database": 13/47

19 March 2002, Tokyo District Court, 4-7 AIPPI Journal 4 = 34 IIC 965 – "Pachinko Slot": 1/127, 13/100

25 March 2002, Supreme Court, 35 IIC (forthcoming) – "Pachinko Device": 13/37

19 September 2002, Tokyo District Court, (unreported) – "Nichia I": 13/47

26 September 2002, Supreme Court, 19 Law & Technology 81 (2003) – "FM Signal Device": 13/28

31 October 2002, Tokyo High Court, 2003 AIPPI Japan English Edition 359 – "Anti-Allergic Agent": 13/14

16 October 2003, Tokyo District Court, (unreported) – "Sango Fossile Powder": 13/29

26 December 2003, Tokyo District Court, 1851 Hanrei Jihô 138 – "Filling Machine": 13/104.

29 January 2004, Tokyo District Court, (unreported) – "Nichia II": 13/47

Korea

1 April 1981, Supreme Court, 89 Hunma 160: 1/186

26 July 1983, Supreme Court, 81 Hu 45, Shindo Mulsan Co., Ltd. *v.* Hanmi Silup Co., Ltd.: 14/8

9 April 1985, Supreme Court, 83 Hu 85, Chevron Research Co. *v.* Jinheung Fine Chemicals Co: 14/5

26 November 1991, Supreme Court, 90 Hu 1499, Bayer AG *v.* Cheil Sugar Co., Ltd.: 14/6

12 October 1993, Supreme Court, 91 Hu 1908, Aktiebolaget Haessle *v.* Boryung Pharmaceutical Co., Ltd.: 14/1

28 September 1996, Constitutional Court, 92 Hunga 11 and No. 93 Hunga 8, 9, 10: 1/32

17 September 1998, Patent Court, 98 Heo 2160, Bayer AG *v.* Union Quimico Pharmaceutica S.A.: 14/3

22 December 1998, Supreme Court, 91 Ma 540, Cheiljedang Corporation *v.* F. Hoffinan La Roche AG: 14/9

28 July 2000, Supreme Court, 97 Hu 2200: 14/4

21 August 2001, Supreme Court, 98 Hu 522, Nissan Chemical *v.* LG Chemical: 14/7

6 September 2002, Supreme Court, 2001 Hu 171, Cheil Jedang *v.* Genetics Institute: 14/2

United States

Advanced Cardiovascular Systems Inc. *v.* C.R. Baird Inc., 5 October 1992, 25 USPQ 2d 1354 (N.D.Cal. 1992): 1/52, 15/106

American Medical Systems Inc. *v.* Medical Engineering Corporation, 4 October 1993, 6 F.3d 1523 (Fed. Cir. 1993): 1/125

Anchor Wall Sys., Inc. *v.* Rockwood Retaining Walls, Inc., 340 F.3d 1298 (Fed. Cir. 2003): 15/117

Aro Manufacturing Co., Inc. *v.* Convertible Top Replacement Co., Inc., 365 U.S. 336 (1961): 15/74, 15/77

Arrowhead Indus. Water, Inc. *v.* Ecolochem, Inc., 846 F.2d 731 (Fed. Cir. 1988): 15/89, 15/90

Atari, Inc. *v.* JS&A Group, Inc., 747 F.2d 1422 (Fed. Cir. 1984): 15/40

Atlas Powder Co. *v.* Ireco Chemicals., 773 F.2d 1230, 1231 (Fed. Cir. 1985): 15/134

Bandag, Inc. *v.* Al Bolser's Tire Stores, Inc., 750 F.2d 903 (Fed. Cir. 1984): 15/76

Beverly Hills Fan Co. *v.* Royal Sovereign Corp., 8 March 1994, 21 F.3d 1558 (Fed. Cir. 1994): 1/97, 15/56

BIC Leisure Products *v.* Windsurfing International, 4 August 1993, 1 F.3d 1214 (Fed. Cir. 1993): 1/120

Blonder-Tongue Labs Inc. *v.* University of Illinois Foundation et al., 420 U.S. 313 (1971): 15/82

Carella *v.* Starlight Archery & ProLine Co., 804 F.2d 135 (Fed. Cir. 1986): 15/136

Cybor Corp. *v.* FAS Tech. Inc., 138 F. 3d 1448 (Fed. Cir. 1998): 15/142

Daubert *v.* Merrell Dow Pharmaceuticals, Inc., 509 U.S. 579 (1993): 15/121

DeGeorge *v.* Bernier, 768 F.2d 1318, 1324 (Fed. Cir. 1985): 15/10

Dubost *v.* United States PTO, 777 F.2d 1561, 1564 (Fed. Cir. 1985): 15/39

Dynacore Holdings Corp. *v.* U.S. Phillips Corp., No. 03-1305 (Fed. Cir. March 31, 2004): 15/80, 15/81

EMC Corp. *v.* Norrand Corp., 89 F.3d 807 (Fed. Cir. 1996): 15/91

Enzo APA & Sons, Inc. *v*. Geapag A. G., 9 January 1998, 134 F.3d 1090, 1093 (Fed. Cir. 1998): 1/99, 15/65

Festo Corp. *v*. Shoketsu Kinzoku Kogyo Kabushiki Co., Ltd., 234 F.3d 558 (Fed. Cir. 1999): 15/128, 15/129

Festo Corp. *v*. Shoketsu Kinzoku Kogyo Kabushiki Co., Ltd., 535 U.S. 722, 152 L. Ed. 2d 944, 122 S. Ct. 1831 (2002): 15/128, 15/130

Festo Corp. *v*. Shoketsu Kinzoku Kogyo Kabushiki Co., Ltd., 344 F.3d 1359, 68 U.S.P.Q.2d (BNA) 1321 (Fed. Cir. 2003): 15/131

Fonar Corporation *v*. General Electric, 25 February 1997, 107 F.3d 1543 (Fed. Cir. 1997): 1/118

Frazier Indus. Co., Inc. *v*. Advance Storage Prods., 33 U.S.P.Q.2d 1702 (C.D.Cal. 1994): 15/107

Fromson *v*. Anitec Printing, Inc., 132 F.3d 1437, 1442 (Fed. Cir. 1997): 15/87

Fromson *v*. Western Litho Plate & Supply Co., 853 F.2d 1568 (Fed. Cir. 1988): 15/109

Genentech Inc. *v*. Eli Lilly & Co., 998 F.2d 931 (Fed. Cir. 1993): 15/92, 15/93, 15/94

General Motors Corporation *v*. Devex Corporation, 24 May 1983, 461 U.S. 648 (1983): 1/124

Georgia-Pacific Corporation *v*. United States Plywood-Champion Papers, 381 F.Supp. 1116 (Southern District of New York 1970): 1/121

Gerber Garment Tech, Inc. *v*. Lectra Systems, Inc., 916 F.2d 683, 686: 15/141, 15/142

Graham *v*. John Deere Co., 383 U.S. 1, 17, 18 (1966): 15/17, 15/18

Gyromat Corp. *v*. Champion Spark Plug Co., 735 F.2d 549 (Fed. Cir. 1984): 15/135

H.H. Robertson *v*. United Steel Deck, 27 May 1987, 820 F.2d 384 (Fed. Cir. 1987): 1/69

Hilton Davis Chem. Co. *v*. Warner-Jenkinson Co., Inc., 62 F.3d 1512 (Fed. Cir. 1995) (in banc): 15/45, 15/124

Hybritech Inc. *v*. Abbott Laboratories, 849 F2d 1446 (Fed. Cir. 1988): 1/65, 1/70

In re Freeman, 30 F.3d 1459, 1466 (Fed. Cir. 1994): 15/83, 15/84

In re Gay, 309 F.2d 769, 774 (C.C.P.A. 1962): 15/8

In re Jackson, 217 U.S.P.Q. 804, 807 (Bd. Pat. App. & Int. 1986): 15/9

In re Spalding Sports Worldwide Inc., 203 F.3d 800 (Fed. Cir. 2000): 15/106

Jansen *v*. Rexall Sundown, Inc., 342 F.3d 1329, 1334 (Fed. Cir. 2003): 15/79

Kahn *v*. General Motors Corp., 889 F.2d 1078, 1081-83 (Fed. Cir. 1989): 15/95

Katz *v*. Lear Siegler, Inc., 909 F.2d 1459, 1464 (Fed. Cir. 1990): 15/75

King Instruments Corp. *v*. Otari Corp., 26 June 1985, 767 F.2d 853 (Fed. Cir. 1985): 1/119

Knorr-Bremse Systeme Fuer Natzfahrzeuge GMBH *v.* Dana Corp., 344 F.3d 1336 (2003): 15/111

KSM Fastening Sys., Inc. *v.* H.A. Jones Co., 776 F.2d 1522 (Fed. Cir. 1985): 15/133

Lucent Information Management, Inc. *v.* Lucent Technologies, Inc., 186 F.3d 311, 318 (3rd Cir. 1999): 15/110

Mahurkar *v.* C.R. Bard, 29 March 1996, 79 F.3d 1572 (Fed. Cir. 1996): 1/122

Markman *v.* Westview Instruments, Inc., 52 F.3d 967 (Fed. Cir. 1995): 15/12, 15/45, 15/115, 15/123, 15/140

Markman *v.* Westview Instruments Inc., 116 S. Ct. 1384 (1996): 1/101, 15/45

Mars Inc. *v.* Kabushiki Kaisha Nippon Conlux, 29 April 1994, 24 F.3d 1368 (Fed.Cir. 1994): 1/105, 15/27

Mas-Hamilton Group *v.* LaGard, Inc., 156 F.3d 1206, 1210 (Fed. Cir. 1998): 15/61

Miles Labs, Inc. *v.* Shandon Inc., 997 F.2d 870 (Fed. Cir. 1993): 15/141

Motorola, Inc. *v.* United States, 729 F.2d 765 (Fed. Cir. 1984): 15/35

New Jersey Mach., Inc. *v.* Alford Indus., Inc., 21 USPQ2d 2033, 2035 (D.N.J. 1991): 15/86

New Jersey Mach., Inc. *v.* Alford Indus., Inc., 983 F.2d 1087 (Fed. Cir. 1992): 15/86

Novartis Pharmaceuticals Corp. *v.* Eon Labs Mfg., Inc., 206 F.R.D. 396, 398 (D. Del. 2002): 15/108

Ortho Pharmaceutical Corporation *v.* Smith, 19 March 1992, 959 F.2d 936 (Fed. Cir. 1992): 1/113

OrthoPharm. Cor. *v.* Genetics, Inst., Inc., 52 F.3d 1026 (Fed. Cir. 1995): 15/63, 15/70, 15/71, 15/72

Paine Weber Jackson & Curtis, Inc. *v.* Merrill Lynch Pierce Fenner & Smith, Inc., 564 F.Supp. 1358, 1371 (D.Del. 1983): 15/86

Palumbo *v.* Don-Joy Co., 762 F.2d 969, 975 (Fed. Cir. 1985): 15/114

Panduit Corp. *v.* Stahlin Brothers Fiberworks, 25 April 1978, 575 F.2d 1152 (6th Circuit 1978): 1/115

Paragon Podiatry Lab, Inc. *v.* KLM Labs, Inc., 984 F.2d 1182 (Fed. Cir. 1993): 15/140

Parker *v.* Prudential Ins. Co. of America, 900 F.2d 772, 775 (4th Cir. 1990): 15/110

Pentec, Inc. *v.* Graphic Controols Corp., 776 F.2d 309, 315-316 (Fed. Cir. 1985): 15/19

Procter & Gamble Co. *v.* Paragon Trade Brands, Inc., 917 F.Supp. 305, 310 (D.Del. 1995): 15/62

Read Corporation *v.* Portec Inc., 10 July 1992, 970 F.2d 816 (Fed. Cir. 1992): 1/113, 1/123

Red Wing Shoe Co. *v.* Hockerson-Halberstadt, Inc., 30 June 1998, 148 F.3d 1355 (Fed. Cir. 1998): 1/96, 15/55

Richardson *v*. Suzuki Motor Company, 16 February 1989, 868 F.2d 1226 (Fed. Cir. 1989): 1/112, 15/132

Rite-Hite Corp. *v*. Kelley Co., 15 June 1995, 56 F.3d 1538 (Fed. Cir. 1995): 1/116, 1/128, 13/97, 15/68, 15/69

Schwartzkopf Dev. Corp. *v*. Ti-Coating, Inc., 800 F.2d 240 (Fed. Cir. 1986): 15/40

Spectra-Physics, Inc. *v*. Coherent, Inc., 827 F.2d 1524, 1536 (Fed. Cir. 1987): 15/11

SRI Int'l *v*. Matsushita Elec. Corp. of Am., 775 F.2d 1107, 1128 (Fed. Cir. 1985) (in banc): 15/43

SRI Int'l *v*. Matsushita Elec. Corp. of Am., 775 F.2d 1130: 15/45

State Industry Inc. *v*. Mor-Flo Industries, 31 August 1989, 883 F.2d 1573 (Fed. Cir. 1989): 1/117

Steelcase, Inc. *v*. Haworth, Inc., 954 F.Supp. 1195, 1199-2000 (W.D. Mich. 1997): 15/108

Tate Access Floors, Inc. *v*. Interface Architectural Resources, Inc., 279 F.3d 1357, 1371 n.3 (Fed. Cir. 2002): 15/85

Texas Digital Sys., Inc. *v*. Telegenix, Inc., 308 F.3d 1193 (Fed. Cir. 2002): 15/116

Texas Instruments *v*. International Trade Commission, 871 F.2d 1054, 1062 (Fed. Cir. 1989): 15/7

Textile Prods., Inc. *v*. Mead Corp., 28 January 1998, 134 F.3d 1481 (Fed. Cir. 1998): 1/99, 15/65, 15/66, 15/67

Thorn EMI North America, Inc. *v*. Micron Technology, Inc., 837 F.Supp. 616, 621 (D. Del. 1993): 15/108

Trojan, Inc. *v*. Shat-R-Shield, Inc., 885 F.2d 854 (Fed. Cir. 1989): 15/35

Underwater Devices Inc. *v*. Morrison-Knudsen Co., 717 F.2d 1380 (Fed. Cir. 1983): 15/109

Unique Concepts, Inc. *v*. Brown, 939 F.2d 1558 (Fed. Cir. 1991): 15/13

United States *v*. Procter & Gamble Co., 356 U.S. 677, 683 (1958): 15/103

Vitronics Corp. *v*. Conceptronic, Inc., 90 F.3d 1576 (Fed. Cir. 1996): 15/118

Warner-Jenkinson Co., Inc. *v*. Hilton Davis Chem. Co., 520 U.S. 17, 117 S.Ct. 1040 (1997): 15/45, 15/125, 15/126, 15/141

Willingham *v*. Lawton, 555 F.2d 1340, 1343 (6th Cir. 1977): 1/98, 15/64

Wilson Sporting Goods Co. *v*. David Geoffrey & Assoc., 904 F.2d 677, 684 (Fed. Cir. 1990): 15/127

Yarway Corp. *v*. Eur-Control USA, Inc., 775 F.2d 268 (Fed. Cir. 1985): 15/40

Zenith Electronics Corp. *v*. Exzec, Inc., 182 F.3d 1340, 1353-54 (Fed. Cir. 1999): 15/78

Argentina

National Federal Civil and Commercial Chamber, Division 3, JA, 1981-IV-240, Antonio Delgado SA *v*. Alvitos, José M. et al.: 16/63

22 December 1932, Federal Capital Chamber of Appeals, JA, 40-348: 16/62

22 August 1977, Federal Appeals Chamber of Córdoba, Civil and Commercial Division, LL, 1980-A-274, Brunello, Américo: 16/59

2 July 1985, National Federal Civil and Commercial Chamber of Appeals, Division 2, LL, 1986-E-703; JA 1986-I-346, Relojes Rolex Argentina SA *v*. Joyería Vía Florida: 16/63

19 September 1985, National Federal Civil and Commercial Chamber of Appeal, Division 3, case 2020: 16/59

29 October 1985, National Federal Civil and Commercial Chamber of Appeal, Division 3, case 3544, Vallejo Jiménez, Félix *v*. Traverso Rossi, Ulises Héctor: 16/59

30 January 1990, National Federal Civil and Commercial Chamber of Appeals., Division 2, case 6147, reg. 6901, Court No. 3, Sec. No. 9, Pezzi, SADI A on litigation: 16/56

7 July 1992, LL, 1992-C-540, Ekmekdjian *v*. Sofovich: 16/29

30 October 1992, case 8072, National Federal Civil and Commercial Chamber of Appeal, Division 2, Ancase SA *v*. Zugolan SA on cessation of use of patent – compensation in Zugolan SA *v*. Ancase SA on invalidity of patent: 16/59

3 March 1995, National Federal Civil and Commercial Chamber of Appeal, Division 3, case 7695/91, Quimarco SAIC *v*. Dimaca SRL et al. on cessation of use of trade mark: 16/60

2 April 1996, National Federal Civil and Commercial Chamber of Appeals, Division 2, case 50 903/95, Benítez, Héctor Pedro *v*. Gaya, Miguel et al. on cessation of use of models and patterns, and on compensation: 16/49

23 December 1996, National Federal Civil and Commercial Chamber, Division 1, DE, 172-453: 16/26

26 November 1997, Heladerías Freddo *v*. Spot Network: 16/27

26 December 1997, National Civil Chamber, Division I, Neyra, José Alberto *v*. Botello, Miguel, DE of 8 July 1998, 6: 16/24

10 February 1998, Federal Civil and Commercial Chamber, Division 1, case 22 524, Order de Jaijel, Fanny et al. *v*. Tesis Grupo Editorial Norma on interim relief: 16/24

20 May 1999, National Federal Civil and Commercial Chamber of Appeals, Division 3, case 1191/98, Continental Plast *v*. Terlizzi SAIC on damages: 16/58

4 June 1999, National Federal Civil and Commercial Court no. 4, Section 8, case 2723/99, Camuzzi de Argentina SA *v*. Arnedo, Juan Pablo on interim relief: 16/27

6 July 1999, National Federal Civil and Commercial Chamber of Appeals, Division 2, case 172/99, American Cyanamid Company et al. *v*. IPESA SA on plea of exploitation: 16/25

30 December 1999, Federal Civil Chamber, Division 2, case 5050/99, Pugliese, Francisco Nicolás *v*. Pérez, Carlos Enrique on interim relief: 16/27

26 December 2000, National Federal Civil and Commercial Appeal Chamber, Division 3, case 10 083, Checkpoint systems SA *v.* Sensormatic Arg. SA on indent of Article 250, National Code of Civil and Commercial Procedure: 16/16

5 April 2001, Federal Civil and Commercial Chamber of Appeals, Division 1, case no. 2024/2001, Mayo Marcos, Daniel *v.* Pelikan SA on Appeal Plea: 16/24

11 July 2001, Federal Civil and Commercial Chamber of Appeals, Division 2, case no. 11 018, Bodega Navarro Correas S.A. on interim relief: 16/24

11 October 2001, National Federal Civil and Commercial Appeal Chamber, Division 1, case 3289/2001, Eli Lilly and Company on interim relief: 16/16, 16/17

12 February 2002, National Federal Civil and Commercial Appeal Chamber Division 2, case 7809/2001, Bayer AG *v.* Agtrol Internac. Arg. SA on interim relief: 16/16, 16/18

9 April 2002, National Federal Civil and Commercial Appeal Chamber, Division 3, case 609/02, Syngenta Participations-AG *v.* Ipesa on interim relief: 16/16

24 January 2003, National Federal Civil and Commercial Appeal Chamber, Feria Division, Merial Limited *v.* Afford Especialidades Veterinarias and/or Ricardo Calvo on cessation of exploitation of patent: 16/16

Brazil

1st Civil Court of Novo Hamburgo, RS, Civil Appeal No. 594 012 478, 13 April 1994 – Vacchi S.A. Ind. e Com. Ltda. *v.* Master Equipamentos Industriais: 17/9

8th Chamber of Private Right of the Justice Court of São Paulo, Civil Appeal No. 5.614-4 (RJTJESP-204/119, 21 May 1998): 17/15

8th Chamber of Private Right of the Justice Court of São Paulo, Civil Appeal No. 28.993-4/0, Ribeirão Preto (DJ, 20 July 1998): 17/14

9th Chamber of Private Right of the Justice Court of the State of São Paulo, in Civil Appeal No. 367824 (RJTJESP-215/149-51, April 1999): 17/10

1st Group of the Federal Regional Court (TRF-2R), Civil Appeal No. 97.02.14696-8 RJ (DJ, 13 April 1999): 17/5, 17/11

5th Group of the Federal Regional Court (TRF-2R), Appeal No. 9202086737 (DJ, 8 February 2000, 217-218): 17/4

Federal Regional Court of Appeals (TRF-2R), 1st Panel, review No. 9902265138 RJ (DJ-2, 20 July 2000, 112): 17/12

Court of Appeals, review No. 200102010152088 (DJ-2, 2 May 2001, 88): 17/12

1st Chamber of Private Right of the Justice Ccurt of the State of São Paulo, Civil Appeal No. 102.573-4, São Paulo (RJTJ 248, 153-159, August 2001): 17/14

Court of Appeals, review No. 200202010327488 (DJ-2, 12 September 2002, 379): 17/12

Superior Court of Justice, Special Appeal No. 423.240-RJ, 15 March 2004: 17/1

Printed in the United Kingdom
by Lightning Source UK Ltd.
103383UKS00001B/223-279